*Oracle Press*™

OCA Oracle Database 11g: Administration I

Exam Guide (Exam 1Z0-052)

John Watson

New York Chicago San Francisco Lisbon London Madrid
Mexico City Milan New Delhi San Juan Seoul Singapore Sydney Toronto

The McGraw·Hill Companies

Cataloging-in-Publication Data is on file with the Library of Congress

McGraw-Hill books are available at special quantity discounts to use as premiums and sales promotions, or for use in corporate training programs. To contact a special sales representative, please visit the Contact Us page at www.mhprofessional.com.

OCA Oracle Database 11g: Administration I Exam Guide (Exam 1Z0-052)

567890   DOC DOC   1 4 3 2

ISBN: Book p/n 978-0-07-159104-1 and CD p/n 978-0-07-159105-8
of set 978-0-07-159102-7
MHID: Book p/n 0-07-159104-4 and CD p/n 0-07-159105-2
of set 0-07-159102-8

Sponsoring Editor Tim Green	**Technical Editor** April Wells	**Composition** International Typesetting and Composition
Editorial Supervisor Patty Mon	**Copy Editor** Bob Campbell	**Illustration** International Typesetting and Composition
Project Manager Harleen Chopra, International Typesetting and Composition	**Proofreader** Sanjukta Chandra	**Art Director, Cover** Jeff Weeks
Acquisitions Coordinator Jennifer Housh	**Indexer** Broccoli Information Management **Production Supervisor** Jean Bodeaux	**Cover Designer** Pattie Lee

I want to thank Silvia for looking after me (and our house, garden, cats, and dogs) while I was working on this. She works much harder than me.

ABOUT THE AUTHOR

John Watson (Oxford, UK) works for BPLC Management Consultants, teaching and consulting throughout Europe and Africa. He was with Oracle University for several years in South Africa, and before that worked for a number of companies, government departments, and NGOs in England and Europe. He is OCP qualified in both database and Application Server administration. John is the author of several books and numerous articles on technology and has twenty-five years of experience in IT.

About the Technical Editor

April Wells (Austin, TX) is an experienced Oracle DBA who holds multiple DBA OCP certifications. She currently manages Oracle databases and Oracle data warehouses at NetSpend corporation in Austin, Texas. Previously, April has worked for Oracle Corporation in Austin, Texas as on-site support at Dell, at Corporate Systems in Amarillo, Texas, and at U.S. Steel in Pennsylvania and Minnesota.

CONTENTS AT A GLANCE

CONTENTS

INTRODUCTION

There is an ever increasing demand for staff with IT industry certification. The benefits to employers are significant—they can be certain that staff have a certain level of competence—and the benefits to the individuals, in terms of demand for their services are equally great. Many employers are now requiring technical staff to have certifications and many IT purchasers will not buy from firms that do not have certified staff. The Oracle certifications are among the most sought after. But apart from rewards in a business sense, knowing that you are among a relatively small pool of elite Oracle professionals and have proved your competence is a personal reward well worth attaining.

There are several Oracle certification *tracks*—this book is concerned with the Oracle Database Administration certification track, specifically for release 11g of the database. There are three levels of DBA certification: Certified Associate (OCA), Certified Professional (OCP), and Certified Master (OCM). The OCA qualification is based on two examinations, the second of which is covered in this book. The OCP qualification requires passing a third examination. These examinations can be taken at any Prometric Center and consists of between sixty and seventy questions to be completed in ninety minutes. The OCM qualification requires completing a further two-day evaluation at an Oracle testing center, involving simulations of complex environments and use of advanced techniques.

To prepare for the second OCA examination, you can attend an Oracle University instructor-led training course, you can study Oracle University online learning material, or you can read this book. In all cases, you should also refer to the Oracle Documentation Library for details of syntax. This book will be a valuable addition to other study methods, but it is also sufficient by itself. It has been designed with the examination objectives in mind, though it also includes a great deal of information that will be useful to you in the course of your work.

However, it is not enough to buy the book, place it under your pillow, and assume that knowledge will permeate the brain by a process of osmosis; you must read it thoroughly, work through the exercises and sample questions, and experiment further with various commands. As you become more familiar with the Oracle environment, you will realize that there is one golden rule:

When it doubt, try it out.

In a multitude of cases, you will find that a simple test that takes a couple of minutes can save hours of speculation and poring through manuals. If anything is ever unclear, construct an example, and see what happens. This book was developed using Windows and Linux, but to carry out the exercises and your further investigations, you can use any platform that is supported for Oracle.

Your study of Oracle database administration is about to begin—you can continue these studies for the rest of your working life. Enjoy!

In This Book

This book is organized to serve as an in-depth review for the OCA Oracle Database 11g: Administration I Exam for Oracle professionals. Each chapter covers a major aspect of the exam; all the OCA official certification objectives are carefully covered in the book.

On the CD-ROM

The CD-ROM contains the entire contents of the book in electronic form, as well as one practice test that simulates the real Oracle Database 11g OCA certification test. For more information on the CD-ROM, please see the appendix. A bonus exam is available for download.

Exam Readiness Checklist

At the end of this introduction, you will find an Exam Readiness Checklist. This table lists the official exam objectives. The checklist also allows you to gauge your level of expertise on each objective at the outset of your studies. This should allow you to check your progress and make sure you spend the time you need on more difficult or unfamiliar sections. Each objective is exactly as Oracle Corporation presents it, including the chapter and page reference.

In Every Chapter

This book includes a set of chapter components that call your attention to important items, reinforce important points, and provide helpful exam-taking hints. Take a look at what you'll find in every chapter:

- **Exam Watch** notes call attention to information about, and potential pitfalls in the exam.

watch

The redo log stream includes all changes: those applied to data | *segments and to undo segments, for both committed and uncommitted transactions.*

- **Exercises** are interspersed throughout the chapters, and they allow you to get the hands-on experience you need in order to pass the exams. They help you master skills that are likely to be an area of focus on the exam. Don't just read through the exercises, they are hands-on practice that you should be comfortable completing. Learning by doing is an effective way to increase your competency with a product.

- **On the Job** notes describe the issues that come up most often in real-world settings. They provide a valuable perspective on certification- and product-related topics. They point out common mistakes and address questions that have arisen from on-the-job discussions and experience.

- **Inside the Exam** sections toward the end of each chapter are designed to anticipate what the exam will emphasize. These are pointers regarding key topics to focus on, based on experience taking many production and beta examinations, and having been on the Oracle internal group that validates examination questions.

- The **Certification Summary** is a succinct review of the chapter and a restatement of salient points regarding the exam.

- The **Two-Minute Drill** at the end of every chapter is a checklist of the main points of the chapter. You can use it for a quick, last-minute review before the test.

- The **Self Test** offers questions similar to those found on the certification exam. The answers to these questions, as well as explanations of the answers, can be found at the end of each chapter. By taking the Self Test after completing each chapter, you'll reinforce what you've learned from that chapter, while becoming familiar with the structure of the exam questions.

- The **Lab Questions** at the end of the Self Test sections offer a unique and challenging question format that, in order to answer correctly, require the reader to understand multiple chapter concepts. These questions are more complex and more comprehensive than the other questions, as they test your ability to take all the knowledge you have gained from reading the chapter and apply it to complicated, real-world situations.

Some Pointers

Once you've finished reading this book, set aside some time to do a thorough review. You might want to return to the book several times and make use of all the methods it offers for reviewing the material before taking the examination.

- **Reread all the Two-Minute Drills or have someone quiz you**   You also can use the drills as a way to do a quick cram before the exam.

- **Reread all the Exam Watch notes**   Remember that these notes are based on the OCA exam. They will draw your attention to what you should expect and what you should be on the lookout for.

- **Retake the Self Tests**   It is a good idea to take the Self Test right after you've read the chapter because the questions help reinforce what you've just learned, then do them again at the end. In the examination, the questions do not come conveniently grouped; you will have to be prepared to jump from one topic to another.

- **Complete the Exercises**   Did you do the chapter Exercises and the Lab Questions when you read each chapter? If not, do them! These exercises are designed to cover exam topics and there's no better way to get to know this material than by practicing. Be sure you understand why you are performing each step in each exercise. If there is something you are not completely clear about, reread that section in the chapter.

- **Take the exam**   You will have only an average of a minute or so for each question. Go through them all, fast, answering the ones you know, and marking the ones you don't know for review. Then go through the marked questions again. That will take up most of the time. If there are still some questions you really don't know, guess; there are no marks deducted for incorrect answers.

Exam 1Z0-052

1
Introduction to the Oracle Server Technologies

This chapter describes the entire Oracle product family, the concepts behind relational databases, the SQL language, and the role of the database administrator (DBA) in the IT environment. The content is not directly tested in the OCP examination, but it is assumed knowledge that provides an essential background to the study of Oracle database administration. It also gives an idea of the scope of a DBA's work. The DBA is often expected to know everything about everything. Well, that isn't possible—but at least he/she should be aware of the whole environment and how the parts link together.

The Oracle server technologies product set is more than a database. There are also the Oracle Application Server and the Oracle Enterprise Manager. Taken together, these are the server technologies that make up the Oracle Grid offering. Grid computing is an emerging environment for managing the complete IT environment and for providing resources to users on demand.

Supplied with the server technologies are the development tools: third-generation languages (3GLs) and rapid application development tools. It is also possible to write software in a wide range of third-party application development environments. Oracle Corporation has a total commitment to supporting international standards for data processing, which means that it is perfectly possible to run third-party products on the Oracle technology stack.

The final part of the Oracle product set is the applications, primarily the Oracle E-Business Suite and the Oracle Collaboration Suite. These are applications written with the Oracle development tools and running on the Oracle servers that can fulfill the needs of virtually any organization for business data processing.

The Oracle database is a relational database management system (RDBMS) with object extensions. Data to be managed by an RDBMS should be *normalized*—converted into two-dimensional tables. Structured query language (SQL, pronounced "sequel") is an international standard for managing data stored in relational databases. Oracle Database 11g offers an implementation of SQL that is generally compliant with the current standard, which is SQL-2003. Full details of the compliance can be found in Appendix B of the "SQL Reference," which is part of the Oracle database documentation set.

The DBA's job is to administer the database. But this tautological definition misses a huge amount. The DBA has a pivotal role in an organization's management and knowledge structure; he/she will usually be expected to be competent in all the topics dealt with here.

This chapter consists of summarized descriptions of the Oracle product family, the concepts behind the relational paradigm and the normalization of data into relational structures, the SQL language, and the role of the DBA.

CERTIFICATION OBJECTIVE 1.01

Position the Oracle Product Family

There are many products developed and marketed by Oracle Corporation. Acquisitions made in recent years have expanded the list substantially. The core products can be grouped as follows:

The server technologies

- The Oracle database
- The Oracle Application Server
- The Oracle Enterprise Manager

The development tools

- The languages
- The Oracle Developer Suite

The applications

- Oracle E-Business Suite
- Oracle Collaboration Suite

The Server Technologies

There is a family of products that make up the Oracle server technology stack. Taken together, they aim to deliver the components of Oracle's Grid computing architecture.

on the job

Oracle Corporation's Grid offering is not always the same as the Grid defined by others. Oracle does tend to emphasize the server technology side of Grid computing.

The concept underlying the Grid is *virtualization*: end users ask for a service, but they neither know nor need to know the source of that service.

The three server technologies that Oracle provides to help deliver the Grid are

- The Oracle Database Server
- The Oracle Application Server
- The Oracle Enterprise Manager

The database is the main concern here: it is the repository for data and the engine that manages access to the data. The Oracle Application Server runs software on behalf of end users: it generates the user interfaces in the form of windows displayed in users' browsers, and submits calls for data retrieval and modification to the database for execution. The Oracle Enterprise Manager is an administration tool for monitoring, managing, and tuning the Oracle processes and also (through plug-ins) many third-party products.

The Oracle Database Server

Chapter 2 deals with the architecture of the Oracle Database Server in detail. For now, all that is necessary is to know that it is a repository for data without effective limits on size, and that is accessed by end users either directly through client-server tools and applications or indirectly through applications running on an application server.

The choice between a two-tier client-server architecture and an architecture consisting of three or more tiers is irrelevant to the database: it can execute SQL invoked by client software running on a PC local to the end user as efficiently as it can execute SQL submitted by an application server running on a middle-tier server on behalf of a remote client using a browser.

The Oracle Application Server

With the emergence of the Web as the de facto standard platform for delivering applications to end users has come the need for application servers. An application server replaces the client-side software traditionally installed on end-user computers: it runs applications centrally, presenting them to users in windows displayed locally in web browsers. The applications make use of data stored in one or more database servers.

Oracle Application Server is a platform for developing, deploying, and managing *web applications*. A web application can be defined as any application with which users communicate via HTTP. Web applications usually run in at least three tiers: a database tier manages access to the data, the client tier (often implemented as a web browser) handles the local window management for communications with the users, and an application tier in the middle executes the program logic that generates the user interface and the SQL calls to the database.

Web applications can be developed with a number of technologies, predominant among which today is Java. Applications written in Java should conform to the J2EE (Java 2 Enterprise Edition) standard, which defines how such applications should be packaged and deployed. J2EE and related standards are controlled by Sun Microsystems and accepted by virtually all software developers. Oracle Application Server is a J2EE-compliant application server. Oracle's implementation of the standards allows for automatic load balancing and fault tolerance across multiple application servers on multiple machines though J2EE clustering. Clustering virtualizes the provision of the application service: users ask for an application, which might be available from a number of locations, and the cluster works out from where any one session or request can best be serviced. If one location fails, others will take up the load, and more resources can be made available to an application as necessary. The ability to separate the request for a service from the location of its provision and to add or remove J2EE servers from a cluster dynamically is a major part of the Oracle Application Server's contribution to the Grid.

It is important to note that Oracle's commitment to international standards is total. Applications running in the Oracle Application Server environment can connect to any databases for which there are Java-compliant drivers: it is not necessary to use an Oracle database. Applications developed with the Oracle Application Server toolkits could be deployed to a third-party J2EE-compliant application server. However, the Oracle product set is particularly powerful and will often be the best choice.

The simplest processing model of web applications is three tier: a client tier that manages the user interface, a middle tier that generates the interface and issues SQL statements to the data tier, and a data tier that manages the data itself. In the Oracle environment, the client tier will be a browser (such as Mozilla or Microsoft Internet Explorer) that handles local window management, handles the keyboard input, and tracks mouse movements. The middle tier will be an Oracle Application Server running the software (probably written in Java) that is generating the windows sent to the client tier for display, and the SQL statements sent to the data tier for execution. The data tier will be an Oracle server: an instance and a database. In this three-tier environment, there are two types of session: end-user sessions from the client tier to the middle tier, and database sessions from the middle tier to the data tier. The end-user sessions will be established with HTTP. The database sessions are client-server sessions consisting of a user process and a server process, as described in the preceding section.

It is possible for an application to use a one-for-one mapping of end-user session to database session: each user, from his/her browser, will establish a session against the application server, and the application server will then establish a session against the database server on the user's behalf. However, this model has been proven to be very inefficient when compared to the *connection pooling* model. With connection pooling, the application server establishes a relatively small number of persistent database sessions and makes them available on demand (queuing requests if necessary) to a relatively large number of end-user sessions against the application server.

From the point of view of the database, it makes no difference whether a SQL statement comes from a client-side process such as SQL*Plus or Microsoft Access or from a pooled session to an application server. In the former case, the user process all happens on one machine; in the latter, the user process has been divided into two tiers: an applications tier that generates the user interface and a client tier that displays it. But the database tier really doesn't care.

on the
Job

DBAs often find themselves pressed into service as Application Server administrators. Be prepared for this. There is a separate OCP curriculum for Application Server, for which it may well be worth studying.

Oracle Enterprise Manager

The increasing size and complexity of IT installations makes management of each given component a challenging task. This is hardly surprising: no one ever said that managing a powerful environment should necessarily be simple. Management tools can make the task easier, and the management staff more productive.

Oracle Enterprise Manager comes in three forms:

- Database Control
- Application Server Control
- Grid Control

Oracle Enterprise Manager Database Control is a graphical tool for managing one database, which may be a Real Application Clusters (RAC) clustered database. RAC databases are covered in more advanced books; they are mentioned here because they can be managed through the tool. Database Control has facilities for real-time management and monitoring, for running scheduled jobs such as backup operations, and for reporting alert conditions interactively and through e-mail. An RAC database will have a Database Control process running on each node where there is a database instance; these processes communicate with each other, so that each has a complete picture of the state of the RAC.

Oracle Enterprise Manager Application Server Control is a graphical tool for managing one application server instance, or a group of instances. The grouping technology is dependent on the version. Up to and including Oracle Application Server 10g release 2, multiple application servers were managed as a *farm*, with a metadata repository (typically residing in an Oracle database) as the central management point. This is an excellent management model and offers superb capabilities for deploying and maintaining applications, but it is proprietary to Oracle. From Application Server 10g release 3 onward, the technology is based on J2EE clustering, which is not proprietary to Oracle.

Both Database Control and Application Server Control consist of a Java process running on the server machine, which listens for HTTP and HTTPS connection requests. Administrators connect to these processes from a browser. Database Control then connects to the local database server, and Application Server Control connects to the local application server. An advantage of using browser access is that remote management should be no problem. Most, though naturally not all, sites will permit incoming HTTP or HTTPS connections through their firewalls.

Oracle Enterprise Manager Grid Control globalizes the management environment. A management repository (residing in an Oracle database) and one or more management servers manage the complete environment: all the databases and application servers, wherever they may be. Grid Control can also manage the nodes, or machines, on which the servers run, and (through plug-ins) a wide range of third-party products. Each managed node runs an agent process, which is responsible for monitoring the managed targets on the node: executing jobs against them and reporting status, activity levels, and alert conditions back to the management server(s).

Grid Control gives a holistic view of the environment, and if well configured makes administration staff far more productive than without. It becomes possible for one administrator to manage effectively hundreds or thousands of targets. All communications are over HTTP or HTTPS. Provided the corporate firewalls are configured to permit these protocols, it becomes possible for the administration staff to connect to the management servers from any location that has a browser. Furthermore, the communications between the agents running on the various nodes and the management server(s) are also HTTP or HTTPS, so an organization's complete environment—even if spread over many geographically separate sites, using the Internet for inter-site communications—can be managed as a whole.

The core functionality of Oracle Enterprise Manager (OEM) is available for no additional charge—it is bundled with the database or application server license. There are, however, additional *packs* that are separately licensed. The packs consist for the most part of wizards that make the work of monitoring, tuning, and general management easier. Some DBAs make extensive use of Oracle Enterprise Manager and rely on the packs. Others (perhaps the older ones) still prefer to work with command-line utilities such as SQL*Plus. There is little doubt that using Oracle Enterprise Manager can make a DBA far more productive, but it is by no means compulsory.

Grid Computing

Critical to the concept of Grid computing is *virtualization*. This means that at all levels there is a layer of abstraction between what is requested and what is provided. In the Oracle Grid environment, end users ask for an application service and let the Grid work out which clustered J2EE application server can best provide it. Application servers ask for database service from an RAC database and let the Grid work out from which RAC instance the data service can best be provided. Within the Grid there is a mapping of possible services to available service providers, and algorithms for assigning the workload and resources appropriately. The result is that end users have neither the need nor the capacity to know from where their computing resources are actually being provided. The analogy often drawn is with delivery of domestic electricity: it is supplied on demand, and the home owner has no way of telling which power station is currently supplying him/her.

The Grid is not exclusive to Oracle. At the physical level, some operating system and hardware vendors are providing Grid-like capabilities. These include the ability to partition servers into virtual machines, and dynamically add or remove CPU(s) and RAM from the virtual machines according to demand. This is conceptually similar to Oracle's approach of dynamically assigning application server and database server resources to logical services. There is no reason why the two approaches cannot be combined. Both are working toward the same goal and can work together. The result should be an environment where adequate resources are always available on demand, without facing the issues of excess capacity at some times and underperformance at others. It should also be possible to design a Grid environment with no single point of failure, thus achieving the goal of 100 percent uptime, which is being demanded by many users.

The Development Tools and Languages

The Oracle server technologies include various facilities for developing applications, some existing within the database, others external to it.

Within the database, it is possible to use three languages:

- SQL
- PL/SQL
- Java

Applications running externally to the database can be written in a wide variety of 3GLs (notably Java) or in the tools shipped with Oracle Application Server. Predominant among these are

- Forms
- Reports
- XML Publisher
- Discoverer

There is also a wide variety of third-party tools and environments that can be used for developing applications that will connect to an Oracle database; in particular .NET from Microsoft, for which Oracle provides a comprehensive developers' toolkit.

Languages Internal to the Database

The one language that is unavoidable is SQL. SQL is used for data access, but it cannot be used just on its own for developing complete applications. It has no real facilities for developing user interfaces, and it also lacks the procedural structures needed for manipulating rows individually. The other two languages available within the database fill these gaps. They are PL/SQL and Java. PL/SQL is a 3GL proprietary to Oracle. It has the usual procedural constructs (such as conditional branching based on if-then-else and iterative looping) and facilities for user interface design. In the PL/SQL code, one can embed calls to SQL. Thus, a PL/SQL application might use SQL to retrieve one or more rows from the database, then perform various actions based on their content, and then issue more SQL to write rows back to the database. Java offers a similar capability to embed SQL calls within the Java code. This is industry-standard technology: any Java programmer should be able write code that will work with an Oracle database (or indeed with any other Java-compliant database.)

All Oracle DBAs must be fully competent with SQL and PL/SQL. This is assumed, and required, knowledge.

Knowledge of Java is not assumed and indeed is rarely required. A main reason for this is that bespoke Java applications are now rarely run within the database.

Early releases of Oracle's application server could not run some of the industry-standard Java application components, such as Java servlets and Enterprise JavaBeans (EJBs). To get around this serious divergence from standards, Oracle implemented a Java engine within the database that did conform to the standards. However, from Oracle Application Server release 9*i*, it has been possible to run servlets and EJBs where they should be run: on the application server middle tier. Because of this, it is becoming less common to run Java within the database.

Some Oracle components, such as Intermedia and Text, are written in Java, and for this reason a DBA will usually need to enable Java in the database, but he/she will not be expected to tune or debug these. The DBA is, however, likely to spend a large amount of time tuning and debugging SQL and PL/SQL. Oracle's model for the division of responsibility here is clear: the DBA identifies code with problems and passes it to the developers for fixing. But in many cases, the developers lack the skills (or perhaps the inclination) to do this and the DBA has to fill this role. He/she will also often become a teacher: spreading knowledge of better techniques among the developers.

on the **!** Job *All DBAs must be fully competent with SQL and with PL/SQL. Knowledge of Java and other languages is not usually required but is often helpful.*

Languages External to the Database

Other languages are available for developing client-server applications that run externally to the database. The most commonly used are C and Java, but it is possible to use most of the mainstream 3GLs. For most languages, Oracle provides the OCI (Oracle Call Interface) libraries that let code written in these languages connect to an Oracle database and invoke SQL commands.

Applications written in C or other procedural languages make use of the OCI libraries to establish sessions against the database server. These libraries are proprietary to Oracle. This means that any code using them will be specifically written for Oracle, and would have to be substantially rewritten before it could run against any other database. Java applications can avoid this problem. Oracle provides database connectivity for both *thick* and *thin* Java clients.

A thick Java client is Oracle aware. It uses the supplied OCI class library to connect to the database. This means that the application can make use of all the database's capabilities, including features that are unique to the Oracle environment. Java-thick client applications can exploit the database to the full. But they can never work with a third-party product, and they require the OCI client software to be installed.

A thin Java client is not aware of the database against which it is running: it works with a virtual database defined according to the Java standard, and it lets the container within which it is running map this virtual database onto the Oracle database. This gives the application portability across database versions and providers: a thin Java client application could be deployed in a non-Oracle environment without any changes. But any Oracle features that are not part of the Java database connectivity standard will not be available.

The choice between thick and thin Java clients should be made by a team of informed individuals and influenced by a number of factors including performance, the need for Oracle-specific features, corporate standards, application portability, programmer productivity. Oracle's JDeveloper tool can be used to develop both thick- and thin-client Java applications.

Oracle Developer Suite

Many organizations will not want to use a 3GL to develop database applications. Oracle Corporation provides rapid application development tools as part of the Oracle Developer Suite. These can make programmers far more productive than if they were working with a 3GL. Like the languages, all these application development tools end up doing the same thing: constructing SQL statements that are sent to the database server for execution.

Oracle Forms Developer builds applications that run on an Oracle Application Server middle tier and display in a Java applet on the user's terminal. The entry point to Forms applications is through a browser. Forms applications are generally much faster to develop than applications written in, say, Java. An advantage for end users is that the client-side intelligence provided by the applet means that Forms applications can have a better user interface than applications with user interfaces generated by Java servlets. Servlet applications are restricted by the limitations of HTML tags, whereas the Forms applet can generate any user interface gadget that may be required. For example, there is no HTML tag for a rolling combo box, but these are no problem for Forms.

Oracle Reports is a tool for generating and formatting reports, either on demand or according to a schedule. Completed reports can be cached for distribution. As with Forms, programmer productivity can be higher than when working with a 3GL. An Oracle Reports application does impose restrictions on the client machine because of the possible output formats; these are commonly HTML or PDF. The restrictions come from the need for the client to be able to display these formats, and the need for the developer to be aware of the clients' capabilities. XML Publisher avoids these issues by formatting a report's output as XML tags. Any client can request an XML Publisher report and (provided it has an XML parser) display the results. This is the key to distributing reports over wireless protocols to any device, such as a cellular telephone.

Oracle Discoverer is an end-user tool for report generation. Oracle Reports and XML Publisher need a programmer to design the report. A well-designed report can be highly customizable by the end user through use of parameters supplied at request time, but a programmer is still needed to design the report definition. Oracle Discoverer empowers end users to develop reports themselves. Once Oracle Discoverer, which runs on an Oracle Application Server middle tier, has been appropriately configured, no more programmer input is needed: the end users do all the development. Discoverer can add immense value for end users, while freeing up programming staff for real development work.

The Oracle Applications

The number of Oracle applications products has increased substantially in recent years due to a large number of corporate acquisitions, but two applications remain predominant. The Oracle E-Business Suite is a comprehensive suite of applications based around an accounting engine and Oracle Collaboration Suite is a set of office automation tools.

The Oracle E-Business Suite, based around a core of financial applications, includes facilities for accounting, human resources, manufacturing, customer relationship management, customer services, and much more. All the components share a common data model. The current release has a user interface written with Oracle Developer Forms and Java, depending on which tool is most suitable for the various modules and the expected users, running on Oracle Application Server. There is a large amount of PL/SQL in the database to enable the business functions. Future releases will merge the functionality of other products acquired recently (such as the Siebel and Peoplesoft applications) into a common Java-based interface.

The Oracle Collaboration Suite includes (among other things) servers for e-mail, diary management, voicemail and fax, web conferencing, and (perhaps most impressive) file serving. There is complete integration between the various components. The applications run on Oracle Application Servers, and can be accessed through a web interface from browsers or made available on mobile wireless devices, such as cellular phones.

EXERCISE 1-1

Investigate DBMSs in Your Environment

This is a paper-based exercise, with no specific solution.

Identify the applications, application servers, and databases used in your environment. Then, concentrating on the databases, try to get a feeling for how big and busy they are. Consider the number of users, the volatility of the data, and the data volumes. Finally, consider how critical they are to the organization: how much downtime or data loss can be tolerated for each application and database? Is it possible to put a financial figure on this?

The result of this study should give an idea of how critical the DBA's role is.

CERTIFICATION OBJECTIVE 1.02

Explain Relational Structures

Critical to an understanding of SQL is an understanding of the relational paradigm, and the ability to *normalize* data into relational structures. Normalization is the work of systems analysts, as they model business data into a form suitable for storing in relational tables. It is a science that can be studied for years, and there are many schools of thought that have developed their own methods and notations.

Rows and Tables

Using the relational paradigm, data is stored in two-dimensional tables. A table consists of a number of rows, each consisting of a set of columns. Within a table, all the rows have the same column structure, though it is possible that in some rows some columns may have nothing in them. An example of a table would be a list of one's employees, each employee being represented by one row. The columns might be employee number, name, and a code for the department in which he/she works. Any employees not currently assigned to a department would have that column blank. Another table could represent the departments: one row per department, with columns for the department's code and the department's name.

A note on terminology: what Oracle refers to as a *table* may also be called a *relation* or an *entity*. Rows are sometimes called *records* or *tuples*, and *columns* may be called *attributes* or *fields*. The number of *rows in the table* is the *cardinality of the tuples*.

Relational tables conform to certain rules that constrain and define the data. At the column level, each column must be of a certain data type, such as numeric, date-time, or character. The "character" data type is the most general, in that it can accept anything. At the row level, usually each row must have some uniquely identifying characteristic: this could be the value of one column, such as the employee number and department number in the examples just given, that cannot be repeated in different rows. There may also be rules that define links between the tables, such as a rule that every employee must be assigned a department code that can be matched to a row in the departments table. Following are examples of the tabulated data definitions.

Departments table:

Column Name	Description	Data Type	Length
DEPTNO	Department number	Numeric	2
DNAME	Department name	Character	14

Employees table:

Column Name	Description	Data Type	Length
EMPNO	Employee number	Numeric	4
ENAME	Employee name	Character	10
DEPTNO	Department number	Numeric	2

The tables could contain the rows shown next.

Departments:

DEPTNO	DNAME
10	ACCOUNTING
20	RESEARCH
30	SALES
40	OPERATIONS

Employees:

EMPNO	ENAME	DEPTNO
7369	SMITH	20
7499	ALLEN	30
7521	WARD	30
7566	JONES	20
7654	MARTIN	30
7698	BLAKE	30
7782	CLARK	10
7788	SCOTT	20

Looking at the tables, the two-dimensional structure is clear. Each row is of fixed length, each column is of fixed length (padded with spaces when necessary), and the rows are delimited with a new line. The rows have been stored in code order, but this would be a matter of chance, not design; relational tables do not impose any particular ordering on their rows. Department number 10 has one employee, and department number 40 has none. Changes to data are usually very efficient with the relational model. New employees can be appended to the employees table, or they can be moved from one department to another simply by changing the DEPTNO value in their row.

Consider an alternative structure, where the data is stored according to the hierarchical paradigm. The hierarchical model was developed before the relational model, for technology reasons. In the early days of computing, storage devices lacked the capability for maintaining the many separate files that were needed for the many relational tables. Note that this problem is avoided in the Oracle database by abstracting the physical storage (files) from the logical storage (tables); there is no direct connection between tables and files, and certainly not a one-to-one mapping. In effect, many tables can be stored in a very few files.

A hierarchical structure stores all related data in one unit. For example, the record for a department would include all that department's employees. The hierarchical paradigm can be very fast and very space efficient. One file access may be all that is needed to retrieve all the data needed to satisfy a query. The employees and departments listed previously could be stored hierarchically as follows:

10,ACCOUNTING,7782,CLARK
20,RESEARCH,7369,SMITH,7566,JONES,7788,SCOTT
30,SALES,7499,ALLEN,7521,WARD,7654,MARTIN,7698,BLAKE
40,OPERATIONS

In this example layout, the rows and columns are of variable length. Columns are delimited with a comma, rows with a new line. Data retrieval is typically very efficient if the query can navigate the hierarchy: if one knows an employee's department, the employee can be found quickly. If one doesn't, the retrieval may be slow. Changes to data can be a problem if the change necessitates movement. For example, to move employee 7566, JONES, from RESEARCH to SALES would involve considerable effort on the part of the database because the move has to be implemented as a removal from one line and an insertion into another. Note that in this example, while it is possible to have a department with no employees (the OPERATIONS department), it is absolutely impossible to have an employee without a department: there is nowhere to put her.

The relational paradigm is highly efficient in many respects for many types of data, but it is not appropriate for all applications. As a general rule, a relational analysis should be the first approach taken when modeling a system. Only if it proves inappropriate should one resort to non-relational structures. Applications where the relational model has proven highly effective include virtually all online transaction processing (OLTP) systems and decision support systems (DSSs). The relational paradigm can be demanding in its hardware requirements and in the skill needed to develop applications around it, but if the data fits, it has proved to be the most versatile model. The problems arise from the need to maintain indexes that give the versatility of access of maintain the links between tables, and the space requirements of maintaining multiple copies of the indexed data in the indexes themselves and in the tables in which the columns reside. Nonetheless, relational design is in most circumstances the optimal model.

A number of software publishers have produced database management systems that conform (with varying degrees of accuracy) to the relational paradigm; Oracle is only one. IBM was perhaps the first company to commit major resources to it, but its product (which later developed into DB2) was not ported to non-IBM platforms for many years. Microsoft's SQL Server is another relational database that has been limited by the platforms on which it runs. Oracle databases, by contrast, have always been ported to every major platform from the first release. It may be this that gave Oracle the edge in the RDBMS market place.

A note on terminology: confusion can arise when discussing relational databases with people used to working with Microsoft products. SQL is a language and SQL Server is a database—but in the Microsoft world, the term "SQL" is often used to refer to either.

Data Normalization

The process of modeling data into relational tables is known as normalization. There are commonly said to be three levels of normalization: the first, second, and third normal forms. There are higher levels of normalization: fourth and fifth normal forms are well defined, but any normal data analyst (and certainly any normal human being) will not need to be concerned with them. It is possible for a SQL application to address un-normalized data, but this will usually be dreadfully inefficient because that is not what the language is designed to do. In most cases, data stored in a relational database and accessed with SQL should be normalized to the third normal form.

As an example of normalization, consider a table called BOOKS storing details of books, authors, and publishers, using the ISBN number as the primary key. A *primary key* is the one attribute that can uniquely identify a record. These are two typical entries:

ISBN	Title	Authors	Publisher
12345	Oracle 11g SQL Fundamentals 1 Exam Guide	John Watson, Roopesh Ramklass	McGraw-Hill, Spear Street, San Francisco, CA
67890	Oracle 11g New Features Exam Guide	Sam Alapati	McGraw-Hill, Spear Street, San Francisco, CA

Storing the data in this table gives rise to several *anomalies*. First, here is the insertion anomaly: it is impossible to enter details of authors who are not yet published, because there will be no ISBN number under which to store them. Second, a book cannot be deleted without losing the details of the publisher: a deletion anomaly. Third, if a publisher's address changes, it will be necessary to update the rows for every book he/she has published: an update anomaly. Furthermore, it will be very difficult to identify every book written by one author. The fact that a book may have several authors means that the "author" field must be multivalued, and a search will have to search all the values. Related to this is the problem of having to restructure the table of a book comes along with more authors tan the original design can handle. Also, the storage is very inefficient due to replication of address details across rows, and the possibility of error as this data is repeatedly entered is high. Normalization should solve all these issues.

The first normal form is to remove the repeating groups. In this case, the multiple authors: pull them out into a separate table called AUTHORS. The data structures will now look like this:

BOOKS

ISBN	Title	Publisher
12345	Oracle 11g SQL Fundamentals 1 Exam Guide	McGraw-Hill, Spear Street, San Francisco, CA
67890	Oracle 11g New Features Exam Guide	McGraw-Hill, Spear Street, San Francisco, CA

AUTHORS

Name	ISBN
John Watson	12345
Roopesh Ramklass	12345
Sam Alapati	67890

One row in the BOOKS table is now linked to two rows in the AUTHORS table. This solves the insertion anomaly (there is no reason not to insert as many unpublished authors as necessary), the retrieval problem of identifying all the books by one author (one can search the AUTHORS table on her name), and the problem of a fixed maximum number of authors for any one book (simply insert as many or as few AUTHORS as are needed).

This is the first normal form: no repeating groups.

The second normal form removes columns from the table that are not dependent on the primary key. In this example, that is the publisher's address details: these depend on the publisher, not the ISBN. The BOOKS table and a new PUBLISHERS table will then look like this:

BOOKS

ISBN	Title	Publisher
12345	Oracle 11g OCP SQL Fundamentals 1 Exam Guide	McGraw-Hill
67890	Oracle 11g New Features Exam Guide	McGraw-Hill

PUBLISHERS

Publisher	Street	City	State
McGraw-Hill	Spear Street	San Francisco	California

All the books published by one publisher will now point to a single record in PUBLISHERS. This solves the problem of storing the address many times, and the consequent update anomalies and also the data consistency errors caused by inaccurate multiple entries.

Third normal form removes all columns that are interdependent. In the PUBLISHERS table, this means the address columns: the street exists in only one city, and the city can be in only one state; one column should do, not three. This could be achieved by adding an address code, pointing to a separate address table:

PUBLISHERS

Publisher	Address Code
McGraw-Hill	123

ADDRESSES

Address Code	Street	City	State
123	Spear Street	San Francisco	California

One characteristic of normalized data that should be emphasized now is the use of primary keys and foreign keys. A *primary key* is the unique identifier of a row in a table, either one column or a concatenation of several columns (known as a *composite* key). Every table should have a primary key defined.

Note that the Oracle database deviates from this standard: it is possible to define tables without a primary key—though this is usually not a good idea, and some other RDBMSs do not permit it.

A *foreign key* is a column (or a concatenation of several columns) that can be used to identify a related row in another table. A foreign key in one table will match a primary key in another table. This is the basis of the *many-to-one relationship*. A many-to-one relationship is a connection between two tables, where many rows in one table refer to a single row in another table. This is sometimes called a parent-child relationship: one parent can have many children. In the books example so far, the keys are as follows:

Table	Keys
BOOKS	Primary key: ISBN Foreign key: Publisher
AUTHORS	Primary key: Name + ISBN Foreign key: ISBN
PUBLISHERS	Primary key: Publisher Foreign key: Address code
ADDRESSES	Primary key: Address code

These keys define relationships such as that one book can have several authors.

There are various standards for documenting normalized data structures, developed by different organizations as structured formal methods. Generally speaking, it really doesn't matter which method one uses as long everyone reading the documents understands it. Part of the documentation will always include a listing of the attributes that make up each entity (also known as the columns that make up each table) and an entity-relationship diagram representing graphically the foreign-to-primary key connections. A widely used standard is that primary keys columns should be identified with a hash (#); foreign key columns with a backslash (\ ); mandatory columns (that cannot be left empty) with an asterisk (*); optional columns with a lowercase o. The books tables can now be described as follows:

Table BOOKS

#*	ISBN	Primary key, required
o	Title	Optional
*	Publisher	Foreign key, link to the PUBLISHERS table

Table AUTHORS

#*	Name	Together with the ISBN, the primary key
#\o	ISBN	Part of the primary key, and a foreign key to the BOOKS table Optional, because some authors may not yet be published

Table PUBLISHERS

#*	Publisher	Primary key
\o	Address code	foreign key, link to the ADDRESSES table

Table ADDRESSES

#*	Address code	Primary key
o	Street	
o	City	
o	State	

The second necessary part of documenting the normalized data model is the *entity-relationship diagram (ERD)*. This represents the connections between the tables graphically. There are different standards for these; Figure 1-1 shows the entity-relationship diagram for the books example using a very simple notation limited to showing the direction of the one-to-many relationships. It can be seen that one BOOK can have multiple AUTHORS, one PUBLISHER can publish many books, and so on. More complex notations can be used to show whether the link is required or optional, information which will match that given in the table columns listings previously.

This is a very simple example of normalization and is not in fact complete. If one author were to write several books, this would require multiple values in the ISBN column of the AUTHORS table. That would be a repeating group, which would have to be removed because repeating groups break the rule for first normal form. A major exercise with data normalization is ensuring that the structures can handle all possibilities. Tables in a real-world application may have hundreds of columns and dozens of foreign keys.

on the Job *Errors in relational analysis can be disastrous for an application. It is very difficult (and expensive) to correct any errors later. By contrast, errors made during the programming stage of development can usually be fixed comparatively quickly and cheaply.*

FIGURE 1-1 An entity-relationship diagram, showing basic one-to-many relationships

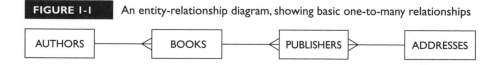

CERTIFICATION OBJECTIVE 1.03

Understand the SQL Language

SQL is defined, developed, and controlled by international bodies. Oracle Corporation does not have to conform to the SQL standard but chooses to do so. The language itself can be thought as being very simple (there are only sixteen commands), but in practice SQL coding can be phenomenally complicated.

What follow are the sixteen SQL commands, separated into commonly used groups. The Data Manipulation Language (DML) commands:

- SELECT
- INSERT
- UPDATE
- DELETE
- MERGE

The Data Definition Language (DDL) commands:

- CREATE
- ALTER
- DROP
- RENAME
- TRUNCATE
- COMMENT

The Data Control Language (DCL) commands:

- GRANT
- REVOKE

The Transaction Control Language (TCL) commands:

- COMMIT
- ROLLBACK
- SAVEPOINT

SQL is a *set-oriented language,* whereas most 3GLs are procedural languages. Programmers working in procedural languages specify what to do with data, one row at a time. Programmers working in a set-oriented language say what they want to do to a group (a *set*) of rows, and let the database work out how to do it to however many rows are in the set.

Procedural languages are usually less efficient than set-oriented languages at managing data, both as regards development and as regards execution. A procedural routine for looping through a group of rows and updating them one by one will involve many lines of code, whereas SQL might do the whole operation with one command: programmer productivity increases. During program execution, procedural code gives the database no options; it must run the code as it has been written. With SQL, the programmer states what he/she wants to do, but not how to do it: the database has the freedom to work out how best to carry out the operation. This will usually give better results.

Where SQL fails is that it is purely a data access language. Most applications will need procedural constructs, such as flow control: conditional branching and iteration. They will also usually need screen control, user interface facilities, and variables. SQL has none of these. SQL is a set-oriented language capable of nothing other than data access. For application development, one will therefore need a procedural language that can invoke SQL calls. It is therefore necessary for SQL to work with a procedural language.

Consider an application that prompts a user for a name, retrieves all the people with that name from a table, prompts the user to choose one of them, and then deletes the chosen person. The procedural language will draw a screen and generate a prompt for a name. The user will enter the name. The procedural language will construct a SQL SELECT statement using the name and submit the statement through a database session to the database server for execution. The server will return a set of rows (all the people with that name) to the procedural language, which will format the set for display to the user, and prompt her to choose one (or more) of them. The identifier for the chosen person (or people) will then be used to construct a SQL DELETE statement for the server to execute. If the identifier is a unique identifier (the primary key), then the set of rows to be deleted will be a set of just one row; if the identifier is nonunique, then the set selected for deletion would be larger. The procedural code will know nothing about the likely size of the sets retrieved or deleted, and the programmer will not know whether the row(s) to be deleted were located by scanning the entire table, or by direct access after searching an index.

CERTIFICATION OBJECTIVE 1.04

Appreciate the DBA's Role

"Database administrator" is often not a very precisely defined job. In many organizations, end users expect the DBA to be an expert on all aspects of the IT environment. If the database crashes, they call the DBA. Fair enough. But they may also call her if the network fails, if the servers crash, or if the application has a bug. Some DBAs believe that end users will call them if the plumbing gets blocked. Perhaps this is because virtually any failure in the IT environment results in end users being unable to use the database, so the DBA is the natural first point of contact.

Apart from these excessive expectations, the DBA is often the only person in the IT management structure who has a holistic view of the environment. Oracle Enterprise Manager Grid Control is a tool specifically intended to aid the DBA with this: it presents a complete picture of the performance and availability of all the databases, application servers, and server machines in the organization. A vital part of the DBA's job is to identify where in a complex information technology environment a failure or a performance issue has occurred, and work with the appropriate support group to fix it. Duties more specifically related to database administration include

- **Sizing applications and server hardware** Accurate forecasts of the necessary main memory, disk space, and CPUs that are needed to ensure that applications will run well without demanding unnecessary resources are an important part of maintaining performance without using excessive budget.

- **Oracle software installation and maintenance** This is a non-trivial task in organizations with many servers. Software installations must be kept up-to-date with critical patches (for security, for instance), and maintenance patches should be applied as they are issued, but before any such update is done to live systems, the DBA must ensure that it is adequately tested.

- **Database physical design** There will usually be many ways to configure the physical storage of a database, some of which may have a large impact on the performance of the system and its manageability. The DBA must also be aware of the impact of different storage structures on devices such as disc and tape systems.

- **Monitoring and tuning performance** This is a continuous activity for production systems. A good DBA will be able to anticipate performance issues and fix them before they arise.

■ **Assisting developers with application design and tuning SQL**   Some DBAs spend eight hours a day tuning SQL. Perhaps this should be the work of the programmers, but at the very least the DBA must identify the problem areas they should be addressing.

■ **Liaising with vendors, end users, developers, senior management, and other support groups**   As the technician with the most complete picture of the environment, the DBA must take a leading role in coordinating planning and action by all parties involved in the IT environment.

■ **Backup, restore, and recovery**   Perhaps the most important part of the job. The DBA must establish routines that will ensure that agreed targets for uptime and data loss (perhaps as demanding as 100 percent and zero respectively) can be met in the face of any possible problem. There is no right or wrong here, only conformance (or lack thereof) to the agreed targets.

■ **User and security management**   Another critical part of the job. As with uptime and data loss, there is no right and wrong in security—only conformance with agreed standards. The DBA must set up procedures that will ensure conformance, and monitor their effectiveness.

Some DBAs believe that they are doing their job perfectly if no one knows they are there. There is a certain amount of truth in this. Database administration is to a large extent support work, and if the work is done well enough with sufficient proactive planning and preventive maintenance, there will never be a reason for users to report a problem. Usually this ideal can't be reached, and a large amount of time will be spent working reactively with different people in different groups to solve issues.

The wide scope of the DBA role requires continual study and personal development, study of the Oracle database itself and also of related technologies. It also requires the inclination to educate and to spread knowledge. This can be the most rewarding part of the job.

CERTIFICATION SUMMARY

This chapter summarized some of the knowledge that is assumed before beginning to study for the OCP examinations: the position of the Oracle database in the Oracle product family, the principles of relational databases and data normalization, the SQL language, and other application development tools. Finally, it considers the DBA's role in the IT environment. A very extensive role indeed.

✓ TWO-MINUTE DRILL

Position the Oracle Product Family

- ❑ The Oracle database stores and manages access to user data.
- ❑ The Oracle Application Server runs applications that connect users to the database.
- ❑ Oracle Enterprise Manager is a tool for managing databases, application servers, and if desired, the entire computing environment.
- ❑ Languages built into the database for application development are SQL, PL/SQL, and Java.

Explain Relational Structures

- ❑ Data must be normalized into two-dimensional tables.
- ❑ Tables are linked through primary and foreign keys.
- ❑ Entity-relationship diagrams represent the tables graphically.

Understand the SQL Language

- ❑ SQL is a set-oriented language.
- ❑ The DML commands are SELECT, INSERT, UPDATE, DELETE, and MERGE.
- ❑ The DDL commands are CREATE, ALTER, DROP, RENAME, TRUNCATE, and COMMENT.
- ❑ The DCL commands are GRANT and REVOKE.
- ❑ The TCL commands are COMMIT, ROLLBACK, and SAVEPOINT.

Appreciate the DBA's Role

- ❑ Sizing applications and server hardware.
- ❑ Oracle software installation and maintenance.
- ❑ Database physical design.
- ❑ Monitoring and tuning performance.
- ❑ Assisting developers with application design and tuning SQL.
- ❑ Liaising with vendors, end users, developers, senior management, and other support groups.
- ❑ Backup, restore, and recovery.
- ❑ User and security management.

SELF TEST

Position the Oracle Product Family

1. Which of these languages can run within the database? (Choose all correct answers.)
   A. C
   B. Java
   C. PL/SQL
   D. SQL
   E. Any other language, if it is linked with the OCI libraries

2. In a web application, on which tier does the application software run? (Choose the best answer.)
   A. In the web browser on the client tier
   B. On the middle tier
   C. Within a Java-enabled database

Explain Relational Structures

3. For what data storage paradigm must data be normalized? (Choose the best answer.)
   A. Hierarchical databases
   B. Network databases
   C. Object-oriented databases
   D. Relational databases

4. What type of relationship should be avoided when normalizing data? (Choose the best answer.)
   A. One-to-many
   B. Many-to-one
   C. Many-to-many
   D. One-to-one

Understand the SQL Language

5. SQL cannot do everything. What functions require another language? (Choose all correct answers.)
   A. User interface design
   B. Branching structures such as IF...THEN...ELSE
   C. Operations that affect many rows at once
   D. Table creation and deletion

6. Which of these is not a SQL command? (Choose the best answer.)

   A. MERGE

   B. UPSERT

   C. COMMENT

   D. SAVEPOINT

   E. All the above are SQL commands

Appreciate the DBA's Role

7. With regard to ensuring that data will not be lost and that security will not be compromised, what would not normally be part of the DBA's duties? (Choose the best answers.)

   A. Designing backup routines

   B. Setting up disk mirroring

   C. Creating and dropping database objects

   D. Testing restore and recovery strategies

LAB QUESTION

A novice DBA needs a system on which to study the Oracle database, and to practice the skills needed to reach the OCA level of competence. Ideally, he/she will have

- A machine with a graphics monitor, 1 GB RAM, and 5 GB free disk space

- The Database 11g installation software, on DVD or downloaded

- The SQL Developer software

- An IP address: either fixed, DHCP, or loopback

- An operating system such as Windows XP or Linux

- Access to the Oracle database documentation

- If permitted, an account on Metalink

Assemble these items.

SELF TEST ANSWERS

Position the Oracle Product Family

1. ☑ **B, C,** and **D.** SQL, PL/SQL, and Java are implemented internally to the database.
   ☒ **A** is wrong because C is not available internally (though with OCI, it can of course be used for writing user processes). **E** is wrong because OCI is used for writing user processes that run externally to the database.

2. ☑ **B.** In a three-tier web application, the application software resides on the middle tier.
   ☒ **A** is wrong because the client tier manages only the user interface. **C** is wrong because the database tier manages only the data access.

Explain Relational Structures

3. ☑ **D.** Normalization is the process of converting data to two-dimensional relational tables.
   ☒ **A, B,** and **C.** Hierarchical, network, and object-oriented databases do not implement normalized data structures.

4. ☑ **C.** Many-to-many relationships should be resolved into one-to-many relationships, by inserting another entity between the two.
   ☒ **A, B,** and **D.** These are all acceptable in the third normal form model.

Understand the SQL Language

5. ☑ **A** and **B.** SQL has no facilities for user interface design or for flow control.
   ☒ **C** is wrong because operations such as this are inherent in SQL's set orientation. **D** is wrong because DDL commands are a part of SQL.

6. ☑ **B.** The UPSERT command does not exist—though some developers refer to a MERGE operation as an UPSERT
   ☒ **A, C, D,** and **E.** MERGE, COMMENT, and SAVEPOINT are all SQL commands.

Appreciate the DBA's Role

7. ☑ **B.** Disk administration is usually the responsibility of the system administrators, not the database administrator.
   ☒ **A, C,** and **D.** These are typically all part of the DBA's work.

LAB ANSWER

Having assembled the necessary items, you are ready to proceed with your studies. Enjoy.

2
Exploring the Database Architecture

An Oracle server consists of two entities: the instance and the database. The instance is memory structures and processes; the database is files on disk. They are separate, but connected. During the creation process (detailed in Chapter 4), the instance is created first, and then the database during the startup process (detailed in Chapter 5) first the instance is started, and then the database is opened. In a typical single-instance environment, the relationship of instance to database is one-to-one, a single instance connected to a single database, but always bear in mind that there are more complex possibilities for distributed environments.

Within the Oracle server, there is complete abstraction of logical storage from physical storage. The logical structures programmers see (such as tables) are not directly related to the physical structures (datafiles) that system administrators see. The relationship between the two is maintained by structures within the controlfile and the data dictionary.

Note that the exercises and the concluding lab question in this chapter require a running database. If you already have a database on which to carry out exercises, then please do them. If not, they will have to wait until the database has been created (Chapter 4).

CERTIFICATION OBJECTIVE 2.01

Describe the Single-Instance Architecture

For the most part in this book, you will be dealing with the most common database environment: one instance on one computer, opening a database stored on local disks. The more complex distributed architectures, involving multiple instances and multiple databases, are beyond the scope of the OCP examination (though not the OCM qualification), but you may realistically expect to see high-level summary questions on distributed architecture.

Single-Instance Database Architecture

The instance consists of memory structures and processes. Its existence is transient, in your RAM and on your CPU(s). When you shut down the running instance, all trace of its existence goes away at the same time. The database consists of physical files on disk. Whether running or stopped, these remain. Thus the lifetime of the instance is only as long as it exists in memory: it can be started and stopped. By contrast, the database, once created, persists indefinitely—until you deliberately delete the files that are associated with the database.

The processes that make up the instance are known as *background* processes, because they are present and running at all times while the instance is active. These processes are for the most part completely self-administering, though in some cases it is possible for the DBA to influence the number of them and their operation.

The memory structures, which are implemented in shared memory segments provided by the operating system, are known as the *system global area*, or SGA. This is allocated at instance startup and released on shutdown. Within certain limits, the SGA in the 11g instance and the components within it can be resized while the instance is running, either automatically or in response the DBA's instructions.

User sessions consist of a user process running locally to the user machine connecting to a server process running locally to the instance on the server machine. The technique for launching the server processes, which are started on demand for each session, is covered in Chapter 6. The connection between user process and server process is usually across a local area network and uses Oracle's proprietary Oracle Net protocol layered on top of an industry-standard protocol (usually TCP). The user process-to-server process split implements the client-server architecture: user processes generate SQL, server processes execute SQL. The server processes are sometimes referred to *foreground* processes, in contrast with the background processes that make up the instance. Associated with each server process is an area of non-shareable memory, called the *program global area*, or PGA. This is private to the session, unlike the system global area, which is available to all the foreground and background processes. Note that background processes also have a PGA. The size of any one session's PGA will vary according to the memory needs of the session at any one time; the DBA can define an upper limit for the total of all the PGAs, and Oracle manages the allocation of this to sessions dynamically.

on the
ⓘob

You will sometimes hear the term shadow process. *Be cautious of using this. Some people use it to refer to foreground processes, others use it for background processes. Never mind which is correct—just make sure you know what they are talking about.*

Memory management in 11g can be totally automatic: the DBA need do nothing more than specify an overall memory allocation for both the SGA and the PGA and let Oracle manage this memory as it thinks best. Alternatively, the DBA can control memory allocations himself. There is an in-between technique, where the DBA defines certain limits on what the automatic management can do.

The physical structures that make up an Oracle database are the datafiles, the redo log, and the controlfile. Within the physical structures of the database, which our system administrators see, are the logical structures that our end users (developers, business analysts, data warehouse architects, and so on) see. The Oracle architecture guarantees abstraction of the logical from the physical: there is no way that a programmer can determine where, physically, a bit of data is located. He/she addresses only logical structures, such as tables. Similarly, it is impossible for a system administrator to know what bits of data are in any physical structure: all he/she can see is the operating system files, not what is within them. It is only you, the database administrator, who is permitted (and required) to see both sides of the story.

The abstraction of logical storage from physical storage is part of the RDBMS standard. If it were possible for a programmer to determine the physical location of a row, then successful execution of the code would be totally dependent on the one environment for which it was written. Any change of platform, movement of datafiles, or even renaming a file would break the application. It is in fact possible to determine where a table (and even one row within a table) actually is, but not through SQL. The language does not permit it. There are tools supplied for the database administrator's use for doing this, should it ever be necessary.

Data is stored in datafiles. There is no practical limit to the number or size of datafiles, and the abstraction of logical storage from physical storage means that datafiles can be moved or resized and more datafiles can be added without the application developers being aware of this. The relationship between physical and logical structures is maintained and documented in the data dictionary, which contains metadata describing the whole database. By querying certain views in the data dictionary, the DBA can determine precisely where every part of every table is.

The data dictionary is a set of tables stored within the database. There is a recursive problem here: the instance needs to be aware of the physical and logical structure of the database, but the information describing this is itself within the database. The solution to this problem lies in the staged startup process, which is detailed in Chapter 5.

A requirement of the RDBMS standard is that the database must not lose data. This means that it must be backed up, and furthermore that any changes made to data between backups must be captured in such a manner that they can be applied to a restored backup. This is the forward recovery process. Oracle implements the capture of changes through the *redo log*. The redo log is a sequential record of all *change vectors* applied to data. A change vector is the alteration made by a DML (Data Manipulation Language: INSERT, UPDATE, or DELETE) statement. Whenever a user session makes any changes, the data itself in the data block is changed, and the change vector is written out sideways to the redo log, in a form that makes it repeatable. Then in the event of damage to a datafile, a backup of the file can be restored and Oracle will extract the relevant change vectors from the redo log and apply them to the data blocks within the file. This ensures that work will never be lost—unless the damage to the database is so extensive as to lose not only one or more datafiles, but also either their backups or the redo log.

The controlfile stores the details of the physical structures of the database and is the starting point for the link to the logical structures. When an instance opens a database, it does so by first reading the controlfile. Within the controlfile is information the instance can then use to connect to the rest of the database, and the data dictionary within it.

The architecture of a single-instance database can be summarized as consisting of four interacting components:

- A user interacts with a user process.
- A user process interacts with a server process.
- A server process interacts with an instance.
- An instance interacts with a database.

Figure 2-1 represents this graphically.

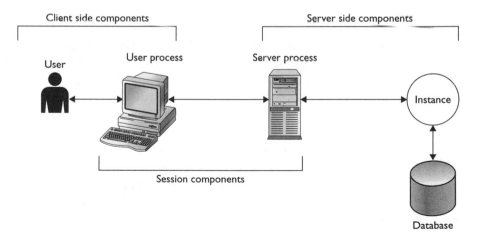

FIGURE 2-1

The indirect connection between a user and a database

It is absolutely impossible for any client-side process to have any contact with the database: all access must be mediated by server-side processes. The client-server split is between the user process (which generates SQL) and the server process (which executes it).

Distributed Systems Architectures

In the single-instance environment, one instance opens one database. In a distributed environment, there are various possibilities for grouping instances and databases. Principally:

- Real Application Clusters (RAC), where multiple instances open one database
- Streams, where multiple Oracle servers propagate transactions between each other
- Data guard, where a primary database updates a standby database

Combinations of these options can (according to the marketing) result in a system that can achieve the goals of one hundred percent uptime and zero percent data loss, with limitless scalability and performance.

Real Application Clusters (RAC)

RAC gives amazing capabilities for performance, fault tolerance, and scalability (and possibly cost savings) and is integral to the Oracle's concept of the Grid. With previous releases, RAC (or its precursor, Oracle Parallel Server) was an expensive add-on option, but from database release 10g onward, RAC is bundled with the standard edition license. This is an indication of how much Oracle Corporation wants to push users toward the RAC environment. Standard edition RAC is limited to a certain number of computers and a certain number of CPUs and cores per computer, but even within these limitations it gives access to a phenomenally powerful environment. RAC is an extra-cost option for the enterprise edition, where the scalability becomes effectively limitless: bounded only by the clustering capacity of the underlying operating system and hardware.

An RAC database can be configured for 100 percent uptime. One instance can be brought down (either for planned maintenance, or perhaps because the computer on which it is running crashes) and the database will remain accessible through a surviving instance on another machine. Sessions against the failed instance can be reestablished against a surviving instance without the end user being aware of any disruption.

Transparent scalability comes from the ability to add instances, running on different machines, to an RAC dynamically. They will automatically take on some of the workload without users needing to be aware of the fact that now more instances are available.

Some applications will have a performance benefit from running on an RAC. But not all. Parallel processing can improve the performance of some work, such as long-running queries and large batch updates. In a single-instance database, assigning multiple parallel execution servers to such jobs will help—but they will all be running in one instance on one machine. In an RAC database, the parallel execution servers can run on different instances, which may get around some of the bottlenecks inherent in single-instance architecture. Other work, such as processing the large number of small transactions typically found in an OLTP (online transaction processing) system, will not get a performance benefit.

on the **job** *Don't convert to RAC just because you can. You need to be certain of what you want to achieve before embarking on what is a major exercise that is usually not necessary.*

Streams

There are various circumstances that make it desirable to transfer data from one database to another. Fault tolerance is one: if an organization has two (or more) geographically separated databases, both containing identical data and both available at all times for users to work on, then no matter what goes wrong at one site, work should be able to continue uninterrupted at the other. Another reason is tuning: the two databases can be configured for different types of work, such as a transaction processing database and a data warehouse.

Keeping the databases synchronized will have to be completely automatic, and all changes made at either site will need to be propagated in real or near-real time to the other site. Another reason could be maintenance of a data warehouse. Data sets maintained by an OLTP database will need to be propagated to the warehouse database, and subsequently these copies will need to periodically refreshed with changes. The data might then be pushed further out, perhaps to a series of data marts each with a subset of the warehouse. Streams is a facility for capturing changes made to tables and applying them to remote copies of the tables that can fill both these requirements.

Streams can be bidirectional: identical tables at two or more sites, with all user transactions executed at each site broadcast to and applied at the other sites. This is the streaming model needed for fault tolerance. An alternative model is used in the data warehouse example, where data sets (and ensuing changes made to them) are extracted from tables in one database and pushed out to tables in another database.

In this model, the flow of information is more likely to be unidirectional, and the table structures may well not be identical at the downstream sites.

Streams can also be used for fault tolerance. It is not uncommon to stream an entire database between multiple instances, with end users working on both sides of the stream. Streams will propagate changes between them, bidirectionally, to keep the two databases synchronized. If one database server fails, work can continue against the surviving database server. When the failed server is brought back online, it will be brought up to date with all the changes done against its partner while it was unavailable.

It is also possible for a session against one instance, through database links, to connect to multiple databases programmatically. Programmers can write code that allows a session against one server to read and update data on another through a database link; there is a fully automated two-phase commit mechanism to ensure transactional consistency in these circumstances.

Data Guard

Data guard systems have one primary database against which transactions are executed, and one or more standby databases used for fault tolerance or for query processing. The standbys are instantiated from a backup of the primary, and updated (possibly in real time) with all changes applied to the primary.

Standbys come in two forms. A *physical* standby is byte-for-byte identical with the primary, for the purpose of zero data loss. Even if the primary is totally destroyed, all data will be available on the standby. The change vectors applied to the primary are propagated to the physical standby in the form of redo records, and applied as though a restored backup database were being recovered. A *logical* standby contains the same data as the primary, but possibly with different data structures. This is for query processing: the primary database will have data structures optimized for transaction processing; the logical standby will have structures optimized for data warehouse type work. Typical differences would be in the indexing. Change vectors are propagated in the form of SQL statements, using the Streams mechanism.

EXERCISE 2-1

Determine if the Database Is Single Instance or Part of a Distributed System

In this exercise, you will run queries to determine whether the database is a self-contained system, or if it is part of a larger distributed environment. Either SQL Developer or SQL*Plus may be used.

1. Connect to the database as user SYSTEM.
2. Determine if the instance is part of an RAC database:

   ```
   select parallel from v$instance;
   ```

   This will return NO if it is a single-instance database.
3. Determine if the database is protected against data loss by a standby database:

   ```
   select protection_level from v$database;
   ```

   This will return UNPROTECTED if the database is indeed unprotected.
4. Determine if Streams has been configured in the database:

   ```
   select * from dba_streams_administrator;
   ```

   This will return no rows, if Streams has never been configured.

CERTIFICATION OBJECTIVE 2.02

Explain the Memory Structures

An Oracle instance consists of a block of shared memory known as the system global area, or SGA, and a number of background processes. At a minimum, the SGA will contain three data structures:

- The database buffer cache
- The log buffer
- The shared pool

It may, optionally, also contain

- A large pool
- A Java pool
- A Streams pool

User sessions also need memory on the server side. This is nonshareable and is known as the program global area, or PGA. Each session will have its own private PGA.

Managing the size of these structures can be largely automatic, or the DBA can control the sizing himself. It is generally good practice to use the automatic management.

The Database Buffer Cache

The database buffer cache is Oracle's work area for executing SQL. When updating data, users' sessions don't directly update the data on disk. The data blocks containing the data of interest are first copied into the database buffer cache. Changes (such inserting new rows and deleting or modifying existing rows) are applied to these copies of the data blocks in the database buffer cache. The blocks will remain in the cache for some time afterward, until the buffer they are occupying is needed for caching another block.

When querying data, the data also goes via the cache. The session works out which blocks contain the rows of interest and copies them into the database buffer cache; the relevant rows are then transferred into the session's PGA for further processing. And again, the blocks remain in the database buffer cache for some time afterward.

Take note of the term *block*. Datafiles are formatted into fixed-sized blocks. Table rows, and other data objects such as index keys, are stored in these blocks. The database buffer cache is formatted into memory buffers each sized to hold one block. Unlike blocks, rows are of variable length; the length of a row will depend on the number of columns defined for the table, whether the columns actually have anything in them, and if so, what. Depending on the size of the blocks (which is chosen by the DBA) and the size of the rows (which is dependent on the table design and usage), there may be several rows per block or possibly a row may stretch over several blocks. The structure of a data block will be described in the section "The Datafiles" later in this chapter.

Ideally, all the blocks containing data that is frequently accessed will be in the database buffer cache, therefore minimizing the need for disk I/O. As a typical use of the database buffer cache, consider an end user retrieving an employee record and updating it, with these statements:

```
select last_name, salary, job_id from employees where employee_id=100;
update employees set salary=salary * 1.1 where employee_id=100;
commit;
```

The user process will have prompted the user for the employee number and constructed the SELECT statement. The SELECT retrieves some details to be sent to the user process, where they will be formatted for display. To execute this statement, the session's server process will read the data block containing the relevant row from a datafile into a buffer. The user process will then initiate a screen dialogue to prompt for some change to be made and verified; then the UPDATE statement and the COMMIT statement will be constructed and sent to the server process for execution. Provided that an excessive period of time has not elapsed, the block with the row will still be available in the cache when the UPDATE statement is executed. In this example, the buffer cache hit ratio will be 50 percent: two accesses of a block in the cache, but only one read of the block from disk. A well-tuned database buffer cache can result in a cache hit ratio well over 90 percent.

A buffer storing a block whose image in the cache is not the same as the image on disk is often referred to as a *dirty* buffer. A buffer will be *clean* when a block is first copied into it: at that point, the block image in the buffer is the same as the block image on disk. The buffer will become dirty when the block in it is updated. Eventually, dirty buffers must be written back to the datafiles, at which point the buffer will be clean again. Even after being written to disk, the block remains in memory; it is possible that the buffer will not be overwritten with another block for some time.

Note that there is no correlation between the frequency of updates to a buffer (or the number of COMMITs) and when it gets written back to the datafiles. The write to the datafiles is done by the database writer background process.

The size of the database buffer cache is critical for performance. The cache should be sized adequately for caching all the frequently accessed blocks (whether clean or dirty), but not so large that it caches blocks that are rarely needed. An undersized cache will result in excessive disk activity, as frequently accessed blocks are continually read from disk, used, overwritten by other blocks, and then read from disk again. An oversized cache is not so bad (so long as it is not so large that the operating system is having to swap pages of virtual memory in and out of real memory) but can cause problems; for example, startup of an instance is slower if it involves formatting a massive database buffer cache.

on the job

Determining the optimal size of the database buffer cache is application specific and a matter of performance tuning. It is impossible to give anything but the vaguest guidelines without making observations, but it is probably true to say that the majority of databases will operate well with a cache sized in hundreds of megabytes up to a few gigabytes. Very few applications will perform well with a cache smaller than this, and not many will need a cache of hundreds of gigabytes.

e x a m

w a t c h   *The size of the database buffer cache can be adjusted dynamically, and can be automatically managed.*

The database buffer cache is allocated at instance startup time. Prior to release 9*i* of the database it was not possible to resize the database buffer cache subsequently without restarting the database instance, but from 9*i* onward it can be resized up or down at any time. This resizing can be either manual, or (from release 10g onward) automatic according to workload, if the automatic mechanism has been enabled.

The Log Buffer

The log buffer is a small, short-term staging area for change vectors before they are written to the redo log on disk. A *change vector* is a modification applied to something; executing DML statements generates change vectors applied to data. The redo log is the database's guarantee that data will never be lost: whenever a data block is changed, the change vectors applied to the block are written out to the redo log, from where they can be extracted and applied to datafile backups if it is ever necessary to restore a datafile.

Redo is not written directly to the redo log files by session server processes. If it were, the sessions would have to wait for disk I/O operations to complete whenever they executed a DML statement. Instead, sessions write redo to the log buffer, in memory. This is much faster than writing to disk. The log buffer (which may contain change vectors from many sessions, interleaved with each other) is then written out to the redo log files. One write of the log buffer to disk may therefore be a batch of many change vectors from many transactions. Even so, the change vectors in the log buffer are written to disk in very nearly real time—and when a session issues a COMMIT statement, the log buffer write really does happen in real time. The writes are done by the log writer background process, the LGWR.

The log buffer is small (in comparison with other memory structures) because it is a very short-term storage area. Change vectors are inserted into it and are streamed to disk in near real time. There is no need for it to be more than a few megabytes at the most, and indeed making it much bigger than the default value can be seriously bad for performance. The default is determined by the Oracle server and is based on the number of CPUs on the server node.

It is not possible to create a log buffer smaller than the default. If you attempt to, it will be set to the default size anyway. It is possible to create a log buffer larger than the default, but this is often not a good idea. The problem is that when a COMMIT statement is issued, part of the commit processing involves writing the contents of the log buffer to the redo log files on disk. This write occurs in real time, and while it is in progress, the session that issued the COMMIT will hang. Commit processing is a critical part of the Oracle architecture. The guarantee that a committed transaction will never be lost is based on this: the commit-complete message is not returned to the session until the data blocks in the cache have been changed (which means that the transaction has been completed) and the change vectors have been written to the redo log on disk (and therefore the transaction could be recovered if necessary). A large log buffer means that potentially there is more to write when a COMMIT is issued, and therefore it may take a longer time before the commit-complete message can be sent, and the session can resume work.

on the **Job** *Raising the log buffer size above the default may be necessary for some applications, but as a rule start tuning with the log buffer on default.*

The log buffer is allocated at instance startup, and it can never be resized subsequently without restarting the instance. It is a circular buffer. As server processes write change vectors to it, the current write address moves around. The log writer process writes the vectors out in batches, and as it does so, the space they occupied becomes available and can be overwritten by more change vectors. It is possible that at times of peak activity, change vectors will be generated faster than the log writer process can write them out. If this happens, all DML activity will cease (for a few milliseconds) while the log writer clears the buffer.

The process of flushing the log buffer to disk is one of the ultimate bottlenecks in the Oracle architecture. You cannot do DML faster than the LGWR can flush the change vectors to the online redo log files.

on the **Job** *If redo generation is the limiting factor in a database's performance, the only option is to go to RAC. In a RAC database, each instance has its own log buffer, and its own LGWR. This is the only way to parallelize writing redo data to disk.*

The Shared Pool

The shared pool is the most complex of the SGA structures. It is divided into dozens of substructures, all of which are managed internally by the

Oracle server. This discussion of architecture will only mention four of the shared pool components, and these only briefly:

- The library cache
- The data dictionary cache
- The PL/SQL area
- The SQL query and PL/SQL function result caches

Some other structures will be described in later chapters. All the structures within the shared pool are automatically managed. Their size will very according to the pattern of activity against the instance, within the overall size of the shared pool. The shared pool itself can be resized dynamically, either in response to the DBA's instructions or through being managed automatically.

The Library Cache

The library cache is a memory area for storing recently executed code, in its parsed form. Parsing is the conversion of code written by programmers into something executable, and it is a process which Oracle does on demand. By caching parsed code in the shared pool so that it can be reused without reparsing, performance can be greatly improved. Parsing SQL code takes time. Consider a simple SQL statement:

```
select * from employees where last_name='KING';
```

Before this statement can be executed, the Oracle server has to work out what it means, and how to execute it. To begin with, what is employees? Is it a table, a synonym, or a view? Does it even exist? Then the "*"—what are the columns that make up the employees table (if it is a table)? Does the user have permission to see the table? Answers to these questions and many others have to be found by querying the data dictionary.

on the job

The algorithm used to find SQL in the library cache is based on the ASCII values of the characters that make up the statement. The slightest difference (even something as trivial as SELECT instead of select) means that the statement will not match but will be parsed again.

Having worked out what the statement actually means, the server has to decide out how best to execute it. Is there an index on the last_name column? If so, would it be quicker to use the index to locate the row, or to scan the whole table? More queries against the data dictionary . . . It is quite possible for a simple one-line query against a user table to generate dozens of queries against the data dictionary, and for the parsing of a statement to take many times longer than eventually executing it. The purpose of the library cache of the shared pool is to store statements in their parsed form, ready for execution. The first time a statement is issued, it has to be parsed before execution—the second time, it can be executed immediately. In a well-designed application, it is possible that statements may be parsed once and executed millions of times. This saves a huge amount of time.

The Data Dictionary Cache

The data dictionary cache is sometimes referred to as the row cache. Whichever term you prefer, it stores recently used object definitions: descriptions of tables, indexes, users, and other metadata definitions. Keeping such definitions in memory in the SGA, where they are immediately accessible to all sessions, rather than each session having to read them repeatedly from the data dictionary on disk, enhances parsing performance.

The data dictionary cache stores object definitions so that when statements do have to be parsed, they can be parsed fast—without having to query the data dictionary. Consider what happens if these statements are issued consecutively:

```
select sum(salary) from employees;
select * from employees where last_name='KING';
```

Both statements must be parsed because they are different statements—but parsing the first SELECT statement will have loaded the definition of the employees table and its columns into the data dictionary cache, so parsing the second statement will be faster than it would otherwise have been, because no data dictionary access will be needed.

on the
Job

Shared pool tuning is usually oriented toward making sure that the library cache is the right size. This is because the algorithms Oracle uses to allocate memory in the SGA are designed to favor the dictionary cache, so if the library cache is correct, then the dictionary cache will already be correct.

The PL/SQL Area

Stored PL/SQL objects are procedures, functions, packaged procedures and functions, object type definitions, and triggers. These are all stored in the data dictionary, as source code and also in their compiled form. When a stored PL/SQL object is invoked by a session, it must be read from the data dictionary. To prevent repeated reading, the objects are then cached in the PL/SQL area of the shared pool.

The first time a PL/SQL object is used, it must be read from the data dictionary tables on disk, but subsequent invocations will be much faster, because the object will already be available in the PL/SQL area of the shared pool.

on the
Job

PL/SQL can be issued from user processes, rather than being stored in the data dictionary. This is called anonymous ***PL/SQL. Anonymous PL/SQL cannot be cached and reused but must compiled dynamically. It will therefore always perform worse than stored PL/SQL. Developers should be encouraged to convert all anonymous PL/SQL into stored PL/SQL.***

The SQL Query and PL/SQL Function Result Cache

The result cache is a release 11*g* new feature. In many applications, the same query is executed many times, by either the same session or many different sessions. Creating a result cache lets the Oracle server store the results of such queries in memory. The next time the query is issued, rather than running the query the server can retrieve the cached result.

The result cache mechanism is intelligent enough to track whether the tables against which the query was run have been updated. If this has happened, the query results will be invalidated and the next time the query is issued, it will be rerun. There is therefore no danger of ever receiving an out-of-date cached result.

The PL/SQL result cache uses a similar mechanism. When a PL/SQL function is executed, its return value can be cached ready for the next time the function is executed. If the parameters passed to the function, or the tables that the function queries, are different, the function will be reevaluated, but otherwise, the cached value will be returned.

By default, use of the SQL query and PL/SQL function result cache is disabled, but if enabled programmatically, it can often dramatically improve performance. The cache is within the shared pool: unlike the other memory areas described previously, it does afford the DBA some control: he/she can specify a maximum size.

Sizing the Shared Pool

Sizing the shared pool is critical for performance. It should be large enough to cache all the frequently executed code and frequently needed object definitions (in the library cache and the data dictionary cache) but not so large that it caches statements that have only been executed once. An undersized shared pool cripples performance because server sessions have repeatedly to grab space in it for parsing statements, which are then overwritten by other statements and therefore have to be parsed again when they are reexecuted. An oversized shared pool can impact badly on performance because it takes too long to search it. If the shared pool is less than the optimal size, performance will degrade. But there is a minimum size below which statements will fail.

Memory in the shared pool is allocated according to an LRU (least recently used) algorithm. When the Oracle server needs space in the shared pool, it will overwrite the object that has not been used for the longest time. If the object is later needed again, it will have to be reloaded—possibly overwriting another object.

on the
Job

Determining the optimal size is a matter for performance tuning, but it is probably safe to say that most databases will need a shared pool of several hundred megabytes. Some applications will need one of more than a gigabyte, and very few will perform adequately with less than a hundred megabytes.

exam
Watch *The shared pool size is dynamic and can be automatically managed.*

The shared pool is allocated at instance startup time. Prior to release 9*i* of the database it was not possible to resize the shared pool subsequently without restarting the database instance, but from 9*i* onward it can be resized up or down at any time. This resizing can be either manual or (from release 10g onward) automatic according to workload, if the automatic mechanism has been enabled.

The Large Pool

The large pool is an optional area that, if created, will be used automatically by various processes that would otherwise take memory from the shared pool. One major use of the large pool is by shared server processes, described in Chapter 6 in the discussion of the shared (or multithreaded) server. Parallel execution servers will also use the large pool, if there is one. In the absence of a large pool, these processes will use memory on the shared pool. This can cause bad contention for the shared pool: if shared servers or parallel servers are being used, a large pool should always be created. Some I/O processes may also make use of the large pool, such as the processes used by the Recovery Manager when it is backing up to a tape device.

Sizing the large pool is not a matter for performance. If a process needs large pool of memory, it will fail with an error if that memory is not available. Allocating more memory than is needed will not make statements run faster. Furthermore, if a large pool exists, it will be used: it is not possible for a statement to start off by using the large pool, and then revert to the shared pool if the large pool is too small.

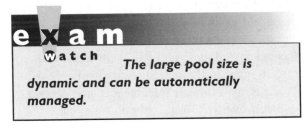

The large pool size is dynamic and can be automatically managed.

From 9i release 2 onward it is possible to create and to resize a large pool after instance startup. With earlier releases, it had to be defined at startup and was a fixed size. From release 10g onward, creation and sizing of the large pool can be completely automatic.

The Java Pool

The Java pool is only required if your application is going to run Java-stored procedures within the database: it is used for the heap space needed to instantiate the Java objects. However, a number of Oracle options are written in Java, so the Java pool is considered standard nowadays. Note that Java code is not cached in the Java pool: it is cached in the shared pool, in the same way that PL/SQL code is cached.

The optimal size of the Java pool is dependent on the Java application, and how many sessions are running it. Each session will require heap space for its objects. If the Java pool is undersized, performance may degrade due to the need to continually reclaim space. In an EJB (Enterprise JavaBean) application, an object such as a stateless session bean may be instantiated and used, and then remain in memory in case it is needed again: such an object can be reused immediately. But if the Oracle server has had to destroy the bean to make room for another, then it will have to be reinstantiated next time it is needed. If the Java pool is chronically undersized, then the applications may simply fail.

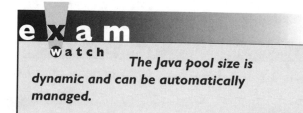

From 10*g* onward it is possible to create and to resize a large pool after instance startup; this creation and sizing of the large pool can be completely automatic. With earlier releases, it had to be defined at startup and was a fixed size.

The Java pool size is dynamic and can be automatically managed.

The Streams Pool

The Streams pool is used by Oracle Streams. This is an advanced tool that is beyond the scope of the OCP examinations or this book, but for completeness a short description follows.

The mechanism used by Streams is to extract change vectors from the redo log and from these reconstruct the statements that were executed—or statements that would have the same effect. These statements are executed at the remote database. The processes that extract changes from redo and the processes that apply the changes need memory: this memory is the Streams pool. From database release 10*g* it is possible to create and to resize the Streams pool after instance startup; this creation and sizing can be completely automatic. With earlier releases it had to be defined at startup and was a fixed size.

The Streams pool size is dynamic and can be automatically managed.

EXERCISE 2-2

Investigate the Memory Structures of the Instance

In this exercise, you will run queries to determine the current sizing of various memory structures that make up the instance. Either SQL Developer or SQL*Plus may be used.

1. Connect to the database as user SYSTEM.

2. Show the current, maximum, and minimum sizes of the SGA components that can be dynamically resized:

```
select COMPONENT,CURRENT_SIZE,MIN_SIZE,MAX_SIZE
from v$sga_dynamic_components;
```

This illustration shows the result on an example database:

```
 db11g@jwlnx1:~                                                          _ □ ✕
SQL>
SQL> select COMPONENT,CURRENT_SIZE,MIN_SIZE,MAX_SIZE from v$sga_dynamic_components;

COMPONENT                    CURRENT_SIZE    MIN_SIZE    MAX_SIZE
-------------------------    ------------  ----------  ----------
shared pool                     226492416   167772160   226492416
large pool                        4194304     4194304     4194304
java pool                        12582912    12582912    12582912
streams pool                            0           0           0
DEFAULT buffer cache            381681664   293601280   436207616
KEEP buffer cache                       0           0           0
RECYCLE buffer cache                    0           0           0
DEFAULT 2K buffer cache                 0           0           0
DEFAULT 4K buffer cache                 0           0           0
DEFAULT 8K buffer cache                 0           0           0
DEFAULT 16K buffer cache                0           0           0
DEFAULT 32K buffer cache                0           0           0
Shared IO Pool                          0           0           0
ASM Buffer Cache                        0           0           0

14 rows selected.

SQL>
SQL>
```

The example shows an instance without Streams, hence a Streams pool of size zero. Neither the large pool nor the Java pool has changed since instance startup, but there have been changes made to the sizes of the shared pool and database buffer cache. Only the default pool of the database buffer cache has been configured; this is usual, except in highly tuned databases.

3. Determine how much memory has been, and is currently, allocated to program global areas:

```
select name,value from v$pgastat
where name in ('maximum PGA allocated','total PGA allocated');
```

CERTIFICATION OBJECTIVE 2.03

Describe the Process Structures

The instance background processes are the processes that are launched when the instance is started and run until it is terminated. There are five background processes that have a long history with Oracle; these are the first five described in the sections that follow: System Monitor (SMON), Process Monitor (PMON), Database Writer (DBWn), Log Writer (LGWR), and Checkpoint Process (CKPT). A number of others have been introduced with the more recent releases; notable among these are Manageability Monitor (MMON) and Memory Manager (MMAN). There are also some that are not essential but will exist in most instances. These include Archiver (ARCn) and Recoverer (RECO). Others will exist only if certain options have been enabled. This last group includes the processes required for RAC and Streams. Additionally, some processes exist that are not properly documented (or are not documented at all). The processes described here are those that every OCP candidate will be expected to know.

There is a platform variation that must be cleared up before discussing processes. On Linux and Unix, all the Oracle processes are separate operating system processes, each with a unique process number. On Windows, there is one operating system process (called ORACLE.EXE) for the whole instance: the Oracle processes run as separate threads within this one process.

SMON, the System Monitor

SMON initially has the task of mounting and opening a database. The steps involved in this are described in detail in Chapter 5. In brief, SMON *mounts* a database by locating and validating the database controlfile. It then *opens* a database by locating and validating all the datafiles and online log files. Once the database is opened and in use, SMON is responsible for various housekeeping tasks, such as collating free space in datafiles.

PMON, the Process Monitor

A user session is a user process that is connected to a server process. The server process is launched when the session is created and destroyed when the session ends. An orderly exit from a session involves the user logging off. When this occurs, any

e x a m

w a t c h *If a session terminates abnormally, what will happen to an active transaction? It will be rolled back, by the PMON background process.*

work he/she was doing will be completed in an orderly fashion, and his/her server process will be terminated. If the session is terminated in a disorderly manner (perhaps because the user's PC is rebooted), then the session will be left in a state that must be cleared up. PMON monitors all the server processes and detects any problems with the sessions. If a session has terminated abnormally, PMON will destroy the server process, return its PGA memory to the operating system's free memory pool, and roll back any incomplete transaction that may have been in progress.

DBWn, the Database Writer

Always remember that sessions do not as a general rule write to disk. They write data (or change to existing data) to buffers in the database buffer cache. It is the database writer that subsequently writes the buffers to disk. It is possible for an instance to have several database writers (up to a maximum of twenty), which will be called DBW0, DBW1, and so on: hence the use of the term DBWn to refer to "the" database writer. The default number is one database writer per eight CPUs, rounded up.

on the

job

How many database writers do you need? The default number may well be correct. Adding more may help performance, but usually you should look at tuning memory first. As a rule, before you optimize disk I/O, ask why there is any need for disk I/O.

DBWn writes dirty buffers from the database buffer cache to the datafiles—but it does not write the buffers as they become dirty. On the contrary: it writes as few buffers as it can get away with. The general idea is that disk I/O is bad for performance, so don't do it unless it really is needed. If a block in a buffer has been written to by a session, there is a reasonable possibility that it will be written to again—by that session, or a different one. Why write the buffer to disk, if it may well be dirtied again in the near future? The algorithm DBWn uses to select dirty buffers for writing to disk (which will clean them) will select only buffers that have not been recently used. So if a buffer is very busy, because sessions are repeatedly reading or writing it, DBWn will not write it to disk. There could be hundreds or thousands of writes to a buffer before DBWn cleans it. It could be that in a buffer cache of a million buffers, a hundred thousand of them are dirty—but DBWn might only write a few hundred of them to disk at a time. These will be the few hundred that no session has been interested in for some time.

DBWn writes according to a very lazy algorithm: as little as possible, as rarely as possible. There are four circumstances that will cause DBWn to write: no free buffers, too many dirty buffers, a three-second timeout, and when there is a checkpoint.

First, when there are no free buffers. If a server process needs to copy a block into the database buffer cache, it must find a *free buffer*. A free buffer is a buffer that is neither dirty (updated, and not yet written back to disk) nor pinned (a pinned buffer is one that is being used by another session at that very moment). A dirty buffer must not be overwritten because if it were the changed, data would be lost, and a pinned buffer cannot be overwritten because the operating system's memory protection mechanisms will not permit this. If a server process takes too long (What is "too long"? This is determined by Oracle internally) to find a free buffer, it signals the DBWn to write some dirty buffers to disk. Once this is done, they will be clean—therefore free, and available for use.

Second, there may be too many dirty buffers—"too many" being another internal threshold. No one server process may have had a problem finding a free buffer, but overall, there could be a large number of dirty buffers: this will cause DBWn to write some of them to disk.

Third, there is a three-second timeout: every three seconds, DBWn will clean a few buffers. In practice, this event may not be significant in a production system because the two previously described circumstances will be forcing the writes, but the timeout does mean that even if the system is idle, the database buffer cache will eventually be cleaned.

Fourth, there may be a checkpoint requested. The three reasons already given will cause DBWn to write a limited number of dirty buffers to the datafiles. When a checkpoint occurs, all dirty buffers are written.

This could mean hundreds of thousands of them. During a checkpoint, disk I/O rates will hit the roof, CPU usage may go to 100 percent, end user sessions will experience degraded performance, and people will start complaining. Then when the checkpoint is complete (which may take several minutes) performance will return to normal. So why have checkpoints? The short answer is, don't have them unless you have to.

The only moment when a checkpoint is absolutely necessary is as the database is closed and the instance is shut down—a full description of this sequence is given in Chapter 5. A checkpoint writes all dirty buffers to disk: this synchronizes the buffer cache with the datafiles, the instance with the database. In normal running, the datafiles are always out of date: they may be missing changes (committed and uncommitted). This does not matter, because the copies of blocks in the buffer cache are up to date, and it is these that the sessions work on. But on shutdown, it is necessary to write everything to disk. Automatic checkpoints only occur on shutdown, but a checkpoint can be forced at any time with this statement:

```
alter system checkpoint;
```

Note that from release 8*i* onward, checkpoints do not occur on log switch (log switches are discussed in Chapter 15).

The checkpoint described so far is a full checkpoint. Partial checkpoints that force DBWn to write all the dirty buffers containing blocks from just one or more datafiles rather than the whole database, occur more frequently: when a datafile or tablespace is taken offline; when a tablespace is put into backup mode; when a tablespace is made read only. These are less drastic than full checkpoints, and occur automatically whenever the relevant event happens.

To conclude, the DBWn writes on a very lazy algorithm: as little as possible, as rarely as possible—except when a checkpoint occurs, when all dirty buffers are written to disk, as fast as possible.

LGWR, the Log Writer

LGWR writes the contents of the log buffer to the online log files on disk. A write of the log buffer to the online redo log files is often referred to as *flushing* the log buffer.

When a session makes any change (by executing INSERT, UPDATE, or DELETE commands) to blocks in the database buffer cache, before it applies the change to the block it writes out the change vector that it is about to apply to the log buffer. In order that no work can be lost, these change vectors must be written to disk with only minimal delay. To this end, the LGWR streams the contents of the log buffer to the online redo log files on disk in very nearly real time. And when a session issues a COMMIT, the LGWR writes in real time: the session hangs, while LGWR writes the buffer to disk. Only then is the transaction recorded as committed, and therefore non-reversible.

LGWR is one of the ultimate bottlenecks in the Oracle architecture. It is impossible to do DML faster than LGWR can write the change vectors to disk. There are three circumstances that will cause LGWR to flush the log buffer: if a session issues a COMMIT; if the log buffer is one-third full; if DBWn is about to write dirty buffers.

First, the write-on-commit. To process a COMMIT, the server process inserts a commit record into the log buffer. It will then hang, while LGWR flushes the log buffer to disk. Only when this write has completed is a commit-complete message returned to the session, and the server process can then continue working. This is the guarantee that transactions will never be lost: every change vector for a committed transaction will be available in the redo log on disk and can therefore be applied to datafile backups. Thus, if the database is ever damaged, it can be restored from backup and all work done since the backup was made can be redone.

It is in fact possible to prevent the LGWR write-on-commit. If this is done, sessions will not have to wait for LGWR when they commit: they issue the command and then carry on working. This will improve performance but can also mean that work can be lost. It becomes possible for a session to COMMIT, then for the instance to crash before LGWR has saved the change vectors. Enable this with caution! It is dangerous, and hardly ever necessary. There are only a few applications where performance is more important than data loss.

Second, when the log buffer is one-third full, LGWR will flush it to disk. This is about performance. If the log buffer is small (as it usually should be) this one-third-full trigger will force LGWR to write the buffer to disk in very nearly real time even if no one is committing transactions. The log buffer for many applications will be optimally sized at only a few megabytes. The application will generate enough redo to fill one third of this in a fraction of a second, so LGWR will be forced to stream the change vectors to disk continuously, in very nearly real time. Then, when a session does COMMIT, there will be hardly anything to write: so the COMMIT will complete almost instantaneously.

Third, when DBWn needs to write dirty buffers from the database buffer cache to the datafiles, before it does so it will signal LGWR to flush the log buffer to the online redo log files. This is to ensure that it will always be possible to reverse an uncommitted transaction. The mechanism of transaction rollback is fully explained in Chapter 11. For now, it is necessary to know that it is perfectly possible for DBWn to write an uncommitted transaction to the datafiles. This is fine, so long as the undo data needed to reverse the transaction is guaranteed to be available. Generating undo data also generates change vectors: as these will be in the redo log files before the datafiles are updated, then the undo data needed to roll back a transaction (should this be necessary) can be reconstructed if necessary.

Note that it can be said that there is a three-second timeout that causes LGWR to write. In fact, the timeout is on DBWR—but because LGWR will always write just before DBWn, in effect there is a three-second timeout on LGWR as well.

CKPT, the Checkpoint Process

The purpose of the CKPT changed dramatically between release 8 and release 8i of the Oracle database. In release 8 and earlier, checkpoints were necessary at regular intervals to make sure that in the event of an instance failure (for example, if the server machine should be rebooted) the database could be *recovered* quickly. These checkpoints were initiated by CKPT. The process of recovery is repairing the damage done by an instance failure; it is fully described in Chapter 15.

In brief, after a crash, all change vectors referring to dirty buffers (buffers that had not been written to disk by DBWn at the time of the failure) must be extracted from the redo log, and applied to the data blocks. This is the recovery process. Frequent checkpoints would ensure that dirty buffers were written to disk quickly, thus minimizing the amount of redo that would have to be applied after a crash and therefore minimizing the time taken to recover the database. CKPT was responsible for signaling regular checkpoints.

From release 8i onward, the checkpoint mechanism changed. Rather than letting DBWn get a long way behind and then signaling a checkpoint (which forces DBWn to catch up and get right up to date, with a dip in performance while this is going on) from 8i onward the DBWn makes *incremental checkpoints* instead of full checkpoints. The incremental checkpoint mechanism instructs DBWn to write out dirty buffers at a constant rate, so that there is always a predictable gap between DBWn (which writes blocks on a lazy algorithm) and LGWR (which writes change vectors in near real time). Incremental checkpointing results in much smoother performance and more predictable recovery times than the older full checkpoint mechanism.

on the job

The faster the incremental checkpoint advances, the quicker recovery will be after a failure. But performance will deteriorate due to the extra disk I/O, as DBWn has write out dirty buffers more quickly. This is a conflict between minimizing downtime and maximizing performance.

The CKPT no longer has to signal full checkpoints, but it does have to keep track of where in the redo stream the incremental checkpoint position is, and if necessary instruct DBWn to write out some dirty buffers in order to push the checkpoint position forward. The current checkpoint position, also known as the RBA (the redo byte address), is the point in the redo stream at which recovery must begin in the event of an instance crash. CKPT continually updates the controlfile with the current checkpoint position.

MMON, the Manageability Monitor

MMON is a process that was introduced with database release 10*g* and is the enabling process for many of the self-monitoring and self-tuning capabilities of the database.

The database instance gathers a vast number of statistics about activity and performance. These statistics are accumulated in the SGA, and their current values can be interrogated by issuing SQL queries. For performance tuning and also for trend analysis and historical reporting, it is necessary to save these statistics to long-term storage. MMON regularly (by default, every hour) captures statistics from the SGA and writes them to the data dictionary, where they can be stored indefinitely (though by default, they are kept for only eight days).

Every time MMON gathers a set of statistics (known as a *snapshot*), it also launches the Automatic Database Diagnostic Monitor, the ADDM. The ADDM is a tool that analyses database activity using an expert system developed over many years by many DBAs. It observes two snapshots (by default, the current and previous snapshots) and makes observations and recommendations regarding performance. Chapter 13 describes the use of ADDM (and other tools) for performance tuning.

As well as gathering snapshots, MMON continuously monitors the database and the instance to check whether any alerts should be raised. Use of the alert system is covered in the second OCP exam. Some alert conditions (such as warnings when limits on storage space are reached) are enabled by default; others can be configured by the DBA.

MMNL, the Manageability Monitor Light

MMNL is a process that assists the MMON. There are times when MMON's scheduled activity is not enough. For example, MMON flushes statistical information accumulated in the SGA to the database according to a schedule: by default, every hour. If the memory buffers used to accumulate this information fill before MMON is due to flush them, MMNL will take responsibility for flushing the data.

MMAN, the Memory Manager

MMAN is a process that was introduced with database release 10g. It enables the automatic management of memory allocations.

Prior to release 9i of the database, memory management in the Oracle environment was far from satisfactory. The PGA memory associated with session server processes was non-transferable: a server process would take memory from the operating system's free memory pool and never return it—even though it might only have been needed for a short time. The SGA memory structures were static: defined at instance startup time, and unchangeable unless the instance were shut down and restarted.

Release 9i changed that: PGAs can grow and shrink, with the server passing out memory to sessions on demand while ensuring that the total PGA memory allocated stays within certain limits. The SGA and the components within it (with the notable exception of the log buffer) can also be resized, within certain limits. Release 10g automated the SGA resizing: MMAN monitors the demand for SGA memory structures and can resize them as necessary.

Release 11g takes memory management a step further: all the DBA need do is set an overall target for memory usage, and MMAN will observe the demand for PGA memory and SGA memory, and allocate memory to sessions and to SGA structures as needed, while keeping the total allocated memory within a limit set by the DBA.

on the Job

The automation of memory management is one of the major technical advances of the later releases, automating a large part of the DBA's job and giving huge benefits in performance and resource utilization. MMAN does it better than you.

ARCn, the Archiver

This is an optional process as far as the database is concerned, but usually a required process for the business. Without one or more ARCn processs (there can be from one to thirty, named ARC0, ARC1, and so on) it is possible to lose data. The process and purpose of launching ARCn to create archive log files is described in detail in Chapter 15. For now, only a summary is needed.

All change vectors applied to data blocks are written out to the log buffer (by the sessions making the changes) and then to the *online* redo log files (by the LGWR). The online redo log files are of fixed size and number: once they have been filled, LGWR will overwrite them with more redo data. The time that must elapse before this happens is dependent on the size and number of the online log files, and the amount of DML activity (and therefore the amount of redo generated) against the database. This means that the online redo log only stores change vectors for recent activity. In order to preserve a complete history of all changes applied to the data, the online log files must be copied as they are filled and before they are reused. The ARCn is responsible for doing this. Provided that these copies, known *archive* redo log files, are available, it will always be possible to recover from any damage to the database by restoring datafile backups and applying change vectors to them extracted from all the archive log files generated since the backups were made. Then the final recovery, to bring the backup right up to date, will come from the online redo log files.

Most production transactional databases will run in *archive log mode,* meaning that ARCn is started automatically and that LGWR is not permitted to overwrite an online log file until ARCn has successfully archived it to an archive log file.

watch   *LGWR writes the online log files; ARCn reads them. In normal running, no other processes touch them at all.*

on the **job**   *The progress of the ARCn processes and the state of the destination(s) to which they are writing must be monitored. If archiving fails, the database will eventually hang. This monitoring can be done through the alert system.*

RECO, the Recoverer Process

A *distributed* transaction is a transaction that involves updates to two or more databases. Distributed transactions are designed by programmers and operate through database links. Consider this example:

```
update employees set salary=salary * 1.1 where employee_id=1000;
update employees@dev set salary=salary * 1.1 where employee_id=1000;
commit;
```

The first update applies to a row in the local database; the second applies to a row in a remote database identified by the database link DEV.

The COMMIT command instructs both databases to commit the transaction, which consists of both statements. A full description of commit processing appears in Chapter 10. Distributed transactions require a *two-phase commit*. The commit in each database must be coordinated: if one were to fail and the other were to succeed, the data overall would be in an inconsistent state. A two-phase commit prepares each database by instructing their LGWRs to flush the log buffer to disk (the first phase), and once this is confirmed, the transaction is flagged as committed everywhere (the second phase). If anything goes wrong anywhere between the two phases, RECO takes action to cancel the commit and roll back the work in all databases.

Some Other Background Processes

It is unlikely that processes other than those already described will be examined, but for completeness descriptions of the remaining processes usually present in an instance follow. Figure 2-2 shows a query that lists all the processes running in an instance on a Windows system. There are many more processes that may exist dependent on enabling certain options, but those shown in the figure will be present in most instances.

The processes not described in previous sections are

- **CJQ0, J000** These manage jobs scheduled to run periodically. The job queue Coordinator, CJQn, monitors the job queue and sends jobs to one of several job queue processes, Jnnn, for execution. The job scheduling mechanism is covered in the second OCP examination.

- **D000** This is a dispatcher process that will send SQL calls to shared server processes, Snnn, if the shared server mechanism has been enabled. This is described in Chapter 6.

- **DBRM** The database resource manager is responsible for setting resource plans and other Resource Manager–related tasks. Using the Resource Manager is covered in the second OCP examination.

- **DIA0** The diagnosability process zero (only one is used in the current release) is responsible for hang detection and deadlock resolution. Deadlocks and their resolution are described in Chapter 10.

FIGURE 2-2

The background
processes
typically present
in a single
instance

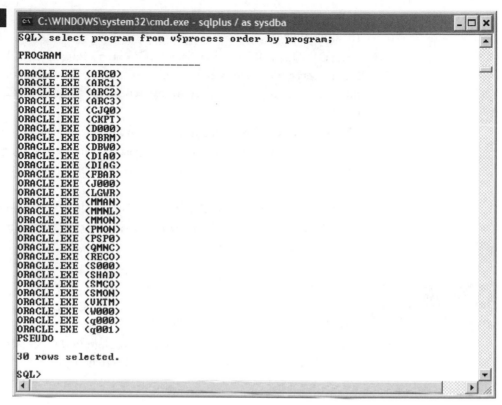

- **DIAG** The diagnosability process (not number zero) performs diagnostic dumps and executes oradebug commands (oradebug is a tool for investigating problems within the instance).

- **FBAR** The flashback data archiver process archives the historical rows of tracked tables into flashback data archives. This is a facility for ensuring that it is always possible to query data as it was at a time in the past.

- **PSP0** The process spawner has the job of creating and managing other Oracle processes, and is undocumented.

- **QMNC, Q000** The queue manager coordinator monitors queues in the database and assigns Qnnn processes to enqueue and dequeue messages to and from these queues. Queues can be created by programmers (perhaps as a means for sessions to communicate) and are also used internally. Streams, for example, use queues to store transactions that need to be propagated to remote databases.

■ **SHAD** This will be called TNS V1-V3 on a Linux system. These processes are the server processes that support user sessions. In the figure there is only one, because only one user is currently connected: the user who issued the query.

■ **SMCO, W000** The space management coordinator process coordinates the execution of various space management–related tasks, such as proactive space allocation and space reclamation. It dynamically spawns slave processes (Wnnn) to implement the task.

■ **VKTM** The virtual keeper of time is responsible for keeping track of time. More complicated than one might think—particularly in a clustered environment.

EXERCISE 2-3

Investigate the Processes Running in Your Instance

In this exercise you will run queries to see what background processes are running on your instance. Either SQL Developer or SQL*Plus may be used.

1. Connect to the database as user SYSTEM.

2. Determine what processes are running, and how many of each:

```
select program from v$session order by program;
select program from v$process order by program;
```

These queries will give similar results: each process must have a session (even the background processes), and each session must have a process. The processes that can occur multiple times will have a numeric suffix, except for the processes supporting user sessions: these will all have the same name.

3. Demonstrate the launching of server processes as sessions are made, by counting the number of server processes (on Linux or any Unix platform) or the number of Oracle threads (on Windows). The technique is different on the two platforms, because on Linux/Unix, the Oracle processes are separate operating system processes, but on Windows they are threads within one operating system process.

A. On Linux, run this command from an operating system prompt:

```
ps -ef|grep oracle|wc -l
```

This will count the number of processes running that have the string oracle in their name; this will include all the session server processes (and possibly a few others).

Launch a SQL*Plus session, and rerun the preceding command: use the host command to launch an operating shell from within the SQL*Plus session. You will see that the number of processes has increased. Exit the session, and you will see that the number has dropped down again. This illustration shows this fact:

```
db11g@jwlnx1:~                                                      _ □ X
[db11g@jwlnx1 ~]$
[db11g@jwlnx1 ~]$ ps -ef | grep oracle | wc -l
4
[db11g@jwlnx1 ~]$ sqlplus system/oracle

SQL*Plus: Release 11.1.0.6.0 - Production on Thu Oct 25 09:51:35 2007

Copyright (c) 1982, 2007, Oracle.  All rights reserved.


Connected to:
Oracle Database 11g Enterprise Edition Release 11.1.0.6.0 - Production
With the Partitioning, OLAP, Data Mining and Real Application Testing options

SQL> host
[db11g@jwlnx1 ~]$ ps -ef | grep oracle | wc -l
5
[db11g@jwlnx1 ~]$ exit
exit

SQL> exit
Disconnected from Oracle Database 11g Enterprise Edition Release 11.1.0.6.0 - Produ
ction
With the Partitioning, OLAP, Data Mining and Real Application Testing options
[db11g@jwlnx1 ~]$ ps -ef | grep oracle | wc -l
4
[db11g@jwlnx1 ~]$ █
```

Observe in the illustration how the number of processes changes from 4 to 5 and back again: the difference is the launching and terminating of the server process supporting the SQL*Plus session.

B. On Windows, launch the task manager. Configure it to show the number of threads within each process: on the View tab, take "Select Columns and tick the Thread Count check box. Look for the ORACLE.EXE process, and note the number of threads. In the next illustration, this is currently at 33.

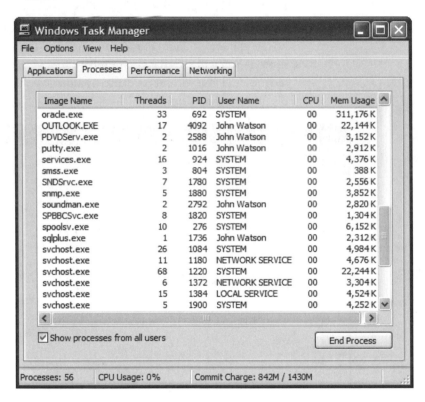

Launch a new session against the instance, and you will see the thread count increment. Exit the session, and it will decrement.

INSIDE THE EXAM

The Relationship Between Processes, Memory Structures, and Files

It is vital to have an understanding of the relationship between the instance and the database. This link is made by the background processes. When an instance starts, the SGA is built in memory. Then the background processes connect to the database files on disk. The processes are the link between the memory structures and the disk structures.

The datafiles will usually be out of date: they will be missing work that has been done in memory, because the DBWn has not yet got around to writing the work to the datafiles. No problem—in memory, the information is real time, and that is what user sessions will see. By contrast, the online redo log files are right up to date, because LGWR writes in very nearly real time—and when a user says COMMIT, it does write in real time.

Always be absolutely clear on which processes are reading and writing memory structures, and which are reading and writing disk structures.

CERTIFICATION OBJECTIVE 2.04

Summarize the Storage Structures

The Oracle database provides complete abstraction of logical storage from physical. The logical data storage is in *segments*. There are various segment types; a typical segment is a table. The segments are stored physically in datafiles. The abstraction of the logical storage from the physical storage is accomplished through tablespaces. The relationships between the logical and physical structures, as well as their definitions, are maintained in the data dictionary.

There is a full treatment of database storage, logical and physical, in Chapter 7.

The Physical Database Structures

There are three file types that make up an Oracle database, plus a few others that exist externally to the database and are, strictly speaking, optional. The required files are the controlfile, the online redo log files, and the datafiles. The external files that

will usually be present (there are others, needed for advanced options) are the initialization parameter file, the password file, the archive redo log files, and the log and trace files.

The Controlfile

First a point of terminology: some DBAs will say that a database can have multiple controlfiles, while others will say that it has one controlfile, of which there may be multiple copies. This book will follow the latter terminology, which conforms to Oracle Corporation's use of phrases such as "multiplexing the controlfile," which means to create multiple copies.

The controlfile is small but vital. It contains pointers to the rest of the database: the locations of the online redo log files and of the datafiles, and of the more recent archive log files if the database is in archive log mode. It also stores information required to maintain database integrity: various critical sequence numbers and timestamps, for example. If the Recovery Manager tool (described in Chapters 16 and 17) is being used for backups, then details of these backups will also be stored in the controlfile. The controlfile will usually be no more than a few megabytes big, but you can't survive without it.

Every database has one controlfile, but a good DBA will always create multiple copies of the controlfile so that if one copy is damaged, the database itself will survive. If all copies of the controlfile are lost, it is possible (though perhaps awkward) to recover, but you should never find yourself in that situation. You don't have to worry about keeping multiplexed copies of the controlfile synchronized—Oracle will take care of that. Its maintenance is automatic—your only control is how many copies to have, and where to put them.

If you get the number of copies, or their location, wrong at database creation time, you can add or remove copies later, or move them around—but you should bear in mind that any such operations will require down time, so it is a good idea to get it right at the beginning. There is no right or wrong when determining how many copies to have. The minimum is one; the maximum possible is eight. All organizations should have a DBA standards handbook, which will state something like "all production databases will have three copies of the controlfile, on three separate devices," three being a number picked for illustration only, but a number that many organizations are happy with. If there are no such guidelines in place, someone should write them (and perhaps the "someone" should be you). There is no rule that says two copies is too few, or seven copies is too many; there are only corporate standards, and the DBA's job is to ensure that the databases conform to these.

Damage to any controlfile copy will cause the database instance to terminate immediately. There is no way to avoid this: Oracle Corporation does not permit operating a database with less than the number of controlfiles that have been requested. The techniques for multiplexing or relocating the controlfile are covered in Chapter 15.

The Online Redo Log Files

The redo log stores a continuous chain in chronological order of every change vector applied to the database. This will be the bare minimum of information required to reconstruct, or redo, all work that has been done. If a datafile (or the whole database) is damaged or destroyed, these change vectors can be applied to datafile backups to redo the work, bringing them forward in time until the moment that the damage occurred. The redo log consists of two file types: the online redo log files (which are required) and the archive log files (which are optional).

Every database has at least two online redo log files, but as with the controlfile, a good DBA creates multiple copies of each online redo log file. The online redo log consists of groups of online redo log files, each file being known as a member. An Oracle database requires at least two groups of at least one member each to function. You may create more than two groups for performance reasons, and more than one member per group for security (an old joke: this isn't just data security, it is job security). The requirement for a minimum of two groups is in order that one group can be accepting the current changes, while the other group is being backed up (or *archived*, to use the correct term).

Every database must have at least two online redo log file groups to function. Each group should have at least two members for safety.

One of the groups is the *current* group: changes are written to the current online redo logfile group by LGWR. As user sessions update data in the database buffer cache, they also write out the minimal change vectors to the redo log buffer. LGWR continually flushes this buffer to the files that make up the current online redo log file group. Log files are fixed size; therefore, eventually the files making up the current group will fill. LGWR will then perform what is called a log switch. This makes the second group current and starts writing to that. If your database is configured appropriately, the ARCn process(es) will then archive (in effect, back up) the log file members making up the first group. When the second group fills, LGWR will switch back to the first group, making it current, and overwriting it; ARCn will then archive the second group. Thus, the online redo log file groups (and therefore the members making them up) are used in a circular fashion, and each log switch will generate an archive redo log file.

As with the controlfile, if you have multiple members per group (and you should!) you don't have to worry about keeping them synchronized. LGWR will ensure that it writes to all of them, in parallel, thus keeping them identical. If you lose one member of a group, as long as you have a surviving member, the database will continue to function.

The size and number of your log file groups are a matter of tuning. In general, you will choose a size appropriate to the amount of activity you anticipate. The minimum size is fifty megabytes, but some very active databases will need to raise this to several gigabytes if they are not to fill every few minutes. A very busy database can generate megabytes of redo a second, whereas a largely static database may generate only a few megabytes an hour. The number of members per group will be dependent on what level of fault tolerance is deemed appropriate, and is a matter to be documented in corporate standards. However, you don't have to worry about this at database creation time. You can move your online redo log files around, add or drop them, and create ones of different sizes as you please at any time later on. Such operations are performed "online" and don't require downtime—they are therefore transparent to the end users.

The Datafiles

The third required file type making up a database is the datafile. At a minimum, you must have two datafiles, to be created at database creation time. With previous releases of Oracle, you could create a database with only one datafile—10g and 11g require two, at least one each for the SYSTEM tablespace (that stores the data dictionary) and the SYSAUX tablespace (that stores data that is auxiliary to the data dictionary). You will, however, have many more than that when your database goes live, and will usually create a few more to begin with.

Datafiles are the repository for data. Their size and numbers are effectively unlimited. A small database, of only a few gigabytes, might have just half a dozen datafiles of only a few hundred megabytes each. A larger database could have thousands of datafiles, whose size is limited only by the capabilities of the host operating system and hardware.

The datafiles are the physical structures visible to the system administrators. Logically, they are the repository for the *segments* containing user data that the programmers see, and also for the segments that make up the data dictionary.

A segment is a storage structure for data; typical segments are tables and indexes. Datafiles can be renamed, resized, moved, added, or dropped at any time in the lifetime of the database, but remember that some operations on some datafiles may require downtime.

At the operating system level, a datafile consists of a number of operating system blocks. Internally, datafiles are formatted into Oracle *blocks*. These blocks are consecutively numbered within each datafile. The block size is fixed when the datafile is created, and in most circumstances it will be the same throughout the entire database. The block size is a matter for tuning and can range (with limits depending on the platform) from 2 KB up to 64 KB. There is no relationship between the Oracle block size and the operating system block size.

on the job

Many DBAs like to match the operating system block size to the Oracle block size. For performance reasons, the operating system blocks should never be larger than the Oracle blocks, but there is no reason not have them smaller. For instance, a 1 KB operating block size and an 8 KB Oracle block size is perfectly acceptable.

Within a block, there is a header section and a data area, and possibly some free space. The header section contains information such as the row directory, which lists the location within the data area of the rows in the block (if the block is being used for a table segment) and also row locking information if there is a transaction working on the rows in the block. The data area contains the data itself, such as rows if it is part of a table segment, or index keys if the block is part of an index segment.

When a user session needs to work on data for any purpose, the server process supporting the session locates the relevant block on disk and copies it into a free buffer in the database buffer cache. If the data in the block is then changed (the buffer is dirtied) by executing a DML command against it, eventually DBWn will write the block back to the datafile on disk.

exam

watch   *Server processes read from the datafiles; DBWn writes to datafiles.*

Datafiles should be backed up regularly. Unlike the controlfile and the online redo log files, they cannot be protected by multiplexing (though they can, of course, be protected by operating system and hardware facilities, such as RAID.) If a datafile is damaged, it can be restored from backup and then *recovered* (to recover a datafile means to bring it up to date) by applying all the redo generated since the backup was made. The necessary redo is extracted from the change vectors in the online and archive redo log files. The routines for datafile backup, restore, and recovery are described in Chapters 16 and 17.

Other Database Files

These files exist externally to the database. They are, for practical purposes, necessary—but they are not strictly speaking part of the database.

- **The Instance Parameter File**   When an Oracle instance is started, the SGA structures build in memory and the background processes start according to settings in the parameter file. This is the only file that needs to exist in order to start an instance. There are several hundred parameters, but only one is required: the DB_NAME parameter. All others have defaults. So the parameter file can be quite small, but it must exist. Creating the parameter file is described in Chapter 4.

- **The Password File**   Users establish sessions by presenting a username and a password. The Oracle server authenticates these against user definitions stored in the data dictionary. The data dictionary is a set of tables in the database; it is therefore inaccessible if the database is not open. There are occasions when a user needs to be authenticated before the data dictionary is available: when he needs to start the database, or indeed to create it. An external password file is one means of doing this. It contains a small number (typically less than half a dozen) of user names and passwords that exist outside the data dictionary, and which can therefore be used to connect to an instance before the data dictionary is available. Creating the password file is described in Chapter 4.

- **Archive Redo Log Files**   When an online redo log file fills, the ARCn process copies it out of the database to an archive redo log file. Once this is done, the archive log is no longer part of the database. It is, however, essential if it is ever necessary to restore a datafile backup, and Oracle docs provide facilities for managing the archive redo log files.

- **Alert Log and Trace Files**   The alert log is a continuous stream of messages regarding certain critical operations affecting the instance and the database. Not everything is logged: only events that are considered to be really important, such as startup and shutdown; changes to the physical structures of the database; changes to the parameters that control the instance. Trace files are generated by background processes when they detect error conditions, and sometimes to report certain actions.

SCENARIO & SOLUTION

You are taking over management of a database, and there is no documentation of the physical or logical storage, or the memory usage. How can you work out how it is configured?	You must run queries against numerous views that describe the database and its contents. There are graphical tools that will help—many are included with Oracle Enterprise Manager—but all these are doing is running queries against views, and formatting the results in a pretty fashion.
Worse still, the database is on an operating system and hardware with which you are not familiar. Does that mean you can't manage it?	No, it doesn't—but you may need some help. In principle, the Oracle architecture is identical on all platforms, and when you are working from within an Oracle tool such as SQL*Plus or SQL Developer, it really doesn't matter what the platform is. That having been said, unless you are reasonably competent at working from the operating system prompt as well, you will need a lot of help from the system administrators.
	Teamwork! A vital skill in IT support.

The Logical Database Structures

The physical structures that make up a database are visible as operating system files to your system administrators. Your users see logical structures such as tables. Oracle uses the term *segment* to describe any structure that contains data. A typical segment is a table, containing rows of data, but there are more than a dozen possible segment types in an Oracle database. Of particular interest (for examination purposes) are table segments, index segments, and undo segments, all of which are investigated in detail later on. For now, you don't need to know more than that tables contain rows of information; that indexes are a mechanism for giving fast access to any particular row; and that undo segments are data structures used for storing the information that might be needed to reverse, or roll back, any transactions that you do not wish to make permanent.

So system administrators see physical datafiles; programmers see logical segments. Oracle abstracts the logical storage from the physical storage by means of the *tablespace*. A tablespace is logically a collection of one or more segments, and physically a collection of one or more datafiles. Put in terms of relational analysis, there is a many-to-many relationship between segments and datafiles: one table may be cut across many datafiles, one datafile may contain bits of many tables. By inserting the tablespace entity between the segments and the files, Oracle resolves this many-to-many relationship.

A number of segments must be created at database creation time: these are the segments that make up the data dictionary. These segments are stored in two tablespaces, called SYSTEM and SYSAUX. The SYSAUX tablespace was new with release 10g: in previous releases, the whole of the data dictionary went into SYSTEM. The database creation process must create at least these two tablespaces, with at least one datafile each, to store the data dictionary.

A segment will consist of a number of blocks. Datafiles are formatted into blocks, and these blocks are assigned to segments as the segments grow. Because managing space one block at a time would be a time-consuming process, blocks are grouped into *extents*. An extent is a series of blocks that are consecutively numbered within a datafile, and segments will grow by adding new extents to them. These extents need not be adjacent to each other, or even in the same datafile; they can come from any datafile that is part of the tablespace within which the segment resides.

Figure 2-3 shows the Oracle data storage hierarchy, with the separation of logical from physical storage.

The figure shows the relationships between the storage structures. Logically, a tablespace can contain many segments, each consisting of many extents. An *extent* is a set of Oracle blocks. Physically, a datafile consists of many operating system blocks assigned by whatever file system the operating system is using. The two sides of the model are connected by the relationships showing that one tablespace can consist of multiple datafiles, and at the lowest level that one Oracle block will consist of multiple operating system blocks.

The Data Dictionary

The data dictionary is metadata: data about data. It describes the database, both physically and logically, and its contents. User definitions, security information, integrity constraints, and (with release 10g and later) performance monitoring information are all part of the data dictionary. It is stored as a set of segments in the SYSTEM and SYSAUX tablespaces.

FIGURE 2-3

The Oracle
logical and
physical storage
hierarchy

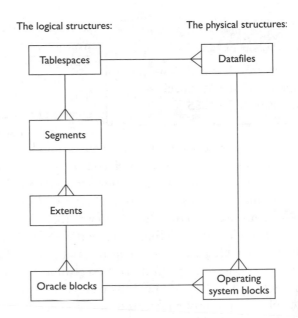

In many ways, the segments that make up the data dictionary are segments like any other: just tables and indexes. The critical difference is that the data dictionary tables are generated at database creation time, and you are not allowed to access them directly. There is nothing to stop an inquisitive DBA from investigating the data dictionary directly, but if you do any updates to it, you may cause irreparable damage to your database, and certainly Oracle Corporation will not support you. Creating a data dictionary is part of the database creation process. It is maintained subsequently by data definition language commands. When you issue the CREATE TABLE command, you are in fact inserting rows into data dictionary tables, as you are with commands such as CREATE USER or GRANT.

To query the dictionary, Oracle provides a set of views. The views come in three forms: prefixed DBA_, ALL_, or USER_. Most of the views come in all three forms. Any view prefixed USER_ will be populated with rows describing objects owned by the user querying the view. So no two people will see the same contents. If user SCOTT queries USER_TABLES, he/she will see information about his/her tables; if you query USER_TABLES, you will see information about your tables. Any view prefixed ALL_ will be populated with rows describing objects to which you have access. So ALL_TABLES will contain rows describing your own tables, plus rows describing tables belonging to any one else that you have been given permission

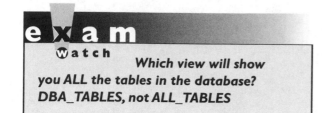

to see. Any view prefixed DBA_ will have rows for every object in the database, so DBA_TABLES will have one row for every table in the database, no matter who created it. These views are created as part of the database creation process, along with a large number of PL/SQL packages that are provided by Oracle to assist database administrators in managing the database and programmers in developing applications. PL/SQL code is also stored in the data dictionary.

The relationship between tablespaces and datafiles is maintained in the database controlfile. This lists all the datafiles, stating which tablespace they are a part of. Without the controlfile, there is no way that an instance can locate the datafiles and then identify those that make up the SYSTEM tablespace. Only when the SYSTEM tablespace has been opened is it possible for the instance to access the data dictionary, at which point it becomes possible to open the database.

SQL code will always refer to objects defined in the data dictionary. To execute a simple query against a table, the Oracle server must first query the data dictionary to find out if the table exists, and the columns that make it up. Then it must find out where, physically, the table is. This requires reading the extent map of the segment. The extent map lists all the extents that make up the table, with the detail of which datafile each extent is in, what block of the datafile the extent starts at, and how many blocks it continues for.

EXERCISE 2-4

Investigate the Storage Structures in Your Database

In this exercise you will create a table segment, and then work out where it is physically. Either SQL Developer or SQL*Plus may be used.

1. Connect to the database as user SYSTEM.

2. Create a table without nominating a tablespace—it will be created in your default tablespace, with one extent:

```
create table tab24 (c1 varchar2(10));
```

3. Identify the tablespace in which the table resides, the size of the extent, the file number the extent is in, and which block of the file the extent starts at:

```
select tablespace_name, extent_id, bytes, file_id, block_id
from dba_extents where owner='SYSTEM' and segment_name='TAB24';
```

4. Identify the file by name: substitute the file_id from the previous query when prompted:

```
select name from v$datafile where file#=&file_id;
```

5. Work out precisely where in the file the extent is, in terms of how many bytes into the file it begins. This requires finding out the tablespace's block size. Enter the block_id and tablespace_name returned by the query in Step 3 when prompted.

```
select block_size * &block_id from dba_tablespaces
where tablespace_name='&tablespace_name';
```

The illustration that follows shows these steps, executed from SQL*Plus:

```
db11g@jwlnx1:~
SQL> create table tab24 (c1 varchar2(10));

Table created.

SQL> select tablespace_name, extent_id, bytes, file_id, block_id
from dba_extents where owner='SYSTEM' and segment_name='TAB24';
  2
TABLESPACE_NAME                      EXTENT_ID       BYTES    FILE_ID    BLOCK_ID
------------------------------------ ---------- ---------- ---------- ----------
SYSTEM                                       0       65536          1       87353

SQL> select name from v$datafile where file#=&file_id;
Enter value for file_id: 1
old    1: select name from v$datafile where file#=&file_id
new    1: select name from v$datafile where file#=1

NAME
----------------------------------------------------------------- -------------
/home/db11g/app/db11g/oradata/orcl/system01.dbf

SQL> select block_size * &block_id from dba_tablespaces
where tablespace_name='&tablespace_name';
  2  Enter value for block_id: 87353
old    1: select block_size * &block_id from dba_tablespaces
new    1: select block_size * 87353 from dba_tablespaces
Enter value for tablespace_name: SYSTEM
old    2: where tablespace_name='&tablespace_name'
new    2: where tablespace_name='SYSTEM'

BLOCK_SIZE*87353
----------------
       715595776

SQL>
```

The illustration shows that the table exists in one extent that is 64 KB large. This extent is in the file `/home/db11g/app/db11g/oradata/orcl/system01.dbf` and begins about 700 MB into the file.

CERTIFICATION SUMMARY

This chapter covers the Oracle instance and database architecture. Many topics will be given a fuller treatment in later chapters, but at this point the overall architecture of the instance (consisting of shared memory structures and processes), the database (consisting of files on disk), and a user session (a user process and a server process) should be clear.

TWO-MINUTE DRILL

Describe the Single-Instance Architecture

- ❑ An Oracle server is an instance connected to a database.
- ❑ An instance is a block of shared memory and a set of background processes.
- ❑ A database is a set of files on disk.
- ❑ A user session is a user process connected to a server process.

Explain the Memory Structures

- ❑ The instance shared memory is the system global area (the SGA).
- ❑ A session's private memory is its program global area (the PGA).
- ❑ The SGA consists of a number of substructures, some of which are required (the database buffer cache, the log buffer, and the shared pool) and some of which are optional (the large pool, the Java pool, and the Streams pool).
- ❑ The SGA structures can be dynamically resized and automatically managed, with the exception of the log buffer.

Describe the Process Structures

- ❑ Session server processes are launched on demand when users connect.
- ❑ Background processes are launched at instance startup and persist until shutdown.
- ❑ Server processes read from the database; background processes write to the database.
- ❑ Some background processes will always be present (in particular SMON, PMON, DBWn, LGWR, CKPT, and MMON); others will run depending on what options have been enabled.

Summarize the Storage Structures

- ❑ There are three required file types in a database: the controlfile, the online redo log files, and the datafiles.
- ❑ The controlfile stores integrity information and pointers to the rest of the database.

❑ The online redo logs store recent change vectors applied to the database.

❑ The datafiles store the data.

❑ External files include the parameter file, the password file, archive redo logs, and the log and trace files.

❑ Logical data storage (segments) is abstracted from physical data storage (datafiles) by tablespaces.

❑ A tablespace can consist of multiple datafiles.

❑ Segments consist of multiple extents, which consist of multiple Oracle blocks, which consist of multiple operating system blocks.

❑ A segment can have extents in several datafiles.

SELF TEST

Describe the Single-Instance Architecture

1. What statements regarding instance memory and session memory are correct? (Choose all correct answers.)
    A. SGA memory is private memory segments; PGA memory is shared memory segments.
    B. Sessions can write to the PGA, not the SGA.
    C. The SGA is written to by all sessions; a PGA is written by one session.
    D. The PGA is allocated at instance startup.
    E. The SGA is allocated at instance startup.

2. How do sessions communicate with the database? (Choose the best answer.)
    A. Server processes use Oracle Net to connect to the instance.
    B. Background processes use Oracle Net to connect to the database.
    C. User processes read from the database and write to the instance.
    D. Server processes execute SQL received from user processes.

Explain the Memory Structures

3. What memory structures are a required part of the SGA? (Choose all correct answers.)
    A. The database buffer cache
    B. The Java pool
    C. The large pool
    D. The log buffer
    E. The program global area
    F. The shared pool
    G. The Streams pool

4. Which SGA memory structure(s) cannot be resized dynamically after instance startup? (Choose all correct answers.)
    A. The database buffer cache
    B. The Java pool
    C. The large pool
    D. The log buffer
    E. The shared pool
    F. The Streams pool
    G. All SGA structures can be resized dynamically after instance startup

5. Which SGA memory structure(s) cannot be resized automatically after instance startup? (Choose all correct answers.)
   A. The database buffer cache
   B. The Java pool
   C. The large pool
   D. The log buffer
   E. The shared pool
   F. The Streams pool
   G. All SGA structures can be resized automatically after instance startup

6. When a session changes data, where does the change get written? (Choose the best answer.)
   A. To the data block in the cache, and the redo log buffer
   B. To the data block on disk, and the current online redo log file
   C. The session writes to the database buffer cache, and the log writer writes to the current online redo log file
   D. Nothing is written until the change is committed

Describe the Process Structures

7. Which of these background processes is optional? (Choose the best answer.)
   A. ARCn, the archive process
   B. CKPT, the checkpoint process
   C. DBWn, the database writer
   D. LGWR, the log writer
   E. MMON, the manageability monitor

8. What happens when a user issues a COMMIT? (Choose the best answer.)
   A. The CKPT process signals a checkpoint.
   B. The DBWn process writes the transaction's changed buffers to the datafiles.
   C. The LGWR flushes the log buffer to the online redo log.
   D. The ARCn process writes the change vectors to the archive redo log.

9. An Oracle instance can have only one of some processes, but several of others. Which of these processes can occur several times? (Choose all correct answers.)
   A. The archive process
   B. The checkpoint process
   C. The database writer process

D. The log writer process

E. The session server process

Summarize the Storage Structures

10. One segment can be spread across many datafiles. How? (Choose the best answer.)

A. By allocating extents with blocks in multiple datafiles

B. By spreading the segment across multiple tablespaces

C. By assigning multiple datafiles to a tablespace

D. By using an Oracle block size that is larger then the operating system block size

11. Which statement is correct regarding the online redo log? (Choose the best answer.)

A. There must be at least one log file group, with at least one member.

B. There must be at least one log file group, with at least two members.

C. There must be at least two log file groups, with at least one member each.

D. There must be at least two log file groups, with at least two members each.

12. Where is the current redo byte address, also known as the incremental checkpoint position, recorded? (Choose the best answer.)

A. In the controlfile

B. In the current online log file group

C. In the header of each datafile

D. In the system global area

LAB QUESTION

Simulate the situation a DBA will find himself/herself in many times: he/she has been asked to take on management of a database that he/she has not seen before, and for which the documentation is woefully inadequate. Using either SQL Developer or SQL*Plus, write a series of queries that will begin to document the system. Following are some of the views that will help: describe each view and then query the relevant columns. To see the views, it will be necessary to connect as a user with high privileges, such as user SYSTEM.

- **V$DATABASE**   On what operating system is the database is running?
- **V$CONTROLFILE**   Where is the controlfile? Is it multiplexed?
- **VLOG, VLOGFILE**   How many online log file groups are there? How many members are in each group, and what are they called? How big are they?
- **V$TABLESPACE, V$DATAFILE**   What tablespaces exist in the database? What datafiles are assigned to each tablespace? What are they called, and how big are they?

SELF TEST ANSWERS

Describe the Single-Instance Architecture

1. ☑ **C** and **E.** The SGA is shared memory, updated by all sessions; PGAs are private to each session. The SGA is allocated at startup time (but it can be modified later).
   ☒ **A** is wrong because it reverses the situation: it is the SGA that exists in shared memory, not the PGA. **B** is wrong because sessions write to both their own PGA and to the SGA. **D** is wrong because (unlike the SGA) the PGA is only allocated on demand.

2. ☑ **D.** This is the client-server split: user processes generate SQL; server processes execute SQL.
   ☒ **A** and **B** are wrong because they get the use of Oracle Net wrong. Oracle Net is the protocol between a user process and a server process. **C** is wrong because it describes what server processes do, not what user processes do.

Explain the Memory Structures

3. ☑ **A, D,** and **F.** Every instance must have a database buffer cache, a log buffer, and a shared pool.
   ☒ **B, C,** and **G** are wrong because the Java pool, the large pool, and the Streams pool are only needed for certain options. **E** is wrong because the PGA is not part of the SGA at all.

4. ☑ **D.** The log buffer is fixed in size at startup time.
   ☒ **A, B, C, E,** and **F** are wrong because these are the SGA's resizable components. **G** is wrong because the log buffer is static.

5. ☑ **D.** The log buffer cannot be resized manually, never mind automatically.
   ☒ **A, B, C, E,** and **F** are wrong because these SGA components can all be automatically managed. **G** is wrong because the log buffer is static.

6. ☑ **A.** The session updates the copy of the block in memory and writes out the change vector to the log buffer.
   ☒ **B** is wrong, because while this will happen, it does not happen when the change is made. **C** is wrong because it confuses the session making changes in memory with LGWR propagating changes to disk. **D** is wrong because all changes to data occur in memory as they are made—the COMMIT is not relevant.

Describe the Process Structures

7. ☑ **A.** Archiving is not compulsory (though it is usually a good idea).
   ☒ **B, C, D,** and **E.** CKPT, DBWn, LGWR, and MMON are all necessary processes.

8. ☑ **C.** On COMMIT, the log writer flushes the log buffer to disk. No other background processes need do anything.

   ☒ **A** is wrong because checkpoints only occur on request, or on orderly shutdown. **B** is wrong because the algorithm DBWn uses to select buffers to write to the datafiles is not related to COMMIT processing, but to how busy the buffer is. **D** is wrong because ARCn only copies filled online redo logs; it doesn't copy change vectors in real time.

9. ☑ **A, C,** and **E.** A and C are correct because the DBA can choose to configure multiple archive and database writer processes. E is correct because one server process will be launched for every concurrent session.

   ☒ **B** and **D.** These are wrong because an instance can have only one log writer process and only one checkpoint process.

Summarize the Storage Structures

10. ☑ **C.** If a tablespace has several datafiles, segments can have extents in all of them.

    ☒ **A** is wrong because one extent consists of consecutive block in any one datafile. **B** is wrong because one segment can only exist in one tablespace (though one tablespace can contain many segments). **D** is wrong because while this can certainly be done, one block can only exist in one datafile.

11. ☑ **C.** Two groups of one member is the minimum required for the database to function.

    ☒ **A** and **B** are wrong because at least two groups are always required. **D** is wrong because while it is certainly advisable to multiplex the members, it is not a technical requirement.

12. ☑ **A.** The checkpoint process writes the RBA to the controlfile.

    ☒ **B, C,** and **D.** The online logs, the datafiles, and SGA have no knowledge of where the current RBA is.

LAB ANSWER

Possible queries follow:

```
select platform_name from v$database;
```

This will return the operating system that database is running on.

```
select name from v$controlfile;
```

This will return one row for each copy of the controlfile. If there is only one row, then it is not multiplexed.

```
select group#,bytes,members from v$log;
select group#,member from v$logfile;
```

The first query will show how many groups exist, their size, and how many members each group has. The second lists the name of each member and the group to which it belongs.

```
select t.name tname,d.name fname,bytes
from v$tablespace t join v$datafile d on t.ts#=d.ts# order by t.ts#;
```

This will list the tablespaces, with their datafile(s). This query is in fact incomplete: it will only list *permanent* tablespaces. To complete your picture of the physical layout of the database, this query must be run too:

```
select t.name tname,d.name fname,bytes
from v$tablespace t join v$tempfile d on t.ts#=d.ts# order by t.ts#;
```

This will show the *temporary* tablespaces. The difference between permanent and temporary tablespaces is covered in Chapter 7.

3
Preparing the Database Environment

A number of tools are available for managing an Oracle database, beginning with the Oracle Universal Installer (the OUI). This is an Oracle product in its own right that is used to manage the installation and maintenance of many other products. The installation of Oracle software has, as far as possible, been standardized for all products on all platforms—but there are platform and product variations. Before installing anything, it is essential to read the product's release notes for the platform concerned. This chapter goes through the process of planning the installation and then installing the Oracle Database 11g software with examples from Linux and Windows.

CERTIFICATION OBJECTIVE 3.01

Identify the Tools for Administering an Oracle Database

Oracle Corporation provides a number of tools for managing the Oracle environment. First (and the main subject of this chapter) there is the OUI, the Oracle Universal Installer. Second, there are tools for creating and upgrading a database. These can be launched from the OUI or run separately (as is done in Chapter 4). Third, the OUI will install a number of other tools for managing a database and related components, notably SQL*Plus. Depending on the installation type chosen, it may install SQL Developer, but iSQL*Plus, a product strongly advocated with database releases 9i and 10g, is no longer supplied.

Oracle Enterprise Manager needs a special mention. It comes in several forms, one of which (the Oracle Enterprise Manager Database Control) will be used extensively in this book.

The Oracle Universal Installer

Historically, managing Oracle software could be a painful task. This was because the DBA was largely responsible for ensuring that incompatible products were kept separate. It was not uncommon to install one product, a second, and a third satisfactorily—then installation of a fourth would break the other three. The problem of incompatibilities lies in the use of the *base libraries*. The base libraries provide facilities that are common to all Oracle products. For example, all Oracle products use the Oracle Net communications protocol; it is impossible to install a product without it. If two products are built on the same version of the base libraries, then (theoretically) they can coexist in the same *Oracle Home*. An Oracle Home is the location of an Oracle product installation: a set of files in a directory structure. Before the Oracle Universal Installer, each product had its own self-contained installation routine, which was sometimes not too clever at identifying incompatibilities with already installed products.

The OUI is written in Java, using JDK/JRE1.5. This means that it is the same on all platforms, with the exception of certain well-know and trivial variations in the Java user interface, such as whether windows have square or rounded corners. The OUI can be installed as a self-contained product in its own Oracle Home, but this is not usually necessary, as it is shipped with every other Oracle product and can be launched from the product installation CD (or DVD); it will install itself into the Oracle Home along with the product. There are different versions of the OUI, and if a product comes with an earlier version than one already installed on the machine, then it will usually be a good idea (and may indeed be necessary) to install the product using the already-installed version, from the existing Oracle Home. When the OUI prompts for the location of a `products.xml` file, specify the DVD with the product you want to install.

on the job

Always use the latest version of the OUI that you have available. There can be issues with updating the OUI inventory if you try to revert to earlier versions after using a later version.

The OUI Inventory

Central to the OUI is the *inventory*. This is a set of files that (ideally) exists outside any Oracle Home. The inventory stores details of all the Oracle products installed on the machine, including the exact version, the location, and in some cases details of patches that have been applied. Every run of the OUI will check the inventory for incompatibilities before permitting an install into an existing Oracle Home to proceed, and will then update the inventory with details of all products installed or upgraded. The location of the Linux inventory can be chosen by the DBA the first time the OUI (any version) is run on the machine. On Windows, the location is always created in

```
%SystemRoot%\Program files\Oracle\Inventory
```

All platforms have a hard-coded, platform-specific technique by which the OUI will find an existing inventory. On Linux this is a file:

```
/etc/oraInst.loc
```

On Solaris it is also a file:

```
/var/opt/oracle/oraInst.loc
```

One Windows it is a key in the registry:

```
HKEY_LOCAL_MACHINE\SOFTWARE\ORACLE\inst_loc
```

When the OUI starts, it will look for this file (or registry key). If it does not exist, OUI assumes that there has never been any Oracle software installed on the machine, and will create the file (or registry key) and write to it the location of the new inventory that is to be created. All subsequent runs of the OUI, no matter what version, will then be able to find the inventory.

This mechanism for creating an inventory pointer does raise an issue with operating system privileges: on Linux or Unix, the user running the installer for the first time will need permission to write to the appropriate directory. Usually only the root user can write to /etc or /var. As it is not acceptable for security reasons to run the OUI as the root user, OUI will generate a script (the orainstRoot.sh script) to be run by the root user that will create the oraInst.loc file. On Windows, the user running the OUI will need privileges that will let him/her create the registry key.

on the *job*

To relocate the inventory, first copy it (the whole directory system to which the inventory pointer is pointing) to the new location, and then edit the pointer file (or registry key). Sometimes, you may want to create a new inventory but keep the old one. On Linux, simply delete the oraInst.loc *file, run the OUI, and choose a location for the new inventory. From then on, edit* oraInst.loc *to switch between the two inventories.*

The Prerequisite Tests

The OUI checks certain requirements on the server machine before it will run. These are platform specific and are given in this file on the installation DVD:

- /install/oraparam.ini (Linux)
- \install\oraparam.ini (Windows)

The requirements are not too demanding, doing little more than checking that the graphics device on which the installer is displaying can show at least 256 colors.

The `oraparam.ini` file also specifies the location on the DVD of the file `products.xml`, which is the file with details of all the products that can be installed from this DVD. Each product will have its own requirements, and these may be demanding (or irritating, if you know they actually don't matter). The product requirements are listed in a set of XML files. Typical of these is

- `/stage/prereq/db/refhost.xml` (Linux)
- `\stage\prereq\db\refhost.xml` (Windows)

The Windows file is usually very simple, specifying little more than a calculation for necessary swap space, and the operating system release:

```
<SYSTEM>
  <MEMORY>
  <PHYSICAL_MEMORY VALUE="256" UNIT="MB"/>
  <!--AVAILABLE_MEMORY VALUE="512" UNIT="MB"/-->
        <SWAP_SIZE>
  <STEP NAME="PHYSICAL_MEMORY" ATLEAST="0" ATMOST="256"
UNIT="MB" MULTIPLE="3"/>
  <STEP NAME="PHYSICAL_MEMORY" GREATER_THAN="256" ATMOST="512"
UNIT="MB" MULTIPLE="2"/>
  <STEP NAME="PHYSICAL_MEMORY" GREATER_THAN="512" ATMOST="2048"
UNIT="MB" MULTIPLE="1.5"/>
  <STEP NAME="PHYSICAL_MEMORY" GREATER_THAN="2048" ATMOST="8192"
UNIT="MB" MULTIPLE="1"/>
  <STEP NAME="PHYSICAL_MEMORY" GREATER_THAN="8192"
UNIT="MB" MULTIPLE="0.75"/>
  </SWAP_SIZE>
  </MEMORY>
  </SYSTEM>
  <CERTIFIED_SYSTEMS>
  <OPERATING_SYSTEM>
  <VERSION VALUE="5.0"/>
  <SERVICE_PACK VALUE="1"/>
  </OPERATING_SYSTEM>
  <OPERATING_SYSTEM>
  <VERSION VALUE="5.1"/>
  <SERVICE_PACK VALUE="1"/>
  </OPERATING_SYSTEM>
  <OPERATING_SYSTEM>
  <VERSION VALUE="5.2"/>
```

```
</OPERATING_SYSTEM>
<!--Microsoft Windows Vista-->
<OPERATING_SYSTEM>
<VERSION VALUE="6.0"/>
</OPERATING_SYSTEM>
</CERTIFIED_SYSTEMS>
```

It is worth noting the swap space calculation, which is based on the amount of main memory detected. For instance, if OUI detects physical memory of 512 MB–2048 MB, it will demand a swap file of 1.5 times the amount of physical memory. OUI is not intelligent enough to realize that Windows can resize its swap file, so that even if the present size is far less than this, it could expand to far more. Also note that the Windows Vista base version (Windows version 6.0) is listed, but not with any service packs.

The Linux prerequisites are more demanding, in that as well as a calculation for required swap space they specify a whole list of packages and kernel settings, with several sections for the various supported Linux distributions. Following is a print of a typical section:

```
<PACKAGES>
  <PACKAGE NAME="make" VERSION="3.81" />
  <PACKAGE NAME="binutils" VERSION="2.17.50.0.6" />
  <PACKAGE NAME="gcc" VERSION="4.1.1" />
  <PACKAGE NAME="libaio" VERSION="0.3.106" />
  <PACKAGE NAME="libaio-devel" VERSION="0.3.106" />
  <PACKAGE NAME="libstdc++" VERSION="4.1.1" />
  <PACKAGE NAME="elfutils-libelf-devel" VERSION="0.125" />
  <PACKAGE NAME="sysstat" VERSION="7.0.0" />
  <PACKAGE NAME="compat-libstdc++-33" VERSION="3.2.3" />
  <PACKAGE NAME="libgcc" VERSION="4.1.1" />
  <PACKAGE NAME="libstdc++-devel" VERSION="4.1.1" />
  <PACKAGE NAME="unixODBC" VERSION="2.2.11" />
  <PACKAGE NAME="unixODBC-devel" VERSION="2.2.11" />
</PACKAGES>
<KERNEL>
  <PROPERTY NAME="semmsl" NAME2="semmsl2" VALUE="250" />
  <PROPERTY NAME="semmns" VALUE="32000" />
  <PROPERTY NAME="semopm" VALUE="100" />
  <PROPERTY NAME="semmni" VALUE="128" />
  <PROPERTY NAME="shmmax" VALUE="536870912" />
  <PROPERTY NAME="shmmni" VALUE="4096" />
  <PROPERTY NAME="shmall" VALUE="2097152" />
  <PROPERTY NAME="file-max" VALUE="65536" />
  <PROPERTY NAME="VERSION" VALUE="2.6.18" />
  <PROPERTY NAME="ip_local_port_range" ATLEAST="1024" ATMOST="65000" />
```

```
      <PROPERTY NAME="rmem_default" VALUE="4194304" />
      <PROPERTY NAME="rmem_max" VALUE="4194304" />
      <PROPERTY NAME="wmem_default" VALUE="262144" />
      <PROPERTY NAME="wmem_max" VALUE="262144" />
   </KERNEL>
```

Obtaining the required packages can be a mission for some Linux and other Unix distributions. Also, some of the kernel settings (such as the `ip_local_port_range`) may conflict with local system administration policies. If you cannot get your system into a state where it will pass the prerequisite tests, you have three options:

First, you can edit the `oraparam.ini` file or the `refhost.xml` file to change the value or to remove the test entirely. This will "fix" the problem permanently. Second, you can run the OUI with a switch that tells it to ignore the prerequisite tests. Third, you can run the OUI and during the run tell it to ignore any failings. This last option can only work when running OUI interactively, not when doing a silent install.

If at all possible, do not do any of these! In practice, often the problem is not that the products will not work. For example, on Linux, some of the kernel settings and packages are not really needed for an entry-level installation. The problem will lie with support. If you ever raise an SR (an SR is a Service Request, passed to Oracle Support Services through Metalink) and your system does not conform to the prerequisites, the support analysts may well refuse to help you. So if you have to break one of the rules to get an installation through, fix it as soon as possible afterward.

Running the OUI

Oracle products are shipped on CDs or DVDs, or can be downloaded from Oracle Corporation's Web site. The installation can be done directly from the CD or DVD, but it us usually better to copy the CD or DVD to disk first, and install from there. This does save time. The downloaded versions are usually ZIP files, or for Linux and Unix compressed TAR or CPIO files. Use whatever operating system utility is appropriate to expand them.

To launch the OUI, on Windows run the `setup.exe` file in the root of the CD or DVD, on Linux and Unix, run the `runInstaller` shell script.

Database Creation and Upgrade Tools

The DBCA, the Database Configuration Assistant, is a graphical tool for creating a database. It is fully described in Chapter 4. Creating a database is not a big deal. You can create twenty databases during a tea break if you have the scripts ready written.

DBCA generates and runs such scripts, and it makes sure that there are no silly mistakes. But it doesn't do anything that couldn't be done from a command-line utility. DBCA can be launched by OUI. First OUI instantiates the Oracle Home, and then it goes on to run DBCA.

As with database creation, database upgrade can be done manually or through a graphical tool. The graphical tool is the DBUA, the Database Upgrade Assistant. It, too, can be called by OUI, if OUI detects an existing database Oracle Home of an earlier version. The DBUA will ensure that no steps are missed, but many DBAs prefer to do upgrades manually. They believe that it gives them more control, and in some cases a manual upgrade can be quicker.

Both DBCA and DBUA are written in Java and therefore require a graphics terminal to display.

Tools for Issuing Ad Hoc SQL: SQL*Plus and SQL Developer

There are numerous tools that can be used to connect to an Oracle database. Two of the most basic are SQL*Plus and SQL Developer. These are provided by Oracle Corporation and are perfectly adequate for much of the work that a database administrator needs to do. The choice between them is partly a matter of personal preference, partly to do with the environment, and partly to do with functionality. SQL Developer undoubtedly offers far more function that SQL*Plus, but it is more demanding in that it needs a graphical terminal, whereas SQL*Plus can be used on character mode devices.

on the job

The iSQL*Plus product that was much trumpeted with database release 9i has now fallen into disuse and is no longer shipped with release 11g. Some old DBAs (who have often been skeptical about the value of graphical tools) predicted this and are using it as an excuse for ignoring SQL Developer. This is not a productive attitude.

SQL*Plus

SQL*Plus is available on all platforms to which the database has been ported, installed into both Oracle database and Oracle client Oracle Homes. On Linux, the executable file is `sqlplus`. The location of this file will be installation specific but will typically be something like

```
/u01/app/oracle/product/db_1/bin/sqlplus
```

Your Linux account should be set up appropriately to run SQL*Plus. There are some environment variables that will need to be set. These are

- ORACLE_HOME
- PATH
- LD_LIBRARY_PATH

The PATH must include the bin directory in the Oracle Home. The LD_LIBRARY_PATH should include the lib directory in the Oracle Home, but in practice you may get away without setting this. Figure 3-1 shows a Linux terminal window and some tests to see if the environment is correct.

In Figure 3-1, first the echo command checks whether the three variables have been set up correctly: there is an ORACLE_HOME, and the bin and lib directories in it have been set as the first elements of the PATH and LD_LIBRARY_PATH variables. Then which confirms that the SQL*Plus executable file really is available, in the PATH. Finally, SQL*Plus is launched with a username, a password, and a connect identifier passed to it on the command line.

Following the logon, the next lines of text display the version of SQL*Plus being used, which is 11.1.0.6.0 and the version of the database to which the connection has been made (which happens to be the same as the version of the SQL*Plus tool) and which options have been installed within the database. The last line is the prompt to the user, SQL>, at which point he/she can enter any SQL*Plus or SQL command.

FIGURE 3-1

Checking the Linux session setup

```
 db11g@jwlnx1:~                                                      _ □ X
[db11g@jwlnx1 ~]$
[db11g@jwlnx1 ~]$ echo $ORACLE_HOME
/u01/app/db11g/product/11.1.0/db_1
[db11g@jwlnx1 ~]$ echo $LD_LIBRARY_PATH
/u01/app/db11g/product/11.1.0/db_1/lib:
[db11g@jwlnx1 ~]$ echo $PATH
/u01/app/db11g/product/11.1.0/db_1/bin:/usr/kerberos/bin:/usr/local/bin:/bin:/us
r/bin:/usr/X11R6/bin:/home/db11g/bin:.
[db11g@jwlnx1 ~]$
[db11g@jwlnx1 ~]$ which sqlplus
/u01/app/db11g/product/11.1.0/db_1/bin/sqlplus
[db11g@jwlnx1 ~]$
[db11g@jwlnx1 ~]$ sqlplus system/oracle@orcl

SQL*Plus: Release 11.1.0.6.0 - Production on Mon Oct 22 02:44:59 2007

Copyright (c) 1982, 2007, Oracle.  All rights reserved.


Connected to:
Oracle Database 11g Enterprise Edition Release 11.1.0.6.0 - Production
With the Partitioning, OLAP, Data Mining and Real Application Testing options

SQL> █
```

Historically, there were always two versions of SQL*Plus for Microsoft Windows: the character version and the graphical version. The character version is the executable file `sqlplus.exe`, the graphical version was `sqlplusw.exe`; with the current release the graphical version no longer exists, but many DBAs will prefer to use it, and the versions shipped with earlier releases are perfectly good tools for working with an 11*g* database. There are no problems with mixing versions: an 11*g* SQL*Plus client can connect to a 9*i* database, and a 9*i* SQL*Plus client can connect to an 11*g* database; changes in Oracle Net may make it impossible to go back further than 9*i*. Following a default installation of either the Oracle database or just the Oracle client on Windows, SQL*Plus will be available as a shortcut on the Windows Start menu.

The tests of the environment and the need to set the variables if they are not correct, previously described for a Linux installation, are not usually necessary on a Windows installation. This is because the variables are set in the Windows registry by the Oracle Universal Installer when the software is installed. If SQL*Plus does not launch successfully, check the registry variables. Figure 3-2 shows the relevant section of the registry, viewed with the Windows `regedit.exe` registry editor utility. Within the registry editor, navigate to the key

```
HKEY_LOCAL_MACHINE\SOFTWARE\ORACLE\KEY_OraDb11g_home1
```

The final element of this navigation path will have a different name if there have been several 11*g* installations on the machine.

FIGURE 3-2	

The Oracle
registry variable

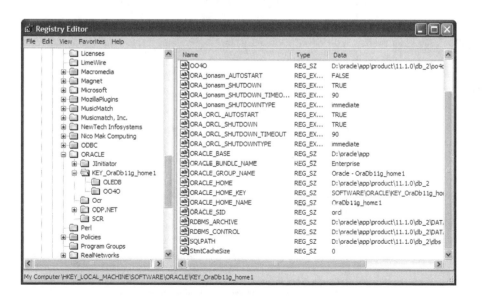

SQL Developer

SQL Developer is a tool for connecting to an Oracle database (or, in fact, some non-Oracle databases too) and issuing ad hoc SQL commands. It can also manage PL/SQL objects. Unlike SQL*Plus, it is a graphical tool with wizards for commonly needed actions. SQL Developer is written in Java, and requires a Java Runtime Environment (a JRE) to run. Being written in Java, SQL Developer is available on all platforms that support the appropriate version of the Java Runtime Environment (the JRE). There are no significant differences between platforms.

SQL Developer need not be installed with the Oracle Universal Installer, which is used to install most other Oracle products. It does not exist in an Oracle Home but is a completely self-contained product. The latest version can be downloaded from Oracle Corporation's Web site.

To install SQL Developer, unzip the ZIP file. That's all. It does require JDK1.5, the Java Runtime Environment release 1.5, to be available: this comes from Sun Microsystems. But if JDK1.5 (or a later release) is not already available on the machine being used, there are downloadable versions of SQL Developer for Windows that include it. For platforms other than Windows, the JDK1.5 must be preinstalled. Download it from Sun Microsystem's Web site, and install it according to the platform-specific directions. To check that the JDK is available and the version, from an operating system prompt run the command

```
java -version
```

This should return something like

```
java version "1.5.0_13"
Java(TM) 2 Runtime Environment, Standard Edition (build 1.5.0_13-b05)
Java HotSpot(TM) Client VM (build 1.5.0_13-b05, mixed mode, sharing)
```

If it does not, using which java may help identify the problem: the search path could be locating an incorrect version.

Once SQL Developer has been unzipped, change your current directory to the directory in which SQL Developer was unzipped, and launch it. On Windows, the executable file is sqldeveloper.exe. On Linux, it is the sqldeveloper.sh shell script. Remember to check that the DISPLAY environment variable has been set to a suitable value (such as127.0.0.1:0.0, if SQL Developer is being run on the system console) before running the shell script.

Any problems with installing the JRE and launching SQL Developer should be referred to your system administrator.

on the
job

Database 11g does ship with a release of SQL Developer, and OUI will unzip it into a directory in the Oracle Home, but this will not be the up-to-date version. As of the time of writing, the version shipped with the production release of the 11g database is version 1.1, but the current version is 1.2.

Figure 3-3 shows the SQL Developer user interface after connecting to a database and issuing a simple query.

The general layout of the SQL Developer window is a left pane for navigation around objects, and a right pane to display and enter information.

In the figure, the left-hand pane shows that a connection has been made to a database. The connection is called orcl_sys. This name is just a label chosen when the connection was defined, but most developers will use some sort of naming convention—in this case, the name chosen is the database identifier, which is orcl, and the name of the user the connection was made as, which was sys. The branches beneath list all the possible object types that can be managed. Expanding the

FIGURE 3-3

The SQL
Developer user
interface

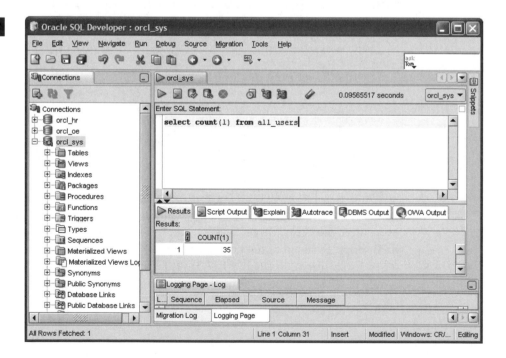

branches would list the objects themselves. The right-hand pane has an upper part prompting the user to enter a SQL statement, and a lower part that will display the result of the statement. The layout of the panes and the tabs visible on them are highly customizable.

The menu buttons across the top menu bar give access to standard facilities:

- **File** A normal Windows-like file menu, from where one can save work and exit from the tool.
- **Edit** A normal Windows-like edit menu, from where one can undo, redo, copy, paste, find, and so on.
- **View** The options for customizing the SQL Developer user interface.
- **Navigate** Facilities for moving between panes, and also for moving around code that is being edited.
- **Run** Forces execution of the SQL statements, SQL script, or PL/SQL block that is being worked on.
- **Debug** Rather than running a whole block of code, step through it line by line with breakpoints.
- **Source** Options for use when writing SQL and PL/SQL code, such as keyword completion and automatic indenting.
- **Tools** Links to external programs, including SQL*Plus.
- **Migrate** Tools for converting applications designed for third-party databases (Microsoft Access and SQL Server, and MySQL) to the Oracle environment.
- **Help** It's pretty good.

SQL Developer can be a very useful tool, and it is very customizable. Experiment with it, read the Help, and set up the user interface the way that works best for you.

EXERCISE 3-1

Install SQL Developer on Windows

In this exercise, you will install SQL Developer on a Windows machine.

1. Download the current version of SQL Developer. The URL is

   `http://www.oracle.com/technology/software/products/sql/index.html`

Click the radio button to accept the license agreement, and then select the file that includes the JDK (if you do not already have this) or without the JDK if it already available on the PC.

The file will be called something like `sqldeveloper-1.2.1.3213.zip`, depending on the version.

2. Move the file to an empty directory, and expand it. You will need WinZip or a similar utility installed to do this. The next illustration shows the contents of the directory into which the file was unzipped, viewed from a command window.

```
C:\WINDOWS\system32\cmd.exe                                          _ □ ×

C:\sqldev\sqldeveloper>dir /ogn
 Volume in drive C is ACER
 Volume Serial Number is 389D-543B

 Directory of C:\sqldev\sqldeveloper

26/10/2007  09:46    <DIR>          .
26/10/2007  09:46    <DIR>          ..
26/10/2007  09:40    <DIR>          ide
26/10/2007  09:40    <DIR>          j2ee
26/10/2007  09:40    <DIR>          jdbc
26/10/2007  09:40    <DIR>          jdev
26/10/2007  09:41    <DIR>          jdk
26/10/2007  09:41    <DIR>          jlib
26/10/2007  09:41    <DIR>          lib
26/10/2007  09:41    <DIR>          rdbms
26/10/2007  09:41    <DIR>          sqldeveloper
21/08/2007  16:55             1,404 icon.png
21/08/2007  16:58            14,154 readme.html
21/08/2007  16:54               489 sqlcli
21/08/2007  16:54               577 sqlcli.bat
21/08/2007  16:55            84,432 sqldeveloper.exe
21/08/2007  16:54                71 sqldeveloper.sh
               6 File(s)        101,127 bytes
              11 Dir(s)   1,569,353,728 bytes free

C:\sqldev\sqldeveloper>_
```

Note the presence of the `readme.html` file. This is the release notes—open it in a browser and read them.

3. Confirm success of *e* installation by running the `sqldeveloper.exe` executable file, either from the command prompt or by double-clicking it in Windows Explorer.

Oracle Enterprise Manager

The version of Oracle Enterprise Manager relevant to the OCP examination is Database Control. This is a tool for managing one database (which can be a RAC database), whereas Grid Control can manage many databases (and more). Database Control is installed into the Oracle Home. It consist of a Java process that monitors a port for incoming connection requests from browsers. If there are several database instances running off the same Oracle Home, each instance will be accessible through Database Control on a different port.

Database Control connects to the database on behalf of the user. It has built-in monitoring capability and will display real-time information regarding alert conditions, activity, and resource usage. It also gives access to many wizards that can make database management and tuning tasks feasible for novice DBAs, and quick to carry out for experienced DBAs.

Starting and stopping the Database Control process is described in Chapter 5; using it for management tasks is demonstrated in every subsequent chapter.

on the *Oracle Enterprise Manager can be a very useful tool, but never use it without*
(job) *understanding what it is doing. Many DBAs like to work from the SQL*Plus or SQL Developer command line to understand out exactly how to do something, and then use Enterprise Manager to make doing it easy. It is also a nice tool for checking syntax for something you've forgotten.*

Other Administration Tools

There are a number of other utilities that will be used in the course of this book. In many cases, there are both graphical and command-line interfaces. All of these are installed into the Oracle Home.

Oracle Net Manager, Oracle Net Configuration Assistant

These are two Java graphical tools for configuring the Oracle networking environment. There is considerable overlap in their functionality, but each does have some capability lacking in the other. Most network administration tasks can also be done through Database Control, and all can be done by editing configuration files by hand.

Historically, manual editing of the Oracle Net configuration files could be an extremely dodgy business: many DBAs believed that the files were very sensitive to trifling variations in format such as use of white spaces, abbreviations, and case. For this reason alone, the graphical tools have always been popular. Recent releases of Oracle Net appear to be less sensitive to such issues, but the graphical tools are still useful for preventing silly syntax errors.

Data Loading and Unloading Utilities

The old utilities for transferring data between Oracle databases were the Export and Import tools. Export runs queries against a database to extract object definitions and data, and writes them out to an operating system file as a set of DDL and

DML commands. Import reads the file and executes the DDL and DML statements to create the objects and enter the data into them. These utilities were very useful for transferring data between databases, because the transfer could go across operating systems and Oracle versions, but because they work through regular user sessions (they are client-server tools), they were not always suitable for large-scale operations. Export files can only be read by Import.

The replacement for Export and Import is Datapump, introduced with release 10g. Functionally, Datapump is very similar: it extracts data from one database, writes it out to a file, and inserts it into another database (possibly a different version, on a different platform). But the implementation is completely different. Datapump uses background processes, not server sessions, to read and write data. This makes it much faster. Launching, controlling, and monitoring Datapump jobs is done through client-server sessions, but the job itself all happens within the instance. Export and Import are still supported, but Datapump is the preferred utility. Datapump-generated files can only be read by Datapump: there is no compatibility with Export and Import.

SQL*Loader is a tool for loading large amounts of data into an Oracle database from operating system files. These files can be laid out in a number of formats. There are restrictions on the formats SQL*Loader can use, but it is a pretty versatile tool and can be configured to parse many file layouts. Typical usage is regular upload of data into an Oracle database from a third-party feeder system: the third-party database will write the data out in an agreed format, and SQL*Loader will then read it.

e x a m

ⓦatch

*Datapump can read only files generated by Datapump, but SQL*Loader can read files generated by any third-party product, so long as the file is formatted in a way that can be parsed.*

Datapump and SQL*Loader are described in Chapter 18. Both have command-line interfaces and a graphical interface through Database Control.

on the job

Export and Import will be useful for a long time to come. Datapump is available only for releases 10g and 11g, so whenever it is necessary to transfer data to or from 9i and earlier databases, the older utilities will still be needed. It is well worth getting familiar with them.

Backup Utilities

It is possible to back up an Oracle database using operating system utilities. Operating system backups (known as *user-managed* backups) are fully supported, and there are circumstances when they may be the best option. But the preferred tool is RMAN, the Recovery Manager. RMAN backups are known as *server-managed* backups. RMAN is introduced and used for simple backup and restore operations in Chapters 16 and 17. It is taken much further in the second OCP examination.

RMAN server-managed backups can do things that user-managed backups cannot. These things include incremental backups, where only the changed blocks of a datafile are backed up; block-level restore and recovery, where if the damage to a file is only to a small part of the file, just that part can be repaired; the application of an incremental backup to full backup, to roll it forward; and validating the datafiles to detect corruptions before end users hit them.

on the *The degree of knowledge of backup and recovery techniques tested by the*
Job *OCP examinations may not be adequate for a DBA to be considered fully competent. Remember that the OCP curriculum is only an introduction to database administration. Backup is a critical task and will require further study.*

The Oracle Secure Backup facility lets the DBA manage backup of the entire environment: Oracle Application Servers, remote clients, and operating system files, as well as the database. It is developed by Oracle in conjunction with operating system and hardware vendors.

CERTIFICATION OBJECTIVE 3.02

Plan an Oracle Database Installation

Before running OUI, it is necessary to confirm adequate hardware and operating system resources, to make a decision about where to install the software, and to consider setting some environment variables.

Choice of Operating System

Some people become almost religiously attached to their favorite operating system. Try to avoid this. All operating systems have good and bad points: none are suitable for all applications. In general, Oracle Corporation supports all the mainstream platforms, including

- Linux on Intel and AMD
- Microsoft Windows on Intel and AMD
- Solaris on SPARC
- AIX on POWER
- HPUX on PA-RISC

These platforms are probably the most common, but there are many others. Some operating systems and CPUs come in both 32-bit and 64-bit versions. Usually, Oracle ports the database to both. When selecting an operating system, the choice should be informed by many factors, including

- Cost
- Ease of use
- Choice of hardware
- Available skills
- Scalability
- Fault tolerance
- Performance

There are other factors, and not only technical ones. Corporate standards will be particularly important.

on the !job *There is some gossip about a supposed rivalry between Oracle and Microsoft (and indeed their respective founders). This is nonsense. Oracle Corporation is fully committed to working with the Microsoft environment. Even the Microsoft client operating systems (such as Windows XP) will usually work, though of course they will never be validated for server applications.*

Linux deserves a special mention. Oracle Corporation has made a huge commitment to Linux, and Linux is used as the development platform for many products (including database release 11g). Linux comes in several distributions. The most popular for Oracle servers are Red Hat and SUSE, but do not ignore the Oracle distribution:

Enterprise Linux. This is very well packaged and fully supported by Oracle Corporation. This means you can have one support line for the entire server technology stack.

Hardware and Operating System Resources

Determining the necessary hardware resources for an Oracle database server requires knowledge of the anticipated data volumes and transaction workload. There are sizing guides available on Metalink. The minimum hardware requirements for a usable system are

- 1 GB RAM
- 1.5 GB swap space
- 400 MB in the TEMP location
- 1.5 GB–3.5 GB for the Oracle Home
- 1.5 GB for the demonstration seed database
- 2.4 GB for the flash recovery area
- A single 1 GHz CPU

The wide range in space for the Oracle Home is because of platform variations. Around 2.5 GB is typical for the Windows NTFS file system, 3.5 GB for the Linux ext3 file system. The flash recovery area is optional. Even if defined, there is no check made as to whether the space is actually available. Machines of a lower specification than that given above can be used for learning or development but would not be suitable for anything else. The TEMP location is a directory specified by the TEMP environment variable.

The server operating system must be checked for compliance with the Oracle certified platforms, bearing in mind these issues:

- That some operating systems come in 32-bit and 64-bit versions
- Correct version and patch level
- Required packages
- Kernel parameters

These factors will be checked by the OUI.

EXERCISE 3-2

Confirm Available Hardware Resources

In this exercise, you will check what resources are available, first for Windows and second for Linux.

Windows:

1. Right-click My Computer, and bring up the Properties dialog box. Note the amount of RAM. This should be at least 512 MB, preferable 1 GB.

2. Take the Advanced tab, and then in the Performance section click the Settings button.

3. In the Performance Options dialog box take the Advanced tab. Note the virtual memory setting. This should be at least one and a half times the memory reported in Step 1.

4. Open a command window, and find the location of your temporary data directory with this command:

```
C:\> echo %TEMP%
```

This will return something like

```
C:\DOCUME~1\JOHNWA~1\LOCALS~1\Temp
```

Check that there is at least 400 MB free space on the file system returned (in this example, it is drive C:).

5. Identify a file system with 5 GB free space for the Oracle Home and a database. This must be a local disk, not on a file server. If you want to copy the installation DVD (you probably do), that will need another 1.5 GB, which can be on a file server.

Linux:

1. From an operating system prompt, run free to show main memory and swap space, which should ideally both be at least 1 GB. These are the values in the total column. In the illustration that follows, they are both about 2 GB.

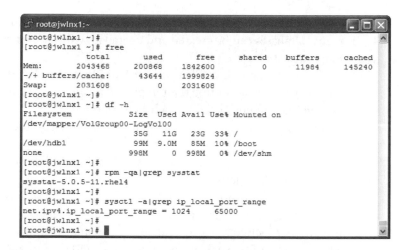

2. Run df -h to show the free space in each mounted file system. Confirm that there is a file system with 5 GB free for the Oracle Home and the database. Confirm that there is 400 MB free in /tmp if it exists as a separate file system; if there is no specific file system for /tmp (as is the case in the illustration), you can assume that it is in the root file system. In the illustration, there is 23 GB free in the root file system.

3. Use rpm to check that all required packages are installed, at the correct (or later) version. In the illustration, the sysstat package is being checked.

4. Use sysctl to check that all the required kernel settings have been made—you may need to have root privilege to do this. In the illustration, the IP port range is being checked.

Optimal Flexible Architecture

The Oracle Home will need a file system into which it can be installed. Oracle Corporation has designed OFA, the Optimal Flexible Architecture, as a file system directory structure that should make maintaining multiple versions of multiple Oracle products straightforward. The heart of OFA is two environment variables: ORACLE_BASE and ORACLE_HOME. The ORACLE_BASE directory is one directory on the server, beneath which all the Oracle software (all products, all versions) should be installed. Each version of each product will then have its own

ORACLE_HOME, beneath the ORACLE_BASE. This structure should ensure that many databases can be created and upgraded without ever ending up with files in inappropriate locations.

The Linux and Unix OFA standard for ORACLE_BASE is that it should be a directory named according the template $/pm/h/u$, where p is a string constant such as u, m is a numeric constant such as 01, h is a standard directory name such as app, and u is the operating system account that will own all the Oracle software, such as oracle.

The Windows OFA standard for ORACLE_BASE is \oracle\app off the root of any suitable drive letter.

The OFA standard for the database ORACLE_HOME is $ORACLE_BASE/ $product/v/db\_n$, where $product$ is a the constant product, v is the release number of the product such as 11.1.0, and db_n is a name derived by the installer based on which product it is, such as db for database, and an incrementing number for each installation of that product, such as 1.

Typical Linux values for ORACLE_BASE and ORACLE_HOME are

```
/u01/app/oracle
/u01/app/oracle/product/11.1.0/db_1
```

and typical Windows values are

```
D:\oracle\app
D:\oracle\app\product\11.1.0\db_1
```

The OFA location for the database itself is ORACLE_BASE/q/d, where q is the string oradata and d is the name of the database. A Linux example for a database called orcl is

```
/u01/app/oracle/oradata/orcl
```

Within the database directory, the controlfile copies, online redo log files, and datafiles should be named as follows:

File Type	Name	Variable	Examples
Controlfile	control*nn*.ctl	*nn* is a unique number	control01.ctl, control02.ctl
Redo log files	redo*nn*.log	*nn* is the online redo log file group number	redo01.log, redo02.log
Datafiles	*tablespacenamenn*.dbf	the datafile's tablespace name and a number	system01.dbf, system02.dbf

OFA does not specify the naming convention for multiplexed online redo log files. Most DBAs will suffix the OFA name with a letter to differentiate members in the same group: redo01a.log, redo01b.log.

Environment Variables

One significant difference between Windows and Unix-like operating systems is in the way in which environment variables are set. Within the Unix family, there are further variations depending on the shell being used. In Windows operating systems, there is the registry: Unix has no equivalent of this.

The Oracle database makes use of several environment variables, some of which can be set before even running the OUI. The OUI will prompt for them, using the preset values as defaults. On Linux, the one variable that must be set before the installer can run is the DISPLAY.

Variables in Windows

Variables can be set at various levels with various degrees of persistence on a Windows system, ranging from permanent, system-wide variables set in the Windows registry to variables set interactively within a command shell. As a general rule, variables set at a higher level (such as within the registry) can be overruled at a lower level (such as within a shell).

The highest level for variables is in the registry. The OUI creates a key in the registry,

```
HKEY_LOCAL_MACHINE\SOFTWARE\ORACLE
```

and defines variables for each installed Oracle product beneath this. Figure 3-2 earlier shows the variables set for the ORACLE key, and then those set one level down, in the key KEY_OraDb11g_home1.

At the ORACLE level, the variable inst_loc defines the location of the OUI inventory, described previously. Beneath this level there are keys for each installed product. In the example shown, there are two products installed: JInitiator (which is Oracle's client-side JVM for running the Forms viewing applet—two versions have been installed on the system) and Database 11*g*. In the key KEY_OraDb11g_home1 there are a number of variables, two of the more significant being the ORACLE_BASE and the ORACLE_HOME. Others specify the locations of various components and the options Windows should use for automatic startup and shutdown of a database instance called ORCL.

There is no easy way to query the value of a Windows registry variable, other than by looking at the registry with a tool such as the regedit.exe *registry editing tool. For this reason, many DBAs like to set variables at the session level, from where they can be easily retrieved and used. Figure 3-4 shows an example of doing this.*

The commands for setting up the environment in the manner desired would usually be specified in a batch file that could be invoked from the command line or as a login script.

Variables in Linux

The syntax for setting and reading environment variables varies from one shell to another. The examples that follow are for the bash shell, because that is possibly the most widely used Linux shell.

Linux environment variables are always session specific. They must all be set up for each session—there is no equivalent of the Windows registry setting up variables with a scope that can include all sessions. To simulate setting what might be thought of as "global" variables applying to all sessions by all users, set them in the /etc/ profile file, which is executed at each logon.

Figure 3-5 shows examples of setting and using bash shell environment variables.

FIGURE 3-4

Setting and using Windows environment variables

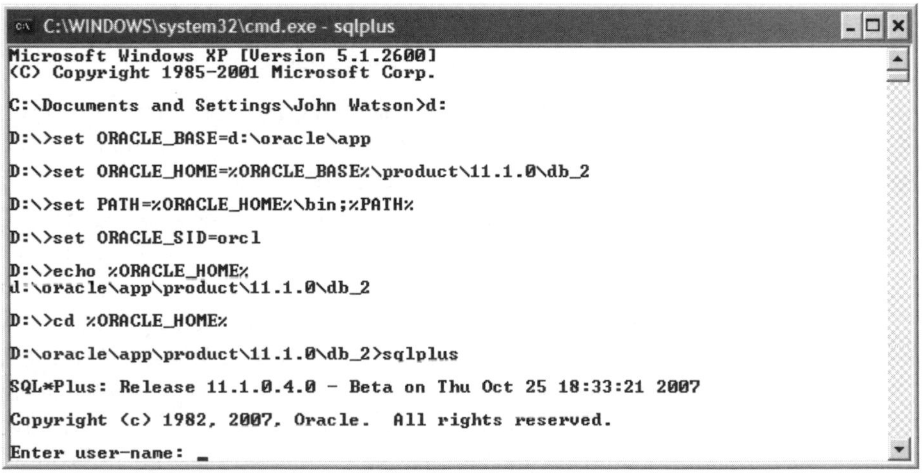

```
C:\WINDOWS\system32\cmd.exe - sqlplus                              _ □ ×
Microsoft Windows XP [Version 5.1.2600]
(C) Copyright 1985-2001 Microsoft Corp.

C:\Documents and Settings\John Watson>d:

D:\>set ORACLE_BASE=d:\oracle\app

D:\>set ORACLE_HOME=%ORACLE_BASE%\product\11.1.0\db_2

D:\>set PATH=%ORACLE_HOME%\bin;%PATH%

D:\>set ORACLE_SID=orcl

D:\>echo %ORACLE_HOME%
d:\oracle\app\product\11.1.0\db_2

D:\>cd %ORACLE_HOME%

D:\oracle\app\product\11.1.0\db_2>sqlplus

SQL*Plus: Release 11.1.0.4.0 - Beta on Thu Oct 25 18:33:21 2007

Copyright (c) 1982, 2007, Oracle.  All rights reserved.

Enter user-name: _
```

FIGURE 3-5

Setting and using environment variables in the bash shell

```
db11g@jwlnx1:~
[db11g@jwlnx1 ~]$
[db11g@jwlnx1 ~]$
[db11g@jwlnx1 ~]$
[db11g@jwlnx1 ~]$ export ORACLE_BASE=/u01/app
[db11g@jwlnx1 ~]$ export ORACLE_HOME=$ORACLE_BASE/db11g/product/11.1.0/db_1
[db11g@jwlnx1 ~]$ export PATH=$ORACLE_HOME/bin:$PATH
[db11g@jwlnx1 ~]$ export LD_LIBRARY_PATH=$ORACLE_HOME/lib:$LD_LIBRARY_PATH
[db11g@jwlnx1 ~]$ export DISPLAY=jwacer.bplc.co.za:0.0
[db11g@jwlnx1 ~]$ export ORACLE_SID=orcl11g
[db11g@jwlnx1 ~]$
[db11g@jwlnx1 ~]$ which sqlplus
/u01/app/db11g/product/11.1.0/db_1/bin/sqlplus
[db11g@jwlnx1 ~]$
[db11g@jwlnx1 ~]$ echo $ORACLE_SID
orcl11g
[db11g@jwlnx1 ~]$
[db11g@jwlnx1 ~]$
```

e x a m

ⓦatch *If the DISPLAY is not set appropriately, OUI will not be able to open any windows and will throw an error.*

Note that in Figure 3-5 two more variables are being set on Linux than in Figure 3-4 on Windows. The LD_LIBRARY_PATH variable should include all dynamically linked libraries that may be needed, and the DISPLAY must be set to point to the terminal on which the user is working.

SCENARIO & SOLUTION

What should go on a checklist before starting an install on Linux or Unix?	You'll need an operating system account, in the group to be used by all DBAs. This account and group will need write permission to the Oracle Base directory. The operating system must be a certified version, including any required packages and kernel settings. There'll need to be a few gigabytes of disk space, plus enough main memory and swap space. A root logon must be available to run the scripts that write to the /etc directory. Unless you are going to do a silent install, you need a graphics terminal for the X Window System, and your DISPLAY variable set to point to it.
Is it the same list for Windows?	No, Windows is easier. There is no need to bother about the equivalent of a root logon because there are no root scripts to run, and no messing about with DISPLAY, because Windows terminals are always graphics devices.

CERTIFICATION OBJECTIVE 3.03

Install the Oracle Software by Using the Oracle Universal Installer (OUI)

To run the OUI for the first time, log on to the server machine as an operating system user with permission to read the CD or DVD (or the directory to which it has been copied) and to write to the directory chosen for the ORACLE_BASE. Then launch the OUI by running

```
setup.exe   (Windows)

runInstaller.sh   (Linux)
```

To bypass the prerequisite checks (not advised, but may be useful), add a switch:

```
runinstaller -ignoreSysPrereqs
```

It is possible to do an installation silently. This will be necessary if there is no graphics device, and is very convenient if you are performing many identical installs on identical machines. Also, it becomes possible to embed an Oracle installation within the routine for installing a complete application. A silent install requires a response file, which includes answers to all the prompts that would otherwise be given. The syntax for running the OUI in this way is

```
runInstaller -silent -reponsefile responsefilename
```

The response file can be created manually (there are examples in the /response directory on the installation DVD), or it can be recorded by OUI from an interactive install:

```
runInstaller -record -destinationFile responsefilename
```

Before doing a silent install, the inventory pointer file (/etc/oraInst.loc on Linux) must have been created, or OUI will not be able to locate (or create if necessary) the inventory.

INSIDE THE EXAM

The Tools and the Prerequisites

Be absolutely clear on what tool installs the software (the OUI) and what tools create a database (the DBCA, or do it from the SQL*Plus command line), but remember that the OUI can call the DBCA. Remember the relationship between the Oracle Base and the Oracle Home and the databases: the whole idea of OFA is that one Oracle Base can contain multiple Oracle Homes

(for different products, and different versions of the same product), and each database Oracle Home can support several databases.

The prerequisites cover hardware requirements and operating system version and configuration. These can be bypassed, but if so, there is no guarantee that the installation will work afterward.

EXERCISE 3-3

Install the Oracle Home

In this exercise, install an Oracle Home on Linux using the OUI. The equivalent exercise for Windows is the lab question at the end of this chapter.

1. Log on to Linux as a user who is a member of the group dba. In the examples following, the user is db11g. Confirm the username and group membership with the id command, as in this illustration:

```
 db11g@jwlnx1:~                                                    [_][□][×]
login as: db11g
Sent username "db11g"
db11g@10.0.0.4's password:
Last login: Sat Oct 27 00:57:19 2007 from 10.0.0.12
[db11g@jwlnx1 ~]$
[db11g@jwlnx1 ~]$ id
uid=501(db11g) gid=501(dba) groups=100(users),501(dba)
[db11g@jwlnx1 ~]$
[db11g@jwlnx1 ~]$ su -
Password:
[root@jwlnx1 ~]# mkdir -p /u02/app/db11g
[root@jwlnx1 ~]# chown db11g:dba /u02/app/db11g
[root@jwlnx1 ~]# chmod 770 /u02/app/db11g
[root@jwlnx1 ~]# exit
logout
[db11g@jwlnx1 ~]$ export DISPLAY=10.0.0.12:0.0
[db11g@jwlnx1 ~]$
[db11g@jwlnx1 ~]$ /home/db11g/db11g_dvd/runInstaller
Starting Oracle Universal Installer...
```

2. Switch to the root user with su and create an OFA-compliant directory for
   the Oracle Base with the mkdir command. In the example, this is /u02/app/
   db11g. Change the ownership and access modes of the directory such that the
   Oracle user has full control of it with the chown and chmod commands, as in
   the preceding illustration, and exit back to the Oracle user.

3. If you are not working on the console machine, set your DISPLAY variable to
   point to an X Window server on the machine on which you are working. In
   the illustration, this is 10.0.0.12:0.0.

4. Launch the OUI by running the runInstaller shell script from the root
   of the installation DVD. In the example, the DVD has been copied into the
   directory /home/db11g/db11g_dvd.

5. The first OUI window will appear, as in the illustration that follows:

   a. Select the Basic Installation radio button.

   b. Specify the Oracle Base as the directory created in Step 2. The Oracle
      Home will default to an OFA-compliant name beneath it.

   c. Select the Enterprise Edition installation type.

   d. Select dba as the Unix DBA group.

   e. Deselect the option to create a database.

   f. Click Next.

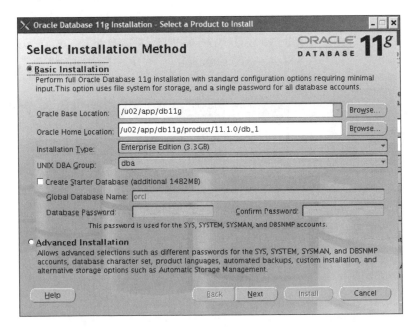

6. If this is the first Oracle install on the machine, the next window will prompt for the location of the OUI inventory. Be sure to specify a directory to which the Oracle user has write permission.

7. The OUI will then make its prerequisite checks. If they pass, click Next to continue. If any fail, take note and fix them if possible. Then use the Retry button to rerun the test. If the check really cannot be fixed, you can click Next to proceed anyway. At your own risk.

8. The next window will be a summary of what the OUI is going to do. Click Next, and it will do it. This should take twenty minutes or so (highly variable, depending on the machine).

9. Toward the end of the install, the window shown in the illustration that follows will appear. This prompts you to run two scripts as the root user: the `orainstRoot.sh` script that will write the `/etc/oraInst.loc` file, and the `root.sh` script that adjusts permissions on files in the new Oracle home. If this is not the first time the OUI has run on the machine, there will not be a prompt for `orainstRoot.sh`. Run the script(s) as root from an operating system prompt (accept defaults for any prompts) and then click OK.

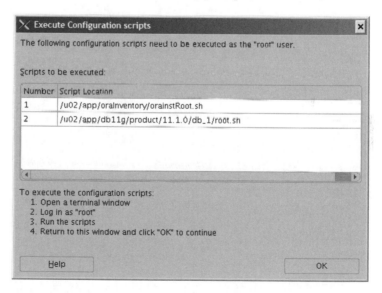

10. The installer will return a message stating that "The installation of Oracle Database 11g was successful." Congratulations! Click Exit.

CERTIFICATION SUMMARY

Most Oracle products are installed with the OUI, the Oracle Universal Installer. The OUI checks the target system to make sure it meets the documented requirements, and then instantiates the Oracle Home. OUI can than invoke the DBCA, Database Configuration Assistant, to create a database. Alternatively, a database can be created later—either with DBCA, or with one of the two provided tools for issuing ad hoc SQL: SQL*Plus, or SQL Developer. SQL Developer is shipped with the database but will usually be installed separately.

There are a number of other tools installed by OUI into the Oracle Home for interacting with a database. These include tools for network administration, backup, and Enterprise Manager Database Control.

TWO-MINUTE DRILL

Identify the Tools for Administering an Oracle Database

- ❏ Installation: the OUI
- ❏ Database creation and upgrade: DBCA, DBUA
- ❏ For issuing ad hoc SQL: SQL*Plus, SQL Developer
- ❏ Backup: RMAN, Oracle Secure Backup
- ❏ Network administration: Oracle Net Manager, Oracle Net Configuration Assistant
- ❏ Data load and unload utilities: Datapump, SQL*Loader
- ❏ Management: Oracle Enterprise Manager, Database Control, and Grid Control

Plan an Oracle Database Installation

- ❏ Hardware requirements
  - ❏ Disk space
  - ❏ Main memory
  - ❏ Swap space
  - ❏ Temporary space
  - ❏ A graphics terminal
- ❏ Operating system requirements
  - ❏ Certified version
  - ❏ Necessary packages
  - ❏ Kernel settings
- ❏ OFA: an appropriate directory for the Oracle Base

Install the Oracle Software by Using the Oracle Universal Installer (OUI)

- ❏ Use a suitable operating system account.
- ❏ Set necessary environment variables (Linux, Unix).
- ❏ Provide access to the root account (Linux, Unix).
- ❏ Make either an interactive or silent install.

SELF TEST

Identify the Tools for Administering an Oracle Database

1. Which of these tools is not usually installed with the Oracle Universal Installer? (Choose the best answer.)
   A. The Oracle Universal Installer itself
   B. SQL*Plus
   C. SQL Developer
   D. Oracle Enterprise Manager Grid Control

2. Which tools can be used to create a database? (Choose all correct answers.)
   A. Database Configuration Assistant
   B. Database Upgrade Assistant
   C. SQL*Plus
   D. Oracle Universal Installer
   E. Oracle Enterprise Manager Database Control

3. Oracle provides the ability to back up the entire environment, not just the Oracle Database. What tool can do this? (Choose the best answer.)
   A. Recovery Manager
   B. Oracle Secure Backup
   C. User-managed backups, carried out with operating system commands

Plan an Oracle Database Installation

4. What statement best describes the relationship between the Oracle Base and the Oracle Home? (Choose the best answer.)
   A. The Oracle Base exists inside the Oracle Home.
   B. The Oracle Base can contain Oracle Homes for different products.
   C. One Oracle Base is required for each product, but versions of the product can exist in their own Oracle Homes within their Oracle Base.
   D. The Oracle Base is created when you run the `orainstRoot.sh` script, and contains a pointer to the Oracle Home.

5. What does Optimal Flexible Architecture (OFA) describe? (Choose the best answer.)
   A. A directory structure
   B. Distributed database systems
   C. Multitier processing architecture
   D. OFA encompasses all the above

Install the Oracle Software by Using the Oracle Universal Installer (OUI)

6. What environment variable must be set on Linux before running the Oracle Universal Installer? (Choose the best answer.)
   A. ORACLE_HOME
   B. ORACLE_BASE
   C. ORACLE_SID
   D. DISPLAY

7. If the OUI detects that a prerequisite has not been met, what can you do? (Choose the best answer.)
   A. You must cancel the installation, fix the problem, and launch OUI again.
   B. A silent install will fail; an interactive install will continue.
   C. Instruct the OUI to continue (at your own risk).
   D. The options will depend on how far into the installation the OUI is when the problem is detected.

8. What type of devices can the OUI install an Oracle Home onto? (Choose all correct answers.)
   A. Regular file systems
   B. Clustered file systems
   C. Raw devices
   D. ASM disk groups

9. Which command-line switch can be used to prevent the OUI from stopping when prerequisite tests fail? (Choose the best answer.)
   A. -silent
   B. -record
   C. -responsefile
   D. -ignoresysprereqs

10. When does an OUI inventory get created? (Choose the best answer.)

    A. Every time a new Oracle Home is created

    B. Every time a new Oracle Base is created

    C. Before the first run of the OUI

    D. During the first run of the OUI

LAB QUESTION

Use the Oracle Universal Installer to instantiate an Oracle Home on a Windows machine. Choose to make an Advanced installation, not a Basic installation, and select the Custom option. This will show all the possibilities. Do not choose to create a database. When presented with a list of all the possible products that can be installed, leave the selection on default. Note that several products are separately licensed, including some of those selected by default. For an installation intended for learning, it is legal to install anything—but for a production installation, only licensed products may be selected.

SELF TEST ANSWERS

Identify the Tools for Administering an Oracle Database

1. ☑ **C.** SQL Developer is not installed with the OUI; it is delivered as a ZIP file that just needs to be unzipped.
☒ **A, B,** and **D.** All other products (even the OUI) are installed with the OUI.

2. ☑ **A, C,** and **D.** DBCA is meant for creating databases, but they can also be created from SQL*Plus or by instructing the OUI to create a database after installing the Oracle Home.
☒ **B** is wrong because DBUA can only upgrade an existing database. **E** is wrong because Database Control is available only after the database is created.

3. ☑ **B.** Oracle Secure Backup is the enterprise backup facility.
☒ **A** and **C.** These are both wrong because they are limited to backing up database files only.

Plan an Oracle Database Installation

4. ☑ **B.** The Oracle Base directory contains all the Oracle Homes, which can be any versions of any products.
☒ **A** is wrong because it inverts the relationship. **C** is wrong because there is no requirement for a separate base for each product. **D** is wrong because it confuses the oraInst.loc file and the OUI with the OFA.

5. ☑ **A.** The rather grandly named Optimal Flexible Architecture is nothing more than a naming convention for directory structures.
☒ **B, C,** and **D.** These are wrong because they go way beyond OFA.

Install the Oracle Software by Using Oracle Universal Installer (OUI)

6. ☑ **D.** Without a DISPLAY set, the OUI will not be able to open any windows.
☒ **A, B,** and **C.** These are wrong because while they can be set before launching the OUI, the OUI will prompt for values for them.

7. ☑ **C.** Perhaps not advisable, but you can certainly do this.
☒ **A** is wrong because while it might be a good idea, it is not something you have to do. **B** is wrong because the interactive installation will halt. **D** is wrong because all prerequisites are checked at the same time.

8. ☑ **A** and **B.** The Oracle Home must exist on a file system, but it can be local or clustered.
☒ **C** and **D.** Raw devices and ASM devices can be used for databases, but not for an Oracle Home.

9. ☑ **D.** The -ignoresysprereqs switch stops OUI from running the tests.
   ☒ **A** is wrong because this will suppress generation of windows, not running tests. **B** is wrong because this is the switch to generate a response file. **C** is wrong because this is the switch to read a response file.

10. ☑ **D.** If the OUI cannot find an inventory, it will create one.
    ☒ **A** and **B** are wrong because one inventory stores details of all Oracle Base and Oracle Home directories. **C** is wrong because it is not possible to create an inventory before running the OUI.

LAB ANSWER

1. Launch the OUI by running the setup.exe file on the installation DVD. On the first window, select the radio button for Advanced Installation and click Next.

2. In the Select Installation Type dialog box, select the radio button for Custom and click Next. This will take you through all the possible options.

3. In the Install Location dialog box, choose directories for the Oracle Base and Oracle Home (following the OFA standard) and a name for the new Oracle Home (the illustration that follows shows possible values) and click Next.

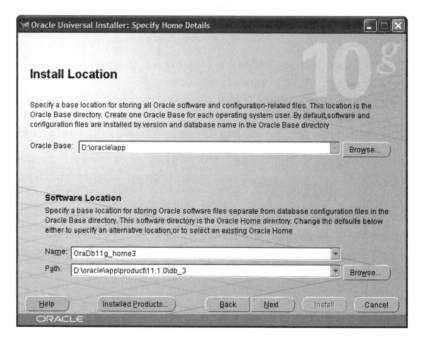

4. The Product-Specific Prerequisite Checks dialog box should report no problems. If there are any, attempt to resolve them and then click Next.

5. The Available Product Components dialog box shows all the products available on the DVD. By default several products that are separately licensed will be selected, such as Advanced Security and Partitioning. Neither of these is free. On this dialog box, for a production system you must select all the options you have paid for, and de-select the others. Click Next.

6. On the Create Database dialog box, select the radio button for Install Database Software Only and click Next.

7. The Summary dialog box will show the products that will be installed. Click Install to proceed with the installation. This should take around a quarter of an hour, depending on the system.

8. When the installation finishes, exit from the installer.

4
Creating an
Oracle Database

This chapter goes through the theory and practice of creating a database: a review of the Oracle server architecture, followed by the mechanics of creation with a look at the relevant tools, both GUI and command line. There is also a description of using database templates. But one objective that must be dealt with immediately is to demystify the process. Creating a database is no big deal. You can create twenty databases during a tea break (and you may well have to do this if you are, for example, supporting an IT teaching institution) once you understand what is required and have prepared appropriate scripts. Furthermore, you really do not have to worry about getting it right. Hardly anything is fixed at database creation time. It certainly makes sense to think about how your database will be structured, its purpose and environment, at creation time, but (with one exception) everything can be changed afterward, though some changes may be awkward. As a general rule, keep things as simple as possible at this stage. Get the thing created and working first; worry about configuring it for use later.

CERTIFICATION OBJECTIVE 4.01

Create a Database by Using the Database Configuration Assistant

This one OCP examination objective is in fact a large task, with several steps. It is not large in terms of the practicalities (creating a database can be quick and simple—a single two-word command will do it, and it may take less than ten minutes), but there are many concepts you should understand:

- The instance, the database, and the data dictionary
- Using the DBCA to create a database
- The instance parameter file
- The CREATE DATABASE command
- Post-creation scripts
- The DBCA's other functions

The Instance, the Database, and the Data Dictionary

An Oracle server is an instance and a database; the two are separate, but connected. The instance is memory structures and processes, in your RAM and on your CPU(s); its existence is transient; it can be started and stopped. The database is files on disk; once created, it persists until it is deleted. Creating an instance is nothing more than building the memory structures and starting the processes. Creating a database is done by the instance as a once-off operation, and the instance can then open and close it many times subsequently. The database is worthless without the instance.

Within the database there is a set of tables and other segments called the *data dictionary*. The data dictionary describes all the logical and physical structures in the database, including all the segments that store user data.

The process of database creation is creating the bare minimum of physical structures needed to store the data dictionary, and then creating the data dictionary within them.

An instance is defined by an instance *parameter file*. The parameter file contains directives that define how the instance should be built in memory: the size of the memory structures, the behavior of the background processes. After building the instance, it is said to be in *no mount* mode. In no mount mode, the instance exists but has not connected to a database. Indeed, the database may not even exist at this point.

All parameters, either specified by the parameter file or implied, have defaults, except for one: the parameter DB_NAME. The DB_NAME parameter names the database to which the instance will connect. This name is also embedded in the controlfile. There is one parameter, CONTROL_FILES, that tells the instance the location of the controlfile. This parameter defines the connection between the instance and the database. When the instance reads the controlfile (which it will find by reading the CONTROL_FILES parameter) if there is a mismatch in database names, the database will not *mount*. In mount mode, the instance has successfully connected to the controlfile. If the controlfile is damaged or non-existent, it will be impossible to mount the database. The controlfile is small, but vital.

Within the controlfile, there are pointers to the other files (the online redo log files and the datafiles) that make up the rest of the database. Having mounted the database, the instance can *open* the database by locating and opening these other files. An open database is a database where the instance has opened all the available online redo log files and datafiles. Also within the controlfile, there is a mapping of datafiles to tablespaces. This lets the instance identify the datafile(s) that make(s) up the SYSTEM tablespace. In the SYSTEM tablespace, it will find the data dictionary. The data dictionary lets the instance resolve references to objects referred to in SQL code to the segments in which they reside, and work out where, physically, the objects are.

The creation of a database server must therefore involve these steps:

- Create the instance.
- Create the database.
- Create the data dictionary.

In practice, the steps are divided slightly differently:

- Create the instance.
- Create the database and the data dictionary objects.
- Create the data dictionary views.

The data dictionary as initially created with the database is fully functional but unusable. It has the capability for defining and managing user data but cannot by used by normal human beings because its structure is too abstruse. Before users (or DBAs) can actually use the database, a set of views must be created on top of the data dictionary that will present it in a human-understandable form.

The data dictionary itself is created by running a set of SQL scripts that exist in the ORACLE_HOME/rdbms/admin directory. These are called by the CREATE DATABASE command. The first is sql.bsq, which then calls several other scripts. These scripts issue a series of commands that create all the tables and other objects that make up the data dictionary.

The views and other objects that make the database usable are generated with more scripts in the ORACLE_HOME/rdbms/admin directory, prefixed with "cat". Examples of these are catalog.sql and catproc.sql, which should always be run immediately after database creation. There are many other optional "cat" scripts that will enable certain features—some of these can be run at creation time; others might be run subsequently to install the features at a later date.

Using the DBCA to Create a Database

These are the steps to follow to create a database:

1. Create a parameter file and (optionally) a password file.
2. Use the parameter file to build an instance in memory.

3. Issue the CREATE DATABASE command. This will generate, as a minimum, a controlfile, two online redo log files, two datafiles for the SYSTEM and SYSAUX tablespaces, and a data dictionary.

4. Run SQL scripts to generate the data dictionary views and the supplied PL/SQL packages.

5. Run SQL scripts to generate the Enterprise Manager Database Control, and any options (such as Java) that the database will require.

On Windows systems, there is an additional step because Oracle runs as a Windows service. Oracle provides a utility, oradim.exe, to assist you in creating this service.

These steps can be executed interactively from the SQL*Plus prompt or through a GUI tool, the Database Configuration Assistant (DBCA). Alternatively, you can automate the process by using scripts or the DBCA with a response file.

Whatever platform you are running on, the easiest way to create a database is through the DBCA. You may well have run this as part of the installation: OUI can launch the DBCA, which prompts you and walks you through the whole process. It creates a parameter file and a password file and then generates scripts that will start the instance; create the database; and generate the data dictionary, the data dictionary views, and Enterprise Manager Database Control. Alternatively, you can create the parameter file and password file by hand, and then do the rest from a SQL*Plus session. Many DBAs combine the two techniques: use the DBCA to generate the files and scripts, and then look at them and perhaps edit them before running them from SQL*Plus.

The DBCA is written in Java—it is therefore the same on all platforms. The only variation is that on Microsoft Windows you must be sitting in front of the machine where you are running it, because that is where the DBCA windows will open. On Unix, you run the DBCA on the machine where you wish to create the database, but you can launch and control it from any machine that has an X server to display the DBCA windows. This is standard X Window System—you set an environment variable DISPLAY to tell the program where to send the windows it opens. For example,

```
export DISPLAY=10.10.10.65:0.0
```

will redirect all X windows to the machine identified by IP address 10.10.10.65, no matter which machine you are actually running the DBCA on.

To launch the DBCA on Windows, take the shortcut on the Start menu. The navigation path will be

1. Start
2. Programs
3. Oracle – OraDB11g_home3
4. Configuration and Migration Tools
5. Database Configuration Assistant

Note that the third part of the path will vary depending on the name given to the Oracle Home at install time.

on the job *It is possible to launch the DBCA from a command prompt, but not even hardened command-line veterans (not even the author of this book) do this, because the command is a little awkward, as can be seen from examining the shortcut.*

To launch the DBCA on Linux, first set the environment variables that should always be set for any Linux DBA session: ORACLE_BASE, ORACLE_HOME, PATH, and LD_LIBRARY_PATH. This is an example of a script that will do this:

```
export ORACLE_BASE=/u02/app/db11g
export ORACLE_HOME=$ORACLE_BASE/product/11.1.0/db_1
export PATH=$ORACLE_HOME/bin:$PATH
export LD_LIBRARY_PATH=$ORACLE_HOME/lib:$LD_LIBRARY_PATH
```

Note that the Base and Home will vary according to choices made at install time. To launch the DBCA, run the dbca shell script, located in the $ORACLE_HOME/bin directory.

on the job *Be sure to have the $ORACLE_HOME/bin directory at the start of your search path, in case there are any Linux executables with the same name as Oracle executables. A well-known case in point is rman, which is both an Oracle tool and a SUSE Linux utility.*

Remember that (with one exception) every choice made at database creation time can be changed later, but that some changes are awkward and will involve down time. It is not therefore vital to get everything right—but the more right it can be, the better.

If the database to be created is going to use Enterprise Manager Database Control, there is an additional step that should be carried out before launching the DBCA: configuring a database listener. This requirement is because Database Control always connects to its database through a listener, and the DBCA checks whether one is available. The configuration is a simple task, described in detail in Chapter 6. For now, do this with the Net Configuration Assistant, accepting defaults all the way.

To launch the Net Configuration Assistant on Windows, take the shortcut on the Start menu. The navigation path will be

1. Start
2. Programs
3. Oracle – OraDB11g_home3
4. Configuration and Migration Tools
5. Net Configuration Assistant

To launch the assistant on Linux, run the `netca` shell script, located in the `$ORACLE_HOME/bin` directory.

EXERCISE 4-1

Use the DBCA to Create a Database

In this exercise, you will create a database listener (if one does not exist already) and then create a database to be called ocp11g using the DBCA, on either Windows or Linux. There is no significant difference between platforms. The illustrations that follow happen to be from Windows.

1. Launch the Net Configuration Assistant. The radio button for Listener Configuration will be selected.
2. Click Next three times. If there is a message stating that a listener already exists, you can exit the tool immediately by clicking Cancel and Finish, and proceed to Step 3. Otherwise, click Next another four times to define the default listener, and then Finish to exit the tool.
3. Launch the Database Configuration Assistant.
4. On the DBCA Welcome dialog box, click Next.

5. The next dialog box has radio buttons for
   - Create a Database
   - Configure Database Options
   - Delete a Database
   - Manage Templates
   - Configure Automatic Storage

   The second and third options will be grayed out, unless the DBCA detects an existing database running off this Oracle Home. Select the Create A Database radio button, and click Next.

6. The Database Templates dialog box has radio buttons for selecting a template on which to base the new database. Select the Custom Database radio button, as this will present all possible options. Click Next.

7. In the Database Identification dialog box, enter a global database name, and a System Identifier (a SID), which will be used as the instance name. These will default to the same thing, which is often what is wanted. For this exercise, enter **ocp11g** for both names. Click Next.

8. The Management Options dialog box has a check box for configuring the database with Enterprise Manager. Select this. Then there are radio buttons for either Grid Control or Database Control. The Grid Control radio button will be grayed out if the DBCA does not detect a Grid Control agent running on the machine. Select Database Control. There are check boxes for Enable Email Notifications and Enable Daily Backup; do not select these. Click Next. It is at this point that the DBCA will give an error if there is no listener available.

9. The Database Credentials dialog box prompts for passwords for four users in the database: SYS (who owns the data dictionary), SYSTEM (used for most DBA work), DBSNMP (used for external monitoring), and SYSMAN (used by Enterprise Manager). Select the radio button for Use The Same Password For All Accounts. Enter **oracle** as the password, twice, and click Next.

10. In the Security Settings dialog box, accept the default, which is 11g security, and click Next.

11. The Storage Options dialog box offers a choice between file system, ASM, or raw devices. Select File System, and click Next.

12. The Database File Locations dialog box prompts for a root directory for the database. Select Use Database File Locations From Template. Click the File Location Variables button to see where the database will be created. It will be the OFA location `ORACLE_BASE/oradata/DB_NAME`. ClickNext.

13. In the Recovery Configuration dialog box, accept the default configuration for the flash recovery area (which will be 2 GB in `ORACLE_BASE/flash_ recovery_area`) and do not enable archiving. Click Next.

14. In the Database Content dialog box, deselect all options except Enterprise Manager Repository. The others are not needed for this database and will make the creation take much longer. Some options will be grayed out; this will be because they have not been installed into the Oracle Home. Click the Standard Database Components button, and deselect these as well. Don't worry about a warning that the XML DB is used by other components. Click Next.

15. The Initialization Parameters dialog box has four tabs. Leave everything on default, but look at all the tabs. The Memory tab shows the memory that will be allocated to the instance, based on a percentage of the main memory detected. The Sizing tab shows the database block size, defaulting to 8 KB. This is the one thing that can never be changed after creation. The Character Sets tab shows the character set to be used within the database, which will have a default value based on the operating system. This can be very awkward to change afterward. The Connection Mode tab determines how user sessions will be managed. Click Next.

16. The Database Storage dialog box shows, via a navigation tree on the left, the files that will be created. Navigate around this, and see the names and sizes of the files. These are nowhere near adequate for a production system but will be fine for now. Click Next.

17. In the Creation Options dialog box, select the check boxes for Create Database and Generate Database Creation Scripts. Note the path for the scripts; it will be `ORACLE_BASE/admin/ocp11g/scripts`. Click Finish.

18. The Confirmation dialog box shows what the DBCA is about to do. Click OK.

19. The DBCA will generate the creation scripts (which should only take a few minutes). Click OK, and the DBCA will create the database. The illustration that follows shows the progress dialog box. Note the location of the DBCA logs—`ORACLE_BASE/cfgtoollogs/dbca/ocp11g`—it may be necessary to

look at the logs if anything fails. The creation will typically take fifteen to forty minutes, depending on the machine.

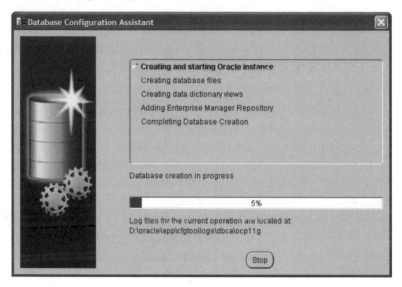

20. When the DBCA completes, it will present the dialog box shown in the illustration that follows. Take note of all the information given, in particular the URL given for database control:

    `http://jwacer.bplc.co.za:1158/em`

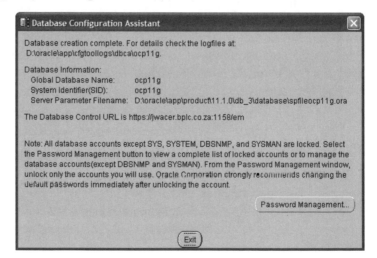

The Scripts and Other Files Created by the DBCA

While the DBCA is creating the database, take a long look at the scripts generated. They will be in the directory ORACLE_BASE/admin/DB_NAME/scripts. In the example that follow, which is from a Windows installation, the ORACLE_BASE is d:\oracle\app and the database name (the global name, without the domain suffix) is ocp11g, so the scripts are therefore in d:\oracle\app\admin\ocp11g\scripts. Navigate to the appropriate directory, and study the files therein.

The Instance Parameter File

The first file to look at is the instance parameter file, named init.ora. This is a print of a typical init.ora file, as generated by the DBCA:

```
###################################################################
# Copyright (c) 1991, 2001, 2002 by Oracle Corporation
###################################################################
##########################################
# Cache and I/O
##########################################
db_block_size=8192
##########################################
# Cursors and Library Cache
##########################################
open_cursors=300
##########################################
# Database Identification
##########################################
db_domain=""
db_name=ocp11g
##########################################
# File Configuration
##########################################
control_files=("D:\oracle\app\oradata\ocp11g\control01.ctl",
"D:\oracle\app\oradata\ocp11g\control02.ctl",
"D:\oracle\app\oradata\ocp11g\control03.ctl")
db_recovery_file_dest=D:\oracle\app\flash_recovery_area
db_recovery_file_dest_size=2147483648
##########################################
# Job Queues
##########################################
job_queue_processes=10
##########################################
# Miscellaneous
##########################################
```

```
compatible=11.1.0.0.0
diagnostic_dest=D:\oracle\app
###########################################
# NLS
###########################################
nls_language="ENGLISH"
nls_territory="UNITED KINGDOM"
###########################################
# Processes and Sessions
###########################################
processes=150
###########################################
# SGA Memory
###########################################
sga_target=318767104
###########################################
# Security and Auditing
###########################################
audit_file_dest=D:\oracle\app\admin\ocp11g\adump
audit_trail=db
remote_login_passwordfile=EXCLUSIVE
###########################################
# Shared Server
###########################################
dispatchers="(PROTOCOL=TCP) (SERVICE=ocp11gXDB)"
###########################################
# Sort, Hash Joins, Bitmap Indexes
###########################################
pga_aggregate_target=105906176
###########################################
# System Managed Undo and Rollback Segments
###########################################
undo_management=AUTO
undo_tablespace=UNDOTBS1
```

Any line beginning with a # symbol is a comment and can be ignored. There are about 300 parameters, but the file generated by the DBCA sets only a few. Most of these are covered in detail in later chapters. Two to emphasize at this point are DB_BLOCK_SIZE and CONTROL_FILES. DB_BLOCK_SIZE determines the size of the buffers in the database buffer cache. When the instance is instructed to create a database, this size will also be used to format the datafiles that make up the SYSTEM and SYSAUX tablespaces. It can never be changed after database creation. CONTROL_FILES is the pointer that allows the instance to find all the multiplexed copies of the database controlfile. At this stage, the controlfile does not exist; this parameter will tell the instance where to create it. Some of the other parameters are self-explanatory and easily related back to the options taken when going through the steps of the exercise, but eventually you must refer to the Oracle Documentation Library (the volume you need is titled "Reference") and read up on all of them. All! Those necessary for examination purposes will be described at the appropriate point.

exam

watch
What is the only instance parameter for which there is no default? It is DB_NAME. A parameter file must exist with at least this one parameter, or you cannot start an instance. The DB_NAME can be up to eight characters long, letters and digits only, beginning with a letter.

The Database Creation Shell Script

This is the file the DBCA executes to launch the database creation process. It is a batch file on Windows, and a shell script on Linux. A Windows example:

```
mkdir D:\oracle\app
mkdir D:\oracle\app\admin\ocp11g\adump
mkdir D:\oracle\app\admin\ocp11g\dpdump
mkdir D:\oracle\app\admin\ocp11g\pfile
mkdir D:\oracle\app\cfgtoollogs\dbca\ocp11g
mkdir D:\oracle\app\flash_recovery_area
mkdir D:\oracle\app\oradata\ocp11g
mkdir D:\oracle\app\product\11.1.0\db_3\database
set ORACLE_SID=ocp11g
set PATH=%ORACLE_HOME%\bin;%PATH%
D:\oracle\app\product\11.1.0\db_3\bin\oradim.exe -new -sid OCP11G
-startmode manual -spfile
D:\oracle\app\product\11.1.0\db_3\bin\oradim.exe -edit -sid OCP11G
-startmode auto -srvcstart system
D:\oracle\app\product\11.1.0\db_3\bin\sqlplus /nolog
 @D:\oracle\app\admin\db11g\scripts\ocp11g.sql
```

First, the script creates a few directories in the Oracle Base. Then it sets the ORACLE_SID environment variable (more of this later) and prepends the ORACLE_HOME/bin directory to the search path.

Because this example is from Windows, there are two commands that will not appear on a Linux system; these use `oradim.exe`. On Windows, an Oracle instance runs as a Windows service. This service must be created. The `oradim.exe` utility is being run twice. The first time will define a new service in the Windows registry, with the system identifier OCP11G, and put the service on manual start. The `-spfile` switch refers to the type of initialization parameter file to be used. The second use of `oradim.exe` edits the service, to set it to automatic start whenever Windows starts. Figure 4-1 shows the resulting service defined in the registry. To see this, use the `regedit.exe` registry editor (or some similar tool) to navigate to the key

`HKEY_LOCAL_MACHINE/SYSTEM/currentControlSet/Services/OracleServiceOCP11G`

Each database instance that can run on a Windows machine will be a service, named after the name of the instance (in this case, OCP11G) that was provided in Exercise 4-1, Step 7.

After the service creation, the script launches SQL*Plus and runs the SQL script `ocp11g.sql` which will control the creation of the database:

```
set verify off
PROMPT specify a password for sys as parameter 1;
DEFINE sysPassword = &1
PROMPT specify a password for system as parameter 2;
DEFINE systemPassword = &2
PROMPT specify a password for sysman as parameter 3;
DEFINE sysmanPassword = &3
PROMPT specify a password for dbsnmp as parameter 4;
```

FIGURE 4-1

The Windows service defining an Oracle instance

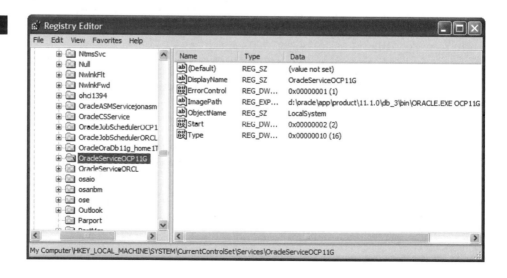

```
DEFINE dbsnmpPassword = &4
host D:\oracle\app\product\11.1.0\db_3\bin\orapwd.exe
file=D:\oracle\app\product\11.1.0\db_3\database\PWDocp11g.ora
password=&&sysPassword force=y
@D:\oracle\app\admin\ocp11g\scripts\CreateDB.sql
@D:\oracle\app\admin\ocp11g\scripts\CreateDBFiles.sql
@D:\oracle\app\admin\ocp11g\scripts\CreateDBCatalog.sql
@D:\oracle\app\admin\ocp11g\scripts\emRepository.sql
@D:\oracle\app\admin\ocp11g\scripts\postDBCreation.sql
```

At the top of the script, there are prompts for passwords for four critical accounts. These will be provided by the password entered in Exercise 4-1, Step 9.

Then, using host to spawn an operating system shell, the script runs the orapwd. exe utility (just called orapwd on Linux.) This will create an external password file for the database. The name of the file must be

```
%ORACLE_HOME%\database\PWD<db_name>.ora
```

on Windows, or

```
$ORACLE_HOME/dbs/orapw<db_name>
```

on Linux, where *<db_name>* is the name of the database. This is the name provided for the global database name in Exercise 4-1, Step 7, but without any domain suffix. Usually, this is the same as the instance name—but they are not the same thing.

The script then calls CreateDB.sql, which will actually create the database.

The CREATE DATABASE Command

This is an example of the CreateDB.sql script:

```
connect "SYS"/"&&sysPassword" as SYSDBA
set echo on
spool D:\oracle\app\admin\ocp11g\scripts\CreateDB.log
startup nomount pfile="D:\oracle\app\admin\ocp11g\scripts\init.ora";
CREATE DATABASE "ocp11g"
MAXINSTANCES 8
MAXLOGHISTORY 1
MAXLOGFILES 16
MAXLOGMEMBERS 3
MAXDATAFILES 100
DATAFILE 'D:\oracle\app\oradata\ocp11g\system01.dbf'
SIZE 300M REUSE AUTOEXTEND ON NEXT  10240K MAXSIZE UNLIMITED
EXTENT MANAGEMENT LOCAL
SYSAUX DATAFILE 'D:\oracle\app\oradata\ocp11g\sysaux01.dbf'
SIZE 120M REUSE AUTOEXTEND ON NEXT  10240K MAXSIZE UNLIMITED
```

```
SMALLFILE DEFAULT TEMPORARY TABLESPACE TEMP TEMPFILE
'D:\oracle\app\oradata\ocp11g\temp01.dbf' SIZE 20M REUSE
AUTOEXTEND ON NEXT  640K MAXSIZE UNLIMITED
SMALLFILE UNDO TABLESPACE "UNDOTBS1" DATAFILE
'D:\oracle\app\oradata\ocp11g\undotbs01.dbf' SIZE 200M REUSE
AUTOEXTEND ON NEXT  5120K MAXSIZE UNLIMITED
CHARACTER SET WE8MSWIN1252
NATIONAL CHARACTER SET AL16UTF16
LOGFILE GROUP 1 ('D:\oracle\app\oradata\ocp11g\redo01.log') SIZE 51200K,
GROUP 2 ('D:\oracle\app\oradata\ocp11g\redo02.log') SIZE 51200K,
GROUP 3 ('D:\oracle\app\oradata\ocp11g\redo03.log') SIZE 51200K
USER SYS IDENTIFIED BY "&&sysPassword"
USER SYSTEM IDENTIFIED BY "&&systemPassword";
spool off
```

The script connects to the instance, using the syntax for password file authentication (this is fully described in Chapter 5). Then, taking the script line by line:

The echo and spool commands cause SQL*Plus to write out a log of everything that happens next.

Then the STARTUP NOMOUNT command builds the instance in memory, using the static parameter file we saw earlier. The significance of "NOMOUNT" will be dealt with in Chapter 5; for now, let it suffice that it is necessary, as there is no database to mount and open. After this completes, there will be an instance running with an SGA and the background processes. The SGA will have been sized according to the parameters in the nominated init.ora file.

And then there is the CREATE DATABASE command, which continues to the semicolon at the end of the file. Following the database name (which is ocp11g), the first section of the command sets some overall limits for the database. They can all be changed subsequently, but if they are clearly inappropriate, it is a good idea to change them now, before creation.

on the job

With the current release, some of these limits (such as the number of datafiles) are only soft limits, and therefore of little significance.

Then there are two datafile specifications: these are the files that will be used for the SYSTEM and SYSAUX tablespaces. Then there are specifications for a TEMPORARY tablespace and an UNDO tablespace (more on this in Chapter 11).

Then there is a specification for the database character set (which is used for the data dictionary and columns of type VARCHAR2, CHAR, and CLOB) and the national character set (which is used for columns of type NVARCHAR2,

NCHAR, and NCLOB). It is possible to change the character set after creation with SQL*Plus. Choice and use of character sets, and other aspects of globalization, are covered in detail in the second OCP examination.

on the
job

Until version 9i of the database, there was no supported means for changing the database character set after creation: it was therefore vital to get this right. With 9i and later, it is possible to change it afterward, but this is not an operation to embark on lightly. Get it right now!

There is then the specification for three log file groups, each consisting of one member. This is an example of the DBCA defaults perhaps not doing a perfect job. It would be better practice to multiplex the redo log: to create at least two members for each group. Not a problem—this can be fixed later (in Chapter 15). The online redo log will always require substantial tuning; the defaults are applicable to virtually no production systems.

Finally, the passwords for database users SYS and SYSTEM are initialized, and the output to the log switched off.

This one file with the CREATE DATABASE command will create a database. After its successful execution, you will have an instance running in memory, and a database consisting of a controlfile and copies as specified by the CONTROL_FILES initialization parameter, and the datafiles and redo logs specified in the CREATE DATABASE command. A data dictionary will have been generated in the SYSTEM tablespace. But although the database has been created, it is unusable. The remaining scripts called by ocp11g.sql make the database usable. The CREATE DATABASE command has many options, all of which have defaults. For example, if you do not specify a datafile for the SYSTEM or SYSAUX tablespace, one will be created anyway. If you do not specify a character set, there is a default, which will depend on the operating system configuration (it may not be a very helpful default— commonly, it is US7ASCII, which is inadequate for many applications). There are also defaults for the online redo log files. There are no defaults for the TEMP and UNDO tablespaces; if these are not specified, the database will be created without them. Not a problem—they can be added later.

exam
watch
The CREATE DATABASE command can be extremely long and complicated—but there are defaults for *everything. You can create a database from a SQL*Plus prompt with two words: CREATE DATABASE.*

Post-Creation Scripts

The other SQL scripts called by `ocp11g.sql` to complete the database creation will depend on the options chosen when going through the DBCA. In this example, as all options except for Enterprise Manager Database control were deselected, there are only four:

■ **CreateDBfiles.sql**   This is of minor significance. It creates a small tablespace, USERS, to be used as the default location for any objects created by users.

■ **CreateDBCatalog.sql**   This is vital. It runs a set of scripts in the `$ORACLE_HOME/rdbms/admin` directory that construct views on the data dictionary and create many PL/SQL packages. It is these views and packages that make it possible to manage an Oracle database.

■ **emRepository.sql**   This runs the script to create the objects needed by Enterprise Manager Database Control. It is run because this was selected in Exercise 4-1, Step 8.

■ **postDBCreation.sql**   This generates a server parameter file from the `init.ora` file (more of this in Chapter 5), unlocks the DBSNMP and SYSMAN accounts used by Enterprise Manager, and runs the Enterprise Manager configuration Assistant (which is `emca.bat` on Windows, `emca` on Linux) to configure Database Control for the new database.

SCENARIO & SOLUTION

You want to create a database for development, and be able to recreate it on demand. How can you do this?	There are two possibilities: create it once through the DBCA and save it as a template, or create it with SQL*Plus and keep copies of the database creation scripts. These scripts could of course be generated by the DBCA.
If you don't really know how a database will be used, is it sensible to create it at all?	Sure, go ahead. Everything can be changed later—except for the database block size. And even this may not be a problem: no one is going to complain about using 8 KB for this, it will be suitable for most databases. If you choose Unicode for the character set, it will be able to store anything. And everything else can be changed later when the usage becomes clear.

The DBCA's Other Functions

The opening screen of the DBCA gives you five options:

- Create a database.
- Configure database options.
- Delete a database.
- Manage templates.
- Configure automatic storage management.

"Configure Database Options" helps you change the configuration of a database you have already created. In the preceding exercise, you deselected all the options: this was to make the creation as quick and simple as possible.

on the **job** *By deselecting all the options, particularly those for "standard database components," creation time is reduced dramatically.*

If you decide subsequently to install some optional features, such as Java or OLAP, running the DBCA again is the simplest way to do it. An alternative method is to run the scripts to install the options by hand, but these are not always fully documented and it is possible to make mistakes—the DBCA is better.

The Delete A Database radio button will prompt you for which database you wish to delete, and then give you one more chance to back out before it deletes all the files that make up the database and (for a Windows system) invokes oradim.exe to delete the instance's service from the Windows registry as well.

on the **job** *Behind the scenes, Delete A Database invokes the SQL*Plus command DROP DATABASE. There is some protection for this command: the database cannot be open at the time; it must be in mount mode.*

Manage Templates is to do with storing database definitions for use later. Remember that in the exercise, you chose to create a "Custom" database. A custom database is not preconfigured—you chose it in order to see all the possibilities as you worked your way through the DBCA. But apart from "Custom," there were options for "Data Warehouse" and "General Purpose or Transaction Processing." If you take either of these, you'll be presented with a version of the DBCA prompts that will create a database with different defaults, at least partly optimized for decision support systems

INSIDE THE EXAM

Creating a Database

Oracle Corporation wants to encourage people to use the graphical tools, and all exam takers must be familiar with them. That having been said, it is a mistake to prepare for the exam without also studying the command-line techniques. The DBCA is a perfect example of how a graphical tool may do nothing more than run commands that can also be invoked from the command line.

Studying the scripts generated by the DBCA makes clear the staged process of database creation: create an initialization parameter file, and use it to start an instance. Use the instance to create the database. Generate a data dictionary within the database. Run additional scripts to install any options.

(DSS, the data warehouse option) or for online transaction processing systems (OLTP, the transaction processing option). These templates do not create a database from the beginning; they expand a set of compressed datafiles and modify these. The final question when you created your database gave you the possibility of saving it as a template—i.e., not to create it at all, but to save the definition for future use. The DBCA will let you manage templates, either the presupplied ones or ones you create yourself, by creating, copying, modifying, or deleting them. Templates can be extremely useful if you are in a position where you are frequently creating and re-creating databases that are very similar.

Finally, Configure Automatic Storage Management launches a wizard that will create an ASM instance. An ASM instance does not open a database; it manages a pool of disks, used for database storage. This is covered in Chapter 6.

CERTIFICATION SUMMARY

A database can be created using the DBCA, or from the SQL*Plus command line. Indeed, the DBCA can generate scripts to run from the SQL*Plus command line. Creation is three distinct steps: create the instance, create the database, create the data dictionary. If using the DBCA, a database listener may be required. The DBCA does not use the listener, but if the option is taken to configure Database Control, the DBCA will check whether a listener is available.

To create an instance, all that is required is a parameter file. Critical parameters are the name of the database and the location of the controlfile(s). Then to create a database, use the CREATE DATABASE command. This will generate as a minimum the controlfile, two online log file groups, the SYSTEM and SYSAUX tablespaces, and a data dictionary. To make the database usable, run a set of scripts that create the data dictionary views and the supplied PL/SQL packages, and then install any options that are required.

✓ TWO-MINUTE DRILL

Create a Database by Using the
Database Configuration Assistant

❑ A database can be created with the DBCA or from the SQL*Plus command line.

❑ The DBCA can create a database from nothing or from a saved template.

❑ The DBCA and SQL*Plus can delete a database.

❑ An instance must be created before the database can be created.

❑ Any options not selected at creation time can be added later.

SELF TEST

Create a Database by Using the Database Configuration Assistant

1. To create a database, in what mode must the instance be? (Choose the best answer.)
   A. Not started
   B. Started in NOMOUNT mode
   C. Started in MOUNT mode
   D. Started in OPEN mode

2. The SYSAUX tablespace is mandatory. What will happen if you attempt to issue a CREATE DATABASE command that does not specify a datafile for the SYSAUX tablespace? (Choose the best answer.)
   A. The command will fail.
   B. The command will succeed, but the database will be inoperable until the SYSAUX tablespace is created.
   C. A default SYSAUX tablespace and datafile will be created.
   D. The SYSAUX objects will be created in the SYSTEM tablespace.

3. Is it necessary to have a database listener created before creating a database? (Choose the best answer.)
   A. No.
   B. Yes.
   C. It depends on whether the database is created with the DBCA or SQL*Plus.
   D. It depends on whether the Database Control option is selected in the DBCA.

4. Several actions are necessary to create a database. Place these in the correct order:
   1. Create the data dictionary views.
   2. Create the parameter file.
   3. Create the password file.
   4. Issue the CREATE DATABASE command.
   5. Issue the STARTUP command.
   (Choose the best answer.)
   A. 2, 3, 5, 4, 1
   B. 3, 5, 2, 4, 1
   C. 5, 3, 4, 2, 1
   D. 2, 3, 1, 5, 4

5. What instance parameter cannot be changed after database creation? (Choose the best answer.)
   A. All instance parameters can be changed after database creation.
   B. All instance parameters can be changed after database creation, if it is done while the instance is in MOUNT mode.
   C. CONTROL_FILES.
   D. DB_BLOCK_SIZE.

6. What files are created by the CREATE DATABASE command? (Choose all correct answers.)
   A. The controlfile
   B. The dynamic parameter file
   C. The online redo log files
   D. The password file
   E. The static parameter file
   F. The SYSAUX tablespace datafile
   G. The SYSTEM tablespace datafile

7. What will happen if you do not run the CATALOG.SQL and CATPROC.SQL scripts after creating a database? (Choose the best answer.)
   A. It will not be possible to open the database.
   B. It will not be possible to create any user tables.
   C. It will not be possible to use PL/SQL.
   D. It will not be possible to query the data dictionary views.
   E. It will not be possible to connect as any users other than SYS and SYSTEM.

8. What tools can be used to manage templates? (Choose all correct answers.)
   A. The Database Configuration Assistant
   B. The Database Upgrade Assistant
   C. SQL*Plus
   D. Database Control
   E. The Oracle Universal Installer

9. At what point can you choose or change the database character set? (Choose all correct answers.)
   A. At database creation time, if you are not using any template
   B. At database creation time, if you are using a template that does not include datafiles
   C. At database creation time, whether or not you are using a template
   D. After database creation, with the DBCA
   E. After database creation, with SQL*Plus

10. If there are several databases created off the same Oracle Home, how will Database Control be configured? (Choose the best answer.)

    A. Database Control will give access to all the databases created from the one Oracle Home through one URL.

    B. Database Control will give access to each database through different ports.

    C. Database Control need only be configured in one database and can then be used to connect to all of them.

    D. Database Control can only manage one database per Oracle Home.

LAB QUESTION

Create a database with the DBCA based on a template and save it as a template. This is to ensure that you have a database suitable for completing the remaining exercises in this book and can quickly create another if necessary.

Use the "General Purpose" template. These changes are to be made from the default:

- Add the sample schemas to the database.
- Use Unicode as the database character set.
- Save the database as a template, as well as creating it.

SELF TEST ANSWERS

Create a Database by Using the Database Configuration Assistant

1. ☑ **B.** The CREATE DATABASE command can only be issued in NOMOUNT mode.
    ☒ **A** is wrong, because if the instance is not started, the only possible command is STARTUP. **C** and **D** are wrong because it is impossible to mount a database if there is no controlfile, and it cannot be opened if there is no redo log and SYSTEM tablespace.

2. ☑ **C.** There are defaults for everything, including the SYSAUX tablespace and datafile definitions.
    ☒ **A** is wrong because the command will succeed. **B** and **D** are wrong because these are not the way the defaults work.

3. ☑ **D.** The only time a listener is required is if the DBCA is used, and Database Control is selected. The DBCA will not continue if it cannot detect a listener.
    ☒ **A** is wrong because there is a circumstance where a listener is required; **B** is wrong because in all other circumstances a listener is not required. **C** is wrong because it does not go far enough: The DBCA will not require a listener, if Database Control is not selected.

4. ☑ **A.** This is the correct sequence (though 2 and 3 could be done the other way round)
    ☒ **B, C,** and **D.** None of these are possible.

5. ☑ **D.** This is the one parameter that can never be changed after creation.
    ☒ **A** and **B** are wrong because DB_BLOCK_SIZE cannot be changed no matter when you try to do it. **C** is wrong because the CONTROL_FILES parameter can certainly be changed, though this will require a shutdown and restart.

6. ☑ **A, C, F,** and **G.** All of these will always be created, by default if they are not specified.
    ☒ **B** and **D** are wrong because these should exist before the instance is started. **E** is wrong because the conversion of the static parameter file to a dynamic parameter file only occurs, optionally, after the database is created.

7. ☑ **D.** The database will function, but without the data dictionary views and PL/SQL packages created by these scripts it will be unusable.
    ☒ **A** is wrong because the database will open; in fact, it must be open to run the scripts. **B** is wrong because tables and other objects can certainly be created. **C** is wrong because PL/SQL will be available; it is the supplied packages that will be missing. **E** is completely irrelevant to these scripts.

8. ☑ **A.** The DBCA is the only tool that can manage templates.
    ☒ **B, C, D,** and **E.** These are all wrong because only the DBCA offers template management.

9. ☑ **C and E.** C is right because the character set can be set at creation time, no matter how the creation is done. E is right because it is possible to change character set after creation (though you don't want to do this unless really necessary).

☒ **A and B** are wrong because templates are not relevant. If the template includes datafiles, the DBCA will change the character set behind the scenes. **D** is wrong because the DBCA does not offer an option to do this.

10. ☑ **B.** Database Control can be used for each database and will be configured with a different port for each one.

☒ **A** is wrong because this is what Grid Control can do. **C** is wrong because Database Control must be installed in every database that will use it. **D** is wrong because while a Database Control is only for one database, every database can have its own.

LAB ANSWER

1. Launch the Net Configuration Assistant. Click Next seven times to create a default listener if there is not one already configured, and exit the tool by clicking Finish. If there is already a default listener, exit the tool immediately with Cancel and Finish.

2. Launch the Database Configuration Assistant. In the Welcome dialog box, click Next.

3. In the Operations dialog box, select the Create A Database radio button and click Next.

4. When prompted to choose a template, select the General Purpose Or Transaction Processing radio button, and click Next.

5. In the Database Identification dialog box, enter the database global name as **orcl11g**. The SID will default to this. If it is customary at your site to use domain suffixes, by all means do so. A commonly used suffix is the name of the server machine, so that databases with the same name on different machines can be distinguished. An example global name using this convention would be

```
orcl11g.jwlnx1.bplc.co.za
```

Click Next.

6. In the Management Option dialog box, select Enterprise Manager and Database Control only. Click Next.

7. When prompted for passwords, use the same password for all accounts: oracle. Click Next.

8. Select File System for the storage. Click Next.

9. In the Database File Locations dialog box, select the Use Database File Locations From Template radio button, and click the File Location Variables button. Note the destination directories. Click Next.

10. Leave the Recovery Configuration dialog box options on default. Click Next.

11. In the Database Content dialog box, select the check box to add the sample schemas to the database. This will not be selected by default. Click Next.

12. In the Initialization Parameters dialog box, in the Memory tab adjust the memory settings if you want—500 MB total for SGA and PGA will be enough. In the Character Sets tab, select the radio button Use Unicode (AL32UTF8). This will not be selected by default. Click Next.

13. Accept the default 11 g security settings. Click Next.

14. In the Automatic Maintenance Tasks dialog box, select Enable Automatic Maintenance Tasks and click Next.

15. In the Database Storage dialog box, click Next.

16. In the Creation Options dialog box, select all the options: Create Database, Save As A Database Template, and Generate Database Creation Scripts. The template name will have defaulted to the SID. In the template description, add a note to the effect that this template uses Unicode and includes the sample schemas. Click Finish.

17. The DBCA will show the progress of the template creation, the script creation, and finally the database creation.

5
Managing the Oracle Instance

After creating a database and an instance, the instance will be started and the database will be open. Assuming that the database was configured with Enterprise Manager Database Control, that too will be running. What may not be running is the database listener (which is fully described in Chapter 6). Before Database Control can connect to the database, the listener must be running too.

The three components (database instance, database listener, and optionally Database Control) have their own command-line utilities that can be used for startup, or once Database Control has been started, it can be used to start the others. Component startup is an area where there may be substantial differences between Windows and other platforms.

Database Control requires no configuration. It only has to be created, and that is done at database creation time. A Database Control instance can be configured later, if it was selected at database creation time. But the database instance will in most cases require substantial configuration after creation. This is done by adjusting initialization parameters.

Basic monitoring of the instance and the database can be done through Database Control or by querying views. There are also various trace files and the instance alert log that should be checked regularly.

CERTIFICATION OBJECTIVE 5.01

Describe the Stages of Database Startup and Shutdown

Oracle Corporation's recommended sequence for starting a database is to start Database Control, then the database listener, and then the database. Starting the database is itself a staged process. There is no necessity to follow this sequence, and in more complex environments such as clustered systems or those managed by Enterprise Manager Grid Control there may well be additional processes too. But this sequence will do for a simple single-instance environment.

Starting and Connecting to Database Control

Database Control is a tool for managing one database (though this database can be clustered). If there are several database instances running off the same Oracle Home, then each instance will have its own Database Control instance. The tool is written in Perl and Java, and accessed from a browser. There is no need to have a Java Runtime Environment or a Perl interpreter installed on the system; both are provided in the Oracle Home and installed by the OUI. All communications with Database Control are over HTTPS, the secure sockets variant of HTTP, and there should therefore be no problems with using Database Control from a browser anywhere in the world—the communications will be secure, and any firewall proxy servers will have no problem routing them. The only configuration needed on the firewall will be making it aware of the port on which Database Control is listening for connection requests.

The configuration of Database Control will have been done at database creation time. This configuration includes two vital bits of information: the host name of the computer on which Database Control is running and the TCP port on which it will be listening. If it is ever necessary to change either of these, Database Control will need to be reconfigured.

To start Database Control, use the emctl utility. This will be located in the ORACLE_HOME/bin directory. The three commands to start or stop Database Control and to check its status are

```
emctl start dbconsole
emctl stop dbconsole
emctl status dbconsole
```

For any of these commands to work, three environment variables must be set: PATH, ORACLE_HOME, and ORACLE_SID. The PATH is needed to allow the operating system to find the emctl utility, which lives in ORACLE_HOME/bin. The ORACLE_HOME and ORACLE_SID are needed so that emctl can find the Database Control configuration files. These are in three places: the directory ORACLE_HOME/sysman/config has general configuration directives that will apply to all Database Control instances running from the Oracle Home (one per database), and also ORACLE_HOME/*hostname_sid*/sysman/config and a similarly named directory beneath ORACLE_HOME/oc4j/j2ee have the details for the Database Control that manages one particular database; hostname is the *hostname* of the machine, and *sid* is the value of the ORACLE_SID variable.

Figure 5-1 shows the startup of Database Control, after a couple of problems.

FIGURE 5-1

Database Control
startup on a
Windows system

In Figure 5-1, the first attempt to query the status of Database Control fails because the ORACLE_SID environment variable is not set. Without this, the `emctl` utility can't find the necessary configuration files. This is further demonstrated by setting the ORACLE_SID to a non-existent instance name; the `emctl status dbconsole` command constructs a directory path based on this that does not exist. After setting the ORACLE_SID correctly, to ocp11g, the status can be queried. The nature of the query can be seen to be nothing more than issuing a URL; this URL can also be issued from any browser as a simple test. As Database Control is not running, the example in the figure continues with starting it, and then again queries the status—this time successfully. Because this example is on a Windows system, the startup involves starting a Windows service, called OracleDBConsoleocp11g; more of this later.

To connect to Database Control, use any reasonably up-to-date browser. The URL is

```
https://hostname:port/em
```

where *hostname* is the name of the machine on which Database Control is running, and *port* is the TCP port on which it is listening for incoming connection requests. If the host has several names or several network interface cards, any will do.

You can even use a loopback address, such as 127.0.0.1, because the Database Control process does listen on all addresses. To identify the port, you can use `emctl`. As shown in Figure 5-1, the output of `emctl status dbconsole` shows the port on which Database Control should be running. Alternatively, you can look in the file `ORACLE_HOME/install/portlist.ini`, which lists all the ports configured by the OUI and DBCA.

As Database Control (the current version, not the one released with 10g) requires the use of HTTPS for security reasons, when you connect from your browser with the URL just given, you may (depending on your local security settings) receive a message regarding the digital certificate that Database Control is returning to your browser. This certificate was generated by Oracle when the Oracle Home was installed and the database created. Figure 5-2 shows such message, as presented by Microsoft's Internet Explorer. Different browsers will respond differently at this point.

The browser is making three checks for the validity of the certificate. The first check is that the certificate is issued by a certificate issuing authority that your browser is prepared to trust. If you click the View Certificate button, you will see that the certificate was issued by the computer on which the Oracle installation was made. Presumably this is a trustworthy source, so that is not a problem. The second check is for the validity dates of the certificate, which (in the example) are fine. The third check is whether the host requested in the URL is the same as the host to which the certificate was issued. These will usually be the same, but if the machine has several hostname aliases or network interface cards, they may not be. For the purposes of forcing this warning in the figure, the connection was made to 127.0.0.1 rather than to the external hostname. To proceed with the connection, click Yes,

An error regarding Database Control's digital certificate

or to prevent this happening again, click View Certificate and then Install Certificate, which will let your browser accept the certificate as genuine from then on. You may also have to follow the link to install the certificate issuing authority (which will also be the host computer) as an accepted authority.

on the job

The mechanism for managing certificates and HTTPS will vary depending on your browser and how it is configured. For Database Control, the certificate really doesn't matter; you do not need secure sockets for authentication, only for encryption.

Once past the SSL certificate issue (which may not arise, depending on local security configuration), if the database listener is running, you will see the Database Control logon window. If it is not, you will see the window in Figure 5-3: the window presented when Database Control cannot detect the listener or the database instance.

FIGURE 5-3

Database Control, failing to detect any other Oracle processes

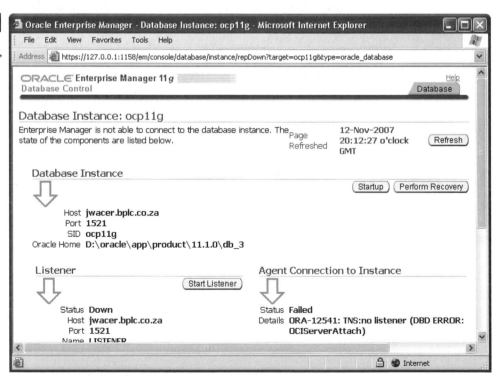

Starting the Database Listener

The database listener is a process that monitors a port for database connection requests. These requests (and all subsequent traffic once a session is established) use Oracle Net, Oracle's proprietary communications protocol. Oracle Net is a layered protocol running over whatever underlying network protocol is in use, probably TCP/IP. Managing the listener is fully described in Chapter 6, but it is necessary to know how to start it now.

There are three ways to start the database listener:

- With the `lsnrctl` utility
- With Database Control
- As a Windows service (Windows only, of course)

The `lsnrctl` utility is in the ORACLE_HOME/bin directory. The key commands are

```
lsnrctl start [listener]
lsnrctl status [listener]
```

where *listener* is the name of listener. This will have defaulted to LISTENER, which is correct in most cases. You will know if you have created a listener with another name. Figure 5-4 shows the output of the `lsnrctl status` command when the listener is running.

FIGURE 5-4

An example of the status of a running database listener

```
 C:\WINDOWS\system32\cmd.exe                                              _ □ ✕

C:\Documents and Settings\John Watson>lsnrctl status

LSNRCTL for 32-bit Windows: Version 11.1.0.4.0 - Beta on 09 NOV 2007 20:46:40

Copyright (c) 1991, 2006, Oracle.  All rights reserved.

Connecting to (DESCRIPTION=(ADDRESS=(PROTOCOL=TCP)(HOST=jwacer.bplc.co.za)(PORT=
1521)))
STATUS of the LISTENER
------------------------
Alias                     LISTENER
Version                   TNSLSNR for 32-bit Windows: Version 11.1.0.4.0 - Beta
Start Date                09-NOV-2007 20:26:25
Uptime                    0 days 0 hr. 20 min. 17 sec
Trace Level               off
Security                  ON: Local OS Authentication
SNMP                      OFF
Listener Parameter File   D:\oracle\app\product\11.1.0\db_3\network\admin\listen
er.ora
Listener Log File         D:\oracle\app\product\11.1.0\db_3\network\log\listener
.log
Listening Endpoints Summary...
  (DESCRIPTION=(ADDRESS=(PROTOCOL=tcp)(HOST=jwacer.bplc.co.za)(PORT=1521)))
  (DESCRIPTION=(ADDRESS=(PROTOCOL=ipc)(PIPENAME=\\.\pipe\EXTPROC1521ipc)))
Services Summary...
Service "PLSExtProc" has 1 instance(s).
  Instance "PLSExtProc", status UNKNOWN, has 1 handler(s) for this service...
Service "ocp11g" has 1 instance(s).
  Instance "ocp11g", status READY, has 1 handler(s) for this service...
Service "ocp11g_XPT" has 1 instance(s).
  Instance "ocp11g", status READY, has 1 handler(s) for this service...
The command completed successfully

C:\Documents and Settings\John Watson>
```

Note the third line of the output in the figure shows the host address and port on which the listener is listening, and the fifth line from the bottom states that the listener will accept connections for a service "ocp11g," which is offered by an instance called "ocp11g." These are the critical bits of information needed to connect to the database. Following a successful database creation with DBCA, it can be assumed that they are correct. If the listener is not running, the output of `lsnrctl status` will make this very clear. Use `lsnrctl start` to start it, or from Database Control click the appropriate button, shown in Figure 5-3.

Starting SQL*Plus

This couldn't be simpler. SQL*Plus is just an elementary process for issuing ad hoc SQL commands to a database. It is a client-server tool. On Windows systems, there used to be a choice between a graphical version and a character-based version, but with release 11g only the character version is being shipped; either launch it from a command prompt, or the standard installation of Oracle will have created a shortcut to the `sqlplus.exe` executable file in your Start menu. On Unix, it is called `sqlplus`. On either operating system you will find the executable program in your `ORACLE_HOME/bin` directory.

A variation you need to be aware of is the NOLOG switch. By default, the SQL*Plus program immediately prompts you for an Oracle username, password, and database connect string. This is fine for regular end users, but useless for database administrators because it requires that the database be already open. To launch SQL*Plus without a login prompt, use the /NOLOG switch:

```
sqlplus /nolog
```

This will give you a SQL prompt, from which you can connect with a variety of syntaxes, to be detailed in the next section. Many DBAs working on Windows will want to modify the Start menu shortcut to include the NOLOG switch.

Database Startup and Shutdown

If one is being precise (always a good idea, if you want to pass the OCP examinations), one does not start or stop a database: an instance may be started and stopped; a database is mounted and opened, and then dismounted and closed. This can be done from either SQL*Plus, using the STARTUP and SHUTDOWN commands, or through Database Control. On a Windows system, it may also be done by controlling the Windows service within which the instance runs. The alert log will give details of all such operations, however they were initiated. Startup and shutdown are critical operations. As such, they are always recorded and can only be carried out by highly privileged users.

Connecting with an Appropriate Privilege

Ordinary users cannot start up or shut down a database. This is because an ordinary user is authenticated against the data dictionary. It is logically impossible for an ordinary user to start up an instance and open (or create) a database, since the data dictionary cannot be read until the database is open. You must therefore connect with some form of external authentication: you must be authenticated either by the operating system, as being a member of the group that owns the Oracle software, or by giving a username/password combination that exists in an external password file. You tell Oracle that you wish to use external authentication by using appropriate syntax in the CONNECT command that you give in your user process.

If you are using SQL*Plus, the syntax of the CONNECT command tells Oracle what type of authentication you wish to use: the default of data dictionary authentication, password file authentication, or operating system authentication. These are the possibilities:

```
connect user/pass[@connect_alias]
connect user/pass[@connect_alias] as sysdba
connect user/pass[@connect_alias] as sysoper
connect / as sysdba
connect / as sysoper
```

In these examples, *user* is the username and *pass* is the password. The *connect_alias* will be resolved to a connect string, as described in Chapter 6. The first example is normal, data dictionary, authentication. Oracle will validate the username/password combination against values stored in the data dictionary. The database must be open, or the connect will fail. Anyone connecting with this syntax cannot—no matter who he/she is—issue startup or shutdown commands. The second two examples instruct Oracle to go to the external password file to validate the username/password combination. The last two examples use operating system authentication; Oracle will go to the host operating system and check whether the operating system user running SQL*Plus is a member of the operating system group that owns the Oracle software, and if the user passes this test, he/she will be logged on as SYSDBA or SYSOPER without any need to give a username and password. A user connecting with any of the bottom four syntaxes will be able to issue startup and shutdown commands and will be able to connect no matter what state the database is in—it may not even have been created yet. Note that the first three examples can include a database connect string; this is necessary if the connection is to be made across a network. Naturally, this is not an option for operating system authentication, because operating system authentication relies on the user being logged on to the machine hosting the Oracle server: he/she must either be working on it directly or have logged in to it with telnet, secure shell, or some similar utility.

on the **job**

From an operating system prompt, you can save a bit of time and typing by combining the launch of SQL*Plus and the CONNECT into one command. Here are two examples:
C:\> sqlplus / as sysdba
C:\> sqlplus sys/oracle@orcl as sysdba

Database Control will by default attempt to connect through a listener, but it can also use operating system authentication. If the situation is that depicted in Figure 5-3, clicking the Startup button will require entering an operating system logon to proceed. If the listener is running, Database Control will present the login window shown in Figure 5-5. The Connect As combo box lets you choose whether to make a normal connection or a SYSDBA connection.

FIGURE 5-5

The Database
Control login
window, when a
listener has been
detected

Oracle Enterprise Manager - Microsoft Internet Explorer

File   Edit   View   Favorites   Tools   Help

Address   https://127.0.0.1:1158/em/console/logon/logon

ORACLE Enterprise Manager 11*g*   Help
Database Control

Login

Login to Database:ocp11g

　　　　　　　 * User Name   [   ]
　　　　　　　 * Password   [   ]
　　　　　　　 Connect As   [Normal ▾]
　　　　　　　　　　　　　　　　　　　 (Login)

Copyright © 1996, 2007, Oracle. All rights reserved.
Oracle, JD Edwards, PeopleSoft, and Retek are registered trademarks of Oracle Corporation and/or its affiliates. Other names
Unauthorized access is strictly prohibited.

SYSOPER and SYSDBA

These are special privileges with special capabilities. They can only be enabled when users are connecting with an external authentication method: either operating system or password file. SYSOPER has the ability to issue these commands:

```
STARTUP
SHUTDOWN
ALTER DATABASE [MOUNT | OPEN | CLOSE | DISMOUNT]
ALTER [DATABASE | TABLESPACE] [BEGIN | END] BACKUP
RECOVER
```

The SYSDBA privilege includes all of these, but in addition has the ability to create a database, to do an incomplete recovery, and to create other SYSOPER and SYSDBA users.

e x a m

ⓦatch

SYSDBA and SYSOPER are not users; they are privileges that can be granted to users. By default, only user

SYS has these privileges until they are deliberately granted to other users.

You may be wondering what Oracle user you are actually logging on as when you use operating system authentication. To find out, from a SQL*Plus prompt connect using the operating system authentication syntax already shown, and then issue the show user command (which can be abbreviate to sho user. Never underestimate the importance of saving keystrokes) as in the examples shown in Figure 5-6.

FIGURE 5-6

Use of operating system and password file authentication

```
C:\WINDOWS\system32\cmd.exe - sqlplus /nolog                    _ □ ×

C:\>set ORACLE_SID=ocp11g

C:\>sqlplus /nolog

SQL*Plus: Release 11.1.0.4.0 - Beta on Mon Nov 12 21:14:02 2007

Copyright (c) 1982, 2007, Oracle.  All rights reserved.

SQL> connect / as sysdba
Connected.
SQL> show user
USER is "SYS"
SQL> conn / as sysoper
Connected.
SQL> sho user
USER is "PUBLIC"
SQL> connect sys/oracle@jwacer.bplc.co.za:1521/ocp11g as sysdba
Connected.
SQL> show user
USER is "SYS"
SQL> conn sys/oracle @ocp11g as sysoper
Connected.
SQL> show user
USER is "PUBLIC"
SQL>
```

So use of the SYSDBA privilege logs you on to the instance as user SYS, the most powerful user in the database and the owner of the data dictionary. Use of the SYSOPER privilege connects you as a user PUBLIC. PUBLIC is not a user in any normal sense—he/she is a notional user with administration privileges, but (by default) with no privileges that let him/her see or manipulate data. You should connect with either of these privileges only when you need to carry out procedures that no normal user can do.

Startup: NOMOUNT, MOUNT, and OPEN

Remember that the instance and the database are separate entities; they can exist independently of each other. The startup process is therefore staged: first you build the instance in memory, second you enable a connection to the database by mounting it, and third you open the database for use. At any moment, a database will be in one of four states:

- SHUTDOWN
- NOMOUNT
- MOUNT
- OPEN

When the database is SHUTDOWN, all files are closed and the instance does not exist. In NOMOUNT mode, the instance has been built in memory (the SGA has been created and the background processes started, according to whatever is specified in its parameter file), but no connection has been made to a database. It is indeed possible that the database does not yet exist. In MOUNT mode, the instance locates and reads the database control file. In OPEN mode, all database files are located and opened and the database is made available for use by end users. The startup process is staged: whenever you issue a startup command, it will go through these stages. It is possible to stop the startup part way. For example, if your control file is damaged, or a multiplexed copy is missing, you will not be able to mount the database, but by stopping in NOMOUNT mode you may be able to repair the damage. Similarly, if there are problems with any datafiles or redo log files, you may be able to repair them in MOUNT mode before transitioning the database to OPEN mode.

At any stage, how does the instance find the files it needs, and exactly what happens? Start with NOMOUNT. When you issue a startup command, Oracle will attempt to locate a parameter file. There are three default filenames. On Unix they are

```
$ORACLE_HOME/dbs/spfileSID.ora
$ORACLE_HOME/dbs/spfile.ora
$ORACLE_HOME/dbs/initSID.ora
```

and on Windows,

```
%ORACLE_HOME%\database\SPFILESID.ORA
%ORACLE_HOME%\database\SPFILE.ORA
%ORACLE_HOME%\database\INITSID.ORA
```

on the **job** *spfileSID.ora is undoubtedly the most convenient file to use as your parameter file. Normally, you will only use spfile.ora in a RAC environment, where one file may be used to start several instances. You will only use an initSID.ora file if for some reason you need to make manual edits; spfiles are binary files and cannot be edited by hand.*

In all cases, *SID* refers to the name of the instance that the parameter file will start. The preceding order is important! Oracle will work its way down the list, using the first file it finds and ignoring the rest. If none of them exist, the instance will not start. The only files used in NOMOUNT mode are the parameter file and the alert log. The parameters in the parameter file are used to build the SGA in memory and to start the background processes. Entries will be written out to the alert log describing this process. Where is the alert log? In the location given by the BACKGROUND_DUMP_DEST parameter, that can be found in the parameter file or by running

```
sho parameter background
```

at a SQL prompt. If the log already exists, it will be appended to. Otherwise, it will be created. If any problems occur during this stage, trace files may also be generated in the same location.

exam **watch** *An "init" file is known as a "static" parameter file or a pfile, because it is only read once, at instance startup. An "spfile" is known as a dynamic parameter file, because Oracle continuously reads and updates it while the instance is running. A parameter file of one sort or the other is essential, because there is one parameter without a default value: the DB_NAME parameter.*

Once the instance is successfully started in NOMOUNT mode, it may be transitioned to MOUNT mode by reading the controlfile. It locates the controlfile by using the CONTROL_FILES parameter, which it knows from having read the parameter file used when starting in NOMOUNT mode. If the controlfile (or any multiplexed copy of it) is damaged or missing, the database will not mount and you will have to take appropriate action before proceeding further. All copies of the controlfile must be available and identical if the mount is to be successful.

As part of the mount, the names and locations of all the datafiles and online redo logs are read from the controlfile, but Oracle does not yet attempt to find them. This happens during the transition to OPEN mode. If any files are missing or damaged, the database will remain in MOUNT mode and cannot be opened until you take appropriate action. Furthermore, even if all the files are present, they must be synchronized before the database opens. If the last shutdown was orderly, with all database buffers in the database buffer cache being flushed to disk by DBWn, then everything will be synchronized: Oracle will know that that all committed transactions are safely stored in the datafiles, and that no uncommitted transactions are hanging about waiting to be rolled back. However, if the last shutdown was disorderly (such as from a loss of power, or the server being rebooted), then Oracle must repair the damage and the database is considered to be in an inconsistent state. The mechanism for this is described in Chapter 15. The process that mounts and opens the database (and carries out repairs, if the previous shutdown was disorderly) is the SMON process. Only once the database has been successfully opened will Oracle permit user sessions to be established.

Shutdown should be the reverse of startup. During an orderly shutdown, the database is first closed, then dismounted, and finally the instance is stopped. During the close phase, all sessions are terminated: active transactions are rolled back by PMON, completed transactions are flushed to disk by DBWn, and the datafiles and redo log files are closed. During the dismount, the controlfile is closed. Then the instance is stopped by deallocating the SGA and terminating the background processes.

on the
Job

If someone were in the middle of a long-running update statement or, for example, were loading tables for a data warehouse, when you had to shut down the database, the rollback phase, and therefore the time it takes the database to close and shut down cleanly, can be a LONG LONG time (sometimes several hours).

Shutdown: NORMAL, IMMEDIATE, TRANSACTIONAL, and ABORT

There are options that may be used on the shutdown command, all of which require either a SYSDBA or a SYSOPER connection:

```
shutdown [normal | transactional | immediate | abort]
```

- **Normal**   This is the default. No new user connections will be permitted, but all current connections are allowed to continue. Only once all users have (voluntarily!) logged off, will the database actually shut down.

on the **Øob**   *Typically, a normal shutdown is useless: there is always someone logged on, even if it is only Database Control itself.*

- **Transactional**   No new user connections are permitted; existing sessions that are not in a transaction will be terminated; sessions currently in a transaction are allowed to complete the transaction and will then be terminated. Once all sessions are terminated, the database will shut down.

- **Immediate**   No new sessions are permitted, and all currently connected sessions are terminated. Any active transactions are rolled back, and the database will then shut down.

- **Abort**   As far as Oracle is concerned, this is the equivalent of a power cut. The instance terminates immediately. Nothing is written to disk, no file handles are closed, and there is no attempt to terminate transactions that may be in progress in any orderly fashion.

on the **Øob**   *A shutdown abort will not damage the database, but some operations (such as backups) are not advisable after an abort.*

The "normal," "immediate," and "transactional" shutdown modes are usually referred to as "clean," "consistent," or "orderly" shutdowns. After all sessions are terminated, PMON will roll back any incomplete transactions. Then a checkpoint is issued (remember the CKPT process from Chapter 2), which forces the DBWn process to write all updated data from the database buffer cache down to the datafiles. LGWR also flushes any change vectors still in memory to the log files. Then the file headers are updated, and the file handles closed. This means that the database is in a "consistent" state: all committed transactions are in the datafiles, there are no uncommitted transactions hanging about that need to be rolled back, and all datafiles and log files are synchronized.

The "abort" mode, sometimes referred to as a "disorderly" shutdown, leaves the database in an "inconsistent" state: it is quite possible that committed transactions have been lost, because they existed only in memory and DBWn had not yet written them to the datafiles. Equally, there may be uncommitted transactions in the datafiles that have not yet been rolled back. This is a definition of a corrupted database: it may be missing committed transactions, or storing uncommitted transactions. These corruptions must be repaired by instance recovery (described in Chapter 15). It is exactly as though the database server had been switched off, or perhaps rebooted, while the database was running.

on the
(j)ob

There is a startup command `startup force` *that can save time. It is two commands in one: a* `shutdown abort` *followed by a* `startup`.

An orderly shutdown is a staged process, and it is theoretically possible to control the stages. The SQL*Plus commands are

```
alter database close;
alter database dismount;
```

These commands will exactly reverse the startup sequence. In practice, however, there is no value to them; a `shutdown` is all any DBA will ever use. They are not even available through Database Control.

EXERCISE 5-1

Conduct a Startup and a Shutdown

Use SQL*Plus to start an instance and open a database, then Database Control to shut it down. If the database is already open, do this in the other order. Note that if you are working on Windows, the Windows service for the database must be running. It will have a name of the form OracleService*SID*, where *SID is the name of the instance*.

1. Log on to the computer as a member of the operating system group that owns the ORACLE_HOME, and set the environment variables appropriately for ORACLE_HOME and PATH and ORACLE_SID, as described in Chapter 4.

2. Check the status of the database listener, and start it if necessary. From an operating system prompt:

```
lsnrctl status
lsnrctl start
```

3. Check the status of the Database Control console, and start it if necessary. From an operating system prompt:

```
emctl status dbconsole
emctl start dbconsole
```

4. Launch SQL*Plus, using the /nolog switch to prevent an immediate logon prompt:

```
sqlplus /nolog
```

5. Connect as SYS with operating system authentication:

```
connect / as sysdba
```

6. Start the instance only:

```
startup nomount;
```

7. Mount the database:

```
alter database mount;
```

8. Open the database:

```
alter database open;
```

9. Confirm that the database is open by querying a data dictionary view:

```
select count(*) from dba_data_files;
```

10. From a browser, connect to the Database Control console. The hostname and port will have been shown in the output of the `emctl status dbconsole` command in Step 3. The URL will be something like `https://jwlnx1 .bplc.co.za:1158/em`.

11. Log on as SYS with the password selected at database creation, and choose SYSDBA from the Connect As drop-down box.

12. On the database home page, click the Shutdown button.

13. The next window prompts for host credentials, which will be your operating system username and password, and database credentials, which will be the SYS username and password. If you want to save these to prevent having to enter them repeatedly, check the box Save As Preferred Credential. Click OK.

INSIDE THE EXAM

Managing the Oracle Instance

The instance opens a database, but the two are separate and need different files. The instance reads only the parameter file to build in memory. It then mounts the database by reading the controlfile, whose location(s) is specified by a parameter. The controlfile has pointers to the rest of the database. So the startup of a database is staged: the NOMOUNT mode requires only a parameter file; the MOUNT mode requires the controlfile(s); the OPEN mode requires the datafiles and the online redo log files.

The instance and the controlfile can be interrogated through dynamic performance views, in NOMOUNT or MOUNT mode. Once the database is in OPEN mode, the data dictionary can also be interrogated, through data dictionary views.

CERTIFICATION OBJECTIVE 5.02

Set Database Initialization Parameters

An instance is defined by the parameters used to build it in memory. It can be changed after startup by adjusting these parameters—if the parameters are ones that can be changed. Some are fixed at startup time and can only be changed by shutting down the instance and starting again.

The parameters used to build the instance initially come from either the parameter file (which may be a static pfile or a dynamic spfile) or from defaults. Every parameter has a default, except for the DB_NAME parameter; this must always be specified. In total there are close on three hundred parameters (the exact number will vary between releases and platforms) that it is acceptable for the DBA to set. There are in fact about another fifteen hundred parameters, known as "hidden" parameters, that the DBA is not supposed to set; these are not usually visible and should only be set on the advice of Oracle Support.

The (approximately) three hundred parameters are divided into "basic" and "advanced." The idea is that most database instances will run well with default values for the advanced parameters. Only about thirty-three (the exact number may vary between versions) are "basic." So setting parameters is not an enormous task. But it is enormously important.

Static and Dynamic Parameters, and the Initialization Parameter File

To view the parameters and their current values, a query such as this will do:

```
select name,value from v$parameter order by name;
```

A query that may give slightly different results is

```
select name,value from v$spparameter order by name;
```

The difference is the view from which the parameter names and values are taken. V$PARAMETER shows the parameter values currently in effect in the running instance. V$SPPARAMETER shows the values in spfile on disk. Usually, these will be the same. But not always. Some parameters can be changed while the instance is running; others, known as static parameters, are fixed at instance startup time. A change made to the changeable parameters will have an immediate effect and can optionally be written out to the spfile. If this is done, then the change will be permanent: the next time the instance is stopped and started, the new value will be read from the spfile. If the change is not saved to the spfile, then the change will only persist until the instance is stopped. To change a static parameter, the change must be written to the spfile, and then it will come into effect at the next startup. If the output of the two preceding queries differs, this will typically be because the DBA has done some tuning work that he has not yet made permanent, or he has found it necessary to adjust a static parameter and hasn't yet restarted the instance.

The other columns in V$PARAMETER and V$SPPARAMETER are self-explanatory. They show such information as whether the parameter can be changed (for a session or for the whole instance), whether it has been changed, and whether it has been specified at all or is on default.

The views can also be seen through Database Control. From the database home page, take the Server tab and the Initialization Parameters link. On the window following, shown in Figure 5-7, there are two subtabs: current shows the values currently in effect, in the running instance and SPFile shows those recorded in the spfile.

The changeable parameters can be adjusted through the same window. The values for the first four parameters shown (CLUSTER_DATABASE, COMPATIBLE, CONTROL_FILES, and DB_BLOCK_SIZE) cannot be changed; they are static. But the next parameter, DB_CREATE_FILE_DEST, can be changed. In the figure,

FIGURE 5-7

Initialization
parameters, as
seen through
Database Control

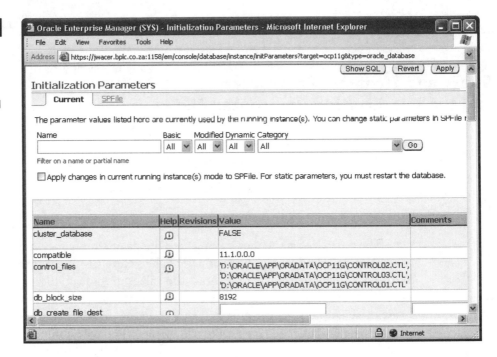

it has not been set—but it can be, by entering a value in the box in the column headed
"Value." To change the static parameters, it is necessary to take the SPFile subtab, and
make the changes there.

To change a parameters with SQL*Plus, use the ALTER SYSTEM command.
Figure 5-8 shows examples.

FIGURE 5-8

Changing
and querying
parameters
with SQL*Plus

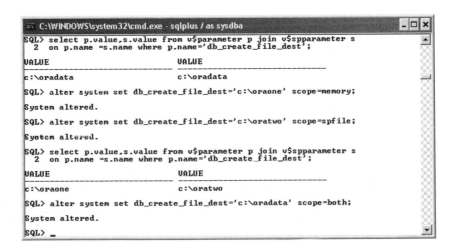

The first query in Figure 5-8 shows that the values for the parameter DB_CREATE_ FILE_DEST are the same in the running instance in memory, and in the spfile on disk. The next two commands adjust the parameter in both places to different values, but using the SCOPE keyword. The results are seen in the second query. The final command uses SCOPE=BOTH to change both the running and the stored value with one command. This BOTH is the default, if the SCOPE is not specified.

e x a m

ⓦatch
An attempt to change a static parameter will fail unless the SCOPE is specified as SPFILE. The default SCOPE is ***BOTH the running instance and the spfile. If the instance is started with a pfile, then SCOPE=SPFILE will fail.***

As was seen in Chapter 4, when a database instance is first created, it will be built with a pfile. This needs to be converted to an spfile. The command is

```
create spfile [='spfilename'] from pfile [='pfilename'];
```

If names are not given for *spfilename* or *pfilename*, then the default names based on the ORACLE_HOME and the SID will be assumed. To reverse-engineer an spfile into a pfile, the command is

```
create pfile [='pfilename'] from spfile [='spfilename'] ;
```

The CREATE PFILE and CREATE SPFILE commands can be run from SQL*Plus at any time, even before the instance has been started.

The Basic Parameters

The instance parameters considered to be "basic" are those that should be considered for every database. In some cases, the default will be fine—but it should still be thought about. To view the basic parameters and their current values, a query such as this will do:

```
select name,value from  v$parameter where isbasic='TRUE' order
by name;
```

A query that may give slightly different results is

```
select s.name,s.value
from v$spparameter s join v$parameter p on s.name=p.name
where p.isbasic='TRUE' order by name;
```

The difference will be because some parameter changes may have been applied to the instance but not the spfile (or vice versa). The necessity for the join is because there is no column on V$SPPARAMETER to show whether a parameter is basic or advanced. Table 5-1 summarizes the basic parameters.

TABLE 5-1   The Basic Parameters

Parameter	Purpose
cluster_database	Is the database an RAC or a single instance? That this is basic indicates that RAC is considered a standard option
Compatible	The version that the instance will emulate. Normally this would be the actual version, but it can look like older versions
control_files	The name and location of the controlfile copies
db_block_size	The default block size for formatting datafiles
db_create_file_dest	The default location for datafiles
db_create_online_log_dest_1	The default location for online redo log files
db_create_online_log_dest_2	The default location for online redo log files multiplexed copies
db_domain	The domain name that can be suffixed to the db_name to generate a globally unique name
db_name	The name of the database (the only parameter with no default)
db_recovery_file_dest	The location of the flash recovery area
db_recovery_file_dest_size	The amount of data that may be written to the flash recovery area
db_unique_name	A unique identifier necessary if two database with the same db_name are on the same machine
instance_number	Used to distinguish two RAC instances opening the same database. Another indication that RAC is considered standard
job_queue_processes	The number of processes available to run scheduled jobs
log_archive_dest_1	The destination for archiving redo log files
log_archive_dest_2	The destination for multiplexed copies of archived redo log files
log_archive_dest_state_1	An indicator for whether the destination is enabled or not
log_archive_dest_state_2	An indicator for whether the destination is enabled or not
nls_language	The language of the instance (provides many default formats)
nls_territory	The geographical location of the instance (which provides even more default formats)
open_cursors	The number of SQL work areas that a session can have open at once

TABLE 5-1	The Basic Parameters (*Continued*)

Parameter	Purpose
pga_aggregate_target	The total amount of memory the instance can allocate to PGAs
processes	The maximum number of processes (including session server processes) allowed to connect to the instance
remote_listener	The addresses of listeners on other machine with which the instance should register; another parameter that is only relevant for an RAC
remote_login_passwordfile	Whether or not to use an external password file, to permit password file authentication
rollback_segments	Almost deprecated—superseded by the UNDO parameters that follow
sessions	The maximum number of sessions allowed to connect to the instance
sga_target	The size of the SGA, within which Oracle will manage the various SGA memory structures
shared_servers	The number of shared server processes to launch, for sessions that are not established with dedicated server processes
star_transformation_enabled	Whether to permit the optimizer to rewrite queries that join the dimensions of a fact table
undo_management	Whether undo data should be automatically managed in an undo tablespace, or manually managed in rollback segments
undo_tablespace	If using automatic undo management, where the undo data should reside

All of these basic parameters are discussed in the appropriate chapters, as well as some of the advanced parameters.

Changing Parameters

The static parameters cannot be changed other than with an ALTER SYSTEM command with a SCOPE=SPFILE clause. Other parameters may apply to the whole system, to individual sessions, or to both.

An example of a static parameter is LOG_BUFFER. If you want to resize the log buffer to 6 MB and issue this command:

```
alter system set log_buffer=6m;
```

it will fail with the message "ORA-02095: specified initialization parameter cannot be modified." It must be changed with the SCOPE=SPFILE clause, and the instance restarted to take effect.

on the
① ob

The default log buffer size is probably correct. If you raise it, you may find that commit processing takes longer. If you make it smaller than default, it will in fact be internally adjusted up to the default size.

An example of a parameter that applies to the whole instance but can be adjusted for individual sessions is OPTIMIZER_MODE. This influences the way in which Oracle will execute statements. A common choice is between the values ALL_ROWS and FIRST_ROWS. ALL_ROWS instructs the optimizer to generate execution plans that will run the statement to completion as quickly as possible, whereas FIRST_ROWS instructs it to generate plans that will get something back to the user as soon as possible, even if the whole statement may then take longer to complete. So if your database is usually used for long DSS-type queries but some users use it for interactive work, you might issue the command

```
alter system set optimizer_mode=all_rows;
```

and let the individual users issue

```
alter session set optimizer_mode=first_rows;
```

if they want to.

There are a few parameters that can only be modified at the session level. Principal among these is NLS_DATE_FORMAT. This parameter, which controls the display of data and time values, can be specified in the parameter file but cannot be changed with ALTER SYSTEM. So it is static, as far as the instance is concerned. But it can be adjusted at the session level:

```
alter session set nls_date_format='dd-mm-yy hh24:mi:ss';
```

This will change the current session's date/time display to the European norm without affecting any other sessions.

EXERCISE 5-2

Query and Set Initialization Parameters

In this exercise, use either SQL*Plus or SQL Developer to manage initialization parameters. The illustrations use SQL*Plus, but only because it is possible to fit more commands in one window than with SQL Developer.

1. Connect to the database (which must be open!) as user SYS, with the SYSDBA privilege. Use either operating system authentication or password file authentication.

2. Display all the basic parameters, checking whether they have all been set or are still on default:

```
select name,value,isdefault from v$parameter where isbasic=-'TRUE'
order by name;
```

3. Any basic parameters that are on default should be investigated to see if the default is appropriate. In fact, all the basic parameters should be considered. Read up on all of them in the Oracle documentation now. The volume you need is titled *Oracle Database Reference. Part 1, Chapter 1 has a paragraph describing every initialization parameter.*

4. Change the PROCESSES parameter to 200. This is a static parameter. The next illustration shows how to do this by specifying a SCOPE and then bouncing the database.

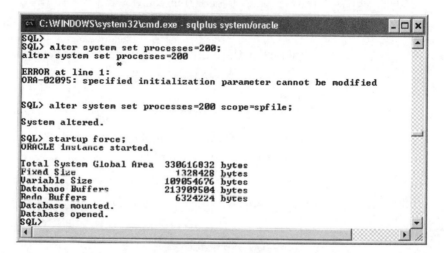

5. Rerun the query from Step 3. Note the new value for PROCESSES, and also for SESSIONS. PROCESSES limits the number of operating system processes that are allowed to connect to the instance, and SESSIONS limits the number of sessions. These figures are related, because each session will require a process. The default value for SESSIONS is derived from PROCESSES, so if SESSIONS was on default, it will now have a new value.

6. Change the value for the NLS_LANGUAGE parameter for your session. Choose whatever mainstream language you want (Oracle supports many languages: 67 at the time of writing), but the language must be specified in English (e.g., use "German," not "Deutsch"):

```
alter session set nls_language=German;
```

7. Confirm that the change has worked by querying the system date:

```
select to_char(sysdate,'day') from dual;
```

You may want to change your session language back to what it was before (such as English) with another ALTER SESSION command. If you don't, be prepared for error messages to be in the language your session is now using.

8. Change the OPTIMIZER_MODE parameter, but restrict the scope to the running instance only; do not update the parameter file. This exercise enables the deprecated rule-based optimizer, which might be needed while testing some old code, but you would not want the change to be permanent:

```
alter system set optimizer_mode=rule scope=spfile;
```

9. Confirm that the change has been effected, but not written to the parameter file:

```
select value from v$parameter where name='optimizer_mode'
union
select value from v$spparameter where name='optimizer_mode';
```

10. Return the OPTIMIZER_MODE to its standard value, in both the running instance and the parameter file:

```
alter system set optimizer_mode=all_rows scope=both;
```

Note that the scope clause is redundant, because BOTH is the default SCOPE.

CERTIFICATION OBJECTIVE 5.03

Use the Alert Log and Trace Files

The alert log is a continuous record of critical operations applied to the instance and the database. Its location is determined by the instance parameter BACKGROUND_DUMP_DEST, and its name is `alert_SID.log`, where *SID* is the name of the instance.

The critical operations recorded in the alert include

- All startup and shutdown commands, including intermediate commands such as ALTER DATABASE MOUNT
- All errors internal to the instance (the ORA-600 errors, about which the DBA can do nothing other than report them to Oracle Support)
- Any detected datafile block corruptions
- Any record locking deadlocks that may have occurred
- All operations that affect the physical structure of the database, such as creating or renaming datafiles and online redo logs
- All ALTER SYSTEM commands that adjust the values of initialization parameters
- All log switches and log archives

The alert log entry for a startup shows all the non-default initialization parameters. This information, together with the subsequent record of changes to the instance with ALTER SYSTEM and to the database physical structures with ALTER DATABASE, means that it is always possible to reconstruct the history of changes to the database and the instance. This can be invaluable when trying to backtrack in order to find the source of a problem.

on the
ô o b

For many DBAs, the first thing they do when they are asked to look at a database for the first time is locate the alert log and scan through it, just to get an Idea of what has been going on.

Trace files are generated by the various background processes, usually when they hit an error. These files will be located in the BACKGROUND_DUMP_ DEST directory, along with the alert log. If a background process has failed because of an error, the trace file generated will be invaluable in diagnosing the problem.

EXERCISE 5-3

Use the Alert Log

In this exercise, locate the alert log and find the entries for the parameter changes made in Exercise 5-2 and the startups and shutdowns in Exercise 5-1.

1. Connect to your database with either SQL*Plus or SQL Developer, and find the value of the BACKGROUND_DUMP_DEST parameter:

```
select value from v$parameter where name='background_dump_dest';
```

Note that this value can also be found with Database Control.

2. Using whatever operating system tool you please (such as the Windows Explorer, or whatever file system browser your Linux session is using), navigate to the directory identified in Step 1.

3. Open the alert log. It will be a file called alert_SID.log, where SID is the name of the instance. Use any editor you please (but note that on Windows, the Notepad is not a good choice because of the way carriage returns are handled. WordPad is much better).

4. Go to the bottom of the file. You will see the ALTER SYSTEM commands of Exercise 5-2 and the results of the startup and shutdowns.

CERTIFICATION OBJECTIVE 5.04

Use Data Dictionary and Dynamic Performance Views

An Oracle database is defined by its data dictionary. The data dictionary is not very comprehensible to normal human beings. For this reason, Oracle provides a set of views onto the data dictionary that should be much easier to understand. These views are the DBA's tool for understanding what is happening in the database. The instance also has a set of tables (which are in fact C data structures) that are not really understandable. These are also externalized as a set of views: the dynamic performance views that are the key to understanding what is happening within the instance.

The Data Dictionary Views

The data dictionary is metadata: data about data. It describes the database, both physically and logically, and its contents. User definitions, security information, integrity constraints, and (from release 10g onward) performance monitoring information are all part of the data dictionary. It is stored as a set of segments in the SYSTEM and SYSAUX tablespaces.

In many ways, the segments that make up the data dictionary are segments like any other: just tables and indexes. The critical difference is that the data dictionary tables are generated at database creation time, and you are not allowed to access them directly. There is nothing to stop an inquisitive DBA from investigating the data dictionary directly, but if you do any updates to it you may cause irreparable damage to your database, and certainly Oracle Corporation will not support you. Creating a data dictionary is part of the database creation process. It is maintained subsequently by Data Definition Language commands. When you issue the CREATE TABLE command, you are in fact inserting rows into data dictionary tables, as you are with commands such as CREATE USER or GRANT.

To query the dictionary, Oracle provides a set of views. The views come in three forms, prefixed DBA_, ALL_, or USER_. Most of the views come in all three forms. Any view prefixed USER_ will be populated with rows describing objects owned by the user querying the view. So no two people will see the same contents. If user SCOTT queries USER_TABLES, he/she will see information about his/her tables; if you query USER_TABLES, you will see information about your tables. Any view prefixed ALL_ will be populated with rows describing objects to which you have access. So ALL_TABLES will contain rows describing your own tables, plus rows describing tables belonging to anyone else that you have been given permission to see. Any view prefixed DBA_ will have rows for every object in the database, so DBA_TABLES will have one row for every table in the database, no matter who created it. These views are created as part of the database creation process, along with a large number of PL/SQL packages that are provided by Oracle to assist database administrators in managing the database and programmers in developing applications. PL/SQL is also stored in the data dictionary.

There are hundreds of data dictionary views. Some of those commonly used by DBAs are

- **DBA_OBJECTS**   A row for every object in the database
- **DBA_DATA_FILES**   A row describing every datafile
- **DBA_USERS**   A row describing each user
- **DBA_TABLES**   A row describing each table
- **DBA_ALERT_HISTORY**   Rows describing past alert conditions

There are many more than these, some of which will be used in later chapters. As well as the views, there are public synonyms onto the views. A query such as this,

```
select object_name,owner, object_type from dba_objects
where object_name='DBA_OBJECTS';
```

will show that in fact there is a view called DBA_OBJECTS owned by SYS, and a public synonym with the same name.

The Dynamic Performance Views

There are more than three hundred dynamic performance views. You will often hear them referred to as the "Vee dollar" views, because their names are prefixed with "V$". In fact, the "Vee dollar" views are not views at all—they are synonyms onto views that are prefixed with "V_$", as shown in Figure 5-9.

FIGURE 5-9

A V$ view (or rather, a view and its V$ synonym)

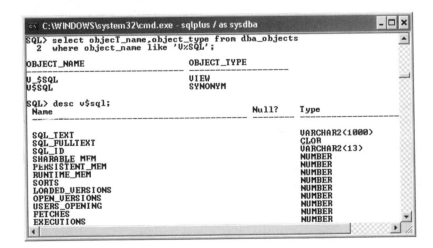

The figure shows V$SQL, which has one row for every SQL statement currently stored in the shared pool, with such information as how often the statement has been executed.

The dynamic performance views give access to a phenomenal amount of information about the instance, and (to a certain extent) about the database. The majority of the views are populated with information from the instance; the remainder are populated from the controlfile. All of them give real-time information. Dynamic performance views that are populated from the instance, such as V$INSTANCE or V$SYSSTAT, are available at all times, even when the instance is in NOMOUNT mode. Dynamic performance views that are populated from the controlfile, such as V$DATABASE or V$DATAFILE, cannot be queried unless the database has been mounted, which is when the controlfile is read. By contrast, the data dictionary views (prefixed DBA, ALL, or USER) can only be queried after the database—including the data dictionary—has been opened.

e x a m
watch
Dynamic performance views are populated from the instance or the controlfile; DBA_, ALL_, and USER_ views are populated from the data dictionary. This difference determines what views can be queried at the various startup stages.

The dynamic performance views are created at startup, updated during the lifetime of the instance, and dropped at shutdown. This means that they will contain values that have been accumulated since startup time; if your database has been open for six months nonstop, they will have data built up over that period. After a shutdown/startup, they will start from the beginning again. While the totals may be interesting, they will not tell you anything about what happened during certain defined periods, when there may have been performance issues. For this reason, it is generally true that the dynamic performance views give you statistics, not metrics. The conversion of these statistics into metrics is a skilled and sometimes time-consuming task, made much easier by the self-tuning and monitoring capabilities of the database.

on the job
There is some overlap between V$ views and data dictionary views. For instance, V$TABLESPACE has a row for every tablespace, as does DBA_TABLESPACES. Note that as a general rule, V$ views are singular and data dictionary views are plural. But there are exceptions.

SCENARIO & SOLUTION

You are taking over administration of a database. How do you start?	Look at the alert log. You can find it by checking the parameter BACKGROUND_DUMP_DEST. Look at all the non-default parameters to see how the instance is being built. Query the views that will show the physical structures: V$DATAFILE, V$LOGFILE.
If you don't even have a login to this database, can you do anything?	Yes, you can. If you have an appropriate operating system logon, as an operating system user who is member of the group that owns the ORACLE_HOME, you can connect as SYS using operating system authentication. Then you can create a normal user, grant him some privileges (such as DBA), and connect as this new user from then on.
On Windows, there always seem to be two ways of starting things: .BAT or .CMD shell scripts, or services. How can you best manage the startup of the Oracle environment?	Yes, there is a choice: start the services defined in the registry, or write a batch file shell script that will start the processes. The exception is the database instance: the service must be started, and then either the service can go on to start the instance, or you can start the instance with a SQL *Plus command called from a batch file. People familiar with defining services, in particular with defining dependencies between them, will prefer that method; people less familiar with services, or who may want visible control of the startup, will use commands in shell scripts.

EXERCISE 5-4

Query Data Dictionary and Dynamic Performance Views

In this exercise, investigate the physical structures of the database by querying views.

1. Connect to the database with SQL*Plus or SQL Developer.

2. Use dynamic performance views to determine what datafile and tablespaces make up the database:

```
select t.name,d.name,d.bytes from v$tablespace t join
v$datafile d on t.ts#=d.ts# order by t.name;
```

3. Obtain the same information from data dictionary views:

```
select t.tablespace_name,d.file_name,d.bytes from
dba_tablespaces t
join dba_data_files d on t.tablespace_name=d.tablespace_name
order by tablespace_name;
```

4. Determine the location of all the controlfile copies. Use two techniques:

```
select * from v$controlfile;
select value from v$parameter where name='control_files';
```

5. Determine the location of the online redo log file members, and their size. As the size is an attribute of the group, not the members, you will have to join two views:

```
select m.group#,m.member,g.bytes from v$log g join v$logfile m
on m.group#=g.group# order by m.group#,m.member;
```

CERTIFICATION SUMMARY

Starting up a database is a staged process. Each stage requires various files to be available. Only when all stages are complete can regular users log on. Before that, only users with SYSDBA or SYSOPER privileges can connect, and they must use a form of authentication other than the data dictionary. The instance is built according to instance parameters stored in a parameter file. Many of these parameters can be adjusted while the instance is running, but others can only be written to the file and will then take effect next time the instance is restarted. In the NOMOUNT and MOUNT modes, various dynamic performance views will be visible. Once in OPEN mode, the data dictionary can also be queried through views.

✓ # TWO-MINUTE DRILL

Describe the Stages of Database Startup and Shutdown

❑ The stages are NOMOUNT, MOUNT, and OPEN.

❑ NOMOUNT mode requires a parameter file.

❑ MOUNT mode requires the controlfile.

❑ OPEN mode requires the datafiles and online redo log files.

Set Database Initialization Parameters

❑ Static parameters cannot be changed without a shutdown/startup.

❑ Other parameters can be changed dynamically, for the instance or a session.

❑ Parameters can be seen in the dynamic performance views V$PARAMETER and V$SPPARAMETER.

Use the Alert Log and Trace Files

❑ The alert log is a continuous stream of messages regarding critical operations.

❑ Trace files are generates by background processes, usually when they hit errors.

Use Data Dictionary and Dynamic Performance Views

❑ The dynamic performance views are populated from the instance or the controlfile.

❑ The data dictionary views are populated from the data dictionary.

❑ Dynamic performance views accumulate values through the lifetime of the instance, and are reinitialized at startup.

❑ Data dictionary views show information that persists across shutdown and startup.

❑ Both the data dictionary views and the dynamic performance views are published through synonyms.

SELF TEST

Describe the Stages of Database Startup and Shutdown

1. You issue the URL https://127.0.0.1:5500/em and receive an error. What could be the problem? (Choose all correct answers.)

   A. You have not started the database listener.

   B. You have not started the dbconsole.

   C. The dbconsole is running on a different port.

   D. You are not logged on to the database server node.

   E. You have not started the Grid Control agent.

   F. You have not started the database.

2. Which files must be synchronized for a database to open? (Choose the best answer.)

   A. Datafiles, online redo log files, and controlfile

   B. Parameter file and password file

   C. All the multiplexed controlfile copies

   D. None—SMON will synchronize all files by instance recovery after opening the database

3. During the transition from NOMOUNT to MOUNT mode, which files are required? (Choose the best answer.)

   A. Parameter file

   B. Controlfiles

   C. Online redologs

   D. Datafiles

   E. All of the above

4. You shut down your instance with SHUTDOWN IMMEDIATE. What will happen on the next startup? (Choose the best answer.)

   A. SMON will perform automatic instance recovery.

   B. You must perform manual instance recovery.

   C. PMON will roll back uncommitted transactions.

   D. The database will open without recovery.

5. You have created two databases on your computer and want to use Database Control to manage them. Which if the following statements are correct? (Choose all correct answers.)

   A. You cannot use Database Control, because it can only manage one database per computer.

   B. You must use Grid Control, as you have multiple databases on the computer.

   C. You can use Database Control, if you contact it on different ports for each database.

   D. You must set the ORACLE_SID variable appropriately before starting each Database Control console.

6. You issue the command SHUTDOWN; and it seems to hang. What could be the reason? (Choose the best answer.)

   A. You are not connected as SYSDBA or SYSOPER.

   B. There are other sessions logged on.

   C. You have not connected with operating system or password file authentication.

   D. There are active transactions in the database; when they complete, the SHUTDOWN will proceed.

7. What action should you take after terminating the instance with SHUTDOWN ABORT? (Choose the best answer.)

   A. Back up the database immediately.

   B. Open the database, and perform database recovery.

   C. Open the database, and perform instance recovery.

   D. None, but some transactions may be lost.

   E. None—recovery will be automatic.

Set Database Initialization Parameters

8. What will be the setting of the OPTIMIZER_MODE parameter for your session after the next startup if you issue these commands:

```
alter system set optimizer_mode=all_rows scope=spfile;
alter system set optimizer_mode=rule;
alter session set optimizer_mode=first_rows;
```

   (Choose the best answer.)

   A. all_rows

   B. rule

   C. first_rows

9. The LOG_BUFFER parameter is a static parameter. How can you change it? (Choose the best answer.)
    A. You cannot change it, because it is static.
    B. You can change it only for individual sessions; it will return to the previous value for all subsequent sessions.
    C. You can change it within the instance, but it will return to the static value at the next startup.
    D. You can change it in the parameter file, but the new value will only come into effect at the next startup.

Use the Alert Log and Trace Files

10. Which of these actions will not be recorded in the alert log? (Choose all correct answers.)
    A. ALTER DATABASE commands
    B. ALTER SESSION commands
    C. ALTER SYSTEM commands
    D. Archiving an online redo log file
    E. Creating a tablespace
    F. Creating a user

11. Which parameter controls the location of background process trace files? (Choose the best answer.)
    A. BACKGROUND_DUMP_DEST
    B. BACKGROUND_TRACE_DEST
    C. DB_CREATE_FILE_DEST
    D. No parameter—the location is platform specific and cannot be changed

Use Data Dictionary and Dynamic Performance Views

12. Which of these views can be queried successfully in nomount mode? (Choose all correct answers.)
    A. DBA_DATA_FILES
    B. DBA_TABLESPACES
    C. V$DATABASE
    D. V$DATAFILE
    E. V$INSTANCE
    F. V$SESSION

13. Which view will list all tables in the database? (Choose the best answer.)

    A. ALL_TABLES

    B. DBA_TABLES

    C. USER_TABLES, when connected as SYS

    D. V$FIXED_TABLE

LAB QUESTION

Prepare scripts for starting the Oracle environment on both Linux and Windows. The scripts should start (though not necessarily in this order) the database instance and open the database, the database listener, and the Database Control console. For the Windows script, consider using services. Remember that some environment variables may be needed.

SELF TEST ANSWERS

Describe the Stages of Database Startup and Shutdown

1. ☑ **B, C,** and **D.** There will always be an error if the database console process has not been started or of it is on a different port, and since the URL used a loopback address, there will be an error if the browser is not running on the same machine as the console.

   ☒ **A** and **F** are wrong because these are not a problem; the listener and the database can both be started if the console is accessible. **E** is wrong because the Grid Control agent is not necessary for Database Control.

2. ☑ **A.** These are the files that make up a database, and all must be synchronized before it can be opened.

   ☒ **B** is wrong because these files are not, strictly speaking, part of the database at all. **C** is wrong because an error with the controlfile will mean the database cannot even be mounted, never mind opened. **D** is wrong because SMON can only fix problems in datafiles, not anything else.

3. ☑ **B.** Mounting the database is the opening of the controlfile (all copies thereof).

   ☒ **A** is wrong because the parameter file is only needed for NOMOUNT. **C, D,** and **E** are wrong because these file types are only needed for open mode.

4. ☑ **D.** An immediate shutdown is clean, so no recovery will be required.

   ☒ **A, B,** and **C.** These are wrong because no recovery or rollback will be required; all the work will have done as part of the shutdown.

5. ☑ **C** and **D.** Database Control will be fine but must be started for each database and contacted on different ports for each database.

   ☒ **A** is wrong because you can use Database Console, but you will need separate instances for each database. **B** is wrong because while Grid Control may be a better tool, it is by no means essential.

6. ☑ **B.** The default shutdown mode is SHUTDOWN NORMAL, which will hang until all sessions have voluntarily disconnected.

   ☒ **A** and **C** are wrong because these would cause an error, not a hang. **D** is wrong because it describes SHUTDOWN TRANSACTIONAL, not SHUTDOWN NORMAL.

7. ☑ **E.** There is no required action; recovery will be automatic.

   ☒ **A** is wrong because this is one thing you should not do after an ABORT. **B** is wrong because database recovery is not necessary, only instance recovery. **C**, instance recovery, is wrong because it will occur automatically in mount mode at the next startup. **D** is wrong because no transactions will ever be lost as a result of an ABORT.

Set Database Initialization Parameters

8. ☑ **B.** the default scope of ALTER SESSION is memory and spfile.
☒ **A** is wrong because this setting will have been replaced by the setting in the second command. **C** is wrong because the session-level setting will have been lost during the restart of the instance.

9. ☑ **D.** This is the technique for changing a static parameter.
☒ **A** is wrong because static parameters can be changed—but only with a shutdown. **B** and **C** are wrong because static parameters cannot be changed for a running session or instance.

Use the Alert Log and Trace Files

10. ☑ **B** and **F.** Neither of these affects the structure of the database or the instance; they are not important enough to generate an alert log entry.
☒ **A, C, D,** and **E.** All of these are changes to physical or memory structures, and all such changes are recorded in the alert log.

11. ☑ **A.** This is the parameter used to determine the location of background traced files.
☒ **B** is wrong because there is no such parameter. **C** is wrong because this is the default location for datafiles, not trace files. **D** is wrong because while there is a platform-specific default, it can be overridden with a parameter.

Use Data Dictionary and Dynamic Performance Views

12. ☑ **E** and **F.** These views are populated from the instance and will therefore be available at all times.
☒ **A** and **B** are data dictionary views, which can only be seen in open mode. **C** and **D** are dynamic performance views populated from the controlfile, and therefore only available in mount mode or open mode.

13. ☑ **B.** The DBA views list every appropriate object in the database.
☒ **A** is wrong because this will list only the tables the current user has permissions on—which might be all the tables. **C** is wrong because it will list only the tables owned by SYS. **D** is wrong because this is the view that lists all the dynamic performance views, not all tables.

LAB ANSWER

A possible Linux shell script is

```
export ORACLE_SID=ocp11g
export ORACLE_BASE=/u01/app/oracle
export ORACLE_HOME=$ORACLE_BASE/product/11.1.0/db_1
export PATH=$ORACLE_HOME/bin:$PATH
export LD_LIBRARY_PATH=$ORACLE_HOME/lib:$LD_LIBRARY_PATH
lsnrctl start listener
sqlplus <<!
connect / as sysdba
startup
!
emctl start dbconsole
```

This script sets the relevant variables to start an instance called ocp11g. The first Oracle process launched is the database listener called LISTENER, which it will be called by default. Then SQL*Plus starts the instance, using the technique for piping in commands. Finally, there is the Database Control console startup.

Using Windows services, the batch file can be much shorter:

```
net start OracleOraDb11g_home1TNSListener
net start OracleServiceOCP11G
net start OracleDBConsoleocp11g
```

This script doesn't need any environment variables because they will be read from the registry by the services, but it does assume that the registry variable ORA_OCP11G_AUTOSTART is set to TRUE. Unless this is done, the script will start the service but not go on to start the instance.

An alternative script is

```
set ORACLE_BASE=d:\app\oracle
set ORACLE_HOME=%ORACLE_BASE%\11.1.0\db_1
set PATH=%ORACLE_HOME%\bin;%PATH%
lsnrctl start listener
net start OracleServiceOCP11G
sqlplus <<!
connect / as sysdba
startup
!
emctl start dbconsole
```

This script explicitly sets environment variables. The instance service must be started with a NET START command, but it is assumed the service does not automatically start the instance itself, and so it is started with SQL*Plus. Starting the database listener and the Database Control console is the same as on Linux.

6

Configuring the Oracle Network Environment

N etworking is an integral part of the client-server database architecture that is
fundamental to all modern relational databases. The Oracle database had the potential
for client-server computing from the beginning (version 1, released in 1978, made
a separation between the Oracle code and the user code), but it was only with version 4 in
1984 that Oracle introduced interoperability between PC and server. True client-server support
came with version 5, in 1986. This chapter Introduces the Oracle Net services. Oracle Net was
previously known as Sqlnet, and you will still hear many DBAs refer to it as such.

The default Oracle Net configuration is a *dedicated server*. In a dedicated server
environment, each user process is connected to its own server process. An
alternative is *shared server*, where a number of user processes make use of a pool
of server processes that are shared by all the sessions. Generally speaking, DBAs
have been reluctant to use shared server, but there are indications that Oracle
Corporation would like more sites to move to it, and certainly knowledge of the
shared server architecture is vital for the OCP examination.

CERTIFICATION OBJECTIVE 6.01

Configure and Manage the Oracle Network

Oracle Net is the enabling technology for Oracle's client-server architecture. It
is the mechanism for establishing sessions against a database instance. There are
several tools that can be used for setting up and administering Oracle Net, though it
can be done with nothing more than an editor such as Windows Notepad. Whatever
tool is used, the end result is a set of files that control a process (the database
listener), which launches server processes in response to connection requests, and
that define the means by which a user process will locate the listener.

Oracle Net and the Client-Server Paradigm

There are many layers between the user and the database. In the Oracle environment,
no user ever has direct access to the database—nor does the process that he/she is
running. Client-server architecture guarantees that all access to data is controlled
by the server.

A user interacts with a user process: this is the software that he/she runs on his/her local terminal. For example, it could be Microsoft Access plus an ODBC driver on a Windows PC; it could be something written in C and linked with the Oracle Call Interface (or OCI) libraries; it could even be your old friend SQL*Plus. Whatever it is, the purpose of the user process is to prompt the user to enter information that the process can use to generate SQL statements. In the case of SQL*Plus, the process merely waits for you to type something in—a more sophisticated user process will paint a proper data entry screen, will validate your input, and then when you click the Submit button will construct the statement and send it off to the server process.

The server process is a process running on the database server machine that executes the SQL it receives from the user process. This is your basic client-server split: a user process generating SQL, a server process executing it. The execution of a SQL statement goes through four stages: parse, bind, execute, and fetch. In the parse phase, your server process works out what the statement actually means, and how best to execute it. Parsing involves interaction with the shared pool of the instance: shared pool memory structures are used to convert the SQL into something that is actually executable. In the bind phase, any variables are expanded to literal values. Then the execute phase will require more use of the instance's SGA, and possibly of the database. During the execution of a statement, data in the database buffer cache will be read or updated and changes written to the redo log buffer, but if the relevant blocks are not in the database buffer cache, your server process will read them from the datafiles. This is the only point in the execution of a statement where the database itself is involved. And finally, the fetch phase of the execution cycle is where the server process sends the result set generated by the statement's execution back to the user process, which should then format it for display.

Oracle Net provides the mechanism for launching a server process to execute code on behalf of a user process. This is establishing a session. Then Oracle Net is responsible for maintaining the session: transmitting SQL from the user process to the server process, and fetching results from the server process back to the user process.

Figure 6-1 shows the various components of a session. A user interacts with a user process; a user process interacts with a server process, via Oracle Net; a server process interacts with the instance; and the instance, via its background processes, interacts with the database. Your client-server split is between the user process generating SQL and the server process executing it. This split will usually be physical as well as logical: there will be a local area network between the machines hosting the user processes and the machine hosting the server side. But it is quite possible for this link to be wide area, or conversely to run the user processes on the server machine. Oracle Net is responsible establishing a session, and then for the ongoing communication between the user process and the server process.

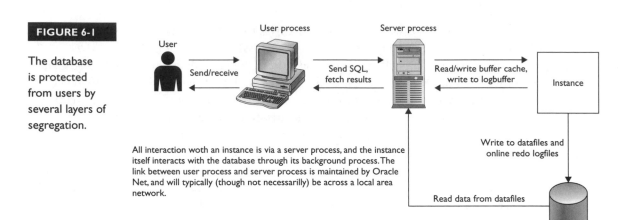

FIGURE 6-1

The database is protected from users by several layers of segregation.

All interaction woth an instance is via a server process, and the instance itself interacts with the database through its background process. The link between user process and server process is maintained by Oracle Net, and will typically (though not necessarilly) be across a local area network.

A Word on Oracle Net and Communication Protocols

Oracle Net is a layered protocol: it runs on top of whatever communications protocol is supported by your operating system. Historically, Sqlnet could work with all the popular protocols (with the exception of NetBIOS/NetBEUI, which has too limited functionality to be used for large database systems: it cannot be routed), but in release 11g Oracle's network support is limited to TCP, TCP with secure sockets, Windows Named Pipes (or NMP), and the newer Sockets Direct Protocol (or SDP) over Infiniband high-speed networks. This reduction in protocol support is in line with industry standards. All operating systems also have an Inter-Process Communication (or IPC) protocol proprietary to the operating system—this is also available to Oracle Net for local connections where the user process is on the same machine as the server.

This layering of Oracle Net on top of whatever is provided by your operating system gives Oracle platform independence. You, as DBA, do not need to know anything about the underlying network; you configure Oracle Net to use whatever protocol has been configured by your network administrators. You need not concern yourself with what is happening beneath. TCP is, for better or worse, undoubtedly the most popular protocol worldwide, so that is the one used in the examples that follow. The use of industry standard protocols means that there need be no dependency between the server-side and the client-side platforms. There is no reason why, for example, a client on Windows cannot talk to a database on Unix. As long as the platform can offer a TCP layer 4 interface, then Oracle Net can use it.

With regard to conformance with the Open Systems Interconnection (or OSI) seven-layer model to which all IT vendors are supposed to comply, Oracle Net maps on to layers five, six, and seven: the session, presentation, and application layers. The protocol adapters installed with the standard Oracle installation provide the crossover to layer four, the transport layer, provided by your operating system. Thus Oracle Net is responsible for establishing sessions between the end systems once TCP (or whatever else you are using) has established a layer four connection. The presentation layer functions are handled by the Oracle Net Two Task Common (or TTC) layer. TCC is responsible for any conversions necessary when data is transferred between the user process and the server process, such as character set changes. Then the application layer functions are the user and server processes themselves.

Establishing a Session

When a user, through his/her user process, wishes to establish a session against an instance, he/she will issue a command something like

```
CONNECT SCOTT/TIGER@ORCL11G
```

Of course, if he/she is using a properly written user interface, he/she won't type in those words but will be prompted to enter the details into a logon screen—but one way or another that is the command the user process will generate. It is now time to go into what actually happens when that command is processed. First, break down the command into its components. There is a database user name ("SCOTT"), followed by a database password ("TIGER"), and the two are separated by a "/" as a delimiter. Then there is an "@" symbol, followed by a connect string, "ORCL11G." The "@" symbol is an indication to the user process that a network connection is required. If the "@" and the connect string are omitted, then the user process will assume that the instance you wish to connect to is running on the local machine, and that the always-available IPC protocol can be used. If the "@" and a connect string are included, then the user process will assume that you are requesting a network connection to an instance on a remote machine—though in fact, you could be bouncing off the network card and back to the machine on to which you are logged.

Connecting to a Local Instance

Even when you connect to an instance running on your local machine, you still use Oracle Net. All Oracle sessions use a network protocol to implement the separation of user code from server code, but for a local connection the protocol is

IPC: this is the protocol provided by your operating system that will allow processes to communicate within the host machine. This is the only type of connection that does not require a database listener; indeed, local connections do not require any configuration at all. The only information needed is to tell your user process which instance you want to connect to. Remember that there could be several instances running on your local computer. You give the process this information through an environment variable. Figure 6-2 shows examples of this in Linux, Figure 6-3 is the same thing on Windows.

Remember that the only difference between platforms is the syntax for setting environment variables, as demonstrated in Figures 6-2 and 6-3.

FIGURE 6-2

Local database connections— Linux

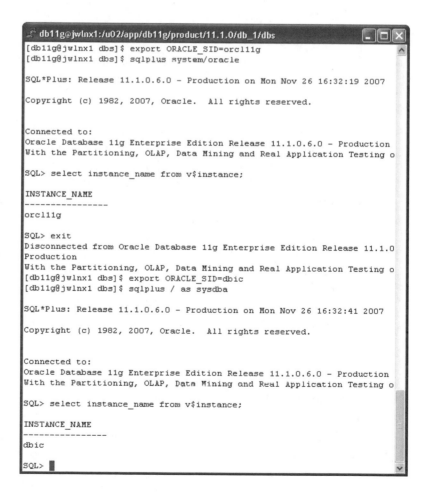

```
db11g@jwlnx1:/u02/app/db11g/product/11.1.0/db_1/dbs

[db11g@jwlnx1 dbs]$ export ORACLE_SID=orcl11g
[db11g@jwlnx1 dbs]$ sqlplus system/oracle

SQL*Plus: Release 11.1.0.6.0 - Production on Mon Nov 26 16:32:19 2007

Copyright (c) 1982, 2007, Oracle.  All rights reserved.


Connected to:
Oracle Database 11g Enterprise Edition Release 11.1.0.6.0 - Production
With the Partitioning, OLAP, Data Mining and Real Application Testing o

SQL> select instance_name from v$instance;

INSTANCE_NAME
----------------
orcl11g

SQL> exit
Disconnected from Oracle Database 11g Enterprise Edition Release 11.1.0
Production
With the Partitioning, OLAP, Data Mining and Real Application Testing o
[db11g@jwlnx1 dbs]$ export ORACLE_SID=dbic
[db11g@jwlnx1 dbs]$ sqlplus / as sysdba

SQL*Plus: Release 11.1.0.6.0 - Production on Mon Nov 26 16:32:41 2007

Copyright (c) 1982, 2007, Oracle.  All rights reserved.


Connected to:
Oracle Database 11g Enterprise Edition Release 11.1.0.6.0 - Production
With the Partitioning, OLAP, Data Mining and Real Application Testing o

SQL> select instance_name from v$instance;

INSTANCE_NAME
----------------
dbic

SQL>
```

FIGURE 6-3

Local database connections—Windows

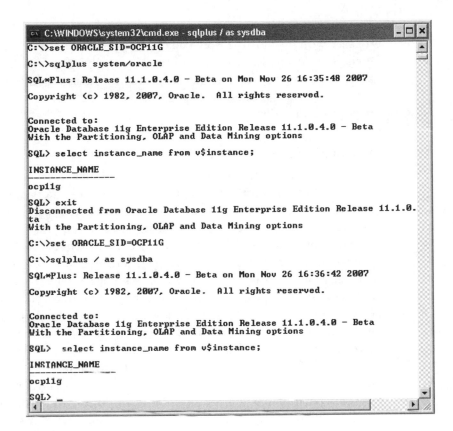

```
C:\>set ORACLE_SID=OCP11G

C:\>sqlplus system/oracle

SQL*Plus: Release 11.1.0.4.0 - Beta on Mon Nov 26 16:35:48 2007

Copyright (c) 1982, 2007, Oracle.  All rights reserved.


Connected to:
Oracle Database 11g Enterprise Edition Release 11.1.0.4.0 - Beta
With the Partitioning, OLAP and Data Mining options

SQL> select instance_name from v$instance;

INSTANCE_NAME
----------------
ocp11g

SQL> exit
Disconnected from Oracle Database 11g Enterprise Edition Release 11.1.0.
ta
With the Partitioning, OLAP and Data Mining options

C:\>set ORACLE_SID=OCP11G

C:\>sqlplus / as sysdba

SQL*Plus: Release 11.1.0.4.0 - Beta on Mon Nov 26 16:36:42 2007

Copyright (c) 1982, 2007, Oracle.  All rights reserved.


Connected to:
Oracle Database 11g Enterprise Edition Release 11.1.0.4.0 - Beta
With the Partitioning, OLAP and Data Mining options

SQL> select instance_name from v$instance;

INSTANCE_NAME
----------------
ocp11g

SQL> _
```

Name Resolution

When connecting using Oracle Net, the first stage is to work out exactly what it is you want to connect to. This is the process of name resolution. If your connect statement includes the connect string "@orcl11g," Oracle Net has to work out what is meant by "orcl11g." This means that the string has to be resolved into certain pieces of information: the protocol you want to use (assume that this is TCP), the IP address on which the database listener is running, the port that the listener is monitoring for incoming connection requests, and the name of the instance (which need not be the same as the connect string) to which you wish to connect. There are variations: rather than an IP address, the connect string can include a hostname, which then gets further resolved to an IP address by a DNS server. Rather than specifying an instance by name, the connect string can include the name of a service, which (in an RAC environment) could be made up of a number of instances. In a single-instance environment, services can still be used—perhaps to assist with tracking the workload imposed on the database by different groups of users. You can configure a number of ways of resolving connect strings to address and instance names, but one way or another the name resolution process gives your user process enough information to go across the network to a database listener and request a connection to a particular instance.

Launching a Server Process

The database listener, running on the server machine, uses one or more protocols to monitor one or more ports on one or more network interface cards for incoming connection requests. You can further complicate matters by running multiple listeners on one machine, and any one listener can accept connection requests for a number of instances. When it receives a connect request, the listener must first validate whether the instance requested is actually available. Assuming that it is, the listener will launch a new server process to service the user process. Thus if you have a thousand users logging on concurrently to your instance, you will be launching a thousand server processes. This is known as the *dedicated server* architecture—later in this chapter you'll see the *shared server* alternative—where each user process is given a server process, dedicated to its session.

In the TCP environment, each dedicated server process launched by a listener will acquire a unique TCP port number. This will be assigned at process startup time by your operating system's port mapping algorithm. The port number gets passed back to the user process by the listener (or on some operating systems the socket already opened to the listener is transferred to the new port number), and the user process can then communicate directly with its server process. The listener has now completed its work and waits for the next connect request.

 **If the database listener is not running, no new server processes can be launched—but this will not affect any existing sessions that have already been established.**

Creating a Listener

A listener is defined in a file: the `listener .ora` file, whose default location is in the `ORACLE_HOME/network/admin` directory. As a minimum, the `listener.ora` file must include a section for one listener, which states its name and the protocol and listening address it will use. You can configure several listeners in the one file, but they must all have different names and addresses.

You can run a listener completely on defaults, without a listener.ora file at all. It will listen on whatever address resolves to the machine's host name, on port 1521. Don't do this; it would be very confusing. Always configure the listener.ora file, to make your Oracle Net environment self-documenting.

As with other files used to configure Oracle Net, the `listener.ora` file can be very fussy about seemingly trivial points of syntax, such as case sensitivity, white spaces, and abbreviations. For this reason, many DBAs do not like to edit it by hand (though there is no reason not to). Oracle provides three graphical tools to manage Oracle Net: Enterprise Manager (Database Control or Grid Control), the Net Manager, and the Net Configuration Assistant. The latter two tools are both written in Java. There is considerable overlap between the functionality of these tools, though there are a few things that can only be done in one or another.

This is an example of a `listener.ora` file:

```
LISTENER =
  (DESCRIPTION =
    (ADDRESS = (PROTOCOL = TCP)(HOST = jwlnx1)(PORT = 1521))
  )
LIST2 =
  (DESCRIPTION =
    (ADDRESS_LIST =
        (ADDRESS = (PROTOCOL = TCP)(HOST = 127.0.0.1)(PORT =
1522))
        (ADDRESS = (PROTOCOL = TCP)(HOST = jwlnx1.bplc
.co.za)(PORT = 1522))
    )
  )
```

The first section of this file defines a listener called LISTENER, monitoring the local hostname on the default port, 1521. The second section defines another listener called LIST2. This listener is monitoring port 1522 on both the hostname address and a loopback address.

To create the listener, you need do nothing more than create an entry in the `listener.ora` file, and start it. Under Windows the listener will run as a Windows service, but there is no need to create the service explicitly; it will be created implicitly the first time the listener is started. From then, if you wish, it can be started and stopped like any other Windows service.

Figure 6-4 shows the Net Manager's view of the listener LIST2, and Figure 6-5 shows it through the Net Configuration Assistant.

FIGURE 6-4

A listener definition as created or viewed with the Net Manager

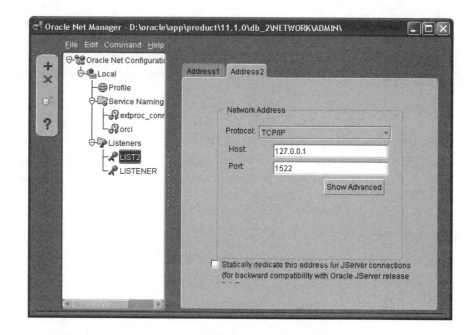

FIGURE 6-5

A listener definition as created or viewed with the Net Configuration Assistant

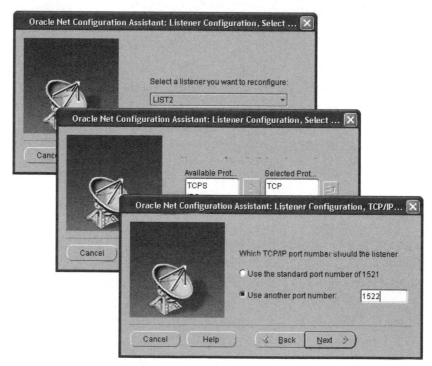

Note that the Net Manager lets you configure multiple listening addresses for a listener (Figure 6-4 shows the loopback address), whereas the Net Configuration Assistant does not: it can only see the one address of the hostname; there is no prompt for creating or viewing any other.

Database Registration

A listener is necessary to spawn server processes against an instance. In order to do this, it needs to know what instances are available on the computer on which it is running. A listener finds out about instances by the process of "registration."

There are two methods for registering an instance with a database: static and dynamic registration. For static registration, you hard-code a list of instances in the listener.ora file. Dynamic registration means that the instance itself, at startup time, locates a listener and registers with it.

<table>
<tr><td>

e x a m

ⓦ a t c h   *The listener and the instance must be running on the same computer, unless you are using RAC. In an RAC environment, any listener on any computer in the cluster can connect you to any instance on any computer.*

</td></tr>
</table>

Static Registration

As a general rule, dynamic registration is a better option, but there are circumstances when you will resort to static registration. Dynamic registration was introduced with release 8i, but if you have older databases that your listener must connect users to, you will have to register them statically. Also some applications may require static registration: typically management tools. To register an instance statically, add an appropriate entry to the listener.ora file:

```
SID_LIST_LIST2 =
  (SID_LIST =
    (SID_DESC =
      (ORACLE_HOME = /u01/oracle/app/product/11.1.0/db_1)
      (SID_NAME = ocp11g)
    )
  )
```

This entry will configure the listener called LIST2 to accept connection requests for an instance called ocp11g. It says nothing about whether the instance is running or even exists at all. The directive ORACLE_HOME is only required if the database listener is not running from the same Oracle Home as the instance. If this is the case, then this directive will let the listener find the executable file that it must run to launch a server process. Usually, this is only necessary if configuring a listener to make connections to instances of a different version, which have to be running off a different home.

Dynamic Instance Registration

This is the preferred method by which an instance will register with a listener. There is an initialization parameter `local_listener`, which tells the instance the network address that it should contact to find a listener with which to register. At instance startup time, the PMON process will user this parameter to locate a listener, and inform it of the instance's name and the names of the service(s) that the instance is offering. The instance name is defined by the `instance_name` parameter, and the `service_names` parameter will have defaulted to this suffixed by the `db_domain` parameter, which will default to null. It is possible to create and start additional services at any time, either by changing the value of the service_names parameter (which can be a comma-delimited list, if the instance is to offer several services) or programmatically using the DBMS_SERVICE package.

Any change to the services must be registered with the local listener. If this is not done, the listener won't know what services are being offered, and will therefore not be able to set up sessions to them. The PMON process will reregister from time to time automatically, but at any time subsequent to instance startup you can force a reregistration by executing the command

```
SQL> alter system register;
```

on the
job

You will need to register your instance with the listener with "alter system register" if you have restarted the listener, or if you started the database instance before starting the listener.

Dynamic registration is a better option than static registration because it ensures that only running instances and available services are registered with the listener, and also that there are no errors in the instance and service names. It is all too easy to make mistakes here, particularly if you are editing the `listener.ora` file by hand. Also, when the instance shuts down, it will deregister from the listener automatically.

From release 9i onward, dynamic registration requires no configuration at all if your listener is running on the default port, 1521. All instances will automatically look for a listener on the local host on that port, and register themselves if they find one. However, if your listener is not running on the default port on the address identified by the hostname, you must specify where the listener is by setting the parameter local_listener and reregistering, for example,

```
SQL> alter system set local_listener=list2;
SQL> alter system register;
```

In this example, the local_listener has been specified by name. This name needs to be resolved into an address in order for the instance to find the listener and register itself, as described in the following section. An alternative technique is to hard-code the listener's address in the parameter:

```
SQL> alter system set
  local_listener='(address=(pro=tcp)(host=127.0.0.1)(port=1522))';
```

This syntax is perfectly acceptable, but the use of a name that can be resolved is better practice, as it places a layer of abstraction between the logical name and the physical address. The abstraction means that if the listening address ever has to be changed, one need only change it in the name resolution service, rather than having to change it in every instance that uses it.

Techniques for Name Resolution

At the beginning of this chapter, you saw that to establish a session against an instance, your user process must issue a connect string. That string resolves to the address of a listener and the name of an instance or service. In the discussion of dynamic instance registration, you saw again the use of a logical name for a listener, which needs to be resolved into a network address in order for an instance to find a listener with which to register. Oracle provides four methods of name resolution: easy connect, local naming, directory naming, and external naming. It is probably true to say that the majority of Oracle sites use local naming, but there is no question that directory naming is the best method for a large and complex installation.

Easy Connect

The Easy Connect name resolution method was introduced with release 10g. It is very easy to use—it requires no configuration at all. But it is limited to one protocol: TCP. The other name resolution methods can use any of the other supported protocols, such TCP with secure sockets, or Named Pipes. Another limitation is that Easy Connect cannot be used with any of Oracle Net's more advanced capabilities, such as load balancing or connect-time failover across different network routes. It is fair to say that Easy Connect is a method you as DBA will find very handy to use, but that it is not a method of much use for your end users. Easy Connect is enabled by default. You invoke it with a syntax such as this as your connect string:

```
SQL> connect scott/tiger@jwlnx1.bplc.co.za:1522/ocp11g
```

In this example, SQL*Plus will use TCP to go to port 1522 on the IP address to which the hostname resolves. Then if there is a listener running on that port and address, it will ask the listener to spawn a server process against an instance that is part of the service called ocp10g. Easy Connect can be made even easier:

```
SQL> connect scott/tiger@jwlnx1.bplc.co.za
```

will also work, but only if the listener is using port 1521, and the service name registered with the listener is jwlnx1.bplc.co.za, the same as the computer name.

Local Naming

With local naming the user supplies an alias, known as an Oracle Net service alias, for the connect string, and the alias is resolved by a local file into the full network address (protocol, address, port, and service or instance name). This local file is the infamous tnsnames.ora file, which has caused DBAs much grief over the years. Consider this example of a tnsnames.ora file:

```
ocp11g =
  (DESCRIPTION =
    (ADDRESS_LIST =
      (ADDRESS = (PROTOCOL = TCP)(HOST = jwlnx1.bplc.co.za)(PORT
= 1522))
    )
    (CONNECT_DATA =
      (service_name = ocp11g)
    )
  )
test =
  (DESCRIPTION =
    (ADDRESS_LIST =
      (ADDRESS = (PROTOCOL = TCP)(HOST = serv2.bplc.co.za)(PORT
= 1521))
    )
    (CONNECT_DATA =
      (sid = testdb)
    )
  )
```

This `tnsnames.ora` file has two Oracle Net service aliases defined within it: ocp11g and test. These aliases are what your users will provide in their connect statements. The first entry, ocp11g, simply says that when the connect string "@ocp11g" is issued, your user process should use the TCP protocol to go the machine jwlnx1.bplc.co.za, contact it on port 1521, and ask the listener monitoring that port to establish a session against the instance with the service name ocp11g. The second entry, test, directs users to a listener on a different machine and asks for a session against the instance called testdb.

on the Job   *There need be no relationship between the alias, the service name, and the instance name, but for the sake of your sanity you will usually keep them the same.*

Local naming supports all protocols and all the advanced features of Oracle Net, but maintaining `tnsnames.ora` files on all your client machines can be an extremely time-consuming task. The `tnsnames.ora` file is also notoriously sensitive to apparently trivial variations in layout. Using the GUI tools will help avoid such problems.

Directory Naming and External Naming

Directory naming points the user toward an LDAP directory server to resolve aliases. LDAP (the Lightweight Directory Protocol) is a widely used standard that Oracle Corporation (and other mainstream software vendors) is encouraging organizations to adopt. To use directory naming, you must first install and configure a directory server somewhere on your network. Oracle provides an LDAP server (the Oracle Internet Directory) as part of the Oracle Application Server, but you do not have to use that—if you already have a Microsoft Active Directory, that will be perfectly adequate. IBM and Novell also sell directory servers conforming to the LDAP standard.

Like local naming, directory naming supports all Oracle Net features—but unlike local naming, it uses a central repository, the directory server, for all your name resolution details. This is much easier to maintain than many `tnsnames.ora` files distributed across your whole user community.

External naming is conceptually similar to directory naming, but it uses third-party naming services such as Sun's Network Information Services (NIS+) or the Cell Directory Services (CDS) that are part of the Distributed Computing Environment (DCE).

The use of directories and external naming services is beyond the scope of the OCP syllabus.

The Listener Control Utility

You can start and stop listeners through Database Control, but there is also a command-line utility `lsnrctl` (it is `lsnrctl.exe` on Windows)—`lsnrctl` commands can be run directly from an operating system prompt, or through a simple user interface. For all the commands, you must specify the name of the listener, if it is not the default name of LISTENER. Figures 6-6 and 6-7 show how to check the status of a listener and to stop and start it, issuing the commands either from the operating system prompt or from within the user interface.

Note that the status command always tells you address on which the listener is accepting connection requests, the name and location of the `listener.ora` file that defines the listener, and the name and location of the log file for the listener. Also, in the examples shown in the figures, the listener LIST2 "supports no services." This is because there are no services statically registered in the `listener.ora` file for

Using lsnrctl commands from the operating system prompt to check the status and then start the listener LIST2

```
C:\>lsnrctl status list2

LSNRCTL for 32-bit Windows: Version 11.1.0.4.0 - Beta on 26-NOV-2007 17:06:59

Copyright (c) 1991, 2006, Oracle.  All rights reserved.

Connecting to (DESCRIPTION=(ADDRESS=(PROTOCOL=TCP)(HOST=jwacer.bplc.co.za)(PORT=
1522)))
TNS-12541: TNS:no listener
 TNS-12560: TNS:protocol adapter error
  TNS-00511: No listener
   32-bit Windows Error: 61: Unknown error

C:\>lsnrctl start list2

LSNRCTL for 32-bit Windows: Version 11.1.0.4.0 - Beta on 26-NOV-2007 17:07:07

Copyright (c) 1991, 2006, Oracle.  All rights reserved.

Starting tnslsnr: please wait...

TNSLSNR for 32-bit Windows: Version 11.1.0.4.0 - Beta
System parameter file is D:\oracle\app\product\11.1.0\db_3\network\admin\listene
r.ora
Log messages written to D:\oracle\app\product\11.1.0\db_3\network\log\list2.log
Listening on: (DESCRIPTION=(ADDRESS=(PROTOCOL=tcp)(HOST=jwacer.bplc.co.za)(PORT=
1522)))

Connecting to (DESCRIPTION=(ADDRESS=(PROTOCOL=TCP)(HOST=jwacer.bplc.co.za)(PORT=
1522)))
STATUS of the LISTENER
------------------------
Alias                     list2
Version                   TNSLSNR for 32-bit Windows: Version 11.1.0.4.0 - Beta
Start Date                26-NOV-2007 17:07:10
Uptime                    0 days 0 hr. 0 min. 3 sec
Trace Level               off
Security                  ON: Local OS Authentication
SNMP                      OFF
Listener Parameter File   D:\oracle\app\product\11.1.0\db_3\network\admin\listen
er.ora
Listener Log File         D:\oracle\app\product\11.1.0\db_3\network\log\list2.lo
g
Listening Endpoints Summary...
  (DESCRIPTION=(ADDRESS=(PROTOCOL=tcp)(HOST=jwacer.bplc.co.za)(PORT=1522)))
The listener supports no services
The command completed successfully

C:\>
```

```
db11g@jwlnx1:~
[db11g@jwlnx1 ~]$ lsnrctl

LSNRCTL for Linux: Version 11.1.0.6.0 - Production on 26-NOV-2007 17:15:34

Copyright (c) 1991, 2007, Oracle.  All rights reserved.

Welcome to LSNRCTL, type "help" for information.

LSNRCTL> status list2
Connecting to (DESCRIPTION=(ADDRESS=(PROTOCOL=TCP)(HOST=jwlnx1.bplc.co.za)
(PORT=1522)))
STATUS of the LISTENER
------------------------
Alias                     list2
Version                   TNSLSNR for Linux: Version 11.1.0.6.0 - Producti
on
Start Date                26-NOV-2007 17:15:29
Uptime                    0 days 0 hr. 0 min. 8 sec
Trace Level               off
Security                  ON: Local OS Authentication
SNMP                      OFF
Listener Parameter File   /u02/app/db11g/product/11.1.0/db_1/network/admin
/listener.ora
Listener Log File         /u02/app/db11g/diag/tnslsnr/jwlnx1/list2/alert/l
og.xml
Listening Endpoints Summary...
  (DESCRIPTION=(ADDRESS=(PROTOCOL=tcp)(HOST=jwlnx1.bplc.co.za)(PORT=1522))
)
The listener supports no services
The command completed successfully
LSNRCTL> stop list2
Connecting to (DESCRIPTION=(ADDRESS=(PROTOCOL=TCP)(HOST=jwlnx1.bplc.co.za)
(PORT=1522)))
The command completed successfully
LSNRCTL> exit
[db11g@jwlnx1 ~]$
```

that listener, and no instances have dynamically registered either. Figure 6-8 uses the
services command to show the state of the listener after an instance has registered
dynamically.

In Figure 6-8, the output of the status command tells you that the listener called
LISTENER supports three services, all available on the instance orcl11g:

- Service orcl11g.jwlnx1.bplc.co.za is the regular database service. The listener
  can launch dedicated server sessions against it (it hasn't launched any yet).

- Service orcl11gXDB.jwlnx1.bplc.co.za is the XML database protocol server.
  This lets users connect to the database with protocols other than Oracle
  NET, such FTP and HTTP.

- Service orcl11g_XPT.jwlnx1.bplc.co.za is to do with Data guard.

FIGURE 6-8

The services command shows the services for which the listener will accept connections.

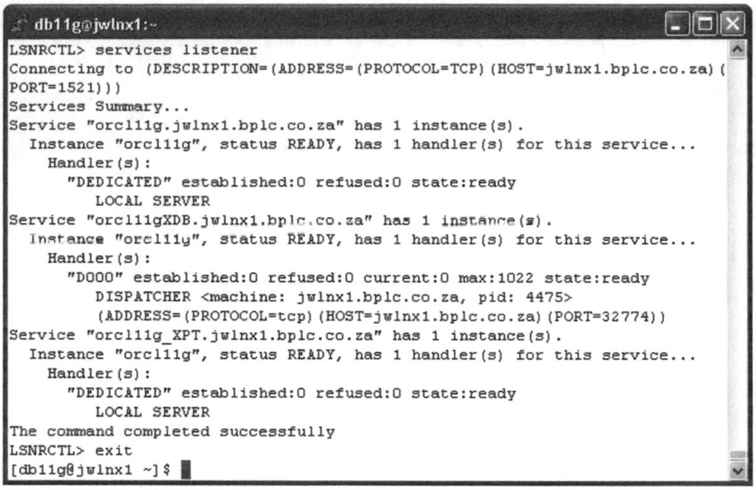

```
db11g@jwlnx1:~                                                    _ □ X
LSNRCTL> services listener
Connecting to (DESCRIPTION=(ADDRESS=(PROTOCOL=TCP)(HOST=jwlnx1.bplc.co.za)(
PORT=1521)))
Services Summary...
Service "orcl11g.jwlnx1.bplc.co.za" has 1 instance(s).
  Instance "orcl11g", status READY, has 1 handler(s) for this service...
    Handler(s):
      "DEDICATED" established:0 refused:0 state:ready
         LOCAL SERVER
Service "orcl11gXDB.jwlnx1.bplc.co.za" has 1 instance(s).
  Instance "orcl11g", status READY, has 1 handler(s) for this service...
    Handler(s):
      "D000" established:0 refused:0 current:0 max:1022 state:ready
         DISPATCHER <machine: jwlnx1.bplc.co.za, pid: 4475>
         (ADDRESS=(PROTOCOL=tcp)(HOST=jwlnx1.bplc.co.za)(PORT=32774))
Service "orcl11g_XPT.jwlnx1.bplc.co.za" has 1 instance(s).
  Instance "orcl11g", status READY, has 1 handler(s) for this service...
    Handler(s):
      "DEDICATED" established:0 refused:0 state:ready
         LOCAL SERVER
The command completed successfully
LSNRCTL> exit
[db11g@jwlnx1 ~]$ █
```

By default, an 11g database instance will register the XDP and XPT services, but they cannot be used without considerable further configuration. The fact that the services are shown to be "status ready" indicates that they were automatically registered by the PMON process: the listener knows they are ready because PMON said they were. If the services has been statically registered, they would be marked as "status unknown," indicating that while they are in the listener.ora file, they may not in fact be working.

To see all the lsnrctl commands, use the HELP command:

```
C:\>lsnrctl help
LSNRCTL for 32-bit Windows: Version 11.1.0.4.0 - Beta
on 26-NOV-2007 17:47:16
Copyright (c) 1991, 2006, Oracle.  All rights reserved.
The following operations are available
An asterisk (*) denotes a modifier or extended command:
start                 stop                  status
services              version               reload
save_config           trace                 change_password
quit                  exit                  set*
show*
```

In summary, this commands are

- **START**   Start a listener.
- **STOP**   Stop a listener.
- **STATUS**   See the status of a listener.

- **SERVICES**   See the services a listener is offering (fuller information than status).
- **VERSION**   Show the version of a listener.
- **RELOAD**   Force a listener to reread its entry in listener.ora.
- **SAVE_CONFIG**   Write any changes made online to the listener.ora file.
- **TRACE**   Enable tracing of a listener's activity.
- **CHANGE_PASSWORD**   Set a password for a listener's administration.
- **QUIT**   Exit from the tool without saving changes to the listener.ora file.
- **EXIT**   Exit from the tool and save changes to the listener.ora file.
- **SET**   Set various options, such as tracing and timeouts.
- **SHOW**   Show options that have been set for a listener.

Note that all these commands should be qualified with the name of the listener to which the command should be applied. If a name is not supplied, the command will be executed against the listener called LISTENER.

Configuring Service Aliases

Having decided what name resolution method to use, your next task is to configure the clients to use it. You can do this through Database Control, but since Database Control is a server-side process, you can only use it to configure clients running on the database server. An alternative is to use the Net Manager. This is a stand-alone Java utility, shipped with all the Oracle client-side products.

To launch the Net Manager, run netmgr from a Unix prompt, or on Windows you will find it on the Start menu.

The Net Manager navigation tree has three branches. The Profile branch is used to set options that may apply to both the client and server sides of Oracle Net and can be used to influence the behavior of all Oracle Net connections. This is where, for example, you can configure detailed tracing of Oracle Net sessions. The Service Naming branch is used to configure client-side name resolution, and the Listeners branch is used to configure database listeners.

When you take the Profile branch as shown in Figure 6-9, you are in fact configuring a file called sqlnet.ora. This file exists in your ORACLE_HOME/network/admin directory. It is optional—there are defaults for every sqlnet.ora directive—but you will usually configure it if only to select the name resolution method.

In the Profile branch, you will see all the available naming methods, with three (TNSNAMES and EZCONNECT and HOSTNAME) selected by default: these are

FIGURE 6-9

Net Manager's
Profile editor

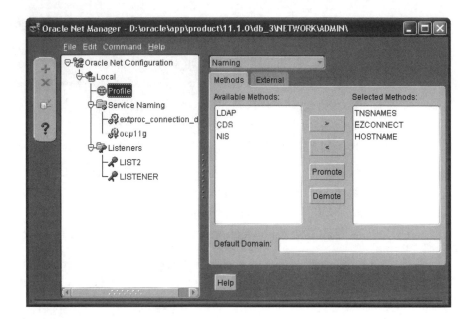

Local Naming and Easy Connect and Host Naming. The external methods are NIS and CDS. LDAP is Directory Naming. Host Naming is similar to Easy Connect and retained for backward compatibility.

Then you need to configure the individual Oracle Net service aliases. This is done in the Service Naming branch, which in fact creates or edits the Local Naming tnsnames.ora file that resides in your ORACLE_HOME/network/admin directory. If you are fortunate enough to be using Directory Naming, you do not need to do this; choosing LDAP in the Profile as your naming method is enough.

A typical entry in the tnsnames.ora file would be

```
OCP11G =
  (DESCRIPTION =
    (ADDRESS_LIST =
      (ADDRESS = (PROTOCOL = TCP)(HOST = jwacer.bplc.co.za)(PORT
= 1521))
    )
    (CONNECT_DATA =
      (SERVICE_NAME = ocp11g)
    )
  )
```

This entry will, if a user enters the connect string "ocp11g," resolve this to a listener running on the address jwlnx1.bplc.co.za monitoring port 1521, and ask the listener for a session against an instance offering the service ocp11g. To connect with this, use

```
sqlplus system/oracle@ocp11g
```

The equivalent with Easy Connect would be

```
sqlplus system/manager@jwacer.bplc.co.uk:1521/ocp11g
```

To test a connect string, use the TNSPING utility. This will accept a connect string, locate the Oracle Net files, resolve the string, and send a message to the listener. If the listener is running and does know about the service requested, the test will return successfully. For example,

```
C:\> tnsping ocp11g
TNS Ping Utility for 32-bit Windows: Version 11.1.0.4.0 - Beta
on 27-NOV-2007 11
:49:55
Copyright (c) 1997, 2006, Oracle.  All rights reserved.
Used parameter files:
D:\oracle\app\product\11.1.0\db_3\network\admin\sqlnet.ora
Used TNSNAMES adapter to resolve the alias
Attempting to contact (DESCRIPTION =
(ADDRESS_LIST = (ADDRESS = (PROTOCOL = TCP)
(HOST = 127.0.0.1)(PORT - 2521))) (CONNECT_DATA = (SERVICE_NAME
= ocp11g)))
OK (40 msec)
```

Note that the output of TNSPING shows the sqlnet.ora file used, the name resolution method used, and then the details of the address contacted. The tool does not go further than the listener; it will not check whether the instance is actually working.

File Names and the TNSADMIN Environment Variable

There are three critical files involved in configuring Oracle Net:

- The listener.ora file is a server-side file that defines database listeners. It includes the protocols, addresses, and ports on which they will listen for incoming connection requests, and (optionally) a hard-coded list of instances against which they will launch sessions.

- The tnsnames.ora file is a client-side file used for name resolution. It is used by user processes to locate database listeners. It may also be used the instance itself, to locate a listener with which to register.

■ The sqlnet.ora file is optional and may exist (possibly with different settings) on the server side, the client side, or both. It contains settings that apply to all connections and listeners, such as security rules and encryption.

The three Oracle Net files by default exist in the directory ORACLE_HOME/ network/admin. It is possible to relocate them with an environment variable: TNSADMIN. An important use of this is on systems that have several Oracle Homes. This is a very common situation. A typical Oracle server machine will have at least three homes: one for the Enterprise Manager Grid Control Agent, one for launching database instances, and one for launching Automatic Storage Management (ASM) instances. (ASM is covered in the second OCP examination.) Client machines may well have several Oracle Homes as well, perhaps one each for the 10g and 11g clients. Setting the TNSADMIN variable to point to one set of files in one of the Oracle home directories (or indeed in a different directory altogether) means that instead of having to maintain multiple sets of files, you need only maintain one set. To set the variable on Windows, you can use the SET command to set it for one session,

```
set TNSADMIN=c:\oracle\net
```

though it will usually be better to set it in the registry, as a string value key in the Oracle Home branch. On Linux and Unix, the syntax will vary depending on the shell, but something like this will usually do:

```
set TNS_ADMIN=/u01/oracle/net; export TNS_ADMIN
```

This command could be placed in each user's .profile file, or in the /etc/ profile where every user will pick it up.

Database Links

So far, Oracle Net has been discussed in the context of users connecting to database instances. Oracle Net can also be used for communications between databases: a user session against one database can execute SQL statements against another database. This is done through a database link. There are several options for creating database links (all to do with security), but a simple example is

```
create database link prodscott
connect to scott identified by tiger using 'prod';
```

This defines a database link from the current database to a remote database identified by the connect string PROD. The link exists in the current user's schema, and only he/she can use it. When he/she issues a statement such as

```
select * from emp@prodscott;
```

INSIDE THE EXAM

Configuring the Oracle Network Environment

Oracle Net is configured with a set of text files: `listener.ora`, `sqlnet.ora`, and (if using local naming, as most sites do) `tnsnames.ora`. But there are defaults for everything: the server side, the listener, can run purely on defaults, and by using Easy Connect, the client side needs no configuration either.

Tools provided to edit these files are the Net Manager, the Net Configuration Assistant, and Enterprise Manager. Experiment with all three to become familiar with navigating around them and with what they can do, and always check the contents of the text files to gain a complete understanding of what has been done.

The dedicated server environment is commonly used, but remember the shared server alternative; it may not be widely used, but it will always be tested in the OCP examinations.

his/her session will launch a session against the remote database, log on to it transparently as user SCOTT, and run the query there. The results will be sent back to the local database and then returned to the user.

Any SQL statements can be executed through a link, provided that the schema to which the link connects has appropriate permissions. For example, consider this scenario:

There is a production database, identified by the connect string PROD, which contains a schema SCOTT, with two tables: EMP and DEPT. There is a link to this database as just defined. There is also a development database, identified by the connect string DEV, which also contains the schema SCOTT. You are connected to a test database. You need to update the development schema with the production data.

First, define a database link to the development database:

```
create database link devscott
connect to scott identified by tiger using 'dev';
```

Then update the development schema to match the production schema:

```
truncate table emp@devscott;
truncate table dept@devscott;
insert into dept@devscott select * from dept@prodscott;
insert into emp@devscott select * from emp@prodscott;
commit;
```

To check whether any rows have been inserted in the production system since the last refresh of development and, if so, insert them into development, you could run this statement:

```
insert into emp@devscott
(select * from emp@prodscott  minus select * from emp@devscott);
```

If it were necessary to change the name of a department, you could do it in both databases concurrently with

```
update dept@prodscott set dname='SUPPORT' where deptid=40;
update dept@devscott set dname='SUPPORT' where deptid=40;
commit;
```

When necessary, Oracle will always implement a two-phase commit to ensure that a distributed transaction (which is a transaction that affects rows in more than one database) is treated as an atomic transaction: the changes must succeed in all databases or be rolled back in all databases. Read consistency is also maintained across the whole environment.

EXERCISE 6-1

Configure Oracle Net

In this exercise, you will set up a complete Oracle Net environment, using graphical and command-line tools. Where there are differences between Windows and Linux, these will be pointed out.

1. Create a directory to be used for the Oracle Net configuration files, and set the TNS_ADMIN variable to point to this. It doesn't matter where the directory is, as long as the Oracle user has permission to create, read, and write it. On Linux:

   ```
   mkdir /u01/oracle/net
   export TNS_ADMIN=/u01/oracle/net
   ```

   Ensure that all work from now is done from a session where the variable has been set.
   On Windows:

   ```
   mkdir d:\oracle\net
   ```

   Create and set the key TNS_ADMIN as a string variable in the registry in the Oracle Home branch. This will typically be

   ```
   HKEY_LOCAL_MACHINE\SOFTWARE\ORACLE\KEY_OraDb1g_home1
   ```

2. Check that the variable is being read by using the TNSPING command from an operating system prompt:

```
tnsping orcl
```

This will return an error "TNS-03505: Failed to resolve name" because there are no files in the TNS_ADMIN directory. On Windows, you may need to launch a new command prompt to pick up the new TNS_ADMIN value from the registry.

3. Start the Net Manager. On Linux, run `netmgr` from an operating system prompt; on Windows, launch it from the Start menu. The top line of the Net Manager window will show the location of the Oracle Net files. If this is not the new directory, then the TNS_ADMIN variable has not been set correctly.

4. Create a new listener: expand the Local branch of the navigation tree, highlight Listeners, and click the +.

5. Enter a listener name, NEWLIST, and click OK.

6. Click Add Address.

7. For Address 1, choose TCP/IP as the protocol and enter **127.0.0.1** as the host, **2521** as the port. The illustration that follows shows the result.

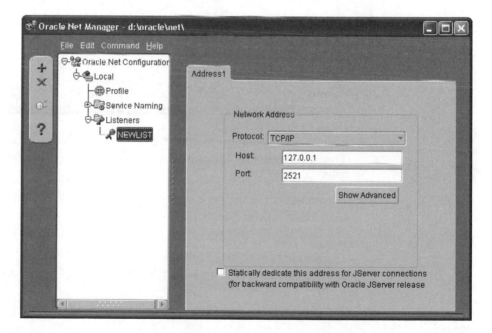

8. Create a new service name: highlight Service Naming in the navigation tree, and click the +.

9. Enter **NEW** as the net service name, and click Next.

10. Select TCP/IP as the protocol, and click Next.

11. Enter **127.0.0.1** as the host name and **2521** as the port and click Next.

12. Enter **SERV1** as the Service Name, and click Next.

13. Click Finish. If you try the test, it will fail at this time. The illustration that follows shows the result.

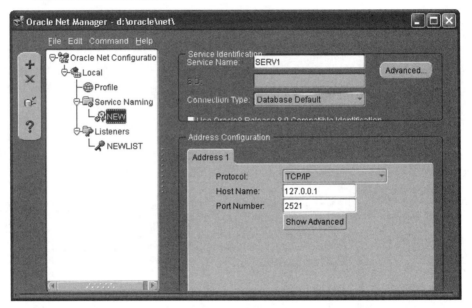

14. Save the configuration by clicking File and Save Network Configuration. This will create the `listener.ora` and `tnsnames.ora` files in the TNS_ADMIN directory.

15. Use an editor to check the two files. They will look like this:
    LISTENER.ORA:

```
NEWLIST =
  (DESCRIPTION =
    (ADDRESS = (PROTOCOL = TCP)(HOST = 127.0.0.1)(PORT = 2521))
  )
```

TNSNAMES.ora:

```
NEW =
  (DESCRIPTION =
    (ADDRESS_LIST =
      (ADDRESS = (PROTOCOL = TCP)(HOST = 127.0.0.1)(PORT =
2521))
    )
    (CONNECT_DATA =
      (SERVICE_NAME = SERV1)
    )
  )
```

16. From an operating system prompt, start the listener with `lsnrctl start newlist`.

17. From an operating system prompt, test the connect string with `tnsping new`.

18. Connect to your database using operating system authentication, bypassing any listener, with `sqlplus / as sysdba`.

19. Set the `service_names` and `local_listener` parameters for the running instance (memory only, not the parameter file) and register the new service name with the new listener:

```
alter system set service_names=serv1 scope=memory;
alter system set local_listener=new scope=memory;
alter system register;
```

20. From an operating system prompt, confirm that the new service has registered with the new listener with `lsnrctl services newlist`.

21. Confirm that the new network environment is functional by logging on:

```
sqlplus system/oracle@new
```

22. There is an optional Exercise 6-2 on shared server to come. If you do not intend to do that, tidy up your environment now:

Restart the database to return the parameters changed in Step 19 to their default values.

Stop the listener with `lsnrctl stop newlist`.

Unset the TNS_ADMIN variable: on Linux, export `TNS_ADMIN=''` or on Windows, remove the TNS_ADMIN registry key.

SCENARIO & SOLUTION

If a database is likely to have many logins per minute, what can be done to scale up the Oracle Net configuration?	Shared server probably won't help—it might help with many concurrent connections, but this issue is different: a high login rate. Setting up several listeners on several addresses and/or ports is likely to be a better answer.
If there are several listeners, or perhaps one listener listening on several addresses or ports, how can you load-balance connections across them?	You can set up Oracle Net to load-balance automatically. In the TNSNAMES.ORA file, list all the addresses, and add the keywords LOAD_BALANCE=ON. This will cause clients to choose addresses randomly, thus balancing traffic across the mall. You can do this in the "Advanced" options of the Net Manager.

CERTIFICATION OBJECTIVE 6.02

Use the Oracle Shared Server Architecture

The standard dedicated server architecture requires that the database listener should spawn a dedicated server process for each concurrent connection to the instance. These server processes will persist until the session is terminated. On Unix-type platforms, the server processes are real operating system processes; on Windows, they are threads within the one ORACLE.EXE process. This architecture can cause problems with scale on some platforms. An alternative is the *shared server* architecture, known as the multithreaded server (or MTS) in earlier releases.

The Limitations of Dedicated Server Architecture

As more users log on to your instance, more server processes get launched. This is not a problem as far as Oracle is concerned. The database listener can launch as many processes as required, though there may be limits on the speed with which it can launch them. If you have a large number of concurrent connection requests, your listener will have to queue them up. You can avoid this by running multiple listeners on different ports, and load-balancing between them. Then once the sessions are established, there is no limit to the number that PMON can manage. But your operating system may well have limits on the number of processes that it can support, limits to do with context switches and with memory.

A computer can only do one thing at once unless it is an SMP machine, in which case each CPU can only do one thing at once. The operating system simulates concurrent processing by using an algorithm to share CPU cycles across all the currently executing processes. This algorithm, often referred to as a time slicing or time-sharing algorithm, takes care of allocating a few CPU cycles to each process in turn. The switch of taking one process off CPU in order to put another process on CPU is called a context switch. Context switches are very expensive: the operating system has to do a lot of work to restore the state of each process as it is brought on to CPU and then save its state when it is switched off the CPU. As more users connect to the instance, the operating system has to context-switch between more and more server processes. Depending on your operating system, this can cause a severe degradation in performance. A decent mainframe operating system can context-switch between tens of thousands of processes without problems, but newer (and simpler) operating systems such as Unix and Windows may not be good at running thousands, or even just hundreds, of concurrent processes. Performance degrades dramatically, because a large proportion of the computer's processing capacity is taken up with managing the context switches, leaving a relatively small amount of processing capacity available for actually doing work.

There may also be memory problems that occur as more sessions are established. The actual server processes themselves are not an issue, because all modern operating systems use shared memory when the same process is loaded more than once. So launching a thousand server processes should take no more memory than launching one. The problem comes with the program global area, or PGA. The PGA is a block of memory associated with each server process, to maintain the state of the session and as a work area for operations such as sorting rows. Clearly, the PGAs cannot be in shared memory: they contain data unique to each session. This is why your system may begin to swap as more users log on: each session will require its own PGA.

So in the dedicated server environment, performance may degrade if your operating system has problems managing a large number of concurrent processes, and the problem will be exacerbated if your server machine has insufficient memory. Note that it doesn't really matter whether the sessions are actually doing anything or not. Even if the sessions are idle, the operating system must still bring them on and off CPU, and possibly page the appropriate PGA into main memory from swap files, according to its time slicing algorithm. There comes a point when, no matter what you do in the way of hardware upgrades, performance begins to degrade because of operating system inefficiencies in managing context switches and paging. These are not Oracle's problems, but to overcome them Oracle offers the option of the shared server architecture. This allows a large number of user processes to be serviced by a relatively small number of shared server processes, thus reducing dramatically the number of processes that the server's operating system has to manage. As a fringe benefit, memory usage may also reduce.

Always remember that the need for a shared server is very much platform and installation specific. Some operating systems will hardly ever need it. For example, a mainframe computer can time-share between many thousands of processes with no problems—it is usually simpler operating systems like Windows or Unix that are more likely to have problems.

The Shared Server Architecture

One point to emphasize immediately is that shared server is implemented purely on the server side. The user process and the application software have no way of telling that anything has changed. The user process issues a connect string that must resolve to the address of a listener and the name of a service (or of an instance). In return, it will receive the address of a server-side process that it will think is a dedicated server. It will then proceed to send SQL statements and receive back result sets; as far as the user process is concerned, absolutely nothing has changed. But the server side is very different.

Shared server is implemented by additional processes that are a part of the instance. They are background processes, launched at instance startup time. There are two new process types: dispatchers and shared servers. There are also some extra queue memory structures within the SGA, and the database listener modifies its behavior for shared server. When an instance that is configured for shared server starts up, in addition to the usual background processes one or more dispatcher processes also start. The dispatchers, like any other TCP process, run on a unique TCP port allocated by your operating system's port mapper: they contact the listener and register with it, using the local_listener parameter (remember that from the earlier section "Database Registration"?) to locate the listener. One or more shared server processes also start. These are conceptually similar to a normal dedicated server process, but they are not tied to one session. They will receive SQL statements, parse and execute them, and generate a result set—but they will not receive the SQL statements directly from a user process, they will read them from a queue that will be populated with statements from any number of user processes. Similarly, the shared servers don't fetch result sets back to a user process directly— instead, they put the result sets onto a response queue.

The next question is, how do the user-generated statements get onto the queue that is read by the server processes, and how do results get fetched to the users? This is where the dispatchers come in. When a user process contacts a listener, rather than launching a server process and connecting it to the user process, the listener passes back the address of a dispatcher. If there is only one dispatcher, the listener will connect it to all the user processes. If there are multiple dispatchers, the listener will load-balance incoming connection requests across them, but the end result is that many user processes will be connected to each dispatcher. Each user process will be under the impression that it is talking to a dedicated server process, but it isn't: it is sharing a dispatcher with many other user processes. At the network level, many user processes will have connections multiplexed through the one port used by the dispatcher.

> **exam**
> **ⓦatch** **A session's connection to a dispatcher persists for the duration of the session, unlike the connection to the listener, which is transient.**

When a user process issues a SQL statement, it is sent to the dispatcher. The dispatcher puts all the statements it receives onto a queue. This queue is called the *common* queue, because all dispatchers share it. No matter which dispatcher a user process is connected to, all statements end up on the common queue.

All the shared server processes monitor the common queue. When a statement arrives on the common queue, the first available shared server picks it up. From then execution proceeds through the usual parse-bind-execute cycle, but when it comes to the fetch phase, it is impossible for the shared server to fetch the result set back to the user process: there is no connection between the user process and the shared server. So instead, the shared server puts the result set onto a *response* queue that is specific to the dispatcher that received the job in the first place. Each dispatcher monitors its own response queue, and whenever any results are put on it, the dispatcher will pick them up and fetch them back to the user process that originally issued the statement.

> **exam**
> **ⓦatch** **There is a common input queue shared by all dispatchers, but each dispatcher has its own response queue.**

A result of the mechanism of dispatchers and queues is that any statement from any user process could be executed by any available shared server. This raises the question of how the state of the session can be maintained. It would be quite possible for a user process to issue, for example, a SELECT FOR UPDATE, a DELETE, and a COMMIT. In a normal dedicated server connection, this isn't a problem because the PGA (which is tied to the one server process that is managing the session) stores information about what the session was doing, and therefore the dedicated server will know what to COMMIT and what locks to release. The PGA for a dedicated server session will store the session's session data, its cursor state, its sort space, and its stack space. But in the shared server environment, each statement might be picked off the common queue by a different shared server process, which will have no idea what the state of the transaction is. To get around this problem, a shared server session stores most of the session data in the SGA, rather than in a PGA. Then whenever a shared server picks a job off the common queue, it will go to the SGA and connect to the appropriate block of memory to find out the state of the session. The memory used in the SGA for each shared server session is known as the user global area (the UGA) and includes all of what would have been in a PGA with the exception of the session's stack space. This is where the memory saving will come from. Oracle can manage memory in the shared pool much more effectively than it can in many separate PGAs.

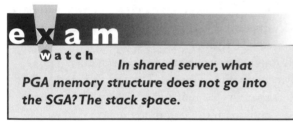

The part of the SGA used for storing UGAs is the large pool. This can be configured manually with the `large_pool_size` parameter, or it can be automatically managed.

Configuring Shared Server

Being a server-side capability, there need be no client configuration at all beyond perfectly normal client-side Oracle Net (the `tnsnames.ora` and `sqlnet.ora` files) as detailed previously. On the server side, shared server is nothing to do with the database—only the instance. The listener will be automatically configured for shared server through dynamic instance registration. It follows that shared server is configured though instance initialization parameters. There are a number of relevant parameters, but two are all that are usually necessary: `dispatchers` and `shared_servers`.

The first parameter to consider is `shared_servers`. This controls the number of shared servers that will be launched at instance startup time. Shared server uses a queuing mechanism, but the ideal is that there should be no queuing: there should always be a server process ready and waiting for every job that is put on the common queue by the dispatchers. Therefore, `shared_servers` should be set to the maximum number of concurrent requests that you expect. But if there is a sudden burst of activity, you don't have to worry too much, because Oracle will launch additional shared servers, up to the value specified for `max_shared_servers`.

By default, shared_servers is one if dispatchers is set. If the parameter max_shared_servers is not set, then it defaults to one-eighth of the processes parameter.

The dispatchers parameter controls how many dispatcher processes to launch at instance startup time, and how they will behave. This is the only required parameter. There are many options for this parameter, but usually two will suffice: how many to start and what protocol they should listen on. Among the more advanced options are ones that allow you to control the port and network card on which the dispatcher will listen, and the address of the listener(s) with which it will register, but usually you can let your operating system's port mapper assign a port, and use the local_listener parameter to control which listener they will register with. The max_dispatchers parameter sets an upper limit to the number of dispatchers you can start, but unlike with shared servers, Oracle will not start extra dispatchers on demand. You can, however, launch additional dispatchers at any time up to this limit.

For example, to enable the shared server architecture, adjust the two critical parameters as follows:

```
SQL> alter system set dispatchers='(dispatchers=2)(protocol=tcp)';
SQL> alter system set shared_servers=20;
```

Tuning the shared server is vital. There should always be enough shared servers to dequeue requests from the common queue as they arrive, and enough dispatchers that they can service incoming requests as they arrive and return results as they are enqueued to the response queues. Memory usage by shared server sessions in the SGA must be monitored. After converting from dedicated server to shared server, the SGA will need to be substantially larger.

When to Use the Shared Server

You will not find a great deal of hard advice in the Oracle documentation on when to use shared server, or how many dispatchers and shared servers you'll need. The main point to hang on to is that shared server is a facility you use because you are forced to, not something you use automatically. It increases scalability, but perhaps at the cost of reducing performance. It is quite possible that any one statement will take longer to execute in a shared server environment than if it were executing on a dedicated server, because it has to go via queues. It may also take more CPU resources because of this enqueuing and dequeuing activity. But overall, the scalability of your system will increase dramatically. Even if each request is marginally slower, you will be able to carry out many more requests per second through the instance.

It is often said that you should think about using shared server when your number of concurrent connections is in the low hundreds. If you have less than one hundred concurrent connections, you almost certainly don't need it. But If you have more than a thousand, you probably do. The critical factor is whether your operating system performance is beginning to degrade.

Consider an OLTP environment, such as hundreds of telephone operators in a call center. Each operator may spend one or two minutes per call, collecting the caller details and entering them into the user process. Then when he/she clicks the Submit button, the user process constructs an insert statement and sends it off to the server process. The server process might go through the whole parse/bind/ execute/fetch cycle for the statement in just a few hundredths of a second. Clearly, no matter how fast the clerks work, their server processes are idle 99.9 percent of the time. But the operating system still has to switch all those processes on and off CPU, according to its time-sharing algorithm. By contrast, consider a data warehouse environment. Here, users submit queries that may run for a long time. The batch uploads of data will be equally long running. Whenever one of these large jobs is submitted, the server process for that session could be working flat out for hours on just one statement.

It should be apparent that shared server is ideal for managing many sessions doing short transactions, where the bulk of the work is on the client side of the client-server divide. In these circumstances, one shared server will be able to service dozens of sessions. But for batch processing work, dedicated servers are much better. If you submit a large batch job through a shared server session, it will work—but it will tie up one of your small pool of shared server processes for the duration of the job, leaving all your other users to compete for the remaining shared servers. The amount of network traffic involved in batch uploads from a user process and in fetching large result sets back to a user process will also cause contention for dispatchers.

A second class of operations that are better done through a dedicated server is database administration work. Index creation, table maintenance operations, and backup and recovery work through the Recovery Manager will perform much better through a dedicated server. And it is logically impossible to issue startup or shutdown commands through a shared server: the shared servers are part of the instance and thus not available at the time you issue a startup command. So the administrator should always have a dedicated server connection.

EXERCISE 6-2 (OPTIONAL)

Set Up a Shared Server Environment

In this exercise, which continues from Step 21 of Exercise 6-1, you will configure the shared server and prove that it is working.

1. Set the `dispatchers` and `shared_servers` parameters and register with the listener as follows:

```
alter system set dispatchers='(pro=tcp)(dis=2)' scope=memory;
alter system set shared_servers=4 scope=memory;
alter system register;
```

2. Confirm that the dispatchers and shared servers have started by querying the view V$PROCESS. Look for processes named S000, S001, S002, S003, D000, and D001:

```
select program from v$process order by program;
```

3. From an operating system prompt, confirm that the dispatchers have registered with the listener:

```
lsnrctl services newlist
```

4. Connect through the listener, and confirm that the connection is through the shared server mechanism:

```
connect system/oracle@ncw;
select d.name,s.name from v$dispatcher d,v$shared_server s,
v$circuit c
where d.paddr=c.dispatcher and s.paddr=c.server;
```

This query will show the dispatcher to which your season is connected, and the shared server process that is executing your query.

5. Tidy up the environment, by returning to the original configuration:

```
alter system set local_listener='' scope=memory;
alter system set service_names='' scope=memory;
alter system set dispatchers='' scope=memory;
alter system set shared_servers=0 scope=memory;
alter system register;
```

Stop the listener from an operating system prompt with `lsnrctl stop newlist`.

Unset the TNS_ADMIN variable: on Linux, `export TNS_ADMIN=''` or on Windows, remove the TNS_ADMIN registry key.

CERTIFICATION SUMMARY

Oracle Net is Oracle Corporation's proprietary network protocol, layered on top of industry standard protocols. When using the dedicated server architecture, the Oracle Net database listener will spawn a server process for each session; when using the shared server architecture; many sessions will share a pool of server processes, via dispatchers that use queues to pass requests and results to and from the servers.

Oracle Net can be configured manually, by editing text files, or with graphical tools. Shared server is implemented purely on the server side, by setting instance parameters.

TWO-MINUTE DRILL

Configure and Manage the Oracle Network

❑ The server-side files are the `listener.ora` and (optionally) `sqlnet.ora` files.

❑ The client-side files are the `tnsnames.ora` and (optionally) `sqlnet.ora` files.

❑ The Oracle Net files live in `ORACLE_HOME`/network/admin, or in whatever directory the TNS_ADMIN variable points to.

❑ Name resolution can be local (with a `tnsnames.ora file`) or central (with an LDAP directory).

❑ Easy Connect does not need any name resolution.

❑ One listener can listen for many databases.

❑ Many listeners can connect to one database.

❑ Instance registration with listeners can be static (by coding details in the `listener.ora` file) or dynamic (by the PMON process updating the listener).

❑ Each user process has a persistent connection to its dedicated server process.

Use the Oracle Shared Server Architecture

❑ User processes connect to dispatchers; these connections are persistent.

❑ All dispatchers place requests on a common queue.

❑ Shared server processes dequeue requests from the common queue.

❑ Each dispatcher has its own response queue.

❑ Shared server processes place results onto the appropriate dispatcher's response queue.

❑ The dispatchers fetch results back to the appropriate user process.

❑ Shared server is configured with (as a minimum) two instance parameters: `dispatchers` and `shared_servers`.

SELF TEST

Configure and Manage the Oracle Network

1. Which protocols can Oracle Net 11g use? (Choose all correct answers.)
   A. TCP
   B. UDP
   C. SPX/IPX
   D. SDP
   E. TCP with secure sockets
   F. Named Pipes
   G. LU6.2
   H. NetBIOS/NetBEUI

2. Where is the division between the client and the server in the Oracle environment? (Choose the best answer.)
   A. Between the instance and the database
   B. Between the user and the user process
   C. Between the server process and the instance
   D. Between the user process and the server process
   E. The client-server split varies depending on the stage of the execution cycle

3. Which of the following statements about listeners are correct? (Choose the best answer.)
   A. A listener can connect you to one instance only.
   B. A listener can connect you to one service only.
   C. Multiple listeners can share one network interface card.
   D. An instance will only accept connections from the listener specified on the local_listener parameter.

4. You have decided to use Local Naming. Which files must you create on the client machine? (Choose the best answer.)
   A. tnsnames.ora and sqlnet.ora
   B. listener.ora only
   C. tnsnames.ora only
   D. listener.ora and sqlnet.ora
   E. None—you can rely on defaults if you are using TCP and your listener is running on port 1521

5. If you stop your listener, what will happen to sessions that connected through it? (Choose the best answer.)

   A. They will continue if you have configured failover.

   B. They will not be affected in any way.

   C. They will hang until you restart the listener.

   D. You cannot stop a listener if it is in use.

   E. The sessions will error out.

6. Study this `tnsnames.ora` file:

```
test =
  (description =
    (address_list =
      (address = (protocol = tcp)(host = serv2)(port = 1521))
    )
    (connect_data =
      (service_name = prod)
    )
  )
prod =
  (description =
    (address_list =
      (address = (protocol = tcp)(host = serv1)(port = 1521))
    )
    (connect_data =
      (service_name = prod)
    )
  )
dev =
  (description =
    (address_list =
      (address = (protocol = tcp)(host = serv2)(port = 1521))
    )
    (connect_data =
      (service_name = dev)
    )
  )
```

Which of the following statements is correct about the connect strings test, prod, and dev? (Choose all correct answers.)

   A. All three are valid.

   B. All three can succeed only if the instances are set up for dynamic instance registration.

    C. The test connection will fail, because the connect string doesn't match the service name.

    D. There will be a port conflict on serv2, because prod and dev try to use the same port.

7. Consider this line from a `listener.ora` file:

```
L1=(description=(address=(protocol=tcp)(host=serv1)(port=1521)))
```

What will happen if you issue this connect string,

`connect scott/tiger@L1` (Choose the best answer.)

    A. You will be connected to the instance L1.

    B. You will only be connected to an instance if dynamic instance registration is working.

    C. You can't tell—it depends on how the client side is configured.

    D. If you are logged on to the server machine, IPC will connect you to the local instance.

    E. The connection will fail if the listener is not started.

Use the Oracle Shared Server Architecture

8. Which of these memory structures is not stored in the SGA for a shared server session? (Choose the best answer.)

    A. Cursor state

    B. Sort space

    C. Stack space

9. Match the object to the function:

Object	Function
a. Common queue	A. Connects users to dispatchers
b. Dispatcher	B. Stores jobs waiting for execution
c. Large pool	C. Executes SQL statements
d. Listener	D. Stores results waiting to be fetched
e. Response queue	E. Receives statements from user processes
f. Shared server	F. Stores UGAs accessed by all servers

10. Which of the following is true about dispatchers? (Choose all correct answers.)

    A. Dispatchers don't handle the work of users' requests; they only interface between user processes and queues.

    B. Dispatchers share a common response queue.

    C. Dispatchers load-balance connections between themselves.

    D. Listeners load-balance connections across dispatchers.

    E. You can terminate a dispatcher, and established sessions will continue.

11. Which of the following statements about shared servers are true? (Choose the best answer.)

    A. All statements in a multistatement transaction will be executed by the same server.

    B. If one statement updates multiple rows, the work may be shared across several servers.

    C. The number of shared servers is fixed by the SHARED_SERVERS parameter.

    D. Oracle will spawn additional shared servers on demand.

LAB QUESTION

Use whatever tool you like (even a text editor) to create two listeners, one listening on address 127.0.0.1, port 2521, the other listening on address 127.0.0.2, port 2521. This will simulate a server with two network cards. Start both listeners.

Use the Net Manager to create a tnsnames entry with both addresses, that will load-balance connections across them and, if one fails, try the other. This is an option visible when you click the Advanced button after defining the second address, as shown in the illustration that follows.

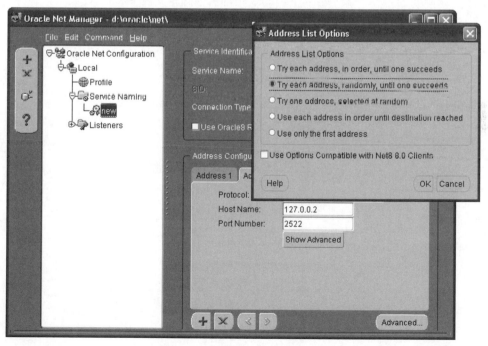

Save the configuration, and test the entry with tnsping. If it works, adjust your instance to use your new tnsnames entry as the value for the `local_listener` parameter.

Test the configuration by connecting with SQL*Plus through the new tnsnames connect string. Prove that there is fault tolerance by shutting down one listener and then the other: you will find that as long as one of them is working, you can still connect.

SELF TEST ANSWERS

Configure and Manage the Oracle Network

1. ☑ **A, D, E,** and **F.** TCP, SDP, TCPS, and NMP are the supported protocols with the current release.

☒ **B** and **H** are wrong because UDP and NetBIOS/NetBEUI have never been supported, **C** and **G** are wrong because SPX and LU6.2 are no longer supported.

2. ☑ **D.** The client-server split is between user process and server process.

☒ **A, B, C,** and **E.** These all misrepresent the client-server architecture

3. ☑ **C.** Many listeners can shared one address, if they use different ports.

☒ **A** is wrong because one listener can launch sessions against many instances. **B** is wrong because a listener can connect you to an registered service. **D** is wrong because the `local_ listener` parameter controls which listener the instance will register with dynamically; it will also accept connections from any listener that has it statically registered.

4. ☑ **C.** This is the only required client-side file for local naming.

☒ **A** is wrong because SQLNET.ORA is not essential. **B** and **D** are wrong because they refer to server-side files. **E** is wrong because some configuration is always necessary for local naming (though not for Easy Connect).

5. ☑ **B.** The listener establishes connections but is not needed for their maintenance.

☒ **A, C, D,** and **E.** These are all incorrect because they assume that the listener is necessary for the continuance of an established session.

6. ☑ **A** and **B.** All three are valid but will only work if the services are registered with the listeners.

☒ **C** is wrong because there need be no connection between the alias used in a connect string and the service name. **D** is wrong because many services can be accessible through a single listening port.

7. ☑ **C.** Some client-side configuration is necessary, and without knowing what it is you have no idea what will happen.

☒ **A** is wrong because the connect string could connect to any instance. **B** is wrong because, while the listener L1 must use dynamic registration, this is not enough. **D** is wrong because the use of IPC to bypass the listener is not relevant. **E** is wrong because (while certainly true) you don't know if it is relevant.

Use the Oracle Shared Server Architecture

8. ☑ **C.** Stack space is not part of the UGA and therefore does not go into the SGA.

☒ **A** and **B.** These are UGA components and therefore do go into the SGA.

9. ☑ a – B, b – E, c – F, d – A, e – D, f – C

These are the correct mappings of objects to functions.

10. ☑ **A** and **D.** Dispatchers maintain the connection to user processes, place requests on the common queue, and retrieve result sets from response queues.

☒ **B** is wrong because each dispatcher has its on response queue. **C** is wrong because it is the listener that load-balances, not the dispatchers. **E** is wrong because the connections to a dispatcher are persistent: if it dies, they will be broken.

11. ☑ **D.** To prevent queueing on the common queue, Oracle will launch additional shared servers—but only up to the `max_shared_servers` value.

☒ **A** is wrong because each statement may be picked up by a different server. **B** is wrong because any one statement can be executed by only one server. **C** is wrong because this parameter controls the number of servers initially launched, which may change later.

LAB ANSWER

The listeners (called, in this example, list2 and list3) will be defined by entries similar to these in the `listener.ora` file:

```
LIST3 =
  (DESCRIPTION =
    (ADDRESS = (PROTOCOL = TCP)(HOST = 127.0.0.2)(PORT = 2521))
  )
LIST2 =
  (DESCRIPTION =
    (ADDRESS = (PROTOCOL = TCP)(HOST = 127.0.0.1)(PORT = 2521))
  )
```

Start the listeners with these commands from an operating system prompt:

```
lsnrctl start list2
lsnrctl start list3
```

The tnsnames.ora entry (in this example called NEW) will look like this:

```
NEW =
  (DESCRIPTION =
    (ADDRESS_LIST =
```

```
      (ADDRESS = (PROTOCOL = TCP)(HOST = 127.0.0.1)(PORT = 2521))
      (ADDRESS = (PROTOCOL = TCP)(HOST = 127.0.0.2)(PORT = 2521))
      (LOAD_BALANCE = yes)
    )
  (CONNECT_DATA =
      (SERVICE_NAME = OCP11G)
    )
  )
```

The SERVICE_NAME directive should be whatever your instance has its service_names parameter set to; this will by default be the instance name.

To test the tnsnames entry and the listeners, from an operating system prompt:

```
tnsping new
```

To register the instance with both listeners, from a SQL prompt:

```
alter system set local_listener=new scope =memory;
alter system register;
```

There is no reason to limit the scope of the change to the running instance, except that if something goes horribly wrong, all you need do is restart the instance to return to the original value.

Then to test the connection, from an operating system prompt:

```
sqlplus system/oracle@new
```

7
Managing Database Storage Structures

T he previous two chapters dealt with the instance and the sessions against it: processes and memory structures. This chapter begins the investigation of the database itself. All data processing occurs in memory, in the instance, but data storage is in the database on disk. The database consists of three file types: the controlfile, the online redo log files, and the datafiles. Data is stored in the datafiles.

Users never see a physical datafile. All they see are logical segments. System administrators never see a logical segment. All they see are physical datafiles. The Oracle database provides complete abstraction of logical storage from physical. This is one of the requirements of the relational database paradigm. As a DBA, you must be aware of the relationship between the logical and the physical storage. Monitoring and administering these structures, a task often described as *space management*, used to be a huge part of a DBA's workload. The facilities provided in recent releases of the database can automate space management to a certain extent, and they can certainly let the DBA set up storage in ways that will reduce the maintenance workload considerably.

CERTIFICATION OBJECTIVE 7.01

Understand Tablespaces and Datafiles

Data is stored logically in segments and physically in datafiles. The *tablespace* entity abstracts the two, one tablespace can contain many segments and be made up of many datafiles. There is no direct relationship between a segment and a datafile. The datafiles can exist as files in a file system or (from release 10g onward) on Automatic Storage Management (ASM) devices.

The Oracle Data Storage Model

The separation of logical from physical storage is a necessary part of the relational database paradigm. It means that programmers have no possibility of finding out where, physically, an item of data is. If they could find out, their software would be tied to the one machine on which it was written. And even then, something as trivial as renaming or moving a file would break the application. The relational paradigm states that programmers should address only logical structures and let the database manage the mapping to physical structures. This means that physical storage can be reorganized, or the whole database moved to completely different hardware and operating system, and the application will not be aware of any change.

Figure 7-1 shows the Oracle storage model sketched as an entity-relationship diagram, with the logical structures to the left and the physical structures to the right.

There is one relationship drawn in as a dotted line: a many-to-many relationship between segments and datafiles. This relationship is dotted, because it shouldn't be there. As good relational engineers, DBAs do not permit many-to-many relationships. Resolving this relationship into a normalized structure is what the storage model is all about. Taking the entities in the figure one by one.

The *tablespace* entity resolves the many-to-many relationship between segments and datafiles. One tablespace can contain many segments and be made up of many datafiles. This means that any one segment may be spread across multiple datafiles, and any one datafile may contain all of or parts of many segments. This solves many storage challenges. Some older database management systems used a one-to-one relationship between segments and files: every table or index would be stored as a separate file. This raised two dreadful problems for large systems. First, an application might well have thousands of tables and even more indexes; managing many thousands of files was an appalling task for the system administrators. Second, the maximum size of a table is limited by the maximum size of a file. Even if modern operating systems do not have any practical limits, there may well be limitations

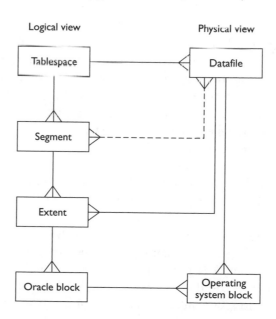

FIGURE 7-1

The Oracle
storage model

imposed by the underlying hardware environment. Use of tablespaces bypasses both these problems. Tablespaces are identified by name, unique in the database.

The *segment* entity represents any database object that stores data and therefore requires space in a tablespace. Your typical segment is a table, but there are other segment types, notably index segments (described in Chapter 9) and undo segments (described in Chapter 11). Any one segment can exist in only one tablespace, but the tablespace can spread it across all the files making up the tablespace. This means that the tables' sizes are not subject to any limitations imposed by the environment on maximum file size. As many segments can share a single tablespace, it becomes possible to have far more segments than there are datafiles. Segments are schema objects, identified by the segment name qualified with the owning schema name. Note that programmatic schema objects (such as PL/SQL procedures, views, or sequences) are not segments: they do not store data, and they exist within the data dictionary.

The *Oracle block* is the unit of I/O for the database. Datafiles are formatted into Oracle blocks, consecutively numbered. The size of the Oracle blocks is fixed for a tablespace (generally speaking, it is the same for all tablespaces in the database); the default (with release 11g) is 8 KB. A row might be only a couple hundred bytes, and so there could be many rows stored in one block, but when a session wants a row, the whole block will be read from disk into the database buffer cache. Similarly, if just one column of one row has been changed in the database buffer cache, the DBWn will (eventually) write the whole block back into the datafile from which it came, overwriting the previous version. The size of an Oracle block can range from 2 KB to 16 KB on Linux or Windows, to 32 KB on some other operating systems. The block size is controlled by the parameter DB_BLOCK_SIZE. This can never be changed after database creation, because it is used to format the datafile(s) that make up the SYSTEM tablespace. If it becomes apparent later on that the block size is inappropriate, the only course of action is to create a new database and transfer everything into it. A block is uniquely identified by its number within a datafile: the block number alone is not enough.

Managing space one block at a time would be a crippling task, so blocks are grouped into *extents*. An extent is a set of consecutively numbered Oracle blocks within one datafile. Every segment will consist of one or more extents, consecutively numbered. These extents may be in any and all of the datafiles that make up the tablespace. An extent can be identified from either the dimension of the segment (extents are consecutively numbered per segment, starting from zero) or the dimension of the datafile (every segment is in one file, starting at a certain Oracle block number).

A *datafile* is, physically, made up of a number of operating system blocks. How datafiles and the operating system blocks are structured is entirely dependent on the operating system's file system. Some file systems have well-known limitations and are therefore not widely used for modern systems (for example, the old MS-DOS FAT file system could handle files up to only 4 GB, and only 512 B of them per directory). Most databases will be installed on file systems with no practical limits, such as NTFS on Windows or ext3 on Linux. The alternatives to file systems for datafile storage are raw devices or ASM. Raw devices are now very rarely used for datafile storage because of manageability issues. ASM is briefly described in the later section of this chapter, Automatic Storage Management (ASM).

An *operating system block* is the unit of I/O for your file system. A process might want to read only one byte from disk, but the I/O system will have to read an operating system block. The operating system block size is configurable for some file systems (for example, when formatting an NTFS file system you can choose from 512 B to 64 KB), but typically system administrators leave it on default (512 B for NTFS, 1 KB for ext3). This is why the relationship between Oracle blocks and operating system blocks is usually one-to-many, as shown in Figure 7-1. There is no reason not to match the operating system block size to the Oracle block size if your file system lets you do this. The configuration that should always be avoided would be where the operating system blocks were bigger than the Oracle blocks.

Segments, Extents, Blocks, and Rows

Data is stored in segments. The data dictionary view DBA_SEGMENTS describes every segment in the database. This query shows the segment types in a simple database—the counts are low because there is no real application installed:

```
SQL> select segment_type,count(1) from dba_segments group by
segment_type
  2  order by segment_type;
SEGMENT_TYPE          COUNT(1)
-------------------- ----------
CLUSTER                     10
INDEX                     3185
INDEX PARTITION            324
LOB PARTITION                7
LOBINDEX                   760
LOBSEGMENT                 760
NESTED TABLE                29
ROLLBACK                     1
TABLE                     2193
TABLE PARTITION            164
TYPE2 UNDO                  10
11 rows selected.
SQL>
```

In brief, and in the order they are most likely to concern a DBA, these segments types are

- **TABLE**   These are the heap-structured tables: variable-length rows, in random order. Even though a typical segment is a table segment, never forget that the table is not the segment, and that there are more complex table organizations that use other segment types.

- **INDEX**   Indexes are sorted lists of key values, each with a pointer, the ROWID, to the physical location of the row. The ROWID specifies which Oracle block of which datafile the row is in, and the row number within the block.

- **TYPE2 UNDO**   These are the undo segments (no one refers to them as "type2 undo" segments) that store the prechange versions of data that are necessary for providing transactional integrity: rollback, read consistency, and isolation.

- **ROLLBACK**   Rollback segments should not be used in normal running from release 9*i* onward. Release 9*i* introduced automatic undo management, which is based on undo segments. There will always be one rollback segment that protects the transactions used to create a database (this is necessary because at that point no undo segments exist), but it shouldn't be used subsequently.

- **TABLE PARTITION**   A table can be divided into many partitions. If this is done, then the partitions will be individual segments, and the table itself will not be a segment at all: it exists only as the total of its partitions. Each table partition of a heap table is itself structured as a heap table, in its own segment. These segments can be in different tablespaces, meaning that it becomes possible to spread one table across multiple tablespaces.

- **INDEX PARTITION**   An index will by default be in one segment, but indexes can be partitioned. If you are partitioning your tables, you will usually partition the indexes on those tables as well.

- **LOBSEGMENT, LOBINDEX, LOB PARTITION**   If a column is defined as a large object data type, then only a pointer is stored in the table itself: a pointer to an entry in a separate segment where the column data actually resides. LOBs can have indexes built on them for rapid access to data within the objects, and LOBs can also be partitioned.

- **CLUSTER**   A cluster is a segment that can contain several tables. In contrast with partitioning, which lets you spread one table across many segments, clustering lets you denormalize many tables into one segment.
- **NESTED TABLE**   If a column of a table is defined as a user-defined object type that itself has columns, then the column can be stored in its own segment, as a nested table.

Every segment has one or more extents. When a segment is created, Oracle will allocate an extent to it in whatever tablespace is specified. Eventually, as data is entered, the extent will fill. Oracle will then allocate a second extent, in the same tablespace but not necessarily in the same datafile. If you know that a segment is going to need more space, you can manually allocate an extent. Figure 7-2 shows how to identify precisely where a segment is.

In the figure, the first command creates the table HR.NEWTAB, relying completely on defaults for the storage. Then a query against DBA_EXTENTS shows that the segment consists of just one extent, extent number zero. This extent is in file number 4 and is 8 blocks long. The first of the 8 blocks is block number 1401. The size of the extent is 64 KB, which shows that the block size is 8 KB. The next

FIGURE 7-2	
Determining the physical location of a segment's extents	

```
C:\WINDOWS\system32\cmd.exe - sqlplus / as sysdba

SQL> create table hr.newtab(c1 date);

Table created.

SQL> select tablespace_name,file_id,extent_id,block_id,blocks,bytes
  2  from dba_extents where owner='HR' and segment_name='NEWTAB';

TABLESPACE_NAME     FILE_ID    EXTENT_ID    BLOCK_ID      BLOCKS       BYTES
--------------- ---------- ---------- ---------- ---------- ----------
USERS                     4          0        1401           8       65536

SQL> alter table hr.newtab allocate extent;

Table altered.

SQL> select tablespace_name,file_id,extent_id,block_id,blocks,bytes
  2  from dba_extents where owner='HR' and segment_name='NEWTAB';

TABLESPACE_NAME     FILE_ID    EXTENT_ID    BLOCK_ID      BLOCKS       BYTES
--------------- ---------- ---------- ---------- ---------- ----------
USERS                     4          0        1401           8       65536
USERS                     4          1        1409           8       65536

SQL> select tablespace_name,file_name from dba_data_files where file_id=4;

TABLESPACE_NAME FILE_NAME
--------------- ---------------------------------------------------
USERS           D:\APP\ORACLE\ORADATA\ORCL11G\USERS01.DBF

SQL>
```

command forces Oracle to allocate another extent to the segment, even though the first extent will not be full. The next query shows that this new extent, number 1, is also in file number 4 and starts immediately after extent zero. Note that it is not clear from this example whether or not the tablespace consists of multiple datafiles, because the algorithm Oracle uses to work out where to assign the next extent does not simply use datafiles in turn. If the tablespace does consist of multiple datafiles, you can override Oracle's choice with this syntax:

```
ALTER TABLE tablename ALLOCATE EXTENT STORAGE (DATAFILE 'filename');
```

on the
Ɵob

Preallocating space by manually adding extents can deliver a performance benefit but is a huge amount of work. You won't do it for more than a very few tables or indexes that have an exceptionally high growth rate, or perhaps before bulk loading operations.

The last query in Figure 7-2 goes to the view DBA_DATA_FILES to determine the name of the file in which the extents were allocated, and the name of the tablespace to which the datafile belongs. To identify the table's tablespace, one could also query DBA_SEGMENTS.

on the
Ɵob

You can query DBA_TABLES to find out in which tablespace a table resides, but this will only work for non-partitioned tables—not for partitioned tables, where each partition is its own segment and can be in a different tablespace. Partitioning lets one table (stored as multiple segments) span tablespaces.

An extent consists of a set of consecutively numbered blocks. Each block will have a header area and a data area. The header is of variable size and grows downward from the top of the block. Among other things, it contains a row directory (that lists where in the block each row begins) and row locking information. The data area fills from the bottom up. Between the two there may (or may not) be an area of free space. Events that will cause a block's header to grow include inserting and locking rows. The data area will initially be empty and will fill as rows are inserted (or index keys are inserted, in the case of a block of an index segment). The free space does get fragmented as rows are inserted, deleted, and updated (which may cause a row's size to change), but that is of no significance because all this happens in memory, after the block has been copied into a buffer in the database buffer cache. The free space is coalesced into a contiguous area when necessary, and always before the DBWn writes the block back to its datafile.

Automatic Storage Management (ASM)

Datafiles can exist on four types of device: local file systems, clustered file systems, ASM disk groups, and raw devices:

- **File on a file local system** These are the simplest datafiles; they exist as normal operating system files in a directory structure on disks directly attached to the computer running the instance. On a PC running Windows or Linux, these could be internal IDE or SATA drives. On more sophisticated hardware, they would usually be SCSI disks, or external drives.

- **Files on a clustered file system** A clustered file system is external disks, mounted concurrently on more than one computer. The clustered file system mediates access to the disks from processes running on all the computers in the cluster. Using clustered file systems is one way of implementing RAC: the database must reside on disks accessible to all the instances that are going to open it. Clustered file systems can be bought from operating system vendors, or Oracle Corporation's OCFS (Oracle Clustered File System) is an excellent alternative. OCFS was first written for Linux and Windows (for which there were no proper clustered file systems) and bundled with database release 9*i*; with 10*g* it was ported to all the other mainstream operating systems.

- **Files on raw devices** It is possible to create datafiles on disks with no file system at all. This is still supported but is really only a historical anomaly. In the bad old days before clustered file systems (or ASM) existed, raw devices were the only way to implement a Parallel Server database. Parallel Server itself was replaced with RAC in database release 9*i*.

- **Files on ASM devices** ASM is a facility introduced with database release 10*g*. This is an alternative to file system–based datafile storage and is covered in the second OCP examination.

on the **Job**

Some people claim that raw devices give the best performance. With contemporary disk and file system technology, this is almost certainly not true. And even if it were true, they are so awkward to manage that no sane DBA wants to use them.

ASM is covered in detail in the second OCP examination, but an understanding of what it can do is expected for the first examination. In summary, ASM is a logical volume manager provided by Oracle and bundled with the database. The general idea is that you take a bunch of raw disks, give them to Oracle, and let Oracle get on with it. Your system administrators need not worry about creating file systems at all.

A logical volume manager provided by the operating system, or perhaps by a third party such as Veritas, will take a set of *physical volumes* and present them to the operating system as *logical volumes*. The physical volumes could be complete disks, or they could be partitions of disks. The logical volumes will look to application software like disks, but the underlying storage of any one logical volume might not be one physical volume but several. It is on these logical volumes that the file systems are then created.

A logical volume can be much larger than any of the physical volumes of which it is composed. Furthermore, the logical volume can be created with characteristics that exploit the performance and safety potential of using multiple physical volumes. These characteristics are striping and mirroring of data. Striping data across multiple physical volumes gives huge performance gains. In principle, if a file is distributed across two disks, it should be possible to read it in half the time it would take if it were all on one disk. The performance will improve geometrically, in proportion to the number of disks assigned to the logical volume. Mirroring gives safety. If a logical volume consists of two or more physical volumes, then every operating system block written to one volume can be written simultaneously to the other volume. If one copy is damaged, the logical volume manager will read the other. If there are more than two physical volumes, a higher degree of mirroring becomes possible, providing fault tolerance in the event of multiple disk failures.

Some operating systems (such as AIX) include a logical volume manager as standard, with other operating systems it is an optional (and chargeable) extra. Historically, some of the simpler operating systems (such as Windows and Linux) did not have much support for logical volume managers at all. If a logical volume manager is available, it may require considerable time and skill to set up optimally.

ASM is a logical volume manager designed for Oracle database files. The definition of "database file" is broad. Apart from the true database files (controlfile, online redo log files, and datafiles) ASM can also store backup files, archived redo log files, and datapump files (all these files will be detailed in later chapters). It cannot be used for the Oracle Home, or for the alert log and trace files.

To set up ASM, the system administrators must provide the physical volumes. These can be actual disks, partitions of disks, or devices provided by a SAN (storage area network) or some form of network-attached storage. The rules

exam

watch　　**ASM can store only database files, not the binaries. The Oracle Home must always be on a conventional file system.**

on what type of devices can be used and how they should be configured are strict, but not unusual. The DBA then groups these physical volumes (known as ASM *disks*) into logical volumes (known as ASM *disk groups*). The disk groups are formatted into *allocation units*, which are contiguous blocks of space on a physical volume. The default allocation unit size is 1 MB, but this can be increased up to 64 MB if the nature of the application is such (typically, a data warehouse) that it would benefit from this. The lowest level of storage is the *physical block*. This will be determined by the geometry of the disks.

Every file created on an ASM disk group will always be striped across all the ASM disks that make up the group. This is not configurable; it is a performance benefit with no downside and is always implemented. Mirroring is configurable but is enabled by default.

Generally speaking, ASM gives far superior performance to any third-party logical volume manager. This is because it is an Oracle-aware system that can stripe the files intelligently. Different file types have different access patterns that make different striping and mirroring strategies appropriate. Because ASM stripes at the file level (rather than the volume level, the way a RAID system does), it can handle this much better than an operating system–dependent logical volume manager. The file-level striping and mirroring also means that additional disks can be added to or removed from a group one at a time if necessary. For example, if a volume group consists of just two disks and a third is added, ASM will automatically launch a *rebalance* operation to bring it into use by restriping the ASM files: it will move a mix of primary and mirrored extents from the existing disks onto the new disk. Similarly, if a disk leaves the group (either because of an administration command or a failure), the disk group will immediately rebalance itself to reinstantiate lost mirrors. Rebalancing operations occur in the background, while the database is in use.

A key feature of ASM is that it can work as a clustered file system. Historically, many operating systems had problems with making a file system available on two or more nodes concurrently (this is not making files available through a file server—it is directly attached storage), as is necessary for RAC database. For operating systems that do support clustered file systems, often they are a chargeable option. ASM is a clustered file system available on all mainstream platforms and bundled with the Oracle database license.

ASM gives fantastic performance. It works for single-instance databases, as well as RAC databases.

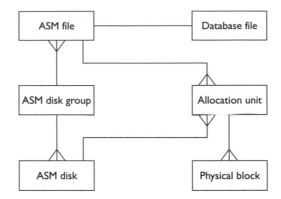

Figure 7-3 sketches the ASM structures as an entity-relationship diagram.
Note the one-to-one mapping of an ASM file to a database file, which could
be any of the file types that ASM supports. One could draw in a many-to-many
relationship between ASM files and ASM disks, but this is resolved via either the
ASM disk groups or the allocation units.

EXERCISE 7-1

Investigate the Database's Data Storage Structures

In this exercise, you will run queries to document a database's physical structure. The
commands could be run interactively from SQL*Plus or Database Control, but it
would make sense to save them as a script that (with suitable refinements for display
format and for site specific customizations) can be run against any database as part of
the regular reports on space usage.

1. Connect to the database as user SYSTEM.

2. Determine the name and size of the controlfile(s):

```
select name,block_size*file_size_blks bytes from
v$controlfile;
```

3. Determine the name and size of the online redo log file members:

```
select member,bytes from v$log join v$logfile using (group#);
```

4. Determine the name and size of the datafiles and the tempfiles:

```
select name,bytes from v$datafile
union all
select name,bytes from v$tempfile;
```

SCENARIO & SOLUTION

You are designing storage structure for a new database that will be administered by junior staff with little knowledge of the operating system or indeed of database administration. How can you make things easier?	Use as much automation as possible. ASM can manage the disks with no OS knowledge needed at all. Enabling OMF, by setting the relevant parameters to point to an ASM disk group, makes file management completely transparent. The database may well run for months without any need for manual intervention for space management—as long as the ASM disk group doesn't fill up.
What can you do to reduce the likelihood of accidentally deleting database files?	This is recurrent nightmare for many DBAs. It happens more often than you can possibly imagine. The only way is to develop operating practices that become ingrained in your habits. For instance, never use wild cards when deleting files; on Linux or Unix, alias commands to safer versions (such as rm to rm -i); do not log on to the operating system as the root (for Unix) or Administrator (for Windows) user but as a much lower-privileged person.

CERTIFICATION OBJECTIVE 7.02

Create and Manage Tablespaces

Tablespaces are repositories for schema data, including the data dictionary (which is the SYS schema). All databases must have a SYSTEM tablespace and a SYSAUX tablespace, and (for practical purposes) a temporary tablespace and an undo tablespace. These four will usually have been created when the database was created. Subsequently, the DBA may create many more tablespaces for user data, and possible additional tablespaces for undo and temporary data.

Tablespace Creation

To create a tablespace with Enterprise Manager Database Control, from the database home page take the Server tab and then the Tablespaces link in the Storage section. Figure 7-4 shows the result for the default database.

FIGURE 7-4

The tablespaces
in the default
ORCL database

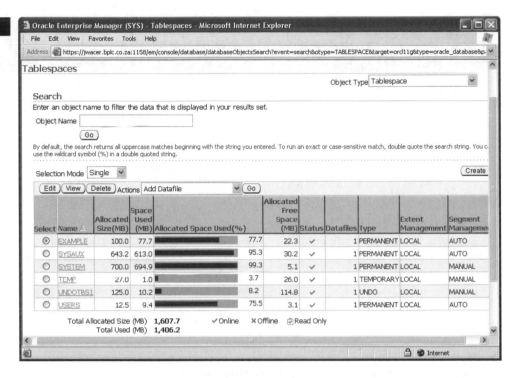

There are six tablespaces shown in the figure. For each tablespace, identified by
name, the window shows:

- **Allocated size** This is the current size of the datafile(s) assigned to the
  tablespace. It is based on the current size, not the maximum size to which it
  may be allowed to expand.
- **Space used** This is the space occupied by segments in the tablespace that
  cannot be reclaimed.
- **Allocated space used (%)** A graphical representation of the previous two
  figures.
- **Allocated free space** The space currently available within the tablespace.
- **Status** A green tick indicates that the tablespace is online, and therefore
  that the objects within it should be accessible. An offline tablespace would be
  indicated with a red cross.

- **Datafiles**   The number of datafiles (or tempfiles for temporary tablespaces, if one is being precise) that make up the tablespace.
- **Type**   The type of objects that can be stored in the tablespace. A permanent tablespace stores regular schema objects, such as tables and indexes. A temporary tablespace stores only system management temporary segments, and an undo tablespace stores only system-managed undo segments.
- **Extent management**   The technique used for allocating extents to segments. LOCAL is the default and should always be used.
- **Segment management**   The technique used for locating blocks into which insertions may be made. AUTO is the default and is recommended for all user data tablespaces.

This information could be also be gleaned by querying the data dictionary views DBA_TABLESPACES, DBA_DATA_FILES, DBA_SEGMENTS, and DB_FREE_SPACE as in this example:

```
SQL> select t.tablespace_name name, d.allocated, u.used, f.free,
  2  t.status, d.cnt, contents, t.extent_management extman,
  3  t.segment_space_management segman
  4  from dba_tablespaces t,
  5  (select sum(bytes) allocated, count(file_id) cnt from dba_data_files
  6  where tablespace_name='EXAMPLE') d,
  7  (select sum(bytes) free from dba_free_space
  8  where tablespace_name='EXAMPLE') f,
  9  (select sum(bytes) used from dba_segments
 10  where tablespace_name='EXAMPLE') u
 11  where t.tablespace_name='EXAMPLE';
```

NAME	ALLOCATED	USED	FREE	STATUS	CNT	CONTENTS	EXTMAN	SEGMAN
EXAMPLE	104857600	81395712	23396352	ONLINE	1	PERMANENT	LOCAL	AUTO

Click the Create button to create a tablespace. The Create Tablespace window prompts for a tablespace name, and the values for Extent Management, Type, and Status. In most circumstances, the defaults will be correct: Local, Permanent, and Read-Write. Then the Add button lets you specify one or more datafiles for the new tablespace. Each file must have a name and a size, and can optionally be set to *autoextend* up to a maximum file size. The autoextend facility will let Oracle increase the size of the datafile as necessary, which may avoid out-of-space errors.

Figures 7-5 and 7-6 show the windows for creating a tablespace NEWTS with one datafile.

Clicking the Show SQL button would display this command (the line numbers have been added manually):

```
1       CREATE SMALLFILE TABLESPACE "NEWTS"
2       DATAFILE 'D:\APP\ORACLE\ORADATA\ORCL11G\newts01.dbf'
3       SIZE 100M AUTOEXTEND ON NEXT 10M MAXSIZE 200M
4       LOGGING
5       EXTENT MANAGEMENT LOCAL
6       SEGMENT SPACE MANAGEMENT AUTO
7       DEFAULT NOCOMPRESS;
```

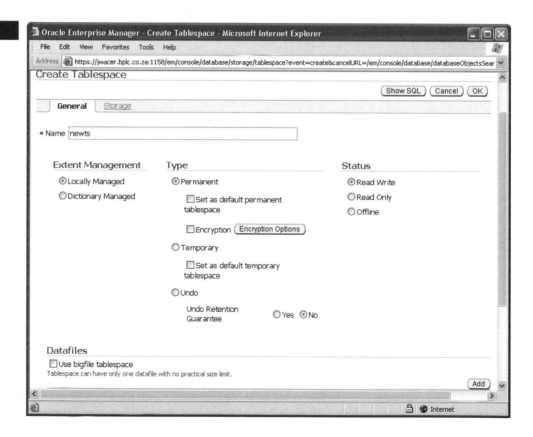

FIGURE 7-5

The Create Tablespace window

FIGURE 7-6

The Add Datafile
window

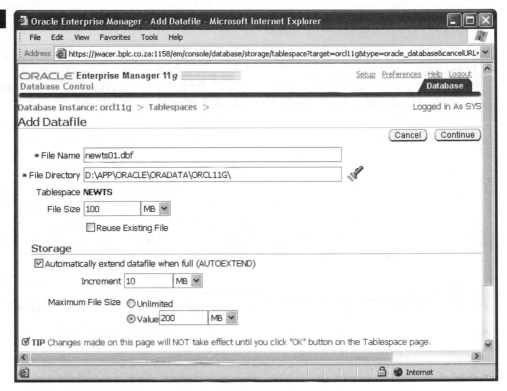

Taking this command line by line:

Line 1	The tablespace is a SMALLFILE tablespace. This means that it can consist of many datafiles. The alternative is BIGFILE, in which case it would be impossible to add a second datafile later (though the first file could be resized.) The Use Bigfile Tablespace check box in Figure 7-5 controls this.
Line 2	The datafile name and location.
Line 3	The datafile will be created as 100 MB but when full can automatically extend in 10 MB increments to a maximum of 200 MB. By default, automatic extension is not enabled.
Line 4	All operations on segments in the tablespace will generate redo; this is the default. It is possible to disable redo generation for a very few operations (such as index generation).
Line 5	The tablespace will use bitmaps for allocating extents; this is the default.
Line 6	Segments in the tablespace will use bitmaps for tracking block usage; this is the default.
Line 7	Segments in the tablespace will not be compressed; this is the default.

Taking the Storage tab shown in Figure 7-5 gives access to options for extent management and compression, as shown in Figure 7-7.

When using local extent management (as all tablespaces should), it is possible to enforce a rule that all extents in the tablespace should be the same size. This is discussed in the following section. If enabling compression, then it can be applied to data only when it is bulk-loaded, or as a part of all DML operations. If logging is disabled, this provides a default for the very few operations where redo generation can be disabled, such as index creation. Whatever setting is chosen, all DML operations will always generate redo.

on the job

All tablespaces should be locally managed. The older mechanism, known as dictionary managed, was far less efficient and is only supported (and only just) for backward compatibility. It has been possible to create locally managed tablespaces, and to convert dictionary-managed tablespaces to locally managed, since release 8i.

FIGURE 7-7

Further options for tablespace creation

Oracle Enterprise Manager - Create Tablespace - Mozilla Firefox

File   Edit   View   History   Bookmarks   Tools   Help

https://jwacer.bplc.co.za:1158/em/console/database/storage/ta | G▼ Google

General   **Storage**

Extent Allocation

⦿ Automatic
○ Uniform
   Size 160   MB ▾

Segment Space Management

⦿ Automatic

Objects in the tablespace automatically manage their free space. It offers high performance for free space management.

○ Manual

Objects in the tablespace will manage their free space using free lists. It is provided for backward compatibility.

Compression Options

Enabling data segment compression can reduce disk usage.

Compression   ⦿ Disabled
              ○ Enabled on direct-path INSERT operations only
              ○ Enabled on all operations

Enable logging

⦿ Yes

Generate redo logs for creation of tables, indexes and partitions, and for subsequent inserts. Recoverable

○ No

Done   jwacer.bplc.co.za:1158

A typical tablespace creation statement as executed from the SQL*Plus command line is shown in Figure 7-8, with a query confirming the result.

The tablespace GLTABS consists of two datafiles, neither of which will autoextend. The only deviation from defaults has been to specify a uniform extent size of 5 MB. The first query in the figure shows that the tablespace is not a bigfile tablespace; if it were, it would not have been possible to define two datafiles.

The second query in the figure investigates the TEMP tablespace, used by the database for storing temporary objects. It is important to note that temporary tablespaces use *tempfiles*, not datafiles. Tempfiles are listed in the views V$TEMPFILE and DBA_TEMP_FILES, whereas datafiles are listed in V$DATAFILE and DBA_DATA_FILES. Also note that the V$ views and the DBA views give different information. As the query shows, you can query V$TABLESPACE to find if a tablespace is a bigfile table and V$TEMPFILE (or V$DATAFILE) to find how big a file was at creation time. This information is not shown in the DBA views. However, the DBA views give the detail of extent management and segment space management. The different information available in the views is because some information is stored only in the controlfile (and therefore visible only in V$ views) and some is stored only in the data dictionary (and therefore visible only in DBA views). Other information is duplicated.

FIGURE 7-8	
Tablespace creation and verification with SQL*Plus	

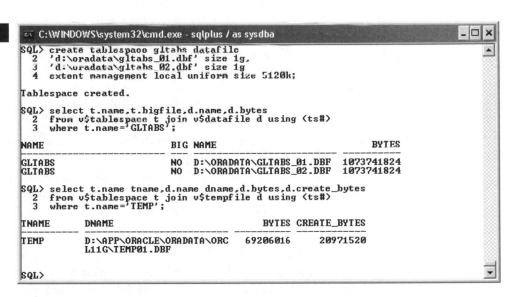

Altering Tablespaces

The changes made to tablespaces after creation are commonly

- Renaming
- Taking online and offline
- Flagging as read-write or read only
- Resizing
- Changing alert thresholds

Rename a Tablespace and Its Datafiles

The syntax is

```
ALTER TABLESPACE tablespaceoldname RENAME TO tablespacenewname;
```

This is very simple but can cause problems later. Many sites rely on naming conventions to relate tablespaces to their datafiles. All the examples in this chapter do just that: they embed the name of the tablespace in the name of the datafiles. Oracle doesn't care: internally, it maintains the relationships by using the tablespace number and the datafile (or tempfile) number. These are visible as the columns V$TABLESPACE.TS# and V$DATAFILE.FILE#. If your site does rely on naming conventions, then it will be necessary to rename the files as well. A tablespace can be renamed while it is in use, but to rename a datafile, the datafiles must be offline. This is because the file must be renamed at the operating system level, as well as within the Oracle environment, and this can't be done if the file is open: all the file handles would become invalid.

Figure 7-9 is an example of the whole process, using the tablespace created in Figure 7-8.

In the figure, the first command renames the tablespace. That's the easy part. Then the tablespace is taken offline (as described in the next section), and two operating system commands rename the datafiles in the file system. Two ALTER DATABASE commands change the filenames as recorded within the controlfile, so that Oracle will be able to find them. Finally the tablespace is brought back online.

Taking a Tablespace Online or Offline

An *online* tablespace or datafile is available for use; an *offline* tablespace or datafile exists as a definition in the data dictionary and the controlfile but cannot be used. It is possible for a tablespace to be online but one or more of its datafiles to be offline.

FIGURE 7-9

Renaming a tablespace and its datafiles

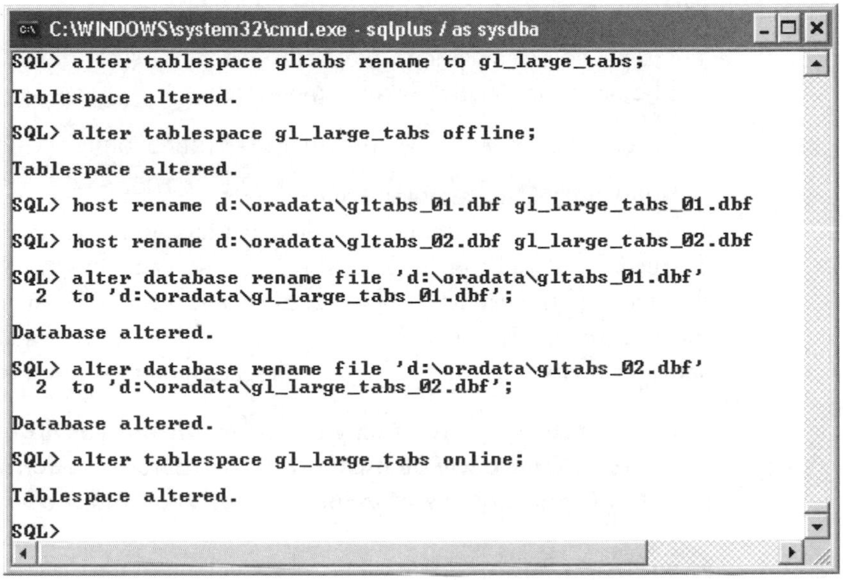

This is a situation that can produce interesting results and should generally be avoided. The syntax for taking a tablespace offline is

```
ALTER TABLESPACE tablespacename OFFLINE [NORMAL | IMMEDIATE | TEMPORARY];
```

A NORMAL offline (which is the default) will force a checkpoint for all the tablespace's datafiles. Every dirty buffer in the database buffer cache that contains a block from the tablespace will be written to its datafile, and then the tablespace and the datafiles are taken offline.

At the other extreme is IMMEDIATE. This offlines the tablespace and the datafiles immediately, without flushing any dirty buffers. Following this, the datafiles will be corrupted (they may be missing committed changes) and will have to be recovered by applying change vectors from the redo log before the tablespace can be brought back online. Clearly, this is a drastic operation. It would normally be done only if a file has become damaged so that the checkpoint cannot be completed. The process of recovery is detailed in Chapter 17.

A TEMPORARY offline will checkpoint all the files that can be checkpointed, and then take them and the tablespace offline in an orderly fashion. Any damaged file(s) will be offlined immediately. If just one of the tablespaces datafiles has been damaged, this will limit the number of files that will need to be recovered.

Mark a Tablespace as Read Only

To see the effect of making a tablespace read only, study Figure 7-10.

The syntax is completely self-explanatory:

```
ALTER TABLESPACE tablespacename [READ ONLY | READ WRITE];
```

Following making a tablespace read only, none of the objects within it can be changed with DML statements, as demonstrated in the figure. But they can be dropped. This is a little disconcerting but makes perfect sense when you think it through. Dropping a table doesn't actually affect the table. It is a transaction against the data dictionary, that deletes the rows that describe the table and its columns; the data dictionary is in the SYSTEM tablespace, and that is not read only.

Making a tablespace read only can have advantages for backup and restore operations. Oracle will be aware that the tablespace contents cannot change, and that it may not therefore be necessary to back it up repeatedly.

Resizing a Tablespace

A tablespace can be resized either by adding datafiles to it or by adjusting the size of the existing datafiles. The datafiles can be resized upward automatically as necessary if the AUTOEXTEND syntax was used at file creation time. Otherwise, you have to do it manually with an alter database command:

```
ALTER DATABASE DATAFILE filename RESIZE n[M|G|T];
```

FIGURE 7-10

Operations
on a read-only
tablespace

```
C:\WINDOWS\system32\cmd.exe - sqlplus / as sysdba                    _ □ ×
SQL>
SQL>
SQL> create table testtab(c1 date) tablespace gl_large_tabs;

Table created.

SQL> alter tablespace gl_large_tabs read only;

Tablespace altered.

SQL> insert into testtab values(sysdate);
insert into testtab values(sysdate)
                    *
ERROR at line 1:
ORA-00372: file 6 cannot be modified at this time
ORA-01110: data file 6: 'D:\ORADATA\GL_LARGE_TABS_01.DBF'


SQL> drop table testtab;

Table dropped.

SQL> _
```

The M, G, or T refer to the units of size for the file: megabytes, gigabytes, or terabytes. For example,

```
alter database datafile '/oradata/users02.dbf' resize 10m;
```

From the syntax, you do not know if the file is being made larger or smaller. An upward resize can only succeed if there is enough space in the file system, a resize downward can only succeed if the space in the file is not already in use by extents allocated to a segment.

To add another datafile of size two gigabytes to a tablespace:

```
alter tablespace gl_large_tabs
add datafile 'D:\ORADATA\GL_LARGE_TABS_03.DBF' size 2g;
```

Clauses for automatic extension can be included, or to enable automatic extension later use a command such as this:

```
alter database datafile 'D:\ORADATA\GL_LARGE_TABS_03.DBF'
autoextend on next 100m maxsize 4g;
```

This will allow the file to double in size, increasing 100 MB at a time.

Changing Alert Thresholds

The use of the server-generated alert system will be described in Chapter 13. For now it is only necessary to know that the MMON process of the instance monitors, in near real time, how full every tablespace is. If a tablespace fills up beyond a certain point, MMON will raise an alert. The default alert levels are to raise a warning alert when a tablespace is over 85 percent full, and a critical alert when it is over 97 percent full. The alerts can be seen in several ways, but the easiest is to look at the database home page of Database Control, where they are displayed in the Alerts section.

To view or change the alert levels, select the tablespace and click the Edit button, visible in Figure 7-4, then in the Edit Tablespace window take the Thresholds tab. Figure 7-11 shows this for the EXAMPLE tablespace.

In the figure, the "Available space" in the tablespace is reported as 32 GB. This is clearly incorrect, because the Allocated Space, as displayed in Figure 7-4, is only 100 MB. The answer lies in datafile autoextension. If AUTOEXTEND is enabled for a datafile and no MAXSIZE is specified, then the file can grow to a platform-dependent limit, in this case 32 GB. Of course, this says nothing about whether the file system has room for a file that size. The alert system uses the maximum possible

FIGURE 7-11

The alert thresholds for the EXAMPLE tablespace

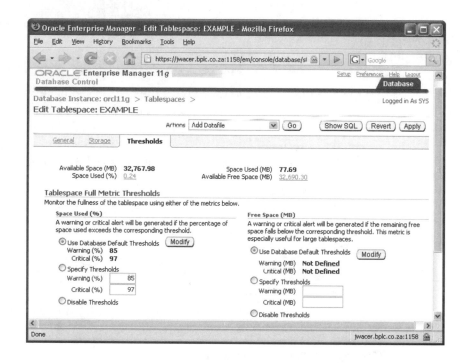

size of the tablespace as the basis for its calculations, which is meaningless if the tablespace's datafiles were created with the syntax AUTOEXTEND ON MAXSIZE UMLIMITED, or if a MAXSIZE was not specified.

It should be apparent that when using automatic extension, it is good practice to set a maximum limit. This can be done from the command line with an ALTER DATABASE command, or through Database Control. That having been done, use of Database Control to set thresholds is self-explanatory.

Dropping Tablespaces

To drop a tablespace, use the DROP TABLESPACE command. The syntax is

```
DROP TABLESPACE tablespacename
[INCLUDING CONTENTS [AND DATAFILES] ] ;
```

If the INCLUDING CONTENTS keywords are not specified, the drop will fail if there are any objects in the tablespace. Using these keywords instructs Oracle to drop the objects first, and then to drop the tablespace. Even this will fail in some circumstances, such as the tablespace containing a table that is the parent in a foreign key relationship with a table in another tablespace.

If the AND DATAFILES keywords are not specified, the tablespace and its contents will be dropped but the datafiles will continue to exist on disk. Oracle will know nothing about them anymore, and they will have to be deleted with operating system commands.

On Windows systems, you may find the datafiles are still there after using the INCLUDING CONTENTS AND DATAFILES clause. This is because of the way Windows flags files as "locked." It may be necessary to stop the Windows Oracle service (called something like OracleServiceORCL) before you can delete the files manually.

Oracle-Managed Files (OMF)

Use of OMF is intended to remove the necessity for the DBA to have any knowledge of the file systems. The creation of database files can be fully automated. To enable OMF, set some or all of these instance parameters:

```
DB_CREATE_FILE_DEST
DB_CREATE_ONLINE_LOG_DEST_1
DB_CREATE_ONLINE_LOG_DEST_2
DB_CREATE_ONLINE_LOG_DEST_3
DB_CREATE_ONLINE_LOG_DEST_4
DB_CREATE_ONLINE_LOG_DEST_5
DB_RECOVERY_FILE_DEST
```

The DB_CREATE_FILE_DEST parameter specifies a default location for all datafiles. The DB_CREATE_ONLINE_LOG_DEST_n parameters specify a default location for online redo log files. DB_RECOVERY_FILE_DEST sets up a default location for archive redo log files and backup files. As well as setting default file locations, OMF will generate filenames and (by default) set the file sizes. Setting these parameters can greatly simplify file-related operations. Having enabled OMF, it can always be overridden by specifying a datafile name on the CREATE TABLESPACE command.

EXERCISE 7-2

Create, Alter, and Drop Tablespaces

In this exercise, you will create tablespaces and change their characteristics. Then enable and use OMF. The exercise can be done through Database Control, but if so, be sure to click the Show SQL button at all stages to observe the SQL statements being generated.

1. Connect to the database as user SYSTEM.

2. Create a tablespace in a suitable directory—any directory on which the Oracle owner has write permission will do:

```
create tablespace newtbs
datafile '/home/db11g/oradata/newtbs_01.dbf' size 10m
extent management local autoallocate
segment space management auto;
```

This command specifies the options that are the default. Nonetheless, it may be considered good practice to do this, to make the statement self-documenting.

3. Create a table in the new tablespace, and determine the size of the first extent:

```
create table newtab(c1 date) tablespace newtbs;
select extent_id,bytes from dba_extents
where owner='SYSTEM' and segment_na me='NEWTAB';
```

4. Add extents manually, and observe the size of each new extent by repeatedly executing this command,

```
alter  table newtabs allocate extent;
```

followed by the query from Step 3. Note the point at which the extent size increases.

5. Take the tablespace offline, observe the effect, and bring it back online. This is shown in the accompanying illustration.

```
db11g@jwlnx1:~                                              _ □ X
SQL>
SQL> alter tablespace newtbs offline;

Tablespace altered.

SQL> insert into newtab values(sysdate);
insert into newtab values(sysdate)
                 *
ERROR at line 1:
ORA-00376: file 6 cannot be read at this time
ORA-01110: data file 6: '/home/db11g/oradata/newtbs_01.dbf'


SQL> alter tablespace newtbs online;

Tablespace altered.

SQL> insert into newtab values(sysdate);

1 row created.

SQL>
```

6. Make the tablespace read only, observe the effect, and make it read-write again. This is shown in the next illustration.

```
db11g@jwlnx1:~                                              _ □ X
SQL>
SQL> alter tablespace newtbs read only;

Tablespace altered.

SQL> insert into newtab values(sysdate);
insert into newtab values(sysdate)
                 *
ERROR at line 1:
ORA-00372: file 6 cannot be modified at this time
ORA-01110: data file 6: '/home/db11g/oradata/newtbs_01.dbf'


SQL> drop table newtab;

Table dropped.

SQL>  alter tablespace newtbs read write;

Tablespace altered.

SQL>
```

7. Enable OMF for datafile creation:

```
alter system set db_create_file_dest='/home/db11g/oradata';
```

8. Create a tablespace, using the minimum syntax now possible:

```
create tablespace omftbs;
```

9. Determine the characteristics of the OMF file:

```
select file_name,bytes,autoextensible,maxbytes,increment_by
from dba_data_files where tablespace_name='OMFTBS';
```

Note the file is initially 100MB, autoextensible, with no upper limit.

10. Adjust the OMF file to have more sensible characteristics. Use whatever system-generated filename was returned by Step 9:

```
alter database datafile
' /oradata/ORCL11G/datafile/o1_mf_omftbs_3olpn462_.dbf'
resize 500m;
alter database datafile
'/home/db11g/oradata/ORCL11G/datafile/o1_mf_omftbs_3olpn462_.dbf'
autoextend on next 100m maxsize 2g;
```

11. Drop the tablespace, and use an operating system command to confirm that the file has indeed gone:

```
drop tablespace omftbs including contents and datafiles;
```

CERTIFICATION OBJECTIVE 7.03

Manage Space in Tablespaces

Space management occurs at several levels. First, space is assigned to a tablespace. This is done by sizing the datafiles, as already described. Second, space within a tablespace is assigned to segments. This is done by allocating extents. Third, space within a segment is assigned to rows. This is done by maintaining bitmaps that track how much space is free in each block.

Extent Management

The extent management method is set per tablespace and applies to all segments in the tablespace. There are two techniques for managing extent usage: *dictionary management* or *local management*. The difference is clear: local management should always be used; dictionary management should never be used. Dictionary-managed extent management is still supported, but only just. It is a holdover from previous releases.

Dictionary extent management uses two tables in the data dictionary. SYS.UET$ has rows describing used extents, and SYS.FET$ has rows describing free extents. Every time the database needs to allocate an extent to a segment, it must search FET$ to find an appropriate bit of free space, and then carry out DML operations against FET$ and UET$ to allocate it to the segment. This mechanism causes bad problems with performance, because all space management operations in the database (many of which could be initiated concurrently) must serialize on the code that constructs the transactions.

Local extent management was introduced with release 8*i* and became default with release 9*i*. It uses bitmaps stored in each datafile. Each bit in the bitmap covers a range of blocks, and when space is allocated, the appropriate bits are changed from zero to one. This mechanism is far more efficient than the transaction-based mechanism of dictionary management. The cost of assigning extents is amortized across bitmaps in every datafile that can be updated concurrently, rather than being concentrated (and serialized) on the two tables.

When creating a locally managed tablespace, an important option is *uniform size*. If uniform is specified, then every extent ever allocated in the tablespace will be that size. This can make the space management highly efficient, because the block ranges covered by each bit can be larger: only one bit per extent. Consider this statement:

```
create tablespace large_tabs datafile 'large_tabs_01.dbf' size 10g
extent management local uniform size 160m;
```

Every extent allocated in this tablespace will be 160 MB, so there will be about 64 of them. The bitmap needs only 64 bits, and 160 MB of space can be allocated by updating just one bit. This is going to be very efficient—provided that the segments in the tablespace are large. If a segment were created that only needed space for a few rows (such as the HR.REGIONS table), it would still get an extent of 160 MB. Small objects need their own tablespace:

```
create tablespace small_tabs datafile 'small_tabs_01.dbf' size 1g
extent management local uniform size 160k;
```

The alternative (and default) syntax would be

```
create tablespace any_tabs datafile 'any_tabs_01.dbf' size 10g
extent management local autoallocate;
```

When segments are created in this tablespace, Oracle will allocate a 64 KB extent. As a segment grows and requires more extents, Oracle will allocate extents of 64 KB up to 16 extents, from which it will allocate progressively larger extents. Thus fast-growing segments will tend to be given space in ever-increasing chunks.

on the

Oracle Corporation recommends AUTOALLOCATE, but if you know how big segments are likely to be and can place them accordingly, UNIFORM SIZE may well be the best option. Many applications are designed in this manner.

It is possible that if a database has been upgraded from previous versions, it will include dictionary-managed tablespaces. Check this with this query:

```
select tablespace_name, extent_management from dba_tablespaces;
```

Any dictionary-managed tablespaces should be converted to local management with this PL/SQL procedure call:

```
execute dbms_space_admin.tablespace_migragte_to_local('tablespacename');
```

on the

Converting tablespaces to local management is quick and easy, except for the SYSTEM tablespace, where some extra steps are required. These are well documented in the System Administrator's guide of the product documentation.

Segment Space Management

The segment space management method is set per tablespace and applies to all segments in the tablespace. There are two techniques for managing segment space usage: *manual* or *automatic*. The difference is clear: automatic management should always be used; manual management should never be used. Manual segment space management is still supported but never recommended. It is a holdover from previous releases.

Automatic segment space management was introduced with release 9*i* and has become default with release 11*g*. Every segment created in an automatic management tablespace has a set of bitmaps that describe how full each block is. There are five bitmaps for each segment, and each block will appear on exactly one bitmap. The bitmaps track the space used in bands: there is a bitmap for full blocks;

and there are bitmaps for blocks that are 75 percent to 100 percent used, 50 percent to 75 percent used, 25 percent to 50 percent used, and 0 percent to 25 percent used. When searching for a block into which to insert a row, the session server process will look at the size of the row to determine which bitmap to search. For instance, if the block size is 4 KB and the row to be inserted is 1500 bytes, an appropriate block will be found by searching the 25 percent to 50 percent bitmap. Every block on this bitmap is guaranteed to have at least 2 KB of free space. As rows are inserted, are deleted, or change size through updates, the bitmaps get updated accordingly.

The old manual space management method used a simple list, known as the *free list,* which stated which blocks were available for insert but without any information on how full they were. This method could cause excessive activity, as blocks had to be tested for space at insert time, and often resulted in a large proportion of wasted space.

To see if any tablespaces are using manual management, run this query:

```
select tablespace_name,segment_space_management from dba_tablespaces;
```

It is not possible to convert tablespace from manual to automatic segment space management. The only solution is to create a new tablespace using automatic segment space management, move the segments into it (at which point the bitmap will be generated), and drop the old tablespaces.

EXERCISE 7-3

Change Tablespace Characteristics

In this exercise, you will create a tablespace using the non-default manual space management, to simulate the need to convert to automatic segment space management after an upgrade.

1. Connect to your database as user SYSTEM.
2. Create a tablespace using manual segment space management. As OMF was enabled in Exercise 7-2, there is no need for any datafile clause:

   ```
   create tablespace manualsegs segment space management manual;
   ```

3. Confirm that the new tablespace is indeed using the manual technique:

   ```
   select segment_space_management from dba_tablespaces
   where tablespace_name='MANUALSEGS';
   ```

4. Create a table and an index in the tablespace:

```
create table mantab (c1 number) tablespace manualsegs;
create index mantabi on mantab(c1) tablespace manualsegs;
```

These segments will be created with freelists, not bitmaps.

5. Create a new tablespace that will (by default) use automatic segment space management:

```
create tablespace autosegs;
```

6. Move the objects into the new tablespace:

```
alter table mantab move tablespace autosegs;
alter index mantabi rebuild online tablespace autosegs;
```

7. Confirm that the objects are in the correct tablespace:

```
select tablespace_name from dba_segments
where segment_name like 'MANTAB%';
```

8. Drop the original tablespace:

```
drop tablespace manualsegs including contents and datafiles;
```

9. Rename the new tablespace to the original name. This is often necessary, because some application software checks tablespaces names:

```
alter tablespace autosegs rename to manualsegs;
```

10. Tidy up by dropping the tablespace, first with this command:

```
drop tablespace manualsegs;
```

Note the error caused by the tablespace not being empty, and fix it:

```
drop tablespace manualsegs including contents and datafiles;
```

INSIDE THE EXAM

Managing Database Storage Structures

It is essential to be absolutely clear on the Oracle storage model: the abstraction of logical storage from physical, which means there is no direct relationship between a table (or any other segment type) and a datafile. Space management is much simpler with the current release than with earlier releases and can indeed be completely automated by using OMF. All that is ever needed, once the parameters have been set, is the simple command:

```
CREATE TABLESPACE tablespacename;
```

and then let Oracle get on with it. The use of bitmaps for extent management and for space management within segments is a huge performance enhancement over earlier releases. The previous techniques are only supported for backward compatibility; converting existing storage structures to the newer methods is possible.

Database Control includes excellent graphical tools for managing tablespaces and datafiles, but for reporting purposes it will usually be necessary to query data dictionary and dynamic performance views.

CERTIFICATION SUMMARY

The relational database paradigm requires a separation of logical storage, as seen by the programmers, from the physical storage seen by the system administrators. Oracle implements this with tablespaces. Within a tablespace, the segments are made of extents that are made up of Oracle blocks.

The current techniques of managing space with bitmaps, both for allocating extents to segments and for identifying blocks within a segment that are suitable for row insertion, are far superior to earlier techniques and should always be used. Combined with OMF and ASM, they can make space management completely automatic.

✓ TWO-MINUTE DRILL

Understand Tablespaces and Datafiles

- ❏ One tablespace can be many datafiles.
- ❏ One tablespace can have many segments.
- ❏ One segment is one or more extents.
- ❏ One extent is many consecutive blocks, in one datafile.
- ❏ One Oracle block should be one or more operating system blocks.
- ❏ The Oracle block is the granularity of database I/O.

Create and Manage Tablespaces

- ❏ SMALLFILE tablespace can have many datafiles, but a BIGFILE tablespace can have only one.
- ❏ Tablespaces default to local extent management, automatic segment space management, but not to a uniform extent size.
- ❏ OMF datafiles are automatically named, initially 100 MB, and can autoextend without limit.
- ❏ A tablespace that contains segments cannot be dropped, unless an INCLUDING DATAFILES clause is specified.
- ❏ Tablespaces can be online or offline, read-write or read only.
- ❏ Tablespaces can store three types of object: permanent objects, temporary objects, or undo segments.

Manage Space in Tablespaces

- ❏ Local extent management tracks extent allocation with bitmaps in each datafile.
- ❏ The UNIFORM SIZE clause when creating a tablespace forces all extents to be the same size.
- ❏ The AUTOALLOCATE clause lets Oracle determine the next extent size, which is based on how many extents are being allocated to a segment.
- ❏ Automatic segment space management tracks the free space in each block of an extent using bitmaps.
- ❏ It is possible to convert a tablespace from dictionary extent management to local extent management, but not from freelist segment management to automatic management.

SELF TEST

Understand Tablespace and Datafiles

1. Examine the exhibit:

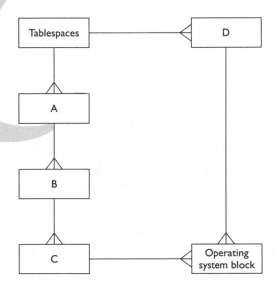

The exhibit shows the Oracle storage model, with four entities having letters for names. Match four of the following entities to the letters A, B, C, D:

DATAFILE
EXTENT
ORACLE BLOCK
ROW
SEGMENT
TABLE

2. What statements are correct about extents? (Choose all correct answers.)

    A. An extent is a grouping of several Oracle blocks.

    B. An extent is a grouping of several operating system blocks.

    C. An extent can be distributed across one or more datafiles.

    D. An extent can contain blocks from one or more segments.

    E. An extent can be assigned to only one segment.

3. Which of these are types of segment? (Choose all correct answers.)

    A. Sequence

    B. Stored procedure

    C. Table

    D. Table partition

    E. View

Create and Manage Tablespaces

4. If a tablespace is created with this syntax:

    ```
    create tablespace tbs1 datafile 'tbs1.dbf' size 10m;
    ```

    which of these characteristics will it have? (Choose all correct answers.)

    A. The datafile will autoextend, but only to double its initial size.

    B. The datafile will autoextend with MAXSIZE UNLIMITED.

    C. The extent management will be local.

    D. Segment space management will be with bitmaps.

    E. The file will be created in the DB_CREATE_FILE_DEST directory.

5. How can a tablespace be made larger? (Choose all correct answers.)

    A. Convert it from a SMALLFILE tablespace to a BIGFILE tablespace.

    B. If it is a SMALLFILE tablespace, add files.

    C. If it is a BIGFILE tablespace, add more files.

    D. Resize the existing file(s).

6. Which of these commands can be executed against a table in a read-only tablespace? (Choose the best answer.)

    A. DELETE

    B. DROP

    C. INSERT

    D. TRUNCATE

    E. UPDATE

7. What operation cannot be applied to a tablespace after creation? (Choose the best answer.)

- **A.** Convert from dictionary extent management to local extent management.
- **B.** Convert from manual segment space management to automatic segment space management.
- **C.** Change the name of the tablespace.
- **D.** Reduce the size of the datafile(s) assigned to the tablespace.
- **E.** All the above operations can be applied.

Manage Space in Tablespaces

8. By default, what thresholds are set for space warnings on a tablespace? (Choose the best answer.)

- **A.** 85 percent and 97 percent.
- **B.** This will depend on whether AUTOEXTEND has been enabled.
- **C.** This will depend on whether it is a SMALLFILE or a BIGFILE tablespace.
- **D.** By default, no warnings are enabled.

9. When the database is in mount mode, what views must be queried to find what datafiles and tablespaces make up the database? (Choose all correct answers.)

- **A.** DBA_DATA_FILES
- **B.** DBA_TABLESPACES
- **C.** DBA_TEMP_FILES
- **D.** V$DATABASE
- **E.** V$DATAFILE
- **F.** V$TABLESPACE

10. Which views could you query to find out about the temporary tablespaces and the files that make them up? (Choose all correct answers.)

- **A.** DBA_DATA_FILES
- **B.** DBA_TABLESPACES
- **C.** DBA_TEMP_TABLESPACES
- **D.** DBA_TEMP_FILES
- **E.** V$DATAFILE
- **F.** V$TABLESPACE
- **G.** V$TEMPTABLESPACE
- **H.** V$TEMPFILE

LAB QUESTION

Create a tablespace with one datafile. Use a uniform extent size of 64 KB. Create two tables in this tablespace, and manually allocate a few extents to each in turn. Run a query to find the exact physical locations of each table: you will see that they are interleaved. Add a second datafile to the tablespace, and allocate a few more extents. Rerunning the query should demonstrate that Oracle is bringing the new file into use.

This exercise can all be done with SQL*Plus if you wish, but Database Control does have a nice graphical representation of the physical placement of a table. To reach this, from the database home page take the Server tab and the Tablespaces link in the Storage section. Select the tablespace, and click the View button. Then in the Actions drop-down box choose Show Tablespace Contents and click the Go button. Expand the "Extent Map" and (at last . . .) you will see the representation of where the extents for the tables are.

If you use Database Control for the whole exercise, be sure to click Show SQL at all points to see the code begin generated.

SELF TEST ANSWERS

Understand Tablespace and Datafiles

1. ☑ **A** is SEGMENT, **B** is EXTENT, **C** is ORACLE BLOCK, **D** is DATAFILE.
   ☒ Neither ROW nor TABLE are included in the model.

2. ☑ **A** and **E.** One extent is several consecutive Oracle blocks, and one segment consists of one or more extents.
   ☒ **B, C,** and **D** are all wrong because they misinterpret the Oracle storage model.

3. ☑ **C** and **D.** A table can be type of segment, as is a table partition (in which case the table itself will not be a segment).
   ☒ **A, B,** and **E** are wrong because they exist only as objects defined within the data dictionary. The data dictionary itself is a set of segments.

Create and Manage Tablespaces

4. ☑ **C** and **D.** With release 11g, local extent management and automatic segment space management are enabled by default.
   ☒ **A** and **B** are both wrong because by default autoextension is disabled. **E** is wrong because providing a filename will override the OMF mechanism.

5. ☑ **B** and **D.** A small file tablespace can have many files, and all datafiles can be resized upward.
   ☒ **A** is wrong because you cannot convert between SMALLFILE and a BIGFILE. **C** is wrong because a BIGFILE tablespace can have only one file.

6. ☑ **B.** Objects can be dropped from read-only tablespaces.
   ☒ **A, C, D,** and **E.** All of these commands will fail because they require writing to the table, unlike a DROP, which only writes to the data dictionary.

7. ☑ **B.** It is not possible to change the segment space management method after creation.
   ☒ **A** and **C** are wrong because a tablespace can be converted to local extent management or renamed at any time. **D** is wrong because a datafile can be resized downward, though only if the space to be freed up has not already been used. **E** is wrong because you cannot change the segment space management without re-creating the tablespace.

Manage Space in Tablespaces

8. ☑ **A.** 85 percent and 97 percent are the database-wide defaults applied to all tablespaces.
   ☒ **B** is wrong because AUTOEXTEND does not affect the warning mechanism (though it may make it pointless). **C** is wrong because the warning mechanism considers only the tablespace, not the files. **D** is wrong because by default the space warning is enabled.

9. ☑ **D** and **E.** Joining these views will give the necessary information.
   ☒ **A** and **B** are wrong because these views will not be available in mount mode. **C** is wrong because there is no relevant information in V$DATABASE.

10. ☑ **B, D, F,** and **H.** V$TABLESPACE and DBA_TABLESPACE will list the temporary tablespaces, and V$TEMPFILE and DBA_TEMP_FILES will list their files.
    ☒ **A** and **E** are wrong because V$DATAFILE and DBA_DATA_FILES do not include tempfiles. **C** and **G** are wrong because there are no views with these names.

LAB ANSWER

A possible solution using SQL*Plus is

```
create tablespace labtbs datafile 'labtbs_01.dbf' size 10m uniform size 64k;
create table tab1(c1 date) tablespace labtbs;
create table tab2 tablespace labtbs as select * from tab1;
alter table tab1 allocate extent;
alter table tab2 allocate extent;
alter table tab1 allocate extent;
alter table tab2 allocate extent;
select segment_name,file_id,extent_id,block_id,blocks from dba_extents
where tablespace_name='LABTBS';
alter tablespace labtbs add datafile 'labtbs_02.dbf' size 10m;
alter table tab1 allocate extent;
alter table tab2 allocate extent;
select segment_name,file_id,extent_id,block_id,blocks from dba_extents
where tablespace_name='LABTBS';
```

The illustration that follows shows Database Control's graphical representation of the layout of extent map. The used extents are in two groups (at the beginning of the tablespace and more in the middle) because the tablespace is two datafiles, and both are being used.

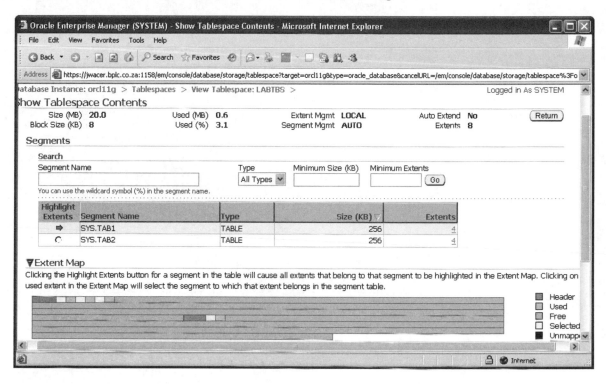

8
Administering User Security

W hen a user logs on to the database, following some means of identification he/she connects to a *user account*. The user account defines his/her initial access permissions and the attributes of the session. Associated with a user account is a *schema*. The terms "user," "user account," and "schema" can often be used interchangeably in the Oracle environment, but they are not always the same thing. A user is a person who connects to a user account by establishing a session against the instance and logging on with the user account name. A schema is a set of objects owned by a user account, and is described in Chapter 9.

There are many facilities for enforcing security within an Oracle database. This chapter deals with those related to user accounts—some others are dealt with in Chapter 12. A user account must be granted privileges before a session (or sessions) connected to the account can do anything. There are many different privileges that can be granted for many different objects and actions, and to manage privileges individually is not practical for any but the simplest systems. Privileges are usually grouped into roles, which make privilege administration much easier.

Finally, this chapter looks at profiles. Profiles can be used to manage passwords and (to limited extent) control the resources that a user is allowed to take up within the instance and the database.

CERTIFICATION OBJECTIVE 8.01

Create and Manage Database User Accounts

To establish a session against an instance and a database, a user must connect to a user account. The account must be specified by name and authenticated by some means. The way the account was created will set up a range of attributes for the session, some of which can be changed later while the session is in progress. There are a number of accounts created at database creation time, and the DBA will usually create many more subsequently.

In some applications, each user will have his/her own database user account. This means that the database is fully aware to whom each session really belongs. This security model works well for small applications but is often impractical for larger systems with many hundreds or thousands of users. For large systems, many users will connect to the same account. This model relies on the application to map the real end user to a database user account, and it can make session-level security and auditing more complex. This chapter assumes that every user is known to the database; they all have their own user accounts.

User Account Attributes

A user account has a number of attributes defined at account creation time. These will be applied to sessions that connect to the account, though some can be modified by the session or the DBA while the session is running. These attributes are

- Username
- Authentication method
- Default tablespace
- Tablespace quotas
- Temporary tablespace
- User profile
- Account status

All of these should be specified when creating the user, though only username and authentication methods are mandatory; the others have defaults.

Username

The username must be unique in the database and must conform to certain rules. A username must begin with a letter, must be no more than 30 characters, and can consist of only letters, digits, and the characters dollar ($) and underscore ( ). A user name may not be a reserved word. The letters are case sensitive but will be automatically converted to uppercase. All these rules (with the exception of the length) can be broken if the username is specified within double quotes, as shown on Figure 8-1.

In the first example in the figure, a username JOHN is created. This was entered in lowercase, but will have been converted to uppercase, as can be seen in the first query. The second example uses double quotes to create the user with a name in lowercase. The third and fourth examples use double quotes to bypass the rules on characters and reserved words; both of these would fail without the double quotes. If a username includes lowercase letters or illegal characters or is a reserved word, then double quotes must always be used to connect to the account subsequently.

FIGURE 8-1

How to create
users with non-
standard names

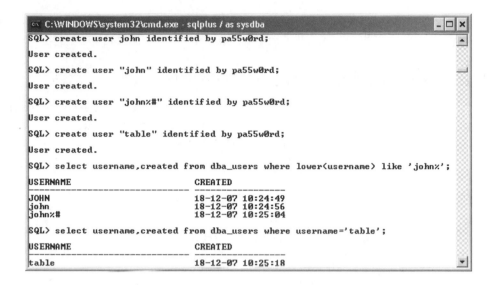

```
C:\WINDOWS\system32\cmd.exe - sqlplus / as sysdba                        _ □ x
SQL> create user john identified by pa55w0rd;
User created.
SQL> create user "john" identified by pa55w0rd;
User created.
SQL> create user "john%#" identified by pa55w0rd;
User created.
SQL> create user "table" identified by pa55w0rd;
User created.
SQL> select username,created from dba_users where lower(username) like 'john%';

USERNAME                       CREATED
------------------------------ ------------------
JOHN                           18-12-07 10:24:49
john                           18-12-07 10:24:56
john%#                         18-12-07 10:25:04
SQL> select username,created from dba_users where username='table';

USERNAME                       CREATED
------------------------------ ------------------
table                          18-12-07 10:25:18
```

on the **job**

It is possible to use non-standard usernames, but this may cause dreadful confusion. Some applications rely on the case conversion; others always use double quotes. It may be considered good practice always to use uppercase and only the standard characters; this means that double quotes can be used or not.

A username can never be changed after creation. If it is necessary to change it, the account must be dropped and another account created. This is a drastic action, because all the objects in the user's schema will be dropped along with the user.

Default Tablespace and Quotas

Every user account has a *default tablespace*. This is the tablespace where any schema objects (such as tables or indexes) created by the user will reside. It is possible for a user to own objects in any tablespace on which he has been given a quota, but unless another tablespace is specified when creating the object, it will go into the user's default tablespace.

There is a database-wide default tablespace that will be applied to all user accounts if a default tablespace is not specified when creating the user. The default can be set when creating the database and changed later with

```
ALTER DATABASE DEFAULT TABLESPACE tablespace_name ;
```

If a default tablespace is not specified when creating the database, it will be set to the SYSTEM tablespace.

on the !
j o b

After creating a database, do not leave the default tablespace as SYSTEM; this is very bad practice. Either change it as soon as you have created another tablespace, or after the CREATE DATABASE command has in fact let you create a default tablespace.

A *quota* is the amount of space in a tablespace that a user is allowed to occupy. He can create objects and allocate extents to them until the quota is reached. If he has no quota on a tablespace, he cannot create any objects at all. Quotas can be changed at any time. If a user's quota is reduced below the size of the objects he already owns (or even reduced to zero), the objects will survive and will still be usable, but they will not be permitted to get any bigger.

Figure 8-2 shows how to investigate and set quotas.

The first query in the figure is against DBA_USERS and determines the default and temporary tablespaces for the user JOHN, created in Figure 8-1. DBA_USERS has one row for every user account in the database. User JOHN has picked up the database defaults for the default and temporary tablespaces, which are shown in the last query against DATABASE_PROPERTIES.

FIGURE 0-2

Managing user quotas

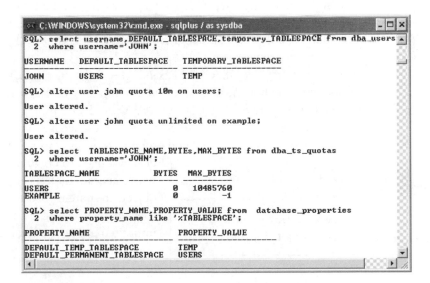

ⓦatch   *Before you can create a table, you must have both permission to execute CREATE TABLE and a quota on a tablespace in which to create it.*

The two ALTER USER commands in Figure 8-2 give JOHN the capability to take up to 10 MB of space in the USERS tablespace, and an unlimited amount of space in the EXAMPLE tablespace. The query against DBA_TS_QUOTAS confirms this; the figure "–1" is how "unlimited" is represented. At the time the query was run JOHN had not created any objects, so the figures for BYTES are zeros, indicating that he is not currently using any space in either tablespace.

on the
ⓘob   *Most users will not need any quotas, because they will never create objects. They will only have permissions against objects owned by other schemas. The few object-owning schemas will probably have QUOTA UNLIMITED on the tablespaces where their objects reside.*

Temporary Tablespace

Permanent objects (such as tables) are stored in permanent tablespaces; temporary objects are stored in temporary tablespaces. A session will need space in a temporary tablespace if it needs space for certain operations that exceed the space available in the session's PGA. Remember that the PGA is the program global area, the private memory allocated to the session. Operations that need temporary space (in memory if possible, in a temporary tablespace if necessary) include sorting rows, joining tables, building indexes, and using temporary tables. Every user account is assigned a temporary tablespace, and all user sessions connecting to the account will share this temporary tablespace.

The query against DBA_USERS in Figure 8-2 shows user JOHN's temporary tablespace, which is the database default temporary tablespace. This is shown by the last query in Figure 8-2, against DATABASE_PROPERTIES.

Space management within a temporary tablespace is completely automatic. Temporary objects are created and dropped as necessary by the database. A user does not need to be granted a quota on his/her temporary tablespace. This is because the objects in it are not actually owned by him/her; they are owned by the SYS user, who has an unlimited quota on all tablespaces.

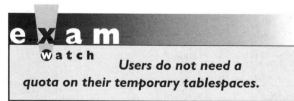

ⓦatch   *Users do not need a quota on their temporary tablespaces.*

To change a user's temporary tablespace (which will affect all future sessions that connect to the account), use an ALTER USER command:

```
ALTER USER username TEMPORARY TABLESPACE tablespace_name;
```

on the Job

If many users are logging on to the same user account, they will share use of one temporary tablespace. This can be a performance bottleneck, which may be avoided by using temporary tablespace groups.

Profile

A user's profile controls his/her password settings and gives a limited amount of control over his/her resource usage. Use of profiles is detailed in the later section Create and Manage Profiles.

Profiles are a useful way of managing passwords and resources but can really only apply in an environment where every application user has his/her own database user account. For example, if many users connect to the same database user account, you would not want the password to be invalidated by one of them, because that would lock out everyone else. Similarly, resource usage will often need to be managed on a per-session basis rather than for the account as a whole.

Account Status

Every user account has a certain status, as listed in the ACCOUNT_STATUS column of DBA_USERS. There are nine possibilities:

- ■ **OPEN**   The account is available for use.
- ■ **LOCKED**   This indicates that the DBA deliberately locked the account. No user can connect to a locked account.
- ■ **EXPIRED**   This indicates that the lifetime has expired. Passwords can have a limited lifetime. No user can connect to an EXPIRED account until the password is reset.
- ■ **EXPIRED & LOCKED**   Not only has the account been locked, but its password has also expired.
- ■ **EXPIRED (GRACE)**   This indicates that the *grace period* is in effect. A password need not expire immediately when its lifetime ends; it may be configured with a grace period during which users connecting to the account have the opportunity to change the password.

- **LOCKED (TIMED)** This indicates that the account is locked because of failed login attempts. An account can be configured to lock automatically for a period after an incorrect password is presented a certain number of times.
- **EXPIRED & LOCKED (TIMED)**
- **EXPIRED (GRACE) & LOCKED**
- **EXPIRED (GRACE) & LOCKED (TIMED)**

To lock and unlock an account, use these commands:

```
ALTER USER username ACCOUNT LOCK ;
ALTER USER username ACCOUNT UNLOCK ;
```

To force a user to change his password, use this command:

```
ALTER USER username PASSWORD EXPIRE;
```

This will immediately start the grace period, forcing the user to change his/her password at his/her next login attempt (or one soon after). There is no such command as "alter...unexpire." The only way to make the account fully functional again is to reset the password.

Authentication Methods

A user account must have an authentication method: some means whereby the database can determine if the user attempting to create a session connecting to the account is allowed to do so. The simplest technique is by presenting a password that will be matched against a password stored within the database, but there are alternatives. The possibilities are

- Operating system authentication
- Password file authentication
- Password authentication
- External authentication
- Global authentication

The first two techniques are used only for administrators; the last requires an LDAP directory server. The LDAP directory server is the Oracle Internet Directory, shipped as a part of the Oracle Application Server.

Operating System and Password File Authentication

To enable operating system and password file authentication (the two go together) for an account, you must grant the user either the SYSDBA or the SYSOPER privilege:

```
GRANT [sysdba | sysoper ] TO username ;
```

Granting either (or both) of these privileges will copy the user's password from the data dictionary into the external password file, where it can be read by the instance even if the database is not open. It also allows the instance to authenticate users by checking whether the operating system user attempting the connection is a member of the operating system group that owns the Oracle Home installation. Following database creation, the only user with these privileges is SYS.

To use password file authentication, the user can connect with this syntax with SQL*Plus:

```
CONNECT username / password [@db_alias] AS [ SYSOPER | SYSDBA ] ;
```

Note that password file authentication can be used for a connection to a remote database over Oracle Net.

To use operating system authentication, the user can connect with this syntax with SQL*Plus:

```
CONNECT / AS [ SYSOPER | SYSDBA ] ;
```

The operating system password is not stored by Oracle, and therefore there are no issues with changing passwords.

The equivalent of these syntaxes is also available when connecting with Database Control, by selecting SYSDBA from the Connect As drop-down box on the Database Control login window. To determine to whom the SYSDBA and SYSOPER privileges have been granted, query the view V$PWFILE_USERS. Connection with operating system or password file authentication is always possible, no matter what state the instance and database are in, and is necessary to issue STARTUP or SHUTDOWN commands.

A third privilege that operates in the same manner as SYSDBA and SYSOPER is SYSASM. This is a privilege that is only applicable to ASM instances.

All user sessions must be authenticated. There is no such thing as an "anonymous" login, and some authentication method must be used.

Password Authentication

The syntax for a connection with password authentication using SQL*Plus is

```
CONNECT username / password [@db_alias] ;
```

Or with Database Control, select NORMAL from the Connect As drop-down box.

When connecting with password authentication, the instance will validate the password given against that stored with the user account in the data dictionary. For this to work, the database must be open; it is logically impossible to issue STARTUP or SHUTDOWN commands when connected with password authentication. The user SYS is not permitted to connect with password authentication; only password file, operating system, or LDAP authentication are possible for SYS.

User names are case sensitive but are automatically converted to uppercase unless specified within double quotes. In previous releases of the database, passwords were not case sensitive at all. With release 11g, passwords are case sensitive and there is no automatic case conversion. It is not necessary to use double quotes; the password will always be read exactly as entered.

When a connection is made across a network, release 11g will always encrypt it using the AES algorithm before transmission. To use encryption for the ongoing traffic between the user process and the server process requires the Advanced Security Option, but password encryption is standard.

Any user can change his/her user account password at any time, or a highly privileged user (such as SYSTEM) can change any user account password. The syntax (whether you are changing your own password or another one) is

```
ALTER USER username IDENTIFIED BY password ;
```

External Authentication

If a user account is created with external authentication, Oracle will delegate the authentication to an external service; it will not prompt for a password. If the Advanced Security Option has been licensed, then the external service can be a Kerberos server, a Radius server, or (in the Windows environment) the Windows native authentication service. When a user attempts to connect to the user account, rather than authenticating the user itself, the database instance will accept (or reject) the authentication according to whether the external authentication service has authenticated the user. For example, if using Kerberos, the database will check that the user does have a valid Kerberos token.

Without the Advanced Security Option, the only form of external authentication that can be used is operating system authentication. This is a requirement for

SYSDBA and SYSOPER accounts (as already discussed) but can also be used for normal users. The technique is to create an Oracle user account with the same name as the operating system user account but prefixed with a string specified by the instance parameter OS_AUTHENT_PREFIX. This parameter defaults to the string OPS$. To check its value, use a query such as

```
select value from v$parameter where name='os_authent_prefix';
```

On Linux or Unix, external operating system authentication is very simple. Assuming that the OS_AUTHENT_PREFIX is on default and that there is an operating system user called jwatson, then create an oracle user and grant him the CREATE SESSION privilege as follows:

```
create user ops$jwatson identified externally;
grant create session to ops$jwatson;
```

Any user logged on to Unix as jwatson will be able to issue this command:

```
sqlplus /
```

from an operating system prompt, and will be connected to the database user account ops$jwatson.

Under Windows, when Oracle queries the operating system to find the identity of the user, Windows will usually (depending on details of Windows security configuration) return the username prefixed with the Windows domain. Assuming that the Windows logon ID is John Watson (including a space) and that the Windows domain is JWACER (which happens to be the machine name) and that the OS_AUTHENT_PREFIX is on default, the command will be

```
create user "OPS$JWACER\JOHN WATSON" identified externally;
```

Note that the user name must be in uppercase, and because of the illegal characters (a backslash and a space) must be enclosed in double quotes.

on the Job *Using external authentication can be very useful, but only if the users actually log on to the machine hosting the database. Users will rarely do this, so the technique is more likely to be of value for accounts used for running maintenance or batch jobs.*

Global Authentication

An emerging standard for identity management is the use of LDAP servers. An LDAP-compliant directory server, the Oracle Internet Directory, is distributed by

Oracle Corporation as part of Oracle Application Server. A *global user* is a user who is defined within the LDAP directory, and *global authentication* is a means of delegating user authentication to the directory.

There are two techniques for global authentication:

■ The users can be defined in the directory, and also in the database. A user will be connected to a user account with the same name as the user's common name in the directory.

■ The users can be defined only in the directory. The database will be aware of the users' global names but connects all users to the same user account.

Neither of these techniques requires the user to present a password to the database. The connection will happen without any prompts if the directory accounts and the database user accounts are set up correctly.

Creating Accounts

The CREATE USER command has only two required arguments: a user name and a method of authentication. Optionally, it can accept a clause to specify a default tablespace and a temporary tablespace, one or more quota clauses, a named profile, and commands to lock the account and expire the password. A typical example (with line numbers added) would be

```
1     create user scott identified by tiger
2     default tablespace users temporary tablespace temp
3     quota 100m on users, quota unlimited on example
4     profile developer_profile
5     password expire
6     account unlock;
```

Only the first line is required; there are defaults for everything else. Taking the command line by line:

1. Provide the username, and a password for password authentication.
2. Provide the default and temporary tablespaces.
3. Set up quotas on the default and another tablespace.
4. Nominate a profile for password and resource management.
5. Force the user to change his password immediately.
6. Make the account available for use (which would have been the default).

Every attribute of an account can be adjusted later with ALTER USER commands, with the exception of the name. To change the password,

```
alter user scott identified by lion;
```

To change the default and temporary tablespaces,

```
alter user scott default tablespace hr_data temporary tablespace
hr_temp;
```

To change quotas,

```
alter user scott quota unlimited on hr_data, quota 0 on users;
```

To change the profile,

```
alter user scott profile prod_profile;
```

To force a password change,

```
alter user scott password expire;
```

To lock the account,

```
alter user scott account lock;
```

Having created a user account, it may be necessary to drop it:

```
drop user scott;
```

This command will only succeed if the user does not own any objects: if the schema is empty. If you do not want to identify all the objects owned and drop them first, they can be dropped with the user by specifying CASCADE:

```
drop user scott cascade;
```

To manage accounts with Database Control, from the database home page take the Schema tab and then the Users link in the Security section. This will show all the user accounts in the database. Figure 8-3 shows these sorted in reverse order of creation. To change the sort order click the appropriate column header.

The first "user" in the figure is PUBLIC. This is a notional user to whom privileges can be granted if you wish to grant them to every user. The Create button will present a window that prompts for all the user account attributes. The Delete button will drop an account, with the CASCADE option if necessary—but it will give an "Are you sure" prompt before proceeding.

FIGURE 8-3

Users shown by
Database Control

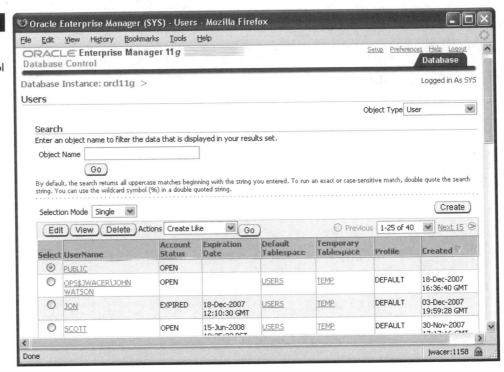

To adjust the attributes of an account, select it and click Edit. This will take you to the Edit User window, shown in Figure 8-4. This window can be used to change all aspects of the account except for tablespace quotas, which have their own tabs. It also has tabs for granting and revoking privileges and roles.

EXERCISE 8-1

Create Users

In this exercise, you will create some users to be used for the remaining exercises in this chapter. It is assumed that there is a permanent tablespace called EXAMPLE

FIGURE 8-4

The Edit User
Database Control
window

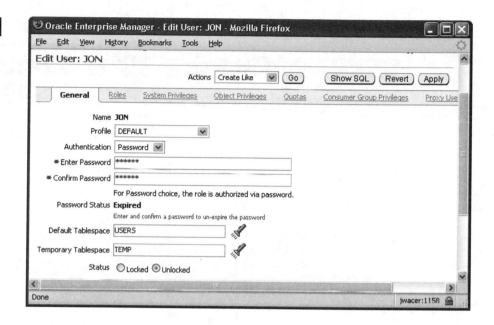

and a temporary tablespace called TEMP. If these don't exist, either create them or use any other suitable tablespaces.

1. Connect to your database with SQL*Plus as a highly privileged user, such as SYSTEM or SYS.

2. Create three users:

```
create user alois identified by alois
default tablespace example password expire;
create user afra identified by oracle;
default tablespace example quota unlimited on example;
create user anja identified by oracle;
```

3. Confirm that the users have been created with Database Control. From the database home page, the navigation path is the Server tab and the Users link

in the Security section. They should look something like those shown in this illustration:

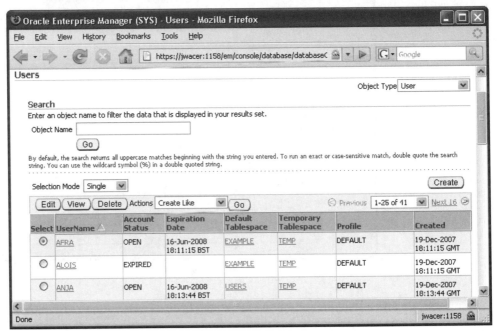

4. From SQL*Plus, attempt to connect as user ALOIS:

```
connect alois/alois
```

5. When prompted, select a new password (such as "oracle"). But it won't get you anywhere, because ALOIS does not have the CREATE SESSION privilege.

6. Refresh the Database Control window, and note that the status of the ALOIS account is no longer EXPIRED but OPEN, because his password has been changed.

Grant and Revoke Privileges

By default, no one can do anything in an Oracle database. A user cannot even connect without being granted a privilege. And once this has been done, he/she still can't do anything useful (or dangerous) without being given more privileges. Privileges are assigned to user accounts with a GRANT command and withdrawn with a REVOKE. Additional syntax can give a user the ability to grant any privileges he/she has to other users. By default only the DBAs (SYS and SYSTEM) have the right to grant any but the most limited privileges.

Privileges come in two groups: system privileges that (generally speaking) let users perform actions that affect the data dictionary and object privileges that let users perform actions that affect data.

System Privileges

There are about two hundred system privileges. Most apply to actions that affect the data dictionary, such as creating tables or users. Others affect the database or the instance, such as creating tablespaces, adjusting instance parameter values, or establishing a session. Some of the more commonly used privileges are

- **CREATE SESSION** This lets the user connect. Without this, he/she cannot even log on to the database.
- **RESTRICTED SESSION** If the database is started with STARTUP RESTRICT, or adjusted with ALTER SYSTEM ENABLE RESTRICTED SESSION, only users with this privilege will be able to connect.
- **ALTER DATABASE** Gives access to many commands necessary for modifying physical structures.
- **ALTER SYSTEM** Gives control over instance parameters and memory structures.
- **CREATE TABLESPACE** With the ALTER TABLESPACE and DROP TABLESPACE privileges, these will let a user manage tablespaces.
- **CREATE TABLE** Lets the grantee create tables in his/her own schema; includes the ability to alter and drop them, to run SELECT and DML commands on them, and to create, alter, or drop indexes on them.

- **GRANT ANY OBJECT PRIVILEGE**   Lets the grantee grant object permissions on objects he/she does not own to others—but not to himself/herself.
- **CREATE ANY TABLE**   The grantee can create tables that belong to other users.
- **DROP ANY TABLE**   The grantee can drop tables belonging to any other users.
- **INSERT ANY TABLE, UPDATE ANY TABLE, DELETE ANY TABLE**   The grantee can execute these DML commands against tables owned by all other users.
- **SELECT ANY TABLE**   The grantee can SELECT from any table in the database.

The syntax for granting system privileges is

```
GRANT privilege [, privilege...] TO username ;
```

After creating a user account, a command such as this will grant the system privileges commonly assigned to users who will be involved in developing applications:

```
grant create session, alter session,
create table, create view, create synonym, create cluster,
create database link, create sequence,
create trigger, create type, create procedure, create operator
to username ;
```

These privileges will let the user connect and configure his/her session, and then create objects to store data and PL/SQL objects. These objects can only exist in his/her own schema; he/she will have no privileges against any other schema. The object creation will also be limited by the quota(s) he/she may (or may not) have been assigned on various tablespaces.

A variation in the syntax lets the grantee pass his/her privilege on to a third party. For example:

```
connect system/oracle;
grant create table to scott with admin option;
connect scott/tiger;
grant create table to jon;
```

This gives SCOTT the ability to create tables in his own schema, and also to issue the GRANT command himself. In this example, he lets use JON create tables too— but JON will only be able to create them in the JON schema. Figure 8-5 shows the result of the grant as depicted by Database Control; the same information could be garnered by querying the view DBA_SYS_PRIVS.

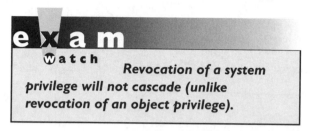

e x a m

ⓦ a t c h *Revocation of a system privilege will not cascade (unlike revocation of an object privilege).*

If a privilege is revoked from a user, any actions he/she performed using that privilege (such as creating tables) remain intact. Also, if he/she had been granted and had used the ADMIN OPTION, any users to whom he/she passed on the privilege will retain it. There is no record kept of the granter of a system privilege, so it is not possible for a REVOKE to cascade. Figure 8-6 illustrates this.

The ANY privileges give permissions against all relevant objects in the database. Thus,

```
grant select any table to scott;
```

FIGURE 8-6

GRANT and
REVOKE from
SQL*Plus

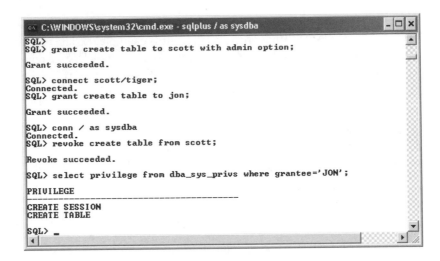

```
C:\WINDOWS\system32\cmd.exe - sqlplus / as sysdba                    _ □ ×
SQL>
SQL> grant create table to scott with admin option;

Grant succeeded.

SQL> connect scott/tiger;
Connected.
SQL> grant create table to jon;

Grant succeeded.

SQL> conn / as sysdba
Connected.
SQL> revoke create table from scott;

Revoke succeeded.

SQL> select privilege from dba_sys_privs where grantee='JON';

PRIVILEGE
----------------------------------------
CREATE SESSION
CREATE TABLE

SQL> _
```

will let SCOTT query every table in every schema in the database. It is often
considered bad practice to grant the ANY privileges to any user other than the
system administration staff.

on the job

*In fact, ANY is not as dangerous now as with earlier releases. It no longer
includes tables in the SYS schema, so the data dictionary is still protected. But
ANY should still be used with extreme caution, as it removes all protection
from user tables.*

Object Privileges

Object privileges give the ability to perform SELECT, INSERT, UPDATE, and
DELETE commands against tables and related objects, and to execute PL/SQL

objects. These privileges do not
exist for objects in the users'
own schemas; if a user has the
system privilege CREATE
TABLE, he/she can perform
SELECT and DML operations
against the tables he/she
creates with no further need for
permissions.

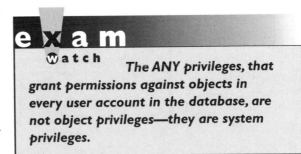

exam

Watch *The ANY privileges, that
grant permissions against objects in
every user account in the database, are
not object privileges—they are system
privileges.*

The object privileges apply to different types of object:

Privilege	Granted on
SELECT	Tables, views, sequences, synonyms
INSERT	Tables, views, synonyms
UPDATE	Tables, views, synonyms
DELETE	Tables, views, synonyms
ALTER	Tables, sequences
EXECUTE	Procedures, functions, packages, synonyms

The syntax is

```
GRANT privilege ON schema.object TO username [WITH GRANT OPTION] ;
```

For example,

```
grant select on hr.regions to scott;
```

Variations include the use of ALL, which will apply all the permissions relevant to the type of object, and nominating particular columns of view or tables:

```
grant select on hr.employees to scott;
grant update (salary) on hr.employees to scott;
grant all on hr.regions to scott;
```

This code will let SCOTT query all columns of HR's EMPLOYEES table but only write to one nominated column, SALARY. Then SCOTT is given all the object privileges (SELECT and DML) on HR's REGIONS table. Figure 8-7 shows the result of this, as viewed in Database Control.

on the **job** *Granting privileges at the column level is often said to be bad practice because of the massive workload involved. If it is necessary to restrict peoples' access to certain columns, creating a view that shows only those columns will often be a better alternative.*

Using WITH GRANT OPTION (or with Database Control, selecting the Grant Option check box shown in Figure 8-7) lets a user pass his/her object privilege on to a third party. Oracle retains a record of who granted object privileges to whom; this allows a REVOKE of an object to cascade to all those in the chain. Consider this sequence of commands:

FIGURE 8-7

Object privilege
management with
Database Control

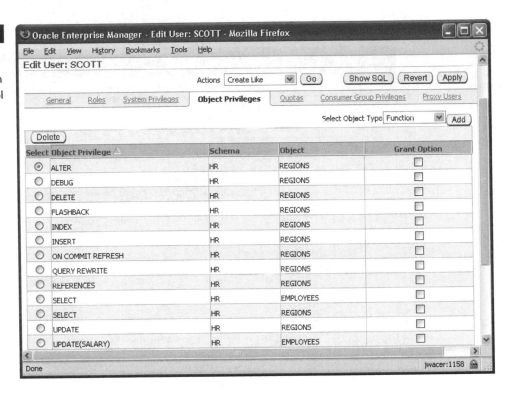

```
connect hr/hr;
grant select on employees to scott with grant option;
connect scott/tiger;
grant select on hr.employees to jon with grant option;
conn jon/jon;
grant select on hr.employees to sue;
connect hr/hr;
revoke select on employees from scott;
```

At the conclusion of these commands,
neither SCOTT nor JON nor SUE has the
SELECT privilege against HR.EMPLOYEES.

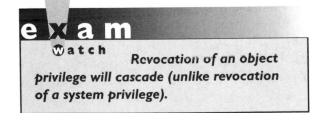

EXERCISE 8-2

Grant Direct Privileges

In this exercise, you will grant some privileges to the users created in Exercise 8-1 and prove that they work.

1. Connect to your database as user SYSTEM with SQL*Plus.
2. Grant CREATE SESSION to user ALOIS:

```
grant create sessions to alois;
```

3. Open another SQL*Plus session, and connect as ALOIS. This time, the login will succeed:

```
connect alois/oracle
```

4. As ALOIS, attempt to create a table:

```
create table t1 (c1 date);
```

This will fail with the message "ORA-01031: insufficient privileges."

5. In the SYSTEM session, grant ALOIS the CREATE TABLE privilege:

```
grant create table to alois;
```

6. In the ALOIS session, try again:

```
create table t1 (c1 date);
```

This will fail with the message "ORA-01950: no privileges on tablespace 'EXAMPLE'."

7. In the SYSTEM session, give ALOIS a quota on the EXAMPLE tablespace:

```
alter user alois quota 1m on example;
```

8. In the ALOIS session, try again. This time, the creation will succeed.
9. As ALOIS, grant object privileges on the new table:

```
grant all on t1 to afra;
grant select on t1 to anja;
```

10. Connect to Database Control as user SYSTEM.

11. Confirm that the object privileges have been granted. The navigation path from the database home page is: on the Schema tab click the Tables link in the Database Objects section. Enter **ALOIS** as the Schema and **T1** as the Table and click the Go button. In the Actions drop-down box, select Object Privileges. As shown in the next illustration, ANJA has only SELECT, but AFRA has everything. Note that the window also shows by whom the privileges were granted, and that none of them were granted WITH GRANT OPTION.

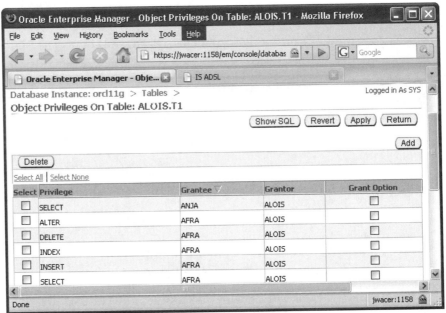

12. With Database Control, confirm which privileges have granted to ALOIS. The navigation path from the database home page is: on the Server tab click the Users link in the Security section. Select the radio button for ALOIS, and click the View button. You will see that he has two system privileges (CREATE SESSION and CREATE TABLE) without the ADMIN OPTION, a 1MB quota and EXAMPLE, and nothing else.

13. Retrieve the same information shown in Steps 11 and 12 with SQL*Plus. As SYSTEM, run these queries:

```
select grantee,privilege,grantor,grantable from dba_tab_privs
where owner='ALOIS' and table_name='T1';
select * from dba_sys_privs where grantee='ALOIS';
```

14. Revoke the privileges granted to AFRA and ANJA:

```
revoke all on alois.t1 from afra;
revoke all on alois.t1 from anja;
```

Confirm the revocations by rerunning the first query from Step 13.

CERTIFICATION OBJECTIVE 8.03

Create and Manage Roles

Managing security with directly granted privileges works but has two problems. First, it can be a huge workload: an application with thousands of tables and users could need millions of grants. Second, if a privilege has been granted to a user, that user has it in all circumstances: it is not possible to make a privilege active only in certain circumstances. Both these problems are solved by using *roles*. A role is a bundle of system and/or object privileges that can be granted and revoked as a unit, and having been granted can be temporarily activated or deactivated within a session.

Creating and Granting Roles

Roles are not schema objects: they aren't owned by anyone and so cannot be prefixed with a username. However, they do share the same namespace as users: it is not possible to create a role with the same name as an already-existing user, or a user with the same name as an already-existing role.

Create a role with the CREATE ROLE command:

```
CREATE ROLE rolename ;
```

Then grant privileges to the role with the usual syntax, including WITH ADMIN or WITH GRANT OPTION of desired.

For example, assume that the HR schema is being used as a repository for data to be used by three groups of staff: managerial staff have full access, senior clerical staff have limited access, junior clerical staff have very restricted access. First create a role that might be suitable for the junior clerk; all they can do is answer questions by running queries:

```
create role hr_junior;
grant create session to hr_junior;
```

```
grant select on hr.regions to hr_junior;
grant select on hr.locations to hr_junior;
grant select on hr.countries to hr_junior;
grant select on hr.departments to hr_junior;
grant select on hr.job_history to hr_junior;
grant select on hr.jobs to hr_junior;
grant select on hr.employees to hr_junior;
```

Anyone granted this role will be able to log on to the database and run SELECT statements against the HR tables. Then create a role for the senior clerks, who can also write data to the EMPLOYEES and JOB_HISTORY tables:

```
create role hr_senior;
grant hr_junior to hr_senior with admin option;
grant insert, update, delete on hr.employees to hr_senior;
grant insert, update, delete on hr.job_history to hr_senior;
```

This role is first granted the HR_JUNIOR role (there is no problem granting one role to another) with the syntax that will let the senior users assign the junior role to others. Then it is granted DML privileges on just two tables. Then create the manager's role, which can update all the other tables:

```
create role hr_manager;
grant hr_senior to hr_manager with admin option;
grant all on hr.regions to hr_manager;
grant all on hr.locations to hr_manager;
grant all on hr.countries to hr_manager;
grant all on hr.departments to hr_manager;
grant all on hr.job_history to hr_manager;
grant all on hr.jobs to hr_manager;
grant all on hr.employees to hr_manager;
```

This third role is given the HR_SENIOR role with the ability to pass it on, and then gets full control over the contents of all the tables. But note that the only system privilege this role has is CREATE_SESSION, acquired through HR_SENIOR, which acquired it through HR_JUNIOR. Not even this role can create or drop tables; that must be done by HR himself, or an administrator with CREATE ANY TABLE and DROP ANY TABLE.

Note the syntax WITH ADMIN OPTION, which is the same as that for granting system privileges. As with system privileges, revocation of a role will not cascade; there is no record kept of who has granted a role to whom.

Finally, grant the roles to the relevant staff. If SCOTT is a manager, SUE is a senior clerk, and JON and ROOP are junior clerks, the flow could be as in Figure 8-8.

FIGURE 8-8

Granting roles
with SQL*Plus

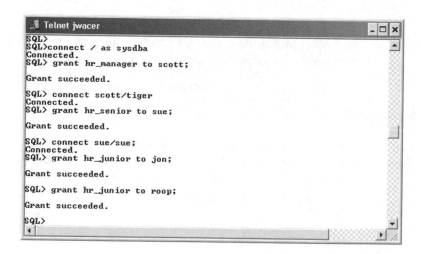

Predefined Roles

There are at least 50 predefined roles in an Oracle database (possibly many more, depending on what options have been installed). Ones that every DBA should be aware of are

- **CONNECT**   This only exists for backward compatibility. In previous releases, it had the system privileges necessary to create data storing objects, such as tables; with the current release, it only has CREATE SESSION.
- **RESOURCE**   Also for backward compatibility, this role can create both data objects (such as tables) and procedural objects (such PL/SQL procedures). It also includes UNLIMITED TABLESPACE.
- **DBA**   Has most of the system privileges, and several object privileges and roles. Any user granted DBA can manage virtually all aspects of the database, except for startup and shutdown.
- **SELECT_CATALOG_ROLE**   Has over 2000 object privileges against data dictionary objects, but no system privileges or privileges against user data. Useful for junior administration staff who must monitor and report on the database but not be able to see user data.
- **SCHEDULER_ADMIN**   Has the system privileges necessary for managing the Scheduler job scheduling service.

There is also a predefined role PUBLIC, which is always granted to every database user account. It follows that if a privilege is granted to PUBLIC, it will be available to all users. So following this command:

```
grant select on hr.regions to public;
```

all users will be able to query the HR.REGIONS table.

on the **job**   *The PUBLIC role is treated differently from any other role. It does not, for example, appear in the view DBA_ROLES. This is because the source code for DBA_ROLES, which can be seen in the `cdsec.sql` script called by the `catalog.sql` script, specifically excludes it.*

Enabling Roles

By default, if a user has been granted a role, then the role will enabled. This means that the moment a session is established connecting to the user account, all the privileges (and other roles) granted to the role will be active. This behavior can be modified by making the role non-default. Following the example given in the preceding section, this query shows what roles have been granted to JON:

```
SQL> select * from dba_role_privs where grantee='JON';
GRANTEE                            GRANTED_ROLE     ADM DEF
---------------------------------- ---------------- --- ---
JON                                HR_JUNIOR        NO  YES
```

JON has been granted HR_JUNIOR. He does not have administration on the role (so he cannot pass it on to anyone else), but it is a default role—he will have this role whenever he connects. This situation may well not be what you want. For example, JON has to be able to see the HR tables (it's his job) but that doesn't mean that you want him to be able to dial in from home, at midnight, and hack into the tables with SQL*Plus. You want to arrange things such that he can only see the tables when he is at a terminal in the Personnel office, running the HR application, in working hours.

To change the default behavior:

```
alter user jon default role none;
```

Now when JON logs on, he will not have any roles enabled. Unfortunately, this means he can't log on at all—because it is only HR_JUNIOR that gives him the CREATE SESSION system privilege. Easily fixed:

```
SQL> grant connect to jon;
Grant succeeded.
SQL> alter user jon default role connect;
```

```
User altered.
SQL> select * from dba_role_privs where grantee='JON';
GRANTEE                           GRANTED_ROLE     ADM DEF
------------------------------    ---------------  --- ---
JON                               HR_JUNIOR        NO  NO
JON                               CONNECT          NO  YES
```

Now when JON connects, only his CONNECT role is enabled—and the current version of CONNECT is not dangerous at all. Within the application, software commands can be embedded to enable the HR_JUNIOR role. The basic command to enable a role within a session is

```
SET ROLE rolename ;
```

which can be issued by the user at any time. So no security yet. But if the role is created with this syntax:

```
CREATE ROLE rolename IDENTIFIED USING procedure_name ;
```

then the role can only be enabled by running the PL/SQL procedure nominated by *procedure_name*. This procedure can make any number of checks, such as that the user is working on a particular TCP/IP subnet; that he/she is running a particular user process (probably not SQL*Plus); that the time is in a certain range; and so on. Embedding calls to the enabling procedures at appropriate points in an application can switch roles on and off as required, while leaving them disabled at all times when a connection is made with a ad hoc SQL tool such as SQL*Plus.

on the job

It can be very difficult to work out how a user can see some data. He/she may have been granted a specific SELECT; he/she may have been granted ALL; he/she may have SELECT ANY; SELECT may have been granted to PUBLIC; he/she may have a role to which SELECT has been granted. He/she may have all of these, in which they would all have to be revoked to stop his/her seeing the data.

EXERCISE 8-3

Create and Grant Roles

In this exercise, you will create some roles, grant them to the users, and demonstrate their effectiveness.

1. Connect to your database with SQL*Plus as user SYSTEM.

2. Create two roles as follows:

```
create role usr_role;
create role mgr_role;
```

3. Grant some privileges to the roles, and grant USR_ROLE to MGR_ROLE:

```
grant create session to usr_role;
grant select on alois.t1 to usr_role;
grant usr_role to mgr_role with admin option;
grant all on alois.t1 to mgr_role;
```

4. As user SYSTEM, grant the roles to AFRA and ANJA:

```
grant mgr_role to AFRA;
```

5. Connect to the database as user AFRA:

```
connect afra/oracle;
```

6. Grant the USR_ROLE to ANJA, and insert a row into ALOIS.T1:

```
grant usr_role to anja;
insert into alois.t1 values(sysdate);
commit;
```

7. Confirm the ANJA can connect and query ALOIS.t1 but do nothing else:

```
connect anja/oracle
select * from alois.t1;
insert into alois.t1 values(sysdate);
```

8. As user SYSTEM, adjust ANJA so that by default she can log on but do nothing else:

```
connect system/oracle
grant connect to anja;
alter user anja default role connect;
```

9. Demonstrate the enabling and disabling of roles:

```
connect anja/oracle
select * from alois.t1;
set role usr_role;
select * from alois.t1;
```

10. Use Database Control to inspect the roles. The navigation path from the database home page is: on the Server tab click the Roles link in the Security section. Click the links for the two new roles to see their privileges. This illustration shows the MGR_ROLE:

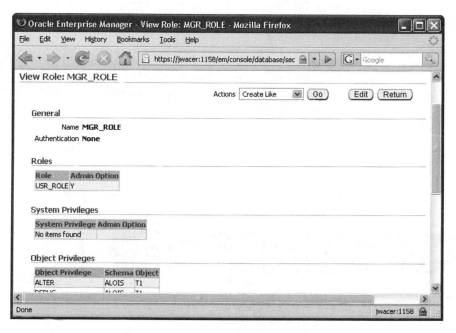

11. To see to whom a role has been granted, in the Actions drop-down box shown in the preceding illustration, select Show Grantees and click the Go button. This illustration shows the result for USR_ROLE:

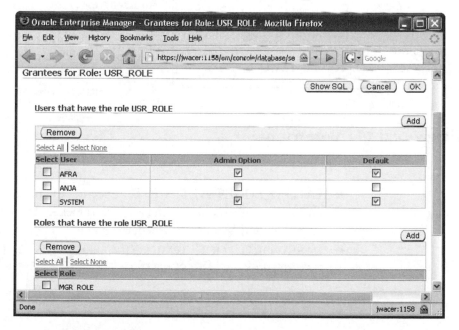

12. Obtain the same information retrieved in Steps 10 and 11 with these queries:

```
select * from dba_role_privs
where granted_role in ('USR_ROLE','MGR_ROLE');
select grantee,owner,table_name,privilege,grantable
from dba_tab_privs where grantee in ('USR_ROLE','MGR_ROLE')
union all
select grantee,to_char(null),to_char(null),privilege,admin_
option
from dba_sys_privs  where grantee in ('USR_ROLE','MGR_ROLE')
order by grantee;
```

CERTIFICATION OBJECTIVE 8.04

Create and Manage Profiles

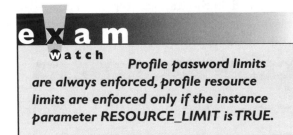

e x a m

ⓦ a t c h *Profile password limits are always enforced, profile resource limits are enforced only if the instance parameter RESOURCE_LIMIT is TRUE.*

A *profile* has a dual function: to enforce a password policy and to restrict the resources a session can take up. Password controls are always enforced; resource limits are only enforced if the instance parameter RESOURCE_LIMIT is on TRUE—by default, it is FALSE. Profiles are used automatically, but the default profile (applied by default to all users, including SYS and SYSTEM) does very little.

Password Management

The limits that can be applied to passwords are

- **FAILED_LOGIN_ATTEMPTS**   Specifies the number of consecutive errors on a password before the account is locked. If the correct password is given before this limit is reached, the counter is reset to zero.
- **PASSWORD_LOCK_TIME**   The number of days to lock an account after FAILED_LOGIN_ATTEMPTS is reached.

- **PASSWORD_LIFE_TIME** The number of days before a password expires. It may still be usable for a while after this time, depending on PASSWORD_ GRACE_TIME.
- **PASSWORD_GRACE_TIME** The number of days following the first successful login after the password has expired that prompts to change the password will be generated. The old password is still usable during this time.
- **PASSWORD_REUSE_TIME** The number of days before a password can be reused.
- **PASSWORD_REUSE_MAX** Then number of times a password can be reused.
- **PASSWORD_VERIFY_FUNCTION** The name of a function to run whenever a password is changed. The purpose of the function is assumed to be checking the new password for a required degree of complexity, but it can do pretty much anything you want.

SCENARIO & SOLUTION

When setting up security structures for an application, when would global authentication be better than password authentication?	Password authentication can only work if all users have database accounts. This is not a good idea if there are hundreds or thousands of users, but for a small application it does mean that the database can enforce security. For large systems, global authentication will be better; it is what enterprise-wide identity management systems are designed to do. The downside is that the programmers may have to do more work to enforce security, because the database won't really know who the users are. So it becomes a matter of scale.
If you suspect that some users are doing relatively unimportant work that is impacting adversely on other (more urgent) work, what can you do?	You can try to use profiles to restrict the time permitted for any one call and the amount of I/O that a session is allowed, but this is very crude. If you have Enterprise Edition licenses, you should consider using the Resource Manager instead. The Resource Manager has very sophisticated facilities for prioritizing work.

Resource Limits

The limits that can be applied to resource usage (also known as *kernel* limits) are

- **SESSIONS_PER_USER** The number of concurrent logins that can be made to the same user account. Sessions attempting to log in with the same user name when this limit is reached will be blocked.
- **CPU_PER_SESSION** The CPU time (in centiseconds) that a session's server process is allowed to use before the session is forcibly terminated.
- **CPU_PER_CALL** The CPU time (in centiseconds) that a session's server process is allowed to use to execute one SQL statement before the statement is forcibly terminated.
- **LOGICAL_READS_PER_SESSION** The number of blocks that can be read by a session (irrespective of whether they were in the database buffer cache or read from disk) before the session is forcibly terminated.
- **LOGICAL_READS_PER_CALL** The number of blocks that can be read by a single statement (irrespective of whether they were in the database buffer cache or read from disk) before the statement is forcibly terminated.
- **PRIVATE_SGA** For sessions connected through the shared server architecture, the number of kilobytes that the session is allowed to take in the SGA for session data.
- **CONNECT_TIME** In minutes, the maximum duration of a session before the session is forcibly terminated.
- **IDLE_TIME** In minutes, the maximum time a session can be idle before the session is forcibly terminated.
- **COMPOSITE_LIMIT** A weighted sum of CPU_PER_SESSION, CONNECT_TIME, LOGICAL_READS_PER_SESSION, and PRIVATE_SGA. This is an advanced facility that requires configuration beyond the scope of the OCP examination.

Resource limits will not be applied unless an instance parameter has been set:

```
alter system set resource_limit=true;
```

This will default to FALSE.

When a session is terminated because a resource limit has been reached, if there was a transaction in progress it will be rolled back. If a statement is terminated, the work done by the statement will be rolled back, but any earlier statements will remain intact and uncommitted.

INSIDE THE EXAM

Administering User Security

The default security in an Oracle database is 100 percent. You can't even log on without being granted permission to do so. There is no way to connect anonymously, though there are several ways of authenticating yourself.

Once connected to a user account, you are restricted by the privileges and roles you have been granted, and by your quota on tablespaces. A role is just a bundle of object and system privileges, but unlike a directly granted privilege, a role can be enabled or disabled within a session.

Granting system privileges, object privileges, and roles is similar in concept but requires slightly different syntax. The syntax for a REVOKE is identical. Revoking an object privilege will cascade but revoking a role or a system privilege will not.

Profiles can be used to enforce rules on passwords and to control the resources users are allowed to take up within the database.

on the
Job

Profiles can be used to limit resource usage, but a much more sophisticated tool is the Resource Manager.

Creating and Assigning Profiles

Profiles can be managed through Database Control or from SQL*Plus. To see which profile is currently assigned to ach user, run this query:

```
select username,profile from dba_users;
```

By default, all users (with the exception of two internal users, DBSNMP and WKSYS) will be assigned the profile called DEFAULT. Then the view that will display the profiles themselves is DBA_PROFILES:

```
select * from dba_profiles where profile='DEFAULT';
```

Or with Database Control, from the database home page take the Server tab, and then click the Users link in the Security section to see which profile each user has. Select a user and click the Edit button to assign a different profile. To see how the profiles are set up, click the Profiles link in the Security section.

The DEFAULT profile has no resource limits at all, but there are some password limits:

Resource Name	Limit
FAILED_LOGIN_ATTEMPTS	10
PASSWORD_LOCK_TIME	1
PASSWORD_LIFE_TIME	180
PASSWORD_GRACE_TIME	7

These restrictions are not too strict: a password can be entered incorrectly ten consecutive times before the account is locked for one day, and a password will expire after about six months with a one-week grace period for changing it after that.

The simplest way to enable more sophisticated password management is to run a supplied script. On Unix or Linux it is

```
$ORACLE_HOME/rdbms/admin/utlpwdmg.sql
```

On Windows it is

```
%ORACLE_HOME%\rdbms\admin\utlpwdmg.sql
```

On either platform, the script creates two functions called VERIFY_FUNCTION and VERIFY_FUNCTION_11G, and runs this command:

```
ALTER PROFILE DEFAULT LIMIT
PASSWORD_LIFE_TIME 180
PASSWORD_GRACE_TIME 7
PASSWORD_REUSE_TIME UNLIMITED
PASSWORD_REUSE_MAX UNLIMITED
FAILED_LOGIN_ATTEMPTS 10
PASSWORD_LOCK_TIME 1
PASSWORD_VERIFY_FUNCTION verify_function_11G;
```

This command will adjust the profile called DEFAULT. Any users with the DEFAULT profile (which is all users, by default) will immediately pick up the new values. Following a standard database creation, the only change will be the specification of the PASSWORD_VERIFY_FUNCTION. The function nominated, VERIFY_FUNCTION_11G, makes a set of simple tests and will reject a password change if it does not pass all of them:

■ The new password must be at least eight characters long.

- The new password cannot be the same as the username (spelled backward or forward) or the name of the database, in upper- or lowercase.
- A few simple and commonly used passwords (such as "oracle") will be rejected.
- The new password must have at least one letter and at least one digit.
- The password must differ in at least three characters from the preceding password.

The script should be viewed as an example script (certainly the function is very elementary) and should be edited to the needs of the organization. Most organizations will need to go further than this and create a set of profiles to be applied to different users.

To create a profile with SQL*Plus, use the CREATE PROFILE command, setting whatever limits are required. Any limits not specified will be picked up from the current version of the DEFAULT profile. For example, it could be that the rules of the organization state that no users should be able to log on more than once, except for administration staff, who can log on as many concurrent sessions as they want and must change their passwords every week with one-day grace, and the programmers, who can log on twice. To do this, first adjust the DEFAULT profile:

```
alter profile default limit sessions_per_user 1;
```

Create a new profile for the DBAs, and assign it:

```
create profile dba_profile limit sessions_per_user unlimited
password_life_time 7 password_grace_time 1;
alter user sys profile dba_profile;
alter user system profile dba_profile;
```

Create a profile for the programmers, and assign it:

```
create profile programmers_profile limit sessions_per_user 2;
alter user jon profile programmers_profile;
alter user sue profile programmers_profile;
```

To let the resource limit take effect, adjust the instance parameter:

```
alter system set resource_limit=true;
```

Assuming that the instance is using an SPFILE, this change will be propagated to the parameter file and will therefore be permanent.

A profile cannot be dropped if it has been assigned to users. They must be altered to a different profile first. Once done, drop the profile with

```
DROP PROFILE profile_name ;
```

Alternatively, use this syntax:

```
DROP PROFILE profile_name CASCADE ;
```

which will automatically reassign all users with *profile_name* back to the DEFAULT profile.

EXERCISE 8-4

Create and Use Profiles

In this exercise, create, assign, and test a profile that will force some password control.

1. Connect to your database with SQL*Plus as user system.
2. Create a profile that will lock accounts after two wrong passwords:

   ```
   create profile two_wrong limit failed_login_attempts 2;
   ```

3. Assign this new profile to ALOIS:

   ```
   alter user alois profile two_wrong;
   ```

4. Deliberately enter the wrong password for ALOIS a few times:

   ```
   connect alois/wrongpassword
   ```

5. As user SYSTEM, unlock the ALOIS account:

   ```
   alter user alois account unlock;
   ```

6. Check that ALOIS can now connect:

   ```
   connect alois/oracle
   ```

   The next illustration shows the sequence of events.

```
C:\WINDOWS\system32\cmd.exe - sqlplus / as sysdba

SQL> create profile two_wrong limit failed_login_attempts 2;

Profile created.

SQL> alter user alois profile two_wrong;

User altered.

SQL> connect alois/wrongpassword
ERROR:
ORA-01017: invalid username/password; logon denied


Warning: You are no longer connected to ORACLE.
SQL> connect alois/wrongpassword
ERROR:
ORA-01017: invalid username/password; logon denied


SQL> connect alois/oracle
ERROR:
ORA-28000: the account is locked


SQL> connect system/oracle
Connected.
SQL> alter user alois account unlock;

User altered.

SQL> connect alois/oracle
Connected.
SQL> _
```

7. Tidy up by dropping the profile, the roles, and the users. Note the use of CASCADE when dropping the profile to remove it from ALOIS, and on the DROP USER command to drop his table as well. Roles can be dropped even if they are assigned to users. The privileges granted on the table will be revoked as the table is dropped.

```
connect system/oracle
drop profile two_wrong cascade;
drop role usr_role;
drop role mgr_role;
drop user alois cascade;
drop user anja;
drop user afra;
```

CERTIFICATION SUMMARY

User accounts define users who can connect to the database and are associated with a schema that stored the objects owned by the account. Privileges must be granted to an account (either directly or via roles) before the account is usable in any way.

Privileges come in two forms: system privileges that control certain actions within the database (typically, actions that involve changes to the data dictionary) and object privileges that control access to data. A role is a bundle of privileges. Unlike a privilege (which is always enabled once granted), a role can be enabled or disabled within a session.

Profiles give control over account passwords and resource usage. All user accounts have a profile, by default the profile called DEFAULT. The DEFAULT profile can be adjusted, and the change will immediately apply to all users with the DEFAULT profile. Or additional profiles can be created and assigned explicitly to certain users.

TWO-MINUTE DRILL

Create and Manage Database User Accounts

- ❏ Users connect to a user account, which is connected to a schema.
- ❏ All users must be authenticated before they can connect.
- ❏ A user must have a quota on a tablespace before he/she can create any objects.
- ❏ A user who owns objects cannot be dropped, unless the CASCADE keyword is used.

Grant and Revoke Privileges

- ❏ By default, a user can do nothing. He/she can't even log on.
- ❏ Direct privileges are always enabled.
- ❏ A revocation of a system privilege does not cascade; a revocation of an object privilege does.

Create and Manage Roles

- ❏ Roles are not schema objects.
- ❏ Roles can contain both system and object privileges, and other roles.
- ❏ A role can be enabled or disabled for a session.

Create and Manage Profiles

- ❏ Profiles can manage passwords and resource limits.
- ❏ Password limits are always enforced; resource limits are dependent on an instance parameter.
- ❏ Every user always has a profile, by default the DEFAULT profile.

SELF TEST

Create and Manage Database User Accounts

1. How can you permit users to connect without requiring them to authenticate themselves? (Choose the best answer.)

   A. Grant CREATE SESSION to PUBLIC.

   B. Create a user such as this, without a password:

   ```
   CREATE USER ANON IDENTIFIED BY '';
   ```

   C. Create a profile that disables password authentication and assign it to the users.

   D. You cannot do this because all users must be authenticated.

2. You create a user with this statement:

   ```
   create user jon identified by oracle default tablespace example;
   ```

   What more must be done before he can create a table in the EXAMPLE tablespace? (Choose all correct answers.)

   A. Nothing more is necessary.

   B. Give him a quota on EXAMPLE.

   C. Grant him the CREATE TABLE privilege.

   D. Grant him the CREATE SESSION privilege.

   E. Grant him the MANAGE TABLESPACE privilege.

3. If a user owns tables in a tablespace, what will be the effect of attempting to reduce his/her quota on the tablespace zero? (Choose the best answer.)

   A. The tables will survive, but INSERTS will fail.

   B. The tables will survive but cannot get bigger.

   C. The attempt will fail unless the tables are dropped first.

   D. The tables will be dropped automatically if the CASCADE keyword is used.

4. If you create a user without specifying a temporary tablespace, what temporary tablespace will be assigned? (Choose the best answer.)

   A. You must specify a temporary tablespace

   B. SYSTEM

   C. TEMP

   D. The database default temporary tablespace

   E. He/she will not have a temporary tablespace

Grant and Revoke Privileges

5. You issue these commands:

A. `grant select on hr.regions to jon;`
B. `grant all on hr.regions to jon;`
C. `grant dba to jon;`
D. `grant select on hr.regions to public;`

Which grants could be revoked to prevent JON from seeing the contents of HR.REGIONS? (Choose all correct answers.)

A. a, b, c, and d
B. a, c, and d
C. b, c, and d
D. c and d
E. a, b, and c

6. Which of these statements about system privileges are correct? (Choose all correct answers.)

A. Only the SYS and SYSTEM users can grant system privileges.
B. If a system privilege is revoked from a user, it will also be revoked from all users to whom he granted it.
C. If a system privilege is revoked from a user, it will not be revoked from all users to whom she granted it.
D. CREATE TABLE is a system privilege.
E. CREATE ANY TABLE is a system privilege.

Create and Manage Roles

7. Study this script (line numbers have been added):

```
1    create role hr_role identified by pass;
2    grant create table to hr_role;
3    grant select table to hr_role;
4    grant connect to hr_role;
```

Which line will cause an error? (Choose the best answer.)

A. Line 1, because only users, not roles, have passwords.
B. Line 2, because only users, not roles, can create and own tables.
C. Line 3, because SELECT TABLE is not a privilege.
D. Line 4, because a role cannot have a system privilege in addition to table privileges.

8. Which of these statements is incorrect regarding roles? (Choose the best answer.)

    A. You can grant object privileges and system privileges and roles to a role.

    B. A role cannot have the same name as a table.

    C. A role cannot have the same name as a user.

    D. Roles can be enabled or disabled within a session.

Create and Manage Profiles

9. You have created a profile with LIMIT SESSIONS_PER_USER 1 and granted it to a user, but you find that he/she is still able to log on several times concurrently. Why could this be? (Choose the best answer.)

    A. The user has been granted CREATE SESSION more than once.

    B. The user has been granted the DBA role.

    C. The RESOURCE_LIMIT parameter has not been set.

    D. The RESOURCE_MANAGER_PLAN parameter has not been set.

10. Which of these can be controlled by a password profile? (Choose all correct answers.)

    A. Two or more users choosing the same password

    B. Preventing the reuse of a password by the same user

    C. Forcing a user to change password

    D. Enabling or disabling password file authentication

LAB QUESTION

For this question, use Database Control where possible if you wish, but it is usually necessary to use SQL*Plus to query views directly when trying to understand what is happening with access rights. There are often several ways of getting to a table, and it can be difficult to work out why a user can see it.

Create a user BERND, and give him the necessary permissions to log on to the database with password authentication and create tables in his own schema. Test this by connecting as BERND and creating a table DATETAB, with a single column of type DATE. Insert a row into DATETAB, and commit the insert.

Create a user CHRISTA. Give her these privileges:

```
CREATE SESSION
SELECT ON BERND.DATETAB
ALL ON BERND.DATETAB
```

Connect as CHRISTA, and check that she can read BERND.DATETAB. Revoke her SELECT privilege, and confirm that she can no longer select from BERND.DATETAB, though she can (perhaps oddly) insert rows into it. Why is this, when she was also granted ALL on BERND.DA-TETAB? Run queries against DBA_TAB_PRIVS at all stages to understand what is happening.

Create a user DORIS, and grant privileges as follows:

```
SELECT ON BERND.DATETAB to DORIS
SELECT ON BERND.DATETAB to PUBLIC
SELECT ANY TABLE to DORIS
DBA to DORIS
```

Confirm that DORIS can now read BERND.DATETAB. What privileges must be revoked before DORIS will no longer be able to see BERND.DATETAB? Check the permissions at all stages by querying DBA_TAB_PRIVS, DBA_SYS_PRIVS, and DBA_ROLE_PRIVS.

Tidy up by dropping the users. Remember to use CASCADE where appropriate.

SELF TEST ANSWERS

Create and Manage Database User Accounts

1. ☑ **D.** All users must be authenticated.
   ☒ **A** is wrong because while this will give all users permission to connect, they will still have to authenticate. **B** is wrong because a NULL is not acceptable as a password. **C** is wrong because a profile can only manage passwords, not disable them.

2. ☑ **B, C,** and **D.** All these actions are necessary.
   ☒ **A** is wrong because without privileges and quota, JON cannot connect and create a table. **E** is wrong because this privilege lets you manage a tablespace, not create objects in it.

3. ☑ **B.** It will not be possible to allocate further extents to the tables.
   ☒ **A** is wrong because inserts will succeed as long as there is space in the extents already allocated. **C** is wrong because there is no need to drop the tables. **D** is wrong because CASCADE cannot be applied to a quota command.

4. ☑ **D.** There is always a database-wide default, which (by default) is SYSTEM. In many cases, it will have been set to TEMP.
   ☒ **A** is wrong because there is a default. **B** is wrong because the default may not be SYSTEM (though it is by default). **C** is wrong because while TEMP is a frequently used default, it may not be. **E** is wrong because all user accounts must have a temporary tablespace.

Grant and Revoke Privileges

5. ☑ **A, B,** and **C.** Any of these will prevent the access.
   ☒ **D** is wrong because the grants in (a) and (b) will remain in effect. **E** is wrong because the grant to PUBLIC in (d) will remain in effect.

6. ☑ **C** is correct because the revocation of a system privilege does not cascade. **D** and **E** are correct because any action that updates the data dictionary is a system privilege.
   ☒ **A** is wrong because system privileges can be granted by any user who has been granted the privilege WITH ADMIN OPTION. **B** is wrong because the revocation of a system privilege does not cascade.

Create and Manage Roles

7. ☑ **C.** There is no such privilege as SELECT TABLE; it is granted implicitly with CREATE TABLE.
   ☒ **A** is wrong because roles can be password protected. **B** is wrong because even though tables

must be owned by users, permission to create them can be granted to a role. **D** is wrong because a role can have any combination of object and system privileges.

8. ☑ **B.** Roles are not schema objects, and so can have the same names as tables.
☒ **A** is wrong because roles can have any combination of system, object, and role privileges. **C** is wrong because roles cannot have the same names as users. **D** is wrong because roles can be enabled and disabled at any time.

Create and Manage Profiles

9. ☑ **C.** The RESOURCE_LIMIT parameter will default to FALSE, and without this resource limits are not enforced.
☒ **A** is wrong because this privilege controls whether uses can connect to the account at all, not how many times. **B** is wrong because no role can exempt a user from profile limits. **D** is wrong because this parameter controls which Resource Manager plan is active, which is not relevant to whether resource limits are enforced.

10. ☑ **B** and **C.** These are both password limits.
☒ **A** is wrong because this cannot be prevented by any means. **D** is wrong because profiles only apply to password authentication; password file authentication is managed separately.

LAB ANSWER

A possible solution is as follows:
To create BERND and the table:

```
conn system/oracle
create user bernd identified by bernd;
alter user bernd default tablespace example quota unlimited on example;
grant create table,create session to bernd;
connect bernd/bernd
create table datetab (c1 date);
insert into datetab values(sysdate);
commit;
```

Then experiment with CHRISTA:

```
connect system/oracle
create user christa identified by christa;
grant create session to christa;
grant select on bernd.datetab to christa;
select * from dba_tab_privs where grantee='CHRISTA';
```

```
grant all on bernd.datetab to christa;
select * from dba_tab_privs where grantee='CHRISTA';
connect christa/christa;
select * from bernd.datetab;
connect system/oracle
revoke select on bernd.datetab from christa;
select * from dba_tab_privs where grantee='CHRISTA';
connect christa/christa;
insert into bernd.datetab values(sysdate);
select * from bernd.datetab;
```

For the experiment with DORIS, the queries to be run to investigate the permissions could include

```
select * from dba_tab_privs where owner='BERND' and table_name='DATETAB';
select * from dba_tab_privs where GRANTEE in ('DORIS','PUBLIC')
and owner='BERND';
select * from dba_sys_privs where GRANTEE in ('DORIS','PUBLIC');
select * from dba_role_privs where grantee='DORIS';
select * from dba_sys_privs where privilege='SELECT ANY TABLE';
```

Note that to gain a full understanding of who can access that data, it is necessary to develop a set of queries that will take account of all possibilities.

9
Managing Schema Objects

D ata in an Oracle database is stored in tables. Constraints, applied to tables, are the means whereby the database can implement some of the business rules defined by your business analysts. Indexes are required for enforcing some constraints, and necessary for performance reasons as well. Tables, constraints, and indexes are schema objects: they cannot exist independently of the user to whom they belong.

The final part of the chapter deals with *temporary* tables (often referred as *global temporary* tables). The content of a temporary table is visible only to one session and is cleared when the session ends. Performance of DML and queries against temporary tables can be many times faster than against permanent tables. Temporary tables are an extremely useful capability that all developers and administrators should be aware of.

Designing the structure of tables, indexes, and constraints should be a cooperative exercise between several parties:

- Business analysts, who model the business processes the system is to implement
- Systems analysts, who normalize the data into an ideal form
- System designers, who adapt the ideal form to the realities of the environment
- Application designers, who write the SQL to implement the design
- Database administrators, who have to make the design work

The content of this chapter therefore crosses several domains, and in terms of the OCP examinations there is a considerable overlap with the SQL curriculum.

CERTIFICATION OBJECTIVE 9.01

Create and Modify Tables

The Oracle database supports several types of permanent table: heap tables, index-organized tables, partitioned tables, and clustered tables. This chapter deals only with the basic heap table. Tables exist within schemas and must conform to the rules for naming schema objects. The columns of a table are defined as being of certain data types.

Users, User Accounts, Schemas, and Schema Objects

A user is a person who logs on to the database from a user process and connects to a user account. Chapter 8 covered the techniques for creating user accounts and giving them the privileges that allow them to connect to the database, and then create and use objects. When a user account is created, a schema is created too. A schema consists of the objects owned by the account. Initially, it will be empty. A schema is a container for tables, views, code, and other database objects. Many people use the terms "user," "user account," and "schema" interchangeably. In the Oracle environment, you can get away with this (though not necessarily with other database management systems).

Some schemas will always be empty: the user will never create any objects, because he/she does not need to and (if he/she is set up correctly) will not have the necessary privileges anyway. Users such as this will have been granted permissions, either through direct privileges or through roles, to use code and access data in other schemas, owned by other users. Other users may be the reverse of this: they will own many objects but will never actually log on to the database. They need not even have been granted the CREATE SESSION privilege, so the account is effectively disabled (or indeed it can be locked). These schemas are used as repositories for code and data, accessed by others.

Schema objects are objects with an owner. The unique identifier for an object of a particular type is not its name—it is its name, prefixed with the name of the schema to which it belongs. Thus the table HR.REGIONS is a table called REGIONS that is owned by user HR. There could be another table, SYSTEM.REGIONS, which would be a completely different table (perhaps different in both structure and contents) owned by user SYSTEM, and residing in that user's schema.

A number of users (and their associated schemas) are created automatically at database creation time. Principal among these are SYS and SYSTEM. User SYS owns the data dictionary: a set of tables (in the SYS schema) that define the database and its contents. SYS also owns several hundred PL/SQL packages: code that is provided for the use of database administrators and developers. Objects in the SYS schema should never be modified with DML commands. If you were to execute DML against the data dictionary tables, you would run the risk of corrupting the data dictionary, with disastrous results. You update the data dictionary by running DDL commands (such as CREATE TABLE), which provide a layer of abstraction between you and the data dictionary itself. The SYSTEM schema stores various additional objects used for administration and monitoring.

Depending on the options selected during database creation, there may be more users created—perhaps up to thirty in total. These others are used for storing the code and data required by various options. For example, the user MDSYS stores the objects used by Oracle Spatial, an option that extends the capabilities of the Oracle database to manage geographical information.

Naming Schema Objects

A schema object is an object that is owned by a user. The database will also contain non-schema objects; these may be objects that have nothing to do with users, such as tablespaces, or in some cases they are objects owned by SYS and directly accessible by all users; examples of the latter include public synonyms and public database links that can be used by all users regardless of privileges.

To view schema objects through Database Control, take the appropriate link for the type of object of interest from the Schema tab on the database home page, as shown in Figure 9-1, and you will be prompted for various search criteria.

All schema object names must conform to certain rules:

- The name may be from one to thirty characters long, with the exception of database link names, which may be up to 128 characters long.
- Reserved words (such as SELECT) cannot be used as object names.
- All names must begin with a letter from A through Z.
- Names can only use letters, numbers, underscore (_), the dollar sign ($), or the hash symbol (#).
- Lowercase letters will be converted to uppercase.

FIGURE 9-1

Schema objects manageable with Database Control

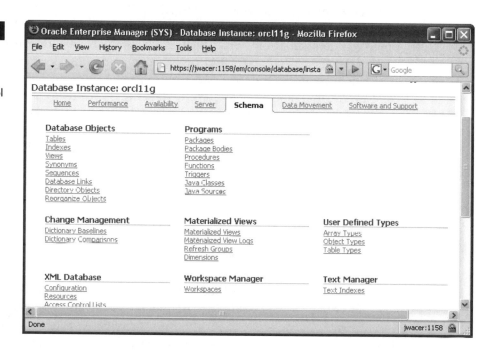

By enclosing the name within double quotes, all these rules (with the exception of the length) can be broken, but to get to the object subsequently it must always be specified with double quotes, as in the examples in Figure 9-2. Note that the same restrictions apply to column names.

Although tools such as SQL*Plus will automatically convert lowercase letters to uppercase, unless the name is enclosed within double quotes, remember that object names are always case sensitive. In this example, the two tables are completely different:

```
ocp10g> create table lower(c1 date);
Table created.
ocp10g> create table "lower"(col1 varchar(2));
Table created.
ocp10g> select table_name from dba_tables where
  2  lower(table_name) = 'lower';
TABLE_NAME
------------------------------
lower
LOWER
```

FIGURE 9-2	

Using double quotes to use non-standard names

```
SQL> create table "with space" ("-Hyphen" date);

Table created.

SQL> insert into "with space" values(sysdate);

1 row created.

SQL> select * from with space;
select * from with space
                   *
ERROR at line 1:
ORA-00903: invalid table name


SQL> select -Hyphen from "with space";
select -Hyphen from "with space"
        *
ERROR at line 1:
ORA-00904: "HYPHEN": invalid identifier


SQL> select "-Hyphen" from "with space";

-Hyphen
---------
23-DEC-07

SQL>
```

While it is possible to use lowercase names and non-standard characters (even spaces), it is considered bad practice because of the confusion it can cause.

Object Namespaces

It is often said that the unique identifier for an object is the object name, prefixed with the schema name. While this is generally true, for a full understanding of naming it is necessary to introduce the concept of a *namespace*. A namespace defines a group of object types, within which all names must be uniquely identified, by schema and name. Objects in different namespaces can share the same name.

These object types all share the same namespace:

- Tables
- Views
- Sequences
- Private synonyms
- Stand-alone procedures
- Stand-alone stored functions
- Packages
- Materialized views
- User-defined types

Thus it is impossible to create a view with the same name as a table—at least, it is impossible if they are in the same schema. And once created, SQL statements can address a view as though it were a table. The fact that tables, views, and private synonyms share the same namespace means that you can set up several layers of abstraction between what the users see and the actual tables, which can be invaluable for both security and for simplifying application development.

These object types each have their own namespace:

- Indexes
- Constraints
- Clusters
- Database triggers
- Private database links
- Dimensions

Thus it is possible (though perhaps not a very good idea) for an index to have the same name as a table, even within the same schema.

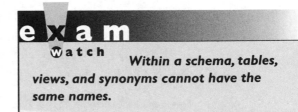

Within a schema, tables, views, and synonyms cannot have the same names.

Datatypes

When creating tables, each column must be assigned a datatype, which determines the nature of the values that can be inserted into the column. These datatypes are also used to specify the nature of the arguments for PL/SQL procedures and functions. When selecting a datatype, you must consider the data that you need to store and the operations you will want to perform upon it. It may be possible to change a column to a different datatype after creation, but this is not always easy. Space is also a consideration: some datatypes are fixed length, taking up the same number of bytes no matter what data is actually in them; others are variable. If a column is not populated, then Oracle will not give it any space at all; if you later update the row to populate the column, then the row will get bigger, no matter whether the datatype is fixed length or variable.

Datatypes for alphanumeric data:

- **VARCHAR2**   Variable-length character data, from 1 byte to 4 KB. The data is stored in the database character set.
- **NVARCHAR2**   As VARCHAR2, but the data is stored in the alternative national language character set: one of the permitted Unicode character sets.
- **CHAR**   Fixed-length character data, from 1 byte to 2 KB, in the database character set. If the data is not the length of the column, then it will be padded with spaces.
- **RAW**   Variable-length binary data, from 1 byte to 2 KB. Unlike the CHAR and VARCHAR datatypes, RAW data is not converted by Oracle Net from the database's character set to the user process's character set on select, or the other way on insert.

Datatypes for numeric data, all variable length:

- **NUMBER**   Numeric data, for which you can specify precision and scale. The precision can range from 1 to 38; the scale can range from –84 to 127.

- **FLOAT**   This is an ANSI datatype, floating-point number with precision of 126 binary (or 38 decimal). Oracle also provides BINARY_FLOAT and BINARY_DOUBLE as alternatives.
- **INTEGER**   Equivalent to NUMBER, with scale zero.

Datatypes for date and time data, all fixed length:

- **DATE**   This is either length zero, if the column is empty, or 7 bytes. All DATE data includes century, year, month, day, hour, minute, and second. The valid range is from January 1, 4712 BC to December 31, 9999 AD.
- **TIMESTAMP**   This is length zero if the column is empty, or up to 11 bytes, depending on the precision specified. Similar to DATE, but with precision of up to nine decimal places for the seconds, six places by default.
- **TIMESTAMP WITH TIMEZONE**   As TIMESTAMP, but the data is stored with a record kept of the timezone to which it refers. The length may be up to 13 bytes, depending on precision. This datatype lets Oracle determine the difference between two times by normalizing them to UTC, even if the times are for different time zones.
- **TIMESTAMP WITH LOCAL TIMEZONE**   As timestamp, but the data is normalized to the database time zone on saving. When retrieved, it is normalized to the time zone of the user process selecting it.
- **INTERVAL YEAR TO MONTH**   Used for recording a period in years and months between two DATEs or TIMESTAMPs.
- **INTERVAL DAY TO SECOND**   Used for recording a period in days and seconds between two DATEs or TIMESTAMPs.

Large object datatypes:

- **CLOB**   Character data stored in the database character set, size effectively unlimited: 4 GB multiplied by the database block size.
- **NCLOB**   As CLOB, but the data is stored in the alternative national language character set: one of the permitted Unicode character sets.
- **BLOB**   As CLOB, but binary data that will not undergo character set conversion by Oracle Net.

- **BFILE**   A locator pointing to a file stored on the operating system of the database server. The size of the files is limited to 4 GB.
- **LONG**   Character data in the database character set, up to 2 GB. All the functionality of LONG (and more) is provided by CLOB; LONGs should not be used in a modern database, and if your database has any columns of this type, they should be converted to CLOB.
- **LONG RAW**   As LONG, but binary data that will not be converted by Oracle Net. Any LONG RAW columns should be converted to BLOBs.

on the

For ISO/ANSI compliance, you can specify a VARCHAR datatype when creating tables, but any columns of this type will be automatically converted to VARCHAR2.

Oracle provides a range of typecasting functions for converting between datatypes, and in some circumstances will do automatic typecasting. Figure 9-3 illustrates both techniques.

In the figure, the first insert uses typecasting functions to convert the character data entered to the datatypes specified for the table columns. The second insert attempts to insert character strings into all three columns, but the insert still succeeds because

FIGURE 9-3	
Use of typecasting functions and automatic typecasting	

```
SQL> create table typecast(dcol date,ncol number,vcol varchar2(20));

Table created.

SQL> alter session set nls_date_format='dd-mm-yy';

Session altered.

SQL> insert into typecast values
  2  (to_date('23-04-05'),to_number(1000),'done correctly');
ERROR:
ORA-01756: quoted string not properly terminated

SQL> insert into typecast values ('24-04-05','1000','automatic casting');

1 row created.

SQL> select * from typecast;

DCOL            NCOL VCOL
--------- ---------- --------------------
24-04-05        1000 automatic casting

SQL>
```

Oracle can convert datatypes automatically if necessary, and if the format of the data is suitable. Note that the accuracy of the typecasting can be dependent on the data. In the example, the date is being interpreted as a European-style date (day-month-year), which might not be intended if the users happen to use American styles (month-day-year), which would throw an error, or African style (year-month-day), which would work but not as intended.

on the **job**

Do not rely on automatic typecasting. It can impact on performance and may not always work. The Oracle environment is strongly typed, and your programmers should respect this.

Creating Tables

The syntax for creating a table requires giving the table a name (which must be unique within the namespace in the schema to which the table belongs) and specifying one or more columns, each with a datatype. It is also possible to specify constraints when creating a table; alternatively, constraints can be added later. There are many examples in this book of creating tables from the SQL*Plus command line (there have already been two examples in this chapter), but it can also be done through Database Control. Database Control provides a fully functional menu-driven interface for creating and editing table structures, and also for managing the constraints, indexes, and views that will be based on the tables.

All tables require storage. Unless specified otherwise, tables will be created with one extent in the creator's default tablespace. Any other tablespace on which the user has a quota can be specified at creation time, or a table can be moved to a different tablespace later.

To reach the table management window of Database Control, from the database home page take the Schema tab, then the Tables link in the Database Objects section, as shown in Figure 9-4. Enter whatever search criteria are needed to locate the table of interest; note that double quotes can be used to find tables with non-standard names and the % wildcard. Click the Actions drop-down box to see what possibilities are available.

The actions are:

CREATE LIKE	Create a new table based on the same structure as the selected table.
CREATE INDEX	Define and generate an index on the table.
CREATE SYNONYM	Create a logical name, or alias, that can be used as a pseudonym for the table.
CREATE TRIGGER	Create a block of PL/SQL code will run automatically whenever DML is executed against the table.
GENERATE DDL	Reverse-engineer the table definition, to produce a CREATE TABLE statement that could be used to reproduce the table.
OBJECT PRIVILEGES	Give users permission to read or alter the data in the table.
MANAGE OPTIMIZER STATISTICS	Analyze the contents of the table, to gather statistics used by the optimizer to work out how best to access the table.
REORGANIZE	Runs a wizard to take you through the process or reorganizing the data in a table to move the table, or to change its structure.
RUN SEGMENT ADVISOR	Use the advisor to generate a recommendation for whether the table should be shrunk.
SHRINK SEGMENT	Use the online reorganization tool to reclaim wasted space from a segment.
SHOW DEPENDENCIES	Display all the objects that are in some way related to the table and so could be affected by any action on the table.
VIEW DATA	This wizard assists with querying and displaying the contents of the table.
FLASHBACK TABLE	Reverse any DML against the table, in reverse chronological order, to take the table back to a previous state.
FLASHBACK VERSIONS QUERY	Query historical data, to display previous versions of rows.
FLASHBACK TRANSACTION	Find and reverse transactions against the table.
LOG MINER	Investigate all DML that has been executed against the table.

The Edit button goes to a window that will display the column structures of the table. From here, columns can be added, dropped, and modified. Examples of the SQL to do this are

```
alter table dept add (started date);
alter table dept modify (started timestamp);
alter table dept drop column started;
```

In this example, the first command adds a column STARTED to the table, datatype DATE. The second command modifies the datatype to TIMESTAMP. The third command drops the column.

FIGURE 9-4

The Database
Control Tables
window

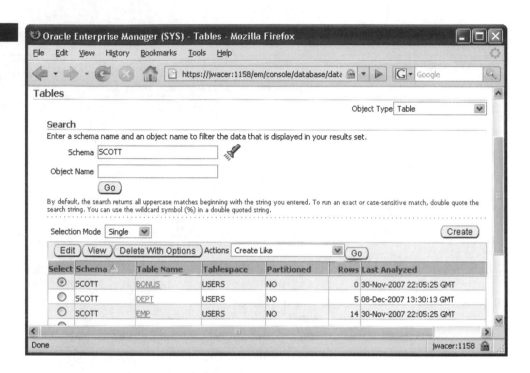

To drop a table, user the DROP TABLE command. Syntactically, this is very simple:

```
DROP TABLE table_name [CASCADE CONSTRAINTS] ;
```

When a table is dropped, all associated indexes and triggers will be dropped as well. Constraints will be dropped, though if the table is the parent table in a foreign key constraint, the drop will fail unless the CASCADE CONSTRAINTS keywords are specified.

EXERCISE 9-1

Create and Modify Tables

In this exercise, use SQL*Plus to create and modify a simple table, and then use Database Control to extract the DDL necessary to recreate it.

1. Connect to your database with SQL*Plus as user HR.

2. Create a table as follows:

```
create table ex_emps as select * from employees where 1=2;
```

This will create an empty table, in HR's default tablespace, intended to store details of staff who have been fired.

3. Remove the columns not relevant to ex-employees:

```
alter table ex_emps drop column email;
alter table ex_emps drop column phone_number;
```

4. Add columns needed in the new table:

```
alter table ex_emps add (fire_date date);
alter table ex_emps add(reason varchar2(20));
```

5. Connect to the database with Database Control as user SYSTEM.

6. Locate the newly created table. The navigation path is to take the Schema tab from the database home page, and click the Tables link in the Database Objects section. Enter **HR** as the search criterion and click Go. This will locate all of HR's tables.

7. Select the radio button for the table EX_EMPS, Generate DDL in the Actions drop-down box, and click Go. The generated DDL will resemble that shown in this illustration:

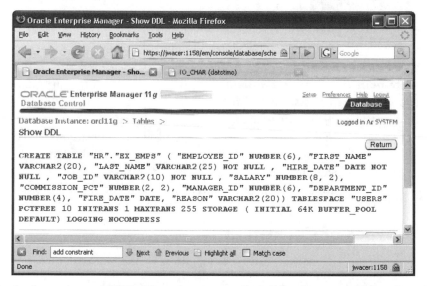

8. Study the generated DDL. Note that it is nothing like that specified in Step 2: double quotes are used around all names; NOT NULL constraints have been copied, but no others; defaults have been applied for tablespace, storage, and the LOGGING and COMPRESS options.

CERTIFICATION OBJECTIVE 9.02

Manage Constraints

Table constraints are a means by which the database can enforce business rules and guarantee that the data conforms to the entity-relationship model determined by the systems analysis that defines the application data structures. For example, the business analysts of your organization may have decided that every customer and every invoice must be uniquely identifiable by number, that no invoices can be issued to a customer before that customer has been created, and that every invoice must have a valid date and a value greater than zero. These would be implemented by creating primary key constraints on the CUSTOMER_NUMBER column of the CUSTOMERS table and the INVOICE_NUMBER column of the INVOICES table, a foreign key constraint on the INVOICES table referencing the CUSTOMERS table, a not null constraint on the DATE column of the INVOICES table (the DATE data type will itself ensure that any dates are valid automatically—it will not accept invalid dates), and a check constraint on the AMOUNT column on the INVOICES table.

A constraint violation will force an automatic rollback of the entire statement that hit the problem, not just the single action within the statement, and not the entire transaction.

When any DML is executed against a table with constraints defined, if the DML violates a constraint then the whole statement will be rolled back automatically. Remember that a DML statement that affects many rows might partially succeed before it hits a constraint problem with a particular row. If the statement is part of a multistatement transaction, then the statements that have already succeeded will remain intact, but uncommitted.

The Types of Constraint

The constraint types supported by the Oracle database are

- UNIQUE
- NOT NULL
- PRIMARY KEY

- FOREIGN KEY
- CHECK

Constraints have names. It is good practice to specify the names with a standard naming convention, but if they are not explicitly named, Oracle will generate names.

Unique Constraints

A unique constraint nominates a column (or combination of columns) for which the value must be different for every row in the table. If the constraint is based on a single column, this is known as the *key* column. If the constraint is composed of more than one column (known as a *composite key* unique constraint), the columns do not have to be the same data type or be adjacent in the table definition.

An oddity of unique constraints is that it is possible to enter a NULL value into the key column(s); it is indeed possible to have any number of rows with NULL values in their key column(s). So selecting rows on a key column will guarantee that only one row is returned—unless you search for NULL, in which can all the rows where the key columns are NULL will be returned.

Unique constraints are enforced by an index. When a unique constraint is defined, Oracle will look for an index on the key column(s), and if one does not exist, it will be created. Then whenever a row is inserted, Oracle will search the index to see if the values of the key columns are already present; if they are, it will reject the insert. The structure these indexes (known as B*Tree indexes) does not include NULL values, which is why many rows with NULL are permitted: they simply do not exist in the index.

While the first purpose of the index is to enforce the constraint, it has a secondary effect: improving performance if the key columns are used in the WHERE clauses of SQL statements. However, selecting WHERE `key_column` IS NULL cannot use the index (because it doesn't include the NULLs) and will therefore always result in a scan of the entire table.

Not Null Constraints

The not null constraint forces values to be entered into the key column. Not null constraints are defined per column; if the business requirement is that a group of columns should all have values, you cannot define one not null constraint for the whole group but must define a not null constraint for each column.

Any attempt to insert a row without specifying values for the not null-constrained columns results in an error. It is possible to bypass the need to specify a value by including a DEFAULT clause on the column when creating the table, as discussed in the previous section "Creating Tables."

Primary Key Constraints

The primary key is the means of locating a single row in a table. The relational database paradigm includes a requirement that every table should have a primary key: a column (or combination of columns) that can be used to distinguish every row. The Oracle database deviates from the paradigm (as do some other RDBMS implementations) by permitting tables without primary keys.

Tables without primary keys are possible, but not a good idea. Even if the business rules do not require the ability to identify every row, primary keys are often needed for maintenance work.

The implementation of a primary key constraint is in effect the union of a unique constraint and a not null constraint. The key columns must have unique values, and they may not be null. As with unique constraints, an index must exist on the constrained column(s). If one does not exist already, an index will be created when the constraint is defined. A table can have only one primary key. Try to create a second, and you will get an error. A table can, however, have any number of unique constraints and not null columns, so if there are several columns that the business analysts have decided must be unique and populated, one of these can be designated the primary key, and the others made unique and not null. An example could be a table of employees, where e-mail address, social security number, and employee number should all be required and unique.

e x a m

⚠ a t c h *Unique and primary key constraints need an index. If one does not exist, one will be created automatically.*

Foreign Key Constraints

A foreign key constraint is defined in the child table in a parent-child relationship. The constraint nominates a column (or columns) in the child table that corresponds to the primary key column(s) in the parent table. The columns do not have to have the same names, but they must be of the same data type. Foreign key constraints define the relational structure of the database: the many-to-one relationships that connect the table, in their third normal form.

If the parent table has unique constraints as well as (or instead of) a primary key constraint, these columns can be used as the basis of foreign key constraints, even if they are nullable.

Just as a unique constraint permits null values in the constrained column, so does a foreign key constraint. You can insert rows into the child table with null foreign key columns—even if there is not a row in the parent table with a null value. This creates *orphan* rows and can cause dreadful confusion. As a general rule, all the columns in a unique constraint and all the columns in a foreign key constraint are best defined with not null constraints as well; this will often be a business requirement.

A foreign key constraint is defined on the child table, but a unique or primary key constraint must already exist on the parent table.

Attempting to inset a row in the child table for which there is no matching row in the parent table will give an error. Similarly, deleting a row in the parent table will give an error if there are already rows referring to it in the child table. There are two techniques for changing this behavior. First, the constraint may be created as ON DELETE CASCADE. This means that if a row in the parent table is deleted, Oracle will search the child table for all the matching rows and delete them too. This will happen automatically. A less drastic technique is to create the constraint as ON DELETE SET NULL. In this case, if a row in the parent table is deleted, Oracle will search the child table for all the matching rows and set the foreign key columns to null. This means that the child rows will be orphaned but will still exist. If the columns in the child table also have a not null constraint, then the deletion from the parent table will fail.

It is not possible to drop or truncate the parent table in a foreign key relationship, even if there are no rows in the child table. This still applies if the ON DELETE SET NULL or ON DELETE CASCADE clauses were used.

A variation on the foreign key constraint is the *self-referencing* foreign key constraint. This defines a condition where the parent and child rows exist in the same table. An example would be a table of employees, which includes a column for the employee's manager. The manager is himself an employee and must exist in the table. So if the primary key is the EMPLOYEE_NUMBER column, and the manager is identified by a column MANAGER_NUMBER, then the foreign key constraint will state that the value of the MANAGER_NUMBER column must refer back to a valid EMPLOYEE_ NUMBER. If an employee is his own manager, then the row would refer to itself.

Check Constraints

A check constraint can be used to enforce simple rules, such as that the value entered in a column must be within a range of values. The rule must be an expression that will evaluate to TRUE or FALSE. The rules can refer to absolute values entered as literals, or to other columns in the same row, and they may make use of some functions. As many check constraints as you want can be applied to one column, but it is not possible to use a subquery to evaluate whether a value is permissible, or to use functions such as SYSDATE.

on the
Job

The not null constraint is in fact implemented as a preconfigured check constraint.

Defining Constraints

Constraints can be defined when creating a table, or added to the table later. When defining constraints at table creation time, the constraint can be defined in line with the column to which it refers, or at the end of the table definition. There is more flexibility to using the latter technique. For example, it is impossible to define a foreign key constraint that refers to two columns or a check constraint that refers to any column other than that being constrained if the constraint is defined in line, but both these are possible if the constraint is defined at the end of the table.

For the constraints that require an index (the unique and primary key constraints), the index will be created with the table if the constraint is defined at table creation time.

Consider these two table creation statements (to which line numbers have been added):

```
1    create table dept(
2    deptno number(2,0) constraint dept_deptno_pk primary key
3    constraint dept_deptno_ck check (deptno between 10 and 90),
4    dname varchar2(20) constraint dept_dname_nn not null);
5    create table emp(
6    empno number(4,0) constraint emp_empno_pk primary key,
7    ename varchar2(20) constraint emp_ename_nn not null,
8    mgr number (4,0) constraint emp_mgr_fk references emp (empno),
9    dob date,
10    hiredate date,
11    deptno number(2,0) constraint emp_deptno_fk references dept(deptno)
12    on delete set null,
13    email varchar2(30) constraint emp_email_uk unique,
```

```
14      constraint emp_hiredate_ck check (hiredate >= dob + 365*16),
15      constraint emp_email_ck
16      check ((instr(email,'@') > 0) and (instr(email,'.') > 0)));
```

Taking these statements line by line:

1. The first table created is DEPT, intended to have one row for each department.

2. DEPTNO is numeric, two digits, no decimals. This is the table's primary key. The constraint is named DEPT_DEPTNO_PK.

3. A second constraint applied to DEPTNO is a check limiting it to numbers in the range 10 to 90. The constraint is named DEPT_DEPTNO_CK.

4. The DNAME column is variable-length characters, with a constraint DEPT_DNAME_NN making it not nullable.

5. The second table created is EMP, intended to have one row for every employee.

6. EMPNO is numeric, up to four digits with no decimals. Constraint EMP_EMPNO_PK marks this as the table's primary key.

7. ENAME is variable-length characters, with a constraint EMP_ENAME_NN making it not nullable.

8. MGR is the employee's manager, who must himself be an employee. The column is defined in the same way as the table's primary key column of EMPNO. The constraint EMP_MGR_FK defines this column as a self-referencing foreign key, so any value entered must refer to an already-extant row in EMP (though it is not constrained to be not null, so it can be left blank).

9. DOB, the employee's birthday, is a date and not constrained.

10. HIREDATE is the date the employee was hired and is not constrained. At least, not yet.

11. DEPTNO is the department with which the employee is associated. The column is defined in the same way as the DEPT table's primary key column of DEPTNO, and the constraint EMP_DEPTNO_FK enforces a foreign key relationship; it is not possible to assign an employee to a department that does not exist. This is nullable, however.

12. The EMP_DEPTO_FK constraint is further defined as ON DELETE SET NULL, so if the parent row in DEPT is deleted, all matching child rows in EMPNO will have DEPTNO set to NULL.

13. EMAIL is variable-length character data and must be unique if entered (though it can be left empty).

14. This defines an additional table level constraint EMP_HIREDATE_CK. The constraint checks for use of child labor, by rejecting any rows where the date of hiring is not at least sixteen years later than the birthday. This constraint could not be defined in line with HIREDATE, because the syntax does not allow references to other columns at that point.

15., 16. An additional constraint EMP_EMAIL_CK added to the EMAIL column, which makes two checks on the e-mail address. The INSTR functions search for "@" and "." characters (which will always be present in a valid e-mail address) and if it can't find both of them, the check condition will return FALSE and the row will be rejected.

The preceding examples show several possibilities for defining constraints at table creation time. Further possibilities not covered are

- Controlling the index creation for the unique and primary key constraints
- Defining whether the constraint should be checked at insert time (which it is by default) or later on, when the transaction is committed
- Stating whether the constraint is in fact being enforced at all (which is the default) or is disabled

It is possible to create tables with no constraints and then to add them later with an ALTER TABLE command. The end result will be the same, but this technique does make the code less self-documenting, as the complete table definition will then be spread over several statements rather than being in one.

Constraint State

At any time, every constraint is either enabled or disabled, and validated or not validated. Any combination of these is syntactically possible:

- **ENABLE VALIDATE** It is not possible to enter rows that would violate the constraint, and all rows in the table conform to the constraint.
- **DISABLE NOVALIDATE** Any data (conforming or not) can be entered, and there may already be non-conforming data in the table.
- **ENABLE NOVALIDATE** There may already be non-conforming data in the table, but all data entered now must conform.
- **DISABLE VALIDATE** An impossible situation: all data in the table conforms to the constraint, but new rows need not. The end result is that the table is locked against DML commands.

The ideal situation (and the default when a constraint is defined) is ENABLE VALIDATE. This will guarantee that all the data is valid, and no invalid data can be entered. The other extreme, DISABLE NOVALIDATE, can be very useful when uploading large amounts of data into a table. It may well be that the data being uploaded does not conform to the business rules, but rather than have a large upload fail because of a few bad rows, putting the constraint in this state will allow the upload to succeed. Immediately following the upload, transition the constraint into the ENABLE NOVALIDATE state. This will prevent the situation from deteriorating further while the data is checked for conformance before transitioning the constraint to the ideal state.

As an example, consider this script, which reads data from a source table of live data into a table of archive data. The assumption is that there is a NOT NULL constraint on a column of the target table that may not have been enforced on the source table:

```
alter table sales_archive modify constraint sa_nn1 disable novalidate;
insert into sales_archive select * from sales_current;
alter table sales_archive modify constraint sa_nn1 enable novalidate;
update sales_archive set channel='NOT KNOWN' where channel is null;
alter table sales_archive modify constraint sa_nn1 enable validate;
```

Constraint Checking

Constraints can be checked as a statement is executed (an IMMEDIATE CONSTRAINT) or when a transaction is committed (a DEFERRED constraint). By default, all constraints are IMMEDIATE and not deferrable. An alternative approach to the previous example would have been possible had the constraint been created as deferrable:

```
set constraint sa_nn1 deferred;
insert into sales_archive select * from sales_current;
update sales_archive set channel='NOT KNOWN' where channel is null;
commit;

    set constraint sa_nn1 immediate;
```

For the constraint to be deferrable, it must have been created with appropriate syntax:

```
    alter table sales_archive add constraint sa_nn1
    check (channel is not null) deferrable initially immediate;
```

It is not possible to make a constraint deferrable later, if it was not created that way. The constraint SA_NN1 will by default be enforced when a row is inserted (or updated), but the check can be postponed until the transaction commits. A common use for deferrable constraints is with foreign keys. If a process inserts or updates rows in both the parent and the child tables, if the foreign key constraint is not deferred the process may fail if rows are not processed in the correct order.

By default, constraints are enabled and validated, and they are not deferrable.

Changing the status of a constraint between ENABLED/DISABLED and VALIDATE/NOVALIDATE is an operation that will affect all sessions. The status is a data dictionary update. Switching a deferrable constraint between IMMEDIATE and DEFERRED is session specific, though the initial state will apply to all sessions.

EXERCISE 9-2

Manage Constraints

In this exercise, use Database Control and SQL*Plus to define and adjust some constraints on the table created in Exercise 9-1.

1. In Database Control, navigate to the listing of HR's tables, as in Exercise 9-1, Steps 5 and 6.

2. Select the radio button for the table EX_EMPS and click the Edit button. This will take you to a window showing the column definitions of the EX_EMPS table.

3. Take the Constraints tab to view the three NOT NULL constraints that were created with the table. Note that their names are not helpful—this will be fixed in Step 10.

4. In the Constraints drop-down box, select Primary and click the Add button.

5. In the Add PRIMARY constraint window, choose the EMPLOYEE_ID column and click Continue, as in the next illustration, to return to the Edit Table window.

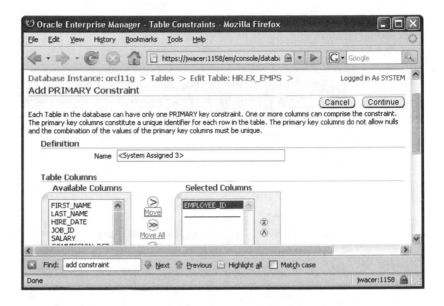

6. Click the Show SQL button to see the constraint creation statement, and then the Return button.

7. Click the Apply button to run the statement.

8. Connect to your database as user HR with SQL*Plus.

9. Run this query to find the names of the constraints:

```
select constraint_name,constraint_type,column_name
from user_constraints natural join user_cons_columns
where table_name='EX_EMPS';
```

10. Rename the constraints to something more meaningful, using the original constraint names retrieved in Step 9, with ALTER TABLE commands:

```
ALTER TABLE ex_emps RENAME CONSTRAINT old_name TO new_name ;
```

The illustration that follows shows this process, using a naming convention based on a "_PK" suffix for the primary key constraint and "_NN" for the not null check constraints.

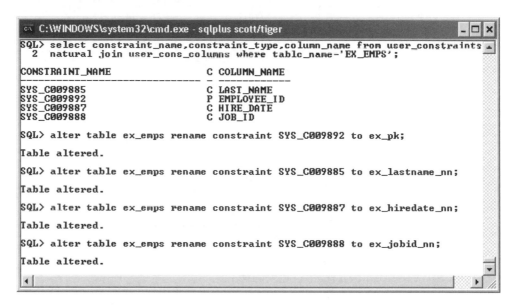

Create Indexes

Indexes have two functions: to enforce primary key and unique constraints, and to improve performance. An application's indexing strategy is critical for performance. There is no clear demarcation of whose domain index management lies within. When the business analysts specify business rules that will be implemented as constraints, they are in effect specifying indexes. The database administrators will be monitoring the execution of code running in the database, and will make recommendations for indexes. The developer, who should have the best idea of what is going on in the code and the nature of the data, will also be involved in developing the indexing strategy.

Why Indexes Are Needed

Indexes are part of the constraint mechanism. If a column (or a group of columns) is marked as a table's primary key, then every time a row is inserted into the table, Oracle must check that a row with the same value in the primary key does not already exist. If the table has no index on the column(s), the only way to do this would be to scan right through the table, checking every row. While this might be acceptable for a table of only a few rows, for a table with thousands or millions (or billions) of rows this is not feasible. An index gives (near) immediate access to key values, so the check for existence can be made virtually instantaneously. When a primary key constraint is defined, Oracle will automatically create an index on the primary key column(s), if one does not exist already.

A unique constraint also requires an index. The difference from a primary key constraint is that the column(s) of the unique constraint can be left null, perhaps in many rows. This does not affect the creation and use of the index: nulls do not go into the B*Tree indexes, as described in the next section, Types of Index.

Foreign key constraints are enforced by indexes, but the index must exist on the parent table, not necessarily on the table for which the constraint is defined. A foreign key constraint relates a column in the child table to the primary key or to a unique key in the parent table. When a row is inserted in the child table, Oracle will do a lookup on the index on the parent table to confirm that there is a matching row before permitting the insert. However, you should always create indexes on the foreign key columns within the child table for performance reasons: a DELETE on the parent table will be much faster if Oracle can use an index to determine whether there are any rows in the child table referencing the row that is being deleted.

Indexes are critical for performance. When executing any SQL statement that includes a WHERE clause, Oracle has to identify which rows of the table are to be selected or modified. If there is no index on the column(s) referenced in the WHERE clause, the only way to do this is with a *full table scan*. A full table scan reads every row of the table, in order to find the relevant rows. If the table has billions of rows, this can take hours. If there is an index on the relevant column(s), Oracle can search the index instead. An index is a sorted list of key values, structured in a manner that makes the search very efficient. With each key value is a pointer to the row in the table. Locating relevant rows via an index lookup is far faster than using a full table scan, if the table is over a certain size and the proportion of the rows to be retrieved is below a certain value. For small tables, or for a WHERE clause that will retrieve a large fraction of the table's rows, a full table scan will be quicker: you can (usually) trust Oracle to make the correct decision regarding whether to use an index, based on information the database gathers about the tables and the rows within them.

A second circumstance where indexes can be used is for sorting. A SELECT statement that includes the ORDER BY, GROUP BY, or UNION keywords (and a few others) must sort the rows into order—unless there is an index, which can return the rows in the correct order without needing to sort them first.

A third circumstance when indexes can improve performance is when tables are joined, but again Oracle has a choice: depending on the size of the tables and the memory resources available, it may be quicker to scan tables into memory and join them there, rather than use indexes. The *nested loop join* technique passes through one table using an index on the other table to locate the matching rows: this is usually a disk-intensive operation. A *hash join* technique reads the entire table into memory, converts it into a hash table, and uses a hashing algorithm to locate matching rows; this is more memory and CPU intensive. A *sort merge join* sorts the tables on the join column and then merges them together: this is often a compromise between disk, memory, and CPU resources. If there are no indexes, then Oracle is severely limited in the join techniques available.

on the **job**

Indexes will assist SELECT statements, and also any UPDATE, DELETE, or MERGE statements that use a WHERE clause—but they will slow down INSERT statements.

Types of Index

Oracle supports several types of index, which have several variations. The two index types of concern here are the B*Tree index, which is the default index type, and the bitmap index. As a general rule, indexes will improve performance for data retrieval but reduce performance for DML operations. This is because indexes must be maintained. Every time a row is inserted into a table, a new key must be inserted into every index on the table, which places an additional strain on the database. For this reason, on transaction processing systems it is customary to keep the number of indexes as low as possible (perhaps no more than those needed for the constraints) and on query-intensive systems such as a data warehouse to create as many as might be helpful.

B*Tree Indexes

A B*Tree index (the "B" stands for "balanced") is a tree structure. The root node of the tree points to many nodes at the second level, which can point to many nodes at the third level, and so on. The necessary depth of the tree will be largely determined by the number of rows in the table and the length of the index key values.

on the **Job**

The B*Tree structure is very efficient. If the depth is greater than three or four, then either the index keys are very long or the table has billions of rows. If neither of these is the case, then the index is in need of a rebuild.

The leaf nodes of the index tree store the rows' keys, in order, each with a pointer that identifies the physical location of the row. So to retrieve a row with an index lookup, if the WHERE clause is using an equality predicate on the indexed column, Oracle navigates down the tree to the leaf node containing the desired key value, and then uses the pointer to find the row. If the WHERE clause is using a non-equality predicate (such as any of the operators LIKE, BETWEEN, >, or <) then Oracle can navigate down the tree to find the first matching key value and then navigate across the leaf nodes of the index to find all the other matching values. As it does so, it will retrieve the rows from the table, in order.

The pointer to the row is the *rowid.* The rowid is an Oracle-proprietary pseudocolumn, which every row in every table has. Encrypted within it is the physical address of the row. As rowids are not part of the SQL standard, they are never visible to a normal SQL statement, but you can see them and use them if you want. This is demonstrated in Figure 9-5.

A row's rowid is globally unique. Every row in every table in the whole database will have a different rowid. The rowid encryption gives the physical address of the row; from it, Oracle can calculate which operating system file, and where in the file the row is, and go straight to it.

FIGURE 9-5

Displaying and using rowids

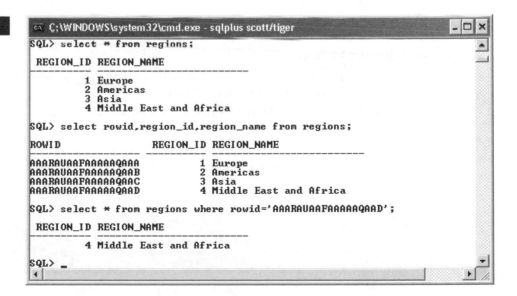

B*Tree indexes are a very efficient way of retrieving rows if the number of rows needed is low in proportion to the total number of rows in the table, and if the table is large. Consider this statement:

```
select count(*) from employees where last_name between 'A%' and 'Z%';
```

This WHERE clause is sufficiently broad that it will include every row in the table. It would be much slower to search the index to find the rowids and then use the rowids to find the rows than to scan the whole table. After all, it is the whole table that is needed. Another example would be if the table were small enough that one disk read could scan it in its entirety; there would be no point in reading an index first.

It is often said that if the query is going to retrieve more than 2 to 4 percent of the rows, then a full table scan will be quicker. A major exception to this is if the value specified in the WHERE clause is NULL. NULLs do not go into B*Tree indexes, so a query such as this:

```
select * from employees where last_name is null;
```

will always result in a full table scan. There is little value in creating a B*tree index on a column with few unique values, as it will not be sufficiently selective: the proportion of the table that will be retrieved for each distinct key value will be too high. In general, B*Tree indexes should be used if

- The cardinality (the number of distinct values) in the column is high,
- The number of rows in the table is high, and
- The column is used in WHERE clauses or JOIN conditions.

Bitmap Indexes

In many business applications, the nature of the data and the queries is such that B*Tree indexes are not of much use. Consider the table of sales for a chain of supermarkets, storing one year of historical data, which can be analyzed in several dimensions. Figure 9-6 shows a simple entity-relationship diagram, with just four of the dimensions.

The cardinality of each dimension could be quite low. Make these assumptions:

SHOP	There are four shops.
PRODUCT	There are two hundred products.
DATE	There are 365 days.
CHANNEL	There are two channels (walk-in and delivery).

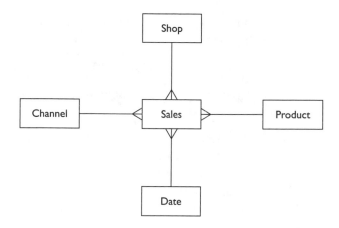

FIGURE 9-6

A fact table with
four dimensions

Assuming an even distribution of data, only two of the dimensions (PRODUCT and DATE) have a selectivity that is better than the commonly used criterion of 2 percent to 4 percent, which makes an index worthwhile. But if queries use range predicates (such as counting sales in a month or of a class of ten or more products), then not even these will qualify. This is a simple fact: B*Tree indexes are often useless in a data warehouse environment. A typical query might want to compare sales between two shops to walk-in customers of a certain class of product in a month. There could well be B*Tree indexes on the relevant columns, but Oracle would ignore them as being insufficiently selective. This is what bitmap indexes are designed for.

A bitmap index stores the rowids associated with each key value as a bitmap. The bitmaps for the CHANNEL index might look like this:

```
WALKIN      11010111000101011101011101.....
DELIVERY    00101000111010100010100010.....
```

This indicates that the first two rows were sales to walk-in customers, the third sale was a delivery, the fourth sale was a walk-in, and so on.

The bitmaps for the SHOP index might be

```
LONDON      11001001001001101001010000.....
OXFORD      00100010011000010001001000.....
READING     00010001000100000100100010.....
GLASGOW     00000100100010000010000101.....
```

This indicates that the first two sales were in the London shop, the third was in Oxford, the fourth in Reading, and so on. Now if this query is received:

```
select count(*) from sales where channel='WALKIN' and shop='OXFORD';
```

Oracle can retrieve the two relevant bitmaps and add them together with a Boolean AND operation:

```
WALKIN              1101011100010101110101101.....
OXFORD              0010001001100001000100110 0.....
WALKIN & OXFORD     0000001000000001000000000 0.....
```

The result of the AND operation shows that only the seventh and sixteenth rows qualify for selection. This merging of bitmaps is very fast and can be used to implement complex Boolean operations with many conditions on many columns using any combination of AND, OR, and NOT operators. A particular advantage that bitmap indexes have over B*Tree indexes is that they include NULLs. As far as the bitmap index is concerned, NULL is just another distinct value, which will have its own bitmap.

In general, bitmap indexes should be used if

- The cardinality (the number of distinct values) in the column is low,
- The number of rows in the table is high, and
- The column is used in Boolean algebra operations.

on the !ob

If you knew in advance what the queries would be, then you could build B*Tree indexes that would work, such as a composite index on SHOP and CHANNEL. But usually you don't know, which is where the dynamic merging of bitmaps gives great flexibility.

Index Type Options

There are six commonly used options that can be applied when creating indexes:

- Unique or non-unique
- Reverse key
- Compressed
- Composite
- Function based
- Ascending or descending

All these six variations apply to B*Tree indexes, but only the last three can be applied to bitmap indexes:

■ A *unique* index will not permit duplicate values. Non-unique is the default. The unique attribute of the index operates independently of a unique or primary key constraint: the presence of a unique index will not permit insertion of a duplicate value even if there is no such constraint defined. A unique or primary key constraint can use a non-unique index; it will just happen to have no duplicate values. This is in fact a requirement for a constraint that is deferrable, as there may be a period (before transactions are committed) when duplicate values do exist.

■ A *reverse key* index is built on a version of the key column with its bytes reversed: rather than indexing "John," it will index "nhoJ." When a SELECT is done, Oracle will automatically reverse the value of the search string. This is a powerful technique for avoiding contention in multiuser systems. For instance, if many users are concurrently inserting rows with primary keys based on a sequentially increasing number, all their index inserts will concentrate on the high end of the index. By reversing the keys, the consecutive index key inserts will tend to be spread over the whole range of the index. Even though "John" and "Jules" are close together, "nhoJ" and "seluJ" will be quite widely separated.

■ A *compressed* index stores repeated key values only once. The default is not to compress, meaning that if a key value is not unique, it will be stored once for each occurrence, each having a single rowid pointer. A compressed index will store the key once, followed by a string of all the matching rowids.

■ A *composite* index is built on the concatenation of two or more columns. There are no restrictions on mixing datatypes. If a search string does not include all the columns, the index can still be used—but if it does not include the left-most column, Oracle will have to use a skip-scanning method that is much less efficient than if the left-most column is included.

■ A *function-based* index is built on the result of a function applied to one or more columns, such as upper(last_name) or to_char(startdate, 'ccyy-m-dd'). A query will have to apply the same function to the search string, or Oracle may not be able to use the index.

By default, an index is *ascending,* meaning that the key are sorted in order of lowest value to highest. A descending index reverses this. In fact, the difference is often not important: the entries in an index are stored as a doubly linked list so it is possible to navigate up or down with equal celerity, but this will affect the order in which rows are returned if they are retrieved with an index range scan.

Creating and Using Indexes

Indexes are created implicitly when primary key and unique constraints are defined, if an index on the relevant column(s) does not already exist. The basic syntax for creating an index explicitly is

```
CREATE [UNIQUE | BITMAP] INDEX [ schema.]indexname
ON [schema.]tablename (column [, column...] ) ;
```

The default type of index is a non-unique, non-compressed, non-reverse key B*Tree index. It is not possible to create a unique bitmap index (and you wouldn't want to if you could—think about the cardinality issue). Indexes are schema objects, and it is possible to create an index in one schema on a table in another, but most people would find this somewhat confusing. A *composite* index is an index on several columns. Composite indexes can be on columns of different data types, and the columns do not have to be adjacent in the table.

on the job

Many database administrators do not consider it good practice to rely on implicit index creation. If the indexes are created explicitly, the creator has full control over the characteristics of the index, which can make it easier for the DBA to manage subsequently.

Consider this example of creating tables and indexes, and then defining constraints:

```
create table dept(deptno number,dname varchar2(10));
create table emp(empno number, surname varchar2(10),
forename varchar2(10), dob date, deptno number);
create unique index dept_i1 on dept(deptno);
create unique index emp_i1 on emp(empno);
create index emp_i2 on emp(surname,forename);
create bitmap index emp_i3 on emp(deptno);
alter table dept add constraint dept_pk primary key (deptno);
alter table emp add constraint emp_pk primary key (empno);
alter table emp add constraint emp_fk
foreign key (deptno) references dept(deptno);
```

The first two indexes created are flagged as UNIQUE, meaning that it will not be possible to insert duplicate values. This is not defined as a constraint at this point but is true nonetheless. The third index is not defined as UNIQUE and will therefore accept duplicate values; this is a composite index on two columns. The fourth index is defined as a bitmap index, because the cardinality of the column is likely to be low in proportion to the number of rows in the table.

When the two primary key constraints are defined, Oracle will detect the precreated indexes and use them to enforce the constraints. Note that the index on DEPT.DEPTNO has no purpose for performance because the table will in all likelihood be so small that the index will never be used to retrieve rows (a scan will be quicker), but it is still essential to have an index to enforce the primary key constraint.

Once they are created, use of indexes is completely transparent and automatic. Before executing a SQL statement, the Oracle server will evaluate all the possible ways of executing it. Some of these ways may involve using whatever indexes are available; others may not. Oracle will make use of the information it gathers on the tables and the environment to make an intelligent decision about which (if any) indexes to use.

on the
()ob

The Oracle server should make the best decision about index use, but if it is getting it wrong, it is possible for a programmer to embed instructions, known as optimizer hints, in code that will force the use (or not) of certain indexes.

Modifying and Dropping Indexes

There is a command ALTER INDEX . . . , but it cannot be used to change any of the characteristics described in this chapter: the type (B*Tree or bitmap) of the index, the columns, or whether it is unique or non-unique. The ALTER INDEX command lies in the database administration domain and would typically be used to adjust the physical properties of the index, not the logical properties that are of interest to developers. If it is necessary to change any of these properties, the index must be dropped and recreated. Continuing the example in the preceding section, to change the index EMP_I2 to include the employees' birthdays,

```
drop index emp_i2;
create index emp_i2 on emp(surname,forename,dob);
```

This composite index now includes columns with different data types. The columns happen to be listed in the same order that they are defined in the table, but this is by no means necessary.

When a table is dropped, all the indexes and constraints defined for the table are dropped as well. If an index was created implicitly by creating a constraint, then dropping the constraint will also drop the index. If the index had been created explicitly and the constraint created later, then if the constraint were dropped the index would survive.

EXERCISE 9-3

Create Indexes

In this exercise, add some indexes to the EX_EMPS table, and modify the one index created when the primary key constraint was added.

1. Connect to your database with SQL*Plus as user HR.

2. Determine the name and some other characteristics of the primary key index by running this query:

```
select index_name,column_name,index_type,uniqueness
from user_indexes natural join user_ind_columns
where table_name='EX_EMPS';
```

3. Create a compound B*Tree index on the employees' names:

```
create index ex_name_i on ex_emps (last_name,first_name);
```

4. Create bitmap indexes on some low-cardinality columns:

```
create bitmap index ex_dept_i on ex_emps(department_id);
create bitmap index ex_mgr_i on ex_emps (manager_id);
```

5. With Database Control, look at the indexes. The navigation path from the database home page is to take the Schema tab, and then click the Indexes link in the Database Objects section. Enter HR as the schema name and EX_EMPS as the object name, and click Go. The indexes (four, including the automatically created primary key index) will be shown.

CERTIFICATION OBJECTIVE 9.04

Create and Use Temporary Tables

A temporary table has a definition that is visible to all sessions, but the rows within it are private to the session that inserted them. The syntax is

```
CREATE GLOBAL TEMPORARY TABLE temp_tab_name
(column datatype [,column datatype…] )
[ON COMMIT {DELETE | PRESERVE} ROWS] ;
```

SCENARIO & SOLUTION

You are taking over administration of a poorly documented system. What do you need to do to build up a picture of the data structures?	This can be very difficult, but it has to be done. Running queries against DBA_CONSTRAINTS with joins to DBA_TABLES should give you an idea of the relational structure. The "Generate DDL" capability of Database Control is also useful.
When should you think about encouraging developers to use temporary tables?	If you see a lot of TRUNCATE commands, it is likely that programmers are loading data into tables, working on it, and then removing it. This is a perfect use for temporary tables. Another case is where many queries have to perform similar work, such as joining and aggregating, but then produce reports with different subsets of data, or perhaps reports that differ only in ordering or levels of subtotaling.

The column definition is the same as a regular table, and can indeed be supplied from a subquery. The optional clause at the end determines the lifetime of any rows inserted. The default is to remove the rows the moment the transaction that inserted them completes, but this behavior can be changed to preserve them until the session that inserted them ends. Whichever option is chosen, the data will be private to each session: different users can insert their own rows into their own copy of the table, and they will never see each other's rows.

In many ways, a temporary table is similar to a permanent table. You can execute any DML or SELECT command against it. It can have indexes, constraints, and triggers defined. It can be referenced in views and synonyms, or joined to other tables. The difference is that the data is transient and private to the session, and that all SQL commands against it will be far faster than commands against permanent tables.

The first reason for the speed is that temporary tables are not segments in permanent tablespaces. Ideally, they exist only in the PGAs of the sessions that are using them, so there is no disk activity or even database buffer cache activity involved. If the PGA cannot grow sufficiently to store the temporary table (which will be the case if millions of rows are being inserted—not unusual in complex report generation), then the table gets written out to a temporary segment in the user's temporary tablespace. I/O on temporary tablespaces is much faster than I/O on permanent tablespaces, because it does not go via the database buffer cache; it is all performed directly on disk by the session's server process.

A second reason for speed is that DML against temporary tables does not generate redo. Since the data only persists for the duration of a session (perhaps only for the duration of a transaction), there is no purpose in generating redo. This gives the dual benefit of fast DML for the session working on the table, and taking the strain off the redo generation system, which can be a bad point of contention on busy multiuser databases.

Figure 9-7 shows the creation and use of a temporary table with SQL*Plus. The Database Control Table Creation Wizard can also create temporary tables.

A typical use of temporary tables is for the reporting systems that run in data warehouses. A large amount of data can be extracted from source tables and loaded into temporary tables, where it can be manipulated into a form suitable for running reports. In systems such as this, the temporary tables may contain billions of rows and occupy many gigabytes of space in temporary tablespaces. But the moment the session exits, all the data will be cleared.

FIGURE 9-7

Creation and use of a temporary table

```
C:\WINDOWS\system32\cmd.exe - sqlplus scott/tiger

SQL> create global temporary table tmp_emp (dept number,salary number);
Table created.
SQL> insert into tmp_emp (select deptno,sal from emp);
14 rows created.
SQL> update tmp_emp set salary=salary*1.1;
14 rows updated.
SQL> select sum(salary) from tmp_emp;

SUM(SALARY)
-----------
    31927.5
SQL> commit;
Commit complete.
SQL> select sum(salary) from tmp_emp;

SUM(SALARY)
-----------

SQL>
```

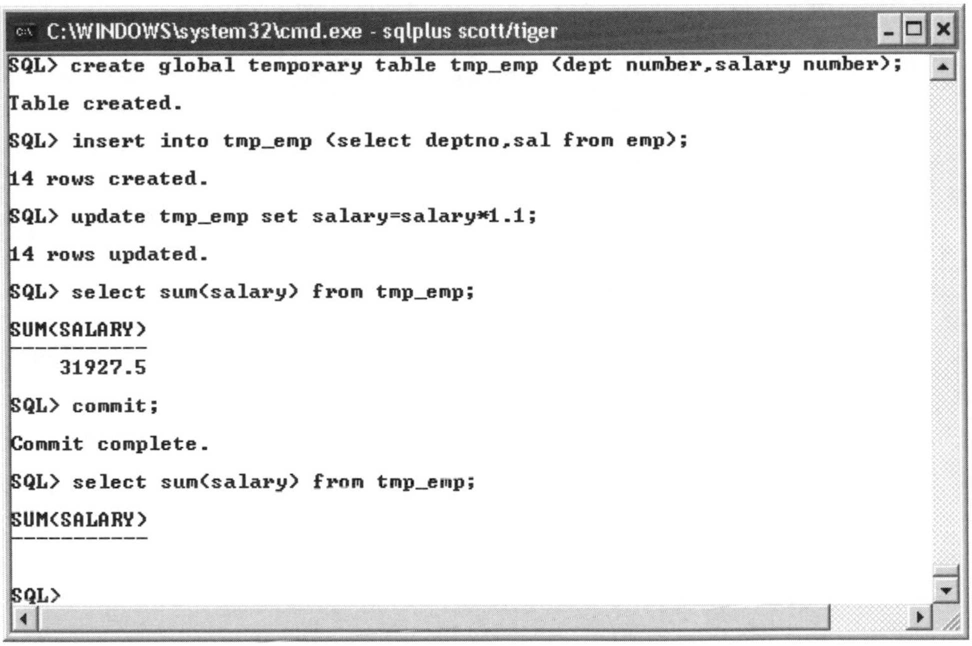

EXERCISE 9-4

Create and Use Temporary Tables

In this exercise, create a temporary table to be used for reporting on current employees. Demonstrate, by using two SQL*Plus sessions, that the data is private to each session.

1. Connect to your database with SQL*Plus as user HR.

2. Create a temporary table as follows:

```
create global temporary table tmp_emps on commit preserve
rowsas select * from employees where 1=2;
```

3. Insert some rows and commit them:

```
insert into tmp_emps select * from employees where
department_id=30;
commit;
```

4. Start a second SQL*Plus session as HR.

5. In the second session, confirm that the first insert is not visible, even though committed, and insert some different rows:

```
select count(*) from tmp_emps;
insert into tmp_emps select * from employees where
department_id=50;
commit;
```

6. In the first session, truncate the table:

```
truncate table tmp_emps;
```

7. In the second session, confirm that there are still rows in that sessions copy of the table:

```
select count(*) from tmp_emps;
```

8. In the second session, demonstrate that terminating the session does clear the rows. This will require disconnecting and connecting again:

```
disconnect;
connect hr/hr
select count(*) from tmp_emps;
```

9. Tidy up the environment by dropping the tables, either with SQL*Plus:

```
drop table tmp_emps;
drop table ex_emps;
```

or with Database Control. The indexes and constraints will have been dropped as well.

INSIDE THE EXAM

Managing Schema Objects

The published examination objectives for the first OCP DBA examination specify only knowledge of permanent and temporary tables, indexes, and constraints. However, candidates may also be expected to be familiar with views, sequences, and synonyms. All six of these schema objects are covered in the first SQL examination: the DBA exams do assume that candidates have already passed this.

The syntax for managing schema objects can be very awkward. For this reason, it may be tempting to use the wizards in Database Control for creating and modifying objects. This is fine, if you always click the Show SQL button to see the SQL statements being generated by the wizards. The syntax will be tested, and it is vital to be familiar with it.

CERTIFICATION SUMMARY

Data is stored in tables. Associated with tables are the constraints that control the relational structure of the tables of the database, which is defined by foreign, unique, and primary key constraints. Together with check constraints (including the NOT NULL constraint), these can enforce business rules.

Constraints can be enforced or held in abeyance, and if enforced there is control over when they are checked. By default, all constraints are enforced and checked at statement execution time. A constraint violation will therefore cause the statement to be rolled back.

Indexes have a dual function: to enforce foreign, unique, and primary key constraints, and to improve the performance of queries. Index creation can be automatic: triggered by creating a constraint. However, if indexes are defined manually there are several options that cam make them more useful.

Temporary tables work in many ways like permanent tables, but data in them is private to a session. Because they do not exist as segments in a permanent tablespace, but only in sessions' PGAs and in temporary segments in a temporary tablespace, operations on them are very much faster.

TWO-MINUTE DRILL

Create and Modify Tables

- ❑ Tables are schema objects, sharing a namespace with views and synonyms.
- ❑ After creation, column definitions can be added, dropped, or modified.

Manage Constraints

- ❑ Constraints can be defined at table creation time, or added later.
- ❑ A primary key is functionally equivalent to unique plus not null.
- ❑ A unique constraint does not stop insertion of many null values.
- ❑ Foreign key constraints define the relationships between tables.

Create Indexes

- ❑ Indexes are required for enforcing unique and primary key constraints.
- ❑ NULLs are not included in B*Tree indexes but are included in bitmap indexes.
- ❑ B*Tree indexes can be unique or non-unique, which determines whether they can accept duplicate key values.
- ❑ B*Tree indexes are suitable for high cardinality columns, bitmap indexes for low cardinality columns.
- ❑ Bitmap indexes can be compound, function based, or descending; B*Tree indexes can also be unique, compressed, and reverse key.

Create and Use Temporary Tables

- ❑ Rows in a temporary table are visible only to the session that inserted them.
- ❑ DML on temporary tables does not generate redo.
- ❑ Temporary tables exist only in sessions' PGAs or in temporary segments.
- ❑ A temporary table can keep rows for the duration of a session or of a transaction, depending on how it was created.

SELF TEST

Create and Modify Tables

1. Which of these statements will fail because the table name is not legal? (Choose all correct answers.)

    A. `create table "SELECT" (col1 date);`

    B. `create table "lower case" (col1 date);`

    C. `create table number1 (col1 date);`

    D. `create table 1number(col1 date);`

    E. `create table update(col1 date);`

2. Several object types share the same namespace and therefore cannot have the same name in the same schema. Which of the following object types is not in the same namespace as the others? (Choose the best answer.)

    A. Index

    B. PL/SQL stored procedure

    C. Synonym

    D. Table

    E. View

3. Which of the following is not supported by Oracle as an internal datatype? (Choose the best answer.)

    A. CHAR

    B. FLOAT

    C. INTEGER

    D. STRING

4. You need to record date-time values, with a precision of one second. What would be a suitable datatype for a single column to store this information? (Choose the best answer.)

    A. DATE.

    B. TIMESTAMP.

    C. Either DATE or TIMESTAMP.

    D. You must develop your own user-defined datatype, because the internal types store either the date or the time.

Manage Constraints

5. Some types of constraint require an index. (Choose all that apply.)
- A. CHECK
- B. NOT NULL
- C. PRIMARY KEY
- D. UNIQUE

6. A transaction consists of two statements. The first succeeds, but the second (which updates several rows) fails part way through because of a constraint violation. What will happen? (Choose the best answer.)
- A. The whole transaction will be rolled back.
- B. The second statement will be rolled back completely, and the first will be committed.
- C. The second statement will be rolled back completely, and the first will remain uncommitted.
- D. Only the one update that caused the violation will be rolled back, everything else will be committed.
- E. Only the one update that caused the violation will be rolled back, everything else will remain uncommitted.

Create Indexes

7. Which of the following statements is correct about indexes? (Choose the best answer.)
- A. An index can be based on multiple columns of a table, but the columns must be of the same datatype.
- B. An index can be based on multiple columns of a table, but the columns must be adjacent and specified in the order that they are defined in the table.
- C. An index cannot have the same name as a table, unless the index and the table are in separate schemas.
- D. None of the above statements is correct.

8. Which of the following options can be applied to B*Tree indexes, but not to bitmap indexes? (Choose all correct answers.)
- A. Compression
- B. Descending order
- C. Function-based key expressions
- D. Reverse key indexing
- E. Uniqueness
- F. Use of compound keys

Create and Use Temporary Tables

9. Data in temporary tables has restricted visibility. If a user logs on as HR and inserts rows into a temporary table, to whom will the rows be visible?

A. To no session other than the one that did the insert

B. To all sessions connected as HR

C. To all sessions, until the session that inserted them terminates

D. To all sessions, until the session that inserted them commits the transaction

10. Where does the data in a temporary table get written to disk? (Choose the best answer.)

A. It is never written to disk

B. To the user's temporary tablespace

C. To the temporary tablespace of the user in whose schema the table resides

D. To a disk local to the session's user process

LAB QUESTION

Figure 9-6 in this chapter shows an entity-relationship diagram for a simple system designed to store and analyze sales. The columns for the fact table SALES are

SALE_ID	system-generated primary key
CHANNEL_ID	foreign key to CHANNELS
PRODUCT_ID	foreign key to PRODUCTS
SHOP_ID	foreign key to SHOPS
DAY_ID	foreign key to DAYS
QUANTITY	the quantity of the product sold

It is expected that there will be several million SALES rows per year. The dimension tables are

PRODUCTS	a list of all products, including price. Cardinality of a few hundred
CHANNEL	possible sales methods, such as walk-in, Internet, and telephone
SHOPS	details of all the shops, including ZIP code—no more than a couple of dozen
DAYS	dates for which sales are being stored: 365, identified by day number

Write code to create the tables, with appropriate indexes and constraints. Consider what type of indexes will be appropriate.

Design a temporary table to be used for reporting purposes. This table should be a denormalized version of the data, which will include all the columns of the SALES fact table plus some columns from the dimension tables that will be useful for analysis: the price of the product, the description of the channel, the ZIP code of the shop, and the date of the sale. A query will be needed to extract data from the source tables and insert it into the temporary table. The work done on the temporary table will include updates, so that reports can be run on projected future changes; the data in it should therefore persist after committing changes.

SELF TEST ANSWERS

Create and Modify Tables

1. ☑ **D and E.** A table name can neither begin with a digit nor be a reserved word.
   ☒ **A and B** are wrong because the use of double quotes means they will not cause errors. **C** is wrong because it is a legal table name.

2. ☑ **A.** Indexes have their own namespace.
   ☒ **B, C, D,** and **E.** Stored procedures, synonyms, tables, and views all shared the same namespace.

3. ☑ **D.** STRING is not an internal datatype.
   ☒ **A, B,** and **C.** CHAR, FLOAT, and INTEGER are all internal datatypes.

4. ☑ **C.** Both DATE and TIMESTAMP can store per-second information.
   ☒ **A and B** are wrong because both would be correct, not one. **D** is wrong because all the date-time datatypes store both the data and the time.

Manage Constraints

5. ☑ **C and D.** Unique and primary key constraints need an index.
   ☒ **A and B.** NOT NULL and CHECK constraints are not enforced with indexes.

6. ☑ **C.** This correctly describes the result of a constraint violation.
   ☒ **A** is wrong because only the one statement is rolled back. **B** is wrong because there will be no COMMIT. **D** is wrong because there will be no COMMIT. **E** is wrong because the whole statement, not just the failing update, will be rolled back.

Create Indexes

7. ☑ **D.** All the statements are wrong.
   ☒ **A** is wrong because compound indexes need not be on columns of the same datatype. **B** is wrong because the columns in a compound index need not be physically adjacent. **C** is wrong because indexes and tables do not share the same namespace.

8. ☑ **A, D,** and **E.** Compression, reverse key, and unique can only be applied to B*Tree indexes.
   ☒ **B, C,** and **F.** Descending, function-based, and compound indexes can be either B*Tree or bitmap.

Create and Use Temporary Tables

9. ☑ **A.** Rows in a temporary table are visible only the inserting session.

☒ **B, C,** and **D.** All these incorrectly describe the scope of visibility of rows in a temporary table.

10. ☑ **B.** If a temporary table cannot fit in a session's PGA, it will be written to the session's temporary tablespace.

☒ **A** is wrong because temporary tables can be written out to temporary segments. **C** is wrong because the location of the temporary segment is session specific, not table specific. **D** is wrong because it is the session server process that writes the data, not the user process.

LAB ANSWER

There will need to be indexes on the primary key columns of all the tables. As there may be a high concurrent insert rate on the SALES table, this should be a reverse key index. The indexes on the foreign key columns of the SALES table should be bitmapped, because they are of relatively low cardinality and will be used in Boolean algebra-type queries.

This is a possible solution:

```
/*create the tables*/
create table sales
(sale_id number, channel_id number, product_id number,
shop_id number, day_id number, quantity number);
create table products (product_id number, pname varchar2(20),price number);
create table channels (channel_id number, cname varchar2(20));
create table shops (shop_id number, address varchar2(20), zip varchar2(10));
create table days (day_id number, day date);
/*pre-create indexes to be used for constraints*/
create unique index prod_pk on products(product_id);
create unique index chan_pk on channels(channel_id);
create unique index shop_pk on shops(shop_id);
create unique index day_id on days(day_id);
create unique index sales_pk on sales(sale_id) reverse;
/*create bitmap indexes on the dimension columns of the fact table*/
create bitmap index sales_chan on sales(channel_id);
create bitmap index sales_prod on sales(product_id);
create bitmap index sales_shop on sales(shop_id);
create bitmap index sales_date on sales(day_id);
/*add the primary key constraints*/
alter table products add constraint prod_pk primary key (product_id);
alter table channels add constraint chan_pk primary key (channel_id);
```

```
alter table shops add constraint shop_pk primary key (shop_id);
alter table days add constraint day_pk primary key (day_id);
alter table sales add constraint sales_pk primary key(sale_id);
/*add the foreign key constraints*/
alter table sales add constraint sales_prod_fk
foreign key (product_id) references products;
alter table sales add constraint sales_chan_fk
foreign key (channel_id) references channels;
alter table sales add constraint sales_shop_fk
foreign key (shop_id) references shops;
alter table sales add constraint sales_day_fk
foreign key (day_id) references days;
/*create the temporary table */
create global temporary table tmp_sales (sale_id number, channel_id number,
cname varchar2(20), product_id number, price number, shop_id number,
zip varchar2(10), day_id number, day date, quantity number)
on commit preserve rows;
/*the query to populate the temporary table */
insert into tmp_sales
select sale_id, channel_id, cname, product_id, price, shop_id, zip,
day_id, day, quantity
from sales natural join channels natural join products natural join shops
natural join days;
```

10
Managing Data and Concurrency

Data in a relational database is managed with the DML (data manipulation language) commands of SQL. These are INSERT, UPDATE, DELETE, and (with more recent versions of SQL) MERGE. Associated with these are the transaction control statements COMMIT and ROLLBACK. These commands are dealt with in detail in the SQL curriculum and tested in the appropriate examinations, but DML is assumed knowledge for the DBA curriculum. It is unlikely that SQL syntax will be tested in the DBA OCP examinations, but a thorough understanding of how DML statements are executed and of commit processing is essential.

SQL is an international standard defined by the ANSI and ISO bodies. It is not designed to be a complete application development language. It is a set-oriented language designed for managing data with declarative commands: you tell SQL what you want it to do, not how to do it. As such, it lacks the necessary procedural constructs and user interface facilities needed for a complete application development environment. Oracle Corporation has designed its own, proprietary, 3GL (third-generation language) to fill the gap. This language is PL/SQL. PL/SQL includes facilities for iteration, conditional branching, variables, and user interface development that application developers need. SQL commands must be embedded in the PL/SQL code whenever the code needs to access data. PL/SQL has the facilities for managing code that are found in any decent 3GL: procedures, functions, and packages. PL/SQL is covered in detail in its own curriculum and PL/SQL syntax is unlikely to be tested in the DBA OCP examinations, but familiarity with managing PL/SQL objects is required.

on the
ⓘ o b
All Oracle database administrators must be fully competent with SQL and PL/SQL. Apart from using these languages to write their own routines for managing the environment, DBAs are usually expected to tune and debug SQL and PL/SQL. They are often required to be better programmers than the programmers.

Most database applications are multiuser. Perhaps they may have thousands of concurrent users. This means that there will be times when two or more sessions need to access the same data at the same time. The Oracle database has row and table locking mechanisms that will manage this, ensuring data integrity. The locking mechanisms can be completely automatic. The database administrator must be aware of locking conflicts, and in some cases take action to solve locking problems.

Manage Data Using DML

The DML commands change data in tables. They will also change data in indexes, but this is automatic and will happen without the programmer's knowledge. The relational database paradigm defines the manner in which one or more DML statements must be grouped into *transactions*. This is not the place to go into detail on the relational database transactional paradigm—there are numerous academic texts on this—but a quick review of transaction theory is necessary before looking at how Oracle has implemented transaction management and DML.

Database Transactions

Oracle's mechanism for assuring transactional integrity is the combination of undo segments and redo log files: this mechanism is undoubtedly the best of any database yet developed and conforms perfectly with the international standards for data processing. Other database vendors comply with the same standards with their own mechanisms, but with varying levels of effectiveness. In brief, any relational database must be able to pass the ACID test: it must guarantee atomicity, consistency, isolation, and durability.

A Is for Atomicity

The principle of *atomicity* states that either all parts of transaction must complete, or none of them complete. For example, if your business analysts have said that every time you change an employee's salary, you must also change his grade, then the *atomic* transaction will consist of two updates. The database must guarantee that both go through, or neither. If only one of the updates were to succeed, you would have an employee on a salary that was incompatible with his grade: a data corruption, in business terms. If anything (anything at all!) goes wrong before the transaction is complete, the database itself must guarantee that any parts that did go through are reversed; this must happen automatically. But although an atomic transaction sounds small (like an atom), it could be enormous. To take another example, it is logically impossible in accountancy terms for the nominal ledger of an accounting suite to be half in August and half in September: the end-of-month rollover is therefore (in business terms) one atomic transaction, which may affect millions of rows in thousands of tables, and take hours to complete (or to roll back, if anything goes wrong). The *rollback* of an incomplete transaction is the reversal process and may be manual (as when you issue the ROLLBACK command), but it must be automatic and unstoppable in the case of an error. Oracle guarantees atomicity absolutely through use of undo segments, dealt with in detail in Chapter 11.

C Is for Consistency

The principle of *consistency* states that the results of a query must be consistent with the state of the database at the time the query started. Imagine a simple query that averages the value of a column of a table. If the table is large, it will take many minutes to pass through the table. If other users are updating the column while the query is in progress, should the query include the new or the old values? Should it include rows that were inserted or deleted after the query started? The principle of consistency requires that the database ensure that changed values are not seen by the query: it will give you an average of the column as it was when the query started, no matter how long the query takes or what other activity is occurring on the tables concerned.

Through the use of undo segments Oracle guarantees that if a query succeeds, the result will be consistent. However, if your undo segments are incorrectly configured, the query may not succeed: there is a famous Oracle error, ORA-1555 "snapshot too old," that is raised. This used to be an extremely difficult problem to fix with earlier releases of the database, but from release 9*i* onward you should always be able to avoid it.

I Is for Isolation

The principle of *isolation* states that an incomplete (that is, uncommitted) transaction must be invisible to the rest of the world. While the transaction is in progress, only the one session that is executing the transaction is allowed to see the changes: all other sessions must see the unchanged data, not the new values. The logic behind this is, first, that the full transaction might not go through (remember the principle of atomicity?) and that therefore no other users should be allowed to see changes that might be reversed. And second, during the progress of a transaction the data is (in business terms) inconsistent: there is a short time when the employee has had his/her salary changed, but not his/her grade. Transaction isolation requires that the database must conceal transactions in progress from other users: they will see the preupdate version of the data, until the transaction completes, when they will see all the changes as a consistent set.

Oracle guarantees transaction isolation through use of undo segments.

D Is for Durable

The principle of *durability* states that once a transaction completes, it must be impossible for the database to lose it. During the time that the transaction is in progress, the principle of isolation requires that no one (other than the session concerned) can see the changes it has made so far. But the instant the transaction completes, it must be broadcast to the world, and the database must guarantee that the change is never lost: a relational database is not allowed to lose data. Oracle fulfils this requirement through the use of log files. Log files come in two forms: online redo log files and archive redo log files. These are dealt with in detail in Chapter 15. For now, remember that it is impossible for a properly configured Oracle database to lose data. Of course, data can be lost through user error: inappropriate DML or dropping objects. But as far as Oracle and the DBA are concerned, such events are transactions like any other: according to the principle of durability, they are absolutely non-reversible.

on the job

If a database ever loses data, management's first reaction is often to fire the DBA. Everyone knows that Oracle won't lose data—that is why people buy it—therefore it must be the administrator's fault. Careers have been broken for this reason.

Executing SQL Statements

The whole of the SQL language is only a dozen or so commands. The ones we are concerned with here are

- SELECT
- INSERT
- UPDATE
- DELETE

Remember that the SQL1999 standard (implemented with Oracle Database release 9*i*) introduced the very powerful MERGE command, which combined INSERT and UPDATE. The SQL2003 standard (introduced with Oracle Database release 10*g*) took MERGE further, by adding a DELETE capability. As far as the database is concerned, a MERGE is nothing more than a combination of INSERT, UPDATE, and DELETE statements that happen to be executed with one pass through the data rather than several—there is no need to consider it separately here.

Executing a SELECT Statement

The SELECT command retrieves data. The execution of a select statement is a staged process: the server process executing the statement will first check whether the blocks containing the data required are already in memory, in the database buffer cache. If they are, then execution can proceed immediately. If they are not, the server must locate them on disk, and copy them into the database buffer cache.

e x a m

ⓦatch　　*Always remember that*　　*blocks from the database buffer cache to servers read blocks from datafiles into*　*the datafiles.*
the database buffer cache, DBWn writes

Once the data blocks required for the query are in the database buffer cache, any further processing (such as sorting or aggregation) is carried out in the PGA of the session. When the execution is complete, the result set is returned to the user process.

How does this relate to the ACID test just described? For consistency, if the query encounters a block that has been changed since the time the query started, the server process will go to the undo segment that protected the change, locate the old version of the data, and (for the purposes of the current query only) roll back the change. Thus any changes initiated after the query commenced will not be seen. A similar mechanism guarantees transaction isolation, though this is based on whether the change has been committed, not only on whether the data has been changed. Clearly, if the data needed to do this rollback is no longer in the undo segments, this mechanism will not work. That is when you get the "snapshot too old" error.

Figure 10-1 shows a representation of the way a SELECT statement is processed.

In the figure, Step 1 is the transmission of the SELECT statement from the user process to the server process. The server will search the database buffer cache to find if the necessary blocks are already in memory, and if they are, proceed to Step 4. If they are not, Step 2 is to locate the blocks in the datafiles, and Step 3 is to copy them into the database buffer cache. Step 4 transfers the data to the server process, where there may be some further processing before Step 5 returns the result of the query to the user process.

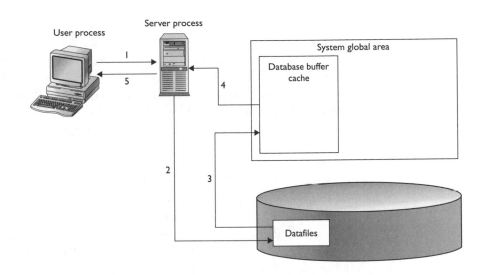

FIGURE 10-1

The stages of
execution of
a SELECT

Executing an UPDATE Statement

For any DML operation, it is necessary to work on both data blocks and undo blocks, and also to generate redo: the A, C, and I of the ACID test require generation of undo; the D requires generation of redo.

---

exam

watch *Undo is not the opposite of redo! Redo protects all block changes, no matter whether it is a change to a block of a table segment, an index segment,* *or an undo segment. As far as redo is concerned, an undo segment is just another segment, and any changes to it must be made durable.*

The first step in executing DML is the same as executing SELECT: the required blocks must be found in the database buffer cache, or copied into the database buffer cache from the datafiles. The only change is that an empty (or *expired*—more of that in Chapter 11) block of an undo segment is needed too. From then on, things are a bit more complicated.

First, locks must be placed on any rows and associated index keys that are going to be affected by the operation. This is covered later in this chapter.

Then the redo is generated: the server process writes to the log buffer the change vectors that are going to be applied to the data blocks. This generation of redo is applied both to table block changes and to undo block changes: if a column of a row is to be updated, then the rowid and the new value of the column are written to the log buffer (which is the change that will be applied to the table block), and also the old value (which is the change that will be applied to the undo block). If the column is part of an index key, then the changes to be applied to the index are also written to the log buffer, together with a change to be applied to an undo block to protect the index change.

Having generated the redo, the update is carried out in the database buffer cache: the block of table data is updated with the new version of the changed column, and the old version of the changed column is written to the block of undo segment. From this point until the update is committed, all queries from other sessions addressing the changed row will be redirected to the undo data. Only the session that is doing the update will see the actual current version of the row in the table block. The same principle applies to any associated index changes.

As a simple example, consider this statement:

```
update emp set sal=sal*1.1 where empno=7934;
```

To execute this statement, the block of table data containing the row for employee number 7934 (and possibly several others rows too, if the rows are smaller than the block) is copied into the database buffer cache, and a block of an undo segment is also copied into the cache. Then your server process writes to the log buffer the old version of the SAL column (which is the change to be applied to the block of undo) and the new version of the SAL column (which is the change to be applied to the block of table data). Lastly, the blocks themselves are updated in the database buffer cache. And remember that because SQL is a set-oriented language, if there are many rows in the EMP table with the same EMPNO, they would all be updated by the one statement. But because EMPNO will be a primary key, that won't happen.

Executing INSERT and DELETE Statements

Conceptually, INSERT and DELETE are managed in the same fashion as an UPDATE. The first step is to locate the relevant blocks in the database buffer cache, or to copy them into it if they are not there.

Redo generation is exactly the same: all change vectors to be applied to data and undo blocks are first written out to the log buffer. For an INSERT, the change vector to be applied to the table block (and possibly index blocks) are the bytes that make up the new row (and possibly the new index keys). The vector to be applied to the undo block is the rowid of the new row. For a DELETE, the change vector to be written to the undo block is the entire row.

A crucial difference between INSERT and DELETE is in the amount of undo generated. When a row is inserted, the only undo generated is writing out the new rowid to the undo block. This is because to roll back an INSERT, the only information Oracle requires is the rowid, so that this statement can be constructed:

```
delete from table_name where rowid=rowid_of_the_new_row ;
```

Executing this statement will reverse the original change.

INSERT generates a minimal amount of undo data; DELETE generates much more.

For a DELETE, the whole row (which might be several kilobytes) must be written to the undo block, so that the deletion can be rolled back if need be by constructing a statement that will insert the complete row back into the table.

Transaction Control: **COMMIT, ROLLBACK, SAVEPOINT**

Oracle's implementation of the relational database paradigm begins a transaction implicitly with the first DML statement. The transaction continues until a COMMIT or ROLLBACK statement. The SAVEPOINT command is not part of the SQL

SCENARIO & SOLUTION

If an application is running slowly and Database Control shows that locking is the problem, what might you do to resolve the problem?	In the short term, you can try killing sessions. But that is no sort of real solution. The answer will usually lie in either poor programming or poor system design. The programming issues should be discussed with the developers—are they taking more locks than necessary, or not releasing them quickly enough? Design problems should be discussed with the business analysts. Perhaps the whole transaction structure could be improved.
If an application is running slowly and the system administrators say that the system is I/O bound, what might you do to resolve the problem?	Disk I/O is never a problem. It is only a symptom of a problem. The question to ask is not "how can I improve the disk I/O?" but "how can I reduce the need for disk I/O?" This will often involve tuning the SQL and tuning memory usage. Tuning disk I/O is the last resort.

standard and is really just an easy way for programmers to back out some statements, in reverse order. It need not be considered separately, as it does not terminate a transaction.

Executing a Rollback

Remember that if anything goes wrong, rollback of transactions in progress is completely automatic and is carried out by background processes. For example, if the session that initiated the transaction fails (perhaps a PC running a user process reboots, or the network link goes down), then PMON will detect that there is a problem with the session, and roll back the transaction. If the server is rebooted while the database is in use, then on startup SMON will detect the problem and initiate a rollback of all active transactions.

A manual rollback requires the user to issue the ROLLBACK command. But however the rollback is initiated, the mechanism is identical: in the case of an UPDATE, the preupdate versions of the columns, as stored in the block of undo segment, are used to construct another UPDATE command that will set the columns of the row in the table block back to their original values. To roll back an insert, Oracle retrieves the rowid of the inserted row from the undo block and uses it as the key for a DELETE statement on the table. To roll back a DELETE, Oracle constructs a complete INSERT statement from the data in the undo block. Thus, Oracle's implementation of the ROLLBACK command is to use undo data to construct and execute another statement that will reverse the effect of the first statement. Then Oracle will issue a COMMIT that will commit both the original change and the rollback change, as one transaction.

on the **job**

A rollback will itself generate more redo as it executes, perhaps rather more than the original statement.

If you issue a DML command and omit a WHERE clause, like this,

```
delete from emp;
```

and so delete all of the several million rows in the table when you meant to delete just one, you can roll back the changes. During the deletion, your server process will have copied the rows to an undo segment as it deleted them from the table: ROLLBACK will insert them back into the table, and no one will ever know you made the mistake. Unless, of course, you typed COMMIT . . .

Executing a Commit

Commit processing is where many people (and even some experienced DBAs) show an incomplete, or indeed completely inaccurate, understanding of the Oracle architecture. When you say COMMIT, all that happens physically is that LGWR flushes the log buffer to disk. DBWn does absolutely nothing. This is one of the most important performance features of the Oracle database.

To make a transaction durable, all that is necessary is that the changes that make up the transaction are on disk: there is no need whatsoever for the actual table data to be on disk, in the datafiles. If the changes are on disk, in the form of multiplexed redo log files, then in the event of damage to the database the transaction can be reinstantiated by restoring the datafiles from a backup taken before the damage occurred and applying the changes from the logs. This process is covered in detail in later chapters—for now, just hang on to the fact that a COMMIT involves nothing more than flushing the log buffer to disk, and flagging the transaction as complete. This is why a transaction involving millions of updates in thousands of files over many minutes or hours can be committed in a fraction of a second. Because LGWR writes in very nearly real time, virtually all the transaction's changes are on disk already. When you say COMMIT, LGWR actually does write in real time: your session will hang until the write is complete. This delay will be the length of time it takes to flush the last bit of redo from the log buffer to disk, which will take milliseconds. Your session is then free to continue, and from then on all other sessions will no longer be redirected to the undo blocks when they address the changed table, unless the principle of consistency requires it.

What does DBWn do when you say COMMIT? Answer: absolutely nothing.

The change vectors written to the redo log are all the change vectors: those applied to data blocks (tables and indexes) and those applied to undo segments.

The redo log stream includes all changes: those applied to data segments and to undo segments, for both committed and uncommitted transactions.

Having said that DBWn has nothing to do with commit processing, it does of course write changed, or "dirty," blocks to disk—eventually. The algorithm used is intended to ensure that while changed blocks do get to disk, they will not be written so quickly as to impact on normal working. If DBWn never wrote blocks to disk, there would be a huge amount of work for it do when a checkpoint is finally needed. The exception is when a checkpoint is issued: these are the rare occasions (typically, only during an orderly shutdown of the database and instance) when CKPT instructs DBWn to write all dirty blocks to the datafiles. The checkpointing process is covered in detail in Chapter 15.

e x a m

w a t c h *In normal running, DBWn writes only a few dirty buffers to disk; when a checkpoint is signaled, it writes all dirty buffers to disk.*

Where there is often confusion is that the stream of redo written out to the log files by LGWR will contain changes for both committed and uncommitted transactions. Furthermore, at any given moment DBWn may or may not have written out changed blocks of data segments or undo segments to the datafiles for both committed and uncommitted transactions. So in principle, your database on disk is corrupted: the datafiles may well be storing uncommitted work, and be missing committed changes. But in the event of a crash, the stream of redo on disk always has enough information to reinstantiate any committed transactions that are not in the datafiles (by use of the changes applied to data blocks), and to reinstantiate the undo segments (by use of the changes applied to undo blocks) needed to roll back any uncommitted transactions that are in the datafiles.

DDL and Transaction Control

The COMMIT and ROLLBACK statements only apply to DML. You cannot roll back a DDL statement: once executed, it is immediately durable. If it were possible to see the source code for (for example) the CREATE TABLE command, it would be obvious why. When you create a table, you are in fact doing a transaction against some data dictionary tables: at the very least, you are inserting a row into SYS.TAB$, which is a data dictionary table with one row to define every table in the database, and one or more rows into SYS.COL$, a data dictionary table with one row for the definition of every column of every table in the database. Then the command concludes with a COMMIT. This is to protect the data dictionary: if the COMMIT were not built into the CREATE TABLE command, the possibility of an incomplete transaction would arise, and an incomplete transaction in the data dictionary could have appalling side effects.

Since it is not possible nest transactions (the SQL standard does not permit it), executing one or more DML commands followed by a DDL command will commit the whole lot: the DML statements as well as the DDL statement.

The So-Called "Autocommit"

To conclude this discussion of commit processing, it is necessary to remove any confusion about what is often called *autocommit*, or sometimes *implicit commit*. You will often hear it said that in some situations Oracle will autocommit. One of these situation is when doing DDL, which is described in the preceding section; another is when you exit from a user process such as SQL*Plus.

Quite simply, there is no such thing as an automatic commit. When you execute a DDL statement, there is a perfectly normal COMMIT included in the source code that implements the DDL command. But what about when you exit from your user process? If you are using SQL*Plus on a Windows terminal (never mind what operating system the database server is running) and you issue a DML statement followed by an EXIT, your transaction will be committed. This is because built into the SQL*Plus EXIT command there is a COMMIT statement; if we could see the source code, it would be obvious. But what if you click in the top-right corner of the SQL*Plus window? The window will close, and if you log in again, you will see that the transaction has been rolled back. This is because the programmers who wrote SQL*Plus for Microsoft Windows included a ROLLBACK statement in the code that is executed when you close the window. The behavior of SQL*Plus on other platforms may well be different; the only way to be sure is to test it. So whether you get an "autocommit" when you exit from a program in various ways is entirely dependent on how your programmers wrote your user process. The Oracle server will simply do what it is told to do.

There is a SQL*Plus command SET AUTOCOMMIT ON. This will cause SQL*Plus to modify its behavior: it will append a COMMIT to every DML statement issued. So all statements are committed immediately as soon as they are executed and cannot be rolled back. But this is happening purely on the user process side; there is still no autocommit in the database, and the changes made by a long-running statement will be isolated from other sessions until the statement completes. Of course, a disorderly exit from SQL*Plus in these circumstances, such as killing it with an operating system utility while the statement is running, will be detected by PMON and the active transaction will always be rolled back.

EXERCISE 10-1

Manage Data Using DML

In this exercise, you will demonstrate transaction isolation and control. Use two SQL*Plus sessions (or SQL Developer if you prefer), each connected as user SYSTEM. Run the commands in the steps that follow in the two sessions in the correct order.

Step	In Your First Session	In Your Second Session
1	`create table t1 as select * from all_users;`	
2	`select count(*) from t1;`	`select count(*) from t1;`
Results are the same in both sessions.		
3	`delete from t1;`	
4	`select count(*) from t1;`	`select count(*) from t1;`
Results differ because transaction isolation conceals the changes.		
5	`rollback;`	
6	`select count(*) from t1;`	`select count(*) from t1;`
Results are the same in both sessions.		
7	`delete from t1;`	
8	`select count(*) from t1;`	`select count(*) from t1;`
9	`create view v1 as select * from t1;`	
10	`select count(*) from t1;`	`select count(*) from t1;`
11	`rollback;`	
12	`select count(*) from t1;`	`select count(*) from t1;`
Oh dear! The DDL statement committed the DELETE, so it can't be rolled back.		
13	`drop view v1;`	
14	`drop table t1;`	

Identify and Administer PL/SQL Objects

PL/SQL is a programming language developed specifically for the Oracle database. It extends the SQL language by providing procedural structures and facilities for generating user interface code. Theoretically, a database administrator may not need to be an expert in PL/SQL—programming work should be done by development staff. But in practice, the more PL/SQL a DBA knows, the better. Furthermore, at most Oracle installations, the DBA will be expected to assist programmers with writing code and when necessary to create PL/SQL objects as well.

SQL and Procedural Languages

The Oracle database, like all ISO-compliant relational databases, supports the use of Structured Query Language, SQL. SQL is a set-oriented language designed for retrieving and manipulating data in client-server environments. It is very efficient at this, but there are many occasions when your programmers will want to manipulate rows one at a time, rather than in groups. SQL alone cannot handle this. Also, SQL does not have any facilities for designing user interfaces. By contrast, procedural languages can manipulate individual rows. They have commands that will allow navigation from one row to another, and can include flow control structures.

To combine the advantages of SQL's set-oriented structures with the control facilities of a procedural language, your programmers need to use a language with elements of both. The universally accepted approach is to embed SQL commands in procedural code. There are two approaches to this. The pure client-server approach is to run the procedural code on a client machine (either a user's terminal or an application server) and send the SQL commands it generates to the database server for execution. An alternative is to run the procedural code, as well as the SQL, within the database. In some ways, the second approach is more efficient: there is no network overhead, and all the code is centrally stored and managed. But it means that the language is proprietary: it will run within the database that is designed to run it, and nowhere else. A second possible problem is that all the processing workload is concentrated within the database.

PL/SQL is Oracle's proprietary 3GL that runs within the database. You can use it to retrieve and manipulate data with SQL, while using procedural constructs such as IF...THEN...ELSE or FOR or WHILE. The PL/SQL code can be stored on a client machine and sent to the server for execution, or it can be stored within the database as a named block of code.

From release 8i of the Oracle database, it is also possible to use Java within the database. Like PL/SQL, Java can be used to provide a blend of procedural code with SQL statements. Since Java can run either on a client machine (typically, an application server) or within the database, it gives you the option of distributing the processing workload—at the cost of increased network traffic. And unlike PL/SQL, it is a non-proprietary industry standard: if your application is written in Java, it should be portable to any Java-compliant database. But Java is a much lower-level language, with a far longer development cycle.

The choice of language is dependent on many factors, but PL/SQL should always be considered in the Oracle environment. It is a very quick and easy language to work with, and all DBAs should be familiar with it—if only to assist programmers.

PL/SQL always executes within the database, no matter where it is stored. Java can run either within the database or on the user machine.

Stored and Anonymous PL/SQL

PL/SQL runs within the database, but it can be stored on either the client or the server. PL/SQL code can also be entered interactively from a SQL*Plus prompt. *Stored* PL/SQL is loaded into the database and stored within the data dictionary as a named PL/SQL object. When it is saved to the database, it is compiled: the compilation process checks for syntactical errors and also picks up errors relating to the data objects the code addresses. This saves time when the code is actually run, and means that programmers should pick up errors at compilation time, before users hit them. Code stored remotely, or ad hoc code issued at the SQL*Plus prompt, is *anonymous* PL/SQL. It is compiled dynamically; this impacts on performance, and it also raises the possibility that unexpected errors might occur.

Figure 10-2 shows an example of running an anonymous PL/SQL block and of creating and running a stored procedure.

The anonymous block in Figure 10-2 creates a variable called INCREASE with the DECLARE statement and sets it to 10. Then the procedural code (within the BEGIN...END statements) uses the variable within a SQL statement that updates a column of a table.

FIGURE 10-2

Anonymous and
stored PL/SQL

```
Telnet jwacer                                                    _ □ ×
SQL>
SQL> declare increase number := 10;
  2   begin
  3   update emp set sal=sal*(100+increase)/100;
  4   commit;
  5   end;
  6   /

PL/SQL procedure successfully completed.

SQL> create procedure inc_sal(increase number) as
  2   begin
  3   update emp set sal=sal*(100+increase)/100;
  4   commit;
  5   end;
  6   /

Procedure created.

SQL> execute inc_sal(10);

PL/SQL procedure successfully completed.

SQL>
```

The second example in the figure creates a procedure called INC_SAL, stored within the data dictionary. It takes a numeric argument called INCREASE and uses this in a SQL UPDATE statement. Then the procedure is invoked with the EXECUTE command, passing in a value for the argument.

These examples are very simple, but they should illustrate how anonymous PL/SQL runs just once and therefore must be compiled at execution time, whereas stored PL/SQL can be compiled in advance and then executed many times.

on the **Ü o b** *Anonymous PL/SQL is less efficient than stored PL/SQL and also causes problems with source code management, as the code may be distributed across many machines.*

PL/SQL Objects

There are six commonly used types of PL/SQL object:

- Procedure
- Function
- Package
- Package body
- Trigger
- Type body

All of these are schema objects stored within the data dictionary. Procedures and functions do things. Packages are collections of procedures and functions, grouped together for manageability. To create these PL/SQL objects, you can use Enterprise Manager Database Control, SQL*Plus, SQL Developer, or various third-party products. Triggers are a category of object that cannot be packaged: they are associated with tables and run whenever an appropriate DML statement is executed against the tables. Object types are beyond the scope of the OCP DBA examinations.

on the

ⓙ o b

*SQL*Plus and Database Control are only suitable for small-scale PL/SQL development. For real work, your programmers will need a proper IDE (integrated development environment) tool that will assist with syntax checking, debugging, and source code management.*

Procedures and Functions

A *procedure* is a block of code that carries out some action. It can, optionally, be defined with a number of arguments. These arguments are replaced with the actual parameters given when the procedure is invoked. The arguments can be IN arguments, meaning that they are used to pass data into the procedure, or OUT arguments, meaning that they are modified by the procedure and after execution the new values are passed out of the procedure. Arguments can also be IN-OUT, where the one variable serves both purposes. Within a procedure, you can define any number of variables that, unlike the arguments, are private to the procedure. To run a procedure, either call it from within a PL/SQL block or use the interactive EXECUTE command.

A function is similar in concept to a procedure, but it does not have OUT arguments and cannot be invoked with EXECUTE. It returns a single value, with the RETURN statement.

Anything that a function can do, a procedure could do also. Functions are generally used for relatively simple operations: small code blocks that will be used many times. Procedures are more commonly used to divide code into modules, and may contain long and complex processes.

Figure 10-3 shows an example of creating and invoking a function.

The first line is an instruction to create the function, or if it already exists to overwrite it. The function takes one numeric argument and will return a varchar2 value. Within the BEGIN...END is the procedural code, which includes the flow control construct IF...THEN...ELSE...END IF.

FIGURE 10-3

Creating and
using a function
with SQL*Plus

```
Telnet jwacer                                                          - □ x
SQL> create or replace function odd_even(v1 number) return varchar2
  2   as begin
  3   if
  4     mod(v1,2)=0
  5   then
  6     return 'even';
  7   else
  8     return 'odd';
  9   end if;
 10   end odd_even;
 11   /

Function created.

SQL> select odd_even(8) from dual;

ODD_EVEN(8)
-----------------
even

SQL> select odd_even(9) from dual;

ODD_EVEN(9)
-----------------
odd

SQL>
```

on the **j o b**

*If you use CREATE, rather than CREATE OR REPLACE, you will have to drop
the object first if it already exists.*

Figure 10-4 shows an example of creating and invoking a procedure that uses an
iteration structure, which calls a user-defined function.

The procedure uses a looping construct to call a statement a variable number of
times, dependent on the value of the parameter passed to the IN argument.

FIGURE 10-4

Creating and
executing a
procedure with
SQL*Plus

```
Telnet jwacer                                                          - □ x
SQL> create or replace procedure ins_ints(v1 in number)
  2   as begin
  3   for i in 1..v1 loop
  4     insert into integers values(i,odd_even(i));
  5   end loop;
  6   end ins_ints;
  7   /

Procedure created.

SQL> execute ins_ints(5);

PL/SQL procedure successfully completed.

SQL> select * from integers;

        C1 C2
---------- -----
         1 odd
         2 even
         3 odd
         4 even
         5 odd

SQL>
```

on the **Job**

Some people get very upset about terminology. To summarize, an "argument" is the variable defined when you create a function or procedure; a "parameter" is the value passed to the argument when you run the function or procedure.

Packages

To group related procedures and functions together, your programmers create packages. A package consists of two objects: a specification and a body. A package specification lists the functions and procedures in the package, with their call specifications: the arguments and their data types. It can also define variables and constants accessible to all the procedures and functions in the package. The package body contains the PL/SQL code that implements the package: the code that creates the procedures and functions.

To create a package specification, use the CREATE PACKAGE command. For example,

```
SQL> create or replace package numbers
  2   as
  3   function odd_even(v1 number) return varchar2;
  4   procedure ins_ints(v1 in number);
  5   end numbers;
  6   /
Package created.
```

Then to create the package body, use the CREATE OR REPLACE PACKAGE BODY statement to create the individual functions and procedures.

There are several hundred PL/SQL packages provided as standard with the Oracle database. These supplied packages are, for the most part, created when you create a database. Some of them are for the use of the database administrator (such as the DBMS_WORKLOAD_REPOSITORY package, which lets you manage the Automatic Workload Repository; this is covered in Chapter 13); others are for your developers (such as the DBMS_OUTPUT package that lets them write to a session's user process).

To invoke a packaged procedure, you must prefix the procedure name with the package name. For example,

```
SQL> exec numbers.odd_even(5);
```

This will run the ODD_EVEN procedure in the NUMBERS package. The package must exist in the schema to which the user is connected, or it would be necessary to prefix the package name with the schema name. The user would also need to have the EXECUTE privilege on the package.

Database Triggers

Database *triggers* are a special category of PL/SQL object, in that they cannot be invoked manually. A trigger runs (or "fires") automatically, when a particular action is carried out, or a certain situation arises; this is the triggering event. There are a number of possible triggering events. For many of them the trigger can be configured to fire either before or after the event. It is also possible to have both before and after triggers defined for the same event. The DML triggers, that fire when rows are inserted, updated, or deleted, can be configured to fire once for each affected row, or once per statement execution.

All triggers have one factor in common: their execution is completely beyond the control of the user who caused the triggering event. He/she may not even know that the trigger fired. This makes triggers admirably suited to auditing user actions and implementing security, as will be described in Chapter 12.

The following table describes the commonly used triggering events.

Event	Before or After?

DML triggers:
 	
   INSERT
   UPDATE
   DELETE
	Before and/or after
	
	Can fire once per statement, or once per row. A MERGE command will fire whatever triggers are appropriate to the action carried out.

DDL triggers:
 	
   CREATE
   ALTER
   DROP
   TRUNCATE
	Before and/or after

Database operations:
 	
   SERVERERROR
   LOGON
   LOGOFF
   STARTUP
   SHUTDOWN
	
	After
	After
	Before
	After
	Before

SUSPEND	After Fires after a resumable operation is suspended because of a space error.

Note that there is no such thing as a trigger on SELECT, though in Chapter 12 you will see how fine-grained auditing can be used to produce a similar effect.

There are numerous uses for triggers. These might include

- **Auditing users' actions** A trigger can capture full details of what was done and who did it, and write them out to an audit table.
- **Executing complex edits** An action on one row may, in business terms, require a number of associated actions on other tables. The trigger can perform these automatically.
- **Security** A trigger can check the time, the user's IP address, the program he/she is running, and any other factors that should limit what the session can do.
- **Enforcing complex constraints** An action may be fine in terms of the constraints on one table but may need to be validated against the contents of several other tables.

Consider an HR system. Before an employee is deleted from the current employees' table, it is necessary to transfer all his/her details from a number of tables to archive tables. This could be enforced by creating a trigger as follows:

```
create or replace trigger archive_emp
before delete on current_emps
for each row
begin
archive_emp(:old.employee_id);
end;
```

Whenever any session deletes rows from the CURRENT_EMPS table, before each row is actually deleted the procedure ARCHIVE_EMP will execute, taking the EMPLOYEE_ID of the row being deleted as its parameter. This procedure will do whatever is necessary to archive an employee's data. This illustrates an important point: it is generally considered good practice to keep triggers small, and to do the bulk of the work with a stored procedure.

EXERCISE 10-2

Create PL/SQL Objects

In this exercise, you will use Database Control to create PL/SQL objects, and execute them with SQL*Plus.

1. Connect to your database as user SYSTEM with SQL*Plus.

2. Create a table to be used for this exercise:

```
create table integers(c1 number, c2 varchar2(5));
```

3. Connect to your database as user SYSTEM with Database Control.

4. From the database home page, take Schema tab then the Packages link in the Programs section. Click Create.

5. In the Create Package window, enter **NUMBERS** as the package name, and the source code for the package as shown in the next illustration. Click OK to create the package.

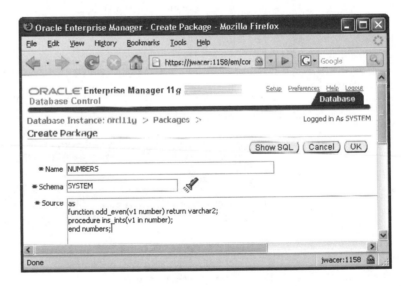

6. From the database home page, take Schema tab and then the Packages Bodies link in the Programs section. Click Create.

7. In the Create Package Body window, enter **NUMBERS** as the package name, and the source code for the package body as in the next illustration. Click OK to create the package body.

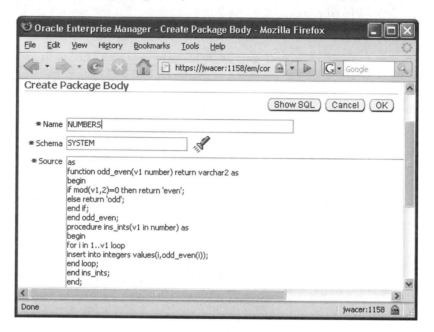

8. In your SQL*Plus session, describe the package, execute the procedure, and check the results, as in this illustration:

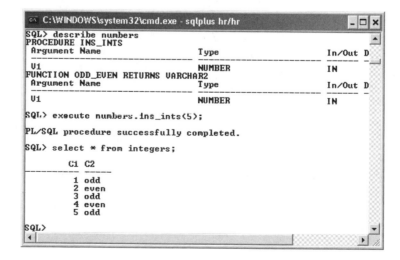

9. Tidy up by dropping the package (the table will be used in the next exercise):

```
drop package numbers;
```

Note that this DROP will COMMIT the insert of the rows.

Monitor and Resolve Locking Conflicts

In any multiuser database application it is inevitable that, eventually, two users will wish to work on the same row at the same time. This is a logical impossibility, and the database must ensure that it is a physical impossibility. The principle of transaction isolation—the I of the ACID test—requires that the database guarantee that one session cannot see or be affected by another session's transaction until the transaction has completed. To accomplish this, the database must serialize concurrent access to data; it must ensure that even though multiple sessions have requested access to the same rows, they actually queue up, and take turns.

Serialization of concurrent access is accomplished by record and table locking mechanisms. Locking in an Oracle database is completely automatic. Generally speaking, problems only arise if software tries to interfere with the automatic locking mechanism with poorly written code, or if the business analysis is faulty and results in a business model where sessions will collide.

Shared and Exclusive Locks

The standard level of locking in an Oracle database guarantees the highest possible level of concurrency. This means that if a session is updating one row, the one row is locked; nothing else. Furthermore, the row is only locked to prevent other sessions from updating it—other sessions can read it at any time. The lock is held until the transaction completes, either with a COMMIT or a ROLLBACK. This is an exclusive lock: the first session to request the lock on the row gets it, and any other sessions requesting write access must wait. Read access is permitted—though if the row has been updated by the locking session, as will usually be the case, then any reads will involve the use of undo data to make sure that reading sessions do not see any uncommitted changes.

Only one session can take an exclusive lock on a row, or a whole table, at a time—but *shared* locks can be taken on the same object by many sessions. It would not make any sense to take a shared lock on one row, because the only purpose of a row lock is to gain the exclusive access needed to modify the row. Shared locks are taken on whole tables, and many sessions can have a shared lock on the same table. The purpose of taking a shared lock on a table is to prevent another session acquiring an exclusive lock on the table: you cannot get an exclusive lock if anyone else already has a shared lock. Exclusive locks on tables are required to execute DDL statements. You cannot issue a statement that will modify an object (for instance, dropping a column of a table) if any other session already has a shared lock on the table.

To execute DML on rows, a session must acquire exclusive locks on the rows to be changed, and shared locks on the tables containing the rows. If another session already has exclusive locks on the rows, the session will hang until the locks are released by a COMMIT or a ROLLBACK. If another session already has a shared lock on the table and exclusive locks on other rows, that is not a problem. An exclusive lock on the table would be, but the default locking mechanism does not lock whole tables unless this is necessary for DDL statements.

on the

iob

It is possible to demand an exclusive lock on a whole table, but this has to be specifically requested, and programmers should have a good reason for doing it.

All DML statements require at least two locks: an exclusive lock on each row affected and a shared lock on the table containing the row. The exclusive lock prevents another session from interfering with the row, and the shared lock prevents another session from changing the table definition with a DDL statement. These locks are requested automatically. If a DML statement cannot acquire the exclusive row locks it needs, then it will hang until it gets them.

To execute DDL commands requires an exclusive lock on the object concerned. This cannot be obtained until all DML transactions against the table have finished, thereby releasing both their exclusive row locks and their shared table locks. The exclusive lock required by any DDL statement is requested automatically, but if it cannot be obtained—typically, because another session already has the shared lock granted for DML—then the statement will terminate with an error immediately.

The Enqueue Mechanism

Requests for locks are queued. If a session requests a lock and cannot get it because another session already has the row or object locked, the session will wait. It may be that several sessions are waiting for access to the same row or object—in that case,

Oracle will keep track of the order in which the sessions requested the lock. When the session with the lock releases it the next session will be granted it, and so on. This is known as the *enqueue* mechanism.

If you do not want a session to queue up if it cannot get a lock, the only way to avoid this is to use the WAIT or NOWAIT clauses of the SELECT...FOR UPDATE command. A normal SELECT will always succeed, because SELECT does not require any locks—but a DML statement will hang. The SELECT...FOR UPDATE command will select rows and lock them in exclusive mode. If any of the rows are locked already, the SELECT...FOR UPDATE statement will be queued and the session will hang until the locks are released, just as a DML statement would. To avoid sessions hanging, use either SELECT...FOR UPDATE NOWAIT or SELECT... FOR UPDATE WAIT <n>, where <n> is a number of seconds. Having obtained the locks with either of the SELECT...FOR UPDATE options, you can then issue the DML commands with no possibility of the session hanging.

on the **Job** *It is possible to append the keywords SKIP LOCKED to a SELECT FOR UPDATE statement, which will return and lock only rows that are not already locked by another session. This command existed with earlier releases but is only supported from release 11g.*

Lock Contention

When a session requests a lock on a row or object and cannot get it because another session has an exclusive lock on the row or object, it will hang. This is lock contention, and it can cause the database performance to deteriorate appallingly as all the sessions queue up waiting for locks. Some lock contention may be inevitable, as a result of normal activity: the nature of the application may be such that different users will require access to the same data. But in many cases, lock contention is caused by program and system design.

The Oracle database provides utilities for detecting lock contention, and it is also possible to solve the problem in an emergency. A special case of lock contention is the *deadlock*, which is always resolved automatically by the database itself.

on the **Job** *Lock contention is a common reason for an application which performs well under test to grind to halt when it goes production, and the number of concurrent users increases. This is not the DBA's fault, but be prepared to detect such problems.*

The Causes of Lock Contention

It may be that the nature of the business is such that users do require write access to the same rows at the same time. If this is a limiting factor in performance of the system, the only solution is business process reengineering, to develop a more efficient business model. But although some locking is a necessary part of business data processing, there are some faults in application design that can exacerbate the problem.

Long-running transactions will cause problems. An obvious case is where a user updates a row and then does not commit the change. Perhaps he/she even goes off to lunch, leaving the transaction unfinished. You cannot stop this happening if users have access to the database with tools such as SQL*Plus, but it should never occur with well-written software. The application should take care that a lock is only imposed just before an update occurs, and released (with a COMMIT or ROLLBACK) immediately afterward.

Poorly written batch processes can also cause problems, if they are coded as long transactions. Consider the case of an accounting suite nominal ledger: it is a logical impossibility in accountancy terms for the ledger to be partly in one period and partly in another, so the end-of-month rollover to the next period is one business transaction. This transaction may involve updating millions of rows in thousands of tables, and take hours to complete. If the rollover routine is coded as one transaction with a COMMIT at the end, millions of rows will be locked for hours—but in accountancy terms, this is what should happen. Good program design would avoid the problem by updating the rows in groups, with regular commits—but the programmers will also have to take care of simulating read consistency across transactions and handle the situation where the process fails part way through. If it were one transaction, this wouldn't be a problem: the database would roll it back. If it is many small transactions, they will have to manage a ledger that is half in one period and half in another. These considerations should not be a problem: your programmers should bear in mind that long transactions impact on the usability of the system and design their systems accordingly.

Third-party user process products may impose excessively high locking levels. For example, there are some application development tools that always do a SELECT... FOR UPDATE to avoid the necessity of requerying the data and checking for changes. Some other products cannot do row-level locking: if a user wants to update one row, the tool locks a group of rows—perhaps dozens or even hundreds. If your application software is written with tools such as these, the Oracle database will simply do what it is told to do: it will impose numerous locks that are unnecessary in business terms. If you suspect that the software is applying more locks than necessary, investigate whether it has configuration options to change this behavior.

Lastly, make sure your programmers are aware of the capabilities of the database. A common problem is repeatable reads. Consider this example:

```
SQL> select * from regions;
 REGION_ID REGION_NAME
---------- -------------------------
         1 Europe
         2 Americas
         3 Asia
         4 Middle East and Africa
SQL> select count(*) from regions;
  COUNT(*)
----------
         5
```

How can this be possible? The first query (the detail report) shows four rows, then the second query (the summary report) shows five. The problem is that during the course of the first query, another session inserted and committed the fifth row. One way out of this would be to lock the tables while running the reports, thus causing other sessions to hang. A more sophisticated way would be to use the SET TRANSACTION READ ONLY statement. This will guarantee (without imposing any locks) that the session does not see any DML on any tables, committed or not, until it terminates the read-only transaction with a COMMIT or ROLLBACK. The mechanism is based on use of undo segments.

Detecting and Resolving Lock Contention

There are views that will tell you what is going on with locking in the database, but this one case where even very experienced DBAs will often prefer to use the graphical tools. To reach the Database Control lock manager, take the Performance tab from the database home page, then the Instance Locks link in the Additional Monitoring Links section. Figure 10-5 shows the Database Locks window, with Blocking Locks selected. There may be any number of locks within the database, but it is usually only the locks that are causing sessions to hang that are of interest. These are known as blocking locks.

In Figure 10-5, there are two problems. Session number 116, logged on as user SCOTT, is holding an exclusive lock on one or more rows of the table HR.EMPLOYEES. This session is not hanging—it is operating normally. But session number 129, logged on as user MPHO, is blocked—it is waiting for an exclusive lock on one or more of the rows locked by session 116. Session 129 is hanging at this moment and will continue to hang until session 116 release its lock(s) by terminating its

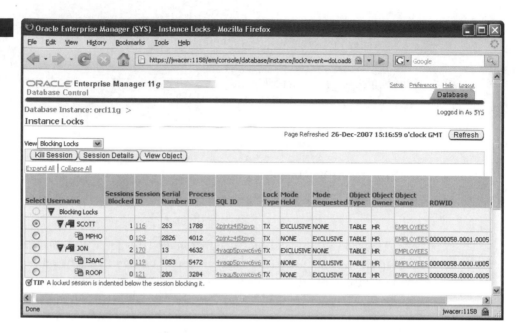

FIGURE 10-5

Showing locks
with database
control

transaction, with a COMMIT or a ROLLBACK. The second problem is worse: JON is blocking two sessions, those of ISAAC and ROOP.

Lock contention is a natural consequence of many users accessing the same data concurrently. The problem can be exacerbated by badly designed software, but in principle lock contention is part of normal database activity. It is therefore not possible for the DBA to resolve it completely—he can only identify that it is a problem, and suggest to system and application designers that they bear in mind the impact of lock contention when designing data structures and programs.

If locks are becoming an issue, as in Figure 10-5, they must be investigated. Database Control gives the necessary information. Double-clicking the values in the "SQL ID" column will let you see what statements being executed caused the lock contention. In the figure, SCOTT and MPHO have both executed one statement. JON, ISAAC, and ROOP have executed another. The "ROWID" column can be used to find the exact row for which the sessions are contending. You cannot drill down to the row from this window, but the rowid can be used in a SELECT statement to retrieve the row in another (unblocked) session. When the code and the rows that cause the contention are known, a solution can be discussed with the system designers and developers.

In an emergency, however, it is possible for the DBA to solve the problem—by terminating the session, or sessions, that are holding too many locks for too long.

When a session is terminated forcibly, any locks it holds will be released as its active transaction is rolled back. The blocked sessions will then become free and can continue.

To terminate a session, either use Database Control, or the ALTER SYSTEM KILL SESSION command. In the example above, if you decided that the SCOTT session is holding its lock for an absurd period of time, you would select the radio button for the session and click the KILL SESSION button. HR's transaction will be rolled back, and MPHO's session will then be able to take the lock(s) it requires and continue working. In the case of the second problem in the figure, killing JON's session would free up ISAAC, who would then be blocking ROOP.

INSIDE THE EXAM

Managing Data and Concurrency

In terms of the commands discussed in this chapter, there is a huge overlap with the SQL and PL/SQL curriculum. Where the subject matter differs is that this chapter gives details of how the commands are actually executed: what happens in memory, on disk, and in the data dictionary when various DML and DDL statements run.

It is vital to have a clear vision of the steps involved in running a SQL statement. The statement must first be generated by the user process. Then it is sent to the server process. The server process must either find the statement in the library cache of the shared pool or parse it (as described in Chapter 2). To execute the statement, there must be I/O on data blocks. If these are not in the database buffer cache, the server process must read them into the cache from the datafiles. If it is a SELECT statement, there may be processing in the session's PGA. If it is a DML statement, there will be change vectors applied to the

blocks, but first the change vectors are written out to the log buffer, from which they are written to the online redo log files in near-real time (and it is real time for a COMMIT). The final stage of execution is to return the results of the statement back to the user process.

In many cases, the SQL statements will be embedded in PL/SQL blocks. These blocks may be stored or generated on the client side (anonymous PL/SQL) or stored within tables in the data dictionary (stored PL/SQL). PL/SQL is Oracle's 3GL and has the features one expects to find in such languages.

Concurrent access to data is managed through the enqueue mechanism. This is a means whereby sessions lock rows as they affected by DML statements. Sessions that request locks on the same rows will serialize on these requests, hanging until they can obtain the lock. The enqueue mechanism ensures that locks are passed on in the order in which they were requested.

Deadlocks

It is possible to construct a position where two sessions block each other in such a fashion that both will hang, each waiting for the other to release its lock. This is a *deadlock*. Deadlocks are not the DBA's problem; they are caused by bad program design and resolved automatically by the database itself. Information regarding deadlocks is written out to the alert log, with full details in a trace file—part of your daily monitoring will pick up the occurrence of deadlocks and inform your developers that they are happening.

If a deadlock occurs, both sessions will hang, but only for a brief moment. One of the sessions will detect the deadlock within seconds, and it will roll back the statement that caused the problem. This will free up the other session, returning the message "ORA-00060 Deadlock detected." This message must be trapped by your programmers in their exceptions clauses, which should take appropriate action.

w a t c h *You can do nothing about deadlocks other than report them—they are resolved automatically by the database.*

It must be emphasized that deadlocks are a program design fault. They occur because the code attempts to do something that is logically impossible. Well-written codes will always request locks in a sequence that cannot cause deadlocks to occur, or will test whether incompatible locks already exist before requesting them.

EXERCISE 10-3

Detect and Resolve Lock Contention

In this exercise, you will first use SQL*Plus to cause a problem, and detect and solve them with Database Control.

1. Using SQL*Plus, connect to your database in two sessions as user SYSTEM.

2. In your first session, lock all the rows in the INTEGERS table, which was created in Exercise 10-1:

```
select * from integers for update;
```

3. In your second session, attempt to update a row. The session will hang:

```
update integers set c2='odder' where c1=1;
```

4. Connect to your database as user SYSTEM with database control.

5. Navigate to the Instance Locks window, by taking the Performance tab from the database home page, and then the Database Locks link in the Additional Monitoring Links section.

6. Observe that the second SYSTEM session is shown as waiting for an EXCLUSIVE lock. Select the radio button for the first blocking session and click Kill Session.

7. In the confirmation window, click Show SQL. This will show a command something like

   ALTER SYSTEM KILL SESSION '120,1318' IMMEDIATE

8. Click Return and Yes to execute the KILL SESSION command.

9. Returning to your SQL*Plus sessions, you will find that the second session is now working, but that the first session can no longer run any commands.

10. Tidy up the environment by dropping the table:

    ```
    drop table integers;
    ```

CERTIFICATION SUMMARY

The DML commands change data. As they write to data bocks in the database buffer cache, the change vectors applied are written out to the redo log stream. Eventually, the DBWn will write the changed buffers back to the disk, overwriting the previous versions of the blocks, but this does not happen in real time. By contrast, the change vectors go to disk almost immediately. The COMMIT processing method ensures that data will never be lost, by writing the change vectors in real time when a COMMIT command is issued. A ROLLBACK is implemented by constructing another statement (or statements) that will reverse the effect of all work done by the transaction so far. The principles of atomicity, consistency, and isolation are enforced by use of undo segments, which store the data needed to construct these reversing statements. Changes to undo segments are protected by the redo mechanism.

PL/SQL blocks can be submitted for execution within the instance as anonymous blocks sent from user processes, or retrieved from stored blocks in the data dictionary. These blocks will usually consist of procedural code with SQL code embedded within it.

Record locking is completely automatic. The default mechanism ensures the highest possible level of concurrency: row-level locking, and no locks for queries.

✓ TWO-MINUTE DRILL

Manage Data Using DML

❑ All DML commands generate undo and redo.

❑ Redo protects all changes to segments—undo segments, as well as data segments.

❑ Server processes read from data files; DBWn writes to data files.

Identify and Administer PL/SQL Objects

❑ Anonymous PL/SQL is stored on the client, stored PL/SQL in the data dictionary.

❑ Procedures and functions can be packaged; triggers cannot be packaged.

❑ PL/SQL code can call SQL code.

Monitor and Resolve Locking Conflicts

❑ The default level of locking is row level.

❑ Locks are required for all DML commands and are optional for SELECT.

❑ A DML statement requires shared locks on the objects involved and exclusive locks on the rows involved.

❑ A DDL lock requires an exclusive lock on the object it affects.

❑ Deadlocks are resolved automatically.

SELF TEST

Manage Data Using DML

1. There are several steps involved in executing a DML statement. Place these in the correct order:
   - A. Apply the change vectors to the database buffer cache.
   - B. Copy blocks from datafiles into buffers.
   - C. Search for the relevant blocks in the database buffer cache.
   - D. Write the change vectors to the log buffer.

2. When a COMMIT is issued, what will happen? (Choose the best answer.)
   - A. All the change vectors that make up the transaction are written to disk.
   - B. DBWn writes the change blocks to disk.
   - C. LGWR writes the log buffer to disk.
   - D. The undo data is deleted, so that the changes can no longer be rolled back.

3. What types of segment are protected by redo? (Choose all correct answers.)
   - A. Index segments
   - B. Table segments
   - C. Temporary segments
   - D. Undo segments

4. Which of these commands will terminate a transaction? (Choose all correct answers.)
   - A. CREATE
   - B. GRANT
   - C. SAVEPOINT
   - D. SET AUTOCOMMIT ON

Identify and Administer PL/SQL Objects

5. What type of PL/SQL objects cannot be packaged? (Choose the best answer.)
   - A. Functions
   - B. Procedures
   - C. Triggers
   - D. All PL/SQL objects can be packaged, except anonymous blocks

6. Which of these statements is not valid in a stored PL/SQL procedure?
    A. CASE
    B. IF
    C. LOOP
    D. RETURN

7. Which of these statement is false regarding PL/SQL? (Choose the best answer.)
    A. Anonymous PL/SQL does not belong to a schema.
    B. Stored PL/SQL is stored in the data dictionary.
    C. Stored PL/SQL is by default stored in the owner's default tablespace.
    D. PL/SQL can call SQL, but SQL cannot call PL/SQL.

Monitor and Resolve Locking Conflicts

8. If several sessions request an exclusive lock on the same row, what will happen? (Choose the best answer.)
    A. The first session will get the lock; after it releases the lock there is a random selection of the next session to get the lock.
    B. The first session will get an exclusive lock, and the other sessions will get shared locks.
    C. The sessions will be given an exclusive lock in the sequence in which they requested it.
    D. Oracle will detect the conflict and roll back the statements that would otherwise hang.

9. If a programmer does not request a type of lock when updating many rows in one table, what lock or locks will he be given? (Choose the best answer.)
    A. No locks at all—the default level of locking is NONE, in order to maximize concurrency
    B. An exclusive lock on the table, because this is the fastest method when many rows are being updated
    C. Shared locks on the table and on each row, because this is the safest (though not the fastest) method
    D. An exclusive lock on each row and a shared lock on the table, because this maximizes concurrency safely

10. What happens if two sessions deadlock against each other? (Choose the best answer.)
    A. Oracle will roll back one session's statement.
    B. Oracle will roll back both sessions' statements.
    C. Both sessions will hang indefinitely.
    D. Oracle will terminate one session.
    E. Oracle will terminate both sessions.

LAB QUESTION

Construct a deadlock situation, and observe Oracle's resolution of this. Create a table as a copy of the HR.REGIONS table, and in one session update region number 1, and in another session update region number 2. Then in the first session update region number 2; the session will hang. Complete the construction of the deadlock by updating region number 1 in the second session:

In Your First Session	In Your Second Session
create table t1 as select * from regions;	
update t1 set region_name='UK' where region_id=1;	update t1 set region_name='EU' where region_id=2;
update t1 set region_name='EC' where region_id=2;	update t1 set region_name='GB' where region_id=1;

Note that an ORA-00060 message is returned to the user session. From the DBA side, deadlocks can be observed in the alert log. Identify the directory where the alert log is by checking the BACKGROUND_DUMP_DEST parameter:

```
select value from v$parameter where name='background_dump_dest';
```

Open the alert log in this directory with any editor. It will be called

```
alert_instancename.log
```

At the bottom of the file there will be an entry stating that a deadlock occurred, with a reference to a trace file that will have full information. Open the trace file and study its contents.

SELF TEST ANSWERS

Manage Data Using DML

1. ☑ **C, B, D, A.** This is the sequence. All others are wrong.

2. ☑ **C.** A COMMIT is implemented by placing a COMMIT record in the log buffer, and LGWR flushing the log buffer to disk.
   ☒ **A** is wrong because many of the change vectors (perhaps all of them) will be on disk already. **B** is wrong because DBWn does not participate in commit processing. **D** is wrong because the undo data may well persist for some time; a COMMIT is not relevant to this.

3. ☑ **A, B,** and **D.** Changes to any of these will generate redo.
   ☒ **D.** Changes to temporary segments do not generate redo.

4. ☑ **A** and **B.** Both DDL and access control commands include a COMMIT
   ☒ **C** and **D.** C is wrong because a savepoint is only a marker within a transaction. D is wrong because this is a SQL*Plus command that acts locally on the user process; it has no effect on an active transaction.

Identify and Administer PL/SQL Objects

5. ☑ **C.** Triggers cannot be packaged.
   ☒ **A** and **B** are wrong because functions and procedures can be packaged. **D** is wrong because neither anonymous blocks nor triggers can be packaged.

6. ☑ **D.** A RETURN is valid in a function, not a procedure.
   ☒ **A, B,** and **C.** These are all valid in both procedures and functions.

7. ☑ **C.** PL/SQL objects are schema objects, but they reside in the data dictionary.
   ☒ **A** is wrong because anonymous PL/SQL is not a schema object. **B** is wrong because PL/SQL is stored in the data dictionary. **D** is wrong because SQL can be embedded in PL/SQL, but not the other way around.

Monitor and Resolve Locking Conflicts

8. ☑ **C.** This correctly describes the operation of the enqueue mechanism.
   ☒ **A** is wrong because locks are granted sequentially, not randomly. **B** is wrong because the shared locks apply to the object; row locks must be exclusive. **D** is wrong because this is more like a description of how deadlocks are managed.

9. ☑ **D.** This correctly describes the DML locking mechanism: a shared lock to protect the table definition, and exclusive locks to protect the rows.

   ☒ **A** is wrong because locks are always imposed. **B** is wrong because exclusive table locks are only applied if the programmer requests them. **C** is wrong because exclusive locks must always be taken on rows.

10. ☑ **A.** One of the statements will be automatically rolled back, allowing the session to continue.

   ☒ **B** is wrong because only one statement will be rolled back. The other will remain in effect, blocking its session. **C** is wrong because this is exactly the effect that is avoided. **D** and **E** are wrong because the deadlock resolution mechanism does not terminate sessions, only statements.

LAB ANSWER

The trace file recording details of the deadlock will have information similar to this:

```
*** 2007-12-28 12:46:04.084
DEADLOCK DETECTED ( ORA-00060 )
[Transaction Deadlock]
The following deadlock is not an ORACLE error. It is a
deadlock due to user error in the design of an application
or from issuing incorrect ad-hoc SQL. The following
information may aid in determining the deadlock:
Deadlock graph:
                ---------Blocker(s)--------  ---------Waiter(s)----
Resource Name   process session holds waits  process session holds waits
TX-0007001f-000005fc39     143     X              27     129          X
TX-00080004-0000061b27     129     X              39     143          X
  session 143: DID 0001-0027-0000000A    session 129: DID 0001-001B-0000003A
session 129: DID 0001-001B-0000003A session 143: DID 0001-0027-0000000A
  Rows waited on:
    Session 143: obj - rowid = 0001187A - AAARh6AAEAAAAIsAAB
    (dictionary objn - 71802, file - 4, block - 556, slot - 1)
    Session 129: obj - rowid = 0001187A - AAARh6AAEAAAAIsAAA
    (dictionary objn - 71802, file - 4, block - 556, slot - 0)
  ----- Information for the OTHER waiting sessions -----
Session 129:
    sid: 129 ser: 2675 audsid: 278286 user: 82/HR flags: 0x45
    pid: 27 O/S info: user: SYSTEM, term: JWACER, ospid: 5624
      image: ORACLE.EXE (SHAD)
    client details:
      O/S info: user: JWACER\John Watson, term: JWACER, ospid: 3848:4236
```

```
   machine: WORKGROUP\JWACER program: sqlplus.exe
   application name: SQL*Plus, hash value=3669949024
 Current SQL Statement:
 update t1 set region_name='GB' where region_id=1
----- End of information for the OTHER waiting sessions -----
 Information for THIS session:
----- Current SQL Statement for this session (sql_id=98x23kx0k87f3) -----
update t1 set region_name='EC' where region_id=2
```

Critical information is the data dictionary object numbers and the rowids of the rows on which the deadlock occurred. In this case, the object number is 71802 in both sessons, and the rowids are AAARh6AAEAAAAIsAAA and AAARh6AAEAAAAIsAAB. Use these to identify where the problem occurred. For example:

```
select owner,object_name from dba_objects where object_id=71802;
select * from owner.object_name where rowid=' AAARh6AAEAAAAIsAAA';
```

Note also that the statements issued by the sessions that caused the deadlock are included in the trace file.

The statements and the rows should be passed to the application developers, who will then fix the problem. Make sure they are aware of the statement toward the top of the trace file:

```
The following deadlock is not an ORACLE error. It is a
deadlock due to user error in the design of an application
or from issuing incorrect ad-hoc SQL.
```

This places the blame right where it belongs: deadlocks are caused by poor design, not by poor administration.

11
Managing
Undo Data

C hapter 10 described what happens in memory, and on disk, when you execute INSERT, UPDATE, or DELETE statements—the manner in which changed data is written to blocks of table and index segments, and the old version of the data is written out to blocks of an undo segment. It also covered the theory behind this, summarized as the ACID test, which every relational database must pass. In this chapter you will see the practicalities of how undo data is managed.

CERTIFICATION OBJECTIVE 11.01

Explain the Purpose of Undo

Undo data is the information needed to reverse the effects of DML statements. It is often referred to as *rollback data,* but try to avoid that term. In earlier releases of Oracle, the terms rollback data and undo data were used interchangeably, but from 9*i* onward they are different: their function is the same, but their management is not. Whenever a transaction changes data, the preupdate version of the data is written out to a rollback segment or to an undo segment. The difference is crucial. Rollback segments can still exist in an 11g database, but with release 9*i* of the database Oracle introduced the undo segment as an alternative. Oracle strongly advises that all databases should use undo segments—rollback segments are retained for backward compatibility, but they are not referenced in the OCP exam and are therefore not covered in this book. But even though "rollback" as a noun should no longer be used in the Oracle environment, "roll back" as a verb is as relevant as ever.

To roll back a transaction means to use data from the undo segments to construct an image of the data as it was before the transaction occurred. This is usually done automatically to satisfy the requirements of the ACID test, but the flashback query capability (introduced with 9*i* and greatly enhanced since) leverages the power of the undo mechanism by giving you the option of querying the database as it was at some time in the past. And of course, any user can use the ROLLBACK command interactively to back out any DML statements that he/she has issued and not committed.

The ACID test requires, first, that the database should keep preupdate versions of data in order that incomplete transactions can be reversed—either automatically in the case of an error or on demand through the use of the ROLLBACK command.

This type of rollback is permanent and published to all users. Second, for consistency, the database must be able to present a query with a version of the database as it was at the time the query started. The server process running the query will go to the undo segments and construct what is called a *read-consistent* image of the blocks being queried, if they were changed after the query started. This type of rollback is temporary and only visible to the session running the query. Third, undo segments are also used for transaction isolation. This is perhaps the most complex use of undo data. The principle of isolation requires that no transaction can be in any way dependent upon another, incomplete, transaction. In effect, even though a multiuser database will have many transactions in progress at once, the end result must be as though the transactions were executing one after another. The use of undo data combined with row and table locks (as described in Chapter 10) guarantees transaction isolation: the impossibility of incompatible transactions. Even though several transactions may be running concurrently, isolation requires that the end result must be as if the transactions were serialized.

From release 9*i* onward, undo data can also be used for flashback queries. This is a completely optional but very powerful tool that allows users to query a past image of the database. For flashback queries, undo data is used to construct a version of one or more tables as they were at some previous time by applying undo data. As with rollback for the purposes of consistency, rollback for flashback purposes is only temporary, and only visible to the session concerned.

As a final word on *rollback* as opposed to *undo*, observe the results of two queries against DBA_SEGMENTS, shown in Figure 11-1. This shows that within the database there is one segment of type ROLLBACK, and ten segments of type TYPE2 UNDO. So rollback segments do still exist in an 11*g* database. Undo segments can only exist in an undo tablespace; this is one of their features. But at database creation time, there may not be an undo tablespace. Therefore, at database creation time, Oracle creates a single old-fashioned rollback segment in the SYSTEM tablespace, along with the data dictionary. This is used during database creation but is never used in normal running. All user transactions will use undo segments, listed in DBA_SEGMENTS as segment type TYPE2 UNDO.

FIGURE 11-1

Segment types
within an 11g
database

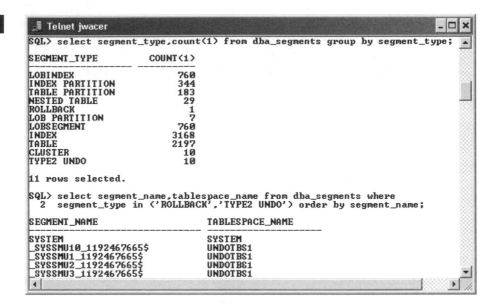

```
 Telnet jwacer                                                        - □ ×
SQL> select segment_type,count(1) from dba_segments group by segment_type;

SEGMENT_TYPE         COUNT(1)
-------------------  --------
LOBINDEX                  760
INDEX PARTITION           344
TABLE PARTITION           183
NESTED TABLE               29
ROLLBACK                    1
LOB PARTITION               7
LOBSEGMENT                760
INDEX                    3168
TABLE                    2197
CLUSTER                    10
TYPE2 UNDO                 10

11 rows selected.

SQL> select segment_name,tablespace_name from dba_segments where
  2  segment_type in ('ROLLBACK','TYPE2 UNDO') order by segment_name;

SEGMENT_NAME                    TABLESPACE_NAME
------------------------------  --------------------
SYSTEM                          SYSTEM
_SYSSMU10_1192467665$           UNDOTBS1
_SYSSMU1_1192467665$            UNDOTBS1
_SYSSMU2_1192467665$            UNDOTBS1
_SYSSMU3_1192467665$            UNDOTBS1
```

EXERCISE 11-1

Use Undo Data

In this exercise, you will investigate the undo configuration and usage in your
database. Use either SQL*Plus or SQL Developer.

1. Connect to the database as user SYSTEM.

2. Determine whether the database is using undo segments or rollback segments
   with this query:

   ```
   select value from v$parameter where name='undo_management';
   ```

   This should return the value AUTO. If it does not, issue this command, and
   then restart the instance:

   ```
   alter system set undo_management=auto scope =spfile;
   ```

3. Determine what undo tablespaces have been created, and which one is being
   used with these two queries:

   ```
   select tablespace_name from dba_tablespaces where
   contents='UNDO';
   select value from v$parameter where name='undo_tablespace';
   ```

4. Determine what undo segments are in use in the database, and how big they are:

```
select tablespace_name,segment_name,segment_id,status from
dba_rollback_segs;
select usn,rssize from v$rollstat;
```

Note that the identifying number for a segment has a different column name in the two views.

5. Find out how much undo data was being generated in your database in the recent past:

```
alter session set nls_date_format='dd-mm-yy hh24:mi:ss';
select begin_time, end_time,
(undoblks * (select value from v$parameter where
name='db_block_size'))
undo_bytes from  v$undostat;
```

CERTIFICATION OBJECTIVE 11.02

Understand How Transactions Generate Undo

When a transaction starts, Oracle will assign it to one (and only one) undo segment. Any one transaction can only be protected by one undo segment—it is not possible for the undo data generated by one transaction to cut across multiple undo segments. This is not a problem, because undo segments are not of a fixed size. So if a transaction does manage to fill its undo segment, Oracle will automatically add another extent to the segment, so that the transaction can continue. It is possible for multiple transactions to share one undo segment, but in normal running this should not occur. A tuning problem common with rollback segments was estimating how many rollback segments would be needed to avoid excessive interleaving of transactions within rollback segments without creating so many as to waste space. One feature of undo management is that Oracle will automatically spawn new undo segments on demand, in an attempt to ensure that it is never necessary for transactions to share undo segments. If Oracle has found it necessary to extend its undo segments or to generate additional segments, when the workload drops Oracle will shrink and drop the segments, again automatically.

As a transaction updates table or index data blocks, the information needed to roll back the changes is written out to blocks of the assigned undo segment. All this happens in the database buffer cache. Oracle guarantees absolutely the A, for atomicity, of the ACID test, meaning that all the undo data must be retained until a transaction commits. If necessary, the DBWn will write the changed blocks of undo data to the undo segment in the datafiles. By default, Oracle does not, however, guarantee the C, for consistency, of the ACID test. Oracle guarantees consistency to the extent that if a query succeeds, the results will be consistent with the state of the database at the time the query started—but it does not guarantee that the query will actually succeed. This means that undo data can be categorized as having different levels of necessity. *Active* undo is undo data that might be needed to roll back transactions in progress. This data can never be overwritten, until the transaction completes. At the other extreme, *expired* undo is undo data from committed transactions, which Oracle is no longer obliged to store. This data can be overwritten if Oracle needs the space for another active transaction. *Unexpired* undo is an intermediate category; it is neither active nor expired: the transaction has committed, but the undo data might be needed for consistent reads, if there are any long-running queries in progress. Oracle will attempt not to overwrite unexpired undo.

The fact that undo information becomes inactive on commit means that the extents of undo segments can be used in a circular fashion. Eventually, the whole of the undo tablespace will be filled with undo data, so when a new transaction starts, or a running transaction generates some more undo, the undo segment will "wrap" around, and the oldest undo data within it will be overwritten—always assuming that this oldest data is not part of a long-running uncommitted transaction, in which case it would be necessary to extend the undo segment instead.

With the old manually managed rollback segments, a critical part of tuning was to control which transactions were protected by which rollback segments. A rollback segment might even be created and brought online specifically for one large transaction. Automatically managed undo segments make all of that unnecessary, because you as DBA have no control over which undo segment will protect any one transaction.

Don't worry about this—Oracle does a better job that you ever could. But if you wish you can still find out which segment has been assigned to each transaction by querying the view V$TRANSACTION, which has join columns to V$SESSION and DBA_ROLLBACK_SEGS, thus letting you build up a complete picture of transaction activity in your database: how many transactions there are currently running, who is running them, which undo segments are protecting those transactions, when the transactions started, and how many blocks of undo each transaction has generated. A related dynamic performance view is V$ROLLSTAT, which gives information on the size of the segments.

on the
J o b

Undo segments are not the same as rollback segments, but the views DBA_ROLLBACK_SEGS and V$ROLLSTAT include rows for both without any flag to say which type of segment they are. The naming convention distinguishes them: undo segment names are automatically generated and prefixed with _SYSSMU.

Figure 11-2 shows queries to investigate transactions in progress. The first query shows that there are currently two transactions. JON's transaction has been assigned to the segment with SEGMENT_ID number 7 and is currently using 277 blocks of undo space. SCOTT's much smaller transaction is protected by segment 2. The second query shows the segment information. The size of each segment will depend on the size of the transactions that happen to have been assigned to them previously. Note that the join column to DBA_ROLLBACK_SEGS is called USN.

FIGURE 11-2

Query showing
details of
transactions in
progress

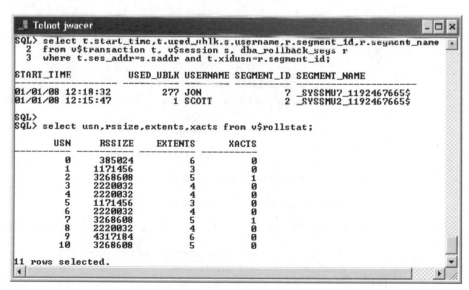

EXERCISE 11-2

Work with Transactions and Flashback Query

In this exercise, demonstrate the manner in which undo data is used to provide transaction isolation and rollback, and to implement flashback query. Use the REGIONS table in the HR demonstration schema.

Connect to the HR schema with two sessions, concurrently. These can be two SQL*Plus sessions, or two SQL Developer sessions, or one of each. The table that follows lists steps to follow in each session.

Step	In Your First Session	In Your Second Session
1	`select * from regions;`	`select * from regions;`
Both sessions see the same data.		
2	`insert into regions` `values(100,'UK');`	`insert into regions` `values(101,'GB');`
3	`select * from regions;`	`select * from regions;`
Both sessions see different results: the original data plus their own changes.		
4	`commit;`	
5	`select * from regions;`	`select * from regions;`
One transaction has been published to the world, the other is still visible to only one session.		
6	`rollback;`	`rollback;`
7	`select * from regions;`	`select * from regions;`
The committed transaction was not reversed because it has already been committed, but the uncommitted one is now completely gone, having been terminated by rolling back the change. With all transactions terminated, both sessions see a consistent view of the table.		

Demonstrate the use of flashback query, using one session connected as user HR:

1. Adjust your time display format to include seconds:

   ```
   alter session set nls_date_format='dd-mm-yy hh24:mi:ss';
   ```

2. Query and record the current time:

   ```
   select sysdate from dual;
   ```

3. Delete the row inserted previously, and commit the deletion:

   ```
   delete from regions where region_id=100;
   commit;
   ```

4. Query the table as it was before the row was deleted:

```
select * from regions
as of timestamp to_timestamp('time_from step_2',
'dd-mm-yy hh24:mi:ss');
```

The deleted row for region 100 will be listed, having been retrieved from an undo segment. The illustration that follows shows Steps 1–4, using SQL*Plus.

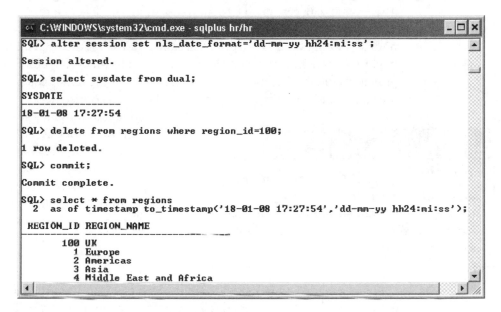

```
C:\WINDOWS\system32\cmd.exe - sqlplus hr/hr
SQL> alter session set nls_date_format='dd-mm-yy hh24:mi:ss';

Session altered.

SQL> select sysdate from dual;

SYSDATE
-----------------
18-01-08 17:27:54

SQL> delete from regions where region_id=100;

1 row deleted.

SQL> commit;

Commit complete.

SQL> select * from regions
  2  as of timestamp to_timestamp('18-01-08 17:27:54','dd-mm-yy hh24:mi:ss');

 REGION_ID REGION_NAME
---------- --------------------------
       100 UK
         1 Europe
         2 Americas
         3 Asia
         4 Middle East and Africa
```

CERTIFICATION OBJECTIVE 11.03

Manage Undo

A major feature of undo segments is that they are managed automatically, but you must set the limits within which Oracle will do its management. After considering the nature and volume of activity in your database, you set certain instance parameters and adjust the size of your undo tablespace in order to achieve your objectives.

Error Conditions Related to Undo

The principles are simple: first, there should always be sufficient undo space available to allow all transactions to continue, and second there should always be sufficient undo data available for all queries to succeed. The first principle requires that your undo tablespace must be large enough to accommodate the worst case for undo demand. It should have enough space allocated for the peak usage of active undo data generated by your transaction workload. Note that this might not be during the highest number of concurrent transactions; it could be that during normal running you have many small transactions, but the total undo they generate might be less than that generated by a single end-of-month batch job. The second principle requires that there be additional space in the undo tablespace to store unexpired undo data that might be needed for read consistency.

If a transaction runs out of undo space, it will fail with the error ORA-30036, "unable to extend segment in undo tablespace." The statement that hit the problem is rolled back, but the rest of the transaction remains intact and uncommitted. The algorithm that assigns space within the undo tablespace to undo segments means that this error condition will only arise if the undo tablespace is absolutely full of active undo data.

e x a m

ⓦatch *If a DML statement runs out of undo space, the portion of it that had already succeeded will be rolled back. The rest of the transaction remains intact, and uncommitted.*

If a query encounters a block that has been changed since the query started, it will go to the undo segment to find the preupdate version of the data. If, when it goes to the undo segment, that bit of undo data has been overwritten, the query fails on consistent read with a famous Oracle error ORA-1555, "snapshot too old."

If the undo tablespace is undersized for the transaction volume and the length of queries, Oracle has a choice: either let transactions succeed and risk queries failing with ORA-1555 or let queries succeed and risk transactions failing with ORA-30036. The default behavior is to let the transactions succeed, to allow them to overwrite unexpired undo.

Parameters for Undo Management, and Retention Guarantee

There are three parameters controlling undo: UNDO_MANAGEMENT, UNDO_TABLESPACE, and UNDO_RETENTION.

UNDO_MANAGEMENT defaults to AUTO with release 11g. It is possible to set this to MANUAL, meaning that Oracle will not use undo segments at all. This is for backward compatibility, and if you use this, you will have to do a vast amount of work creating and tuning rollback segments. Don't do it. Oracle Corporation strongly advises setting this parameter to AUTO, to enable use of undo segments. This parameter is static, meaning that if it is changed the change will not come into effect until the instance is restarted. The other parameters are dynamic—they can be changed while the running instance is running.

If you are using UNDO_MANAGEMENT=AUTO, you must also specify UNDO_TABLESPACE. This parameter nominates a tablespace, which must have been created as an undo tablespace, as the active undo tablespace. All the undo segments within it will be brought online (that is, made available for use) automatically.

Lastly, UNDO_RETENTION, set in seconds, is usually optional. It specifies a target for keeping inactive undo data and determines when it becomes classified as expired rather than unexpired. If, for example, your longest running query is thirty minutes, you would set this parameter to 1800. Oracle will then attempt to keep all undo data for at least 1800 seconds, and your query should therefore never fail with ORA-1555. If, however, you do not set this parameter, or set it to zero, Oracle will still keep data for as long as it can anyway. The algorithm controlling which expired undo data is overwritten first will always choose to overwrite the oldest bit of data; therefore, UNDO_RETENTION is always at the maximum allowed by the size of the tablespace.

on the
ᶿob

Some queries can be very long-running indeed. Queries lasting several days are not unheard of. You will need an undo tablespace the size of Jupiter if you are going to run such queries successfully during normal transaction processing. You may want to consider limiting the DML workload during long reporting runs.

Where the UNDO_RETENTION parameter is not optional is if you have configured guaranteed undo retention. The default mode of operation for undo is that Oracle will favor transactions over queries. If the sizing of the undo tablespace is such that a choice has to be made between the possibility of a query failing with ORA-1555 and the certainty of a transaction failing with ORA-30036, Oracle will choose to let the transaction continue by overwriting undo data that a query might need. In other words, the undo retention is only a target that Oracle will try to achieve. But there may be circumstances when successful queries are considered more important than successful transactions. An example might be the end-of-month billing run for a utilities company, when it might be acceptable to risk transactions being blocked for a few hours while the reports are generating. Another case is if you are making use of flashback queries, which rely on undo data.

Guaranteed undo retention, meaning that undo data will never be overwritten until the time specified by the undo retention has passed, is enabled at the tablespace level. This attribute can be specified at tablespace creation time, or an undo tablespace can altered later to enable it. Once you activate an undo tablespace for which retention guarantee has been specified, all queries will complete successfully, provided they finish within the undo retention time; you will never have "snapshot too old" errors again. The downside is that transactions may fail for lack of undo space.

If the UNDO_RETENTION parameter has been set, and the datafile(s) making up the undo tablespace is set to autoextend, then Oracle will increase the size of the datafile automatically if necessary to keep to the undo retention target. This combination of guaranteed undo retention and autoextending datafiles means that both queries and transactions will always succeed—assuming you have enough disk space. If you don't, the automatic extension will fail.

A database might have one tablespace used in normal operations where undo retention is not guaranteed, and another to be used during month-end reporting where retention is guaranteed. Such a system could be set up as shown in Figure 11-3.

```
C:\WINDOWS\system32\cmd.exe - sqlplus system/oracle

SQL>
SQL> --create the tablespaces
SQL> create undo tablespace undo_noguarantee datafile size 10m;

Tablespace created.

SQL> create undo tablespace undo_guarantee datafile size 10m;

Tablespace created.

SQL> --then for normal running
SQL> alter system set undo_tablespace=undo_noguarantee;

System altered.

SQL> --and for the end of reporting period
SQL> alter system set undo_tablespace=undo_guarantee;

System altered.

SQL>
```

Sizing and Monitoring the Undo Tablespace

The undo tablespace should be large enough to store the worst case of all the undo generated by concurrent transactions, which will be active undo, plus enough unexpired undo to satisfy the longest running query. In an advanced environment, you may also have to add space to allow for flashback queries as well. The algorithm is simple: calculate the rate at which undo is being generated at your peak workload and multiply by the length of your longest query.

There is a view, V$UNDOSTAT, that will tell you all you need to know. There is also an advisor within Database Control that will present the information in an immediately comprehensible way.

Figure 11-4 shows the undo management screen of Database Control. To reach this, take the Server tab from the database home page, then the Automatic Undo Management link in the Database Configuration section.

The configuration section of the screen shows that the undo tablespace currently in use is called UNDO1, and it is 100 MB in size. Undo guarantee has not been set, but the datafile(s) for the tablespace is autoextensible. Making your undo datafiles autoextensible will ensure that transactions will never run out of space, but Oracle will not extend them merely to meet the UNDO_RETENTION target; it is therefore still possible for a query to fail with "snapshot too old." However, you

FIGURE 11-4

Undo management settings through Database Control

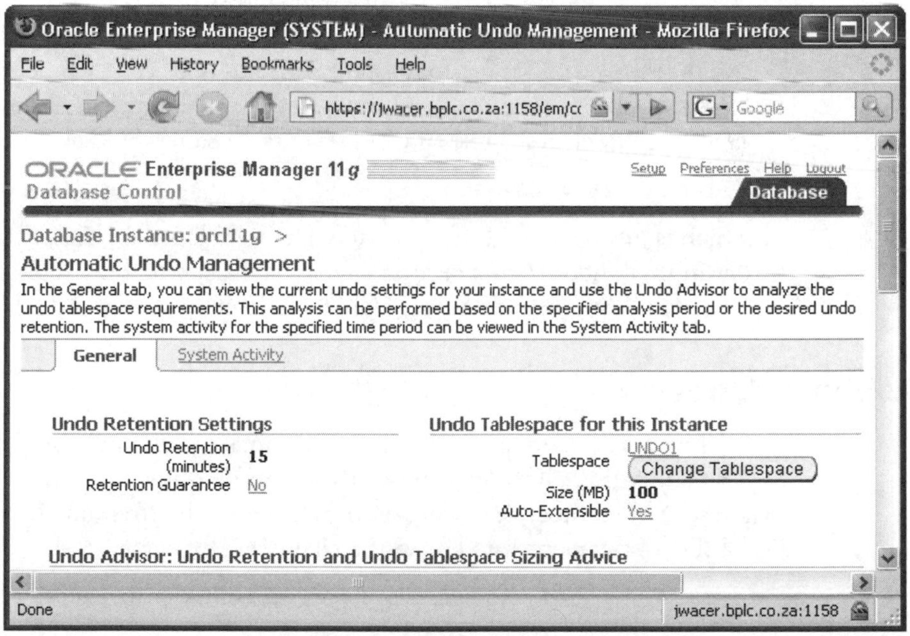

FIGURE 11-5

Undo activity
summarized by
Database Control

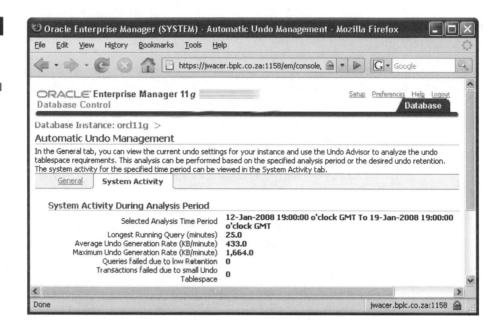

should not rely on the autoextend capability; your tablespace should be the correct
size to begin with. The Change Tablespace button will issue an ALTER SYSTEM
command to activate an alternative undo tablespace.

Further information given on the System Activity tab, shown in Figure 11-5, tells
you that the peak rate for undo generation was only 1664 KB per minute, and the
longest running query was 25 minutes. It follows that the minimum size of the undo
tablespace to be absolutely sure of preventing errors would be, in kilobytes,

```
1664 * 25 = 40265
```

which is just over 40 M. If the current size were less than that, this would be pointed
out in the Undo Advisor section. There have been no transaction errors caused by
lack of undospace, and no query failures caused by lack of undo data.

Flashback Query

Flashback query can place additional demands on the undo system. Flashback query
is a facility that allows users to see the database as it was at a time in the past. There
are several methods of making flashback queries, but the simplest is a straightforward
SELECT statement with an AS OF clause. For example:

```
select * from scott.emp as of timestamp (systimestamp - 1/1440);
```

This statement will return all the rows in the SCOTT.EMP table that were there ten minutes ago. Rows that have been deleted will be seen, rows that have been inserted will not be seen, and rows that have been updated will be seen with their old values. This is the case whether or not the DML statements have been committed. To execute a flashback query, undo data is used to roll back all the changes: the rows that have been deleted are extracted from the undo segments and inserted back into the result set; rows that have been inserted are deleted from the result set.

This statement attempts to see the table as it was a day ago:

```
select * from scott.emp as of timestamp (systimestamp - 1);
```

The first statement will probably succeed—this second statement will probably fail with a "snapshot too old" error. The failure will be because the undo data needed to reconstruct a version of the table as it was a whole day ago will (almost certainly) have been overwritten.

SCENARIO & SOLUTION

Sometimes users make awful mistakes. They delete data, they make inappropriate updates, they do things twice instead of once, and so on. What facilities should you consider to correct these mistakes?	There are several approaches for correcting user error. The most drastic is an "incomplete recovery," which puts the database back to the state it was in before the error, but this will lose all work done subsequently and may take a long (long!) time. A "database flashback" has the same result but will be much faster. A flashback query will often be the best solution—but you'll have to be quick, or the undo data will have expired.
How can you ensure that neither queries nor transactions ever fail because of undo problems?	You'll have to work out how long the longest query is ever going to be. Looking at the MAXQUERYLEN column of the $UNDOSTAT view will help. Set your UNDO_RETENTION parameter to at least this value. Then set the undo tablespace's datafile(s) to autoextend, and enable RETENTION GUARANTEE for the tablespace. But remember that this does raise the possibility of filling your disk space, which may have disastrous results. You must monitor the situation.

Flashback query can be a very valuable tool. For example, if due to some mistake a deletion has occurred (and been committed) at some time in the last hour, this command will reverse it by inserting all deleted rows back into the table:

```
insert into scott.emp
(select from * scott.emp as of timestamp (systimestamp - 1/24)
minus
select * from scott.emp);
```

If flashback query is likely to be used, then the undo system must be configured to handle it by setting the UNDO_RETENTION parameter to an appropriate value. If you want the ability to flash back a day, it must be set to 86400 seconds. The undo tablespace must be appropriately sized. Then to be certain of success, either enable automatic extension for the undo tablespace's datafile(s), or enable the retention guarantee for the tablespace.

Creating and Managing Undo Tablespaces

So far as datafile management is concerned, an undo tablespace is the same as any other tablespace: files can be added, resized, taken online and offline, and moved or renamed. But it is not possible to specify any options regarding storage: you cannot specify automatic segment space management, you cannot specify a uniform extent size. To create an undo tablespace, use the keyword UNDO:

```
CREATE UNDO TABLESPACE tablespace_name
DATAFILE datafile_name SIZE size
  [ RETENTION NOGUARANTEE | GUARANTEE ] ;
```

By default, the tablespace will not guarantee undo retention. This characteristic can be specified at tablespace creation time, or set later:

```
ALTER TABLESPACE tablespace_name
retention [ GUARANTEE | NOGUARANTEE ] ;
```

It is not possible to create segments in an undo tablespace, other than the undo segments that will be created automatically. Initially, there will be a pool of ten undo segments created in an undo tablespace. More will be created if there are more than ten concurrent transactions. Oracle will monitor the concurrent transaction rate and adjust the number of segments as necessary.

No matter how many undo tablespaces there may be in a database, generally speaking only one will be in use at a time. The undo segments in this tablespace will have a status of *online* (meaning that they are available for use); the segments in any other undo tablespaces will have status *offline*, meaning that they will not be used. If the undo tablespace is changed, all the undo segments in the old undo tablespace will be taken offline, and those in the new undo tablespace will be brought online. There are two exceptions to this:

- In a RAC database, every instance opening the database must have its own undo tablespace. This can be controlled by setting the UNDO_TABLESPACE parameter to a different value for each instance. Each instance will bring its own undo segments online.

- If the undo tablespace is changed by changing the UNDO_TABLESPACE parameter, any segments in the previously nominated tablespace that were supporting a transaction at the time of the change will remain online until the transaction finishes.

EXERCISE 11-3

Work with Undo Tablespaces

In this exercise, you will create an undo tablespace with Database Control, and then verify the configuration with SQL*Plus.

1. Connect to your instance as user SYSTEM with Database Control.
2. From the Server tab, in the Storage section take the Tablespaces link.
3. Click Create.
4. Enter **UNDO2** as the tablespace name, and set the radio buttons for Locally Managed, Undo, and Read Write.
5. At the bottom of the screen, click Add to specify a datafile.

6. Enter **UNDO2-01.DBF** as the File Name, leave everything else on default, and click Continue.

7. On the Create Tablespace screen, click Show SQL, and study the statement used to create your undo tablespace. Click Return to return to the Create Tablespace screen, and click OK to create the tablespace.

8. Connect to your instance as user SYSTEM with SQL*Plus.

9. Run this query, which will return one row for each tablespace in your database:

```
select tablespace_name,contents,retention from
dba_tablespaces;
```

Note that your new tablespace has contents UNDO, meaning that it can only be used for undo segments, and that retention is NOGUARANTEE.

10. Run this query, which will return one row for each rollback or undo segment in your database:

```
select tablespace_name, segment_name, status from
dba_rollback_segs;
```

Note that a number of undo segments have been created automatically in your new undo tablespace, but that they are all offline.

11. Adjust your instance to use the new undo tablespace. Use a SCOPE clause to ensure that the change will not be permanent:

```
alter system set undo_tablespace=undo2 scope=memory;
```

12. Rerun the query from Step 9. You will see that the undo segments in the new tablespace have bee brought online, and those in the previously active undo tablespace are offline.

INSIDE THE EXAM

Managing Undo Data

The Oracle database implements transaction atomicity and isolation and read consistency through the use of undo segments. The older rollback segments can still be used (and one rollback segment will always exist, used when creating the database), but this is very bad practice.

Undo segments are created automatically in an undo tablespace: a tablespace that can contain no other objects. The database creates undo segments on demand, attempting to match the number of segments to the number of concurrent transactions. Each segment expands as necessary to accommodate its transaction. As DBA, all you need do is ensure that the undo tablespace is big enough for the anticipated workload.

The automatic undo management mechanism will by default favor transactions over queries. If the undo tablespace is undersized, transactions will continue even they have to overwrite unexpired undo, therefore risking query failure with ORA-1555 "snapshot too old" errors. This behavior can be modified to guarantee that queries will succeed, perhaps at the risk of failing transactions.

Monitoring undo usage is simple through the Database Control undo advisor, or by querying the view V$UNDOSTAT.

CERTIFICATION SUMMARY

Undo data is generated to enable atomic transactions, read consistency, and transaction isolation. The Oracle database guarantees transactional integrity absolutely, but not necessarily read consistency. If the undo system is not appropriately configured, queries may fail because a lack on undo data—but if a query succeeds, it will be consistent. This behavior can be modified by enabling the RETENTION GUARANTEE, though this may mean that transaction fail.

Undo data is stored in a undo tablespace that can contain nothing other than automatically generated and managed undo segments. There may be more than one undo tablespaces in a database, but only one will be in use at any given moment; this is controlled by a dynamic instance parameter, UNDO_TABLESPACE.

✓ TWO-MINUTE DRILL

Explain the Purpose of Undo

❑ All DML statements generate undo data.

❑ Undo data is used for transaction rollback and isolation and to provide read consistency, and also for flashback queries.

❑ Automatic undo management using undo segments is the default with release 11g.

Understand How Transactions Generate Undo

❑ Undo data will always be kept until the transaction that generated it completes with a COMMIT or a ROLLBACK. This is *active* undo.

❑ Undo data will be retained for a period after it become inactive to satisfy any read consistency requirements of long running queries; this is *unexpired* undo.

❑ *Expired* undo is data no longer needed for read consistency and may be overwritten at any time as space in undo segments is reused.

Manage Undo

❑ An instance will use undo segments in one nominated undo tablespace.

❑ More undo tablespaces may exist, but only one will be used at a time.

❑ The undo tablespace should be large enough to store take account of the maximum rate of undo generation and the longest running query.

❑ Undo tablespace datafiles are datafiles like any others.

SELF TEST

Explain the Purpose of Undo

I. When a DML statement executes, what happens? (Choose the best answer.)

A. Both the data and the undo blocks on disk are updated, and the changes are written out to the redo stream.

B. The old version of the data is written to an undo segment, and the new version is written to the data segments and the redo log buffer.

C. Both data and undo blocks are updated in the database buffer cache, and the updates also go to the log buffer.

D. The redo log buffer is updated with information needed to redo the transaction, and the undo blocks are updated with information needed to reverse the transaction.

2. If you suspect that undo generation is a performance issue, what can you do to reduce the amount of undo data generated? (Choose the best answer.)

A. Convert from use of rollback segments to automatic undo management.

B. Set the UNDO_MANAGEMENT parameter to NONE.

C. Reduce the size of the undo segments.

D. There is nothing you can do, as all DML statements must generate undo.

Understand How Transactions Generate Undo

3. If an undo segment fills up, what will happen? (Choose the best answer.)

A. Another undo segment will be created automatically.

B. The undo segment will increase in size.

C. The undo tablespace will extend, if its datafiles are set to autoextend.

D. Transactions will continue in a different undo segment.

4. Which of the following statements are correct about undo? (Choose all correct answers.)

A. One undo segment can protect many transactions.

B. One transaction can use many undo segments.

C. One database can have many undo tablespaces.

D. One instance can have many undo tablespaces.

E. One undo segment can be cut across many datafiles.

F. Undo segments and rollback segments cannot coexist.

5. Even though you are using automatic undo segments, users are still getting "snapshot too old" errors. What could you do? (Choose all correct answers.)

   A. Increase the UNDO_RETENTION parameter.

   B. Set the RENTENTION_GUARANTEE parameter.

   C. Tune the queries to make them run faster.

   D. Increase the size of the undo tablespace.

   E. Enable RETENTION GUARANTEE.

   F. Increase the size of your undo segments.

6. Your undo tablespace has ten undo segments, but during a sudden burst of activity you have twenty concurrent transactions. What will happen? (Choose the best answer.)

   A. Oracle will create another ten undo segments.

   B. The transactions will be automatically balanced across the ten undo segments.

   C. Ten transactions will be blocked until the first ten commit.

   D. What happens will depend on your UNDO_RETENTION setting.

Manage Undo

7. Your users are reporting "ORA-1555: Snapshot too old" errors. What might be the cause of this? (Choose the best answer.)

   A. You are not generating snapshots frequently enough.

   B. The undo data is too old.

   C. There is not enough undo data.

   D. Your undo tablespace is retaining data for too long.

8. First, user JOHN initiates a query. Second, user ROOPESH updates a row that will be included in the query. Third, JOHN's query completes. Fourth, ROOPESH commits his change. Fifth, JOHN runs his query again. Which of the following statements are correct? (Choose all correct answers.)

   A. The principle of consistency means that both JOHN's queries will return the same result set.

   B. When ROOPESH commits, the undo data is flushed to disk.

   C. When ROOPESH commits, the undo becomes inactive.

   D. JOHN's first query will use undo data.

   E. JOHN's second query will use undo data.

   F. The two queries will be inconsistent with each other.

9. Your undo tablespace consists of one datafile on one disk, and transactions are failing for lack of undo space. The disk is full. You have enabled retention guarantee. Any of the following options could solve the problem, but which would cause down time for your users? (Choose the best answer.)

   A. Create another, larger, undo tablespace and use "alter system set undo_tablespace= . . ." to switch to it.

   B. Move the datafile to a disk with more space, and use "alter database resize datafile . . ." to make it bigger.

   C. Reduce the undo_retention setting with "alter system set undo_retention= . . . ."

   D. Disable retention guarantee with "alter tablespace . . . retention guarantee."

10. Examine this query and result set:

```
SQL> select BEGIN_TIME,END_TIME,UNDOBLKS,MAXQUERYLEN from V$UNDOSTAT;
BEGIN_TIME        END_TIME            UNDOBLKS MAXQUERYLEN
----------------- ----------------- ---------- -----------
02-01-08:11:35:55 02-01-08:11:41:33     14435           29
02-01-08:11:25:55 02-01-08:11:35:55    120248          296
02-01-08:11:15:55 02-01-08:11:25:55    137497           37
02-01-08:11:05:55 02-01-08:11:15:55    102760         1534
02-01-08:10:55:55 02-01-08:11:05:55    237014          540
02-01-08:10:45:55 02-01-08:10:55:55    156223         1740
02-01-08:10:35:55 02-01-08:10:45:55    145275          420
02-01-08:10:25:55 02-01-08:10:35:55     99074          120
```

The blocksize of the undo tablespace is 4 KB. Which of the following would be the optimal size for the undo tablespace? (Choose the best answer.)

   A. 1 GB

   B. 2 GB

   C. 3 GB

   D. 4 GB

LAB QUESTION

Simulate a problem with undo. You will need to be connected as user SYSTEM, or some other user to whom you have granted the DB role. The figures used on this exercise will be valid if the database block size is 8 KB.

   Create an undo tablespace with a single datafile of only 256 KB. Do not set the file to autoextend. Confirm that an undo segments has been created in this tablespace, and that it is online by querying the views DBA_ROLLBACK_SEGS and V$ROLLSTAT. Why do you think that only one undo segment was created?

Create an empty table based on the ALL_OBJECTS view with this statement:

```
create table undotest as select * from all_objects where 1=2;
```

Populate this table with the contents of the ALL_OBJECTS view:

```
insert into undotest select * from all_objects;
```

The statement will fail with an error "ORA-30036: unable to extend segment by 8 in undo tablespace." Query the new table, and you will find that it is still empty. Why is this?

Adjust the undo tablespace's data file to autoextend, and attempt to insert the contents of the ALL_OBJECTS view into the new table. This time, the insertion will succeed. Find out how many blocks of undo are needed to support the transaction so far by querying V$TRANSACTION, and how big the new datafile is by querying V$DATAFILE.

Delete every row in the new table, and repeat the queries against V$TRANSACTION and V$DATAFILE. You will see that the deletion generated many more blocks of undo and required a much larger extension of the undo datafile than the insertion. Why is this?

Tidy up by switching back to the original undo tablespace, and dropping the test table and tablespace.

SELF TEST ANSWERS

Explain the Purpose of Undo

1. ☑ **C.** All DML occurs in the database buffer cache, and changes to both data block and undo blocks are protected by redo.

   ☒ **A** is wrong because writing to disk is independent of executing the statement. **B** and **D** are incomplete: redo protects changes to both data blocks and undo blocks.

2. ☑ **D.** All DML generates undo, so the only way to reduce undo generation would be to redesign the application.

   ☒ **A** is wrong because while automatic undo is more efficient, it cannot reduce undo. **B** is wrong because there is no parameter setting that can switch off undo. **C** is wrong because the size of the segments will only affect how quickly they are reused, not how much undo is generated.

Understand How Transactions Generate Undo

3. ☑ **B.** Undo segments extend as a transaction generates more undo data.

   ☒ **A** is wrong because another undo segment will be created only if there are more concurrent transactions than segments. **C** confuses the effect of a segment filling up with that of the tablespace filling up. **D** is impossible because one transaction can only be protected by one undo segment.

4. ☑ **A, C,** and **E.** A is correct, though Oracle will try to avoid this. C is correct, though only one will be made active at any moment by the instance. E is correct, because when it comes to storage an undo segment is like any other segment: the tablespace abstracts the physical storage from the logical storage.

   ☒ **B** is wrong because one transaction is protected by one undo segment. **D** is wrong because one instance can only use one undo tablespace. **F** is wrong because undo and rollback segments can coexist—but a database can only one or the other.

5. ☑ **C, D,** and **E.** C is correct because making the queries complete faster will reduce the likelihood of snapshot too old. D is correct because it will allow more unexpired undo to be stored. E will solve the problem completely, though it may cause problems with transactions.

   ☒ **A** is wrong because it won't help by itself—it is just a target, unless combined with E. **B** is wrong because there is no such parameter. **F** is wrong because this cannot be done manually—Oracle will already be doing its best automatically.

6. ☑ **A.** Undo segments are spawned according to demand.

   ☒ **B** is wrong because more segments will be created. **C** is wrong because there is no limit imposed by the number of undo segments. **D** is wrong because this parameter is not relevant to transactions, only to queries.

Manage Undo

7. ☑ **C.** An ORA-1555 "snapshot too old" error is a clear indication that undo data is not being kept for long enough to satisfy the query workload: there is no enough undo data available.

☒ **A** is wrong because it doesn't refer to undo at all—it refers to snapshots, which existed in earlier versions of the database but are now called materialized views. **B** and **D** are both wrong because they describe the opposing situation: where undo data is being retained for longer than necessary. This is not a problem, but it may be a waste of space.

8. ☑ **C, D,** and **F.** C is correct because undo becomes inactive on commit (though it does not necessarily expire). D is correct because the query will need undo data to construct a result consistent with the state of the data at the start of the query. F is correct because Oracle guarantees consistency within a query, not across queries.

☒ **A** is wrong because Oracle guarantees consistency within a query, not across queries. **B** is wrong because there is no correlation between a COMMIT and a write to the datafiles. **E** is wrong because the second query is against a table that is not changed during the course of the query.

9. ☑ **B.** This is the option that would require downtime, because the data file would have to taken offline during the move and you cannot take it offline while the database is open.

☒ **A, C,** and **D** are wrong because they are all operations that can be carried out during normal running without end users being aware.

10. ☑ **C.** To calculate, take the largest figure for UNDBLKS, which is for a ten-minute period. Divide by 600 to get the rate of undo generation in blocks per second, and multiply by the block size to get the figure in bytes. Multiply by the largest figure for MAXQUERYLEN, to find the space needed if the highest rate of undo generation coincided with the longest query, and divide by a billion to get the answer in gigabytes:
237014 / 600 * 4192 * 1740 = 2.9 (approximately)

☒ **A, B,** and **D.**

LAB ANSWER

This is a possible solution:

```
create undo tablespace smallundo
datafile 'D:\ORADATA\SMALLUNDO.DBF' size 200k;
alter system set undo_tablespace=smallundo;
select segment_id, segment_name, tablespace_name,
status from dba_rollback_segs;
```

There is only one undo segment in the new tablespace, because the datafile is too small to store more than one.

```
create table undotest as select * from all_objects where 1=2;
insert into undotest select * from all_objects;
select count(*) from undotest;
```

There are no rows in the table because the insertion was rolled back.

```
alter database datafile 'D:\ORADATA\SMALLUNDO.DBF' autoextend on;
insert into undotest select * from all_objects;
select xidusn,USED_UBLK from v$transaction;
select bytes from v$datafile where name='D:\ORADATA\SMALLUNDO.DBF';
delete from undotest;
```

A deletion generates much more undo (in this example, perhaps sixty times as much) than an insertion, because whereas an insertion only needs to write the new row ID to the undo segments, a deletion must write out the complete row.

Tidy up:

```
alter system set undo_tablespace=undotbs1;
drop table undotest;
drop tablespace smallundo including contents and datafiles;
```

12

Implementing Oracle Database Security

S
ecurity is an issue of vital concern at all sites. All organizations should have a security manual documenting rules and procedures. If your organization does not have such a manual, someone should be writing it—perhaps that someone should be you. In security, there is no right or wrong; there is only conformance or non-conformance to agreed procedures. If administrators follow the rules and advise on what those rules should be, then any breach of security is not their fault. But unfortunately, history shows that when something goes wrong in the security arena, there is a great desire to blame individuals. It is vitally important that administration staff should be able to point to a rule book that lays down the procedures they should follow, and to routines and logs that demonstrate that they did indeed follow them. This devolves the responsibility to the authors of the rule book, the security manual. If no such manual exists, then any problems are likely to be dumped on the most convenient scapegoat. This is often the database administrator(DBA). You have been warned.

The Oracle product set provides many facilities for enforcing security up to and beyond the highest standards specified by any legislation. Many of the facilities (such as data encryption) are beyond the scope of the first OCP examination, where the treatment of security is limited to use of privileges and auditing.

CERTIFICATION OBJECTIVE 12.01

Database Security and Principle of Least Privilege

The safest principle to follow when determining access to computer systems is that of *least privilege*: no one should have access to anything beyond the absolute minimum needed to perform their work, and anything not specifically allowed is forbidden. The Oracle database conforms to this, in that by default no one can do anything at all, with the exception of the two users SYS and SYSTEM. No other users can even connect, not even those created by the standard database creation routines.

In addition to the use of password profiles described in Chapter 8, there are best practices that should be followed to assist with implementing the least-privilege principle, particularly regarding privileges granted to the PUBLIC account and certain instance parameters.

Public Privileges

There is a role called PUBLIC, which is implicitly granted to every user. Any privileges granted to PUBLIC have, in effect, been granted to everyone who can connect to the database; every account you create will have access to these privileges. By default, the public user has a large number of privileges. In particular, he/she has execute permission on a number of PL/SQL utility packages, as shown in Figure 12-1.

You should always consider revoking the execution privileges on the UTL packages, but remember that application software may assume that the privilege is there. Revoke the privilege as follows:

```
SQL> revoke execute on utl_file from public;
```

Some of the more dangerous packages listed in Figure 12-1 are

■ **UTL_FILE** This allows users to read and write any file and directory that is accessible to the operating system Oracle owner. This includes all the database files, and the ORACLE_HOME directory. On Windows systems, this is particularly dangerous, as many Windows databases run with Administrator privileges. The package is to a certain extent controlled by the UTL_FILE_DIR instance parameter, discussed in the next section.

■ **UTL_TCP** This allows users to open TCP ports on the server machine for connections to any accessible address on the network. The interface provided in the package only allows connections to be initiated by the PL/SQL program; it does not allow the PL/SQL program to accept connections initiated outside

---

FIGURE 12-1

Privileges granted to PUBLIC

```
C:\WINDOWS\system32\cmd.exe - sqlplus / as sysdba

SQL>
SQL> select count(*) from dba_tab_privs where grantee='PUBLIC';

  COUNT(*)
----------
     27477

SQL> select table_name from dba_tab_privs where grantee='PUBLIC'
  2  and privilege='EXECUTE' and table_name like 'UTL%';

TABLE_NAME
------------------------------
UTL_TCP
UTL_HTTP
UTL_FILE
UTL_INADDR
UTL_SMTP
UTL_URL
UTL_ENCODE
UTL_GDK
UTL_COMPRESS
```

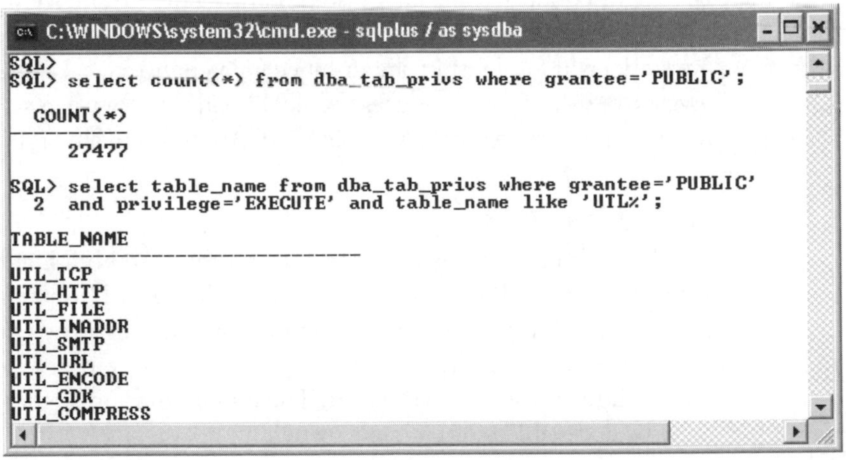

the program. Nonetheless, it does allow malicious users to use your database as the starting point for launching attacks on other systems, or for transmitting data to unauthorized recipients.

- ■ **UTL_SMTP**   Written using UTL_TCP calls, this package lets users send mail messages. It is restricted by the SMTP_OUT_SERVER instance parameter, which gives the address of the outgoing mail server, but even so you probably do not want your database to be used for exchange of mail messages without your knowledge.

- ■ **UTL_HTTP**   This too is written with UTL_TCP calls. It allows users to send HTTP messages and receive responses—in effect, converting your database into a web browser.

Always remember that, by default, these packages are available to absolutely anyone who has a logon to your database, and furthermore that your database may have a number of well-known accounts with well-known passwords.

PUBLIC is a role that is granted to everyone—but when connecting to the instance using the AS SYSOPER syntax, you will appear to be connected to an account PUBLIC.

Security-Critical Instance Parameters

Some parameters are vital to consider for securing the database. The defaults are usually fine, but in some circumstances (for which there should always be a good business case), you may need to change them. All of the parameters described here are static: you must restart the instance for a change to take effect. This is intended to give extra security, as it reduces the likelihood that they can be changed temporarily to an inappropriate setting without the DBA being aware of it.

UTL_FILE_DIR

The UTL_FILE_DIR instance parameter defaults to NULL and is therefore not a security problem. But if you need to set it, take care. This parameter gives PL/SQL access to the file system of the server machine, through the UTL_FILE supplied package. The package has procedures to open a file (either a new file or an existing one) and read from and write to it. The only limitation as that the directories listed must be accessible to the Oracle owner.

The difficulty with this parameter is that, being set at the instance level, it offers no way to allow some users access to some directories and other users access to other directories. All users with execute permission on the UTL_FILE package have access to all the directories listed in the UTL_FILE_DIR parameter.

The parameter takes a comma-separated list of directories and is static. To set it, follow the syntax in this example, which will gives access to two directories following the next restart of the instance:

```
SQL> alter system set utl_file_dir='/oracle/tmp','/oracle/interface' scope=spfile;
```

The UTL_FILE_DIR parameter can include wildcards. Never set it to "*", because that will allow all users access to everything that the database owner can see, including the ORACLE_HOME and all the database files.

REMOTE_OS_AUTHENT and OS_AUTHENT_PREFIX

The REMOTE_OS_AUTHENT instance parameter defaults to FALSE. This controls whether a user can connect to the database from a remote computer without the need to give a password. The reasons for wanting to do this have largely disappeared with modern computer systems, but the capability is still there.

In the days before all users had intelligent terminals, such as PCs, it was customary for users to log on directly to the database server machine and therefore to be authenticated by the server's operating system. They would then launch their user process on the server machine and connect to the database. In order to avoid the necessity for users to provide usernames and passwords twice (once for the operating system logon and again for the database logon), it was common to create the Oracle users with this syntax:

```
SQL> create user jon identified externally;
```

This delegates responsibility for authentication to the server's operating system. Any person logged on to the server machine as operating system user "jon" will be able to connect to the database without the need for any further authentication:

```
$ sqlplus /
Connected to:
Oracle Database 11g Enterprise Edition Release 11.1.0.6.0 - Production
SQL> show user;
USER is "JON"
SQL>
```

This is secure, as long as your server's operating system is secure. As networking became more widespread, it became common to separate the user process workload from the server process workload by having users log on to a different machine dedicated to running user processes, which would connect to the server over Oracle Net (or SQL*Net, as it was then known). Since the user no longer logs on to the server's operating system, external authentication can't be used, unless you use the REMOTE_OS_AUTHENT parameter. Setting this to TRUE means that user JON can connect without a password from any machine where he is logged on as operating system user "jon". An example of the syntax is

```
sqlplus connect /@orcl11g
```

This will log the user on to the database identified in the connect string ORCL11G, passing through his operating system username on his local machine as the database username. This is only secure if you trust the operating systems of all machines connected to the network. An obvious danger is PCs: it is common for users to have administration rights on their PCs, and they can therefore create user accounts that match any Oracle account name.

on the **job**

It is generally considered bad practice to enable remote operating system authentication.

The OS_AUTHENT_PREFIX instance parameter is related to external authentication, either local or remote. It specifies a prefix that must be applied to the operating system username before it can be mapped onto an Oracle username. The default is "OPS$". In the preceding example, it is assumed that this parameter has been cleared, with

```
SQL> alter system set os_authent_prefix='' scope=spfile;
```

Otherwise, the Oracle username would have had to be OPS$JON.

O7_DICTIONARY_ACCESSIBILITY

The O7_DICTIONARY_ACCESSIBILITY instance parameter controls the effect of granting object privileges with the ANY keyword. It defaults to FALSE. You can give user JON permission to see any table in the database with

```
SQL> grant select any table to jon;
```

but do you want him to be able to see the data dictionary tables as well as user tables? Probably not, some of them contain sensitive data, such as unencrypted passwords or source code that should be protected.

O7_DICTIONARY_ACCESSIBILITY defaults to false, meaning that the ANY privileges exclude objects owned by SYS, thus protecting the data dictionary; JON can see all the user data, but not objects owned by SYS. If you change the parameter to TRUE, then ANY really does mean ANY—and JON will be able to see the data dictionary as well as all user data.

It is possible that some older application software may assume that the ANY privileges include the data dictionary, as was always the case with release 7 of the Oracle database (hence the name of the parameter). If so, you have no choice but to change the parameter to TRUE until the software is patched up to current standards.

Data dictionary accessibility is sometimes a problem for application installation routines. You may have to set O7_DICTIONARY_ACCESSIBILITY to true while installing a product, and then be able to put it back on default when the installation is finished.

If you have users who really do need access to the data dictionary, rather than setting O7_DICTIONARY_ACCESSIBILITY to true, consider granting them the SELECT ANY DICTIONARY privilege. This will let them see the data dictionary and dynamic performance views, but they will not be able to see any user data— unless you have specifically granted them permission to do so. This might apply, for example, to the staff of an external company you use for database administration support: they need access to all the data dictionary information, but they have no need to view your application data.

REMOTE_LOGIN_PASSWORDFILE

The remote REMOTE_LOGIN_PASSWORDFILE instance parameter controls whether it is possible to connect to the instance as a user with the SYSDBA or SYSOPER privilege over the network. With this parameter on its default of NONE, the only way to get a SYSDBA connection is to log on to the operating system of the server machine as a member of the operating system group that owns the Oracle software. This is absolutely secure, as long as your server operating system is secure, which it should be.

Setting this parameter to either EXCLUSIVE or SHARED gives users another way in: even if they are not logged on to the server as a member of the Oracle owning group, or even if they are coming in across the network, they can still connect as SYSDBA if they know the appropriate password. The passwords are embedded, in encrypted form, in an operating system file in the Oracle home directory: $ORACLE_HOME/dbs on Unix, or %ORACLE_HOME%\database on Windows. A setting of SHARED means that all instances running of the same Oracle home directory will share a common password file. This will have just one password within it for the SYS user that is common to all the instances. EXCLUSIVE means that the instance will look for a file whose name includes the instance name: PWD`instance_name`.ora on Windows, orapw`instance_name` on Unix, where `instance_name` is the instance name. This file will have instance-specific passwords.

The password file is initially created by running the orapwd utility from an operating system prompt. This will create the file and embed within it a password for the SYS user. Subsequently, you can add other users' passwords to the file, thus allowing them to connect as SYSDBA or SYSOPER as well. Review the scripts in Chapter 3 for an example of the syntax for creating a password file. To add another user to the file, grant him/her either the SYSDBA or SYSOPER privilege, as in Figure 12-2. The V$PWFILE_USERS view shows you which users have their passwords entered in the password file, and whether they have the SYSOPER privilege, the SYSDBA privilege, or both.

Note that when connecting as SYSDBA, even though you use a username and password, you end up connected as user SYS; when connecting as SYSOPER, you are in fact connected as the PUBLIC user.

FIGURE 12-2

Managing the password file with SQL*Plus

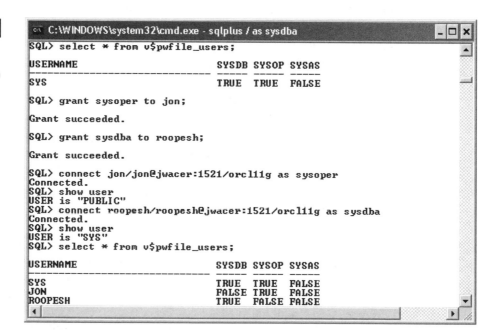

Enabling a password file does not improve security; it weakens it, by giving users another way of obtaining a privileged connection (in addition to local operating system authentication, which is always available). It is, however, standard practice to enable it, because without a password file it may be very difficult to manage the database remotely.

on the
ᵒ Job

Some computer auditors do not understand operating system and password file authentication. They may even state that you must create a password file, to improve security. Just do as they say—it is easier than arguing.

EXERCISE 12-1

Remove Some Potentially Dangerous Privileges

In this exercise, you will generate a script that could be used (possibly after edits, depending on local requirements) to remove some of the more dangerous privileges from PUBLIC. Use SQL*Plus.

1. Connect to your database as user SYSTEM.

2. Adjust SQL*Plus to remove extraneous characters from its output:

```
set headers off
set pagesize 0
sct feedback off
```

3. Start spooling output to a file in a suitable directory. Following are examples for Unix and Windows:

```
spool $HOME/oracle/scripts/clear_public_privs.sql
spool c:\oracle\scripts\clear_public_privs.sql
```

4. Generate the SQL command file by running this statement:

```
select 'revoke execute on '||table_name||' from public;'
from dba_tab_privs where table_name like 'UTL_%';
```

5. Stop the spooling of output:

```
spool off
```

6. Open the generated file with the editor of your choice. Note that there would be a couple of edits needed before it could be run to remove the first and last lines, and also site variations would determine which (if any) privileges could not actually be revoked.

CERTIFICATION OBJECTIVE 12.02

Work with Standard Database Auditing

No matter how good your security policies are, there will be occasions when a policy is not enough. You will have to accept that users have privileges that could be dangerous. All you can do is monitor their use of those privileges, and track what they are actually doing with them. The most extreme example of this is you—the DBA. Anyone with the SYSDBA privilege can do anything at all within the database. For your employers to have confidence that you are not abusing this power (which cannot be revoked, or you couldn't do your job), it is necessary to audit all SYSDBA activity. For regular users, you may also wish to track what they doing. You may not be able to prevent them from breaking company rules on access to data, but you can track the fact that they did it.

Apart from SYSDBA auditing, Oracle provides three auditing techniques:

- Database auditing can track the use of certain privileges, the execution of certain commands, access to certain tables, or logon attempts.
- Value-based auditing uses database triggers. Whenever a row is inserted, updated, or deleted, a block of PL/SQL code will run that can (among other things) record complete details of the event.
- Fine-grained auditing(FGA) allows tracking access to tables according to which rows (or which columns of the rows) were accessed. It is much more precise than either database auditing or value-based auditing, and it can limit the number of audit records generated to only those of interest.

 Auditing of any type increases the amount of work that the database must do. In order to limit this workload, you should focus your auditing closely and not track events of minimal significance.

Auditing SYSDBA Activity

There is an instance parameter AUDIT_SYS_OPERATIONS. If set to TRUE (the default is FALSE), then every statement issued by a user connected AS SYSDBA or AS SYSOPER is written out to the operating system's audit trail. This gives a complete record of all work done by the DBA. Clearly, the audit trail must be protected; if it were possible for the DBA to delete the audit records, there would be no point in creating them.

This brings up the question of *separation of duties*. Your system needs to be configured on such a way that the DBA has no access to the audit records that track his/her activity; they should only be accessible to the computer's system administrator. If the DBA were also the system administrator, then the auditing would be useless. For this reason, a decent computer auditor will always state that the DBA must not have the Unix "root" password (or the Windows "Administrator" password).

The destination of the SYS audit records is platform specific. On Windows, it is the Windows Application log, on Unix it is controlled by the AUDIT_FILE_DEST parameter. This parameter should point to a directory on which the Oracle owner has write permission (so that the audit records can be written by the instance) but that the Unix ID used by the DBA does not, so that he/she cannot adjust the audit records by hand.

Database Auditing

Before setting up database auditing, an instance parameter must be set: AUDIT_TRAIL. This has four possible values:

- **NONE (or FALSE)** Database auditing is disabled, no matter what auditing you attempt to configure.
- **OS** Audit records will be written to the operating system's audit trail—the Application Log on Windows, or the AUDIT_FILE_DEST directory on Unix.
- **DB** The audit records are written to a data dictionary table, SYS.AUD$. There are views that let you see the contents of this table.
- **DB_EXTENDED** As DB, but including the SQL statements with bind variables that generated the audit records.
- **XML** As OS, but formatted with XML tags.
- **XML_EXTENDED** As XML, but with the SQL statements and bind variables.

Having set the AUDIT_TRAIL parameter, you can use database auditing to capture login attempts, use of system and object privileges, and execution of SQL commands. Furthermore, you can specify whether to audit these events when they succeeded, when they failed because of permissions, or both. Auditing commands that did not succeed can be particularly valuable: any records produced will tell you that users are attempting to break their access rights.

Database auditing is configured using the AUDIT command.

Use of privileges can be audited with, for example,

```
SQL> audit create any trigger;
SQL> audit select any table by session;
```

Your programmers will have been granted the CREATE ANY TRIGGER privilege because they will be creating triggers on other schemas' tables as part of their work, but it is a dangerous privilege that could be used maliciously. So you certainly need to know when they use it, in order that you can demand to see the code. Similarly, some staff will need the SELECT ANY TABLE and UPDATE ANY TABLE privileges in order to sort out problems with transactions that have gone wrong, but whenever they use these privileges, a record must be kept so that they will be deterred from accessing data unless they have a legitimate reason.

By default, auditing will generate one audit record for every session that violates an audit condition, irrespective of the number of times it violates the condition. This is equivalent to appending BY SESSION to the AUDIT command. Appending the keywords BY ACCESS to the AUDIT command will generate one record for every violation.

on the
job

The default BY SESSION will often not be what you want, but it does reduce the volume of audit records produced to a more manageable number.

Auditing can also be oriented toward objects:

```
SQL> audit insert on ar.hz_parties whenever successful;
SQL> audit all on ar.ra_interface_lines_all;
```

The first of these commands will generate audit records if a session inserts a row into the named table. The WHENEVER SUCCESSFUL keywords restrict audit records to those where the operation succeeded; the alternative syntax is WHENEVER NOT SUCCESSFUL. By default, all operations (successful or not) are audited. The second example will audit every session that executes DDL statements against the named table.

Database Control has a graphical interface to the auditing system. Figure 12-3 shows the interface after executing the two preceding commands. Note that the window has tabs for displaying, adding, and removing auditing of privileges, objects, and statements. In the figure, you can see the auditing of objects owned by user AR.

FIGURE 12-3

Managing standard
auditing with
Database Control

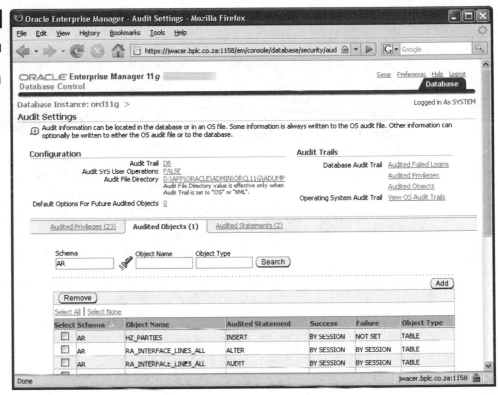

In the Configuration section of the window shown in Figure 12-3, there are links
for setting the audit parameter previously described.

Logons are audited with AUDIT SESSION. For example,

```
SQL> audit session whenever not successful;
```

This is equivalent to auditing the use of the CREATE SESSION privilege. Session
auditing records each connection to the database. The NOT SUCCESFUL
keywords restrict the output to only failed attempts. This can be particularly useful:
recording failures may indicate if attempts are being made to break into the database.

If auditing is to the operating system (because the AUDIT_TRAIL instance
parameter is set to OS or XML), then view the files created in the operating system
audit trail to see the results of the audits with an appropriate editor. If auditing is
directed to the database (AUDIT_TRAIL=DB or DB_EXTENDED), then the
audit records are written to a table in the data dictionary: the SYS.AUD$ table. It
is possible to query this directly, but usually you will go through views. The critical

view is the DBA_AUDIT_TRAIL view. This will show all audit trail entries, no matter whether the audited event was use of a privilege, execution of a statement, or access to an object. Of necessity, the view is very generic, and not all columns (forty-one in all) will be populated for each audit trail entry. The table that follows lists the more commonly used columns.

Column	Description
OS_USERNAME	Operating system name of the user performing the action
USERNAME	Oracle username of the user performing the action
USERHOST	The name of the machine running the user process
TIMESTAMP	When the audited event occurred
OWNER, OBJ_NAME	Schema and name of the object affected
ACTION_NAME	The action audited
PRIV_USED	System privilege used (if any)
SQL_TEXT	The statement executed

INSIDE THE EXAM

Database Security

Database security is critical for virtually all sites. Security is covered in various places in the Oracle database curriculum, at various levels. The general principle all DBAs must be aware of that of *least privilege*: everything not specifically permitted should be forbidden. The Oracle security structures do conform to this, in that unless a privilege is granted it is not available. However, certain grants made by default at database creation time to the PUBLIC role should be considered as potential security risks.

Settings for a number of instance parameters are vital for implementing a secure system. In general, the default settings are safe, but they should always be checked and their values documented.

It is generally accepted that users (particularly DBA staff) will need privileges that could be abused. Auditing is the means for managing this: you accept that users could breach security, but you record the fact that they did it. This should act as a deterrent, and will certainly allow you to catch any such actions. Separation of the duties of the system administrator and the DBA mean that the DBA himself can also be audited.

The other audit views (DBA_AUDIT_OBJECT, DBA_AUDIT_STATEMENT, and DBA_AUDIT_SESSION) each show a subset of the DBA_AUDIT_TRAIL view, only displaying certain audit records and the columns relevant to them.

Value-Based Auditing with Triggers

The database auditing just described can catch the fact that a command was executed against a table, but not necessarily the rows that were affected. For example, issuing AUDIT INSERT ON HR.EMPLOYEES will cause an audit record to be generated whenever a row is inserted into the named table, but the record will not include the actual values of the row that was inserted. On occasion, you may want to capture these. This can be done by using database triggers.

A *database trigger* is a block of PL/SQL code that will run automatically whenever an INSERT, UPDATE, or DELETE is executed against a table. A trigger can do almost anything—in particular, it can write out rows to other tables. These rows will be part of the transaction that caused the trigger to execute, and they will be committed when the rest of the transaction is committed. There is no way that a user can prevent the trigger from firing: if you update a table with an update trigger defined, that trigger will execute.

Consider this trigger creation statement:

```
SQL> CREATE OR REPLACE TRIGGER system.creditrating_audit
  2  AFTER UPDATE OF creditrating
  3  ON oe.customers
  4  REFERENCING NEW AS NEW OLD AS OLD
  5  FOR EACH ROW
  6  BEGIN
  7  IF :old.creditrating != :new.creditrating THEN
  8  INSERT INTO system.creditrating_audit
  9  VALUES (sys_context('userenv','os_user'),
 10  sys_context('userenv','ip_address'),
 11  :new.cust_id ||' credit rating changed from
 12  '||:old.creditrating||
 13  ' to '||:new.creditrating);
 14  END IF;
 15  END;
 16  /
```

The first line names the trigger, which is in the SYSTEM schema. Lines 2 and 3 give the rule that determines when the trigger will execute: every time the CREDITRATING column of a row in OE's CUSTOMERS table is updated. There could be separate triggers defined to manage inserts and deletes, or actions on other columns. Line 7 supplies a condition: if the CREDITRATING column were not actually changed, then the trigger will exit without doing anything. But if the CREDITRATING column were updated, then a row is inserted into another table designed for trapping audit events. Lines 9 and 10 use the SYS_CONTEXT function to record the user's operating system user name and the IP address of the terminal he was using when he executed the update. Lines 11, 12, and 13 record the employee number of the row updated, and the old and new values of the CREDITRATING column. Database auditing as described in the preceding section could have captured all this information, except for the actual values: which employee was updated, and what the change actually was.

Auditing through triggers is a slower process than database auditing, but it does give you more information and let you implement sophisticated business rules.

Fine-Grained Auditing (FGA)

Database auditing can capture all accesses to a table, whether SELECT or for DML. But it cannot distinguish between rows, even though it might well be that only some rows contain sensitive information. Using database auditing, you may have to sift through a vast number of audit records to find the few that have significance. FGA can be configured to generate audit records only when certain rows are accessed, or when certain columns of certain rows are accessed. It can also run a block of PL/SQL code when the audit condition is breached.

FGA is configured with the package DBMS_FGA. To create an FGA audit policy, use the ADD_POLICY procedure, which takes these arguments:

Argument	Description
OBJECT_SCHEMA	The name of the user who owns the object to be audited. This defaults to the user who is creating the policy.
OBJECT_NAME	The name of the table to be audited.
POLICY_NAME	Every FGA policy created must be given a unique name.
AUDIT_CONDITION	An expression to determine which rows will generate an audit record. If left NULL, access to any row is audited.
AUDIT_COLUMN	A list of columns to be audited. If left NULL, then access to any column is audited.
HANDLER_SCHEMA	The username that owns the procedure to run when the audit condition is met. The default is the user who is creating the policy.
HANDLER_MODULE	A PL/SQL procedure to execute when the audit condition is met.
ENABLE	By default, this is TRUE: the policy will be active and can be disabled with the DISABLE_POLICY procedure. If FALSE, then the ENABLE_POLICY procedure must be used to activate the policy.
STATEMENT_TYPES	One or more of SELECT, INSERT, UPDATE, or DELETE to define which statement types should be audited. Default is SELECT only.
AUDIT_TRAIL	Controls whether to write out the actual SQL statement and its bind variables to the FGA audit trail. The default is to do so.
AUDIT_COLUMN_OPTS	Determines whether to audit if a statement addresses any or all of the columns listed in the AUDIT_COLUMNS argument. Options are DBMS_FGA.ANY_COLUMNS, the default, or DBMS_FGA_ALL_COLUMNS.

The other DBMS_FGA procedures are to enable, disable, or drop FGA policies. To see the results of FGA, query the DBA_FGA_AUDIT_TRAIL view:

```
SQL> describe dba_fga_audit_trail;
 Name                                      Null?    Type
 ----------------------------------------- -------- --------------------------
 SESSION_ID                                NOT NULL NUMBER
 TIMESTAMP                                          DATE
 DB_USER                                            VARCHAR2(30)
 OS_USER                                            VARCHAR2(255)
```

```
USERHOST                    VARCHAR2(128)
CLIENT_ID                   VARCHAR2(64)
EXT_NAME                    VARCHAR2(4000)
OBJECT_SCHEMA               VARCHAR2(30)
OBJECT_NAME                 VARCHAR2(128)
POLICY_NAME                 VARCHAR2(30)
SCN                         NUMBER
SQL_TEXT                    NVARCHAR2(2000)
SQL_BIND                    NVARCHAR2(2000)
COMMENT$TEXT                VARCHAR2(4000)
STATEMENT_TYPE              VARCHAR2(7)
EXTENDED_TIMESTAMP          TIMESTAMP(6) WITH TIME ZONE
PROXY_SESSIONID             NUMBER
GLOBAL_UID                  VARCHAR2(32)
INSTANCE_NUMBER             NUMBER
OS_PROCESS                  VARCHAR2(16)
TRANSACTIONID               RAW(8)
STATEMENTID                 NUMBER
ENTRYID                     NUMBER
```

This procedure call will create a policy POL1 that will capture all SELECT statements that read the SALARY column of the HR.EMPLOYEES table, if at least one of the rows retrieved is in department 80:

```
SQL>  execute dbms_fga.add_policy(-
> object_schema=>'HR',-
> object_name=>'EMPLOYEES',-
> policy_name=>'POL1',-
> audit_condition=>'department_id=80',-
> audit_column=>'SALARY');
```

In addition to the DBA_AUDIT_TRAIL view, which shows the results of standard database auditing, and the DBA_FGA_AUDIT_TRAIL view, which shows the results of FGA, there is a view DBA_COMMON_AUDIT_TRAIL. This shows audit events from both types of auditing.

Use Standard Database Auditing

In this exercise, you will enable standard database auditing and see the results, using either Database Control or SQL*Plus. If you use Database Control, be sure to click the Show SQL button whenever possible to see the SQL statements being generated.

1. Connect to your database as user SYSTEM and create a user and a table to be used for the exercise:

```
create user sabine identified by oracle;
create table system.audi as select * from all_users;
grant create session, select any table to sabine;
grant select on audi to sabine;
```

2. Enable auditing of SABINE's use of her SELECT ANY PRIVILEGE, and of all accesses to the table AUDI. With SQL*Plus:

```
audit select any table by access;
audit all on system.audi by access;
```

With Database Control, this can be done from the Audit Settings window.

3. Connect to the database as user SYS. This is necessary, as this step involves restarting the instance. Set the audit trail destination to DB and enable auditing of privileged users, and bounce the instance. Using SQL*Plus:

```
alter system set audit_trail='DB_EXTENDED' scope=spfile;
alter system set audit_sys_operations=true scope =spfile;
startup force;
```

Using Database Control, a possible navigation path from the database home page is to take the Server tab, and then the Audit Settings link in the Security section. Clicking the link labeled Audit Trail in the Configuration section will take you to a window where you can modify the parameter settings in the spfile. Alternatively, go directly to the Initialization Parameters window from the Server tab by taking the Initialization Parameters link in the Database Configuration section.

Set the two parameters in the spfile, and then from the database home page shut down and restart the database.

4. While connected as SYS, all statements will be audited. Run this statement:

```
select count(*) from system.audi;
```

5. If using Linux or Unix, identify the location of the system audit trail by querying the parameter AUDIT_FILE_DEST. This will be used for the auditing of SYS operations, irrespective of the setting for AUDIT_DEST. With SQL*Plus:

```
select value from v$parameter where name='audit_file_dest';
```

Using an operating system utility, navigate to this directory and open the most recently created file.

If using Microsoft Windows, open the Application Log in the Event Viewer. Either way, you will see the SELECT statement that you executed as SYS, with detail of the operating system user and hostname.

6. Connect to the database as SABINE, and run these queries:

```
select count(*) from system.audi;
select count(*) from system.product_user_profile;
```

7. As user SYSTEM, run this query to see the audit events:

```
select sql_text,priv_used,action_name from dba_audit_trail
where username='SABINE';
```

Note that she uses the lowest possible privilege: her access to the AUDI table was through her object privilege, not through the much more powerful system privilege that was needed to get to PRODUCT_USER_PROFILE.

8. Tidy up:

```
drop user sabine;
drop table system.audi;
```

SCENARIO & SOLUTION

If you are told that your system will shortly be the subject of a computer security audit, what should you do?	Nothing! At least, not beforehand. The auditors will want to see the system as it is in normal running. You should cooperate fully with the auditors, with the attitude that they are there to help you. A good computer audit will be very useful. Implementing any recommendations may be a lot of work—but that is what you are being paid for.
Enabling standard database auditing can impact in performance by generating a huge amount of audit data. How can this be controlled?	Try to focus the auditing as tightly as possible, so that you only get audit records for events that really matter. If possible, audit by session, not by access. If auditing to the database, the SYS.AUD$ table may grow to many gigabytes: it will need to be deleted or truncated periodically.

CERTIFICATION SUMMARY

The principles of least privilege and separation of duties should be applied at all Oracle installations. That having been said, there will be situations where users (including the DBAs) can abuse the privileges they require to do their work. Auditing is designed to manage this: you can't stop people from breaking the rules, but you can trap the fact that they did it.

Database auditing can capture events related to use of privileges, to execution of certain statements, and access to certain objects. FGA is more precise: it can focus down to access to particular rows and columns. Auditing with DML triggers can be much more sophisticated: it can take any desired action when DML commands are executed.

✓ **TWO-MINUTE DRILL**

Database Security and Principle of Least Privilege

- ❑ Everything not specifically permitted should be forbidden.
- ❑ The DBA and the system administrator should not be the same person.
- ❑ Privileges granted to the PUBLIC role must be monitored.
- ❑ Security-critical instance parameters must be monitored and cannot be changed without restarting the instance.

Work with Standard Database Auditing

- ❑ Database auditing can be oriented toward privileges, commands, or objects.
- ❑ Audit records can be directed toward a database table or the operating system.
- ❑ Database audit records are stored in the SYS.AUD$ data dictionary table.
- ❑ FGA can be directed toward particular rows and columns.
- ❑ Auditing can also be implemented with database triggers.

SELF TEST

Database Security and Principle of Least Privilege

1. Under what circumstances should you set the REMOTE_LOGIN_PASSWORDFILE instance parameter to EXCLUSIVE? (Choose all correct answers.)

    A. You will need a SYSDBA connection when you are logged onto a machine other than the server.

    B. You want to disable operating system authentication.

    C. You want to add users to the password file.

    D. You want to prevent other users from being added to the password file.

2. If you executed this command as user SYSTEM, it will fail. Why? (Choose the best answer.)

    ```
    alter system set audit_sys_operations=false;
    ```

    A. The parameter can only be changed by the SYS user.

    B. The parameter can only be adjusted in NOMOUNT or MOUNT mode, and SYSTEM can only connect when the database is OPEN.

    C. The principle of "separation of duties" means that only the system administrator, not the DBA, can change this parameter.

    D. The parameter is a static parameter.

3. What conditions must hold before a database session can create a file stored by the operating system of the server? (Choose all correct answers.)

    A. The session must be connected to a database account with execute permission on the package UTL_FILE.

    B. The session must be connected to a database account with execute permission on the package DBMS_OUTPUT.

    C. The parameter UTL_FILE_DIR must have been set.

    D. The parameter DB_WRITER_PROCESSES must be set to greater than zero.

    E. The parameter DB_CREATE_FILE_DEST must be set.

    F. The operating system account under which the Oracle instance is running must have write permission on the directory that will store the file.

Work with Standard Database Auditing

4. If you want a block of PL/SQL code to run whenever certain data is accessed with SELECT, what auditing technique could you use? (Choose the best answer.)

A. Database auditing

B. FGA

C. Database triggers

D. You cannot do this

5. What is necessary to audit actions done by a user connected with the SYSDBA privilege? (Choose the best answer.)

A. Set the AUDIT_SYS_OPERATIONS instance parameter to TRUE.

B. Use database auditing to audit use of the SYSDBA privilege.

C. Set the REMOTE_LOGIN_PASSWORDFILE instance parameter to NONE, so that SYSDBA connections can only be made with operating system authentication. Then set the AUDIT_TRIAL parameter to OS, and make sure that the DBA does not have access to it.

D. This is not possible: any user with SYSDBA privilege can always bypass the auditing mechanisms.

6. Where can you see the results of standard database auditing? (Choose all correct answers.)

A. In the DBA_AUDIT_TRAIL view, if the AUDIT_TRAIL parameter is set to DB

B. In the DBA_COMMON_AUDIT_TRAIL view, if the AUDIT_TRAIL parameter is set to DB

C. In the operating system audit trail, if the AUDIT_TRAIL parameter is set to OS

D. In the operating system audit trail, if the AUDIT_TRAIL parameter is set to XML

7. You issue this statement:

```
audit select on hr.emp by access;
```

but when you issue the command

```
select * from hr.emp where employee_id=0;
```

no audit record is generated. Why might this be? (Choose the best answer.)

A. You are connected as SYS, and the parameter AUDIT_SYS_OPERATIONS is set to FALSE.

B. The AUDIT_TRAIL parameter is set to NONE.

C. The statement did not access any rows; there is no row with EMPLOYEE_ID equal to zero.

D. The instance must be restarted before any change to auditing comes into effect.

LAB QUESTION

Investigate the effects of auditing with standard database auditing and FGA. This exercise assumes that the HR schema is present; the HR.EMPLOYEES table is to be the subject.

Determine the current setting of the AUDIT_TRAIL parameter, using Database Control or with this statement:

```
select value from v$parameter where name='audit_trail';
```

If it is not set to DB_EXTENDED (which directs audit records to the database, including the SQL statements), set it accordingly and restart the instance:

```
connect / as sysdba;
alter system set audit_trail=db_extended scope=spfile;
startup force;
```

Enable auditing of all SELECT and DML statements against HR.EMPLOYEES. Connect as user SYSTEM, and from SQL*Plus issue this command:

```
audit select,insert,update,delete on hr.employees by access;
```

Alternatively, use Database Control. The illustration that follows shows the Add Audited Object window, with settings that will generate the appropriate command.

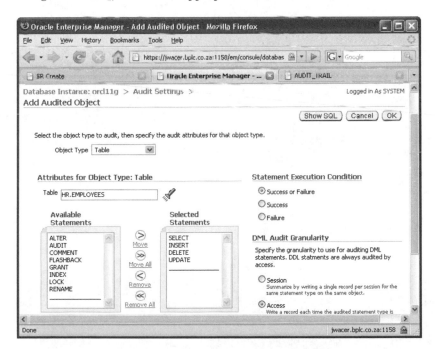

Set up a FGA policy that will only capture statements that read or write the SALARY column of the table. Using SQL*Plus:

```
execute dbms_fga.add_policy(object_schema=>'HR', object_name=>'EMPLOYEES',-
policy_name=>'HR_EMP_SIUD',-
audit_column=>'SALARY',-
statement_types=>'SELECT,INSERT,UPDATE,DELETE');
```

Remove all existing audit records. This must be done as SYS, with SQL*Plus:

```
connect / as sysdba;
truncate table sys.aud$;
```

Experiment with various SELECT, INSERT, UPDATE, and DELETE commands against the table, run as various users, and query the views DBA_AUDIT_TRAIL, DBA_FGA_AUDIT_TRAIL, and DB_COMMON_AUDIT_TRAIL to see the audit records.

SELF TEST ANSWERS

Database Security and Principle of Least Privilege

1. ☑ **A** and **C.** Password file authentication is necessary if SYSDBA connections need to be made across a network, and if you want to grant SYDBA or SYSOPER to any other database users.
   ☒ **B** is wrong because operating system authentication can never be disabled. **D** is wrong because EXCLUSIVE doesn't exclude users; it means one password file per instance.

2. ☑ **D.** No matter who are connected as, the parameter is static and will therefore require a SCOPE=SPFILE clause when changing it.
   ☒ **A** is wrong because SYSTEM can adjust the parameter (as can anyone to whom the ALTER SYSTEM privilege has been granted). **B** is wrong because the parameter can be changed in any mode—if the SCOPE is SPFILE. **C** is wrong because the system administrator cannot change parameters: only a DBA can do this.

3. ☑ **A, C,** and **F.** The necessary conditions are that the session must be able to execute the UTL_FILE procedures, and that the UTL_FILE_DIR parameter must point to a directory on which the Oracle user has the necessary permissions.
   ☒ **B** is wrong because DBMS_OUTPUT is used to write to the user process, not to the operating system. **D** is wrong because DB_WRITER_PROCESSES controls the number of database writers. **E** is wrong because DB_CREATE_FILE_DEST sets a default location for datafiles.

Work with Standard Database Auditing

4. ☑ **B.** An FGA policy can nominate a PL/SQL function to run whenever the audit condition is violated.
   ☒ **A** is wrong because database auditing can do no more than record events. **C** is wrong because database triggers can only be defined for DML statements, not for SELECT. **D** is wrong because FGA can indeed do this.

5. ☑ **A.** Setting this parameter is all that is necessary, though on Unix and Linux you may want to adjust AUDIT_FILE_DEST as well.
   ☒ **B** is wrong because this is a privilege whose use cannot be audited, because it can apply before the database is open. **C** is wrong because the method of gaining SYSDBA is not relevant to whether it is audited. **D** is wrong because SYS cannot bypass this audit technique.

6. ☑ **A, B, C,** and **D.** These are all correct.
   ☒ None.

7. ☑ **B.** If AUDIT_TRAIL is set to NONE, then there will be no standard database auditing.
   ☒ **A** is wrong because auditing the SYS user is in addition to standard database auditing. **C** is

wrong because standard database auditing will record access to the object, never mind whether any rows were retrieved. **D** is wrong because it is auditing parameter changes that requires an instance restart, not audit commands.

LAB ANSWER

Some SELECT statements that will generate FGA audit records, visible in DBA_FGA_AUDIT_ TRAIL, are

```
select * from hr.employees;
select sum(salary) from hr.employees;
```

Any DELETE statement will generate an FGA record, as will any INSERT statement—even if the INSERT does not specify a value for SALARY.

All SELECT and DML statements will generate records in DBA_AUDIT_TRAIL.

13
Database Maintenance

Performance of SQL statements is critically dependent on statistics that the optimizer uses to design efficient execution plans. Collection of statistics can be manual or automatic. If, after gathering statistics, performance is still an issue, then various metrics can be used to drill down to the cause of the problem.

Performance monitoring can take two general forms: reactive or proactive. The "reactive" approach means taking some action when or after a problem manifests itself, while "proactive" means to identify pending issues before they become problems. Clearly, proactive monitoring is the ideal technique to minimize the impact of problems on end users, but reactive monitoring is also necessary in many cases.

The manageability infrastructure provided with Oracle Database 10g can be used to automate a significant amount of the database administrator's (DBA) day-to-day work. With earlier releases, monitoring the database in order to pick up developing problems before they become critical took much time. Identifying and diagnosing performance issues was not only time consuming but also required much skill. Use of the alert system and the diagnostic advisors, installed as standard in every 11g database, frees the DBA from the necessity of devoting a large amount of effort to this work.

CERTIFICATION OBJECTIVE 13.01

Use and Manage Optimizer Statistics

Any one SQL statement may be executable in a number of different ways. For example, it may be possible to join tables in different orders; there may be a choice of whether to use indexes or table scans, or some execution methods may be more intensive in their use of disk I/O as against CPU resources.

The choice of execution plan is critical for performance. In an Oracle database, execution plans are developed dynamically by the optimizer. The optimizer relies heavily on statistics to evaluate the effectiveness of many possible execution plans, and to choose which plan to use. For good performance, it is vital that these statistics are accurate. There are many types of statistics, but chief among these are the object statistics that give details of the tables that the SQL statements address.

Statistics are not relevant to PL/SQL, only to SQL—so gathering statistics will not improve PL/SQL performance. But most PL/SQL will include calls to SQL statements; statistics are as important for these statements as for any others.

Object Statistics

Analyzing a table gathers statistics on the table that will be of use to the optimizer. The statistics are visible in the DBA_TABLES view; they include

- The number of rows in the table
- The number of blocks (used and never used) allocated to the table
- The amount of free space in the blocks that are being used
- The average length of each row
- The number of "chained" rows—rows that cut across two or more blocks, either because they are very long or because of poor storage settings

Apart from statistics regarding the table as a whole, each column of the table is also analyzed. Column statistics are visible in the DBA_TAB_COLUMNS view; they include

- The number of distinct values
- The highest and lowest values
- The number of nulls
- The average column length

When a table is analyzed, its indexes are also examined. The statistics on indexes are shown on the DBA_INDEXES view; they include

- The depth of the index tree
- The number of distinct key values
- The clustering factor—how closely the natural order of the rows follows the order of the keys

These statistics, which are stored within the data dictionary, give the optimizer the information it needs to make vital decisions about how best to execute statements. If statistics are missing or incorrect, performance may degrade dramatically.

It is also possible to gather statistics on indexes explicitly. These statistics (additional to those gathered along with the table statistics) are displayed in the INDEX_STATS view; they include

- The number of index entries referring to extant rows
- The number of index entries referring to deleted rows

This information is of value because of the manner in which indexes are maintained: when rows are deleted, the index keys remain. After a prolonged period, indexes can become inefficient due to the amount of space occupied by these references to deleted rows.

exam

Watch   *In addition to the table*   *DBA_TAB_COLUMNS are also gathered*
statistics shown in DBA_TABLES, the index   *whenever you analyze a table. Analyzing an*
and column statistics in DBA_INDEXES and   *index populates INDEX_STATS.*

Gathering Statistics Manually

Object statistics are not real-time; they are static, which means that they become out of date as DML operations are applied to the tables. It is therefore necessary to gather statistics regularly, to ensure that the optimizer always has access to statistics that reflect reasonably accurately the current state of the database. Statistics can be gathered manually, or the process can be automated. Manual statistics gathering can done with either the ANALYZE command or by executing procedures in the DBMS_STATS package, as in Figure 13-1, or through Database Control.

In Figure 13-1, first the table REGIONS is analyzed, using the ANALYZE command. The keywords COMPUTE STATISTICS instruct Oracle to analyze the whole table, not just a proportion of it. The following query shows that there are four rows in the table. Then there is a row inserted, but the statistics haven't been updated in real time; the number of rows is incorrect, until the table is analyzed again—this time with the DBMS_STATS.GATHER_TABLE_STATS procedure. Numerous arguments can be supplied to the GATHER_TABLE_STATS procedure to control what it does—this is the simplest form of its use.

on the job   *The ANALYZE command is easy to use but has limited functionality. DBMS_*
STATS has many more options and is the recommended tool.

FIGURE 13-1

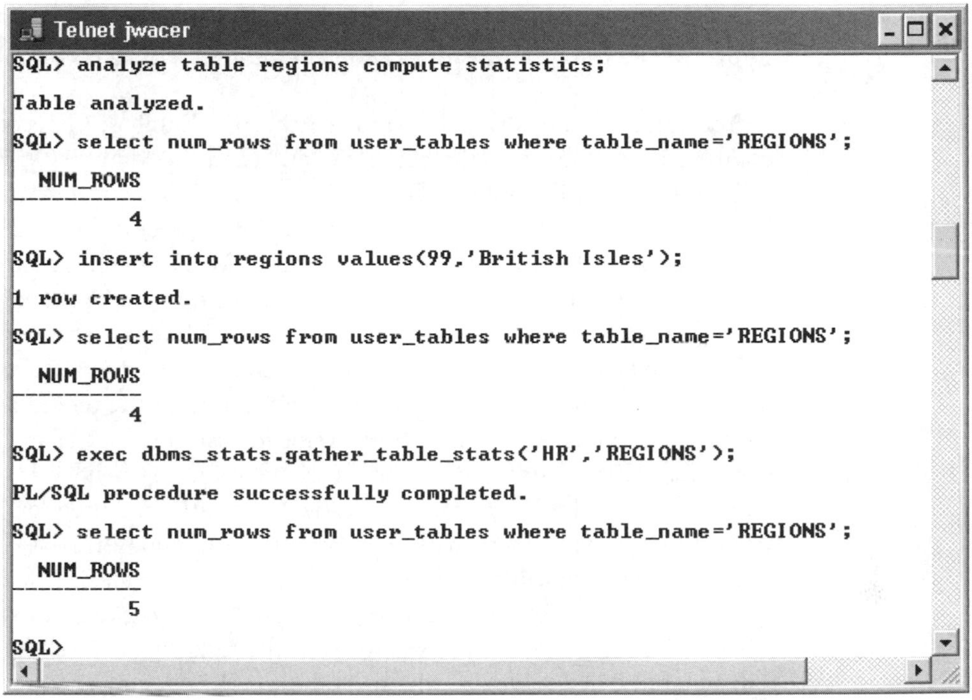

Gathering statistics from the SQL*Plus prompt

```
Telnet jwacer

SQL> analyze table regions compute statistics;
Table analyzed.
SQL> select num_rows from user_tables where table_name='REGIONS';

   NUM_ROWS
----------
         4

SQL> insert into regions values(99,'British Isles');
1 row created.
SQL> select num_rows from user_tables where table_name='REGIONS';

   NUM_ROWS
----------
         4

SQL> exec dbms_stats.gather_table_stats('HR','REGIONS');
PL/SQL procedure successfully completed.
SQL> select num_rows from user_tables where table_name='REGIONS';

   NUM_ROWS
----------
         5

SQL>
```

e x a m

w a t c h   *Object statistics are not real time; they are static until refreshed by a new analysis. If this is not done with sufficient frequency, they will be seriously out of date and the optimizer may consequently develop inappropriate execution plans.*

Gathering statistics will improve performance, but the actual gathering may impose a strain on the database that will have a noticeable effect on performance while the analysis is in progress. This paradoxical situation raises two questions. First, how frequently should statistics be gathered? The more frequently this is done, the better performance may be—but if it is done more frequently than necessary, performance will suffer needlessly. Second, what proportion of an object needs to be analyzed to gain an accurate picture of it?

Analyzing a huge table will be a long and resource-intensive process—it may well be that analyzing a representative sample of the object would be enough for the optimizer and would not impose such a strain on the database.

The DBMS_STATS procedures can take many arguments to influence the depth of the analysis, far more than the older ANALYZE command.

You can also manually gather statistics through Database Control. From the database home page, take the Server tab and then the Manage Optimizer Statistics link in the Query Optimizer section. Then take the Gather Optimizer Statistics link to run a wizard that will take you through the process. The first window of the wizard includes this information message: "For 11, Oracle recommends you enable automated maintenance task (Optimizer Statistics Gathering) to generate optimizer statistics regularly within maintenance windows. This wizard should only be used for cases where the task is inappropriate or disabled. For example, you may want to gather optimizer statistics immediately, or the task failed to execute within a maintenance window, or you want to customize options to gather optimizer statistics." This is a strong hint that Oracle Corporation believes you should automate the gathering of statistics, rather than gathering them on an ad hoc basis. If the database was created with the Database Configuration Assistant, automatic statistics gathering will have been configured, as a job managed by the Scheduler.

The wizard prompts you through the process of setting the various options for what and how to analyze, and when to run the task. Figure 13-2 shows a procedure call generated by the wizard, which can be seen by clicking the Show SQL button on the Review page.

The example in Figure 13-2 shows the use of the GATHER_SCHEMA_STATS procedure, which will analyze all the objects belonging to one user. Taking the arguments in turn:

- OWNNAME specifies the schema to be analyzed.
- CASCADE will analyze indexes as well as tables. The setting given lets Oracle decide which indexes (if any) should be analyzed.
- ESTIMATE_PERCENT controls how much of each table to analyze. The setting given instructs Oracle to make an intelligent guess at the amount needed for a meaningful sample.
- DEGREE specifies whether to perform the analysis with parallel processing. The setting given lets Oracle decide the number of parallel processes according to the environment and the size of each table.
- NO_INVALIDATE controls whether to reparse any SQL with dependencies on the objects analyzed immediately or not. The setting given lets Oracle decide.

FIGURE 13-2

A DBMS_STATS procedure call generated by the Gather Optimizer Statistics Wizard

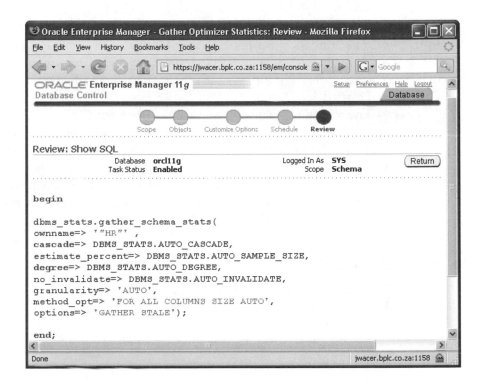

- GRANULARITY refers to how best to analyze objects consisting of a number of subobjects, such as a table that is divided into partitions. The setting given lets Oracle decide.

- METHOD_OPT controls for which columns to build up histograms, and how many buckets they should have. The setting given lets Oracle decide, according to the nature of the SQL being executed and the distribution of values in the data.

- OPTIONS determines which objects to analyze. The setting given instructs Oracle to analyze all objects where Oracle considers the statistics to be out of date.

The example shown in Figure 13-2 illustrates that you can delegate all decisions on what needs to be analyzed, in what way, and to what depth to Oracle itself. If a command such as that shown in the figure is run sufficiently frequently, it should ensure that the optimizer always has the statistics it needs, without overburdening the database by gathering statistics unnecessarily.

Whether using the DBMS_STATS procedure calls from the SQL*Plus prompt or generating the procedure calls with Database Control, there are options for analyzing individual tables and indexes, complete schemas, or the entire database. The arguments that can be passed to the procedure calls control how the analyses will carried out.

The remaining point to consider is how frequently to run the command. There is an automatic statistics gathering task configured by the DBCA that will do this every day, during the *maintenance window*. The maintenance window runs for four hours every weekday night (starting at 2200) and for twenty hours on Saturday and Sunday (starting at 0600), though usually only a very small proportion of this time will be needed. Many databases will run well with statistics gathered by the automatic task, obviating any need to gather statistics manually.

The STATISTICS_LEVEL Instance Parameter

The gathering and visibility of statistics can be controlled by the STATISTICS_LEVEL instance parameter. This has three possible settings:

- BASIC
- TYPICAL
- ALL

The parameter controls the automatic gathering of statistics at two levels: statistics accumulated within the instance regarding activity and object statistics within the database. The instance statistics are accumulated in memory and flushed to the Automatic Workload Repository (the AWR) by the MMON (Manageability Monitor) background process. The object statistics are those gathered by analyzing objects with DBMS_STATS procedure calls.

The default is setting is TYPICAL, which will be suitable for most databases in normal running mode. The TYPICAL setting will gather all the statistics needed by the self-management and tuning capabilities of the database and will also enable the automatic object analysis task that runs daily in the maintenance window. The BASIC setting disables computation of AWR statistics and disables the daily analysis. With this setting, the various performance and tuning advisors will not be available, and the alert system will not function. The ALL setting gathers all possible statistics. These include operating system activity statistics and very detailed statistics on SQL statement execution. It is possible that gathering statistics at this level will impact adversely on performance.

TYPICAL will gather all the statistics that any normal human being needs, but none whose gathering would make the database run more slowly. BASIC cripples your tuning ability and delivers no performance benefit. ALL should be enabled for short periods when you are actively tuning SQL statements. Usually, leave STATISTICS_LEVEL on default.

EXERCISE 13-1

Gather Optimizer Statistics with Various Tools

In this exercise, you will use various techniques for gathering optimizer statistics.

1. Connect to your database as user SYSTEM with SQL*Plus.

2. Create a table and an index to be used for the exercise, and set your session's date format:

```
create table st as select * from all_users;
create index sti on st(username);
alter session set nls_date_format='dd-mm-yy hh24:mi:ss';
```

3. Investigate the statistics on the table and indexes:

```
select count(*) from st;
select num_rows,last_analyzed from user_tables where
table_name='ST';
select distinct_keys,last_analyzed from user_indexes where
index_name='STI';
```

Note that the statistics count of the rows in the table is wrong, because the table has never been analyzed. The number of distinct values recorded in the index is reported correctly (for now), because indexes are automatically analyzed on creation.

4. Analyze the table using the ANALYZE command:

```
analyze table st compute statistics;
```

5. Rerun the queries from Step 3. All the figures are now correct.

6. Insert some more rows into the table:

```
insert into st select * from st;
```

7. Rerun the queries from Step 3. Note that the statistics are wrong.

8. Analyze the table with the DBMS_STATS API:

```
exec dbms_stats.gather_table_stats('SYSTEM','ST');
```

9. Rerun the queries from Step 3. All the figures are now correct.

10. Delete all the rows from the table, and commit:

```
delete from st;
commit;
```

11. Connect to your database as user SYSTEM with Database Control.

12. Take the Server tab from the database home page, and the Manage Optimizer Statistics link in the Query Optimizer section. Then click the Gather Optimizer Statistics link in the Related Links section.

13. In the Object Statistics window, enter **SYSTEM** and **ST** in the Schema and Object boxes and click Go, as shown here:

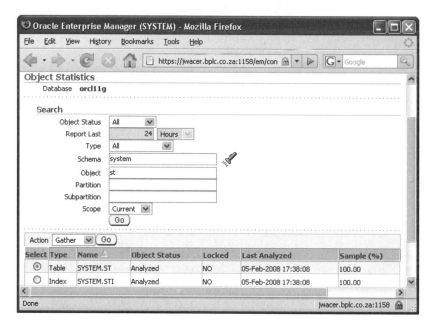

14. Select the radio button for the table ST and "Gather" in the Action box (as shown in the illustration) and click Go. This will launch the Gather Optimizer Statistics Wizard.

15. Click Next, leaving everything on default, until you reach the Review window. Click Show SQL to see the procedure call that has been generated.

16. Click Return to return to the Review window, and Submit to run the job.

17. Return to your SQL*Plus session, and rerun the queries from Step 3. All the figures are now correct.

18. Tidy up:

```
drop table st;
```

CERTIFICATION OBJECTIVE 13.02

Use and Manage the Automatic Workload Repository

Oracle collects a vast amount of statistical information regarding performance and activity. This information is accumulated in memory and periodically written to disk: to the tables that make up the AWR. The AWR exists as a set of tables and other objects in the SYSAUX tablespace. The AWR is related to the data dictionary, but unlike the data dictionary, the AWR is not essential for the database to function (though it may be necessary for it to function well). Data is written to the AWR, stored for a while, and eventually overwritten with more recent information. Note that the optimizer statistics described in the preceding section are gathered and used in a completely different fashion from the AWR statistics described here.

Gathering AWR Statistics

The level of statistics gathered is controlled by the instance parameter STATISTICS_LEVEL. This can be set to BASIC, or to TYPICAL (which is the default), or to ALL. The TYPICAL level will force the collection of all the statistics that are needed for normal tuning, without collecting any whose collection would impact adversely on performance. The BASIC level will disable virtually all statistics, with no appreciable performance benefit. The ALL level will collect extremely detailed statistics on SQL statement execution; these may occasionally be necessary if you are doing advanced SQL statement tuning, but they may cause a slight performance drop while being collected.

Statistics are accumulated in memory, in data structures within the SGA. This causes no performance impact, because the statistics merely reflect what the instance is doing anyway. Periodically (by default, once an hour) they are flushed to disk, to the AWR. This is known as an AWR *snapshot*. The flushing to disk is done by a background process: the Manageability Monitor, or MMON. This use of a background process is the key to the efficiency of the statistics collection process. In earlier releases of the database, accessing performance tuning statistics was only possible by running queries against various views—the dynamic performance V$ views. Populating these views was an expensive process. The DBA had to launch a session against the database and then issue a query. The query forced Oracle to extract data from the SGA and present it to the session in a view. This approach is still possible—all the old views, and many more, are still available—but the AWR approach is far more efficient.

on the job

No third-party tool can ever have the direct memory access to the instance that MMON has. If your instance is highly stressed, you should think carefully before using any tuning products other than those provided by Oracle itself.

The MMON has direct access to the memory structures that make up the SGA, and therefore the statistics within them. It can extract data from the SGA without the need to go via a session. The only overhead is the actual writing the snapshot of the data to the AWR. By default this occurs only once an hour and should not therefore have a noticeable effect on runtime performance.

exam watch

AWR statistics are saved as a snapshot to the AWR by the MMON process, by default every sixty minutes. By default, the snapshots are stored for eight days before being overwritten.

The AWR is a set of tables located in the SYSAUX tablespace—these tables cannot be relocated. They exist in the SYSMAN schema. You can log on to the database with tools such as SQL*Plus as user SYSMAN, but this should never be necessary, and indeed Oracle Corporation does not support access to the AWR tables with SQL*Plus, or with any tools other than the various APIs provided in the form of DBMS packages or through various views. The most straightforward way to access AWR information is through Enterprise Manager; both Enterprise Manager Database Control and Enterprise Manager Grid Control log on to the database as SYSMAN, using a password that is encrypted in their configuration files. This is why changing the SYSMAN password requires more than executing an ALTER USER SYSMAN IDENTIFIED BY . . . command; in addition to this, you must also use the EMCTL utility:

```
emctl setpasswd dbconsole
```

which will update the encrypted password in the appropriate file.

An AWR snapshot can be thought of as a copy of the contents of many V$ views at the time the snapshot was taken, but never forget that the mechanism for copying the information is not to query the V$ views: the information is extracted directly from the data structures that make up the instance. The process that makes the copy is MMON. In addition to information from the dynamic performance (or V$) views, the AWR stores information otherwise visible in the DBA views, populated from the data dictionary. This category of information includes a history of object statistics. Without the AWR, the database would have no long-term record of how objects were changing. The statistics gathered with DBMS_STATS give current information, but it may also be necessary to have a historical picture of the state of the database objects. The AWR can provide this.

Managing the AWR

Snapshots of statistics data are kept in the AWR, by default, for eight days. This period is configurable. As a rough guide for sizing, if the snapshot collection is left on every hour and the retention time is left on eight days, then the AWR may well require between 200 MB and 300 MB of space in the SYSAUX tablespace. But this figure is highly variable and will to a large extent depend on the number of sessions.

To administer the AWR with Database Control, from the database home page take the Server tab, then the AWR link in the Statistics Management section. The AWR window, as in Figure 13-3, shows the current settings for snapshot collection and retention and for the STATISTICS_LEVEL and lets you adjust them.

Adjusting the AWR settings to save snapshots more frequently will make problem diagnosis more precise. If the snapshots are several hours apart, you may miss peaks of activity (and consequent dips in performance). But gathering snapshots too frequently will increase the size of the AWR and could possibly impact performance due to the increased workload of collecting and saving the information.

on the job

It is important to monitor the size and growth of the SYSAUX tablespace and the AWR within it. The Alert System will assist with the first task, and the view V$SYSAUX_OCCUPANTS should be used for the second.

exam

watch   *By default, AWR snapshots are taken every hour and saved for eight days. The AWR is located in the SYSAUX*   *tablespace and cannot be relocated to anywhere else.*

FIGURE 13-3

The AWR
administration
window

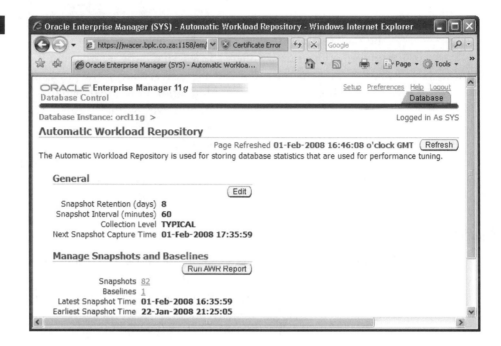

FIGURE 13-3

The AWR
administration
window

Statistics, Metrics, and Baselines

AWR snapshots contain statistics. What Oracle calls a *statistic* is a raw figure, which is meaningless in itself. To be useful, statistics must be converted into *metrics*. A metric is two or more statistics correlated together. For example, the number of disk reads is a statistic; perhaps the number is two billion. By itself, this is useless information. What the DBA needs to know is disk reads per second; disk reads per transaction; disk reads per SQL statement; disk reads per session. These figures are metrics. He/she will also need to do further correlations. For example, disk reads per transaction is very useful; it will identify the transactions that are stressing the I/O system and perhaps should be tuned. But he/she will need to observe this metric over time and see how it changes—perhaps as the SQL is rewritten or indexing structures are changed, the I/O workload will reduce. This introduces the *baseline*. A baseline is a stored set of statistics (and metrics) that can be used for comparisons across time.

As the MMON process saves an AWR snapshot, it generates a large number of metrics from the statistics. This happens automatically. Creating baselines must be done by the DBA. Snapshots are purged after a certain period—by default, after eight days. A baseline is a pair (possibly several pairs) of snapshots that will be kept indefinitely: until the baseline is deliberately dropped. The metrics derived from the baseline can then be compared with the metrics derived from current activity levels, assisting you with identifying changes in activity and behavior.

Baselines need to be created for specific events and for normal running. For example, if the database has regular end-of-month processing, it would make sense to store the AWR snapshots gathered during each month end as baselines so that throughout the year you can observe how the month end processing activity is changing and determine whether any problems are appearing. It also makes sense to store baselines for periods of normal, satisfactory running so that if performance degrades at a later time, information will be available that will help identify what might have changed.

To create a baseline with Database Control, take the link next to "Baselines" shown in Figure 13-3. In the figure, this link is "1", indicating that at the moment there is only one baseline. This link will take you to the AWR Baselines window. From there, you can define periods to store as baselines.

The DBMS_WORKLOAD_REPOSITORY Package

Database Control has interfaces for managing the AWR, but it does so by invoking procedures in a PL/SQL package: DBMA_WORKLOAD_REPOSITORY. The procedures can adjust the frequency and persistence of snapshots, generate an ad hoc snapshot (additional to those generated by MMON), create and manipulate baselines, and generate reports on activity between any two snapshots. Figure 13-4 shows the use of some of the procedures in the package.

FIGURE 13-4

Use of the DBMS_ WORKLOAD_ REPOSITORY package

```
Select C:\WINDOWS\system32\cmd.exe - sqlplus / as sysdba

SQL> execute dbms_workload_repository.create_snapshot;

PL/SQL procedure successfully completed.

SQL> execute dbms_workload_repository.modify_snapshot_settings(-
> retention=>43200,interval=>30);

PL/SQL procedure successfully completed.

SQL> execute dbms_workload_repository.create_baseline(-
> start_snap_id=>487,end_snap_id=>488,baseline_name=>'FridayPM');

PL/SQL procedure successfully completed.

SQL> select snap_id,begin_interval_time from dba_hist_snapshot
  2  order by begin_interval_time desc;

   SNAP_ID BEGIN_INTERVAL_TIME
---------- --------------------------------
       490 01-FEB-08 20.46.16.750
       489 01-FEB-08 20.00.06.796
       488 01-FEB-08 19.00.43.515
```

The first procedure call is to force the MMON process to gather a snapshot immediately, additional to its normal scheduled snapshots. This would typically be used just before and after launching a job of some kind, so that reports can be generated focusing on a particular time frame. The second procedure call adjusts the snapshot management, such that snapshots will be retained for thirty days and gathered by MMON every half hour (the units are minutes). The third procedure call nominates two snapshots to be stored indefinitely as a named baseline. Finally, the query lists all snapshots in the repository; note that in addition to the snapshots gathered automatically on the hour, there is also the ad hoc snapshot gathered by the first procedure call.

EXERCISE 13-2

Monitor the Automatic Workload Repository

In this exercise, you will determine the size of the AWR and monitor its growth as it stores more snapshots.

1. Connect to your database with SQL*Plus as user SYSTEM.
2. The view V$SYSAUX_OCCUPANTS shows all the components installed into the SYSAUX tablespace. Find out how much space the AWR is taking up:

```
select occupant_desc,space_usage_kbytes from v$sysaux_occupants
where occupant_name='SM/AWR';
```

Note the size returned.

3. Gather an AWR snapshot:

```
execute dbms_workload_repository.create_snapshot;
```

4. Rerun the query from Step 2, and calculate the increase in size caused by taking the manual snapshot.
5. Find out how many snapshot there are, and what date range they cover:

```
select min(begin_interval_time), max(begin_interval_time),
count(snap_id) from dba_hist_snapshot;
```

6. Connect to your database as user SYSTEM with Database Control.
7. Navigate to AWR window, shown in Figure 13-3: from the database home page take the Server tab, and then the AWR link in the Statistics Management section. You will see figures corresponding to the results of the query in Step 5.

CERTIFICATION OBJECTIVE 13.03

Use the Advisory Framework

The database comes preconfigured with a set of advisors. First among these is the Automatic Database Diagnostic Monitor, or ADDM. Studying ADDM reports, which are generated automatically whenever an AWR snapshot is taken, will usually be a regular part of the DBA's routine. The ADDM reports are of great value in themselves and will highlight problems within the database and suggest solutions, but in many cases, its recommendations will include suggesting that you run one or more other advisors. These advisors can give much more precise diagnostic information and advice than the ADDM.

To use the advisors, in Database Control take the Advisor Central link in the Related Links section. The Advisor Central window gives you the options of viewing the results of previous advisor tasks, or of using any of the other advisors:

- The ADDM
- The Memory Advisors
- The SQL Access, Tuning, and Repair Advisors
- The Automatic Undo Advisor
- The Mean Time to Recover (MTTR) advisor
- The Data Recovery Advisor
- The Segment Advisor

At this stage, it is only necessary to be aware of the advisors' capabilities. More detailed use of the advisors is required for the second OCP examination.

The Automatic Database Diagnostic Monitor

The ADDM is run automatically by the MMON whenever a snapshot is taken. As with all the advisors, it takes statistics and other information from the AWR. The automatically generated ADDM reports always cover the period between the current snapshot and the previous one—so by default, you will have access to reports covering every hour. You can invoke the ADDM manually to generate a report covering the period between any two snapshots, if you want to span a greater period. The ADDM is triggered both by automatic snapshots and also if you gather a snapshot manually. The reports are purged by default after thirty days.

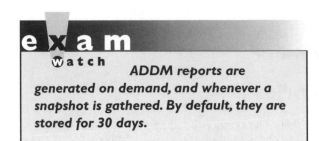

ADDM reports are generated on demand, and whenever a snapshot is gathered. By default, they are stored for 30 days.

To view the ADDM reports with Database Control, take the Advisor Central link in the Related Links section of the database home page. The Advisor Central window will show you the most recent runs of each advisor, as in Figure 13-5.

Select the report's radio button and click View Result to see the summary of recent activity, as in Figure 13-6. In the figure, this shows that overall the database has seen very little activity since the previous evening, but that there were distinct spikes at about 2300 and 0700, as well as in the last hour since 1400, which will be the period covered by this report.

The lower part of the ADDM window shows the results of the analysis. In the figure, these are that ADDM has detected issues with virtual memory, with the SQL being executed, and it disk I/O. Clicking the links would show detail of the finding.

The ADDM will often recommend running another advisor. In the example shown in Figure 13-6, selecting the Top SQL By DB Time link shows the result in Figure 13-7, which identifies the SQL statements that were stressing the system and may recommend running the SQL Tuning advisor against them.

FIGURE 13-5

The Advisor Central

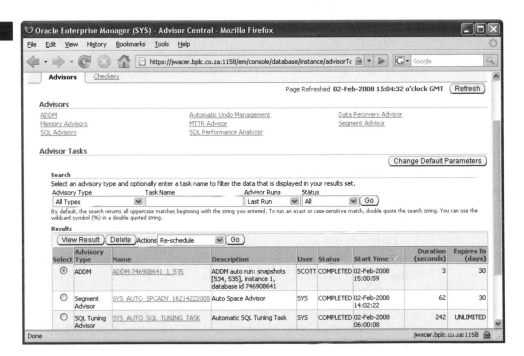

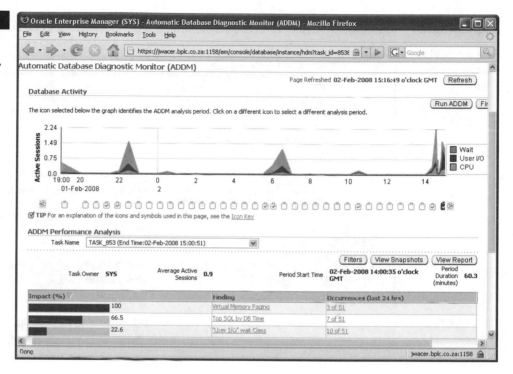

FIGURE 13-6

The ADDM report summary

The Advisors

The ADDM is the starting point for performance analysis and problem resolution, and it may well give all the advice needed. Its recommendations may be

- Hardware changes (such as adding CPUs)
- Database configuration (such as instance parameter settings)
- Schema changes (such as use of table and index partitioning)
- Application changes (such as using bid variables)
- Using other advisors (for more detailed analysis and recommendations)

Other chapters describe some of the other advisors in greater detail. Following are summary descriptions.

FIGURE 13-7

A recommendation
to apply another
advisor

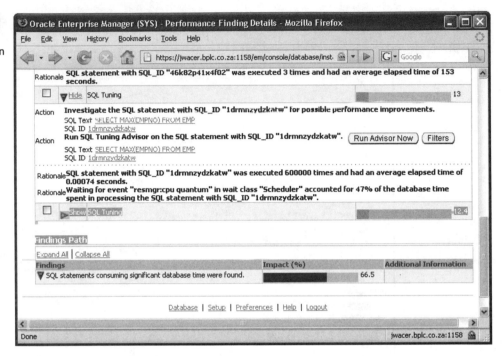

The Memory Advisors

The memory advisors predict the effect of varying the size of memory structures, reporting the estimates in terms of processing time saved (the Shared Pool, Java Pool, and Streams Pool advisors), disk activity reduced (the Database Buffer Cache advisor), or both (the PGA advisor). There is no advisor for the Large Pool. There is, however, an SGA advisor, which will report on the effect of varying the size of the entire SGA. If memory management has been automated by setting the parameter MEMORY_TARGET and leaving all other memory parameters on default, there is an overall memory advisor which gives a single point from which to gauge whether allocating more memory to the instance would improve performance.

The SQL Advisors

There are three SQL advisors: the SQL Access Advisor, the SQL Tuning Advisor, and the SQL Repair Advisor.

The SQL Access Advisor will observe a workload of SQL statements and make recommendations regarding segments that would mean that the workload would run more quickly. The workload can be a hypothetical workload, or it can be derived from the SQL actually executed during a certain time frame. The recommendations can be to create or drop indexes and materialized views, and to make use of segment partitioning.

The SQL Tuning Advisor can analyze individual statements, as well as recommending schema changes (as the Access Advisor does). It can recommend generating additional statistics on the statement's execution that will assist the optimizer in choosing the best execution plan, and rewriting the statement to eliminate some inefficiencies that are inherent in some SQL structures.

Occasionally, an SQL statement can fail because of an internal Oracle error. This will be reported with the "ORA-600" error message. If the error condition (which is a polite name for a "bug") is only encountered when following a particular execution plan, it follows that using a different execution plan could avoid the failure.

The SQL Repair Advisor can investigate this and generate a patch to the statement that will force the optimizer to choose a safe plan, rather than a plan that hits the problem.

The Automatic Undo Advisor

As discussed in Chapter 11, the Undo Advisor will observe the rate of undo data generation and the length of queries being run, and it will recommend a minimum size for the undo tablespace, which will ensure that queries do not fail with a "snapshot too old" error.

The Mean Time to Recover (MTTR) advisor

The mechanism for instance recovery after a failure is detailed in Chapter 15. In summary, if the instance terminates in a disorderly fashion (such as a power cut or server reboot while the database was open, or just a SHUTDOWN ABORT), then on the next startup it is necessary to reinstate all work in progress that had not been written to the datafiles at the time of the crash. This will happen automatically, but until it is done, users cannot log on. The MTTR advisor estimates how long this period of downtime for crash recovery will be, given the current workload.

The Data Recovery Advisor

If the database has been damaged in some way (such as files deleted or data blocks corrupted), it may take some time to identify the problem. Then there will often be several way of recovering from the situation. For example, if a number of datafiles have been damaged by corruptions appearing on a disk, it will be necessary to find out which files, and which blocks. Then a decision must be made as to whether to restore entire files, or only the damaged blocks. If the database is protected by a physical standby, switching over to that would also be a possibility.

Following a failure, any DBA (no matter how experienced) will need time to determine the nature and extent of the problem, and then more time to decide upon the course of action that will repair the damage with the minimum disruption to work. The Data Recovery Advisor follows an expert system to advise the DBA on this. The expert system is essentially what the DBA would follow anyway, but the advisor can do it much faster.

The Segment Advisor

Segments grow automatically. As rows are inserted into table segments and index keys are inserted into index segments, the segments fill—and then Oracle will allocate more extents as necessary. But segments do not shrink automatically as data is removed or modified with DELETE and UPDATE commands; this only happens when the segment is deliberately reorganized. The segment advisor observes tables and indexes, both their current state and their historical patterns of use, and recommends appropriate reorganization when necessary.

Automatic Maintenance Jobs

If the database is to run well, it is vital that the optimizer has access to accurate object statistics; that the tables and indexes are operating efficiently, without a large amount of wasted space and fragmentation; and that the high-load SQL statements have been tuned. The gathering of statistics and the running of the Segment Advisor and the SQL Tuning Advisor are, by default, automatic in an 11*g* database.

A facility introduced with release 10*g* of the database was the *Scheduler*. The Scheduler runs jobs automatically, at certain times and repeatedly at certain intervals. The jobs will usually be defined by the DBA, but following creation of a database with the DBCA, there will be three tasks configured within what is called the AutoTask system. These AutoTasks are

- Gathering optimizer statistics
- Running the Segment Advisor
- Running the SQL Advisor

The AutoTasks run within the Scheduler's *maintenance window*. A Scheduler *window* is a repeating time period. The maintenance windows are defined to open at 2200 every weeknight and to close four hours later, at 0200, and on Saturday and

Sunday to open at 0600, closing twenty hours later, at 0200. The Scheduler is linked to another database facility: the Resource Manager. The Resource Manager allocates resources to different database sessions. The Resource Manager plan that is activated during the maintenance window is one that ensures that no more than 25 percent of machine resources are dedicated to the AutoTask jobs, meaning that running these tasks should not impact adversely on other work. If the maintenance window time frames are not suitable for your database workload, they are adjustable; if the maximum of 25 percent resource usage is too high and causes performance for other work to degrade, this too can be changed. The underlying assumption is that the AutoTasks will run at a time and with a priority that is unlikely to cause problems for regular work for end users.

e x a m

ⓦ a t c h

There are three automated maintenance tasks: gathering optimizer statistics, the Segment Advisor, the SQL Tuning Advisor. The advisors run automatically, but the recommendations must be accepted (or ignored) manually. The tasks run in the maintenance window, which by default opens for four hours every weeknight at 2200 and for twenty hours on Saturday and Sunday, opening at 0600.

For any of the AutoTasks to run, the STATISTICS_LEVEL parameter must be set to TYPICAL (the default) or ALL. The simplest way to manage the scheduling of the AutoTask jobs is through Database Control. Take the Server tab from the Database Home page, then the Automated Maintenance Tasks link on the Scheduler section. The Automated Maintenance Tasks window, shown in Figure 13-8, displays the window for the next run (which opens at 0600, because the figure was taken on a Saturday evening) with links for the results of the last two advisor runs. Taking these links will show the recommendations (if any) with an option to implement them (implementing the recommendations is not automatic).

The segment advisor task relies on the history of object statistics built up by the daily running of the gather optimizer statistics task. By observing these, the Segment Advisor can see not only how much unused space there is in the tables and indexes, but also whether this space is likely to be needed again, and if not advise that the segments should be reorganized. The SQL Tuning Advisor task relies on the AWR statistics gathered by the MMON process. These statistics include figures on which SQL statements are being execute many times, perhaps millions of times an hour;

FIGURE 13-8

The Automated
Maintenance
Tasks window

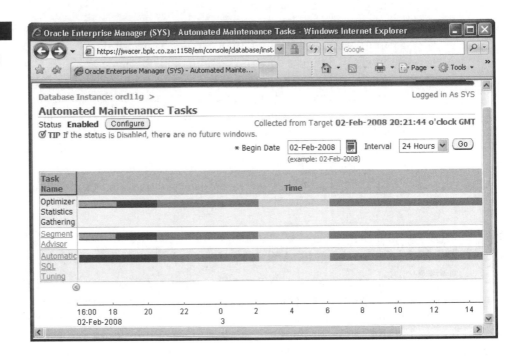

which statements are responsible for a large amount of disk and memory I/O; which statements are taking a long time to run. These are the high-load statements that will be subjected to tuning analysis.

To view and adjust the window schedule, click Configure. This will take you to the window shown in Figure 13-9, where there are radio buttons for enabling or disabling the jobs; buttons for configuring Optimizer Statistics Gathering and Automatic SQL Tuning jobs; links for editing the opening and closing times of the daily windows; and check boxes for selecting in which windows the various jobs will run.

on the
job

The default settings for the maintenance window may well not be appropriate for you. In many Middle Eastern countries, for example, Saturday and Sunday are working days. Also, many databases support global organizations: just because it is the middle of the night for you, that doesn't mean it is for many of your end users.

FIGURE 13-9

The Database
Control window
for managing the
AutoTask system

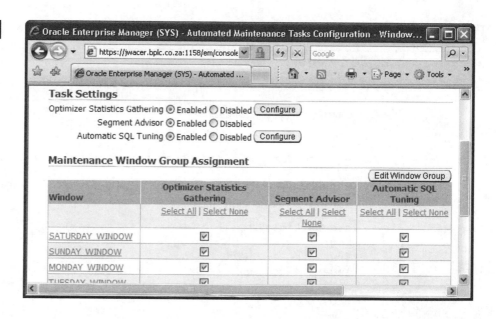

FIGURE 13-9

SCENARIO & SOLUTION	
Are their any restrictions on using the tuning and diagnosis wizards?	There certainly are. The Oracle database standard edition license does not include most of the self-management facilities, and even with an Enterprise Edition license you need some extra, separately licensed, products. You must check with your account manager before using any of them.
Okay, we have all the necessary licenses. When should I use the automatic facilities, and when should I manage things the hard way?	Always use the self-management capabilities and the tuning wizards and advisors, but use your brain as well. You should know the data, the environment, and the patterns of activity of your database better than any wizard. All the tools can do is apply rules and heuristics that are applicable to most systems. Use your site knowledge to question the recommendations, and improve on them.

EXERCISE 13-3

Generate an ADDM Report

In this exercise, you will generate an ADDM report on activity between two snapshots.

1. Connect to your database as user SYSTEM with SQL*Plus.

2. Force the creation of an AWR snapshot

```
execute dbms_workload_repository.create_snapshot;
```

3. Simulate a workload by creating a table and running an anonymous PL/SQL block to generate some activity:

```
create table tmptab as select * from all_objects;
begin
for i in 1..10 loop
insert into tmptab select * from all_objects;
delete from tmptab;
end loop;
commit;
end;
/
```

4. Force the creation of an AWR snapshot, using the command in Step 2. This illustration shows Steps 2–4:

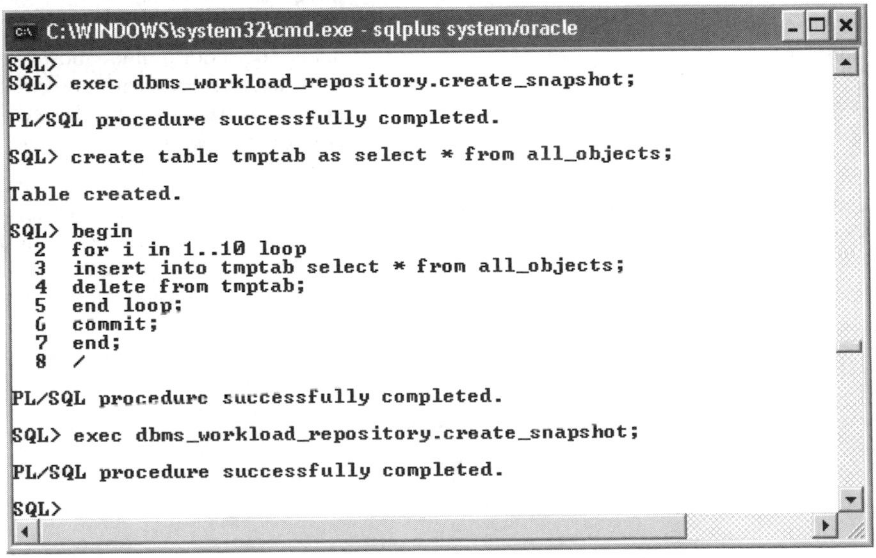

5. Connect to your database as user SYSTEM using Database Control.

6. Take the Advisor Central link in the Related Links section on the database home page. The first report listed will be the ADDM report generated as a result of the snapshot, as shown here:

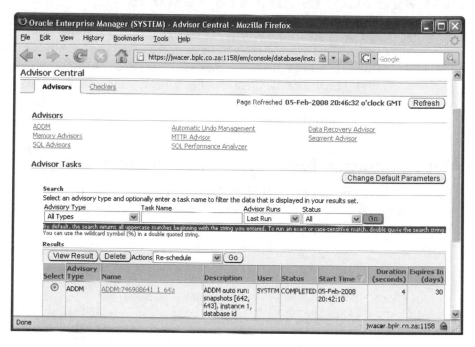

7. Take the Advisor Central link in the Related Links section on the database home page. The first report listed will be the ADDM report generated as a result of the snapshot.

8. Select the radio button for the latest ADDM report, and click the View Result button. Study the report: it will show a spike of activity in the last few minutes, with a number of "Findings" beneath. Click the findings to see the nature of the activity and the statements that caused it.

9. To tidy up, drop the table from your SQL*Plus session:

```
drop table tmptab;
```

CERTIFICATION OBJECTIVE 13.04

Manage Alerts and Thresholds

The Alert system is why, from release 10g onward, the Oracle database can be described as *self-managing*. In earlier releases, the DBA had to spend a great deal of effort on humdrum work that was essential but not always that interesting. He/she also had to devise methods of picking up exceptional conditions as they occurred.

The Alert system can automate a large amount of work that previously fell into the DBA domain.

Alert Condition Monitoring and Notifications

A typical example of the humdrum work is space management: at its most basic, monitoring tablespaces to see when they are about to fill up. This could be done with scripts, such as this one:

```
SQL> select d.tablespace_name,sum(d.bytes) total,sum(f.bytes) free
  2  from dba_data_files d left outer join dba_free_space f
  3  on d.tablespace_name=f.tablespace_name
  4  group by d.tablespace_name;
TABLESPACE_NAME                          TOTAL       FREE
------------------------------------ ---------- ----------
SYSAUX                                807337984   38928384
USERS                                  24641536    1507328
SMALL                                    401408
SYSTEM                               1509949440    4390912
EXAMPLE                               314572800   23396352
UNDO1                                 209715200  208338944
```

But these scripts are prone to error, or at least, misinterpretation. For example, the view DBA_FREE_SPACE has one row for every bit of free space in every tablespace. But if a tablespace were full, there would be no rows at all; hence the need for the OUTER JOIN, without which the SMALL tablespace would not be listed, even though it is in a critical state. Then consider the effect of enabling AUTOEXTEND on the datafiles. Also, an UNDO tablespace will usually be 100 percent full, but this is not a problem, because a large part of the undo data will be inactive and can be overwritten. And what about temporary tablespaces? The query would have to be in a UNION with another query against DBA_TEMP_FILES.

Many DBAs have written suites of SQL code to report on space usage and raise warnings before error conditions occurred. Fine, but the scripts had to be written, they had to be run regularly, and they had to be updated to take account of changes in technology. Many companies have written and marketed tools to do the same thing.

The Alert system replaces a vast amount of this humdrum work. It will monitor many conditions that can cause problems, and will send notifications by a variety of methods. With regard to space management, it is by default configured to raise a warning alert when a tablespace reaches 85 percent full and a critical alert when a tablespace is 97 percent full, with account being taken of autoextension and the nature of the contents.

Alerts comes in two forms. *Stateful* alerts are based on conditions that persist and can be fixed. Tablespace space usage is an example, or the number of sessions hanging, or the average time it is taking to complete an SQL statement execution. *Stateless* alerts are based on events; they happen and are gone. A query failing with "snapshot too old" or two transactions deadlocking are examples.

To configure the Alert system, you set thresholds. The thresholds are stored in the AWR. Then the MMON background process will monitor the database and the instance, in real time, and compare the current state with the thresholds. If a threshold is crossed, it will raise the alert. The mechanism by which an alert is raised is simply to put an entry on the alert queue. A queue is a table of messages that other processes can read. What happens to the alert message next is a matter for further configuration. The default behavior is that Enterprise Manager (either Database Control or Grid Control) will dequeue the message and display it on the database home page, but Enterprise Manager can be configured to send e-mails or SMS messages when it finds that an alert has been raised. You can also view the alerts by querying the view DBA_OUTSTANDING_ALERTS, and it is possible to write an alert handler that will dequeue the messages and take any action desired.

watch *Alerts are raised by the MMON process, not by Enterprise Manager. Enterprise Manager reads alerts, as can other event handlers written by you or by third parties.*

Setting Thresholds

There are over two hundred metrics for which you can set thresholds. They are documented in the view V$METRICNAME, which gives the name of the metric and the units in which it is measured, and the ID number by which it is identified.

There is an API (the DBMS_SERVER_ALERT package) for setting thresholds. For example:

```
1     execute dbms_server_alert.set_threshold(-
2     metrics_id=>dbms_server_alert.redo_generated_sec,-
3     warning_operator=>dbms_server_alert.operator_ge,-
4     warning_value=>'1000000',-
5     critical_operator=>dbms_server_alert.operator_ge,-
6     critical_value=>'2000000',-
7     observation_period=>1,-
8     consecutive_occurrences=>5,-
9     instance_name=>'ORCL11G',-
10    object_type=>dbms_server_alert.object_type_system,-
11    object_name=>null);
```

Taking this PL/SQL execution call line by line:

1. The procedure SET_THRESHOLD will create or update an alert threshold.
2. The metric being set is the rate of redo generation, measured in bytes per second.
3. The comparison operator for the warning level, which is "greater than or equal to."
4. The value for a warning alert, which is 1 MB a second.
5. The comparison operator for the critical level, which is "greater than or equal to."
6. The value for a critical alert, which is 2 MB a second.
7. The observation period, in minutes.
8. The number of consecutive occurrences before the alert is raised.
9. The instance for which the alert is being configured.
10. The type of object to which the alert refers.
11. The name of the object to which the alert refers.

Note that not all the arguments are relevant for all alerts.

The preceding example configures an alert for the rate of redo generation; a warning will be raised if this exceeds 1 MB a second, and a critical warning if it goes over 2 MB a second. The observation period is set to a minute and consecutive occurrences to five; this means that if the redo generation happens to hit a high level just a couple of times, it will not be reported—but if it stays at a high level consistently (for five consecutive minutes), then it will be reported. As this metric is

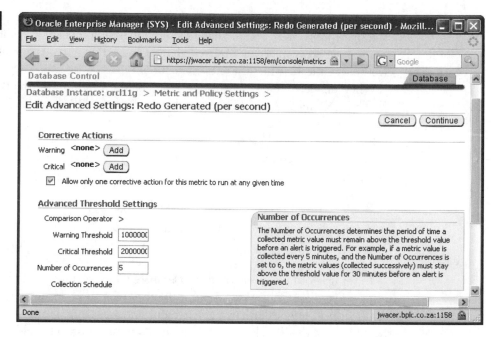

FIGURE 13-10

Setting thresholds with Database Control

one that could vary between instances in an RAC environment, the instance name must be specified, but the object name is not relevant. If the alert were for tablespace usage, then the instance name would not be specified, the object type would be tablespace, and the object name would be set to the name of the tablespace.

To reach the graphical interface for setting thresholds, take the Metric And Policy Settings link in the Related Links section on the database home page. This will show all the metrics with their settings. Clicking the Edit symbol for a metric will take you to the window where the thresholds can be set. Figure 13-10 shows this for the "Redo Generated (per second)" metric, after executing the procedure call just described. The graphical interface does not give access to all the settings for all the metrics; in this case, you cannot specify an observation period (it always set to one minute) and have no choice of comparison operators.

The Notification System

The default notification mechanism for stateful alerts is nothing more than displaying them in Enterprise Manager on the database home page, and writing them to the DBA_OUTSTANDING_ALERTS view. They will remain visible until they are cleared. They may be cleared because the DBA has fixed the problem, or in some cases the problem will go away in the natural course of events. For instance, a tablespace-usage alert would usually require DBA action (such as adding another datafile), whereas an activity-related alert such the rate of redo generation might clear automatically when the activity reduces.

When an alert is cleared, within the database it is removed from the DBA_OUTSTANDING_ALERTS view and written to the DBA_ALERT_HISTORY view. Stateless alerts go straight to the history view.

If any notification beyond the default is needed, this must be configured within Enterprise Manager. The Enterprise Manager notification system requires configuration at three levels:

- A notification method must be configured.
- A rule must be created to catch the event.
- An administrator must subscribe to the rule.

To set up notification methods in Database Control, take the Setup link visible in most Database Control windows at the top right and bottom center, and then the Notification Methods link in the left-hand side menu bar. From here, you specify the address of the SMTP server to which Database Control should send e-mail notifications, with authentication details and a reply address. From this window, shown in Figure 13-11, you can also define additional notification methods.

The alternative notification methods can be seen at the bottom of Figure 13-11: operating system commands or scripts, PL/SQL procedures, or an SNMP trap (which lets Database Control integrate with any SNMP management system that may be available).

Having defined the notification method, create a rule. Take the Preferences link visible in most Database Control windows at the top right and bottom center, then the Rules link in the left-hand side menu bar. There are several preconfigured rules. To create a new one, click Create and give the rule a name; select the Public check box to make it available to other uses. Then click the Metrics button, if the rule is for a metric, and select which metrics the rule should monitor. Figure 13-12 shows adding the "Redo Generation (per second)" metric to a rule.

The final step is for a user to subscribe to the notifications. From the Setup link again, choose Administrators on the left-hand side menu bar. There will by

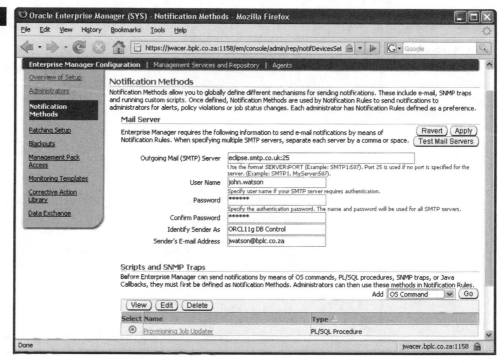

FIGURE 13-11

Defining the server address for Database Control to send e-mail notifications

default be three administrators: SYS, SYSMAN, and SYSTEM. A site making use of Enterprise Manager would usually have created additional users. Select the radio button for the user who is to subscribe to one or more rules, click the Edit button to make sure he/she has an e-mail address set up, and then click the Subscribe To Rules button to reach a list of all the public rules, where the ones for which the user is to receive notifications by e-mail can be selected. Notifications sent with any of the other methods (PL/SQL, OS command, or SNMP) do not need this step; the code written to implement the PL/SQL procedure, the operating system script, or the SNMP trap should handle the propagation of the notification.

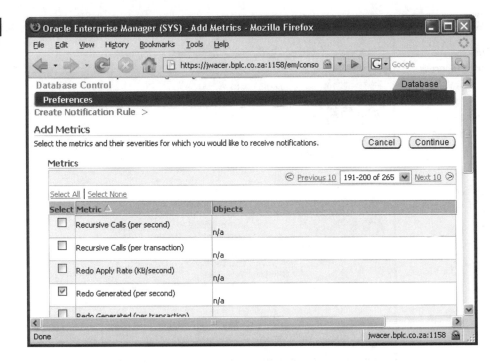

FIGURE 13-12

Adding a metric
to a Database
Control
notification rule

EXERCISE 13-4

Configure Alerts

In this exercise, you will enable an alert for the commit rate and demonstrate its use.

1. Connect to your database with Database Control as user SYSTEM.

2. From the database home page, take the Metric And Policy Settings link in the Related Links section.

3. Make sure that the View box is set to All Metrics, and scroll down to the User Commit (per second) metric.

4. Set the "Warning" and "Critical" thresholds to 1 and 4 respectively. These are artificially low thresholds that it will be simple to cross. Click the OK button to save this change.

5. Connect to your database as user SYSTEM with SQL*Plus, and issue the COMMIT command a few times quickly:

```
SQL> commit;
Commit complete.
SQL> /
Commit complete.
SQL> /
Commit complete.
SQL> /
Commit complete.
SQL> /
Commit complete.
```

6. In your Database Control session, within a few seconds you will see that the alert has been raised, as shown here:

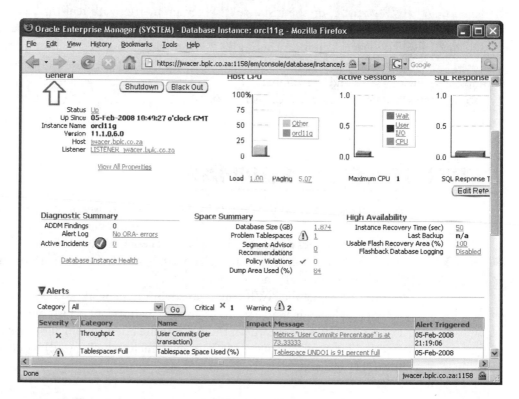

7. Tidy up, by returning to the Edit Thresholds window and clearing the threshold values.

INSIDE THE EXAM

The Self-Managing Database

Many of the topics in this chapter are covered in greater detail elsewhere in the OCP curriculum. However, a general knowledge of the self-managing systems is required for this exam.

At the core of the self-management capabilities is the statistics-gathering mechanism: optimizer statistics on database objects, and AWR statistics on the instance and the database. These are gathered and used automatically. There are APIs for gathering and using both types of statistics, but the automatic mechanisms and the graphical interface presented by Enterprise Manager

make using these optional. The configuration installed in a database created with DBCA may well be all that is required.

Statistics are stored in the AWR, gathered and maintained by the MMON background process. The MMON process is also responsible for raising alerts. The Alert system compares preconfigured threshold values for certain metrics with real-time activity figures and, if a threshold is crossed, raises an alert. Alerts can be notified by Enterprise Manager, or by any other tool that subscribes to the alert queue.

CERTIFICATION SUMMARY

Accurate statistics on the objects in the database are essential if the optimizer is to be allowed to generate efficient SQL execution plans. Gathering of these optimizer statistics can be (and is by default) completely automatic. The AWR stores another class of statistics: instance and database activity and performance statistics. Gathering these is also automatic.

Built on top of the AWR data is an advisor framework: wizards that will analyze activity and recommend actions to improve performance. First among the advisors is the ADDM. Also reliant on the AWR is the Alert system. This consists of thresholds for any of hundreds of metrics, which (when passed) will cause the MMON process to raise an alert message.

TWO-MINUTE DRILL

Use and Manage Optimizer Statistics

❑ Object statistics are gathered automatically, unless STATISTICS_LEVEL is BASIC.

❑ Object statistics are not maintained in real time.

❑ The AWR stores a history of object statistics; the current statistics are stored in the data dictionary.

Use and Manage the Automatic Workload Repository

❑ By default, snapshots are taken every hour and stored for eight days.

❑ Additional snapshots can be taken on demand.

❑ Snapshots can be preserved indefinitely if nominated for a baseline.

❑ MMON is responsible for creating snapshots and launching the ADDM.

❑ The AWR consists of tables (and related objects) in the SYSMAN schema, in the SYSAUX tablespace.

Use the Advisory Framework

❑ The ADDM runs automatically whenever a snapshot is taken, and manually on demand.

❑ ADDM reports will give advice directly and may recommend running other advisors.

❑ By default, the SQL Tuning Advisor and the Segment Advisor will run automatically in the maintenance windows.

❑ Setting STATISTICS_LEVEL to BASIC will disable gathering snapshots and running the advisors.

Manage Alerts and Thresholds

❑ Stateful alerts must be configured with thresholds.

❑ If a stateful alert is raised, it will remain until the situation is cleared; stateless alerts are reported and do not need to be cleared.

❑ Thresholds are stored in the AWR.

❑ It is the MMON background process that raises an alert, and (usually) Enterprise Manager that reports it.

SELF TEST

Use and Manage Optimizer Statistics

1. How can you best automate the collection of optimizer statistics? (Choose the best answer.)

   A. The MMON process will collect them if STATISTICS_LEVEL is set to TYPICAL or to ALL.

   B. An automatic maintenance job will collect them if STATISTICS_LEVEL is set to TYPICAL or to ALL.

   C. Enterprise Manager (Database Control or Grid Control) will collect them if STATISTICS_LEVEL is set to TYPICAL or to ALL.

   D. Execute the DBMS_STATS.GATHER_DATABASE_STATISTICS procedure with OPTIONS=>'GATHER AUTO'.

2. You notice that the statistics on a table are not correct: the NUM_ROWS figure does not include any rows inserted in the day so far. Why might this be? (Choose the best answer.)

   A. The STATISTICS_LEVEL parameter is not set to TYPICAL or ALL.

   B. The statistics have been locked by executing the DBMS_STATS.LOCK_TABLE_STATS procedure.

   C. The statistics will not change until the table is next analyzed.

   D. The automatic maintenance tasks are not running.

3. Where are the object statistics used by the query optimizer stored? (Choose the best answer.)

   A. With the objects themselves

   B. In the data dictionary

   C. In the AWR

   D. They are accumulated in the shared pool of the SGA

Use and Manage the Automatic Workload Repository

4. The AWR is located in the SYSAUX tablespace. If you suspect that it is growing to such a size that it will fill the SYSAUX tablespace, what actions could you take to reduce the likelihood of this happening? (Choose all correct answers.)

   A. Relocate the AWR to a tablespace created specifically for storing it.

   B. Reduce the time between snapshots, so that less data will generated by each one.

   C. Increase the time between snapshots, so that fewer snapshots will be generated.

   D. Adjust the scheduling of the automatic maintenance tasks, so that they will run less frequently.

5. By default, snapshots are removed from the AWR on a regular basis, making comparisons of activity over a long period of time (such as contrasting this year's year-end processing with last year's) impossible. What should you do to make this possible? (Choose the best answer.)

   A. Save the year-end snapshots as a baseline.

   B. Adjust the snapshot retention period to the whole period: a little over a year.

   C. Set the datafile(s) that make up the SYSAUX tablespace to AUTOEXTEND, so that snapshots will not be purged.

   D. Disable purging of snapshots by setting STATISTICS_LEVEL to ALL.

Use the Advisory Framework

6. When does the ADDM run? (Choose all correct answers.)

   A. Whenever a snapshot is taken by MMON

   B. Whenever a snapshot is taken by the DBA

   C. On demand

   D. When the automatic tasks run in the maintenance windows

   E. When triggered by the Alert system

7. Which advisors are run by the auto-task system in the maintenance windows? (Choose all correct answers.)

   A. The ADDM

   B. The memory advisors

   C. The Segment Advisor

   D. The SQL Access Advisor

   E. The SQL Tuning Advisor

   F. The Undo Advisor

8. With regard to the collection of monitoring information, put these steps in the correct order:

   A. Data accumulates in the SGA.

   B. MMON generates an ADDM report.

   C. MMON writes data to the AWR.

   D. Reports are purged.

   E. Snapshots are purged.

Manage Alerts and Thresholds

9. Which process raises alerts? (Choose the best answer.)

   A. MMON, the Manageability Monitor

   B. Enterprise Manager (Database Control or Grid Control)

    C. The server process that detects the problem

    D. SMON, the System Monitor

10. End users are complaining that they receive "snapshot too old" error messages when running long queries. You look at the DBA_OUTSTANDING_ALERTS view, and don't see any. Why might this be? (Choose the best answer.)

    A. The STATISTICS_LEVEL parameter is set to BASIC.

    B. The snapshots for the periods when the errors occurred have been purged.

    C. No alert has been configured for "snapshot too old."

    D. "Snapshot too old" is reported in DBA_ALERT_HISTORY.

LAB QUESTION

Using either SQL*Plus or Database Control, create a tablespace called SMALLTS with a single datafile that is 10 MB, using a uniform extent size of 1 MB. Make sure that it will not autoextend.

Set the thresholds for the warning and the critical space usage alerts to 70% and 80%.

This can be done with SQL*Plus but is much easier with Database Control, as shown here:

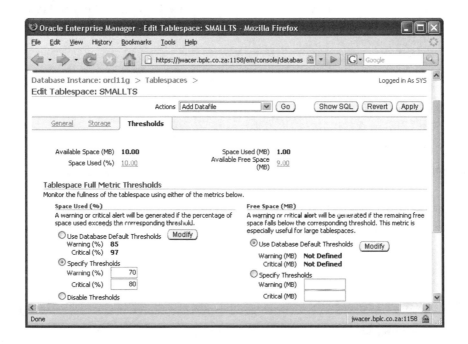

Create a table in the new tablespace, and manually allocate extents to it. This will produce an error once nine extents have been allocated.

Observe the alert that has been raised in Database Control, and as an entry in the DBA_OUTSTANDING_ALERTS view. Note that it may take a few minutes before the alert is raised; this is because the space usage alert is only monitored every ten minutes.

Fix the problem! Think of several techniques. Observe that the alert has been cleared in Database Control and removed from DBA_OUTSTANDING_ALERTS to DBA_ALERT_HISTORY.

Tidy up by dropping the tablespace.

SELF TEST ANSWERS

Use and Manage Optimizer Statistics

1. ☑ **B.** A job will run in the maintenance windows unless STATISICS_LEVEL is set to BASIC.
   ☒ **A** and **C** are wrong because they specify the wrong component to carry out the task. **D** is wrong because the 'GATHER AUTO' option controls what objects to analyze, not whether to analyze at all.

2. ☑ **C.** Optimizer statistics are not maintained in real time, only refreshed when the object is analyzed.
   ☒ **A** and **D** are wrong because they would affect the nightly refresh of the statistics, not a refresh during the day. **B** is wrong because it would freeze the statistics permanently, not just for the day.

3. ☑ **B.** The optimizer uses the latest statistics, which are stored in the data dictionary.
   ☒ **A** is wrong because the statistics are stored independently of the actual segments. **C** is wrong because the AWR stores historical values, which are not used for real-time parsing. **D** is wrong because the SGA stores the execution plan itself, not the information used to generate it.

Use and Manage the Automatic Workload Repository

4. ☑ **C.** Increasing the time between snapshots will reduce the number stored, and therefore the space needed.
   ☒ **A** is wrong because it is not possible to relocate the AWR. **B** is wrong because the space needed to store a snapshot is not related to the snapshot frequency; this would actually have the opposite effect to that desired. **D** is wrong because the automatic maintenance tasks do not control snapshots, and it is snapshots that take up the bulk of the space in the AWR.

5. ☑ **A.** This is exactly the type of situation for which baselines are intended.
   ☒ **B** would work, but you would need a SYSAUX tablespace the size of Jupiter; it is not a good solution. **C** is wrong because the available space has no effect on the retention time. **D** is wrong because STATISTICS_LEVEL controls how much information is gathered, not for how long it is kept.

Use the Advisory Framework

6. ☑ **A, B,** and **C.** MMON will always generate an ADDM report when a snapshot is taken (whether automatically or manually), and the DBA can request a report at any time.
   ☒ **D** is wrong because the auto-tasks do not include running the ADDM. **E** is wrong because the Alert system signals real-time problems: it is not used to launch ADDM, which reports on activity after the events have occurred.

7. ☑ **C** and **E.** These run in every maintenance window, but implementing the recommendations is up to the DBA.
    ☒ **A** is wrong because MMON invokes the ADDM. **B, D,** and **F** are wrong because they are advisors that must be invoked manually.

8. ☑ **A, C, B, E,** and **D.** This is the correct sequence.
    ☒ All other sequences are wrong.

Manage Alerts and Thresholds

9. ☑ **A.** MMON raises alerts.
    ☒ **B** is wrong because Enterprise Manager does not raise alerts; it reports them. **C** and **D** are wrong because neither server sessions nor the SMON are part of the Alert system.

10. ☑ **D.** "Snapshot too old" is a stateless alert and so goes directly to the alert history.
    ☒ **A** is wrong because the STATISTICS_LEVEL refers to statistics, not alerts. **B** is wrong because outstanding alerts do not get purged on any schedule, only by being resolved. **C** is wrong because "snapshot too old" is a stateless alert, and thresholds can only apply to stateful alerts.

LAB ANSWER

This is a solution using SQL*Plus:

1. Create the tablespace:

```
create tablespace smallts datafile '/u01/oradata/orcl11g/smallts1.dbf';
size 10m autoextend off uniform size 1m;
```

2. Set the thresholds:

```
execute
dbms_server_alert.set_threshold(9000,4,'70',4,'80',1,1,null,5,'SMALLTS');
```

3. Create the table:

```
create table toobig (c1 date) tablespace smallts;
```

4. Allocate an extent:

```
alter table toobig allocate extent;
```

5. Observe the alert:

```
select object_name,reason,suggested_action from dba_outstanding_alerts;
```

6. Fix the problem—three possibilities:

```
alter tablespace smallts add datafile '/u01/oradata/orcl11g/smallts2.dbf'
size 10m;
alter database datafile '/u01/oradata/orcl11g/smallts1.dbf' resize 20m;
alter database datafile '/u01/oradata/orcl11g/smallts1.dbf' autoextend on
maxsize 20m;
```

7. Observe the clearance:

```
select reason,resolution from dba_alert_history where object_name='SMALLTS';
```

8. Tidy up:

```
drop tablespace smallts including contents and datafiles;
```

14
Performance Management

Memory usage in an Oracle instance is critical for performance. If the amount of memory allocated to the various structures is not optimal, performance may degrade dramatically: the amount of memory should neither be too little, nor too much. With earlier releases of the database, tuning memory usage required a great deal of skill and time on the part of the DBA, but with release 11g memory tuning can be largely automatic.

Also critical for performance is the state of various objects within the database. If indexes are not usable, SQL statements may execute with methods that are far slower and more resource intensive than the methods they might otherwise use. If PL/SQL objects are invalid, this may impact adversely on performance or it may cause errors. All unusable and invalid objects should be identified, investigated, and repaired.

CERTIFICATION OBJECTIVE 14.01

Use Automatic Memory Management

Memory usage in the Oracle instance falls into two categories: Program Global Areas (PGAs) that are private to each session, and the System Global Area (SGA) that is shared by all the Oracle processes. From release 9i it has been possible to automate the management of the PGA. From release 10g it has been possible to automate the management of the SGA. Release 11g can manage both PGA and SGA together.

on the **job**

All Oracle memory usage is virtual memory. The Oracle processes have no way of knowing if the memory to which they are connecting is in RAM or has been swapped (or paged) to disk. However, swapping is going to cripple performance and should be avoided.

PGA Memory Management

A user session against an Oracle instance consists of a user process connected to a server process. The user process generates SQL statements and sends them to the server process for execution: this is the client-server split. Associated with the server process is a block of non-sharable memory: the PGA. When executing SQL, the server process makes use of the PGA to store session specific data, including

- Temporary tables
- Sorting rows
- Merging bitmaps
- Variables
- The call stack

For some data in the PGA, use of memory is non-negotiable. For example, if the session needs memory for its call stack, that memory must be made available. For other structures (such as temporary table storage) use of PGA is nice but not essential, because if necessary the data can be written out to a disk-based storage structure—though this will impact adversely on performance.

Every SQL statement uses memory in the SGA (specifically, the shared SQL area, in the shared pool) and also will require a minimum amount of PGA memory (sometimes referred to as the private SQL area), without which it cannot execute. Making more PGA memory available will often reduce execution time, but the reduction is not linear. Typically, there will be three stages of memory allocation: these are known as *optimal*, *one-pass*, and *multipass*. The optimal memory allocation is that which will allow the statement to execute purely in memory, with no requirement to make use of temporary storage on disk. The optimal memory allocation is sufficient to accommodate all the input data and any auxiliary data structures that the statement must create. The one-pass memory allocation is insufficient for optimal execution and therefore forces an extra pass over the data. The multipass memory allocation is even smaller and means that several passes over the data will be needed. As an example, consider a sort operation. The ideal situation is that all the rows to be sorted can be read into the PGA and sorted there. The memory required for this is the optimal memory allocation. If the optimal memory allocation is not available, then the rows must be separated into batches. Each batch will be read into memory, sorted, and written out to disk. This results in a set of sorted batches on disk, which must then be read back into memory and merged into a final sorted list of all the rows. The PGA memory needed for this is the one-pass allocation: the sort operation has had to become multiple sorts followed by a merge. If the one-pass memory allocation is not available, then the merge phase as well as the sort phase will require use of temporary disk storage. This is a multipass execution.

A statement's shared SQL area is in the shared pool of the SGA; its private SQL area is in the session's PGA.

The ideal situation is that all SQL statements should execute optimally, but this goal may be impossible to reach. In data warehouse operations, the optimal memory allocation can be many gigabytes if the queries are addressing vast tables. In such environments, one-pass executions may be the best that can be achieved. Multipass executions should be avoided if at all possible. For example, to sort 10 GB of data may require something over 10 GB of memory to run optimally, but only 40 MB to run with one pass. Only if less than 40 MB is available will the sort become multipass, and execution times will then increase substantially.

Managing PGA memory can be automatic, and Oracle Corporation strongly recommends that it should be. The older manual management techniques are supported only for backward compatibility and will not be discussed here. To implement automatic PGA memory management, you set a target for the total PGA memory allocation, summed up for all sessions. The Oracle instance will then pass out memory from this total to sessions on demand. When a session has finished executing its statement, the PGA it was using can be allocated to another session. This system relies on the fact that at any one moment only some of the connected sessions will need any negotiable PGA memory. They will all need a certain amount of PGA memory to retain the state of the session even when the session is idle, but this will leave enough from the total so that those sessions actually running statements can have what they need. At least, that is what one hopes.

on the ⓙob *It is sometimes impossible to achieve optimal memory allocations, because the memory requirements can be huge. One-pass executions are bad but may be unavoidable. Multipass executions are disastrous, and if these are occurring, you should talk to the system administrators about available hardware and to the programmers about tuning their SQL.*

Automatic PGA memory management is enabled with two instance parameters:

- WORKAREA_SIZE_POLICY
- PGA_AGGREGATE_TARGET

The WORKAREA_SIZE_POLICY will default to AUTO, meaning that Oracle can assign PGA to sessions on demand, while attempting to keep the total allocated PGA within the PGA_AGGREGATE_TARGET. This parameter defaults to the greater of 10 MB or 20 percent of the size of the SGA and should be adjusted upward until a satisfactory proportion of statements are executing optimally, but not set so high that memory is over-allocated and the operating system has to page virtual memory to disk.

on the **Job**

For many systems, the default for PGA_AGGREGATE_TARGET will be far too low for optimal performance. Some DBAs set it equal to the size of the SGA, and tune from there.

SGA Memory Management

The SGA contains several memory structures, which can be sized independently. These are

- The shared pool
- The database buffer cache
- The large pool
- The Streams pool
- The Java pool
- The log buffer

As a general rule, the memory allocation to the large pool, the Java pool, and the Streams pool is not a matter for negotiation —either the memory is needed or it isn't. If these structures are undersized, there will be errors; if they are oversized, there will be no performance improvement. The memory allocation to the shared pool, the database buffer cache, and the log buffer is negotiable: if less than optimal, there will not be errors but performance will degrade. The exception is the shared pool: if this is chronically undersized, there will be errors.

on the **Job**

Do not throw memory at Oracle unnecessarily. An oversized shared pool or log buffer is seriously bad for performance. An oversized buffer cache is less likely to be a problem, unless it is so oversized that the system is having to swap.

SGA memory management can be automatic (and Oracle Corporation advises that it should be) with the exception of the log buffer. The DBA sets a total size for the SGA, and the instance will apportion this total to the various structures, ensuring that there are no errors from undersizing of SGA components and that memory above this minimum is allocated where it will do most good. The components will be resized on demand, so that if a component needs more memory, it will be taken from a component that can spare it. The log buffer is the one SGA component whose size is fixed at instance startup and that cannot be automatically managed.

The parameters for manual management of the SGA are

- SHARED_POOL_SIZE
- DB_CACHE_SIZE
- LARGE_POOL_SIZE
- STREAMS_POOL_SIZE
- JAVA_POOL_SIZE

To enable automatic SGA management, leave all of these on default (or set to zero) and set one parameter to enable automatic shared memory management (ASSM):

- SGA_TARGET

When using ASSM, the instance will monitor demand for memory in the various SGA components and pass out memory to the components as required, downsizing components if this is necessary to keep the total allocated memory within the target. Also included within the target is the log buffer. This is sized with the LOG_BUFFER parameter, which is static: the log buffer is created at instance startup and cannot be resized subsequently.

on the **Job**

The default for LOG_BUFFER is probably correct. You can set the parameter to higher than default, but this will often cause a degradation in performance. If you set it to less than the default, your setting will be ignored.

Automatic Memory Management

The Automatic Memory Management mechanism lets the Oracle instance manage server memory usage as a whole, by setting one parameter: MEMORY_TARGET. This takes the automatic PGA management (enabled with PGA_AGGREGATE_TARGET) and the automatic shared memory management (enabled with SGA_TARGET) a step further, by letting Oracle transfer memory between PGAs and SGA on demand.

Automatic memory management is not just a tool to make database administration easy. It will often give big performance benefits as well. Many databases will experience different patterns of activity at different times, which could benefit from different memory configurations. For example, it is not uncommon for a database used for order processing to experience a very heavy transaction processing workload during most of the month, and then a heavy query processing workload during month end reporting runs. Transaction processing will typically not be demanding on PGA memory but will require a large database buffer cache. Query processing will often require large PGA allocations, but not much buffer cache.

Manually transferring memory between SGA and PGA in response to changing patterns of activity is not a practical option, and many systems will not be able to allocate enough memory to both concurrently to satisfy their peak demands. Automatic memory management is able to transfer memory between SGA and PGA as necessary to optimize performance within an overall memory constraint. This overall constraint must be determined by the DBA and the system administrator together. There is little point in the DBA setting an upper limit that is so large that the operating system has to page SGA and PGA to a swap device; the system administrator will be able to advise on a suitable maximum value.

on the Job

To enable automatic memory management, set the one parameter MEMORY_ TARGET, and do not set any of the other parameters listed previously, with the exception of LOG_BUFFER—though this too can often be left on default.

The MEMORY_TARGET parameter is dynamic—it can be adjusted without shutting down the instance—but only within a limit set by another parameter: MEMORY_MAX_TARGET. This is static, so it can only be raised by adjusting with the SCOPE=SPFILE clause and restarting the instance.

EXERCISE 14-1

Set the Memory Management Parameters

In this exercise, you will disable Automatic Memory Management (if it is enabled) and set the SGA and PGA targets independently. Make all the changes using syntax that will only affect the running instance: do not propagate the changes to the spfile, unless you are prepared to reverse them later.

I. Connect to your database with SQL*Plus as user SYSTEM.

2. Ensure that none of the parameters for managing SGA memory structure manually are set:

```
alter system set db_cache_size=0 scope=memory;
alter system set shared_pool_size=0 scope=memory;
alter system set large_pool_size=0 scope=memory;
alter system set java_pool_size=0 scope=memory;
```

3. Disable Automatic Memory Management:

```
alter system set memory_target=0 scope=memory;
```

4. Set the parameters to size PGA and SGA independently, using the lowest permitted values:

```
alter system set pga_aggregate_target=10m scope=memory;
alter system set sga_target=64m scope=memory;
```

The second command may take a few minutes to complete, and it may fail if Oracle cannot reduce the SGA to the requested value.

5. Determine the actual size of the currently allocated PGAs, by summing up the value for the statistic "session pga memory" across all sessions:

```
select sum(value) from v$sesstat natural join v$statname
where name='session pga memory';
```

The figure will be significantly in excess of the 10 MB requested in Step 4. This is because 10 MB is a value that is so low that Oracle cannot keep to it. The PGA target is only a target, not a hard limit.

6. Determine the actual size of the SGA:

```
select sum(bytes) from v$sgastat;
```

This figure too may be greater than that requested in Step 4.

CERTIFICATION OBJECTIVE 14.02

Use Memory Advisors

The Oracle instance collects a vast amount of information regarding activity and performance. These statistics are accumulated in memory and flushed to the Automatic Workload Repository on a regular basis by the MMON background process, as described in Chapter 13. These statistics enable the memory advisors. These are tools that will calculate the effect of varying the sizes of the SGA and PGA memory structures. The Automatic Memory Management facility uses the advisors to make decisions about memory allocation, and they are also visible to the DBA through various views and through Enterprise Manager. Figure 14-1 shows three queries that display memory advisor information.

FIGURE 14-1

The memory
advisors, queried
with SQL*Plus

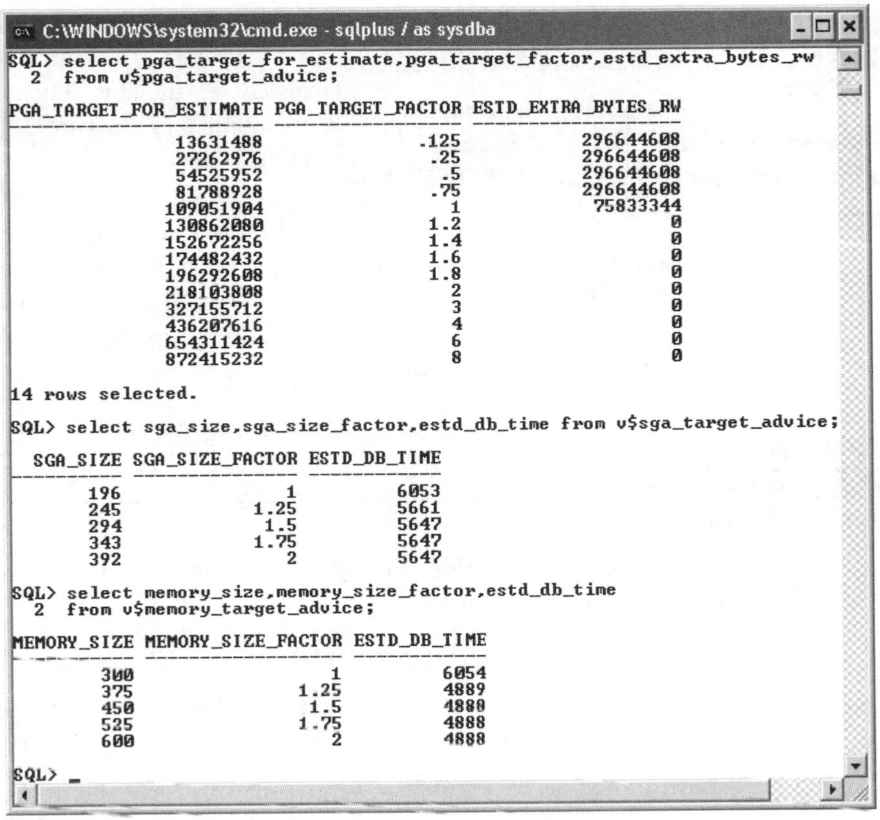

```
C:\WINDOWS\system32\cmd.exe - sqlplus / as sysdba                          _ □ x
SQL> select pga_target_for_estimate,pga_target_factor,estd_extra_bytes_rw
  2  from v$pga_target_advice;

PGA_TARGET_FOR_ESTIMATE PGA_TARGET_FACTOR ESTD_EXTRA_BYTES_RW

               13631488              .125           296644608
               27262976               .25           296644608
               54525952                .5           296644608
               81788928               .75           296644608
              109051904                 1            75833344
              130862080               1.2                   0
              152672256               1.4                   0
              174482432               1.6                   0
              196292608               1.8                   0
              218103808                 2                   0
              327155712                 3                   0
              436207616                 4                   0
              654311424                 6                   0
              872415232                 8                   0

14 rows selected.

SQL> select sga_size,sga_size_factor,estd_db_time from v$sga_target_advice;

  SGA_SIZE SGA_SIZE_FACTOR ESTD_DB_TIME

       196               1         6053
       245            1.25         5661
       294             1.5         5647
       343            1.75         5647
       392               2         5647

SQL> select memory_size,memory_size_factor,estd_db_time
  2  from v$memory_target_advice;

MEMORY_SIZE MEMORY_SIZE_FACTOR ESTD_DB_TIME

        300                  1         6054
        375               1.25         4889
        450                1.5         4888
        525               1.75         4888
        600                  2         4888

SQL> _
```

The first query in Figure 14-1 shows the PGA advisor. The third selected column show an estimate for the amount of disk I/O that would be needed if the PGA target were set to the figure shown in the first column. The second column expresses this figure as a proportion of the actual setting. The fifth row of the output is the current setting: a PGA_TARGET_FACTOR of 1. It can be seen that if another 30 MB of memory were added to the target, less I/O would be needed but that adding more than this would give no further benefit.

The second query in Figure 14-1 shows the SGA advisor. This relates the size of the SGA to a projected value for DB_TIME. DB_TIME is an overall figure for the amount of time spent taken within the database to execute SQL; minimizing DB_TIME is the overall objective of all tuning. It can be seen that if the SGA were raised from its current value of 196 MB to 294 MB, DB_TIME would reduce but that there would be no point in going further.

The advisors will not be enabled unless the STATISTICS_LEVEL parameter is set to TYPICAL or ALL.

The third query is against the memory target advisor, which gives advice on the total (SGA plus PGA) memory allocation. This shows that the optimal value is 450 MB, as opposed to the current value of 300 MB. If using automatic Memory Management (enabled with the MEMORY_TARGET parameter), then this last query is all that need be used. It can be seen that virtually all of the DB_TIME saving could be achieved by raising the target to 375 MB, and if the system administrators say sufficient memory is not available to allocate the optimal amount, then this is what the DBA should ask for.

EXERCISE 14-2

Use the Memory Advisors

In this exercise, you will gather advice about memory allocation using the advisors through Database Control.

1. Connect to your database as user SYS with Database control.

2. From the database home page, click the Advisor Central link in the Related Links section. Then on the Advisors tab, take the Memory Advisors link in the Advisors section.

3. On the SGA tab, in the Current Allocation section you will the current SGA memory usage, which will be the same total as that returned for the query in Exercise 14-1, Step 4, and the breakdown into the individual components.

4. Click Advice, to see a graphical representation of a query against the V$SHARED_POOL_ADVICE view. The following illustration is an example, which shows that the optimal SGA would be nearly 200 MB.

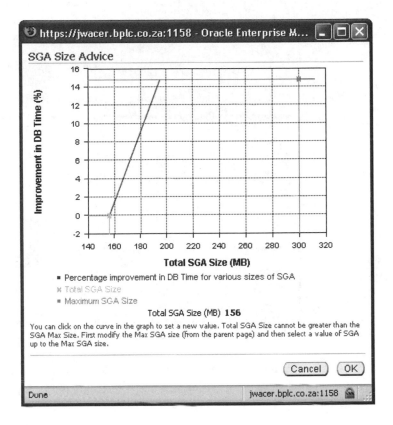

5. On the PGA tab, you will see the target (set to 10 MB) and the actual allocated PGA, which will be higher. The Advice button will show a graphical representation of a query against V$PGA_TARGET_ADVICE.

6. Enable Automatic Memory Management by clicking the Enable button at the top of the Memory Advisors window. This will display the value of MEMORY_MAX_TARGET, along with a possible memory size, and suggest a value for MEMORY_TARGET. In the following illustration, these values are 300 MB and 166 MB.

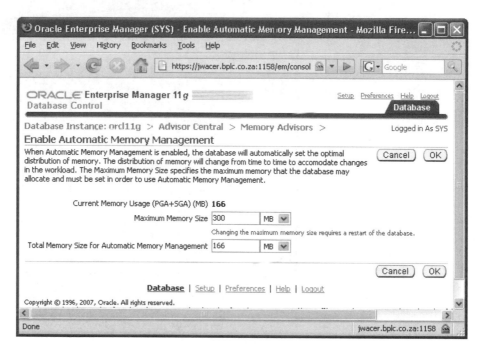

7. Leave the memory parameters on default, and click OK.

8. The memory advisor will now be available: click the Advice button to see the suggested value for the target.

9. Return the instance to the original memory configuration (as it was before Exercise 14-1) by shutting it down and restarting.

CERTIFICATION OBJECTIVE 14.03

Troubleshoot Invalid and Unusable Objects

First, the terminology. Ideally, all objects have a status of *valid*. PL/SQL objects, and views can become *invalid*; indexes can become *unusable*. Depending on the reason for an object becoming invalid, it may become valid automatically when next accessed. Unusable indexes must be made valid by rebuilding, which does not occur automatically.

Invalid Objects

Stored PL/SQL is code stored and compiled within the data dictionary, as PL/SQL objects. These can be

- Procedures
- Functions
- Triggers
- Packages
- Object types

Most, if not all, of these procedural objects will refer to data objects, such as tables. When a procedural object is compiled, the compiler checks the data objects to which it refers in order to confirm that the definition is correct for the code. For example, if the code refers to a column, the column must exist or the code will not compile. If any of the data objects to which a procedural object refers change after the procedural object has been compiled, then the procedure will be marked INVALID. Procedural objects may also be invalid for more mundane reasons: perhaps the programmer made a simple syntactical mistake. In that case, the object will be created INVALID and will be useless.

Oracle will always attempt to recompile invalid PL/SQL objects and views automatically, but this may not succeed. You do not have to do it manually—though it may be advisable to do so.

The same situation can occur with views. When created, they may be fine, but they will be invalidated if the detail tables on which they are based have their definitions changed.

Objects can be created invalid because of programmer error, or they can become invalid some time after creation. The view DBA_OBJECTS (and the derived views ALL_OBJECTS and USER_OBJECTS) has a column, STATUS, which should ideally always be VALID. To identify all invalid objects in the database, as user SYSTEM run the query

```
select owner,object_name,object_type from dba_objects
where status='INVALID';
```

If any objects are listed by this query, the first question to ask is whether the object was ever valid. It may never have worked and not be needed, in which case the best thing to do may be to drop it. But if, as is likely, you do not know if the object was ever valid, then a sensible first step is to attempt to compile it. The first time an invalid object is accessed, Oracle will attempt to compile it automatically— but if the compilation fails, the user will receive an error. Clearly, it is better for the DBA to compile it first; then, if there is an error, he/she can try to fix it before a user notices. Even if the object does compile when it is accessed, there may be a delay while the compilation takes place; it is better for perceived performance if this delay is taken by the DBA in advance.

To repair invalid objects, attempt to compile them. The syntax is

```
ALTER object_type object_name COMPILE ;
```

For example, the statement

```
SQL> alter procedure hr.add_reg compile;
```

will attempt to compile the procedure ADD_REG in the HR schema, and the statement

```
SQL> alter view rname compile;
```

will compile the view RNAME. If the compilation succeeds, you have no further problems. If it fails, then you need to work out why. If a procedure does not compile, use the SQL*Plus command SHOW ERRORS to see why not (unfortunately, SHOW ERRORS is not supported for views).

Often a useful starting point in identifying the cause of compilation errors is to use the DBA_DEPENDENCIES view, described here:

```
SQL> desc dba_dependencies;
 Name                              Null?    Type
 -------------------------------- -------- -------------
 OWNER                            NOT NULL VARCHAR2(30)
 NAME                             NOT NULL VARCHAR2(30)
 TYPE                                      VARCHAR2(17)
 REFERENCED_OWNER                          VARCHAR2(30)
 REFERENCED_NAME                           VARCHAR2(64)
 REFERENCED_TYPE                           VARCHAR2(17)
 REFERENCED_LINK_NAME                      VARCHAR2(128)
 DEPENDENCY_TYPE                           VARCHAR2(4)
```

For every object, identified by NAME, there will be rows for each object on which it depends. For example, if a view retrieves columns from a dozen tables, they will each be listed as a REFERENCED_NAME. If a view does not compile, then investigating these tables would be sensible.

There will be occasions when you are faced with the need to recompile hundreds or thousands of invalid objects. Typically, this occurs after an upgrade to an application, or perhaps after applying patches. Rather than recompiling them individually, use the supplied utility script. On Unix,

```
SQL> @?/rdbms/admin/utlrp
```

or in Windows,

```
SQL> @?\rdbms\admin\utlrp
```

This script, which should be run when connected AS SYSDBA, will attempt to compile all invalid objects. If after running it there are still some invalid objects, you can assume that they have problems that should be addressed individually.

Unusable Indexes

If a procedural object, such as a stored PL/SQL function or a view, becomes invalid, the DBA does not necessarily have to do anything: the first time it is accessed, Oracle will attempt to recompile it—and this may well succeed. But if an index becomes unusable for any reason, it must always be repaired explicitly before it can be used.

An index consists of the index key values, sorted into order, each with the relevant rowid. The rowid is the physical pointer to the location of the row to which the index key refers. If the rowids of the table are changed, then the index will be marked as unusable. This could occur for a number of reasons. Perhaps the most common is that the table has been moved, with the ALTER TABLE . . . MOVE command. This will change the physical placement of all the rows, and therefore the index entries will be pointing to the wrong place. Oracle will be aware of this and will therefore not permit use of the index.

In earlier releases of the Oracle database, it was more than likely that users would detect unusable indexes because their sessions would return errors. When executing SQL statements, if the session attempted to use an unusable index, it would immediately return an error, and the statement would fail. From release 10g and higher the database changes this behavior. If a statement attempts to use an unusable index, the statement will revert to an execution plan that does not require the index. Thus, statements will always succeed—but perhaps at greatly reduced performance. This behavior is controlled by the instance parameter SKIP_UNUSABLE_INDEXES, which defaults to TRUE. The exception to this is if the index is necessary to enforce a constraint: if the index on a primary key column becomes unusable, the table will be locked for DML.

If you wish your database to react as earlier releases, where unusable indexes would cause errors, issue the command `ALTER SYSTEM SET SKIP_UNUSABLE_INDEXES=FALSE;`.

To detect indexes that have become unusable, query the DBA_INDEXES view:

```
SQL> select owner, index_name from dba_indexes where
status='UNUSABLE';
```

Indexes are marked unusable if the rowid pointers are no longer correct. To repair the index, it must be recreated with the ALTER INDEX . . . REBUILD command. This will make a pass through the table, generating a new index with correct rowid pointers for each index key. When the new index is completed, the original, unusable index is dropped.

While an index rebuild is in progress, additional storage space is required; plan ahead to make sure it is available.

INSIDE THE EXAM

Performance Management

Performance management is another topic that is dealt with in detail in the second OCP examination. For the first, only summary knowledge is tested. It is important to have an understanding of how Automatic Memory Management works: that the DBA need do nothing more than set an overall target within which Oracle will pass out memory, on demand, to the various SGA and PGA memory structures, and that there is an advisor that will recommend an appropriate setting. If this mechanism is not enabled, there are separate advisors for the PGA and the SGA. The worst case is where not only is Automatic Memory Management disabled, but the automatic management of PGA and SGA is disabled too. This would be a reversion to the behavior of earlier releases and is not advised.

Indexes can become unusable; procedural objects can become invalid. This is usually a result of DDL commands executed against the tables on which they depend. The DBA should monitor the status of all objects and investigate any problems. The database will attempt to fix problems with dynamic recompilation, but this may fail and will certainly not attempt to rebuild unusable indexes.

The syntax of the REBUILD command has several options. The more important ones are TABLESPACE, ONLINE, and NOLOGGING. By default, the index will be rebuilt within its current tablespace, but by specifying a tablespace with the TABLESPACE keyword, it can be moved to a different one. Also by default, during the course of the rebuild the table will be locked for DML. This can be avoided by using the ONLINE keyword. The NOLOGGING keyword instructs Oracle not to generate redo for the index rebuild operation. This will make the rebuild proceed much faster, but it does mean that the tablespace containing the index should be backed up immediately. Until the tablespace is backed up, the index will not survive media damage requiring use of restore and recovery.

> *Rebuilding indexes may also be necessary as part of normal database administration. Indexes become inefficient with time—particularly if there are many deletions, or updates that affect the key values of rows.*

watch *NOLOGGING disables redo generation only for the index rebuild; all subsequent DML against the index will generate redo as normal. Unless ONLINE is specified, the table will be locked for DML while the rebuild is going on.*

EXERCISE 14-3

Repair Invalid Objects and Unusable Indexes

In this exercise, you will create some objects, break them, and repair them.

1. Using SQL*Plus, connect to your database as user SYSTEM.

2. Create a table to be used for the exercise:

```
create table valid_t as select * from all_users;
```

3. Create some objects dependent on this table:

```
create index valid_i on valid_t (username);
create view valid_v as select * from valid_t;
create procedure valid_p as begin
insert into valid_t values ('name',99,sysdate);
end;
/
```

4. Confirm the status of the objects:

```
select object_name,object_type,status from user_objects
where object_name like 'VALID%';
select status from user_indexes where index_name ='VALID_I';
```

They will all have the STATUS of VALID, and the index will be USABLE.
Steps 2, 3, and 4 are shown here:

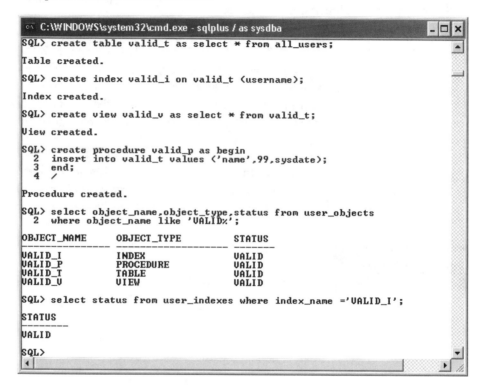

```
C:\WINDOWS\system32\cmd.exe - sqlplus / as sysdba

SQL> create table valid_t as select * from all_users;

Table created.

SQL> create index valid_i on valid_t (username);

Index created.

SQL> create view valid_v as select * from valid_t;

View created.

SQL> create procedure valid_p as begin
  2  insert into valid_t values ('name',99,sysdate);
  3  end;
  4  /

Procedure created.

SQL> select object_name,object_type,status from user_objects
  2  where object_name like 'VALID%';

OBJECT_NAME        OBJECT_TYPE          STATUS
-----------------  -------------------  -------
VALID_I            INDEX                VALID
VALID_P            PROCEDURE            VALID
VALID_T            TABLE                VALID
VALID_V            VIEW                 VALID

SQL> select status from user_indexes where index_name ='VALID_I';

STATUS
-------
VALID

SQL>
```

5. Perform DDL command on the table that will break the objects:

```
alter table valid_t drop column created;
alter table valid_t move;
```

6. Rerun the queries from Step 4. Note that the procedure and the view are now
   INVALID, and the index is UNUSABLE.

7. Attempt to use the invalid objects:

```
execute valid_p;
select * from valid_v;
```

8. Attempt to correct the errors:

```
alter view valid_v compile;
alter procedure valid_p compile;
alter index valid_i rebuild online nologging;
```

The compilations will fail, because the table has been changed, but the index will rebuild: it was never INVALID, merely UNUSABLE because the table move had changed all the rowids.

9. Correct the errors by adding the column back to the table:

```
alter table valid_t add (created date);
```

10. Repeat Step 7. The statements will succeed.

11. Rerun the queries in Step 4. All the objects are fine now, because the attempts to use them forced an automatic recompilation.

12. Tidy up by dropping the objects:

```
drop table valid_t;
drop procedure valid_p;
drop view valid_v;
```

SCENARIO & SOLUTION

If I enable Automatic Memory Management, can I really just let Oracle get on with it?	Pretty much. The only thing you need to do is monitor the memory advisor to see if the target is set appropriately, always remembering that the pattern of activity against the database may change over time. And to give yourself the ability to raise the target if necessary, make sure that the MEMORY_MAX_TARGET parameter is set higher than your current need—perhaps by a few hundred megabytes.
If a lot of objects are repeatedly going invalid, what can I do about it? Is there a better way than continually recompiling them?	You need to try to work out why the invalidations are occurring. A common reason is that development staff members are messing about on the production system, doing work on it that should only be done during maintenance periods. If this is happening, you need to enforce better change control procedures. Another possibility is circular dependencies between objects: A needs B, B needs C, and C needs A. This means that compiling A will break C, and so on. Again, it's the developers: they shouldn't design code like that.

CERTIFICATION SUMMARY

In an 11g database, memory management can (and usually should) be completely automatic: the DBA sets a total and Oracle builds its memory structures within this total, resizing them as necessary for optimal performance. There are advisors that make recommendations regarding sizes of memory structures.

Procedural objects (such as PL/SQL objects, synonyms, and views) can become invalid. This is usually because of DDL applied to the tables on which they depend. Invalid objects will be recompiled automatically when they are next used, but this recompilation can only succeed if the underlying problem has been fixed. Indexes can become unusable. This will usually happen because their table has been relocated. Unusable indexes must be rebuilt, which will not happen automatically. Index rebuilds will, by default, require a table lock and will generate redo—but this behavior can be changed.

TWO-MINUTE DRILL

Use Automatic Memory Management

❑ Automatic Shared Memory Management can be enabled with the parameter SGA_TARGET.

❑ Automatic PGA Management can be enabled with the parameter PGA_AGGREGATE_TARGET.

❑ Automatic Memory Management can be enabled with the parameter MEMORY_TARGET.

Use Memory Advisors

❑ There are advisors for PGA, SGA, and total memory usage.

❑ The advisors can be accessed by querying dynamic performance views, or through Enterprise Manager.

Troubleshoot Invalid and Unusable Objects

❑ Procedural objects will become invalid if the objects on which they depend are changed.

❑ Indexes will become unusable if their table is moved.

❑ Oracle will attempt to recompile invalid procedural object automatically.

❑ Unusable indexes must be rebuilt manually.

❑ Oracle will not attempt to use an unusable index, so there will be no errors.

SELF TEST

Use Automatic Memory Management

1. Where are private SQL areas stored? (Choose the best answer.)
   A. In each session's PGA, always
   B. In each session's PGA, unless a PGA Aggregate Target has been set
   C. In the PGA, unless Automatic Memory Management has been enabled
   D. In the shared pool of the SGA, always

2. Which memory structure is fixed in size at instance startup? (Choose the best answer.)
   A. The shared pool
   B. The large pool
   C. The Java pool
   D. The log buffer
   E. None are fixed, if Automatic Memory Management has been enabled

3. When Automatic Memory Management is enabled, what is not possible? (Choose the best answer.)
   A. Transfer of memory between sessions' PGAs
   B. Transfer of memory between structures within the SGA
   C. Transfer of memory from SGA to PGA, and vice versa
   D. Increasing the total memory usage after instance startup
   E. All of the above are possible

4. Storage of what structures can exist in the PGA? (Choose all correct answers.)
   A. Shared SQL areas
   B. Private SQL areas
   C. Global temporary tables
   D. Sort areas
   E. Bitmap merge areas
   F. Cached object definitions

Use Memory Advisors

5. Which instance parameter can disable the memory advisors? (Choose the best answer.)
   A. DB_CACHE_ADVICE
   B. MEMORY_TARGET

C. STATISTICS_LEVEL

D. TIMED_STATISTICS

6. Which of these parameters cannot be changed without an instance restart? (Choose all correct answers.)

A. MEMORY_MAX_TARGET

B. MEMORY_TARGET

C. PGA_AGGREGATE_TARGET

D. SGA_TARGET

Troubleshoot Invalid and Unusable Objects

7. If you create a table and a procedure that refers to it, and then change the definition of the table, what will happen when you try to run the procedure? (Choose the best answer.)

A. The procedure will recompile automatically and run successfully.

B. The procedure will fail until you recompile it.

C. The procedure will run with reduced performance until you analyze the table.

D. The procedure may or may not compile, depending on the nature of the change.

8. If a SELECT statement attempts to use an UNUSABLE index, what will happen? (Choose the best answer.)

A. The statement will fail.

B. The statement will succeed, but at reduced performance.

C. The index will be rebuilt automatically if possible.

D. It depends on the SKIP_UNUSABLE_INDEXES parameter.

9. You determine that an index is unusable, and decide to rebuild it. Which of the following statements, if any, are correct? (Choose all correct answers.)

A. The NOLOGGING and ONLINE keywords cannot be used together when rebuilding the index.

B. A rebuild may require double the disk space while it is in progress.

C. If you do not use the ONLINE keyword during a rebuild, the table will be unavailable for SELECT and DML statements.

D. The NOLOGGING keyword applied to a rebuild means that DML against the index will not generate redo.

10. If a primary key index becomes unusable, what will the effect be upon an application that uses it? (Choose the best answer.)

   A. SELECT will succeed, but perhaps at reduced performance.

   B. DML commands will succeed, but perhaps at reduced performance.

   C. The primary key constraint can no longer be enforced.

   D. The table may be locked for DML.

LAB QUESTION

Investigate the effect of indexes becoming unusable on SELECT and DML statements by creating a table with a constraint, and then moving the table.

Connect to your database as user SYSTEM, and create a user for this exercise:

```
create user lab identified by lab;
grant dba to lab;
```

Connect as the new user, and create a table, an index, and a primary key constraint:

```
connect lab/lab;
create table lab1 as select * from all_users;
create index lab1i on lab1 (username);
alter table lab1 add constraint lab1_pk primary key (username);
```

Now render the index unusable by moving the table:

```
alter table lab1 move;
```

Attempt to run a SELECT statement using the indexed column, and attempt to insert a row:

```
select username, user_id, created from lab1 where username='SYSTEM';
insert into lab1 values ('New user',99,sysdate);
```

Check the values of two parameters:

```
show parameters skip_unusable_indexes;
show parameters optimizer_mode;
```

Experiment with executing various SELECT and DML statements on different columns with SKIP_UNUSABLE_INDEXES set to TRUE and FALSE, and with OPTIMIZER_MODE set to FIRST_ROWS and to RULE. These are both parameters that can be set at the session level with this command:

```
ALTER SESSION SET parameter_name = value ;
```

What conclusions can you draw about use of unusable indexes and these parameters?

SELF TEST ANSWERS

Use Automatic Memory Management

1. ☑ **A.** Private SQL areas are private to each session, in the session's PGA.
☒ **B** is wrong because automatic PGA management is not relevant to where the private SQL area is stored, only to how it is managed. **C** and **D** are wrong because private SQL areas are always in the PGA.

2. ☑ **D.** The log buffer cannot be changed after startup.
☒ **A, B,** and **C** are wrong because all these structures can be resized. **E** is wrong because not even Automatic Memory Management makes the log buffer resizable.

3. ☑ **E.** Memory can be transferred between all structures (except the log buffer), and the total can be increased.
☒ **A, B, C,** and **D.** There are wrong because all are possible—though D, the increase of total memory usage, is only possible up to the value specified by the MEMORY_MAX_TARGET parameter.

4. ☑ **B, C, D,** and **E.** These are all PGA memory structures, though they may spill to a temporary segment in the users' temporary tablespace.
☒ **A** and **F** are wrong because these structures both exist in the shared pool of the SGA.

Use Memory Advisors

5. ☑ **C.** STATISTICS_LEVEL must be on TYPICAL or FULL, or the advisors will not run.
☒ **A** and **D** are wrong, because these parameters (which still exist only for backward compatibility) are controlled by STATISTICS_LEVEL. **B** is wrong because MEMORY_TARGET determines whether implementing the advice is automatic or manual.

6. ☑ **A.** MEMORY_MAX_TARGET is a static parameter: it cannot be changed without restarting the instance.
☒ **B, C,** and **D.** All these parameters are dynamic, meaning that they can be change without restarting the instance.

Troubleshoot Invalid and Unusable Objects

7. ☑ **D.** Oracle will attempt recompilation, but this may not succeed.
☒ **A** is wrong because this will not necessarily succeed if the nature of the change is such that the procedure needs to be rewritten. **B** is wrong because manual recompilation is not necessary (though it may be a good idea). **C** is wrong because it refers to object statistics, which are not relevant to a problem of this kind.

8. ☑ **D.** The SKIP_UNUSABLE_INDEXES parameter will control whether the statement produces an error or reverts to an alternative plan.
    ☒ **A** and **B** are both wrong because they make an assumption about the SKIP_UNUSABLE_ INDEXES parameter: A assumes it is FALSE; B assumes it is true. **C** is wrong because indexes are never rebuilt automatically.

9. ☑ **B.** A rebuild requires additional space, as the new index is built before the original index is dropped.
    ☒ **A** is wrong because NOLOGGING and ONLINE can be used together. **C** is wrong because without ONLINE the index is locked for DML, but not for SELECT. **D** is wrong because DML always generates redo—it is only the DDL that will not generate redo.

10. ☑ **D.** Loss of a primary key index means that DML against the constrained column(s) will be impossible.
    ☒ **A** is wrong because this is not certain—it is dependent on the SKIP_UNUSABLE_INDEXES setting. **B** is wrong because DML commands will fail if they affect the constrained column(s). **C** is wrong because the constraint will be enforced—by locking the table.

LAB ANSWER

The cost-based optimizer (enabled when OPTIMIZER_MODE is set to FIRST_ROWS, which it will be by default) may decide to ignore the index for SELECT statements, because the table is too small. The rule-based optimizer (enabled when OPTIMIZER_MODE is set to RULE) will not.

When SKIP_UNUSABLE_INDEXES is set to TRUE (which it will be by default), SELECT statements that use the indexed column in their WHERE clause can still succeed because the optimizer can then revert to plans that do not require a broken index, but this cannot help with INSERT and DELETE statements because these will always impact on the indexed column. UPDATE commands will succeed so long as they do not update the indexed column or (depending on the parameter settings) use the index for row selection.

Tidy up by dropping the schema:

```
drop user lab cascade;
```

15
Backup and Recovery Concepts

Perhaps the most important aspect of a database administrator's job is to ensure that the database does not lose data. The mechanisms of redo and undo ensure that it is impossible to corrupt the database no matter what the DBA does, or does not, do (always assuming that there is no physical damage). After working through the section of this chapter headed Instance Recovery, you will be able to prove this. However, it is possible for an Oracle database to lose data if the DBA does not take appropriate precautions.

From release 9*i* onward, an Oracle database can be configured so that no matter what happens, the database will never lose a single row of committed data. It is also possible to configure an environment for one hundred percent availability. This ideal configuration requires use of Data Guard and RAC (or possibly Streams). A single-instance, non-distributed environment cannot achieve this—but it can get very close.

This chapter will go through the concepts behind Oracle's backup and recovery mechanisms: the enabling structure within which you will configure whatever level of data security and availability is demanded by your organization. The next two chapters will cover the practicalities of backup, restore, and recovery. But always be aware that this is a superficial treatment; the second OCP examination deals with backup and recovery in much greater detail. And even after passing that, you will not necessarily be fully competent. This is an area where you cannot do enough studying, research, and (most importantly) practice.

CERTIFICATION OBJECTIVE 15.01

Identify the Types of Failure That Can Occur in an Oracle Database

Failures can be divided into a few broad categories. For each type of failure, there will be an appropriate course of action to resolve it. Each type of failure may well be documented in a service level agreement; certainly the steps to be followed should be documented in a procedures manual.

Statement Failure

An individual SQL statement can fail for a number of reasons, not all of which are within the DBA's domain—but even so, he/she must be prepared to fix them. The first level of fixing will be automatic. Whenever a statement fails, the server process executing the statement will detect the problem and roll back the statement. Remember that a statement might attempt to update many rows, and fail part way through execution; all the rows that were updated before the failure will have their changes reversed through use of undo. This will happen automatically. If the statement is part of a multistatement transaction, all the statements that have already succeeded will remain intact, but uncommitted. Ideally, the programmers will have included exceptions clauses in their code that will identify and manage any problems, but there will always be some errors that get through the error handling routines.

A common cause of statement failure is invalid data, usually a format or constraint violation. A well-written user process will avoid format problems, such as attempting to insert character data into a numeric field, but they can often occur when doing batch jobs with data coming from a third-party system. Oracle itself will try to solve formatting problems by doing automatic typecasting to convert data types on the fly, but this is not very efficient and shouldn't be replied upon. Constraint violations will be detected, but Oracle can do nothing to solve them. Clearly, problems caused by invalid data are not the DBA's fault, but you must be prepared to deal with them by working with the users to validate and correct the data, and with the programmers to try to automate these processes.

A second class of non-DBA-related statement failure is logic errors in the application. Programmers may well develop code that in some circumstances is impossible for the database to execute. A perfect example is the deadlock described in Chapter 10: the code will run perfectly, until through bad luck two sessions happen to try do the same thing at the same time to the same rows. A deadlock is not a database error; it is an error caused by programmers writing code that permits an impossible situation to arise.

Space management problems are frequent, but they should never occur. A good DBA will monitor space usage proactively and take action before problems arise. Space-related causes of statement failure include inability to extend a segment because the tablespace is full, running out of undo space, insufficient temporary space when running queries that use disk sorts or working with temporary tables, a user hitting his/her quota limit, or an object hitting its maximum extents limit. Database Control includes the undo advisor, the segment advisor, the Automatic Database Diagnostic Monitor, and the alert mechanism, all described in previous chapters, which will help to pick up space-related problems before they happen. The effect of space problems that slip through can perhaps be alleviated by setting datafiles to autoextend, or by enabling resumable space allocation, but ideally space problems should never arise in the first place.

on the **!** job

Issue the command "alter session enable resumable" and from then on the session will not show errors on space problems but instead hang until the problem is fixed. You can enable resumable for the whole instance with the RESUMABLE_TIMEOUT parameter.

e x a m

ⓦ**a t c h** *If a statement fails, it will be rolled back. Any other DML statements will remain intact and uncommitted.*

Statements may fail because of insufficient privileges. Remember from Chapter 8 how privileges let a user do certain things, such as select from a table or execute a piece of code. When a statement is parsed, the server process checks whether the user executing the statement has the necessary permissions. This type of error indicates that the security structures in place are inappropriate, and the DBA (in conjunction with the organization's security manager) should grant appropriate system and object privileges.

Figure 15-1 shows some examples of statement failure: a data error, a permissions error, a space error, and a logic error.

FIGURE 15-1

Examples of statement failures

```
Telnet jwacer.bplc.co.za                                         -□×
SQL> --invalid data: there is already a department 10
SQL> insert into dept values (10,'Sales','UK');
insert into dept values (10,'Sales','UK')
*
ERROR at line 1:
ORA-00001: unique constraint (SCOTT.PK_DEPT) violated


SQL> --insufficient privileges: no insert privilege on hr.regions
SQL> insert into hr.regions values (99,'British Isles');
insert into hr.regions values (99,'British Isles')
                *
ERROR at line 1:
ORA-00942: table or view does not exist


SQL> --space problem: insufficient quota
SQL> create table too_big (c1 varchar2(10)) storage (initial 1000m);
create table too_big (c1 varchar2(10)) storage (initial 1000m)
*
ERROR at line 1:
ORA-01536: space quota exceeded for tablespace 'USERS'


SQL> --logic problem: the code can't handle two Taylors:
SQL> declare v_sal number;
  2  begin
  3  select salary into v_sal from hr.employees where last_name='Taylor';
  4  end;
  5  /
declare v_sal number;
*
ERROR at line 1:
ORA-01422: exact fetch returns more than requested number of rows
ORA-06512: at line 3


SQL> _
```

User Process Failure

A user process may fail for any number of reasons, including the user exiting abnormally instead of logging out, the terminal rebooting, or the program causing an address violation. Whatever the cause of the problem, the outcome is the same. The PMON background process periodically polls all the server processes, to ascertain the state of the session. If a server process reports that it has lost contact with its user process, PMON will tidy up. If the session were in the middle of a transaction, PMON will roll back the transaction and release any locks. Then it will terminate the server process and release the PGA back to the operating system.

If a session terminates abnormally, an active transaction will be rolled back automatically.

This type of problem is beyond the DBA's control, but he/she should watch for any trends that might indicate a lack of user training, badly written software, or perhaps network or hardware problems.

Network Failure

In conjunction with the network administrators, it should be possible to configure Oracle Net such that there is no single point of failure. The three points to consider are listeners, network interface cards, and routes.

A database listener is unlikely to crash, but there are limits to the amount of work that one listener can do. A listener can service only one connect request at a time, and it does take an appreciable amount of time to launch a server process and connect it to a user process. If your database experiences high volumes of concurrent connection requests, users may receive errors when they try to connect. You can avoid this by configuring multiple listeners, each on a different address/port combination.

At the operating system and hardware levels, network interfaces can fail. Ideally, your server machine will have at least two network interface cards, for redundancy as well as performance. Create at least one listener for each card.

Routing problems or localized network failures can mean that even though the database is running perfectly, no one can connect to it. If your server has two or more network interface cards, they should ideally be connected to physically separate subnets. Then on the client side configure connect time fault tolerance by listing multiple addresses in the ADDRESS_LIST section of the TNS_NAME.ORA entry. This will permits the user processes to try a series of routes until they find one that is working.

on the job

The network fault tolerance for a single-instance database is only at connect time; a failure later on will disrupt currently connected sessions, and they will have to reconnect. In a RAC environment, it is possible for a session to fail over to a different instance, and the user may not even notice.

User Errors

Historically, *user errors* were undoubtedly the worst errors to manage. Recent releases of the database improve the situation dramatically. The problem is that user errors are not errors as far as the database is concerned. Imagine a conversation on these lines:

User: "I forgot to put a WHERE clause on my UPDATE statement, so I've just updated a million rows instead of one."
DBA: "Did you say COMMIT?"
User: "Of course."
DBA: "Um . . ."

As far as Oracle is concerned, this is a transaction like any other. The *D* for "Durable" of the ACID test states that once a transaction is committed, it must be immediately broadcast to all other users, and be absolutely non-reversible. But at least with DML errors such as the one dramatized here, the user does get the chance to roll back his/her statement if he realizes that it was wrong before committing. But DDL statements don't give you that option. For example, if a programmer drops a table believing he/she is logged onto the test database but is actually logged onto the production database, there is a COMMIT built into the DROP TABLE command. That table is gone—you can't roll back DDL.

on the job

Never forget that there is a COMMIT built into DDL statements that will include any preceding DML statements.

The ideal solution to user errors is to prevent their occurring in the first place. This is partly a matter of user training, but more importantly of software design: no user process should ever let a user issue an UPDATE statement without a WHERE clause. But even the best-designed software cannot prevent users from issuing SQL that is inappropriate to the business. Everyone makes mistakes. Oracle provides a number of ways whereby you as DBA may be able to correct user errors, but this is often extremely difficult—particularly if the error isn't reported for some time. The possible techniques (details of which are beyond the scope of this book) include flashback query, flashback drop, the Log Miner, incomplete recovery, and flashback database.

Flashback query is running a query against a version of the database as at some time in the past. The read-consistent version of the database is constructed, for your session only, through use of undo data.

Figure 15-2 shows one of many uses of flashback query. The user has "accidentally" deleted every row in the EMP table, and committed the delete. Then he/she retrieves the rows with a subquery against the table as it was five minutes previously.

Flashback drop reverses the effect of a DROP TABLE command. In previous releases of the database, a DROP command did what it says: it dropped all references to the table from the data dictionary. There was no way to reverse this. Even flashback query would fail, because the flashback query mechanism does need the data dictionary object definition. But from release 10*g* the implementation of the DROP command has changed: it no longer drops anything; it just renames the object so that you will never see it again, unless you specifically ask to. Figure 15-3 illustrates the use of flashback drop to recover a table.

The Log Miner is an advanced tool that extracts information from the online and archived redo logs. Redo includes all changes made to data blocks. By extracting the changes made to blocks of table data, it is possible to reconstruct the changes that were made—thus, redo can be used to bring a restored backup forward in time.

FIGURE 15-2	
Correcting user error with flashback query	

```
Telnet jwacer.bplc.co.za                                    _ □ ✕

SQL> delete from emp;
14 rows deleted.
SQL> commit;
Commit complete.
SQL> select count(*) from emp;

  COUNT(*)
----------
         0
SQL> insert into emp (select * from emp as of timestamp(sysdate - 5/1440));
14 rows created.
SQL> commit;
Commit complete.
SQL> select count(*) from emp;

  COUNT(*)
----------
        14
```

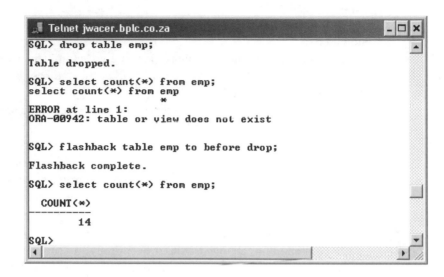

FIGURE 15-3

Correcting
user error with
flashback drop

But the redo stream also has all the changes made to undo blocks, and it is therefore possible to construct the changes that would be needed to reverse transactions, even though they have been committed. Conceptually, the Log Miner is similar to flashback query: the information to reverse a change is constructed from undo data, but whereas flashback query uses undo data that is currently in the undo segments, Log Miner extracts the undo data from the redo logs. This means that Log Miner can go back in time indefinitely, if you have copies of the relevant logs. By contrast, flashback query can only go back as far as your undo tablespace will allow.

Incomplete recovery and flashback database are much more drastic techniques for reversing user errors. With either tool, the whole database is taken back in time to before the error occurred. The other techniques that have been described let you reverse one bad transaction, while everything else remains intact. But if you ever do an incomplete recovery, or a flashback of the whole database, you will lose all the work done from time you go back to—not just the bad transaction.

Media Failure

Media failure means damage to disks, and therefore the files stored on them. This is not your problem (it is something for the system administrators to sort out), but you must be prepared to deal with it. The point to hang on to is that damage to any number of any files is no reason to lose data. With release 9*i* and later, you can survive the loss of any and all of the files that make up a database without losing any committed data—if you have configured the database appropriately. Prior to 9*i*, complete loss of the machine hosting the database could result in loss of data; the Data Guard facility, not covered in the OCP curriculum, can even protect against that.

Included in the category of "media failure" is a particular type of user error: system or DBAs accidentally deleting files. This is not as uncommon as one might think (or hope).

on the **Job**

On Unix systems, the rm *command has been responsible for any number of appalling mistakes. You might want to consider, for example, aliasing the* rm *command to* rm -i *to gain a little piece of mind.*

When a disk is damaged, one or more of the files on it will be damaged, unless the disk subsystem itself has protection through RAID. Remember that a database consists of three file types: the control file, the online redo logs, and the datafiles. The control file and the online logs should always be protected through multiplexing. If you have multiple copies of the control file on different disks, then if any one of them is damaged, you will have a surviving copy. Similarly, multiple copies of each online redo log mean that you can survive the loss of any one. Datafiles can't be multiplexed (other than through RAID, at the hardware level); therefore, if one is lost the only option is to *restore* it from a backup. To restore a file is to extract it from wherever it was backed up, and put it back where it is meant to be. Then the file must be *recovered*. The restored backup will be out of date; recovery means applying changes extracted from the redo logs (both online and archived) to bring it forward to the state it was in at the time the damage occurred.

Recovery requires the use of archived redo logs. These are the copies of online redo logs, made after each log switch. After restoring a datafile from backup, the changes to be applied to it to bring it up-to-date are extracted, in chronological order, from the archive logs generated since the backup was taken. Clearly, you must look after your archive logs because if any are lost, the recovery process will fail. Archive logs are initially created on disk, and because of the risks of using disk storage they, just like the controlfile and the online log files, should be multiplexed: two or more copies on different devices.

So to protect against media failure, you must have multiplexed copies of the controlfile, the online redo log files, and the archive redo log files. You will also take backups of the controlfile, the data files, and the archive log files. You do not back up the redo logs—they are, in effect, backed up when they are copied to the archive logs. Datafiles cannot be protected by multiplexing; they need to be protected by hardware redundancy—either conventional RAID systems, or Oracle's own Automatic Storage Management (ASM).

Instance Failure

An *instance failure* is a disorderly shutdown of the instance, popularly referred to as a crash. This could be caused by a power cut, by switching off or rebooting the server machine, or by any number of critical hardware problems. In some circumstances, one of the Oracle background processes may fail—this will also trigger an immediate instance failure. Functionally, the effect of an instance failure, for whatever reason, is the same as issuing the SHUTDOWN ABORT command. You may hear people talking about "crashing the database" when they mean issuing a SHUTDOWN ABORT command.

After an instance failure, the database may well be missing committed transactions and storing uncommitted transactions. This is the definition of a corrupted database. This situation arises because the server processes work in memory: they update blocks of data and undo segments in the database buffer cache, not on disk. DBWn then, eventually, writes the changed blocks down to the datafiles. The algorithm the DBWn uses to select which dirty buffers to write is oriented toward performance and results in the blocks that are least active getting written first—after all, there would be little point in writing a block that is being changed every second. But this means that at any given moment there may well be committed transactions that are not yet in the datafiles and uncommitted transactions that have been written: there is no correlation between a COMMIT and a write to the datafiles. But of course, all the changes that have been applied to both data and undo blocks are already in the redo logs.

Remember the description of commit processing detailed in Chapter 10: when you say COMMIT, all that happens is that LGWR flushes the log buffer to the current online redo log files. DBWn does absolutely nothing on COMMIT. So for performance reasons, DBWn writes as little as possible as rarely as possible—this means that the database is always out of date. But LGWR writes with a very aggressive algorithm indeed. It writes as nearly as possible in real time, and when you (or anyone else) say COMMIT, it really does write in real time. This is the key to instance recovery. Oracle accepts the fact that the database will be corrupted after an instance failure, but there will always be enough information in the redo log stream on disk to correct the damage.

EXERCISE 15-1

Correct Statement Failures

In this exercise, you will install demonstrate the automatic rollback of statements after failures.

1. Connect to the database as user SYSTEM with SQL*Plus, and create a table to use for this exercise:

```
create table failures as select * from all_users where 1=2;
```

2. Insert some rows (don't COMMIT) and check the number:

```
insert into failures select * from all_users;
select count(*) from all_users;
```

3. Using either Database Control or another SQL*Plus session, connect to the database as SYS and terminate the instance with ABORT.

4. Your SYSTEM session will have been ended. Reconnect, and count the rows in the FAILURES table. The INSERT from Step 2 will have been rolled back.

5. Repeat Step 2.

6. Terminate the SQL*Plus user process: use the Unix or Linux kill command, or on Windows use the task manager.

7. Reconnect as SYSTEM: again, your INSERT will have been rolled back.

8. Tidy up:

```
drop table failures;
```

CERTIFICATION OBJECTIVE 15.02

Describe Ways to Tune Instance Recovery

The rules to which a relational database must conform, as formalized in the ACID test, require that it may never lose a committed transaction and never show an uncommitted transaction. Oracle conforms to the rules perfectly. If the database is corrupted, Oracle will detect the fact and perform instance recovery to remove the corruptions. It will reinstate any committed transactions that had not been saved to the datafiles at the time of the crash, and roll back any uncommitted transactions that had been written to the datafiles. This instance recovery is completely automatic—you can't stop it, even if you wanted to. If the instance recovery fails, which will only happen if there is media failure as well as instance failure, you cannot open the database until you have used media recovery techniques to restore and recover the damaged files. The final step of media recovery is automatic instance recovery.

The Mechanics of Instance Recovery

Because instance recovery is completely automatic, it can be dealt with fairly quickly, unlike media recovery, which will take a whole chapter just for the simplest technique. In principle, instance recovery is nothing more than using the contents of the online log files to rebuild the database buffer cache to the state it was in before the crash. This will replay all changes extracted from the redo logs that refer to blocks that had not been written to disk at the time of the crash. Once this has been done, the database can be opened. At that point, the database is still corrupted—but there is no reason not to allow users to connect, because the instance (which is what users see) has been repaired. This phase of recovery, known as the roll forward, reinstates all changes—changes to data blocks and changes to undo blocks—for both committed and uncommitted transactions. Each redo record has the bare minimum of information needed to reconstruct a change: the block address, and the new values. During roll forward, each redo record is read, the appropriate block loaded from the datafiles into the database buffer cache, and the change is applied. Then the block is written back to disk.

Once the roll forward is complete, it is as though the crash had never occurred. But at that point, there will be uncommitted transactions in the database—these must be rolled back, and Oracle will do that automatically in the rollback phase of instance recovery. However, that happens after the database has been opened for use. If a user connects and hits some data that needs to be rolled back and hasn't yet been, this is not a problem—the roll forward phase will have populated the undo segment that was protecting the uncommitted transaction, so the server can roll back the change in the normal manner for read consistency.

Instance recovery is automatic, and unavoidable—so how do you invoke it? By issuing a STARTUP command. Remember from Chapter 5, on starting an instance, the description of how SMON opens a database. First, it reads the controlfile when the database transitions to mount mode. Then in the transition to open mode, SMON checks the file headers of all the datafiles and online redo log files. At this point, if there had been an instance failure, it is apparent because the file headers are all out of sync. So SMON goes into the instance recovery routine, and the database is only actually opened after the roll forward phase has completed.

on the
job

You never have anything to lose by issuing a STARTUP command. After any sort of crash, try a STARTUP and see how far it gets. It might get all the way.

The Impossibility of Database Corruption

It should now be apparent that there is always enough information in the redo log stream to reconstruct all work done up to the point at which the crash occurred, and furthermore that this includes reconstructing the undo information needed to roll back transactions that were in progress at the time of the crash. But for the final proof, consider this scenario.

User JOHN has started a transaction. He has updated one row of a table with some new values, and his server process has copied the old values to an undo segment. But before these updates were done, his server process wrote out the changes to the log buffer. User ROOPESH has also started a transaction. Neither has committed; nothing has been written to disk. If the instance crashed now, there would be no record whatsoever of either transaction, not even in the redo logs. So neither transaction would be recovered—but that is not a problem. Neither was committed, so they should not be recovered: uncommitted work must never be saved.

Then user JOHN commits his transaction. This triggers LGWR to flush the log buffer to the online redo log files, which means that the changes to both the table and the undo segments for both JOHN's transaction and ROOPESH's transaction are now in the redo log files, together with a commit record for JOHN's transaction. Only when the write has completed is the "commit complete" message returned to JOHN's user process. But there is still nothing in the datafiles. If the instance fails at this point, the roll forward phase will reconstruct both the transactions, but when all the redo has been processed, there will be no commit record for ROOPESH's update; that signals SMON to roll back ROOPESH's change but leave JOHN's in place.

But what if DBWR has written some blocks to disk before the crash? It might be that JOHN (or another user) was continually requerying his data, but that ROOPESH had made his uncommitted change and not looked at the data again. DBWn will therefore decide to write ROOPESH's changes to disk in preference to JOHN's; DBWn will always tend to write inactive blocks rather than active blocks. So now, the datafiles are storing ROOPESH's uncommitted transaction but missing JOHN's committed transaction. This is as bad a corruption as you can have. But think it through. If the instance crashes now—a power cut, perhaps, or a SHUTDOWN ABORT—the roll forward will still be able to sort out the mess. There will always be enough information in the redo stream to reconstruct committed changes; that is obvious, because a commit isn't completed until the write is done. But because LGWR flushes *all* changes to *all* blocks to the log files, there will also be enough information to reconstruct the undo segment needed to roll back ROOPESH's uncommitted transaction.

So to summarize, because LGWR always writes ahead of DBWn, and because it writes in real time on commit, there will always be enough information in the redo stream to reconstruct any committed changes that had not been written to the datafiles, and to roll back any uncommitted changes that had been written to the data files. This instance recovery mechanism of redo and rollback makes it absolutely impossible to corrupt an Oracle database—so long as there has been no physical damage.

Tuning Instance Recovery

A critical part of many service level agreements as the MTTR—the *mean time to recover* after various events. Instance recovery guarantees no corruption, but it may take a considerable time to do its roll forward before the database can be opened. This time is dependent on two factors: how much redo has to be read and how many read/write operations will be needed on the datafiles as the redo is applied. Both these factors can be controlled by checkpoints.

A checkpoint guarantees that as of a particular time, all data changes made up to a particular SCN, or System Change Number, have been written to the datafiles by DBWn. In the event of an instance crash, it is only necessary for SMON to replay the redo generated from the last checkpoint position. All changes, committed or not, made before that position are already in the datafiles; so clearly, there is no need to use redo to reconstruct the transactions committed prior to that. Also, all changes made by uncommitted transactions prior to that point are also in the datafiles—so there is no need to reconstruct undo data prior to the checkpoint position either; it is already available in the undo segment on disk for the necessary rollback.

The more up-to-date the checkpoint position is, the faster the instance recovery. If the checkpoint position is right up-to-date no roll forward will be needed at all—the instance can open immediately and go straight into the rollback phase. But there is a heavy price to pay for this. To advance the checkpoint position, DBWn must write changed blocks to disk. Excessive disk I/O will cripple performance. But on the other hand, if you let DBWn get too far behind, so that after a crash SMON has to process hundreds of megabytes of redo and do millions of read/write operations on the datafiles, the MTTR following an instance failure can stretch into hours.

Tuning instance recovery time used to be largely a matter of experiment and guesswork. It has always been easy to tell how long the recovery actually took—just look at your alert log, and you will see the time when the STARTUP command was issued and the time that the startup completed, with information about how many blocks of redo were processed—but until release 9*i* of the database it was almost impossible to calculate in advance. Release 9*i* introduced a new parameter, FAST_START_MTTR_TARGET, that makes controlling instance recovery time a trivial exercise. You specify it in seconds, and Oracle will then ensure that DBWn writes out blocks at a rate sufficiently fast that if the instance crashes, the recovery will take no longer than that number of seconds. So the smaller the setting, the harder DBWn will work in an attempt to minimize the gap between the checkpoint position and real time. But note that it is only a target—you can set it to an unrealistically low value, which is impossible to achieve no matter what DBWn does. Database Control also provides an MTTR advisor, which will give you an idea of how long recovery would take if the instance failed. This information can also be obtained from the view V$INSTANCE_RECOVERY.

The MTTR Advisor and Checkpoint Auto-Tuning

The parameter FAST_START_MTTR_TARGET defaults to zero. This has the effect of maximizing performance, with the possible cost of long instance recovery times after an instance failure. The DBWn process will write as little as it can get away with, meaning that the checkpoint position may be a long way out of date and that therefore a large amount of redo would have to be applied to the datafiles in the roll forward phase of instance recovery.

Setting FAST_START_MTTR_TARGET to a non-zero value has two effects. First, it sets a target for recovery, as described in the preceding section. But there is also a secondary effect: enabling *checkpoint auto-tuning*. The checkpoint auto-tuning mechanism inspects statistics on machine utilization, such as the rate of disk I/O and CPU usage, and if it appears that there is spare capacity, it will use this capacity to write out additional dirty buffers from the database buffer cache, thus pushing the checkpoint position forward. The result is that even if the FAST_START_ MTTR_TARGET parameter is set to a high value (the highest possible is 3600 seconds—anything above that will be rounded down), actual recovery time may well be much less.

on the *Job*

Enabling checkpoint auto-tuning with a high target should result in your instance always having the fastest possible recovery time that is consistent with maximum performance.

Database Control has an interface to the parameter. From the database home page, take the Advisor Central link, and then the MTTR advisor to get a window that displays the current estimated recovery time (this is the advisor) and gives the option of adjusting the parameter. More complete information can be gained from querying the V$INSTANCE_RECOVERY view, described here:

```
SQL> desc v$instance_recovery;
 Name                                      Null?    Type
 ----------------------------------------- -------- -----------
 RECOVERY_ESTIMATED_IOS                             NUMBER
 ACTUAL_REDO_BLKS                                   NUMBER
 TARGET_REDO_BLKS                                   NUMBER
 LOG_FILE_SIZE_REDO_BLKS                            NUMBER
 LOG_CHKPT_TIMEOUT_REDO_BLKS                        NUMBER
 LOG_CHKPT_INTERVAL_REDO_BLKS                       NUMBER
 FAST_START_IO_TARGET_REDO_BLKS                     NUMBER
 TARGET_MTTR                                        NUMBER
 ESTIMATED_MTTR                                     NUMBER
 CKPT_BLOCK_WRITES                                  NUMBER
 OPTIMAL_LOGFILE_SIZE                               NUMBER
 ESTD_CLUSTER_AVAILABLE_TIME                        NUMBER
 WRITES_MTTR                                        NUMBER
 WRITES_LOGFILE_SIZE                                NUMBER
 WRITES_LOG_CHECKPOINT_SETTINGS                     NUMBER
 WRITES_OTHER_SETTINGS                              NUMBER
 WRITES_AUTOTUNE                                    NUMBER
 WRITES_FULL_THREAD_CKPT                            NUMBER
```

The critical columns are

Column	Meaning
recovery_estimated_ios	The number of read/write operations that would be needed on datafiles for recovery if the instance crashed now
actual_redo_blocks	The number of OS blocks of redo that would need to be applied to datafiles for recovery if the instance crashed now
estimated_mttr	The number of seconds it would take to open the database if it crashed now
target_mttr	The setting of fast_start_mttr_target
writes_mttr	The number of times DBWn had to write, in addition to the writes it would normally have done, to meet the target mttr
writes_autotune	The number of writes DBWn did that were initiated by the auto-tuning mechanism

on the job

Tracking the value of the ESTIMATED_MTTR will tell you if you are keeping to your service level agreement for crash recovery time; WRITES_MTTR tells you the price you are paying for demanding a fast recovery time.

EXERCISE 15-2

Monitor Instance Recovery Times

In this exercise, you will observe the effect of checkpointing on instance recovery times.

1. Connect to your database with SQL*Plus as user SYSTEM.

2. Create a table to use for the exercise:

```
create table cptest as select * from all_users;
```

3. Determine the work involved in recovery, if the instance were to crash now:

```
select recovery_estimated_ios, actual_redo_blks, estimated_mttr
from v$instance_recovery;
```

Note the figures: they should show a recovery time estimated to be only a few seconds.

4. Start a large transaction by running this statement a dozen or so times:

```
insert into cptest select * from cptest;
```

5. Rerun the query from Step 3. You should see that the figures have increased—though this is a matter of luck, as the database will be attempting to push the checkpoint position forward.

6. COMMIT the transaction, and rerun the query from Step 2. There should be no difference: this demonstrates that a COMMIT does not force DBWn to do anything.

7. Force a checkpoint:

```
alter system checkpoint;
```

8. Rerun the query from Step 2. Now, the figures should have dropped back down to near zero, because the checkpoint forced DBWn to write all dirty buffers to the datafiles.

9. Tidy up by dropping the table:

```
drop table ctptest;
```

SCENARIO & SOLUTION

It is often said that production databases should run in archivelog mode, and that test and development systems don't need to. Is that right?	People who say that have never lost a development or test system. The idea is that they aren't "real" systems, so if you lose days' work it doesn't matter. Well, if your testing and development team is a dozen consultants at US$2000 a day, it probably does matter.
Databases don't crash very often, so should the DBA really worry about recovery time?	Recovery time is only important if it is important. Many applications can stand downtime, and if the database has crashed, then the part of the downtime that is the instance recovery may not matter. But for some databases, every second is important. Downtime means no transactions, and if no transactions means no revenue, then if tuning the recovery time can save a few minutes, you must do it.

CERTIFICATION OBJECTIVE 15.03

Identify the Importance of Checkpoints, Redo Log Files, and Archived Log Files

Checkpointing is the process of forcing the DBWn to write dirty buffers from the database buffer cache to the datafiles. There are circumstances when this must be done to ensure that the database could be recovered. Also necessary for recovery are the online redo logs, and the archive redo logs.

Checkpointing

As discussed in the preceding section, the checkpoint position (the point in the redo stream from which instance recovery must start following a crash) is advanced automatically by the DBWn. This process is known as *incremental* checkpointing. In addition, there may be *full checkpoints* and *partial checkpoints*.

A full checkpoint occurs when all dirty buffers are written to disk. In normal running, there might be a hundred thousand dirty buffers, but the DBWn would write just a few hundred of them for the incremental checkpoint. For a full checkpoint, it will write the lot. This will entail a great deal of work: very high CPU and disk usage while the checkpoint is in progress, and reduced performance for user sessions. Full checkpoints are bad for business. Because of this, there will never be a full checkpoint except in two circumstances: an orderly shutdown, or at the DBA's request.

When there database is shut down with the NORMAL, IMMEDIATE, or TRANSACTIONAL option, there is a checkpoint: all dirty buffers are flushed to disk by the DBWn before the database is closed and dismounted. This means that when the database is opened again, no recovery will be needed. A clean shutdown is always desirable and is necessary before some operations (such as enabling the archivelog mode or the flashback database capability). A full checkpoint can be signaled at any time with this command:

```
alter system checkpoint;
```

A partial checkpoint is necessary and occurs automatically as part of certain operations. Depending on the operation, the partial checkpoint will affect different buffers. These are

Operation	What Buffers Will Be Flushed from the Cache
Taking a tablespace offline	All blocks that are part of the tablespace
Taking a datafile offline	All blocks that are part of the datafile
Dropping a segment	All blocks that are part of the segment
Truncating a table	All blocks that are part of the table
Putting a tablespace into backup mode	All blocks that are part of the tablespace

Manually initiated checkpoints should never be necessary in normal running, though they can be useful when you want to test the effect of tuning. There is no checkpoint following a log switch. This has been the case since release 8i, though to this day many DBAs do not realize this.

Protecting the Online Redo Log Files

Remember that an Oracle database requires at least two online log file groups to function, so that it can switch between them. You may need to add more groups for performance reasons, but two are required. Each group consists of one or more members, which are the physical files. Only one member per group is required for Oracle to function, but at least two members per group are required for safety.

Always have at least two members in each log file group, for security. This is not just data security—it is job security, too.

The one thing that a DBA is not allowed to do is to lose all copies of the current online log file group. If that happens, you will lose data. The only way to protect against data loss when you lose all members of the current group is to configure a Data Guard environment for zero data loss, which is not a trivial exercise. Why is it so critical that you do not lose all members of the current group? Think about instance recovery. After a crash, SMON will use the contents of the current online log file group for roll forward recovery, to repair any corruptions in the database. If the current online log file group is not available, perhaps because it was not multiplexed and media damage has destroyed the one member, then SMON cannot do this. And if SMON cannot correct corruptions with roll forward, you cannot open the database.

Just as with multiplexed copies of the controlfile, the multiple members of an online log file group should ideally be on separate disks, on separate controllers. But when considering disk strategy, think about performance as well as fault tolerance. In the discussion of commit processing in Chapter 10, it was made clear that when a COMMIT is issued, the session will hang until LGWR has flushed the log buffer to disk. Only then is "commit complete" returned to the user process, and the session allowed to continue. This means that writing to the online redo log files is one of the ultimate bottlenecks in the Oracle environment: you cannot do DML faster than LGWR can flush changes to disk. So on a high-throughput system, make sure that your redo log files are on your fastest disks served by your fastest controllers.

The online redo log can be reconfigured while the database is open with no downtime, whereas operations on the controlfile can only be carried out when the database is in nomount mode or completely shut down.

If a member of a redo log file group is damaged or missing, the database will remain open if there is a surviving member. This contrasts with the controlfile, where damage to any copy will crash the database immediately. Similarly, groups can be added or removed and members of groups can be added or moved while the database is open, as long as there are always at least two groups, and each group has at least one valid member.

If you create a database with DBCA, by default you will have three groups, but they will have only one member each. You can add more members (or indeed whole groups) either through Database Control or from the SQL*Plus command line. There are two views that will tell you the state of your redo logs. V$LOG will have one row per group, and V$LOGFILE will have one row per log file member. Figure 15-4 shows an example of online redo log configuration.

The first query shows that this database has three log file groups. The current group—the one LGWR is writing to at the moment—is group 2; the other groups are inactive, meaning first that the LGWR is not writing to them, and second that

FIGURE 15-4

Online redo log file configuration

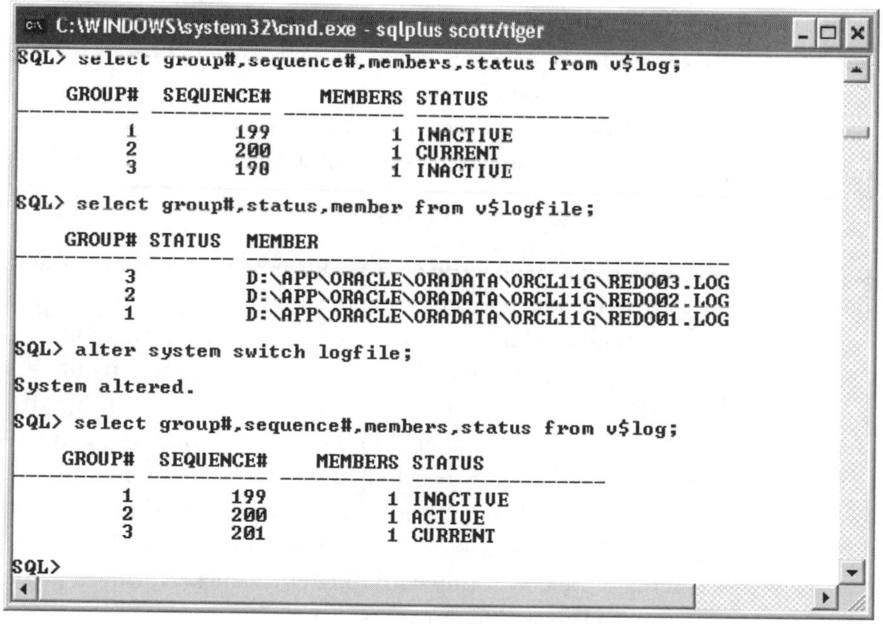

```
C:\WINDOWS\system32\cmd.exe - sqlplus scott/tiger

SQL> select group#,sequence#,members,status from v$log;

    GROUP#  SEQUENCE#     MEMBERS STATUS
    ------  ---------     ------- ------
         1        199           1 INACTIVE
         2        200           1 CURRENT
         3        198           1 INACTIVE

SQL> select group#,status,member from v$logfile;

    GROUP# STATUS  MEMBER
    ------ ------  ------
         3         D:\APP\ORACLE\ORADATA\ORCL11G\REDO03.LOG
         2         D:\APP\ORACLE\ORADATA\ORCL11G\REDO02.LOG
         1         D:\APP\ORACLE\ORADATA\ORCL11G\REDO01.LOG

SQL> alter system switch logfile;

System altered.

SQL> select group#,sequence#,members,status from v$log;

    GROUP#  SEQUENCE#     MEMBERS STATUS
    ------  ---------     ------- ------
         1        199           1 INACTIVE
         2        200           1 ACTIVE
         3        201           1 CURRENT

SQL>
```

in the event of an instance failure, SMON would not require them for instance recovery. In other words, the checkpoint position has advanced into group 2. The SEQUENCE# column tells us that there have been 200 log switches since the database was created. This number is incremented with each log switch. The MEMBERS column shows that each group consists of only one member—seriously bad news, which should be corrected as soon as possible.

The second query shows the individual online redo log files. Each file is part of one group (identified by GROUP#, which is the join column back to V$LOG) and has a unique name. The STATUS column should always be null, as shown. If the member has not yet been used, typically because the database has only just been opened and no log switches have occurred, the status will be STALE; this will only be there until the first log switch. If the status is INVALID, you have a problem.

on the job

As with the controlfile, Oracle does not enforce any naming convention for log files, but most organizations will have standards for this.

Then there is a command to force a log switch:

```
alter system switch logfile;
```

The log switch would happen automatically, eventually, if there were any DML in progress.

The last query shows that after the log switch, group 3 is now the current group that LGWR is writing to, at log switch sequence number 201. The previously current group, group 2, has status ACTIVE. This means that it would still be needed by SMON for instance recovery if the instance failed now. In a short time, as the checkpoint position advances, it will become INACTIVE. Issuing an

```
alter system checkpoint;
```

command would force the checkpoint position to come up-to-date, and group 2 would then become inactive immediately.

The number of members per group is restricted by settings in the controlfile, determined at database creation time. Turn back to Chapter 4, and the CREATE DATABASE command called by the `CreateDB.sql` script; the MAXLOGFILES directive limits the number of groups that this database can have, and the MAXLOGMEMBERS directive limits the maximum number of members of each group. The DBCA defaults for these (sixteen and three, respectively) may well be suitable for most databases, but if they prove to be inappropriate, it is possible to recreate the controlfile with different values. However, as with all controlfile operations, this will require downtime.

To protect the database against loss of data in the event of damage to an online redo log file group, multiplex it. Following the example in Figure 15-4, to add multiplexed copies to the online log, one would use a command such as this:

```
alter database add logfile member
'D:\APP\ORACLE\ORADATA\ORCL11G\REDO01A.log' to group 1;
```

or it can also be done through Database Control.

Archivelog Mode and the Archiver Process(es)

Oracle guarantees that your database is never corrupted, through use of the online redo log files to repair any corruptions caused by an instance failure. This is automatic and unavoidable. But to guarantee no loss of data following a media failure, it is necessary to have a record of all changes applied to the database since the last backup of the database; this is not enabled by default. The online redo log files are overwritten as log switches occur, so the history of change vectors is by default not kept—but the transition to *archivelog mode* ensures that no online redo log file is overwritten unless it has been copied as an archive log file first. So there will be a series of archive log files that represent a complete history of all changes ever applied to the database. If a datafile is damaged at any time, it will then be possible to restore a backup of the datafile and apply the changes from the archive log redo stream to bring it up-to-date.

exam

ⓦatch *An online redo log file can be overwritten only if it is inactive, and (if the database is in archivelog mode) if it has been archived.*

By default, a database is created in *noarchivelog mode*; this means that online redo log files are overwritten by log switches with no copy being made first. It is still impossible to corrupt the database, but data would be lost if the datafiles were damaged by media failure. Once the database is transitioned to archivelog mode, it is impossible to lose data—provided that all the archive log files generated since the last backup are available.

Once a database is converted to archivelog mode, a new background process will start, automatically. This is the archiver process, ARCn. By default Oracle will start four of these processes, but you can have up to thirty. In earlier releases of the database it was necessary to start this process either with a SQL*Plus command or by setting the initialization parameter LOG_ARCHIVE_START, but from release 10g onward Oracle will automatically start the archiver if the database is in archivelog mode.

In archivelog mode, recovery is possible with no loss of data up to and including the last commit. As a general rule, all databases where you cannot afford to lose data should run in archivelog mode. Don't exclude test and development systems from this rule; they are important too.

The archiver will copy the online redo log files to an archive log file after each log switch, thus generating a continuous chain of log files that can be used for recovering a backup. The name and location of these archive log files is controlled by initialization parameters. For safety the archive log files can be multiplexed, just as the online log files can be multiplexed—but eventually, they should be migrated to offline storage, such as a tape library. The Oracle instance takes care of creating the archive logs with the ARCn process, but the migration to tape must be controlled by the DBA, either through operating system commands or by using the recovery manager utility RMAN (described in later chapters).

Archiver processes launch automatically if the database is in archivelog mode.

The transition to archivelog mode can only be done while the database is in mount mode after a clean shutdown, and it must be done by a user with a SYSDBA connection. It is also necessary to set the initialization parameters that control the names and locations of the archive logs generated. Clearly, these names must be unique or archive logs could be overwritten by other archive logs. To ensure unique filenames, it is possible to embed variables such the log switch sequence number in the archive log filenames. These variables may be used to embed unique values in archive log filenames:

Variable	Description
%d	A unique database identifier, necessary if multiple databases are being archived to the same directories.
%t	The thread number, visible as the THREAD# column in V$INSTANCE. This is not significant, except in a RAC database.
%r	The incarnation number. This is important if an incomplete recovery has been done, which will reset the log switch sequence number.
%s	The log switch sequence number. This will guarantee that the archives from any one database incarnation do not overwrite each other.

The minimum archiving necessary to ensure that recovery from a restored backup will be possible is to set one archive destination. But for safety, it will usually be a requirement to multiplex the archive log files by specifying two or more destinations, ideally on different disks served by different controllers. From 9*i* onward, it is possible to specify up to ten archive destinations, giving you ten copies of each filled online redo log file. This is perhaps excessive for safety:

One archive destination? Good idea. Two destinations? Sure, why not. But *ten*?

The reason for ten possible destinations is Data Guard. For the purposes of this book and the OCP exam, an archive log destination will always be a directory on the machine hosting the database—and two destinations on local disks will usually be sufficient. But the destination can be an Oracle Net alias, specifying the address of a listener on a remote computer. This is the key to zero data loss: the redo stream can be shipped across the network to a remote database, where it can be applied to give a real-time backup. Furthermore, the remote database can (if desired) be configured and opened as a data warehouse, meaning that all the query processing can be offloaded from the primary database to a secondary database optimized for such work.

EXERCISE 15-3

Investigate the Redo Log Configuration

In this exercise, you will investigate the configuration of the redo log.

1. Connect to your database as user SYSTEM using SQL*Plus.

2. Document the configuration of redo log with this commands:

```
select * from v$log join v$logfile on v$log.group#=v$logfile
.group#;
```

This will show the log file members, their status, their size, and the group to which they belong. If your database is the default database, it will have three groups each of one member, 50MB big.

3. Determine the archivelog mode of the database, and whether ARCn is running, with these commands:

```
select log_mode from v$database;
select archiver from v$instance;
```

Note that the mode is an attribute of the database, but archiving is an attribute of the instance.

4. Connect to your database as user SYSTEM with Database Control, and view the redo log configuration. Take the Server tab on the database home page, and then the Redo Log Groups link in the Storage section.

5. Then in database control, check the archivelog mode. Take the Availability tab on the database home page, and then the Recovery Settings link in the Backup/recovery section. Here you will see the estimated mean time to recovery, and also the archivelog mode.

CERTIFICATION OBJECTIVE 15.04

Overview of Flash Recovery Area

The flash recovery area is a disk destination used as the default location for recovery-related files. It is controlled with two instance parameters:

- db_recovery_file_dest
- db_recovery_file_dest_size

The first of these parameters nominates the location. This can be a file system directory, or an ASM disk group. It is possible for several databases to share a common destination; each database will have its own directory structure (created automatically) in the destination. The second parameter limits the amount of space in the destination that the database will occupy; it says nothing about how much space is actually available in the destination.

The files that will be written to the flash recovery area (unless specified otherwise) include

- Recovery Manager backups
- Archive redo log files
- Database flashback logs

RMAN, the Recovery Manager, can manage space within the flash recovery area: it can delete files that are no longer needed according to its configured policies for retaining copies and backup of files. In an ideal situation, the flash recovery area will be large enough to store a complete copy of the database, plus any archive logs and incremental backups that would be necessary to recover the copy if necessary.

The database backup routines should also include backing up the flash recovery area to tape, thus implementing a strategy of primary, secondary, and tertiary storage:

- Primary storage is the live database, on disk.
- Secondary storage is a copy of the database plus files needed for fast recovery.
- Tertiary storage is long-term backups in a tape library.

RMAN can manage the whole cycle: backup of the database from primary to secondary and migration of backups from secondary to tertiary storage. Such a system can be implemented in a fashion that will allow near-instant recovery following a failure, combined with the ability to take the database back in time if this is ever necessary.

EXERCISE 15-4

Investigate the Flash Recovery Area Configuration

In this exercise, you will investigate the configuration of the flash recovery area. Using your Database Control session, continue from the last step in Exercise 15-3.

1. Navigate to the bottom part of the Recovery Settings window, which shows the flash recovery area configuration, as shown in this illustration:

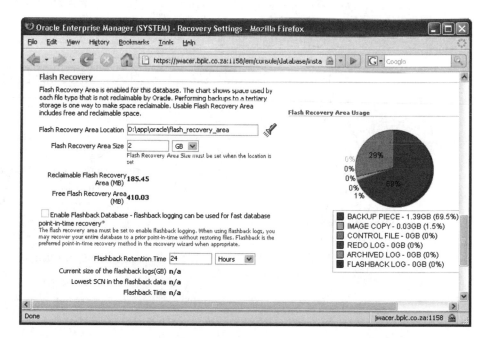

2. Interpret the display: note the settings for the instance parameters DB_RECOVERY_FILE_DEST and DB_RECOVERY_FILE_DEST_SIZE. These are D:\app\oracle\flash_recovery_area and 2 GB in the illustration. Note the space free and the space reclaimable: 410 MB and 185 MB in the illustration. Note the allocation of space: in the illustration, 69 percent of the flash recovery area is taken up with backup pieces, 1.5 percent with image copies.

3. If the flash recovery area parameters are not set, set them now. The directory must be one on which the operating system account that owns the Oracle software has full permissions, and the size should be at least 2 GB.

CERTIFICATION OBJECTIVE 15.05

Configure ARCHIVELOG Mode

A database is by default created in noarchivelog mode. The transition to archivelog mode is straightforward, but it does require downtime. The process is

- Shut down the database, cleanly.
- Start up in mount mode.
- Issue the command ALTER DATABASE ARCHIVELOG.
- Open the database.
- Perform a full backup.

This sequence can be followed either with SQL*Plus (as shown in Figure 15-5) or with Database Control. Generally, more configuration will be required. Following a default installation, the archive logs will be written to only one destination, which will be the flash recovery area. If the parameters that enable the flash recovery area have not been set, they will go to a platform specific destination (the $ORACLE_HOME/dbs directory for Unix systems.) the final command in Figure 15-5, ARCHIVE LOG LIST, shows summary information about the archiving

Transitioning
a database to
archivelog mode
with SQL*Plus

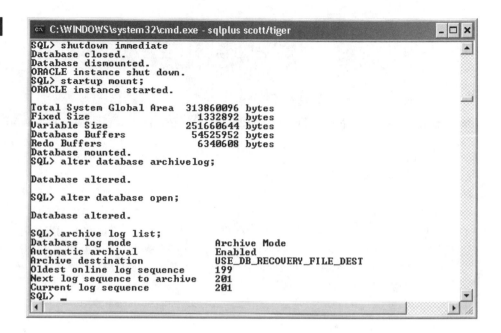

```
C:\WINDOWS\system32\cmd.exe - sqlplus scott/tiger
SQL> shutdown immediate
Database closed.
Database dismounted.
ORACLE instance shut down.
SQL> startup mount;
ORACLE instance started.

Total System Global Area   313860096 bytes
Fixed Size                    1332892 bytes
Variable Size               251660644 bytes
Database Buffers             54525952 bytes
Redo Buffers                  6340608 bytes
Database mounted.
SQL> alter database archivelog;

Database altered.

SQL> alter database open;

Database altered.

SQL> archive log list;
Database log mode              Archive Mode
Automatic archival             Enabled
Archive destination            USE_DB_RECOVERY_FILE_DEST
Oldest online log sequence     199
Next log sequence to archive   201
Current log sequence           201
SQL> _
```

configuration: that the database is running in archivelog mode; that the ARCn process is running; and that the archive log files are being written to the flash recovery area.

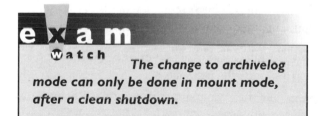

Additional changes would usually include adjusting instance parameters to set up a second archive log file destination for multiplexed copies, and defining a naming template for generating archive log file names.

A full backup is an essential step for the transition to archivelog mode. Following the transition, all backups made earlier are useless. The backup can be made while the database is open or closed, but until it is made, the database is not protected at all.

The change to archivelog mode can only be done in mount mode, after a clean shutdown.

on the job

If the shutdown is not clean (for instance, SHUTDOWN ABORT), the transition will fail. Not a problem—open the database, and shut it down again: this time, cleanly.

INSIDE THE EXAM

Backup and Recovery Concepts

Backup, restore, recovery, and flashback (in all their forms) are covered in much greater detail in the second DBA OCP examination. At this stage, all that should be required is an understanding of the architecture and the general principles. However, do not skimp on this, because the usual rule applies: if you understand the architecture, you can work out the rest.

So, you must be absolutely clear on the memory structures and the processes involved.

The foundation for this is an understanding of the mechanisms of rollback and redo: how they are implemented in the SGA, and in the redo log and the datafiles. Related to this is COMMIT processing.

The content of this chapter is not demanding, but it is the foundation on which the next two chapters (and much of the content of the next examination) are built.

EXERCISE 15-5

Enable Archivelog Mode

In this exercise, you will transition your database into archivelog mode. This is an essential procedure for completing the next two chapters on backup and recovery.

1. Connect to your database with Database Control as user SYS. (Why SYS? Because you will have to stop and start the instance.)

2. From the database home page, take the Availability tab and then Recovery Settings link in the Backup/Recovery section.

3. In the Media Recovery section, select the check box ARCHIVELOG Mode, set the Log Archive Filename Format to **ARC%s_%R.%T**, and set the tenth "Archive Log Destination" to USE_DB_RECOVERY_FILE_DEST. This state is shown in this illustration:

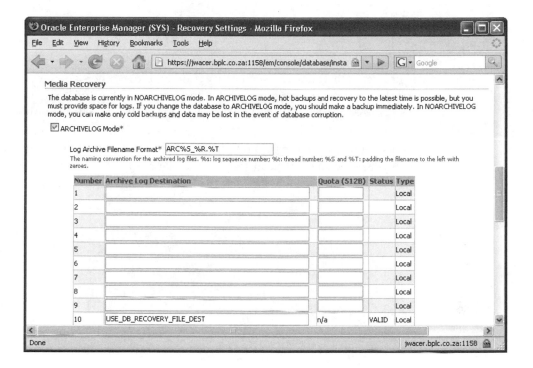

4. Click Apply. There will be a prompt to restart the database.

5. After the restart, confirm the mode change with SQL*Plus. Connect with the SYSDBA role and run the ARCHIVE LOG LIST command:

```
connect / as sysdba
archive log list
```

6. Confirm that archiving is working by forcing a log switch and an archive:

```
alter system archive log current;
```

7. Confirm that the archive log file has been generated, in the flash recovery area:

```
select name,is_recovery_dest_file from v$archived_log;
```

CERTIFICATION SUMMARY

There are many types of failure that can occur. Some of them will be repaired automatically (such as instance or session failures); others are not failures at all as far as the database is concerned (such as user errors). There are techniques for repairing user errors, which may need DBA intervention. Where DBA involvement is always needed is in configuring the database for recoverability in the event of media failure. This requires enabling the archivelog mode, and establishing routines for backup. The flash recovery area can simplify the management of all recovery-related files; it is a single storage point, with self-management capabilities for space usage.

TWO-MINUTE DRILL

Identify the Types of Failure That Can Occur in an Oracle Database

❏ Instance failure results in automatic instance recovery on the next startup.

❏ Session failures are managed automatically by the PMON process.

❏ User errors can be reversed using a number of techniques.

❏ Recovering from media failures requires use of backups and archive logs.

Describe Ways to Tune Instance Recovery

❏ Instance recovery is automatic and unstoppable.

❏ Instance recovery applies change vectors from the online redo log files, since the last incremental checkpoint position.

❏ The time taken for instance recovery is dependent on the amount of redo to be applied, and the number of I/Os on datafiles needed to apply it.

❏ The FAST_START_MTTR_TARGET parameter sets a maximum time for recovery, using a self-tuning mechanism.

❏ If FAST_START_MTTR_TARGET is set, it will also enable the checkpoint auto-tuning process to reduce recovery time further.

Identify the Importance of Checkpoints, Redo Log Files, and Archived Log Files

❏ Full checkpoints occur only on orderly shutdown, or on demand.

❏ Partial checkpoints occur automatically when necessary.

❏ Incremental checkpoints advance the point in the redo stream from which recovery must begin after an instance failure.

❏ The redo log consists of the disk structures for storing change vectors. The online log is essential for instance recovery.

❏ The archive log consists of copies of online log file members, created as they are filled. These are essential for datafile recovery after media failure.

Overview of Flash Recovery Area

❏ The flash recovery area is configured with the instance parameters DB_RECOVERY_FILE_DEST and DB_RECOVERY_FILE_DEST_SIZE.

❏ The flash recovery area is a default destination for all recovery-related files.

Configure ARCHIVELOG Mode

❏ In archivelog mode, an online log file member cannot be overwritten until it has been archived.

❏ Archive processes start automatically when archivelog mode is enabled.

❏ The mode can only be changed when the database is mounted.

SELF TEST

Identify the Types of Failure That Can Occur in an Oracle Database

1. Different errors require different actions for recovery. Match these types of failure (a) through (d) to the appropriate recovery process A through D:

   (a) Server machine reboots
   (b) Client machine reboots
   (c) Statement causes a constraint violation
   (d) Datafile damaged
   A. PMON
   B. RMAN
   C. Session server process
   D. SMON

Describe Ways to Tune Instance Recovery

2. What instance parameter must be set to enable the checkpoint auto-tuning capability? (Choose the best answer.)
   A. dbwr_io_slaves
   B. fast_start_mttr_target
   C. log_checkpoint_interval
   D. statistics_level

3. Which redo log files may be required for instance recovery? (Choose the best answer.)
   A. Only the current online redo log file
   B. Only the active online redo file(s)
   C. Both current and active online redo log file(s)
   D. Current and active online redo log files, and possibly archive redo log files

Identify the Importance of Checkpoints, Redo Log Files, and Archived Log Files

4. When will a full checkpoint occur? (Choose all correct answers.)
   A. As part of a NORMAL shutdown
   B. As part of an IMMEDIATE shutdown

   C. When a tablespace is taken offline

   D. When a log switch occurs

5. Which of these operations cannot be accomplished while the database is open? (Choose all correct answers.)

   A. Adding a controlfile copy

   B. Adding an online log file member

   C. Changing the location of the flash recovery area

   D. Changing the archivelog mode of the database

6. How can you use checkpointing to improve performance?

   A. Frequent checkpoints will reduce the workload on the DBWn.

   B. Enabling checkpoint auto-tuning will optimize disk I/O.

   C. Reducing the MTTR will reduce disk I/O.

   D. Increasing the MTTR will reduce disk I/O.

Overview of Flash Recovery Area

7. What file types will, by default, be stored in the flash recovery area if it has been defined? (Choose all correct answers.)

   A. Archive redo log files

   B. Background process trace files

   C. RMAN backup sets

   D. RMAN image copies

   E. Undo data

Configure ARCHIVELOG Mode

8. There are several steps involved in transitioning to archivelog mode. Put these in the correct order:

   1   alter database archivelog

   2   alter database open

   3   alter system archive log start

   4   full backup

   5   shutdown immediate

   6   startup mount

A. 5, 6, 1, 2, 4; 3 not necessary

B. 5, 4, 6, 1, 2, 3

C. 6, 1, 3, 5, 4, 2

D. 1, 5, 4, 6, 2; 3 not necessary

E. 5, 6, 1, 2, 3; 4 not necessary

9. What conditions must hold before an online log file member can be reused if the database is operating in archivelog mode? (Choose all correct answers.)

A. It must be inactive.

B. It must be multiplexed.

C. It must be archived.

D. The archive must be multiplexed.

10. If the database is in archivelog mode, what will happen if the archiving fails for any reason? (Choose the best answer.)

A. The instance will abort.

B. All non-SYSDBA sessions will hang.

C. DML operations will hang.

D. The database will revert to noarchivelog mode.

LAB QUESTION

Check whether your database is configured for recoverability. These are the points to look at:

- Online redo log files should be multiplexed.
- The controlfile should be multiplexed.
- The database should be in archivelog mode.
- Archiver processes should be running.
- Archive logs should be multiplexed.
- Checkpoint auto-tuning should be enabled.
- The flash recovery area should be enabled.

SELF TEST ANSWERS

Identify the Types of Failure That Can Occur in an Oracle Database

1. ☑ **A** – b: PMON releases resources of failed sessions. **B** – d: RMAN manages media recovery. **C** – c: the server process rolls back failed statements. **D** – a: SMON performs instance recovery.
   ☒ All other combinations.

Describe Ways to Tune Instance Recovery

2. ☑ **B.** If FAST_START_MTTR_TARGET is set to a non-zero value, then checkpoint auto-tuning will be in effect.
   ☒ **A** is wrong because DBWR_IO_SLAVES is for simulating asynchronous disk I/O. **C** is wrong because LOG_CHECKPOINT_INTERVAL will disable the self-tuning mechanism. **D** is wrong because STATISTICS_LEVEL is not relevant to checkpoint auto-tuning.

3. ☑ **C.** Instance recovery will always require the current online redo log file, and if any others were active, it will need them as well.
   ☒ **A** and **B** are wrong because they are not sufficient. **D** is wrong because instance recovery never needs an archive redo log file.

Identify the Importance of Checkpoints, Redo Log Files, and Archived Log Files

4. ☑ **A** and **B.** Any orderly shutdown will trigger a full checkpoint.
   ☒ **C** is wrong because this would trigger only a partial checkpoint. **D** is wrong because log switches do not trigger checkpoints.

5. ☑ **A** and **D.** Anything to do with the controlfile can only be done in nomount or shutdown modes. Changing the archivelog mode can only be done in mount mode.
   ☒ **B** is wrong because the online redo log can be configured while the database is open. **C** is wrong because DB_RECOVERY_FILE_DEST is a dynamic parameter.

6. ☑ **D.** Setting a longer FAST_START_MTTR_TARGET, or not setting it at all, will reduce the need for DBWn to write dirty buffers to disk, which should improve performance.
   ☒ **A** and **C** are both wrong because they describe the opposite effect. **B** is wrong because the auto-tuning capability does not affect performance, though it will reduce recovery time after instance failure.

Overview of Flash Recovery Area

7. ☑ **A, C,** and **D.** These will go to the flash recovery area, unless directed elsewhere.

☒ **B** is wrong because background trace files will go to a directory in the DIAGNOSTIC_DEST directory. **E** is wrong because undo data is stored in the undo tablespace.

Configure ARCHIVELOG Mode

8. ☑ **A.** This is the correct sequence.

☒ **B, C,** and **D** are wrong because enabling archiving is not necessary (it will occur automatically). **E** is wrong because a backup is a necessary part of the procedure.

9. ☑ **A** and **C.** These are the two conditions.

☒ **B** and **D.** While these are certainly good practice, they are not requirements.

10. ☑ **C.** Once all the online log files need archiving, DML commands will be blocked.

☒ **A** is wrong because the instance will remain open. **B** is wrong because only sessions that attempt DML will hang; those running SELECTs can continue. **D** is wrong because this cannot happen automatically.

LAB ANSWER

The information can be obtained using SQL*Plus, or with Database Control. Using SQL*Plus, these queries would do:

```
select group#,members from v$log;
select count(*) from v$controlfile;
select log_mode from v$database;
select archiver from v$instance;
select count(*) from v$parameter where name like 'log\_archive\_dest\__'
or name like 'log\_archive\_dest\___' escape '\' and value is not null;
select value from v$parameter where name='fast_start_mttr_target';
select value from v$parameter where name='db_recovery_file_dest';
```

If the database is the default database created by DBCA and the exercises have been completed as written, the results of these queries will show that there are two problems: the online redo log file groups are not multiplexed and neither are the archive redo log files.

16

Performing
Database Backups

Backups can be made with operating system utilities such as `cp`, `tar`, or `cpio` on Unix or `copy` or `winzip32.exe` on Windows. Backups made in this fashion are known as *user-managed* backups. Alternatively, backups can be made with RMAN, the Recovery Manager. Backups made in this fashion are known as *server-managed* backups. When making a database backup, you have three basic choices. Will the backup be

- **Offline or online?**   Also known as: open or closed, hot or cold, and consistent or inconsistent. Will you make the backup while users are logged on and working, or is the database going to shut down while you make the backup?
- **Whole or partial?**   A whole backup means the complete database: the entire set of datafiles and the controlfile. A partial backup is a subset of the database: one or more datafiles and/or the controlfile.
- **Full or incremental?**   A full backup is complete, self-contained, and usable by itself. An incremental backup is those blocks changed since the last backup; it is useless unless you have the last backup too.

All combinations of these options are valid if your database is in archivelog mode and you make server-managed backups. If your database is in noarchivelog mode, your choice is restricted to closed-whole-full or (if you use RMAN) closed-whole-incremental; you cannot make open or partial backups in noarchivelog mode. If you do not use RMAN, you cannot make incremental backups: user-managed backups can be open or closed and whole or partial, but they must be full.

The second DBA OCP examination goes into much greater detail regarding backup and restore and recovery operations. For the first examination, only basic knowledge is tested—no advanced options, and testing is largely done with the Database Control graphical interface. One point that may well be tested is using Database Control to automate backups.

on the **Job** *Some Linux distributions include a utility called rman. If you get bizarre messages when running server-managed backups, it could be that your search path is finding this utility, not the Oracle utility. Make sure that your search path has $ORACLE_HOME/bin at the beginning to avoid this.*

CERTIFICATION OBJECTIVE 16.01

Create Consistent Database Backups

An *offline* backup is backup taken while the database is closed. You may hear offline backups referred to as *closed, cold,* or *consistent* backups. The term "closed" is self-explanatory and "cold" is just slang, but "consistent" requires an understanding of the Oracle architecture. For a datafile to be consistent, every block in the datafile must have been checkpointed, and the file closed by the operating system. In normal running, the datafiles are inconsistent: there will be a number of blocks that have been copied into the database buffer cache, updated, and not yet written back to disk. The datafile itself, on disk, is therefore not consistent with the real-time state of the database; some parts of it will be out of date. To make a datafile consistent, all changed blocks must be flushed to disk, and the datafile closed. As a general rule, this happens only when the database is shut down cleanly, with the IMMEDIATE, TRANSACTIONAL, or NORMAL shutdown options.

An *online* backup is a backup taken while the database is in use. Other terms for online backups are *open, hot,* or *inconsistent* backups. A datafile that is backed up online will not be synchronized with any particular SCN, nor is it synchronized with the other datafiles or the controlfile. It is backed up while it is in use—being read from by server processes and written to by DBWn.

User-Managed Consistent Backups

To make a consistent backup with operating system commands, there are three steps:

- Copy the controlfile(s).
- Copy the datafiles.
- Copy the online redo log files.

Optionally, copy the online redo log files as well and the tempfiles. And don't forget the parameter file, though strictly speaking that is not part of the database. This SQL*Plus script (run while the database is open) will generate a Windows shell script that will perform the backup using operating system commands:

```
spool cold_backup.bat
select 'copy '||name||' d:\backup' from v$datafile
union all
```

```
select 'copy '||name||' d:\backup' from v$controlfile
union all
select 'copy '||member||' d:\backup' v$logfile;
create pfile='d:\backup\spfile_backup.ora' from spfile;
spool off
```

This example generates a Windows batch file that will copy all the database files and then generate a text file version of the server parameter file. Including the online redo log file members in the backup is, strictly speaking, optional. This is because they will never be needed if the database is shut down cleanly. A clean shutdown includes a checkpoint, which makes the database consistent; there will be no need for recovery, and therefore no need for the online redo log files. Most DBAs will always include the online redo log file members in the backup, because it makes restore simpler and also means that if something goes wrong with the shutdown script such that it is not in fact a clean shutdown, then they will be available for recovery.

If your database is in noarchivelog mode, you cannot do open backups. Backups may only be made with operating system commands when the database is shut down, or with RMAN when it is mounted.

The preceding script does not back up the tempfiles (remember that tempfiles make up the temporary tablespaces). There is no necessity ever to back up the tempfiles because they contain no data that has any persistence beyond the lifetime of the session that created them. If a tempfile gets damaged, the quickest recovery method is to drop it and recreate it; the recreation will be much quicker than a restore, and so there is no point in backing them up.

An example of an operating system script that could be launched by the operating system job scheduler to automate the backup is

```
sqlplus <<!
connect / as sysdba
@generate_cold_backup_bat.sql
shutdown immediate
!
cold_backup.bat
sqlplus <<!
connect / as sysdba
startup

!
```

This script performs these functions:

- Launch SQL*Plus, reading as input the text between the exclamation marks.
- Connect with the SYSDBA privilege.
- Run a SQL*Plus script to generate an operating system backup script.
- Shut down the database.
- Run the generated script.
- Connect with SQL*Plus again, and start up the database.

on the
Job

A whole offline backup couldn't be simpler. Shut down the database and copy it. But always use scripts to make sure that it is shut down cleanly, and that every necessary file is copied.

Server-Managed Consistent Backups

An RMAN offline consistent backup has one crucial difference from an operating system offline consistent backup: it can be accomplished only when the database is in mount mode. This is because RMAN needs to read the controlfile in order to find the datafiles. If an operating system backup were attempted in mount mode, it would be invalid (though the DBA wouldn't realize this until he/she tried to restore) because even in mount node the controlfile might be written to while being copied. The copy would then be inconsistent, and therefore useless. RMAN avoids the problem by taking a read-consistent snapshot of the controlfile and backing that up.

An RMAN backup is launched from the RMAN executable. The RMAN executable is a tool supplied by Oracle and installed into the Oracle Home. RMAN logs on to the database (like any other user process) and then launches additional server processes to copy files. In general, there are three techniques for using RMAN: an interactive interface, for performing ad hoc tasks; a script interface, for running jobs through the operating system's scheduler; and an Enterprise Manager interface, for generating scripts and defining jobs to be scheduled by Enterprise Manager.

This is an RMAN script for performing an offline whole full backup:

```
run {
shutdown immediate;
startup mount;
allocate channel d1 type disk;
backup as backupset database
format 'd:\backup\offline_full_whole.bus';
alter database open;
}
```

The first two commands within the `run{}` block perform a clean shutdown and then bring the database back up in mount mode. Then the script launches a server process to perform the backup. This is known as a channel. In this case, the channel is a disk channel because the backup is being directed to disk; the alternative channel type is SBT_TAPE, which is used for backups directed to a tape device. The next command launches a backup operation. This will be of type BACKUPSET. Backup sets are an RMAN-proprietary structure that can combine many input files into one output file. Backup sets have other advantages, such as compression (not enabled in this example) and the ability to reduce the size of the backup by ignoring blocks in the input datafiles that have never been used. The keyword DATABASE instructs RMAN to back up the entire set of datafiles and the controlfile. RMAN will never back up online redo log file members or tempfiles. The FORMAT keyword names the file that will contain the backup set. Finally, the script opens the database.

RMAN will never back up the online redo log files, or the tempfiles. It will back up datafiles, archivelog files, the controlfile, and the spfile.

An operating system command that could be scheduled to run this script is

```
rman target sys/oracle@orcl11g @offline_full_whole.rman
```

This command launches the RMAN executable, with the SYS login (necessary because of the SHUTDOWN and STARTUP commands) and then the name of the script, which must be preceded by an "@" symbol.

RMAN can generate three types of backup:

- A *backup set* is a proprietary format that can contain several files and will not include never-used blocks.

- A *compressed backup set* has the same content as a backup set, but RMAN will apply a compression algorithm as it writes out the backup set.

- An *image copy* is a backup file that is identical to the input file. An image copy is immediately interchangeable with its source, whereas to extract a file from a backup set requires an RMAN restore operation.

EXERCISE 16-1

Managing Consistent User- and Server-Managed Backups

In this exercise, you will perform a full offline backup using operating system commands, and then a second backup using RMAN.

1. While the database is open, using either SQL*Plus or Database Control determine the names of the datafiles, the controlfile copies, and the online log file members. They will probably all be in one directory, but (depending on what exercises and other work you have done) this may not be the case. Suitable SQL*Plus queries have been given earlier, or in Database Control from the database home page take the Server tab, and then the appropriate links in the Storage section.

2. Using either SQL*Plus or Database Control, connect as user SYS with the SYSDBA privilege, and shut down the database with the IMMEDIATE option. With Database control you can do this with the Shutdown button on the database home page; with SQL*Plus issue SHUTDOWN IMMEDIATE.

3. Using whatever operating system utility you wish (even a GUI drag-and-drop), copy the files identified in Step 1 to a safe location.

4. Using SQL*Plus or Database Control, start the database in mount mode. Using Database Control, you will need to provide operating system login details, and then click the Advanced Options button and select the radio button for Mount The database. If using SQL*Plus, just STARTUP MOUNT will do.

5. From an operating system prompt, launch the RMAN executable (it is called `rman` on Unix and Linux, `rman.exe` on Windows) and connect using operating system authentication. The command is

   ```
   rman target /
   ```

6. Perform a full backup. The command is

   ```
   backup database;
   ```

This will, by default, back up the entire database to the flash recovery area. The next illustration shows the command on a Windows system.

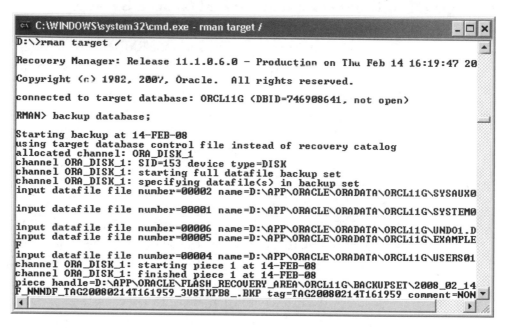

7. Study the feedback in the RMAN session, some of which is shown in the illustration. Note the launching of a channel, the identification of the datafiles, the destination in the flash recovery area, and (not visible in the illustration) the creation of a second backup set for the controlfile and the spfile.

8. Using SQL*Plus or RMAN or Database Control, open the database. With SQL*Plus or RMAN, the command is

```
alter database open;
```

9. Exit from the RMAN utility with the command exit.

CERTIFICATION OBJECTIVE 16.02

Back Up Your Database Without Shutting It Down

There is no reason to shut down the database for backups. An Oracle database can remain open indefinitely and be perfectly adequately protected by hot online backups—provided that it is running in archivelog mode. It is not possible to take an online backup in noarchivelog mode.

User-Managed Open Backups

An open backup with operating system commands is three steps:

- Back up the controlfile with ALTER DATABASE BACKUP CONTROLFILE.
- Copy the datafiles, while they are in backup mode.
- Archive the online redo log files.

To back up the controlfile while it is open, use an ALTER DATABASE command. There are two versions:

```
alter database backup controlfile to 'file_name' ;
alter database backup controlfile to trace as 'file_name' ;
```

The first of these command will take a read-consistent snapshot of the controlfile and back that up to the *file_name* specified. This is often referred to as a *binary* copy. It will be byte-for-byte the same as the live controlfile, and the snapshot mechanism ensures that it is consistent. The second command constructs a CREATE CONTROLFILE command and saves it in a script called *file_name*. This script can be executed while the instance is in NOMOUNT mode to create a new controlfile, with the same contents as the original controlfile from which it was generated. This script is an ASCII file that can be viewed (and edited) with any test editor.

on the
Job

if you don't specify a name for the trace file, it will be generated in the directory specified by the USER_DUMP_DEST instance parameter and will be named according to the name of the instance and the operating system process ID of the server process supporting your session. This is not very useful.

The datafiles can be copied with any operating system utility, but before making the copy they must be put into *backup mode* with an ALTER TABLESPACE command:

```
alter tablespace tablespace_name begin backup;
```

This command has two effects. First, it forces a partial checkpoint: all the dirty buffers in the database buffer cache that contain blocks from the tablespace's datafiles are written to disk. Second, it adjusts the redo generation mechanism for changes made to blocks from those datafiles. This is necessary to manage the situation where a block is updated while it is being copied, and it requires some explanation.

Consider what actually happens if you copy a file with an operating system utility while the file is in use. Take an example where the operating system block size is 512 bytes (the default on many Unix and Windows systems) but the Oracle block size, as determined by the DB_BLOCK_SIZE parameter, is 8 KB. Each Oracle block will be sixteen operating system blocks.

In this scenario, you initiate an operating system copy, perhaps using the Windows copy command. If the file is many megabytes big, this copy will take several seconds or minutes to complete, and during that time it is more than likely that DBWn will flush some changed blocks from the database buffer cache to the datafile; the file will be changed while it is being copied. The granularity of the operating system copy is the operating system block, but the granularity of the DBWn write is the Oracle block. It is thus possible that the copy command will take the first part of an Oracle block, then DBWn will overwrite the whole Oracle block, and the copy command will then take the remaining part of the Oracle block. You have no control over this; the operating system's preemptive multitasking algorithm will bring the processes on and off CPU as it pleases. So in the output file produced by the copy, there will be what is called a *fractured* block: parts of it will be as of different versions. Such a block is completely useless; you have a data corruption in your backup. Of course, you might be lucky and have no fractured blocks—but never rely on that.

If you are using operating system utilities to perform online backups, you avoid the fractured block problem by putting the tablespace containing the datafile into backup mode, with an ALTER TABLESPACE...BEGIN BACKUP command, for the duration of the copy. From that point on, whenever a server process updates a block in the database buffer cache, rather than writing out the minimal change vector to the log buffer it will write out the complete block image to the log buffer. This block image will be read-consistent. Then if it is ever necessary to restore the datafile, any fractured blocks can be replaced with a read-consistent image of the block extracted from the redo logs. Thus you accept that an online backup will have fractured blocks, but Oracle can repair them if necessary. The downside of this is that the rate of redo generation may accelerate astronomically while the tablespace is in backup mode: 8KB for each change, instead of just a few bytes. You may find that you are log-switching thirty times an hour rather than thirty times a day when you put tablespaces into backup mode, with a consequent drop in performance.

This SQL*Plus script will generate a script that will perform full online backup of the database:

```
set serveroutput on
declare
    cursor ts_cursor is
    select * from dba_tablespaces where contents <> 'TEMPORARY';
    cursor df_cursor (ts_name varchar2) is
    select * from dba_data_files where tablespace_name = ts_name;
begin
  for t in ts_cursor loop
  dbms_output.put_line(
  'alter tablespace '||t.tablespace_name||' begin backup;');
  for f in df_cursor(t.tablespace_name) loop
    dbms_output.put_line('host cp -p ''' || f.file_name  || ''' /backup/');
  end loop;
  dbms_output.put_line(
  'alter tablespace '||t.tablespace_name||' end backup;');
  end loop;
  dbms_output.put_line('alter database backup controlfile to trace as
  ''/backup/controlfile.trace'';');
  dbms_output.put_line(
  'alter database backup controlfile to ''/backup/controlfile.binary'';');
  dbms_output.put_line('create pfile=''/backup/spfile_backup.ora''
  from spfile;');
end;
/
```

The logic is to loop through a cursor containing all the permanent tablespaces, putting each tablespace into backup mode, copying its datafiles (listed in another cursor), and then taking it out of backup mode. At the end there are commands to perform both types of controlfile backup, and to back up the server parameter file.

on the
job

Open backups with operating system commands are perfectly reliable, but your scripts must be bulletproof. They must copy every datafile, and the copies must be made while the tablespace is in backup mode. The script must also take the tablespaces out of backup mode once the copies are completed.

As well as backing up the database, the archivelog files should also be backed up and deleted from the disk destination where ARCn created them.

Server-Managed Open Backups

An absolutely reliable open backup can be made with RMAN with a two-word command: BACKUP DATABASE. This command relies on configured defaults for the destination of the backup (disk or tape library), the names of the backup files generated, the number of server channels to launch to carry out the backup, and the type of backup (image copies of the files, backup sets, or compressed backup sets).

This RMAN script performs a full whole online backup of the database and the archive log files:

```
run {
allocate channel t1 type sbt_tape;
allocate channel t2 type sbt_tape;
backup as compressed backupset filesperset 4 database;
backup as compressed backupset archivelog all delete all input;
}
```

The script launches two channels that will write to the tape library. The device driver for the tape library (supplied by the hardware vendor) must have been installed. The use of multiple channels (possible related to the number of tape drives in the library) will parallelize the backup operation, which should make it run faster. The first backup command backs up the complete database, but rather than putting every file into one huge (even though compressed) backup set, it instructs RMAN to divide the database into multiple backup sets of four files each; this can make restore operations faster than if all the files are in one backup set. The second backup command will back up all the archive log files, removing them from disk as it does so.

When using RMAN for open backups, there is no requirement to put the tablespaces into backup mode. This is because RMAN, being an Oracle-aware tool, will detect fractured blocks if they occur, and will retry the block copy until it gets a consistent version. To obtain a read-consistent version of the controlfile, RMAN uses a similar method to the ALTER DATABASE command: it creates a read-consistent snapshot.

e x a m

⑭ a t c h   *When creating backup sets, or compressed backup sets, RMAN will never back up blocks that have never been used. This results in considerable space savings.*

EXERCISE 16-2

Perform Server-Managed and User-Managed Open Backups

In this exercise, you will perform a hot backup of a datafile with operating system commands and with RMAN.

1. Connect to your database as user SYSTEM with SQL*Plus.

2. Identify the file (or files) that makes up your SYSAUX tablespace:

```
select file_name from dba_data_files where
tablespace_name='SYSAUX';
```

3. Put the SYSAUX tablespace into backup mode:

```
alter tablespace sysaux begin backup;
```

4. Using an operating system utility, copy the file(s) identified in Step 2 to a safe location. If working on Windows, note that some Windows utilities have problems copying open files. If this is an issue, use the Oracle-supplied utility ocopy.exe, which has the same syntax as the Windows copy command and has no problem with open files.

5. In the SQL*Plus session, take the tablespace out of backup mode:

```
alter tablespace sysaux end backup;
```

6. Connect to the database using RMAN:

```
rman target /
```

7. Back up the tablespace:

```
backup tablespace sysaux;
```

8. Study the output of Step 7. An example (showing Steps 6, 7, and 8) is in the next illustration.

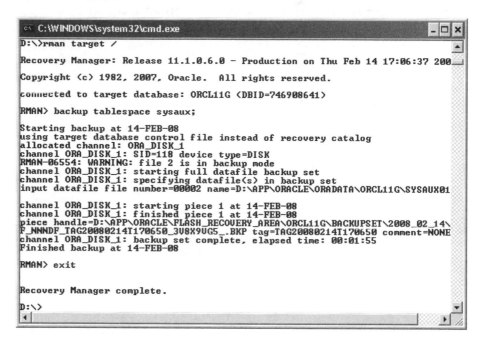

9. Exit from the RMAN utility.

CERTIFICATION OBJECTIVE 16.03

Create Incremental Backups

Incremental backups can be made with server-managed backups, but not with user-managed backups. As far as an operating system utility is concerned, the granularity of the backup is the datafile: an operating system utility cannot look inside the datafile to extract changed blocks incrementally. Incremental backups must always be as backup sets or compressed backup sets. It is logically impossible to make an image copy incremental backup, because an incremental backup can never be identical to the source file. If it were, it wouldn't be incremental.

An incremental backup relies on a starting point that contains all blocks: this is known as the *incremental level 0* backup. Then an *incremental level 1* backup will extract all blocks that have changed since the last level 1 backup, or the last level 0 backup if there have been no intervening level 1 backups. A *cumulative* backup will extract all blocks that have changed since the last level 0 backup, irrespective of whether there have been any level 1 backups in the meantime.

An RMAN command to make a level 0 backup is

```
backup as backupset incremental level 0 database;
```

This command relies on configured defaults for launching channels, for the number of files to place in each backup set, and to where the backup set will be written. The backup set will contain all blocks that have ever been used. Many sites will make an incremental level 0 backup every weekend. Then a level 1 backup can be made with this command:

```
backup as backupset incremental level 1 database;
```

This command could be run daily, to extract all blocks changed since the last level 1 (or, the first time it is run, the level 0) backup. A cumulative incremental backup might be run mid-week:

If there is no level 0 backup, then the first level 1 or cumulative backup will in fact perform a level 0 backup.

```
backup as backupset cumulative database;
```

This will extract all blocks changed since the level 0 backup.

on the **job** *You can specify incremental levels higher than 1, but they don't have any effect and are permitted only for backward compatibility. Earlier releases of RMAN made use of them.*

EXERCISE 16-3

Make an Incremental Backup

In this exercise, you will make incremental backups, first using the RMAN utility and then using Database Control.

1. Connect to the database with the RMAN executable, make an incremental backup of the SYSTEM tablespace, and exit from the utility. The commands are

```
rman target /
backup incremental level 1 tablespace system;
exit
```

2. Study the output of Step 1. Note that the controlfile and spfile were backed up too; this is automatic whenever the SYSTEM tablespace is backed up. This will have been a level 0 backup, because there was no level 0 on which to base a level 1.

3. Connect to the database with Database Control as user SYS.

4. From the database home page, take the Availability tab and then the Schedule Backup link in the Manage section.

5. Select the radio button for Tablespaces, and click the Scheduled Customized Backup button.

6. In the Schedule Customized Backup: Tablespaces window, click the Add button, the check box for the SYSTEM tablespace, and Select. Click Next.

7. In the Schedule Customized Backup: Options window, select the radio button for Incremental Backup, and deselect the Also Backup All Archived Logs In Disk check box. Click Next.

8. In the Schedule Customized Backup: Settings window, accept the defaults, which will direct the backup to the flash recovery area, and click Next.

9. In the Schedule Customized Backup: Schedule window, accept the defaults, which will run the job immediately, and click Next.

10. In the Schedule Customized Backup: Review window, study the RMAN script that has been generated, and click Submit Job.

11. Click OK to exit from the wizard.

CERTIFICATION OBJECTIVE 16.04

Automate Database Backups

Enterprise Manager can schedule backups. The mechanism is not related to the operating system's job scheduler, nor to the job scheduling system within the database. It is purely an Enterprise Manager facility and is available whether you are using Grid Control or Database Control. The Enterprise Manager agent runs the job according to a specified schedule. The backups can be of any type (online or offline, whole or partial, and full or incremental) but will always be server managed: using RMAN.

EXERCISE 16-4

Define an Automatic Backup Job

In this exercise, you will define a repeating backup job.

1. Connect to the database with Database Control as user SYS.
2. From the database home page, take the Availability tab and then the Schedule Backup link in the Manage section.
3. Select the radio button for Whole Database, and click the Schedule Customized Backup button.
4. In the Schedule Customized Backup: Options window, select the radio buttons for Incremental Backup, and Online Backup and the check boxes to back up

and delete archive log files and delete obsolete backups (as shown in the next illustration). Click Next.

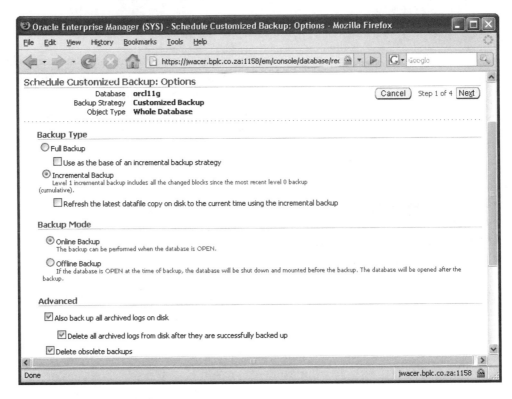

5. In the Schedule Customized Backup: Settings window, accept the defaults, which will direct the backup to the flash recovery area. Click Next.

6. In the Schedule Customized Backup: Schedule window, select the radio button for Repeating and set a schedule and time, such as daily at 02:00. Select the radio button for Repeat Until Specified Date, and enter tomorrow's date. Click Next.

7. In the Schedule Customized Backup: Review window, study the RMAN script that has been generated. This will be more complex than any seen previously, but it is still self-explanatory. Click Submit Job.

8. To confirm the creation of the job, return to the database home page, and take the Jobs link in the Related Links section. You will see the backup job scheduled.

SCENARIO & SOLUTION

What is the best way to automate backup routines? With Oracle facilities, or with operating system facilities?	Within the Oracle environment, you can automate backup jobs with Enterprise Manager. If you are confident that the relevant processes (the Database Control processes, or the Grid Control agent) will always be running, then use them. Otherwise, the operating system job scheduler may be a better option.
Is it best to use RMAN? My system administrators insist that their backups (based on disk technology for creating snapshots) are faster and better.	RMAN backups can do things that user-managed backups can't. In particular, they can be incremental (vital for large databases). Also, the automation of restore and recovery is fantastic. But you will often find a lot of opposition to RMAN coming from your system administrators. Historically, they were the people who did backups, and they are very good at finding reasons why their techniques are better. Their reasoning is not always fully informed and may be influenced by office politics.

CERTIFICATION OBJECTIVE 16.05

Manage Backups, View Backup Reports, and Monitor the Flash Recovery Area

RMAN uses a repository to store details of all the backup operations it has carried out. This repository is the key to automated restore and recovery, and the source of reports on backups. By default, server-managed backups will go to the flash recovery area. RMAN will attempt to manage space in the flash recovery area, but the DBA must monitor it as well.

The RMAN Repository

During a backup operation, RMAN will write to its repository all detail of the backup: what was backed up, where the backup files are, the time and system change number of certain events, and so on.

For a datafile restore operation, RMAN must determine the most recent backup (either full or level 0) from which to extract the file should be extracted. Then to recover it, RMAN must determine which incremental backups (if any) are available and then extract and apply them. Then it must determine what archive log files are needed and (if they are no longer available on disk) restore them too from backups, and apply them. Finally, it will apply change vectors from the online log files to bring the restored file right up to date.

The repository is the source of the information RMAN needs. Whenever it does anything, it will consult the repository. The repository is stored in the database's controlfile. This does raise the question of what to do if the controlfile itself needs to be restored. There are techniques to cover this situation (dealt with in the second OCP examination) by creating a separate database known as the Recovery Manager Catalog, and by creating automatic backups of the controlfile to a well-known location. At this stage, the assumption is that the controlfile is protected by multiplexing, so there will always be at least one copy of it available.

e x a m

ⓦatch   *The RMAN repository is always stored in the target database's controlfile—though it is possible to have a copy of it in a separate database, known as the Recovery Manager Catalog.*

INSIDE THE EXAM

Performing Database Backups

The first database administration OCP examination does not demand great knowledge of making backups. However, an understanding of the architecture and basic techniques may well be tested.

Architecturally, remember that the RMAN executable is a user process like any other: it connects to the database via a server session. To do work, it launches additional server processes known as channels. This is why RMAN backups are called "server managed":

all the work is done by server processes. RMAN uses a repository, stored in the target database's controlfile. This repository has details of all backups made.

User-managed backups are accomplished with operating system and SQL*Plus commands. You should be familiar with the techniques for user-managed backups, both open and closed, and with creating server-managed backup jobs with Database Control.

Reports on Backups

RMAN has two commands that will tell you the state of your backup: LIST will tell you what backups there are, REPORT will tell you what backups are needed. Examples from the RMAN command line are

```
list backup of database;
list backup of archivelog all;
report need backup;
report obsolete;
```

The first of these commands will list all the backups that have been made and are still recorded in the repository. The second command lists all backups of archived red log files. The third command lists everything that needs to be backed up according to the Recovery Manager's configured retention policy (such as three backups of every file). The final command lists all backups that are no longer needed according to the Recovery Manager's configured retention policy.

To see the same information with Database Control, from the database home page take the Availability tab, and then the Backups Reports link in the Manage section. Figure 16-1 shows the Backup Reports window, listing two incremental backups. These were of the same file.

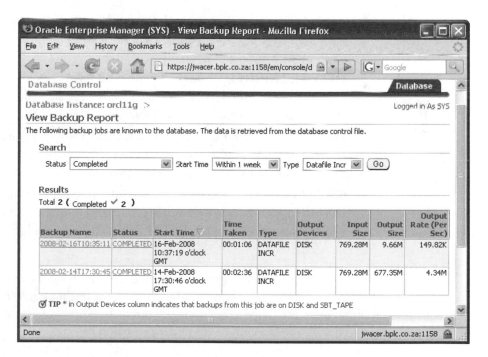

FIGURE 16-1

Some backups listed in Database Control

In the figure, note the values in the columns for "Input Size" and "Output Size." The earlier backup was incremental, but as it was a level 0, the size of the output is a large proportion of the size of the input—although it does not equal that size, because backup sets do not include blocks that have never been used. The more recent backup set is much smaller, because it was an incremental level 1 backup, capturing only the blocks changed since the level 0.

Managing Backups

Using server-managed backups, management should be largely automatic. That's the whole idea. But there are circumstances where intervention will be necessary—typically, when something has been done that RMAN doesn't know about. If backup files are removed or destroyed, or if additional user-managed backups are made, then RMAN must be informed of what has happened.

Backups will usually reside on tape, in an automated tape library. The tape library will often have a retention policy: it will automatically delete all files over a certain age. The RMAN repository will not know that this has happened. If the tape library is not deleting old files, then RMAN must do it. From the RMAN command line, there are four critical commands:

- **CROSSCHECK** A crosscheck forces RMAN to compare its repository with the real world. It will check that all the backups it has made do still exist, on disk or tape. Any that it finds to be missing are flagged as EXPIRED.
- **DELETE EXPIRED** This will remove all references from the repository to expired backups. If the backups have merely been moved (off site, perhaps), an alternative is to mark them as UNAVAILABLE.
- **DELETE OBSOLETE** This will force RMAN to apply its retention policy. It will delete all backups that it considers to be no longer necessary from disk or tape, and remove the references to them from its repository.
- **CATALOG** This command lets you inform RMAN about additional user-managed backups, so that RMAN can include them in its repository. If backups have been moved, CATALOG can also be used to tell RMAN the new locations.

To use these commands through Database Control, from the database home page take the Availability tab, then the Manage Current Backups link in the Manage section. Figure 16-2 shows the Manage Current Backups window: note the buttons that give access to the commands in the preceding list.

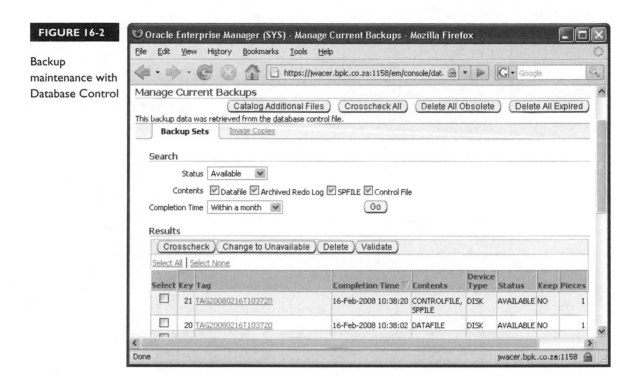

FIGURE 16-2

Backup maintenance with Database Control

Monitoring the Flash Recovery Area

Once use of a flash recovery area has been configured, it is vital to monitor how much space is being taken up within it. Figure 16-3 shows the Database Control Monitoring window. To reach this, from the database home page take the Availability tab, and then the Recovery Settings link in the Setup section. The flash recovery area is shown in the bottom part of the window.

In the figure, first note on the left-hand side the values for the two parameters that manage the flash recovery area: DB_RECOVERY_FILE_DEST is set to /u01/ app/oracle/flash_recovery_area and DB_RECOVERY_FILE_DEST_SIZE is set to 3.5 GB. Beneath these, note that there is 40 MB of reclaimable space: this is space occupied by backups that the Recovery Manager can reuse when necessary, or that could be cleared manually with the DELETE OBSOLETE command. The pie chart on the right-hand side of the figure shows the contents of the flash recovery area: the bulk of the space used is backup sets (stored as pieces) and image copies, with a small amount of space taken up by archived logs.

FIGURE 16-3

The flash recovery area, monitored with Database Control

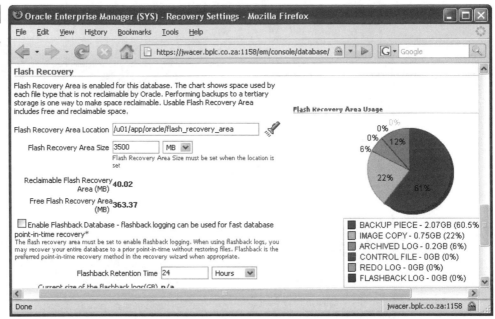

The same information could be obtained by querying the views V$RECOVERY_FILE_DEST and V$FLASH_RECOVERY_AREA_USAGE, as in Figure 16-4.

FIGURE 16-4

The flash recovery area, monitored with SQL*Plus

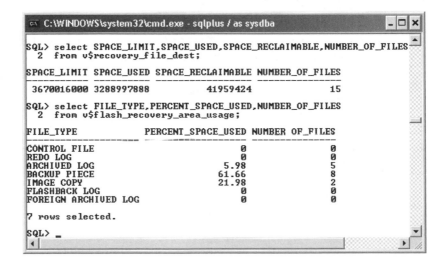

Manage RMAN Backups

In this exercise, you will use the RMAN utility to manage the backups made in previous exercises.

1. Connect to the database with the RMAN executable, from an operating system prompt using operating system authentication:

```
rman target /
```

2. Query the server-managed backups made so far:

```
list backup of database;
```

This will list at least four backup sets: the full backup of the whole database made in Exercise 16-1, the full partial backup (just the SYSAUX datafile) made in Exercise 16-2, and the two incremental partial backups of the SYSTEM tablespace made in Exercise 16-3.

3. Catalog the user-managed backup of SYSAUX tablespace made in Exercise 16-2. Use this command, substituting the path and name you used when making the copy:

```
catalog datafilecopy '/u01/app/oracle/oradata/orcl11g/
sysaux01.dbf.bak';
```

4. Confirm the success of the catalog with this command:

```
list copy of tablespace sysaux;
```

5. Exit from the RMAN executable:

```
exit;
```

CERTIFICATION SUMMARY

A user-managed backup is made with operating system commands and with SQL*Plus commands. Server-managed backups are made with the Recovery Manager, controlled either through the RMAN executable or Enterprise Manager.

Backups can be open or closed, whole or partial, full or incremental. But the full range of choices is available only if the database is in archivelog mode and you use RMAN. In noarchivelog mode, if making a user-managed backup, the only option is closed-whole-full. A server-managed backup can also be closed-whole-incremental. In archivelog mode, open and partial backups are a possibility with both server- and user-managed backups—but only server-managed backups can be incremental.

TWO-MINUTE DRILL

Create Consistent Database Backups

- ❑ A consistent backup is one made after the database has been shut down.
- ❑ A user-managed consistent backup is three steps:
    - ❑ Copy the online redo log files.
    - ❑ Copy the controlfile(s).
    - ❑ Copy the datafiles.
- ❑ A server-managed consistent backup is also three steps:
    - ❑ Mount the database.
    - ❑ Back up the control file.
    - ❑ Back up the datafiles.
- ❑ RMAN will never back up online log files or tempfiles.

Back Up Your Database Without Shutting It Down

- ❑ A user-managed open backup is three steps:
    - ❑ Archive the online redo log files.
    - ❑ ALTER DATABASE BACKUP CONTROLFILE TO . . . .
    - ❑ Copy the datafiles, while their tablespace is in backup mode.
- ❑ A server-managed open backup is also three steps:
    - ❑ Archive the online redo log files.
    - ❑ Back up the controlfile.
    - ❑ Back up the datafiles, without the need to enable backup mode.

Create Incremental Backups

- ❑ User-managed backups cannot be incremental, but server-managed backups can be.
- ❑ The starting point for an incremental strategy must be an incremental level 0 backup. A full backup cannot be used.
- ❑ The incremental levels are 0, 1, or cumulative.
- ❑ Incremental backups can be made in archivelog or noarchivelog mode.

Automate Database Backups

❑ User- or server-managed backup jobs can be scheduled with the operating system scheduler.

❑ The Enterprise Manager job system can schedule server-managed backups of all types.

Manage Backups, View Backup Reports, and Monitor the Flash Recovery Area

❑ Server-managed backups are recorded in a repository, in the target database's controlfile.

❑ The repository can checked with reality with the CROSSCHECK command, and modified if necessary.

❑ User-managed backups can be recorded in the repository and thus brought under RMAN control by using the CATALOG command.

❑ If backing up to the flash recovery area, its usage must be monitored.

SELF TEST

Create Consistent Database Backups

1. What file types can be backed up by RMAN? (Choose all correct answers.)
   A. Archive log files
   B. Controlfile
   C. Online log files
   D. Password file
   E. Permanent tablespace datafiles
   F. Server parameter file
   G. Static parameter file
   H. Temporary tablespace tempfiles

2. If your database is in noarchivelog mode, which of the following is possible? (Choose the best answer.)
   A. Online backups
   B. Partial backups
   C. Incremental backups
   D. All of the above, but only if you use RMAN

3. RMAN backup sets are smaller than RMAN image copies because . . . (Choose the best answer.)
   A. They always use compression.
   B. They always skip include unused blocks.
   C. They never include tempfiles.
   D. They can be written directly to tape.

Back Up Your Database Without Shutting It Down

4. Which of the following statements is correct about RMAN offline backup? (Choose all correct answers.)
   A. The database must be in NOMOUNT mode.
   B. The database must be in MOUNT mode.
   C. The backup will fail if the shutdown mode was SHUTDOWN IMMEDIATE.
   D. Noarchivelog databases can only be backed up offline.
   E. Archivelog databases cannot be backed up offline.
   F. Offline backups can be incremental.

5. You need to back up the control file while the database is open. What will work? (Choose the best answer.)

   A. The controlfile can be included in an RMAN backup set, but not backed up as an image copy.

   B. The ALTER DATBASE BACKUP CONTROLFILE TO TRACE command will make an image copy of the controlfile.

   C. You cannot back up the controlfile while it is in use —it is protected by multiplexing.

   D. None of the above.

Create Incremental Backups

6. You perform a full backup on Sunday, an incremental level 0 backup on Monday, an incremental level 1 differential backup on Tuesday, an incremental level 1 cumulative backup on Wednesday, and an incremental level 1 cumulative backup on Thursday. Which blocks will be included in the Thursday backup? (Choose the best answer.)

   A. All blocks changed since Sunday

   B. All blocks changed since Monday

   C. All blocks changed since Tuesday

   D. All blocks changed since Wednesday

7. If you issue this RMAN command,

   ```
   backup incremental level 1;
   ```

   and there is no level 0 backup, what will happen? (Choose the best answer.)

   A. The command will fail.

   B. The incremental backup will be based on the most recent full backup.

   C. RMAN will perform a level 0 backup.

   D. RMAN will perform a level 1 cumulative backup of all blocks that have ever been changed.

Automate Database Backups

8. What processes must be running if an RMAN backup scheduled within the Oracle environment is to run? (Choose all correct answers.)

   A. The database instance processes must be running, in MOUNT or OPEN mode.

   B. The database instance processes must be running, in at least NOMOUNT mode.

   C. The Enterprise Manager processes (either Database Control or the Grid Control agent) must be running.

   D. The operating system scheduler must be running.

Manage Backups, View Backup Reports, and Monitor the Flash Recovery Area

9. What is true about the crosscheck command? (Choose the best answer.)
    A. Crosscheck will check the validity of the backup pieces.
    B. Crosscheck will delete references to files that no longer exist.
    C. Crosscheck will verify the existence of backup set pieces.
    D. Crosscheck only works with backup sets, not image copies.

10. If the volume of data in the flash recovery area has reached the limit defined by DB_RECOVERY_FILE_DEST_SIZE, what will happen when RMAN attempts to write more data to it? (Choose the best answer.)
    A. If AUTOEXTEND has been enabled and the MAXSIZE has not been reached, the flash recovery area will extend as necessary.
    B. The operation will fail.
    C. This will depend on whether warning and critical alerts have been enabled for the flash recovery area.
    D. RMAN will automatically delete OBSOLETE backups.
    E. RMAN will automatically delete EXPIRED backups.

LAB QUESTION

Investigate some of the merits of backup sets when compared to image copies. Use either the RMAN command-line interface or scheduled jobs created with Database Control to generate the backups, and determine the size of the output files and how long the operation took. If you hit errors because your flash recovery area fills up, either increase it by adjusting the DB_RECOVERY_FILE_DEST SIZE parameter, or clear out space by deleting backups already made.

To make the backups with Database Control, from the database home page take the Availability tab, and then the Schedule Backup link in the Manage section. In the Settings window of Schedule Customized Backup Wizard, click the Override Current Settings button to reach the window where you can choose whether the backup should be as a backup set, a compressed backup set, or an image copy.

Using the command-line interface, suitable commands to create backups would be

```
backup as backupset database incremental level 0;
backup as compressed backupset database incremental level 0;
backup as copy database;
backup as backupset database incremental level 1;
```

The command to see the size and duration of the backups is

```
list backup of database;
list copy of database;
```

What conclusions can you draw regarding the merits of backup sets?

Finally, tidy up by deleting backups that are no longer needed. The default RMAN retention policy is to have one backup of everything, so deleting obsolete backups should remove several of the backups created in this chapter. Either use the Delete All Obsolete button shown in Figure 16-2, or from the command line use this command:

```
delete obsolete;
```

Observe the effect on space usage in the flash recovery area.

SELF TEST ANSWERS

Create Consistent Database Backups

1. ☑ **A, B, E,** and **F.** These are the database file types that the Recovery Manager can back up and restore.
   ☒ **C, D, G,** and **H.** RMAN will never back up online redo logs or tempfiles because it is not necessary to back them up, and it cannot back up a static parameter file or the external password file.

2. ☑ **C.** RMAN can make incremental backups no matter what the database is in.
   ☒ **A, B,** and **D.** Whatever tool method you use, backups of a noarchivelog-mode database cannot be either partial or online.

3. ☑ **B.** A backup set will never include blocks that have never been used.
   ☒ **A** is wrong because compression is an option, not enabled by default. **C** is wrong because it applies to image copies as well as backup sets. **D** is wrong because it is not relevant: an image copy can't go to tape, because if it did, it wouldn't be an image.

Back Up Your Database Without Shutting It Down

4. ☑ **B, D,** and **F.** Offline backups must be done in mount mode. This is the only backup type for a noarchivelog mode database, but it can be incremental.
   ☒ **A** is wrong because the database must be mounted, or RMAN won't be able to connect to its repository or find the location of the datafiles. **C** is wrong because an IMMEDIATE shutdown is clean—it is only an ABORT that would cause problems. **E** is wrong because an archivelog mode database can certainly be backed up offline—it just isn't necessary.

5. ☑ **D.** A, B, and C are all incorrect.
   ☒ **A** is wrong because a copy of the controlfile can be created while the database is open, via a read-consistent snapshot. **B** is wrong because this command will generate a CREATE CONTROLFILE script, not a file copy. **C** is wrong because the file multiplexing is an additional precaution, not the only one.

Create Incremental Backups

6. ☑ **B.** A cumulative backup will include all blocks changed since the last level 0 backup.
   ☒ **A** is wrong because the full backup cannot be used as a base for an incremental backup. **C** and **D** are wrong because cumulative backups always go back to the most recent level 0 backup.

7. ☑ **C.** RMAN will revert to level 0 in this circumstance.
   ☒ **A** is wrong because the backup will succeed—though perhaps not in the way you wanted. **B** is wrong because no incremental backup can be based on a full backup. **D** is wrong because although the effect described is correct, it will not be recorded as a cumulative backup but as a level 0 backup.

Automate Database Backups

8. ☑ **A** and **C.** The Enterprise Manager processes will run the backup, and the database must be mounted or RMAN will not be able to connect to the repository.
   ☒ **B** is wrong because NOMOUNT mode is not enough. **D** is wrong because Oracle-scheduled backups do not use the operating system scheduler.

Manage Backups, View Backup Reports, and Monitor the Flash Recovery Area

9. ☑ **C.** The crosscheck command verifies that the repository does accurately reflect reality.
   ☒ **A** is wrong because crosscheck does not validate whether the backups are good—only whether they exist. **B** is wrong because crosscheck doesn't delete references to missing backups; it only flags them as expired. **D** is wrong because crosscheck confirms the existence of both backup sets and image copies.

10. ☑ **D.** Backups that are OBSOLETE according to RMAN's retention policy will be removed.
    ☒ **A** is wrong because this describes datafiles, not the flash recovery area. **B** is wrong because the operation will not necessarily fail—it may be possible to free up space automatically. **C** is wrong because the alert system will only report the problem; it won't fix it. **E** is wrong because EXPIRED refers to the status of the backup record in the repository, not the backup itself.

LAB ANSWER

As a general rule, backup sets will always be significantly smaller than image copies. This is because they do not include never-used blocks. If you enable compression, they will be smaller still. The elapsed time for a backup set operation is also shorter.

17

Performing Database Recovery

CERTIFICATION OBJECTIVES

T
he terms *restore* and *recover* have precise meanings in the Oracle environment. To restore a file is to extract it from a backup and return it to the place where it was made. If a datafile is damaged or missing, a restore operation will replace it with a copy from the backup. So far so good, but the restored file will be out of date compared to the rest of the database. To recover the file, extract the relevant change vectors from the redo log stream and apply them to bring the file forward in time until it is synchronized with the rest of the database.

Restoration and recovery constitute a major topic, and there are many possibilities, depending on the nature of the fault. In the first OCP examination, only limited knowledge is tested: diagnosis and repair of straightforward problems, using the Data Recovery Advisor.

CERTIFICATION OBJECTIVE 17.01

Overview of Data Recovery Advisor

The Data Recovery Advisor (the DRA) is a facility for diagnosing and repairing problems with a database. There are two interfaces: the RMAN executable and Enterprise Manager. The DRA is capable of generating scripts to repair damage to datafiles and (in some circumstances) the controlfile: it does not advise on problems with the spfile or with the online redo log files. It is dependent on Automatic Diagnostic Repository (the ADR) and the Health Monitor. The information the Health Monitor gathers and the advice the DRA gives follow the same diagnosis and repair methods that the DBA would follow without them—but they make the process quicker and less prone to error.

Loss of database files is no reason to lose data—provided that appropriate precautions have been taken:

- Multiplex the controlfile.
- Multiplex the online redo log files.
- Back up the controlfile and the datafiles.
- Run the database in archivelog mode.

Depending on the type of file that is lost, there are different techniques for recovery.

Recovery from Loss of the Controlfile

A point to emphasize is that the controlfile should never be completely lost: it should be multiplexed, so that if one copy of it is lost, another copy will still be available. If any copy of the controlfile is damaged, the database instance will abort immediately. If you attempt a startup, the instance will go nomount mode but will stop there: it will not mount the database unless all copies of the controlfile, as specified by the CONTROL_FILES instance parameter, are valid.

watch *Damage to any controlfile copy will abort the instance immediately. It will not be possible to mount the database until the problem has been fixed.*

To confirm that the controlfile is multiplexed, when in mount mode or open mode issue this query:

```
select name from v$controlfile;
```

which will list all copies of the controlfile. If this query returns only one row, the controlfile is not multiplexed. Correct this situation during the next period of scheduled downtime, and if no downtime is scheduled, you should schedule a period as soon as possible. The process is

- Shut down the database.
- Copy the controlfile.
- Start up the instance in nomount mode.
- Change the CONTROLFILES parameter to include the new copy.
- Shut down again.
- Start up the database in open mode.

Running the query given previously will now list both copies. The necessity for a shutdown is to obtain a consistent copy of the controlfile. If it were copied when the database was open or mounted, the copy would not be valid.

If the startup stops in nomount mode because the database cannot be mounted, determine what controlfile copies it is looking for with this query:

```
select value from v$parameter where name='control_files';
```

To find which copy is damaged or missing, look in the alert log. This is the file alert_*instancename*.ora in the directory specified by the BACKGROUND_DUMP_DEST parameter. The last few lines will be something like this:

```
ALTER DATABASE     MOUNT
ORA-00210: cannot open the specified control file
ORA-00202: control file: 'D:\APP\ORACLE\ORADATA\ORCL11G\CONTROL02.CTL'
ORA-27041: unable to open file
OSD-04002: unable to open file
O/S-Error: (OS 2) The system cannot find the file specified.
Mon Fe:b 18 09:01:10 2008
Checker run found 1 new persistent data failures
ORA-205 signalled during: ALTER DATABASE     MOUNT...
```

To repair the damage, copy a surviving file (one of the files listed in the query against V$PARAMETER) over the damaged file (the file mentioned in the alert log).

This method of recovery, although it is manual, is usually the fastest. But be absolutely certain that you do not accidentally copy the damaged file over the good one. Do not laugh! It is very easy to make a mistake like that, particularly when working in a hurry.

Recovery from Loss of an Online Redo Log File Member

If your online redo log file groups are multiplexed, loss of a single member is not a problem. As long as there is at least one valid member of each online redo log file group, the database will continue running, and if it is shut down, it will open without a problem. But Oracle will not be happy: there will be many messages written out to the alert log.

A missing redo log file member will not be reported by the Server Alert system.

The situation where all members of a group are lost (in which case the instance will abort and cannot be opened) is beyond the scope of the first OCP examination, though it is tested extensively in the second examination.

To confirm whether the online redo log file members are multiplexed and to see the status of each file, run this query:

```
select * from v$logfile;
```

If any members have a STATUS of INVALID, you should take immediate action to correct the situation. The status STALE may be reported—this is not a problem;

it only shows that the file has not yet been used. To repair a damaged member, the simplest technique is to use the CLEAR command. This will instruct Oracle to delete and recreate all the members of log file group 3:

```
alter database clear logfile group 3;
```

watch *Damage to online redo log file members will not cause the instance to abort or prevent opening the database, as long as there is at least one functioning member for each group.*

If the log file group is current, active, or (in archivelog mode) unarchived, the CLEAR will fail with an appropriate error message. These commands will fix these issues:

```
alter system switch logfile;
alter system checkpoint;
alter system archive log all;
```

Loss of Any Datafile in Noarchivelog Mode

In noarchivelog mode, there can be no concept of recovery: the redo needed to bring a restored backup forward in time isn't available. It is not possible to open a database with a datafile that is out of date. If it were, the integrity of the system would be compromised. So if any file is

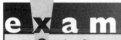

watch *In noarchivelog mode, the only restore possible is of the whole database. There can be no recovery.*

damaged, the only options are to instruct Oracle never to look for the file again by dropping the tablespace of which it is a part, or to restore the entire database: the complete set of datafiles and the controlfile from the last backup. If you have the online redo log files as well (which you will usually have if you are doing user-managed backups), restore these too and open the database. If you do not have backups of the online redo log files, recreate them by opening the database with this command:

```
alter database open resetlogs;
```

Loss of a Datafile in Archivelog Mode

The datafiles that make up the SYSTEM and UNDO tablespaces are *critical*. If any of these is damaged while the database is open, it will abort. The other datafiles are *non-critical*: the database will take them offline automatically, and the database will remain open. If the database is shut down, if the damaged or missing datafile is critical it will not be possible to open the database until it has been restored and recovered. If the datafile is non-critical, it must be taken offline manually before the database can be opened, and then it can be restored and recovered while the database is open.

During the period that the database is open but a non-critical file is offline, applications may behave in unexpected ways. Any indexes with extents in the offline file will be unusable, which can lead to performance degradation and also table locks caused by the impossibility of checking constraints. Any tables with extents in the offline file will be unusable—though queries that can be satisfied with columns included in indexes may still work.

To diagnose damage to datafiles, run this query in either mount or open mode:

```
select name,online_status,error
from v$datafile join v$recover_file using (file#);
```

If the database is shut down, the steps to repair a damaged non-critical datafile are

- Mount the database.
- Take the damaged file(s) offline.
- Open the database.
- Restore the damaged file(s).
- Recover it (them).
- Bring the damaged file(s) online.

Step 3 could be postponed to the end if you don't mind prolonging the period of downtime. If the database is open, only the last three steps are necessary.

Damage to a critical datafile can only be repaired in mount mode, so there are four steps:

- Mount the database.
- Restore the damaged file(s).
- Recover it (them).
- Open the database.

The Health Monitor and the ADR

The Health Monitor is a set of checks that run automatically when certain error conditions arise, or manually in response to the DBA's instructions. The results of the checks are not stored in the database, but in the file system. This is because the nature of some errors is such that the database is not available: it is therefore essential to have an external repository for the Health Monitor results. This repository is the ADR, which is located in the directory specified by the DIAGNOSTIC_DEST instance parameter.

Different Health Monitor checks can run only at various stages:

- In nomount mode, only the "DB Structure Integrity" check can run, and it can only check the integrity of the controlfile.

- In mount mode, the "DB Structure Integrity" check will check the integrity of the controlfile, and of the online redo log file and the datafile headers. The "Redo Integrity Check" can also run, which will check the online and archive log files for accessibility and corruption.

- In open mode, it is possible to run checks that will scan every data block for corruption, and check the integrity of the data dictionary and the undo segments.

The interfaces that will allow manual running of Health Monitor checks are available only when the database is open. There are two interfaces: using SQL*Plus to invoke procedures in the DBMS_HM PL/SQL package, and Database Control. Figure 17-1 shows the Database Control interface. To reach this window, from the database home page take the Advisor Central link in the Related Links section, and then the Checkers tab.

From the window shown in Figure 17-1, you can see the results of all Health Monitor runs (runs in reaction to errors and manual runs) and also run checks on demand.

The Capabilities and Limitations of the DRA

The DRA can do nothing unless the instance is in nomount mode, or higher. It follows that it cannot assist if there is a problem with the initialization file. In nomount mode, it can diagnose problems with the controlfile and generate scripts to restore it, either by using an existing valid copy or (if none is available) by extracting a copy from a backup set—provided it can find one. Once the database

FIGURE 17-1

The Database
Control interface
to the Health
Monitor

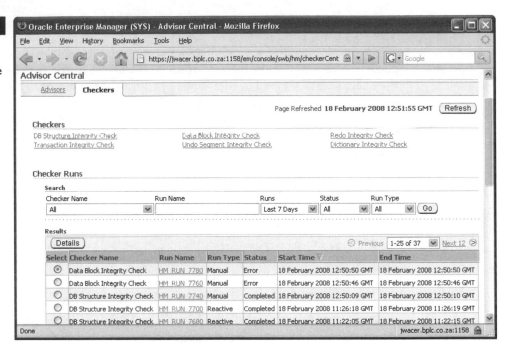

can reach mount mode, the DRA can diagnose problems with missing or damaged datafiles and missing online log file groups, and generate repair scripts.

The DRA (in the current release) only supports single-instance databases. If a fault brings down a RAC database, you can mount it in single-instance mode, use the DRA to repair the damage, and then shut it down and reopen it in RAC mode. This technique may not be able to repair damage that is local to one instance. The DRA cannot repair failures on a primary database by using blocks or files from a standby database, and neither can it repair failures on a standby database.

*The DRA will only function
for a single-instance database. It cannot*
*work with a RAC clustered database, nor
with a Data Guard standby database.*

SCENARIO & SOLUTION

If there is extensive damage, can the DRA handle this? What if I lose a whole disk, and the disk contains a controlfile copy, and some datafiles, and some online redo log file members?	The DRA can handle this situation, but only in stages. The database won't mount, because of the controlfile problem: the DRA will generate a script to fix this. Then the database won't open because of the datafile problem: run DRA again, and it will generate a script to fix this. If a whole online log file group is gone, the script will fix that too—but it won't do anything about a individual log file group member if the group is still functioning.
Is it better to rely on the Health Monitor and the DRA, or to do things by hand?	The Health Monitor will pick up errors—but you should be watching for them anyway. The DRA will fix them— but not necessarily in the most efficient manner. They won't make mistakes, but sometimes you can do better. So use these facilities, but always run your own checks as well, and always consider whether the advice is the best.

EXERCISE 17-1

Use the DRA to Diagnose and Advise Upon Problems

In this exercise, you will cause a problem with the database, and use the DRA to report on it.

1. From an operating system prompt, launch the RMAN executable:

```
rman target /
```

2. Confirm that there is a whole full backup of the SYSAUX tablespace:

```
list backup of tablespace sysaux;
```

If this does not return at least one backup set of type FULL, repeat Exercise 16-2, Steps 6–8.

3. Shut down the instance and exit from RMAN:

```
shutdown immediate;
exit;
```

4. Using an operating system utility, delete the datafile(s) for the SYSAUX tablespace that were listed in Step 2. If using Windows, you may have to stop the Windows service under which the instance is running to release the Windows file lock before the deletion is possible.

5. Connect to the database with SQL*Plus, and attempt a startup:

   ```
   startup;
   ```

   This will stop in mount mode, with an error regarding the missing file. If using Windows, make sure the service has been started.

6. Launch the RMAN executable and connect, as in Step 1.

7. Diagnose the problem:

   ```
   list failure;
   ```

   This will return a message to the effect that one or more non-system datafiles are missing.

8. Generate advice on the failure:

   ```
   advise failure;
   ```

   This will suggest that you should restore and recover the datafile, and generate a repair script. Open the script with any operating system editor, and study its contents.

CERTIFICATION OBJECTIVE 17.02

Use Data Recovery Advisor to Perform Recovery (Control File, Redo Log File, and Data File)

The DRA makes use of information gathered by the Health Monitor to find problems, and then it constructs RMAN scripts to repair them. As with any RMAN-based utility, the instance must be started. To start an instance in nomount mode, all that is required is a parameter file. RMAN is in fact capable of starting an instance without a parameter file, using the ORACLE_SID environment variable as a default for the one parameter for which there is no default value: the DB_NAME parameter. This ability may mean that is possible to bootstrap a restore and recovery operation from nothing.

The flow for using the DRA is as follows:

- **Assess data failures** The Health Monitor, running reactively or on demand, will write error details to the ADR.
- **List failures** The DRA will list all failures, classified according to severity.

- **Advise on repair**   The DRA will generate RMAN scripts to repair the damage.
- **Execute repair**   Run the scripts.

The commands can be run from the RMAN executable, or through Database Control. The advice will only be generated for errors previously listed and still open. No advice will be generated for additional errors that have occurred since the listing, or for errors fixed since the listing.

If one or more failures exist, then you should typically use `LIST FAILURE` *to show information about the failures and then use* `ADVISE FAILURE` *in the same RMAN session to obtain a report of your repair options. Finally,* `REPAIR FAILURE` *will fix the problem.*

Figure 17-2 shows a DRA session, launched from the RMAN executable. The situation is that the instance started and mounted the database, but failed to open.

The first command in the figure launches the RMAN executable, from an operating system prompt. The connection succeeds, but RMAN reports that the database is not open.

The second command lists all current failures: there is one non-system datafile missing. If this step were omitted, the next step would not return anything.

The third command generates advice on fixing the failure. The first suggestion is that some error by the system administrators could be responsible for the problem and could be fixed manually. Then there is an automatic repair involving restore

INSIDE THE EXAM

Restore and Recovery

Restore and recovery are topics of vital importance, but for the first OCP examination they are dealt with only superficially. Candidates will be expected to understand the concepts and the basic techniques: what can be done in noarchivelog and in archivelog modes, and the effects of damage to the various database file types. The practicalities of restore and recovery are unlikely to be tested.

An understanding of the capabilities of the DRA will be expected, and the flow of list-to-advise-to-repair.

FIGURE 17-2

A DRA
session, using
the Recovery
Manager

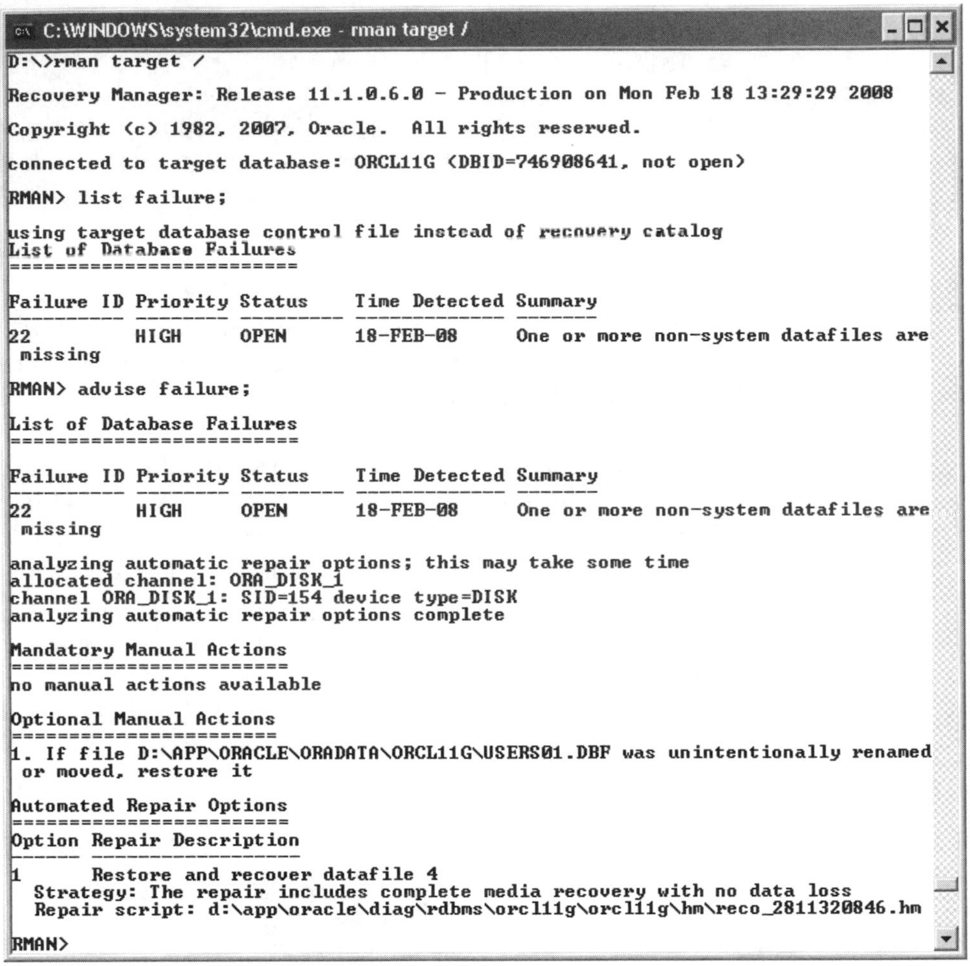

```
C:\WINDOWS\system32\cmd.exe - rman target /                              - □ x

D:\>rman target /

Recovery Manager: Release 11.1.0.6.0 - Production on Mon Feb 18 13:29:29 2008

Copyright (c) 1982, 2007, Oracle.  All rights reserved.

connected to target database: ORCL11G (DBID=746908641, not open)

RMAN> list failure;

using target database control file instead of recovery catalog
List of Database Failures
=========================

Failure ID Priority Status    Time Detected  Summary
---------- -------- ------    -------------  -------
22         HIGH     OPEN      18-FEB-08      One or more non-system datafiles are
 missing

RMAN> advise failure;

List of Database Failures
=========================

Failure ID Priority Status    Time Detected  Summary
---------- -------- ------    -------------  -------
22         HIGH     OPEN      18-FEB-08      One or more non-system datafiles are
 missing

analyzing automatic repair options; this may take some time
allocated channel: ORA_DISK_1
channel ORA_DISK_1: SID=154 device type=DISK
analyzing automatic repair options complete

Mandatory Manual Actions
========================
no manual actions available

Optional Manual Actions
=======================
1. If file D:\APP\ORACLE\ORADATA\ORCL11G\USERS01.DBF was unintentionally renamed
 or moved, restore it

Automated Repair Options
========================
Option Repair Description
------ ------------------
1      Restore and recover datafile 4
  Strategy: The repair includes complete media recovery with no data loss
  Repair script: d:\app\oracle\diag\rdbms\orcl11g\orcl11g\hm\reco_2811320846.hm

RMAN>
```

and recovery. This is in the form of an RMAN script. The contents of the script (not shown in the figure) were:

```
# restore and recover datafile
restore datafile 4;
recover datafile 4;
```

To run the script, the command would be

```
repair failure;
```

Following this, the database could be opened.

on the

ó ob

The DRA works, but you can often do better. For example, it does not generate scripts that will minimize downtime by opening the database before doing the restore and recovery (which would be possible in the example).

e x a m

ⓦatch

The DRA will not generate any advice if you have not first asked it to list failures. Any failures occurring since the last listing, or fixed since the last listing, will not be advised upon.

On connecting with Database Control to a damaged database, there will always be a button named Perform Recovery. Figure 17-3 shows the window this will produce for the same situation shown in Figure 17-2.

The Information section seen in Figure 17-3 shows that there is one failure, and that the database is mounted. The Advise And Recover button will launch a wizard that will list details of the failure, generate the repair script, and then submit it as a job to the Enterprise Manager job system, and finally prompt for opening the database.

The DRA can generate scripts to restore a missing or damaged controlfile copy and to rebuild a missing online log file group and to restore and recovery missing or damaged datafiles. It will not take any action if a member of a multiplexed log file group is damaged.

FIGURE 17-3

The Database Control interface to the DRA

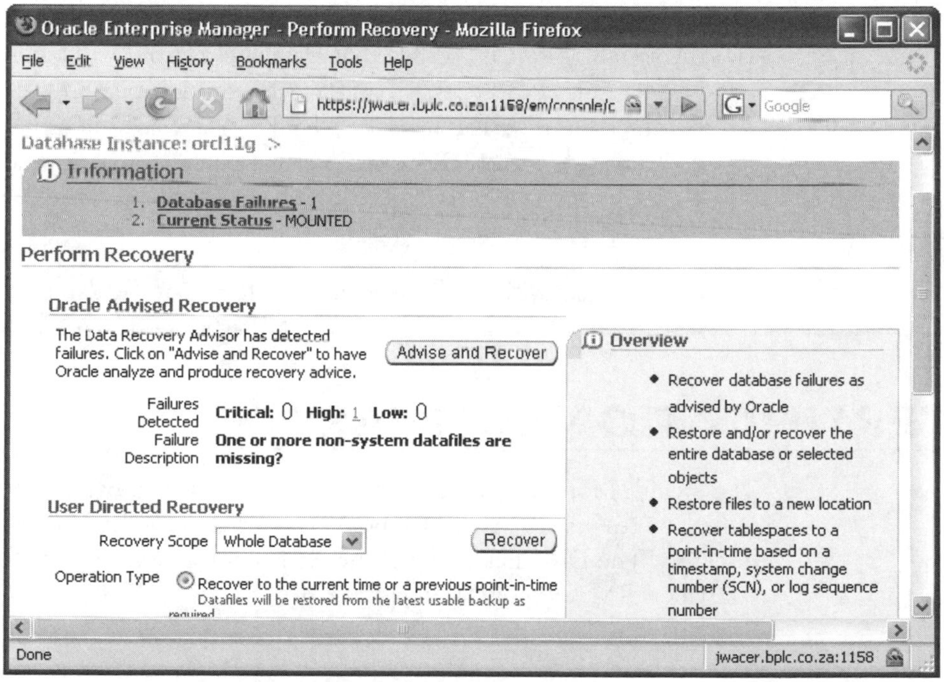

EXERCISE 17-2

Repair a Fault with the DRA

In this exercise, you will diagnose and repair the problem caused in Exercise 17-1 using Database Control.

1. Using a browser, attempt to connect to Database Control. This will present a window stating that the database is mounted, with buttons for Startup and Perform Recovery.

2. Click the Startup button. Enter operating system and database credentials and follow the prompts to open the database. This will fail, so click the Perform Recovery button.

3. In the Perform Recovery window, click the Advise And Repair button to enter the DRA Wizard.

4. In the View And Manage Failures window, click Advise.

5. In the Manual Actions window, click Continue With Advice.

6. In the Recovery Advice window, observe the script and click Continue.

7. In the Review window, click Submit Recovery Job.

8. When the job completes, use either Database Control or SQL*Plus to open the database. It is possible that Database Control will have gotten confused as a result of this exercise, and may have trouble determining what state the database is in. If this appears to be the case, close the browser and restart the Database Control processes. From an operating system prompt:

```
emctl stop dbconsole;
emctl start dbconsole;
```

Reconnect with the browser, and confirm that the database is now open.

CERTIFICATION SUMMARY

The Health Monitor is a set of checks that run automatically when error conditions arise. The results are written to the ADR, stored in the DIAGNOSTIC_DEST directory. The DRA makes use of the ADR information to identify failures, and then constructs RMAN scripts to repair them.

TWO-MINUTE DRILL

Overview of Data Recovery Advisor

❑ The ADR is a set of files in the DIAGNOSTIC_DEST directory.

❑ The DRA can repair damage to datafiles and controlfile, and replace missing log file groups.

❑ Restore and recovery of the controlfile or a critical datafile can be done only in mount mode.

❑ Restore and recovery of a non-critical datafile can be done while the database is open.

Use Data Recovery Advisor to Perform Recovery (Control File, Redo Log File, and Data File)

❑ Failures must be listed before they can be advised upon.

❑ The DRA can be accessed through the RMAN executable or with Enterprise Manager.

❑ The DRA is available in all modes: in nomount mode it can repair the controlfile; in mount or open mode it can repair datafiles.

SELF TEST

Overview of Data Recovery Advisor

1. Loss of which of these files will cause an open database to crash? (Choose all correct answers.)
   A. A multiplexed controlfile
   B. A multiplexed online log file
   C. A multiplexed archive log file
   D. An active undo tablespace datafile
   E. An active temporary tablespace tempfile
   F. A datafile from the SYSAUX tablespace
   G. A datafile from the SYSTEM tablespace
   H. A datafile containing critical user data

2. You issue the command ALTER DATABASE CLEAR LOGFILE GROUP 2, and it fails with the message "ORA-01624: log 2 needed for crash recovery of instance orcl11g (thread 1)." What could be an explanation for this? (Choose the best answer.)
   A. Log file group 2 has not been archived.
   B. Log file group 2 is being used for recovery.
   C. The database has not been checkpointed.
   D. The group is not multiplexed.

3. Your database is in noarchivelog mode, and you lose a non-critical datafile. What can you do to minimize loss of data? (Choose the best answer.)
   A. Restore the one damaged file, and leave the rest of the database up to date.
   B. Restore all the datafiles, but leave the controlfile up to date.
   C. Restore the whole database, and clear the online redo logs.
   D. Restore the one damaged file, and apply the online redo logs.

4. In noarchivelog mode, what restore and recover options are available to you? (Choose all correct answers.)
   A. Whole database restore
   B. Partial restore
   C. Online restore of non-critical datafiles
   D. Offline restore of critical datafiles
   E. Automatic recovery after an instance crash

5. What sequence will allow you to add a multiplexed controlfile copy? (Choose the best answer.)

    1: Adjust the CONTROL_FILES parameter.

    2: Copy the controlfile.

    3: Mount the database.

    4: Open the database.

    5: Recover the controlfile.

    6: Recover the database.

    7: Shut down the database.

    A. 7, 2, 1, 3, 4 (5 and 6 not necessary)

    B. 7, 1, 3, 2, 6, 4 (5 not necessary)

    C. 2, 1, 5 (3, 4, 6 and 7 not necessary)

    D. 7, 1, 6, 3, 4 (2 and 5 not necessary)

Use Data Recovery Advisor to Perform Recovery (Control File, Redo Log File, and Data File)

6. These are three DRA commands:

    ADVISE FAILURE;

    LIST FAILURE;

    REPAIR FAILURE;

    In what order must they be run in to fix a problem? (Choose the best answer.)

    A. ADVISE, LIST, REPAIR

    B. LIST, ADVISE, REPAIR

    C. LIST, REPAIR (ADVISE is not necessary)

    D. ADVISE, REPAIR (LIST is not necessary)

7. On what type or state of database can the DRA not be used? (Choose all correct answers.)

    A. A single-instance database that is shut down

    B. A single-instance database in nomount mode

    C. A single-instance database in mount mode

    D. An open RAC database

    E. A mounted standby database

8. Where is the ADR stored? (Choose the best answer.)

    A. In the Automatic Workload Repository

    B. In the SYSAUX tablespace

     C. In the data dictionary

     D. In operating system files

     E. In the Enterprise Manager repository

9. If you issue the LIST FAILURE command with the DRA and then another failure occurs, when you run ADVISE FAILURE for what will you receive advice? (Choose the best answer.)

     A. For the original failures only

     B. For the new failure only

     C. For all the failures

     D. For none of the failures until you run a new LIST FAILURES

10. Which file types can be repaired while the database is open? (Choose the best answer.)

     A. A damaged multiplexed controlfile copy

     B. A current multiplexed online log file

     C. A damaged non-critical datafile, if the database is in archivelog mode

     D. All of the above, if the DRA is used and server-managed backups are available

LAB QUESTION

Prepare for this extended exercise by taking a full backup of the database with RMAN. Run this backup from the RMAN command line or as a Database Control scheduled job, but be absolutely certain that you do have a backup. Also confirm that you have at least two copies of the controlfile, and that your online redo log files are multiplexed.

Abort the database and simulate a major failure by deleting a datafile and a controlfile copy and a redo log file member.

Repair the situation, using the DRA if you want. To begin with, the instance will not be able to mount the database. In nomount mode, the DRA will be able to generate a script to copy a surviving controlfile to the missing location. If not using the DRA, copy it by hand. The database can then be mounted but will not open until the missing datafile has been restored and recovered. The missing online redo log file member can be replaced by clearing the log file group after the database has been opened.

SELF TEST ANSWERS

Overview of Data Recovery Advisor

1. ☑ **A, D,** and **G.** If any files of these types is lost, the instance will abort immediately.
   ☒ **B** is wrong because the whole purpose of multiplexing the redo log is to survive a failure. **C** is wrong because nothing that happens to an archived log file can affect the instance. **E, F,** and **H** are wrong because the instance can take these file types offline automatically and so remain open.

2. ☑ **C.** A log file group will remain active until the checkpoint position has advanced through it, and it cannot be cleared until this has happened.
   ☒ **A** is wrong because this would give a different error message. **B** is wrong because the message does not indicate that file is being used for recovery, but that it would be needed for recovery. **D** is wrong because multiplexing is not relevant to the status of the log file member.

3. ☑ **C.** This is the sequence for restoring a database in noarchivelog mode.
   ☒ **A** and **B** are wrong because both options would result in a database with unsynchronized files that could not be opened. **D** is wrong because recovery cannot be done in noarchivelog mode.

4. ☑ **A** and **E.** The only option for restore is a complete restore, and instance recovery is always available.
   ☒ **B, C,** and **D.** These are all partial restores, which are not possible in noarchivelog mode.

5. ☑ **A.** This is the only valid sequence.
   ☒ **B** is wrong because the controlfile must be copied before it can be mounted. **C** is wrong because controlfile copies cannot be added without downtime (and there no such command as "recover controlfile"). **D** is wrong because a database recovery will not generate a controlfile—though a restore could.

Use Data Recovery Advisor to Perform Recovery
(Control File, Redo Log File, and Data File)

6. ☑ **B.** This is the only sequence that will work.
   ☒ **A** is wrong because the sequence is incorrect. **C** is wrong because ADVISE is necessary to generate the repair script. **D** is wrong because LIST is necessary to identify the problem.

7. ☑ **A, D,** and **E.** The DRA can only work with single-instance databases, with the instance running.
   ☒ **B** and **C.** These are wrong because the DRA can work on a single-instance database, so long as the instance is running.

8. ☑ **D.** The ADR resides in files in the DIAGNOSTIC_DEST directory.
   ☒ **A, B,** and **C** are wrong because they all imply storage within the database, which is not correct. **E** is wrong because although Enterprise Manager can read the ADR, it does not manage it.

9. ☑ **A.** The already populated list of failures will be used for generating advice.
   ☒ **B** and **C** are wrong because the new failure will not be in the list and so will not be advised upon. **D** is wrong because the generated list is still valid—just out of date.

10. ☑ **C.** A non-critical datafile can be restored and recovered in open mode.
    ☒ **A** is wrong because controlfile damage will always abort the instance. **B** is wrong because members of the current group cannot be repaired. **D** is wrong because unfortunately not even the DRA can do everything.

LAB ANSWER

If using Database Control, the wizard should walk you through the whole process—except the online log file member repair.

If using command-line utilities, once in nomount mode connect with RMAN. Use LIST FAILURE, ADVISE FAILURE, and REPAIR FAILURE. At this stage, this will only detect and repair the controlfile problem, but you can now mount the database. Repeat the LIST-ADVISE-REPAIR cycle to repair the datafile damage, and open the database.

Finally, clear the damaged log file group to rebuild the missing member.

If you find that your database cannot be recovered no matter what you try, the last resort is a full restore. From the RMAN prompt, use these commands:

```
restore database force;
recover database;
```

In the real world, this would be a bad option because of the downtime involved in a complete restore.

18

Moving Data

CERTIFICATION OBJECTIVES

Th.ere are many situations where bulk transfers of data into a database or between databases are necessary. Common cases are populating a data warehouse with data extracted from transaction processing systems, or copying data from live systems to test or development environments. As entering data with standard INSERT statements is not always the best way to do large-scale operations, the Oracle database comes with facilities for designed for bulk operations. These are SQL*Loader and Data Pump. There is also the possibility of reading data without ever actually inserting it into the database; this is accomplished through use of external tables.

Describe and Use Methods to Move Data (SQL Loader, Directory Objects, External Tables)

SQL*Loader is a tool for inserting data into an Oracle database. There are restrictions on the layout of the data, but SQL*Loader can be configured to read a wide variety of formats. It is user process, which establishes a session against the database. Use of external tables lets data in SQL*Loader–compatible files be read interactively by sessions, as though the data were stored in an internal table. It is also possible to write data out to an external table. Directory objects are required when using external tables (and also when using Data Pump, dealt with in a later section) to provide a layer of abstraction between the storage of the source data by the operating system, and the reading of the data by the Oracle database sessions.

SQL*Loader

In many cases, you will be faced with a need to do a bulk upload of datasets generated from some third-party system. This is the purpose of SQL*Loader. The input files may be generated by anything, but as long as the layout conforms to something that SQL*Loader can understand, it will upload the data successfully. Your task as DBA is to configure a SQL*Loader control file that can interpret the contents of the input data files; SQL*Loader will then insert the data.

Architecturally, SQL*Loader is a user process like any other: it connects to the database via a server process. To insert rows, it can use two techniques: *conventional* or *direct* path. A conventional insert uses absolutely ordinary INSERT statements. The SQL*Loader user process constructs an INSERT statement with bind variables in the VALUES clause and then reads its source data file to execute the INSERT once for each row to be inserted. This method uses the database buffer cache and generates undo and redo data: these are INSERT statements like any others, and normal commit processing makes them permanent.

The direct path bypasses the database buffer cache. SQL*Loader reads the source data file and sends its contents to the server process. The server process then assembles blocks of table data in its PGA and writes them directly to the datafiles. The write is above the *high water mark* of the table and is known as a *data save*. The high water mark is a marker in the table segment above which no data has ever been written: the space above the high water mark is space allocated to the table that has not yet been used. Once the load is complete, SQL*Loader shifts the high water markup to include the newly written blocks, and the rows within them are then immediately visible to other users. This is the equivalent of a COMMIT. No undo is generated, and if you wish, you can switch off the generation of redo as well. For these reasons, direct path loading is extremely fast, and furthermore it should not impact on your end users, because interaction with the SGA is kept to a minimum.

Direct path loads are very fast, but they do have drawbacks:

- Referential integrity constraints must be dropped or disabled for the duration of the operation.
- Insert triggers do not fire.
- The table will be locked against DML from other sessions.
- It is not possible to use direct path for clustered tables.

These limitations are a result of the lack of interaction with the SGA while the load is in progress.

exam

ⓦatch Only UNIQUE, PRIMARY KEY, and NOT NULL constraints can be enforced by a direct path load; INSERT triggers do not fire; the table is locked for DML.

SQL*Loader uses a number of files. The *input data files* are the source data that it will upload into the database. The *control file* is a text file with directives telling SQL*Loader how to interpret the contents of the input files, and what to do with the rows it extracts from them. *Log files* summarize the success (or otherwise) of the job, with detail of any errors. Rows extracted from the input files may be rejected by SQL*Loader (perhaps because they do not conform to the format expected by the control file) or by the database (for instance, insertion might violate an integrity constraint); in either case they are written out to a *bad file*. If rows are successfully extracted from the input but rejected because they did not match some record selection criterion, they are written out to a *reject file*.

The control file is a text file instructing SQL*Loader on how to process the input data files. It is possible to include the actual data to be loaded on the control file, but you would not normally do this; usually, you will create one control file and reuse it, on a regular basis, with different input data files. The variety of input formats that SQL*Loader can understand is limited only by your ingenuity in constructing a control file.

Consider this table:

```
SQL> desc dept;
 Name                                      Null?    Type
 ---------------------------------------- -------- ---------------
 DEPTNO                                    NOT NULL NUMBER(2)
 DNAME                                              VARCHAR2(14)
 LOC                                                VARCHAR2(13)
```

And this source data file, named DEPTS.TXT:

```
50, SUPPORT, LONDON
60, HR, OXFORD
70, EDUCATION
```

A SQL*Loader control file to load this data is DEPTS.CTL:

```
1       load data
2       infile 'depts.txt'
3       badfile 'depts.bad'
4       discardfile 'depts.dsc'
5       append
6       into table dept
7       fields terminated by ','
8       trailing nullcols
9       (deptno integer external(2),
10       dname,
11       loc)
```

To perform the load, from an operating system prompt run this command:

```
sqlldr userid=scott/tiger control=depts.ctl direct=true
```

This command launches the SQL*Loader user process, connects to the local database as user SCOTT password TIGER, and then performs the actions specified on the control file DEPTS.CTL. The DIRECT=TRUE argument instructs SQL*Loader to use the direct path rather than conventional insert (which is the default). Taking the control file line by line:

Line	Purpose
1	Start a new load operation.
2	Nominate the source of the data.
3	Nominate the file to write out any badly formatted records.
4	Nominate the file to write out any unselected records.
5	Add rows to the table (rather than, for example, truncating it first).
6, 7	Specify the field delimiter in the source file.
8	If there are missing fields, insert NULL values.
9, 10, 11	The columns into which to insert the data.

This is a very simple example. The syntax of the control file can handle a wide range of formats with intelligent parsing to fix any deviations in format such as length or data types. In general you can assume that it is possible to construct a control file that will understand just about any input data file. However, do not think that it is always easy.

on the **Job**

It may be very difficult to get a control file right, but once you have it, you can use it repeatedly, with different input data files for each run. It is then the responsibility of the feeder system to produce input data files that match your control file, rather than the other way around.

Directory Objects

In many applications it is necessary for a database session to read or write operating system files. The supplied PL/SQL package UTL_FILE has procedures for doing this. Using these procedures, programmers can specify an operating system directory (or a logical drive and directory on Windows systems) on the database server machine and open or create files, and read data from and write data to them. There are restrictions on the directories and files that can be opened in this way, but they are not very fine-grained.

The operating system directories that can be accessed by UTL_FILE are only those listed in UTL_FILE_DIR instance parameter. This parameter defaults to NULL (meaning that no directories can be accessed) but would usually be set to a comma-separated list of all the directories where such access is necessary. It is possible to use a "*" wildcard, which means that every directory on the server will be accessible. It is not possible to limit access to particular users: the UTL_FILE_DIR parameter is a system-level parameter, and once set all the directories listed will be visible to all sessions. The operating system itself will enforce some security: only those directories and files which are accessible to the operating system user who owns the Oracle instance will be accessible.

Setting UTL_FILE_DIR to "*" can be a serious security risk.

If the parameter is set as follows:

```
alter system set utl_file_dir='/tmp' scope = spfile;
```

then any user with execute permission on the UTL_FILE package (which is everyone, because EXCUTE on UTL_FILE is by default granted to PUBLIC) will be able to work with files in the /tmp directory. Note the use of the SCOPE=SPFILE clause: the parameter is a static parameter and so cannot be changed without restarting the instance. This is to give a measure of auditability to such changes, as they have security implications.

Oracle directories give a layer of abstraction between the user and the operating system: you as DBA create a directory within the database, which points to a physical path. Permissions on these Oracle directories can then be granted to individual users. This gives much more finely grained access control than the UTL_FILE_DIR parameter. At the operating system level, the Oracle user will need permissions against the operating system directories to which the Oracle directories refer.

Directories can be created either from a SQL*Plus prompt or from within Database Control. To see information about directories, query the view DBA_DIRECTORIES. Each directory has a name, an owner, and the physical path to which it refers. Note that Oracle does not verify whether the path exists when you create the directory—if it does not, or if the operating system user who owns the Oracle software does not

exam @atch *Directories are always owned by user SYS, but to create them you must have been granted the appropriate privilege.*

have permission to read and write to it, you will only get an error when you actually use the directory. Having created a directory, you must give the Oracle user who will be running Data Pump permission to read from and write to it, just as your system administrators must give the operating system user permission to read from and write to the physical path.

Figure 18-1 demonstrates how to create directories, using SQL*Plus. In the figure, user SCOTT attempts to create a directory pointing to his operating system home directory on the database server machine. This fails because, by default, users do not have permission to do this. After being granted permission, he tries again. As the directory creator, he will have full privileges on the directory. He then grants read permission on the directory (and therefore any files within it) to all users, and write permission to one user. The query against ALL_DIRECTORIES shows that the directory (like all directories) is owned by SYS: directories are not schema objects. This is why SCOTT cannot drop the directory, even though he created it.

FIGURE 18-1

Creating
directories with
SQL*Plus

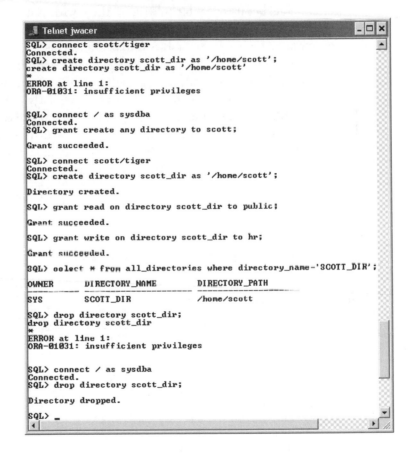

Directory objects can be used by the UTL_FILE procedures, and they are also a requirement for external tables and for the Data Pump utility.

External Tables

Tables are usually stored as segments within a database, but it is also possible to use *external* tables. An external table exists as an object defined in the data dictionary, but not as a segment; the storage is an operating system file. External tables can be queried as any other table. It is not possible to execute DML operations against an external table, but it is possible to write to them with Data Pump. In all cases, access to external tables is through Oracle directories.

A common use of external tables is to avoid the necessity to use SQL*Loader to read tables into the database. This can give huge savings in the ETL (extract-transform-load) cycle typically used to update a DSS system with data from a feeder system. Consider the case where a feeder system regularly generates a dataset as a flat ASCII file, which should be merged into existing database tables. One approach would be to use SQL*Loader to load the data into a staging table, and then a separate routine to merge the rows from the staging table into the DSS tables. This second routine cannot start until the load is finished. Using external tables, the merge routine can read the source data from the operating system file(s) without having to wait for it to be loaded.

To create an external table, use the CRATE TABLE command with the keywords ORGANIZATION EXTERNAL. These tell Oracle that the table does not exist as a segment. Then specify the layout and location of the operating system file. For example,

```
create table new_dept
  (deptno number(2),
  dname varchar2(14),
  loc varchar2(13))
organization external (
  type oracle_loader
  default directory scott_dir
  access parameters
    (records delimited by newline
    badfile 'depts.bad'
    discardfile 'depts.dsc'
    logfile 'depts.log'
    fields terminated by ','
    missing field values are null)
  location ('depts.txt'));
```

This command will create an external table that will be populated by the DEPTS. TXT file shown in the section "SQL*Loader" earlier in this chapter. The syntax for the ACCESS PARAMETERS is virtually identical to the SQL*Loader control file syntax and is used because the TYPE has been set to ORACLE_LOADER. The specification for the DEFAULT DIRECTORY gives the Oracle directory where Oracle will look for the source data file, and where it will write the log and other files.

External tables can be queried in exactly the same way as internal tables. They can be used in joins, views, and subqueries. They cannot have indexes, and (as they cannot be written to with DML commands) they do not have constraints or triggers.

It is possible to write to an external table with Data Pump. This can only be done as part of a CREATE TABLE . . . AS SELECT . . . operation. For example,

```
create table dept_ext (deptno, dname)
  organization external (
  type oracle_datapump
  default directory scott_dir
  location ('dept_ext.dp'))
as select deptno,dname from dept;
```

SCENARIO & SOLUTION

I need to transfer large volumes of data on a regular basis into an Oracle database from a third-party database. What options do I have?	You only have one supplied tool: SQL*Loader. This can read virtually any format but can be very difficult to set up. But you have no option: it is the only tool. You do have an option with how to use it: direct path load or conventional load. The former will be faster, but the target tables will be locked while the load is in progress, and therefore the application may not be usable. This is not a decision you can take: it is up to your end users to decide whether they are more concerned about speed or uptime.
If I can read external tables or load them SQL*Loader, which should I use?	If speed is of the essence, then external tables are probably better because they can cut out a whole stage of the ETL cycle. But SQL*Loader is a very powerful and has excellent facilities for "cleaning" data as it is processed. So there is no straight answer—keep an open mind.

The specification for the TYPE is DATAPUMP. This is the only permitted value; it instructs Oracle to write out the data in the Data Pump format. Once generated, the table can be queried as though it were an internal table, or copied to another system and queried there.

Use SQL*Loader and External Tables

In this exercise, you will install use SQL*Loader to insert data into a table, and also to generate the CREATE TABLE script for an external table.

1. Connect to your database as user SYSTEM (in the examples, the SYSTEM password is ORACLE) with SQL*Plus.

2. Create a table to use for the exercise:

```
create table names(first varchar2(10),last varchar2(10));
```

3. Using any editor that will create plain text files, create a file `names.txt` with these values (or similar):

```
John,Watson
Roopesh,Ramklass
Sam,Alapati
```

4. Using the editor, create a control file `names.ctl` with these settings:

```
load data
infile 'names.txt'
badfile 'names.bad'
truncate
into table names
fields terminated by ','
trailing nullcols
(first,last)
```

This control will truncate the target file before carrying out the insert.

5. From an operating system prompt, run SQL*Loader as follows:

```
sqlldr system/oracle control=names.ctl
```

6. Study the log file `names.log` that will have been generated.

7. With SQL*Plus, confirm that the rows have been inserted:

```
select * from names;
```

8. To generate a statement that will create an external table, you can use SQL*Loader and an existing control file:

```
sqlldr userid=system/oracle control=names.ctl external_
table=generate_only
```

9. This will have generated another log file, `names.log`, which will include a create table statement, something like this:

```
CREATE TABLE "SYS_SQLLDR_X_EXT_NAMES"
(
  "FIRST" VARCHAR2(10),
  "LAST" VARCHAR2(10)
)
ORGANIZATION external
(
  TYPE oracle_loader
  DEFAULT DIRECTORY SYS_SQLLDR_XT_TMPDIR_00000
  ACCESS PARAMETERS
  (
    RECORDS DELIMITED BY NEWLINE CHARACTERSET WE8MSWIN1252
    BADFILE 'SYS_SQLLDR_XT_TMPDIR_00000':'names.bad'
    LOGFILE 'names.log_xt'
    READSIZE 1048576
    FIELDS TERMINATED BY "," LDRTRIM
    MISSING FIELD VALUES ARE NULL
    REJECT ROWS WITH ALL NULL FIELDS
    (
      "FIRST" CHAR(255)
        TERMINATED BY ",",
      "LAST" CHAR(255)
        TERMINATED BY ","
    )
  )
  location
  (
    'names.txt'
  )
)REJECT LIMIT UNLIMITED
```

10. From your SQL*Plus session, create an Oracle directory pointing to the operating system directory where your `names.txt` file is. For example,

```
create directory system_dmp as '/home/oracle';
```

11. Make any edits you wish to the command shown in Step 9. For example, you might want to change the name of the table being created ("SYS_SQLLDR_X_EXT_NAMES" isn't very useful) to something more meaningful. You will need to change both the DEFAULT DIRECTORY and BADFILE settings to point to the directory created in Step 10.

12. Run the statement created in Step 11 from your SQL*Plus session.

13. Query the table with a few SELECT and DML statements. You will find that a log file is generated for every SELECT, and that DML is not permitted.

14. Tidy up: delete the `names.txt` and `names.ctl` files; drop the tables.

INSIDE THE EXAM

Moving Data

Using the SQL DML commands is not always the best technique for moving large amounts of data. Two characteristics in particular may make them inappropriate for large-scale data insertion: they are always run in a client-server model and they always generate redo and undo.

The client-server paradigm has the problem of network communications. Even if the user process that generates the SQL and the server process that executes the SQL are running on the same machine, all the data being inserted must be transmitted between them by a network protocol. Undo and redo generation are not a problem—they are a very necessary feature—but their generation does impose extra work on the database.

For large-scale data insertion, Oracle provides the SQL*Loader utility. This is a tool that can read data in a wide variety of formats and can insert it efficiently using the direct path (which largely bypasses the SGA) if desired. This method does not require undo generation, and redo can be switched off too. But it is still a client-server tool. The fastest possible way to insert data is Data Pump; this uses server-side processes and so bypasses the network communications issue. But Data Pump can only work with its own proprietary file format; SQL*Loader can read anything.

Explain the General Architecture of Oracle Data Pump

In the normal course of events, ordinary SELECT and DML commands are used to extract data from the database and to insert data into it, but there are occasions when you will need a much faster method for bulk operations. For many reasons it may be desirable to extract a large amount of data and the associated object definitions from a database in a form that will allow it to be easily loaded into another. One obvious purpose for extracting large amounts of data is for backups, but there are others, such as archiving of historical data before deleting it from the live system, or to transfer data between production and test environments, or between an online system and a data warehouse.

Data Pump and Export/Import

Historically, Oracle provided the Export and Import utilities. These were effective (and they are still available with release 11g), but they suffer from the limitation of being client-server tools; they are just user processes, like any other. The Export utility connects to the database via a server process and issues SELECT statements: the data retrieved by the server process is passed back to the Export user process, where it is formatted and written out to a disk file. Similarly, the Import utility user process logs onto the instance via a server process; then it reads the disk file produced by Export and constructs DDL and insert statements to create tables and load the data into them. Release 10g introduced the Data Pump facility. Functionally, the results are the same as the old Export/Import utilities: large amounts of data can be extracted from one database and transferred into another. But the implementation is totally different, and far superior. Note also that the Data Pump file format and the Export/Import file format are completely different: the old Import utility cannot read files generated with Data Pump, and Data Pump cannot read files generated by the old Export utility.

Syntactically, the operating system utilities to manage Data Pump have been kept as similar as possible to the Export and Import utilities. This is deliberate and is meant to encourage DBAs to move to the newer (and better) technique. However, there are enough differences that it is not realistic to expect scripts designed for one tool to work the other.

In most environments, it is not possible to use only Data Pump. There are two main reasons for this: first, Data Pump can only work with releases 10*g* and 11*g*. When it is necessary to transfer data between these releases and an older database, Export/Import is the only tool. Second, there is one thing that Export/Import can do but Data Pump cannot do: write to the operating system of the user process. This is a critical architectural difference: Export/Import are user processes that use files local to the user; Data Pump is a server-side facility that uses files on the database server.

on the job

The Export/Import utilities are not tested in the OCP examinations, but all DBAs should be familiar with them.

Data Pump Architecture

Data Pump is a server-side utility. You initiate Data Pump jobs from a user process, either SQL*Plus or through Enterprise Manager, but all the work is done by server processes. This improves performance dramatically over the old Export/Import utilities, because the Data Pump processes running on the server have direct access to the datafiles and the SGA; they do not have to go via a session. Also, it is possible to launch a Data Pump job and then detach from it, leaving it running in the background. You can reconnect to the job to monitor its progress at any time.

There are a number of processes involved in a Data Pump job, two queues, a number of files, and one table. First, the processes:

The user processes are expdp and impdp (for Unix) or expdp.exe and impdp.exe (Windows). These are used to launch, control, and monitor Data Pump jobs. Alternatively, there is an Enterprise Manager interface, more on which later. The expdp or impdp user process establishes a session against the database through a normal server process. This session then issues commands to control and monitor Data Pump jobs. When a Data Pump job is launched, at least two processes are started: a Data Pump Master process (the DMnn) and one or more worker processes (named DWnn). If multiple Data Pump jobs are running concurrently, each will have its own DMnn process, and its own DWnn processes. As the name implies, the master process controls the workers. If you have enabled parallelism, then each DWnn may make use of two or more parallel execution servers (named Pnnn).

Two queues are created for each Data Pump job: a control queue and a status queue. The DMnn divides up the work to be done and places individual tasks that make up the job on the control queue. The worker processes pick up these tasks and execute them—perhaps making use of parallel execution servers. This queue operates on a deliver-exactly-once model: messages are enqueued by the DMnn and dequeued by the worker that picks them up. The status queue is for monitoring purposes: the DMnn places messages on it describing the state of the job. This queue operates on a publish-and-subscribe model: any session (with appropriate privileges) can query the queue to monitor the job's progress.

The files generated by Data Pump come in three forms: SQL files, dump files, and log files. SQL files are DDL statements describing the objects included in the job. You can choose to generate them (without any data) as an easy way of getting this information out of the database, perhaps for documentation purposes or as a set of scripts to recreate the database. Dump files contain the exported data. This is formatted with XML tags. The use of XML means that there is a considerable overhead in dump files for describing the data. A small table like the REGIONS table in the HR sample schema will generate a 94 KB dump file, but while this overhead may seem disproportionately large for a tiny table like that, it becomes trivial for larger tables. The log files describe the history of the job run.

Lastly, there is the control table. This is created for you by the DMnn when you launch a job, and is used both to record the job's progress and to describe it. It is included in the dump file as the final item of the job.

Directories and File Locations

Data Pump always uses Oracle directories. These are needed to locate the files that it will read or write, and its log files. One directory is all that is needed, but often a job will use several. If the amount of data is many gigabytes to be written out in parallel to many files, you may want to spread the disk activity across directories in different file systems.

If a directory is not specified in the Data Pump command, there are defaults. Every 11g database will have an Oracle directory that can be used. This is named DATA_PUMP_DIR. If the environment variable ORACLE_BASE has been set at database creation time, the operating system directory will be the directory admin/*database_name*/dpdump beneath this. If ORACLE_BASE is not set, the directory will be admin/*database_name*/dpdump beneath the ORACLE_HOME directory (where *database_name* is the name of the database). To identify the location in your database, query the view DBA_DIRECTORIES. However, the fact that this Oracle directory exists does not mean it can be used; any user wishing to use Data Pump will have to be granted read and/or write permissions on it first.

Specifying the directory (or directories) to use for a Data Pump job can be done at four levels. In decreasing order of precedence, these are

- A per-file setting within the Data Pump job
- A parameter applied to the whole Data Pump job
- The DATA_PUMP_DIR environment variable
- The DATA_PUMP_DIR directory object

So it is possible to control the location of every file explicitly, or a single Oracle directory can be nominated for the job, or an environment variable can be used, or failing all of these Data Pump will use the default directory. The environment variable should be set on the client side but will be used on the server side. An example of setting it on Unix is

```
DATA_PUMP_DIR=SCOTT_DIR; export DATA_PUMP_DIR
```

or on Windows,

```
set DATA_PUMP_DIR=SCOTT_DIR
```

Direct Path or External Table Path?

Data Pump has two methods for loading and unloading data: the direct path and the external table path. The direct path bypasses the database buffer cache. For a direct path export, Data Pump reads the datafiles directly from disk, extracts and formats the content, and writes it out as a dump file. For a direct path import, Data Pump reads the dump file, uses its content to assemble blocks of table data, and writes them directly to the datafiles. The write is above the "high water mark" of the table. The high water mark is a marker in the table above which no data has ever been written. Once the load is complete, Data Pump shifts the high water mark up to include the newly written blocks, and the rows within them are then visible to other users. This is the equivalent of a COMMIT. No undo is generated, and if you wish, you can switch off the generation of redo as well. Direct path is therefore extremely fast, and furthermore it should not impact on your end users because interaction with the SGA is kept to a minimum.

The external table path uses the database buffer cache. Even though Data Pump is manipulating files that are external to the database, it uses the database buffer cache as though it were reading and writing an internal table. For an export, Data Pump reads blocks from the datafiles into the cache through a normal SELECT process.

From there, it formats the data for output to a dump file. During an import, Data Pump constructs standard insert statements from the content of the dump file and executes them by reading blocks from the datafiles into the cache, where the insert is carried out in the normal fashion. As far as the database is concerned, external table Data Pump jobs look like absolutely ordinary (though perhaps rather large) SELECT or INSERT operations. Both undo and redo are generated, as they would be for any normal DML statement. Your end users may well complain while these jobs are in progress. Commit processing is absolutely normal.

So what determines whether Data Pump uses the direct path or the external table path? You as DBA have no control; Data Pump itself makes the decision based on the complexity of the objects. Only simple structures, such as heap tables without active triggers, can be processed through the direct path; more complex objects such as clustered tables force Data Pump to use the external table path because it requires interaction with the SGA in order to resolve the complexities. In either case, the dump file generated is identical.

EXERCISE 18-2

Perform a Data Pump Export

In this exercise, you will carry out a Data Pump export using Database Control.

1. Connect to your database as user SYSTEM with SQL*Plus, and create a table to use for the exercise:

   ```
   create table ex182 as select * from all_users;
   ```

2. Connect to your database as user SYSTEM with Database Control. Navigate to the Export Wizard: take the Data Movement tab from the database home page, then the Export To Export Files link in the Move Row Data section.

3. Select the radio button for Tables. Enter your operating system username and password for host credentials (if these have not already been saved as preferred credentials) and click Continue.

4. In the Export: Tables window, click Add and find the table SYSTEM.EX182. Click Next.

5. In the Export: Export Options window, select the directory SYSTEM_DMP (created in Exercise 18-1) as the Directory Object for Optional Files. Click Next.

6. In the Export: Files window, choose the directory SYSTEM_DMP and click Next.

7. In the Export: Schedule window, give the job a name and click Next to run the job immediately.

8. In the Review window, click Submit Job.

9. When the job has completed, study the log file that will have been created in the operating directory mapped onto the Oracle directory SYSTEM_DMP.

CERTIFICATION OBJECTIVE 18.03

Use Data Pump Export and Import to Move Data Between Oracle Databases

Data Pump is commonly used for extracting large amounts of data from one database and inserting it into another, but it can also be used to extract other information such as PL/SQL code or various object definitions. There are several interfaces: command-line utilities, Enterprise Manager, and a PL/SQL API. Whatever purpose and technique are used, the files are always in the Data Pump proprietary format. It is not possible to read a Data Pump file with any tool other than Data Pump.

Capabilities

Fine-grained object and data selection facilities mean that Data Pump can export either the complete database or any part of it. It is possible to export table definitions with or without their rows, PL/SQL objects, views, sequences, or any other object type. If exporting a table, it is possible to apply a WHERE clause to restrict the rows exported (though this may make direct path impossible) or to instruct Data Pump to export a random sample of the table expressed as a percentage.

Parallel processing can speed up Data Pump operations. Parallelism can come at two levels: the number of Data Pump worker processes, and the number of parallel execution servers each worker process uses.

An estimate facility can calculate the space needed for a Data Pump export, without actually running the job.

The Network Mode allows transfer of a Data Pump data set from one database to another without ever staging it on disk. This is implemented by a Data Pump export job on the source database writing the data over a database link to the target database, where a Data Pump import job reads the data from the database link and inserts it.

Remapping facilities mean that objects can be renamed or transferred from one schema to another and (in the case of data objects) moved from one tablespace to another as they are imported.

When exporting data, the output files can be compressed and encrypted.

Using Data Pump with the Command-Line Utilities

The executables expdb and impdp are installed into the ORACLE_HOME/bin directory. Following are several examples of using them. Note that in all cases the command must be a single one-line command; the line breaks are purely for readability.

To export the entire database,

```
expdp system/manager@orcl11g full=y
parallel =4
dumpfile=datadir1:full1_%U.dmp,
         datadir2:full2_%U.dmp,
         datadir3:full3_%U.dmp,
         datadir4:full4_%U.dmp,
filesize=2G
compression=all
```

This command will connect to the database as user SYSTEM and launch a full Data Pump export, using four worker processes working in parallel. Each worker will generate its own set of dump files, uniquely named according to the %U template, which generates strings of eight unique characters. Each worker will break up its output into files of 2 GB (perhaps because the directories are on Samba devices) of compressed data.

A corresponding import job (which assumes that the files generated by the export have all been placed in one directory) would be

```
impdb system/manager@dev11g full=y
directory=samba_dir
parallel=4
dumpfile=full1_%U.dmp,full2_%U.dmp,full3_%U.dmp,full4_%U.dmp
```

This command makes a selective export of the PL/SQL objects belonging to two schemas:

```
expdp system/manager schemas=hr,oe
directory=code_archive
dumpfile=hr_oe_code.dmp
include=function,include=package,include=procedure,include-type
```

This command will extract everything from a Data Pump export that was in the HR schema, and import it into the DEV schema:

```
impdp system/manager
directory=usr_data
dumpfile=usr_dat.dmp
schema=hr
remap_schema=hr:dev
```

This last example does a network mode import:

```
impdp system/manager@orcl11g
directory=db_dir
schema=hr
network_link=prod.ebs.ac.za
```

The job will connect to the database identified by the database link prod.ebs.mf.za. This link will need to have a username and password with appropriate permissions embedded within it. The entire HR schema will be extracted from this database and transferred with Oracle Net to the database identified by the TNS alias ORCL11G, where it will be imported. Note that even a network-mode import, which does need to write data to disk, will still require a directory to write its log file.

Using Data Pump with Database Control

The Database Control interface to Data Pump generates the API calls that are invoked by the expdp and impdp utilities, but unlike the utilities it makes it possible to see the scripts and if desired copy, save, and edit them. To reach the Data Pump facilities, from the database home page take the Data Movement tab. In the Move Row Data section, there are five links that will launch wizards:

- **Export to Export Files**   Define Data Pump export jobs
- **Import from Export Files**   Define Data Pump import jobs
- **Import from Database**   Define a Data Pump network mode import
- **Monitor Export and Import Jobs**   Attach to running jobs to observe their progress, to pause or restart them, or to modify their operation

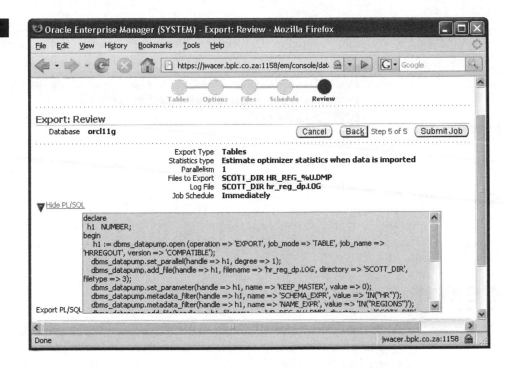

FIGURE 18-2

The final step of the Database Control Data Pump Export Wizard

The final stage of each wizard gives the option to see the PL/SQL code that is being generated. The job is run by the Enterprise Manager job system, either immediately or according to a schedule. Figure 18-2 shows this final step of scheduling a simple export job of the HR.REGIONS table.

EXERCISE 18-3

Use Data Pump in Network Mode

In this exercise, you will use Data Pump to transfer a table through a database link. The exercise assumes that Oracle Net is configured with a functioning TNS names alias.

1. Connect to your database as user SYSTEM with SQL*Plus.

2. Create a database link, using the username SYSTEM. In this example, the SYSTEM password is ORACLE, and the TNS names alias that connect to the database is ORCL11G:

```
create database link l1
connect to system identified by oracle using 'orcl11g';
```

3. From an operating system prompt, use Data Pump to export and import the table created in Exercise 18-2. Because the database refers back to the same database, it will be necessary to specify a different name for the imported table:

```
impdp userid=system/oracle tables=system.ex182
remap_table=system.ex182:system.imported network_link=l1
```

4. From your SQL*Plus session, confirm that the table has been imported to a different name:

```
select * from imported;
```

5. Tidy up:

```
drop table ex182;
drop table imported;
```

CERTIFICATION SUMMARY

An Oracle directory is a pointer to an operating system directory. Users can be given read or write permissions on different Oracle directories. SQL*Loader is a client-server tool for inserting large amounts of data. Direct load inserts do not generate undo, and redo can be switched off. Data Pump always does direct load if possible—but complex objects may have to be read or written via the database buffer cache, as external tables. The Data Pump processes are background processes. Server sessions are only used to control Data Pump jobs, not to do the work.

TWO-MINUTE DRILL

Describe and Use Methods to Move Data (Directory Objects, SQL*Loader, External Tables)

❑ Directory objects map an Oracle directory to an operating system directory.

❑ Directory objects are owned by SYS, and read or write permissions can be granted to users.

❑ SQL*Loader is a client-server tool that works over normal database sessions.

❑ The SQL*Loader control file can read a wide variety of formats, if configured correctly.

❑ External tables in the ORACLE_LOADER format can be queried from within the database as though they were normal heap tables.

❑ It is not possible to perform DML on external tables, but they can be created and populated by Data Pump format using CREATE TABLE . . . AS SELECT . . . .

Explain the General Architecture of Oracle Data Pump

❑ Data Pump uses server-side processes; the client tools manage jobs, they do not execute them.

❑ Data Pump will always use direct path, unless the complexity of the objects precludes this.

Use Data Pump Export and Import to Move Data Between Oracle Databases

❑ A Data Pump dump file can only be read by Data Pump.

❑ The network mode of Data Pump copies data between databases without staging it on disk.

❑ Data Pump always reads and writes Oracle directories; it is not aware of the operating system directory structure.

SELF TEST

Describe and Use Methods to Move Data
(Directory Objects, SQL*Loader, External Tables)

1. Which of these statements accurately describes Oracle directory objects? (Choose the best answer.)

   A. Directories are owned by users, and permissions to access them can be granted to others users.

   B. The server will not confirm that the operating system directory exists and is accessible to the Oracle processes when the Oracle directory is created.

   C. Directory objects must be listed in the UTL_FILE_DIR parameter before PL/SQL can read or write files in them.

   D. All users can create private directories; public directories can only be created by uses with the CREATE ANY DIRECTORY privilege.

2. What distinguishes a SQL*Loader direct load from a conventional load? (Choose all correct answers.)

   A. A direct load is performed by background processes, not through a session.

   B. Tables are locked during a direct load.

   C. Direct loads do not generate UNDO data.

   D. Direct loads do not maintain indexes.

3. When you query an external table, what happens? (Choose the best answer.)

   A. The data is read from an operating system file to a temporary segment in the session's temporary tablespace.

   B. The data is read into the session's PGA, bypassing the SGA.

   C. The data is read into the database buffer cache.

   D. Whether the data has to go via the database buffer cache will depend on how complex the table's structure is.

4. Which of the following is not a SQL*Loader file? (Choose the best answer.)

   A. Bad file

   B. Control file

   C. Discard file

   D. Good file

   E. Log file

Explain the General Architecture of Oracle Data Pump

5. You are using Data Pump to upload rows into a table, and wish to use the direct path. Which of the following statements is correct? (Choose all correct answers.)

   A. You must include the DIRECT keyword in the Data Pump control file.

   B. This is not possible if the table is in a cluster.

   C. You must disable insert triggers on the table first.

   D. You must enable insert triggers on the table first.

   E. You have no control over this—Data Pump will use the direct path automatically if it can.

   F. Direct path is slower than the external table path, because it doesn't cache data in memory.

6. Which of the following is not a Data Pump file type? (Choose the best answer.)

   A. Dump file

   B. Log file

   C. Control file

   D. SQL file

7. You want to transfer a large amount of data from one database to another; both databases are on the same machine. What should be the quickest method? (Choose the best answer.)

   A. Use the Export/Import utilities.

   B. Use Data Pump to write out the data, and a SQL*Loader direct load to bring it in.

   C. Use Data Pump in network mode.

   D. Use Data Pump export to write out the data then Data Pump import to read it in.

Use Data Pump Export and Import to Move Data Between Oracle Databases

8. You create a directory with this statement:

   ```
   create directory dp_dir as 'c:\tmp';
   ```

   but when you try to use it with Data Pump, there is an error. Which of the following could be true? (Choose all correct answers.)

   A. The Oracle owner has no permissions on `c:\tmp`.

   B. The Oracle user has no permissions on `dp_dir`.

   C. The path `c:\tmp` does not exist.

   D. The path `c:\tmp` must exist, or the "create directory" statement would have failed.

   E. If you use Data Pump in network mode, then there would be no need for a directory.

   F. Issuing the command `grant all on dp_dir to public;` may solve some permission problems.

9. You launch a Data Pump job with `expdp` and then exit from the session. Which of the following is true? (Choose all correct answers.)

   A. The job will terminate.

   B. The job will continue running in the background.

   C. You cannot monitor the job once you have exited.

   D. You can reattach to the job to monitor it.

   E. The job will pause but can be restarted.

10. When running a Data Pump import using the `impdp` facility on your PC, where should the source dump file(s) be? (Choose the best answer.)

    A. The dump file(s) must be on your PC.

    B. The dump file(s) must be on the server.

    C. The direct path is only possible if the dump file(s) are on the server; if they are local, then Data Pump must revert to the external table path.

    D. Data Pump will use network mode if the dump file(s) are not local to the database.

LAB QUESTION

In this exercise, create a copy of the HR schema. Do the work as user SYSTEM. The examples that follow use the command-line utilities, but Enterprise Manager can be used instead.

The first step will be to perform a Data Pump export of the entire schema. You can use the default directory DATA_PUMP_DIR (query the data dictionary view DBA_DIRECTORIES to find to where this is mapped) or create your own. From an operating system prompt, the command will be something like this:

```
expdp userid=system/oracle schemas=hr directory=data_pump_dir file=hr.dmp
```

While the export is in progress, from a SQL*Plus session run this query:

```
select program from v$process order by program;
```

You will see two Data Pump processes listed, DM00 and DW00. These will persist for the duration of the Data Pump job. Once the job has completed, study the log file that will have been generate in the nominated directory.

To import the schema, use a command similar to this:

```
impdp userid=system/oracle schemas=hr directory=data_pump_dir
dumpfile=hr.dmp remap_schema=hr:dev
```

Confirm that the schema has been imported into a newly created schema by connecting to the new schema (in the example, called DEV). The password will be the same as that for HR (which is HR, by default). You will find that the HR tables exist.

SELF TEST ANSWERS

Describe and Use Methods to Move Data (Directory Objects, SQL*Loader, External Tables)

1. ☑ **B.** The server validates the operating system directory and permissions only when the directory is used.
☒ **A** is wrong because directories are not schema objects: they are owned by SYS. **C** is wrong because it describes the older technique of writing directly to the operating system. **D** is wrong because the privilege is needed to create any directory at all—there is no such thing as a private directory.

2. ☑ **B and C.** A direct load will lock a table against DML and does not generate UNDO data.
☒ **A** is wrong because SQL*Loader must use a database session. **D** is wrong because indexes are maintained.

3. ☑ **C.** External tables are read via the database buffer cache.
☒ **A, B,** and **D.** These are all wrong because external tables are permanent objects visible to all sessions and therefore cannot be stored only in the private structures of the PGA and temporary segments.

4. ☑ **D.** SQL*Loader does not have a "Good" file.
☒ **A, B, D,** and **E.** These are the four file types that SQL*Loader uses, in addition to the source data file(s).

Explain the General Architecture of Oracle Data Pump

5. ☑ **B, C,** and **E.** Clustered tables and tables with active triggers are too complex for a direct path load; Data Pump will automatically choose the external table path if necessary.
☒ **A** is wrong because DIRECT is a SQL*Loader keyword, not a Data Pump keyword. **D** describes the reverse of what must be done and **F** misinterprets the purpose of a direct path load.

6. ☑ **C.** It is SQL*Loader that uses a control file, not Data Pump.
☒ **A, B,** and **D.** These are the Data Pump file types.

7. ☑ **C.** Network mode will always be fastest, even on the same machine, because the export and import run concurrently.
☒ **A** is wrong because these older utilities are always slower because they use client-server architecture. **B** is impossible because only Data Pump can read a Data Pump dump. **D** is wrong because, while perfectly possible, is as not as fast as network mode import.

Use Data Pump Export and Import to Move Data Between Oracle Databases

8. ☑ **A, B,** and **C.** Any of these would cause a Data Pump operation to fail.
   ☒ **D** is wrong because the existence of the path is not validated at creation time. **E** is wrong because even a network-mode operation will need a directory for the log file. **F** is wrong syntactically; the command should be `grant all on directory dp_dir to public;`

9. ☑ **B** and **D.** Data Pump jobs execute independently of the session that launched them, and it is possible to reattach to a job to observe its progress.
   ☒ **A** will not happen; the job can continue. **C** is wrong because reattaching is always possible. **E** is wrong because while a job can be paused, this is not the default behavior.

10. ☑ **B.** Data Pump uses server-side process, so all files must be on the server.
   ☒ **A** is wrong because it assumes Data Pump is a client-server tool, like SQL*Loader. **C** and **D** are wrong because they misunderstand the use of direct path and of network mode.

LAB ANSWER

To run the exercise with Database Control, from the database home page take the Data Movement tab and then the Export To Export Files link in the Move Row Data section. Select the radio button to export a schema, and follow the wizard to choose the HR schema and a directory, and then to schedule the job.

To import the schema, follow the Import From Export Files Wizard and choose a schema into which to import the HR objects.

19
Intelligent Infrastructure Enhancements

T his final chapter covers describes mechanisms for using Oracle Support Services, and how to apply database patches. A prerequisite is that you must have an account with MetaLink associated with a CSI (Customer Support Identifier) number issued by Oracle Corporation. MetaLink is the external interface of Oracle Support Services: a searchable database containing millions of articles on technical issues, and facilities for locating and downloading patches and for raising SRs (Service Requests.) An SR is a request for an Oracle Support Services analyst to assist with a problem.

This material is not extensively examined, but it is possible that general knowledge of procedures could be tested. If you do not have a MetaLink account, you will not be able to complete the exercises for this chapter—for this reason, it includes screen shots of every step in using Database Control to set up a job to download and apply a patch.

on the **Job** *SRs used to be called TARs (Technical Assistant Requests), and you will still hear many DBAs using phrases such as "raising a tar."*

SCENARIO & SOLUTION

How can I get a MetaLink username and password?	You need to speak to the nominated MetaLink administrator for your organization. He/she will generate a username and password for you, linked to the correct CSI number. Oracle Corporation does not permit people to share accounts.
Where can I find advice on how to get the best out of Oracle Support Services?	Once you have your MetaLink account, log on and on the Headlines tab take the News, Events, and Training subtab. There will be many links for articles and online courses on how best to use MetaLink and how best to work with Oracle Support Services.

CERTIFICATION OBJECTIVE 19.01

Use the Enterprise Manager Support Workbench

The Enterprise Manager Support Workbench is a graphical tool giving access to the Automatic Diagnostic Repository (the ADR) with facilities for gathering information, packaging it, and sending it to Oracle Support Services.

The Automatic Diagnostic Repository (ADR)

The ADR is a central storage point for all diagnostic information. This includes various dumps and trace files, the alert log, and health monitor reports. It is a file-based repository. All instances (RDBMS instances and also ASM instances) create their own directory structure within the ADR.

The location of the ADR is determined by the instance parameter DIAGNOSTIC_DEST. This will default to the ORACLE_BASE environment variable (which is a registry variable on Windows systems) or, if this has not been set, to the ORACLE_HOME/log directory. Within the DIAGNOSTIC_DEST, there will be a directory for the ADR_BASE: this is DIAGNOSTIC_DEST/diag. In the ADR_BASE there are directories for each Oracle product, such as the RDBMS, or database listeners. Within each product directory, there will be directories for each instance of the product: this is the ADR_HOME for the instance. For a database instance, the ADR_HOME is

```
ORACLE_BASE/diag/database_name/instance_name
```

where *database_name* is the name of the database and *instance_name* is the name of the instance. For example:

```
/u01/app/oracle/orcl11g/orcl11g
```

Within the ADR_HOME there will be a directory structure for the various files that make up the ADR for the instance. Some of the files are formatted with XML tags and are not intended to be viewed directly with editors; some are binary data, others are plain text. The directory ADR_HOME/trace is used as the default value for the instance parameters USER_DUMP_DEST (trace files generated by user sessions) and BACKGROUND_DUMP_DEST (the alert log and trace files generated by background processes). There is another copy of the alert log, formatted with XML tags, in ADR_HOME/alert.

Problems and Incidents

A *problem* is a critical error in the database or the instance. Examples include internal Oracle errors (errors reported with the error code ORA-600) and operating system errors. Each problem has a problem key, which is a text string including the error code and any parameters.

An *incident* is an occurrence of a problem. Incidents are considered to have the same root cause if their problem keys match. When an incident occurs, it is reported in the alert log and Enterprise Manager gathers diagnostic data about the incident in the form of dump files (incident dumps) and stores these in an ADR subdirectory created for that incident.

An *incident package* is a collection of data regarding one or more incidents and problems, formatted for upload to Oracle Support Services as part of an SR.

The ADR Command-Line Interface (ADRCI)

There is a command-line tool for managing the ADR: the ADRCI. This tool can display details of all problems and incidents, and generate reports and incident packages. Figure 19-1 shows the launching of the ADCRI on Windows, and then running the HELP command.

In Figure 19-1, note that ADRCI has detected the ADR_BASE. A simple ADRCI session might use these commands:

```
set home diag/rdbms/orcl1g/orcl11g
show problem
ips create package problem 8
```

The SET HOME command points the ADRCI toward one ADR_HOME, the path being relative to the ADR_BASE. The SHOW PROBLEM command will list all known problems for that ADR_HOME, identified by PROBLEM_ID number. The IPS CREATE PACKAGE command will generate an incident package for the nominated problem in the directory ADR_HOME/incpkg.

In most cases, the ADRCI will not be needed: Database Control has an interface to the ADR that is usually easier to use.

The Support Workbench

Enterprise Manager Database Control database home page displays all critical alerts. Clicking any of them will take you to the Support Workbench, shown in Figure 19-2.

FIGURE 19-1

The ADRCI utility

```
C:\WINDOWS\system32\cmd.exe - adrci                                    _ □ ×
D:\>adrci

ADRCI: Release 11.1.0.6.0 - Beta on Tue Mar 11 12:39:49 2008

Copyright (c) 1982, 2007, Oracle.  All rights reserved.

ADR base = "d:\app\oracle"
adrci> help

 HELP [topic]
    Available Topics:
            CREATE REPORT
            ECHO
            EXIT
            HELP
            HOST
            IPS
            PURGE
            RUN
            SET BASE
            SET BROWSER
            SET CONTROL
            SET ECHO
            SET EDITOR
            SET HOMES | HOME | HOMEPATH
            SET TERMOUT
            SHOW ALERT
            SHOW BASE
            SHOW CONTROL
            SHOW HM_RUN
            SHOW HOMES | HOME | HOMEPATH
            SHOW INCDIR
            SHOW INCIDENT
            SHOW PROBLEM
            SHOW REPORT
            SHOW TRACEFILE
            SPOOL

 There are other commands intended to be used directly by Oracle, type
 "HELP EXTENDED" to see the list

adrci> _
```

FIGURE 19-2

The Support
Workbench

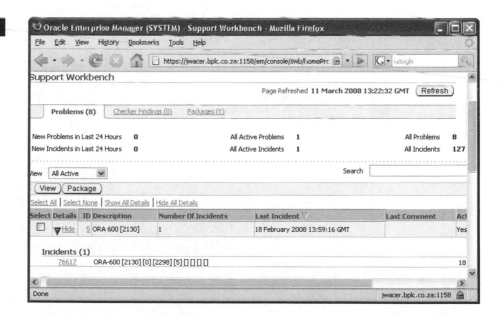

```
Oracle Enterprise Manager (SYSTEM) - Support Workbench - Mozilla Firefox      _ □ ×
File  Edit  View  History  Bookmarks  Tools  Help

     https://jwacer.bplc.co.za:1158/em/console/swb/homePrc          Google

Support Workbench

                                    Page Refreshed 11 March 2008 13:22:32 GMT   [Refresh]

    Problems (8)     Checker Findings (0)   Packages (1)

New Problems in Last 24 Hours    0              All Active Problems   1         All Problems    8
New Incidents in Last 24 Hours   0              All Active Incidents  1         All Incidents   127

View  All Active                                            Search

[View] [Package]
Select All | Select None | Show All Details | Hide All Details

Select Details  ID Description        Number Of Incidents  Last Incident          Last Comment    Act
  □    ▼Hide    5 ORA 600 [2130]      1                    18 February 2008 13:59:16 GMT           Yes

       Incidents (1)
       76617          ORA-600 [2130] [0] [2298] [5] □□□□                                          18

Done                                                              jwacer.bplc.co.za:1158
```

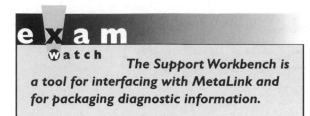

Figure 19-2 shows that there have been eight problems with a total of 127 incidents, but only one problem is still active. This is the problem number 5, which generated an ORA-600 error. From the Support Workbench, you can select a problem, view the details, and create an incident package by clicking the appropriate buttons.

To create an SR regarding a problem, select problem's check box and click View to reach Problem Details window, shown in Figure 19-3.

The links shown in the Oracle Support tab of the Problem Details window will launch wizards for creating an incident package, and then raising an SR to which the package can be attached.

FIGURE 19-3

Problem Details, with links for using MetaLink

Oracle Enterprise Manager (SYSTEM) - Problem Details: ORA 600 [2130] - Mozilla Firefox

File   Edit   View   History   Bookmarks   Tools   Help

https://jwacer.bplc.co.za:1158/em/conso   G▾ Google

Problem Details: ORA 600 [2130]

Page Refreshed **11 March 2008 13:34:02 GMT**   (Refresh)

Investigate and Resolve

(Go to Metalink)   (Quick Package)

<u>Self Service</u>   **Oracle Support**

Summary

SR#   --   (Edit)

Bug#   --   (Edit)

Active   **Yes**

Packaged   **No**

Number of Incidents   **1**

Collect and Send Diagnostic Data

<u>Create a Service Request with Metalink</u>
<u>Record Service Request Number to Problem</u>
<u>Generate Additional Dumps and Test Cases</u>
<u>Package the Problem</u>

Last Incident

Timestamp   <u>18 February 2008 13:59:16 GMT</u>

Incident Source   **System Generated**

Impact

Checkers Run   **0**

Checker Findings   **0**

Track and Close

<u>Check the Service Request Status with Metalink</u>
<u>Close the problem</u>

Done   jwacer.bplc.co.za:1158

EXERCISE 19-1

Use the Support Workbench

In this exercise, you will investigate any problems that may have been recorded in the ADR.

1. Connect to your database with Database control as user SYSTEM.

2. Open the Support Workbench: from the database home page, take the Software And Support tab, then the Support Workbench link in the Support section.

3. The default display is to show problems in the last 24 hours. In the View drop-down box, choose All to see all problems that are known to the ADR, as shown here:

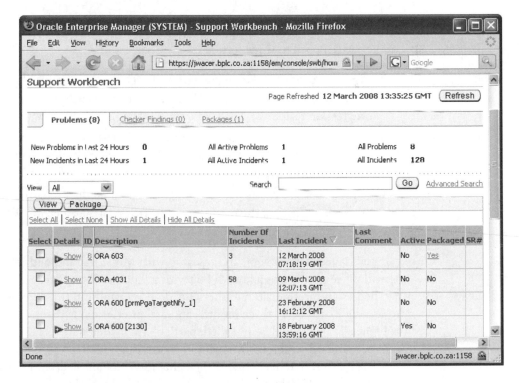

4. Investigate any problems shown by clicking the links to show the details of the problem.

CERTIFICATION OBJECTIVE 19.02

Manage Patches

In some environments, patching can take up a considerable amount of time. It is, however, a vital task. Some patches will be to fix problems in the Oracle code that causes some features not to work as documented: applying these is optional, only necessary if your installation happens to have hit the problem. Others are to fix security issues and are not optional at all. Patches can be applied using a command-line utility, or with Enterprise Manager.

Types of Patch

Patches are shipped in three forms:

- **Interim patches**   These are written to fix one specific problem, for an exact release level of the database. They are not necessarily fully integration or regression tested.

- **CPU (Critical Patch Update) patches**   These are cumulative patches for a specific release level and include all dependent patches. CPUs are fully integration and regression tested.

- **Patch sets**   A patch set is a cumulative set of product fixes that will increment the release level of the product (as reported by a query against V$VERSION), for instance, from 11.1.0.6 to 11.1.0.7.

If you have hit a problem, and research with MetaLink and with other sources identifies the problem as a known bug with a patch to fix it, this patch can be installed as an interim patch. Otherwise, do not install interim patches. CPUs are usually issued every three months and will often include patches for security problems. These should be installed, particularly if your systems have to comply with security standards enforced by local jurisdictions. Applying a patch set is a much bigger operation that may change the behavior of the product, rather than merely fixing problems. Applying patch sets should not be embarked upon without testing.

To apply patches, use the Opatch utility. This can be invoked from the command line, or through Database Control.

on the
job

Many DBAs try to avoid installing interim patches. They will fix a problem, but applying several may be problematic because of the lack of integration testing. CPUs and patch sets are much safer.

Integration with MetaLink and the Patch Advisor

Database Control includes a Patch Advisor that will identify what CPUs and any Oracle-recommended patches should be applied to the database. This requires configuring a connection to MetaLink and scheduling a job to make the check. An account with MetaLink and an Internet connection from the server machine are prerequisites for doing this.

To configure MetaLink integration, take the Setup link at the top right of the Database Control database home page and then the Patching Setup link in the Overview Of Setup section. In the Patching Setup window, enter your MetaLink username and password. These will be associated with the username you used when connecting to Database Control. If there is a proxy server between the database server and the Internet, the Proxy And Connection Settings tab will let you configure this.

To schedule a job for checking what patches are needed, from the database home page take the Jobs link in the Related Links section. In the Create Job drop-down

---

INSIDE THE EXAM

Selecting the Right Edition

The material in this chapter is unlikely to be examined in any detail, but general principles may be tested.

Working with Oracle Support Services is a vital part of a DBA's job. The contacts will usually be one of two kinds: proactive work intended to stop future problems, and reactive work when dealing with problems. Database Control can be configured to run a job (the REFRESHFROMMETALINK

job) that will contact MetaLink regularly and download lists of patches, CPUs, and patch sets that are considered relevant for your installation. Applying everything listed will keep the system up to date with fixes for known problems, one hopes before they occur. Using Database Control interactively, you can raise SRs, and download and apply patches in response to particular problems.

box choose Refresh From Metalink and click Go. Give the job a name, schedule it to run with whatever frequency you think appropriate, and submit the job. Once the job has run, the Patch Advisor should be available.

To reach the Patch Advisor, from the database home page take the Software and Support tab, then the Patch Advisor link in the Database Software Patching section. This will show all the recommended patches for the database, as of the last time the job was run.

Applying Patches

Patches can be applied with the Opatch utility, or with Database Control; the Database Control method in fact uses Opatch behind the scenes. The Opatch utility is installed into the directory ORACLE_HOME/Opatch and launched by running the executable file opatch (or opatch.bat on Windows). The prerequisites are that the ORACLE_HOME environment variable must be set (note that on Windows it is not sufficient to have this as a registry variable, it must be set within the operating system session); the Java Runtime Environment 1.4 or later must be available; a few standard operating system utilities must be available. To test the prerequisites, use the LSINVENTORY command as in Figure 19-4.

FIGURE 19-4

Using Opatch to inspect the inventoried software

```
C:\WINDOWS\system32\cmd.exe                                          _ □ x

D:\>%ORACLE_HOME%\Opatch\opatch lsinventory
Invoking OPatch 11.1.0.6.0

Oracle Interim Patch Installer version 11.1.0.6.0
Copyright (c) 2007, Oracle Corporation.  All rights reserved.

Oracle Home       : D:\app\oracle\product\11.1.0\db_1
Central Inventory : C:\Program Files\Oracle\Inventory
   from           : n/a
OPatch version    : 11.1.0.6.0
OUI version       : 11.1.0.6.0
OUI location      : D:\app\oracle\product\11.1.0\db_1\oui
Log file location : D:\app\oracle\product\11.1.0\db_1\cfgtoollogs\opatch\opatch2
008-03-11_18-14-22PM.log

Lsinventory Output file location : D:\app\oracle\product\11.1.0\db_1\cfgtoollogs
\opatch\lsinv\lsinventory2008-03-11_18-14-22PM.txt

--------------------------------------------------------------------------------

Installed Top-level Products (2):

Oracle Database 11g                                            11.1.0.6.0
Oracle Database 11g Examples                                  11.1.0.6.0
There are 2 products installed in this Oracle Home.

There are no Interim patches installed in this Oracle Home.

--------------------------------------------------------------------------------

OPatch succeeded.

D:\>_
```

In Figure 19-4, Opatch is being run on a Windows system. The utility was invoked by specifying the full path, using the ORACLE_HOME environment variable, and the LSINVENTORY command. This shows summary information regarding what has been installed, including any interim patches (none, in the example). To obtain much more detailed information, use the –detail switch:

```
%ORACLE_HOME%\Opatch\opatch lsinventory -detail
```

All patches will come with a README.TXT file of instructions detailing how to install the patch. These instructions will include detail on whether the database should be open or shut down while the patch is applied. To apply a patch once it is downloaded from MetaLink and expanded (it will have come as a ZIP file), run Opatch as follows:

```
opatch apply path_to_patch
```

where *path_to_patch* is the directory where the patch was expanded.

To apply a patch with Database Control, the patch must first be downloaded to a *staging area*. The staging area is a location where the patch is *staged*—stored locally, prior to application. To reach the wizard that will stage and apply the patch, from the database home page take the Software And Support tab, and then the Stage Patch link in the Database Software Patching section. This will launch a six-step wizard:

- Select patch
- Select destination
- Set credentials
- Stage or apply
- Schedule
- Summary

The wizard will connect to MetaLink using stored credentials, download the patch, and create a job to apply the patch. The illustrations that follow show examples of using the wizard to apply a patch.

1. First, enter the patch number and operating system (some patches come in versions that are operating system specific).

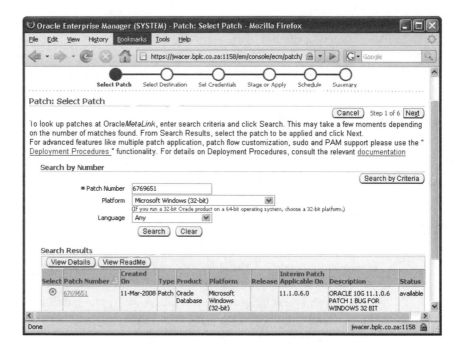

2. Choose the targets to which the patch should be applied. The choice will be limited to targets appropriate for the patch (in the example, database instances).

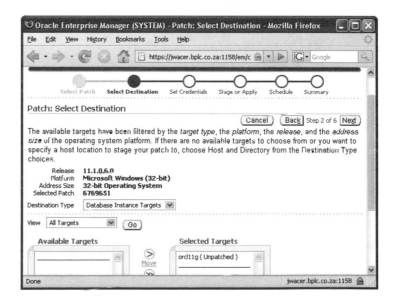

3. Provide credentials. These will be either operating system credentials, database credentials, or both depending on the patch.

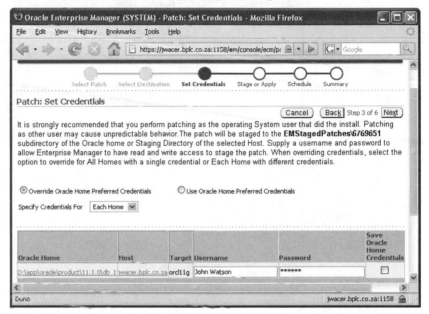

4. Decide whether to apply the patch or only stage it for future use.

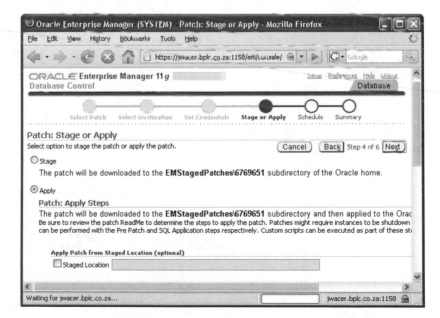

5. Schedule the job that will download and apply the patch.

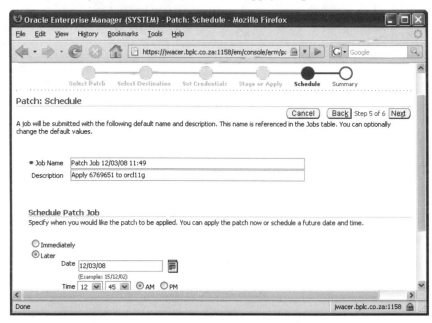

6. The final step is to view a summary of the operation.

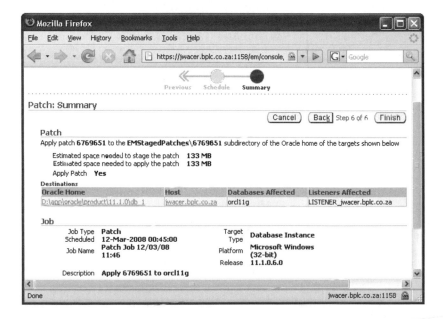

EXERCISE 19-2

Download and Apply a Patch

In this exercise, you will download a patch and apply it. Oracle Corporation provides a dummy patch for this purpose. At the time of writing, this is only available for 32-bit Linux. If you are working on another operating system, don't worry—you will get practice in patching soon enough when you start working on a live database.

1. Log in to MetaLink.

2. Take the Patches & Updates tab, and then the Simple Search link.

3. When prompted for a Patch Number/Name, enter **6198642**. When prompted for a Platform Or Language, select Linux x86 from the drop-down box. Click Go.

4. Click the Download button, shown in the next illustration, to download the patch from MetaLink to an appropriate directory.

5. From an operating system prompt, unzip the patch. It will unzip into a directory named 6198642.

6. Shut down the database and the listener: Opatch will not proceed if these are running.

7. Apply the patch:

```
$ORACLE_HOME/OPatch/opatch apply patch_directory
```

where *patch_directory* is the directory into which the patch was unzipped. The next illustration shows this step, and the start of the output.

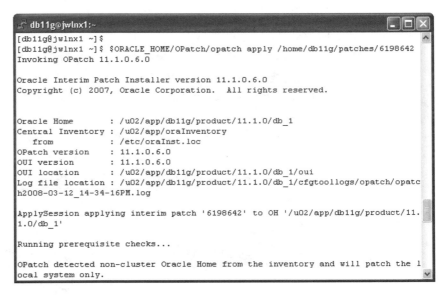

8. Confirm the patch application with this command:

```
$ORACLE_HOME/OPatch/opatch lsinventory
```

CERTIFICATION SUMMARY

The Support Workbench is an interface between you, the database, and MetaLink. Using the Support Workbench, you can identify problems, gather all relevant information into a package, and raise an SR with Oracle Support Services. Sometimes problems will require installing patches. These are installed with the Opatch utility, either from the command line or through the Database Control interface.

TWO-MINUTE DRILL

Use the Enterprise Manager Support Workbench

❑ Database Control can connect to MetaLink and identify lists of advised patches.

❑ The Support Workbench can classify errors into named problems, each consisting of one or more incidents.

❑ Diagnostic information is stored in files in the ADR, located by default in the ORACLE_BASE.

❑ All diagnostic information in the ADR relevant to a problem can be packaged for transmission to Oracle Support Services.

Manage Patches

❑ Interim patches fix one problem.

❑ CPUs are bundled patches, often including security fixes.

❑ Patch sets raise the release level of the product.

❑ The Opatch utility installs patches, and updates the inventory.

SELF TEST

Use the Enterprise Manager Support Workbench

1. If the system is behind a firewall proxy server, where must the proxy server be defined before the REFRESHFROMMETALINK job can run? (Choose the best answer.)

   A. In the browser.

   B. In Database Control.

   C. In both the browser and Database Control.

   D. It is necessary to configure the firewall to allow a direct connection from the. database server to the Internet.

2. Where is the Automatic Diagnostic Repository? (Choose the best answer.)

   A. In the location specified by the ADR_BASE environment variable.

   B. In the flash recovery area.

   C. In the location specified by the DIAGNOSTIC_DEST instance parameter.

   D. In the location specified by the oraInst.loc file on Unix systems, or the INST_LOC registry variable on Windows systems.

Manage Patches

3. If your database release level is at 11.1.0.6, application of what type of patch will raise this level?

   A. An interim patch

   B. A critical patch update

   C. A patch set

   D. Any patch installation will raise the reported level

4. What tool(s) can you use to install patches? (Choose all correct answers.)

   A. Database Control

   B. The Opatch utility

   C. The Oracle Universal Installer

   D. The Automatic Diagnostic Repository Command-Line Interface tool (the ADRCI)

5. What are the prerequisites for running the Opatch utility? (Choose all correct answers.)

   A. The ORACLE_HOME must be set as an environment variable.

   B. MetaLink credentials must be either stored or entered at run time.

   C. A Java Runtime Environment must be available.

   D. The database must be in NOMOUNT mode.

LAB QUESTION

Investigate the state of your database installation, with regard to patch levels. Query V$VERSION to determine the release level, and use the Opatch utility to determine what patches have been applied (if any).

Configure Database Control to run the REFRESHFROMMETALINK job, and see if there are any recommended patches or CPUs that should be installed. If there are, download and install them.

SELF TEST ANSWERS

Use the Enterprise Manager Support Workbench

1. ☑ **B.** Database Control must be able to make an outbound HTTP connection to MetaLink.
   ☒ **A** and **C** are wrong because the browser does not make the connection to MetaLink—it makes a connection to Database Control. **D** is wrong because while this would work, it is not necessary.

2. ☑ **C.** The DIAGNOSTIC_DEST parameter specifies the directory used as the root of the ADR.
   ☒ **A** is wrong because ADR_BASE is not an environment variable. **B** is wrong because the flash recovery area stores backup and recovery data, not problem diagnosis data. **D** is wrong because it confuses the ADR with the OUI Inventory.

Manage Patches

3. ☑ **C.** Patch sets raise the fourth digit of the release level.
   ☒ **A, B,** and **D.** Interim patches and critical patch updates apply within a release level and cannot raise it.

4. ☑ **A** and **B.** Opatch (either invoked from the command line or through Database Control) is the tool to install patches.
   ☒ **C** is wrong because the OUI doesn't install patches—it installs or upgrades an Oracle Home, which is a much larger operation. **D** is wrong because the ADRCI uses the ADR to investigate problems, it doesn't install patches to fix them.

5. ☑ **A** and **C.** Opatch needs the ORACLE_HOME environment variable (the Windows registry variable is not enough) and a JRE.
   ☒ **B** is wrong because MetaLink is not needed to apply a patch, only to download it. **D** is wrong because (in most cases) the database should be shut down before applying patches.

LAB ANSWER

The query against V$VERSION is nothing more than this:

```
select * from v$version;
```

Note that if the software is 32 bit, V$VERSION does not explicitly say this. If it is 64 bit, this is stated in the first row of the output.

The Opatch command to list details of everything installed including patches is

```
opatch lsinventory -detail
```

To download and install patches, you can use the Database Control wizard to automate the whole process, or you can use a browser to connect to MetaLink and download patches interactively, and then use Opatch to install them.

Appendix

About the CD

The CD-ROM included with this book comes complete with MasterExam and an electronic version of the book. The software is easy to install on any Windows 98/NT/2000/XP/Vista computer and must be installed to access the MasterExam feature. You may, however, browse the electronic book directly from the CD without installation. To register for a second bonus MasterExam, simply click the Online Training link on the Main page and follow the directions to the free online registration.

System Requirements

Software requires Windows 98 or higher and Internet Explorer 5.0 or above and 20 MB of hard disk space for full installation. The electronic book requires Adobe Acrobat Reader.

Installing and Running MasterExam

If your computer CD-ROM drive is configured to autorun, the CD-ROM will automatically start up upon inserting the disk. From the opening screen you may install MasterExam by pressing the MasterExam button. This will begin the installation process and create a program group named "LearnKey." To run MasterExam, use Start | Programs | LearnKey. If the autorun feature did not launch your CD, browse to the CD and click the LaunchTraining.exe icon.

MasterExam

MasterExam provides you with a simulation of the actual exam. The number of questions, the type of questions, and the time allowed are intended to be an accurate representation of the exam environment. You have the option to take an open book exam, including hints, references, and answers, a closed book exam, or the timed MasterExam simulation.

When you launch MasterExam, a digital clock display will appear in the upper left-hand corner of your screen. The clock will continue to count down to zero unless you choose to end the exam before the time expires.

Electronic Book

The entire contents of the Study Guide are provided in PDF. Adobe's Acrobat Reader has been included on the CD.

Help

A help file is provided through the Help button on the main page in the lower left-hand corner. An individual help feature is also available through MasterExam.

Removing Installation(s)

MasterExam is installed to your hard drive. For *best* results for removal of programs use the Start | Programs | LearnKey | Uninstall option to remove MasterExam.

Technical Support

For questions regarding the technical content of the electronic book or MasterExam, please visit www.osborne.com or e-mail customer.service@mcgraw-hill.com. For customers outside the 50 United States, e-mail international_cs@mcgraw-hill.com.

LearnKey Technical Support

For technical problems with the software (installation, operation, removing installations), please visit www.learnkey.com or e-mail techsupport@learnkey.com.

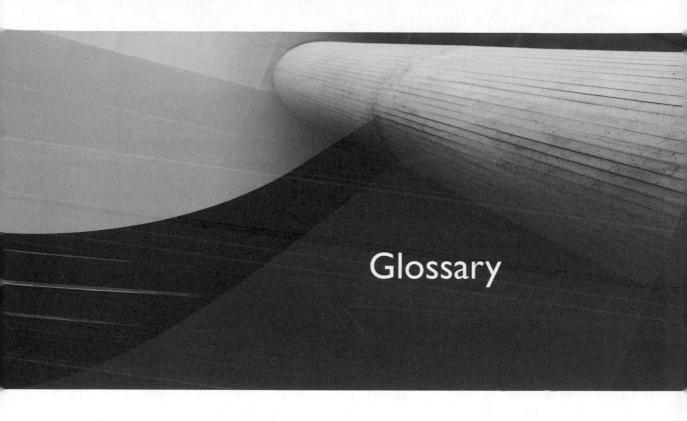

Glossary

A

ACID Atomicity, Consistency, Isolation, and Durability. Four characteristics that a relational database must be able to maintain for transactions.

ADDM Automatic Database Diagnostic Monitor. A tool that generates performance tuning reports based on snapshots in the AWR.

ADR Automatic Diagnostic Repository. The default location for the alert log, trace files, and other information useful for fault finding.

ADRCI The ADR command-line interface.

AES Advanced Encryption Standard. A widely used data encryption method.

AL16UTF16 A Unicode fixed-width two-byte character set, commonly specified for the NLS character set used for NVARCHAR2, NCHAT, and NCLOB data types.

Alias   In Oracle Net, a pointer to a connect string. An alias must be resolved into the address of a listener and the name of a service or instance.

ANSI   American National Standards Institute. A U.S. body that defines a number of standards relevant to computing.

API   Application programming interface. A defined method for manipulating data, typically implemented as a set of PL/SQL procedures in a package.

ASCII   American Standard Code for Information Interchange. A standard (with many variations) for coding letters and other characters as bytes.

ASH   Active session history. A category of information in the AWR, that records details of session activity.

ASM   Automatic storage management. An LVM provided with the Oracle database.

ASSM   Automatic segment space management. The method of managing space within segments by use of bitmaps.

Attribute   One element of a tuple (aka a column).

AWR   Automatic Workload Repository. A set of tables in the SYSAUX tablespace, populated with tuning data gathered by the MMON process.

B

Background process   A process that is part of the instance: launched at startup.

BFILE   A large object data type that is stored as an operating system file. The value in the table column is a pointer to the file.

Bind variable   A value passed from a user process to a SQL statement at statement execution time.

BLOB   Binary large object. A LOB data type for binary data, such as photographs and video clips.

Block   The units of storage into which datafiles are formatted. The size can be 2 KB, 4 KB, 8 KB, 16 KB, 32 KB, or 64 KB. Some platforms will not permit all these sizes.

BMR   Block media recovery. An RMAN technique for restoration and recovery of individual data blocks, rather than complete data files.

C

CET   Central European Time. A time zone used in much of Europe (though not Great Britain) that is 1 hour ahead of UTC, with daylight saving time in effect during the summer months.

Character set   The encoding system for representing data within bytes. Different character sets can store different characters and may not be suitable for all languages. Unicode character sets can store any character.

Check constraint   A simple rule enforced by the database that restricts the values that can be entered into a column.

Checkpoint   An event that forces the DBWn to write all dirty buffers from the database buffer cache to the datafiles.

CKPT   The checkpoint process. The background process responsible for recording the current redo byte address—the point in time up to which the DBWn has written changed data blocks to disk—and for signaling checkpoints, which force DBWn to write all changed blocks to disk immediately.

Client-server architecture   A processing paradigm where the application is divided into client software that interacts with the user and server software that interacts with the data.

CLOB   Character large object. A LOB data type for character data, such as text documents, stored in the database character set.

Cluster   A hardware environment where more than one computer shares access to storage. A RAC database consists of several instances on several computers opening one database on the shared storage.

Cluster segment   A segment that can contain one or more tables, denormalized into a single structure.

Column   An element of a row: tables are two-dimensional structures, divided horizontally into rows and vertically into columns.

Commit   To make a change to data permanent.

Complete recovery   Following a restore of damaged database files, a complete recovery applies all redo to bring the database up to date with no loss of data.

Connect identifier   An Oracle Net alias.

Connect role   A preseeded role retained only for backward compatibility.

Connect string   The database connection details needed to establish a session: the address of the listener and the service or instance name.

Consistent backup   A backup made while the database is closed.

Constraint   A mechanism for enforcing rules on data: that a column value must be unique, or may only contain certain values. A primary key constraint specifies that the column must be both unique and not null.

Control file   The file containing pointers to the rest of the database, critical sequence information, and the RMAN repository.

CPU   Central processing unit. The chip that provides the processing capability of a computer, such as an Intel Pentium or a Sun SPARC.

CTWR   Change Tracking Writer. The optional background process that records the addresses of changed blocks, to enable fast incremental backups.

D

Data blocks   The units into which datafiles are formatted, made up of one of more operating system blocks.

Data dictionary   The tables and views owned by SYS in the SYSTEM tablespace that define the database and the objects within it.

Data dictionary views   Views on the data dictionary tables that let the DBA investigate the state of the database.

Data Guard   A facility whereby a copy of the production database is created and updated (possibly in real time) with all changes applied to the production database.

Data Pump   A facility for transferring large amounts of data at high speed into, out of, or between databases.

Database buffer cache   An area of memory in the SGA used for working on blocks copied from datafiles.

Database link   A connection from one database to another, based on a username and password and a connect string.

Datafile   The disk-based structure for storing data.

DBA   Database administrator. The person responsible for creating and managing Oracle databases, this could be you.

DBA role   A preseeded role in the database provided for backward compatibility that includes all the privileges needed to manage a database, except that needed to start up or shut down.

DBCA   The Database Configuration Assistant. A GUI tool for creating, modifying, and dropping instances and databases.

DBID   Database identifier. A unique number for every database, visible in the DBID column of the V$DATABASE dynamic performance view.

DBMS   Database management system, often used interchangeably with RDBMS.

DBWn or DBWR   The Database Writer. The background process responsible for writing changed blocks from the database buffer cache to the datafiles. An instance may have up to ten database writer processes, DBW0 through DBW9.

DDL Data Definition Language. The subset of SQL commands that change object definitions within the data dictionary: CREATE, ALTER, DROP, and TRUNCATE.

Deadlock A situation where two sessions block each other, such that neither can do anything. Deadlocks are detected and resolved automatically by the DIA0 background process.

DHCP Dynamic Host Configuration Protocol. The standard for configuring the network characteristics of a computer, such as its IP address, in a changing environment where computers may be moved from one location to another.

DIA0 The diagnosability process that detects hang and deadlock situations.

DIAG The diagnosability process that generates diagnostic dumps.

Direct path A method of I/O on datafiles that bypasses the database buffer cache.

Directory object An Oracle directory: a object within the database that points to an operating system directory.

Dirty buffer A buffer in the database buffer cache that contains a copy of a data block that has been updated and not yet written back to the datafile.

DMnn Data Pump Master process. The process that controls a data pump job, one will be launched for each job that is running.

DML Data Manipulation Language. The subset of SQL commands that change data within the database: INERT, UPDATE, DELETE, and MERGE.

DNS Domain Name Service. The TCP mechanism for resolving network names into IP addresses.

Domain The set of values an attribute is allowed to take. Terminology: tables have rows, rows have columns with values. Or: relations have tuples, tuples have attributes with values taken from their domain.

DSS Decision Support System. A database, such as a data warehouse, optimized for running queries as opposed to OLTP work.

DWnn   Data Pump Worker process. There will be one or more of these launched for each data pump job that is running.

E

Easy connect   A method of establishing a session against a database by specifying the address on the listener and the service name, without using an Oracle Net alias.

EBCDIC   Extended Binary Coded Decimal Interchange Code. A standard developed by IBM for coding letters and other characters in bytes.

Environment variable   A variable set in the operating system shell that can be used by application software and by shell scripts.

Equijoin   A join condition using an equality operator.

F

Fact table   The central table in a star schema, with columns for values relevant to the row and columns used as foreign keys to the dimension tables.

FGA   Fine-grained auditing. A facility for tracking user access to data, based on the rows that are seen or manipulated.

Flash recovery area   A default location for all recovery-related files.

Full backup   A backup containing all blocks of the files backed up, not only those blocks changed since the last backup.

G

GMT   Greenwich Mean Time. Now referred to as UTC, this is the time zone of the meridian through Greenwich Observatory in London.

Grid computing   An architecture where the delivery of a service to end users is not tied to certain server resources but can be provided from anywhere in a pool of resources.

GUI   Graphical user interface. A layer of an application that lets users work with the application through a graphical terminal, such as a PC with a mouse.

H

HTTP   Hypertext Transfer Protocol. The protocol that enables the World Wide Web (both invented at the European Organization for Nuclear Research in 1989)—this is a layered protocol that runs over TCP/IP.

HWM   High water mark. This is the last block of a segment that has ever been used, blocks above this are part of the segment but are not yet formatted for use.

I

I/O   Input/output. The activity of reading from or writing to disks, often the slowest point of a data processing operation.

IBM   International Business Machines. A well-known computer hardware, software, and services company.

Image copy   An RMAN copy of a file.

Inconsistent backup   A backup made while the database was open.

Incremental backup   A backup containing only blocks that have been changed since the last backup was made.

Instance recovery   The automatic repair of damage caused by a disorderly shutdown of the database.

IOT   Index-organized table. A table type where the rows are stored in the leaf blocks of an index segment.

IP   Internet Protocol. Together with the Transmission Control Protocol, TCP/IP: the de facto standard communication protocol used for client/server communication over a network.

IPC   Inter-Process Communications protocol. The platform-specific protocol, provided by your OS vendor, used for processes running on the same machine to communicate with each other.

ISO   International Organization for Standardization. A group that defines many standards, including SQL.

J

J2EE   Java 2 Enterprise Edition. The standard for developing Java applications.

Join   The process of connecting rows in different tables, based on common column values.

JVM   Java Virtual Machine. The runtime environment needed for running code written in Java. Oracle provides a JVM within the database, and there will be one provided by your operating system.

L

Large pool   A memory structure within the SGA used by certain processes: principally shared server processes and parallel execution servers.

LDAP   Lightweight Directory Access Protocol. The TCP implementation of the X25 directory standard, used by the Oracle Internet Directory for name resolution, security, and authentication. LDAP is also used by other software vendors, including Microsoft and IBM.

LGWR   The Log Writer. The background process responsible for flushing change vectors from the log buffer in memory to the online redo log files on disk.

Library cache   A memory structure within the shared pool, used for caching SQL statements parsed into their executable form.

Listener   The server-side process that listens for database connection requests from user processes and launches server processes to establish sessions.

LOB   Large object. A data structure that is too large to store within a table. LOBs (Oracle supports several types) are defined as columns of a table but physically are stored in a separate segment.

Log switch   The action of closing one online logfile group and opening another: triggered by the LGWR process filling the first group.

LRU   Least recently used. LRU lists are used to manage access to data structures, using algorithms that ensure that the data that has not been accessed for the longest time is the data that will be overwritten.

LVM   Logical Volume Manager. A layer of software that abstracts the physical storage within your computer from the logical storage visible to an application.

M

MMAN   The Memory Manager background process, which monitors and reassigns memory allocations in the SGA for automatically tunable SGA components.

MML   Media Management Layer. Software that lets RMAN make use of automated tape libraries and other SBT devices.

MMNL   Manageability Monitor Light. The background process responsible for flushing ASH data to the AWR, if MMON is not doing this with the necessary frequency.

MMON   The Manageability Monitor is a background process that is responsible for gathering performance monitoring information and raising alerts.

Mounted database   A situation where the instance has opened the database controlfile, but not the online redo logfiles or the datafiles.

MTBF   Mean time between failures. A measure of the average length of running time for a database between unplanned shutdowns.

MTS   Multi-Threaded Server. Since release 9i, renamed to Shared Server. This is the technique whereby a large number of sessions can share a small pool of server processes, rather than requiring one server each.

MTTR   Mean time to recover. The average time it takes to make the database available for normal use after a failure.

Multiplexing   To maintain multiple copies of files (particularly controlfiles and redo log files).

N

Namespace   A logical grouping of objects within which no two objects may have the same name.

NCLOB   National character large object. A LOB data type for character data, such as text documents, stored in the alternative national database character set.

NetBEUI   NetBIOS Extended User Interface. An enhanced version of NETBIOS.

NetBIOS   Network Basic Input Output System. The network communications protocol that was burnt onto the first network card that IBM ever produced.

NLS   National Language Support. The capability of the Oracle database to support many linguistic, geographical, and cultural environments, now usually referred to as Globalization.

Node   A computer attached to a network.

Null   The absence of a value, indicating that the value is not known, missing, or inapplicable.

O

OC4J   Oracle Containers for J2EE. The control structure provided by the Oracle Internet Application Server for running Java programs.

OCA
Oracle Certified Associate.

OCI Oracle Call Interface. An API, published as a set of C libraries, that programmers can use to write user processes that will use an Oracle database.

OCP Oracle Certified Professional. The qualification you are working toward at the moment.

ODBC Open Database Connectivity. A standard developed by Microsoft for communicating with relational databases. Oracle provides an ODBC driver that will allow clients running Microsoft products to connect to an Oracle database.

Offline backup A backup made while the database is closed.

OLAP Online analytical processing. Selection-intensive work involving running queries against a (usually) large database. Oracle provides OLAP capabilities as an option, in addition to the standard query facilities.

OLTP Online transaction processing. A pattern of activity within a database typified by a large number of small, short transactions.

Online backup A backup made while the database is open.

Online redo log The files to which change vectors are streamed by the LGWR.

Oracle Net Oracle's proprietary communications protocol, layered on top of an industry-standard protocol.

ORACLE_BASE The root directory into which Oracle products are installed.

ORACLE_HOME The root directory of any one Oracle product.

OS Operating system. Typically, in the Oracle environment, this will be a version of Unix (perhaps Linux) or Microsoft Windows.

P

Parse To convert SQL statements into a form suitable for execution.

PGA   Program global area. The variable-sized block of memory used to maintain the state of a database session. PGAs are private to the session and controlled by the session's server process.

PL/SQL   Procedural Language / Structured Query Language. Oracle's proprietary programming language, which combines procedural constructs, such as flow control, and user interface capabilities with SQL.

PMON   The Process Monitor. The background process responsible for monitoring the state of user's sessions against an instance.

Primary key   The column (or combination of columns) whose value(s) can be used to identify each row in a table.

R

RAC   Real Application Clusters. Oracle's clustering technology, which allows several instances in different machines to open the same database for scalability, performance, and fault tolerance.

RAID   Redundant Array of Inexpensive Disks. Techniques for enhancing performance and/or fault tolerance by using a volume manager to present a number of physical disks to the operating system as a single logical disk.

RAM   Random access memory. The chips that make up the real memory in your computer hardware, as against the virtual memory presented to software by the operating system.

Raw device   An unformatted disk or disk partition.

RDBMS   Relational database management system, often used interchangeably with DBMS.

Referential integrity   A rule defined on a table specifying that the values in a column (or columns) must map onto those of a row in another table.

Relation   A two-dimensional structure consisting of tuples with attributes (aka a table).

RMAN   Recovery Manager. Oracle's backup and recovery tool.

Rowid   The unique identifier of every row in the database, used as a pointer to the physical location of the row. The rowid datatype is proprietary to Oracle Corporation, not part of the SQL standard.

RVWR   The Recovery Writer background process, an optional process responsible for flushing the flashback buffer to the flashback logs.

S

SBT   System backup to tape. An RMAN term for a tape device.

Schema   The objects owned by a database user.

SCN   System change number. The continually incrementing number used to track the sequence and exact time of all events within a database.

Segment   A database object within a schema that stores data.

Sequence   A database object within a schema that can generate consecutive numbers.

Service name   A logical name registered by an instance with a listener, which can be specified by a user process when it issues a connect request. A service name will be mapped onto a SID by the listener when it establishes a session.

Session   A user process and a server process, connected to the instance.

SGA   System global area. The block of shared memory that contains the memory structures that make up an Oracle instance.

SID   Either: System Identifier. The name of an instance, which must be unique on the computer the instance is running on. Users can request a connection to a named SID, or to a logical service and let the listener choose an appropriate SID.
   Or: Session Identifier. The number used to identify uniquely a session logged on to an Oracle instance.

SMON The System Monitor. The background process responsible for opening a database and monitoring the instance.

Spfile The server parameter file: the file containing the parameters used to build an instance in memory.

SQL Structured Query Language. An international standard language for extracting data from and manipulating data in relational databases.

SSL Secure Sockets Layer. A standard for securing data transmission, using encryption, checksumming, and digital certificates.

Synonym An alternative name for a database object.

Sysdba The privilege that lets a user connect with operating system or password file authentication, and create or start up and shut down a database.

Sysoper The privilege that lets a user connect with operating system or password file authentication, and start up and shut down (but not create) a database.

System A preseeded schema used for database administration purposes.

T

Table A logical two-dimensional data storage structure, consisting of rows and columns.

Tablespace The logical structure that abstracts logical data storage in tables from physical data storage in datafiles.

TCP Transmission Control Protocol. Together with the Internet Protocol, TCP/IP: the de facto standard communication protocol used for client/server communication over a network.

TCPS TCP with SSL. The secure sockets version of TCP.

Tempfile The physical storage that makes up a temporary tablespace, used for storing temporary segments.

TNS   Transparent Network Substrate. The heart of Oracle Net, a proprietary layered protocol running on top of whatever underlying network transport protocol you choose to use, probably TCP/IP.

Transaction   A logical unit of work, which will complete in total or not at all.

Tuple   A one-dimensional structure consisting of attributes (aka a row).

U

UGA   User global area. The part of the PGA that is stored in the SGA for sessions running through shared servers.

UI   User interface. The layer of an application that communicates with end users, nowadays, frequently graphical: a GUI.

URL   Uniform Resource Locator. A standard for specifying the location of an object on the Internet, consisting of a protocol, a host name and domain, an IP port number, a path and filename, and a series of parameters.

UTC   Coordinated Universal Time, previously known as Greenwich Mean Time (GMT). UTC is the global standard time zone; all others relate to it as offsets, ahead or behind.

X

X   As in the X Window System, the standard GUI environment used on most computers—except those that run Microsoft Windows instead.

XML   Extensible Markup Language. A standard for data interchange using documents, where the format of the data is defined by tags within the document.

INDEX

C

J

M

P

S

T

GET YOUR FREE SUBSCRIPTION
TO ORACLE MAGAZINE

Oracle Magazine is essential gear for today's information technology professionals. Stay informed and increase your productivity with every issue of *Oracle Magazine*. Inside each free bimonthly issue you'll get:

IF THERE ARE OTHER ORACLE USERS AT YOUR LOCATION WHO WOULD LIKE TO RECEIVE THEIR OWN SUBSCRIPTION TO ORACLE MAGAZINE, PLEASE PHOTOCOPY THIS FORM AND PASS IT ALONG.

ORACLE
MAGAZINE

- Up-to-date information on Oracle Database, Oracle Application Server, Web development, enterprise grid computing, database technology, and business trends
- Third-party vendor news and announcements
- Technical articles on Oracle and partner products, technologies, and operating environments
- Development and administration tips
- Real-world customer stories

Three easy ways to subscribe:

① Web
Visit our Web site at otn.oracle.com/oraclemagazine.
You'll find a subscription form there, plus much more!

② Fax
Complete the questionnaire on the back of this card and fax the questionnaire side only to +1.847.763.9638.

③ Mail
Complete the questionnaire on the back of this card and mail it to P.O. Box 1263, Skokie, IL 60076-8263

ORACLE

FREE SUBSCRIPTION

○ **Yes, please send me a FREE subscription to *Oracle Magazine*.**   ○ **NO**
To receive a free subscription to *Oracle Magazine*, you must fill out the entire card, sign it, and date it (incomplete cards cannot be processed or acknowledged). You can also fax your application to +1.847.763.9638.
Or subscribe at our Web site at otn.oracle.com/oraclemagazine

○ From time to time, Oracle Publishing allows our partners exclusive access to our e-mail addresses for special promotions and announcements. To be included in this program, please check this circle.

○ Oracle Publishing allows sharing of our mailing list with selected third parties. If you prefer your mailing address not to be included in this program, please check here. If at any time you would like to be removed from this mailing list, please contact Customer Service at +1.847.647.9630 or send an e-mail to oracle@halldata.com.

signature (required)   date

X

name   title

company   e-mail address

street/p.o. box

city/state/zip or postal code   telephone

country   fax

YOU MUST ANSWER ALL TEN QUESTIONS BELOW.

① WHAT IS THE PRIMARY BUSINESS ACTIVITY OF YOUR FIRM AT THIS LOCATION? (check one only)
- ☐ 01 Aerospace and Defense Manufacturing
- ☐ 02 Application Service Provider
- ☐ 03 Automotive Manufacturing
- ☐ 04 Chemicals, Oil and Gas
- ☐ 05 Communications and Media
- ☐ 06 Construction/Engineering
- ☐ 07 Consumer Sector/Consumer Packaged Goods
- ☐ 08 Education
- ☐ 09 Financial Services/Insurance
- ☐ 10 Government (civil)
- ☐ 11 Government (military)
- ☐ 12 Healthcare
- ☐ 13 High Technology Manufacturing, OEM
- ☐ 14 Integrated Software Vendor
- ☐ 15 Life Sciences (Biotech, Pharmaceuticals)
- ☐ 16 Mining
- ☐ 17 Retail/Wholesale/Distribution
- ☐ 18 Systems Integrator, VAR/VAD
- ☐ 19 Telecommunications
- ☐ 20 Travel and Transportation
- ☐ 21 Utilities (electric, gas, sanitation, water)
- ☐ 98 Other Business and Services

② WHICH OF THE FOLLOWING BEST DESCRIBES YOUR PRIMARY JOB FUNCTION? (check one only)
Corporate Management/Staff
- ☐ 01 Executive Management (President, Chair, CEO, CFO, Owner, Partner, Principal)
- ☐ 02 Finance/Administrative Management (VP/Director/ Manager/Controller, Purchasing, Administration)
- ☐ 03 Sales/Marketing Management (VP/Director/Manager)
- ☐ 04 Computer Systems/Operations Management (CIO/VP/Director/ Manager MIS, Operations)
IS/IT Staff
- ☐ 05 Systems Development/ Programming Management
- ☐ 06 Systems Development/ Programming Staff
- ☐ 07 Consulting
- ☐ 08 DBA/Systems Administrator
- ☐ 09 Education/Training
- ☐ 10 Technical Support Director/Manager
- ☐ 11 Other Technical Management/Staff
- ☐ 98 Other

③ WHAT IS YOUR CURRENT PRIMARY OPERATING PLATFORM? (select all that apply)
- ☐ 01 Digital Equipment UNIX
- ☐ 02 Digital Equipment VAX VMS
- ☐ 03 HP UNIX
- ☐ 04 IBM AIX
- ☐ 05 IBM UNIX
- ☐ 06 Java
- ☐ 07 Linux
- ☐ 08 Macintosh
- ☐ 09 MS-DOS
- ☐ 10 MVS
- ☐ 11 NetWare
- ☐ 12 Network Computing
- ☐ 13 OpenVMS
- ☐ 14 SCO UNIX
- ☐ 15 Sequent DYNIX/ptx
- ☐ 16 Sun Solaris/SunOS
- ☐ 17 SVR4
- ☐ 18 UnixWare
- ☐ 19 Windows
- ☐ 20 Windows NT
- ☐ 21 Other UNIX
- ☐ 98 Other
- 99 ☐ None of the above

④ DO YOU EVALUATE, SPECIFY, RECOMMEND, OR AUTHORIZE THE PURCHASE OF ANY OF THE FOLLOWING? (check all that apply)
- ☐ 01 Hardware
- ☐ 02 Software
- ☐ 03 Application Development Tools
- ☐ 04 Database Products
- ☐ 05 Internet or Intranet Products
- 99 ☐ None of the above

⑤ IN YOUR JOB, DO YOU USE OR PLAN TO PURCHASE ANY OF THE FOLLOWING PRODUCTS? (check all that apply)
Software
- ☐ 01 Business Graphics
- ☐ 02 CAD/CAE/CAM
- ☐ 03 CASE
- ☐ 04 Communications
- ☐ 05 Database Management
- ☐ 06 File Management
- ☐ 07 Finance
- ☐ 08 Java
- ☐ 09 Materials Resource Planning
- ☐ 10 Multimedia Authoring
- ☐ 11 Networking
- ☐ 12 Office Automation
- ☐ 13 Order Entry/Inventory Control
- ☐ 14 Programming
- ☐ 15 Project Management
- ☐ 16 Scientific and Engineering
- ☐ 17 Spreadsheets
- ☐ 18 Systems Management
- ☐ 19 Workflow

Hardware
- ☐ 20 Macintosh
- ☐ 21 Mainframe
- ☐ 22 Massively Parallel Processing
- ☐ 23 Minicomputer
- ☐ 24 PC
- ☐ 25 Network Computer
- ☐ 26 Symmetric Multiprocessing
- ☐ 27 Workstation
Peripherals
- ☐ 28 Bridges/Routers/Hubs/Gateways
- ☐ 29 CD-ROM Drives
- ☐ 30 Disk Drives/Subsystems
- ☐ 31 Modems
- ☐ 32 Tape Drives/Subsystems
- ☐ 33 Video Boards/Multimedia
Services
- ☐ 34 Application Service Provider
- ☐ 35 Consulting
- ☐ 36 Education/Training
- ☐ 37 Maintenance
- ☐ 38 Online Database Services
- ☐ 39 Support
- ☐ 40 Technology-Based Training
- ☐ 98 Other
- 99 ☐ None of the above

⑥ WHAT ORACLE PRODUCTS ARE IN USE AT YOUR SITE? (check all that apply)
Oracle E-Business Suite
- ☐ 01 Oracle Marketing
- ☐ 02 Oracle Sales
- ☐ 03 Oracle Order Fulfillment
- ☐ 04 Oracle Supply Chain Management
- ☐ 05 Oracle Procurement
- ☐ 06 Oracle Manufacturing
- ☐ 07 Oracle Maintenance Management
- ☐ 08 Oracle Service
- ☐ 09 Oracle Contracts
- ☐ 10 Oracle Projects
- ☐ 11 Oracle Financials
- ☐ 12 Oracle Human Resources
- ☐ 13 Oracle Interaction Center
- ☐ 14 Oracle Communications/Utilities (modules)
- ☐ 15 Oracle Public Sector/University (modules)
- ☐ 16 Oracle Financial Services (modules)
Server/Software
- ☐ 17 Oracle9i
- ☐ 18 Oracle9i Lite
- ☐ 19 Oracle8i
- ☐ 20 Other Oracle database
- ☐ 21 Oracle9i Application Server
- ☐ 22 Oracle9i Application Server Wireless
- ☐ 23 Oracle Small Business Suite

Tools
- ☐ 24 Oracle Developer Suite
- ☐ 25 Oracle Discoverer
- ☐ 26 Oracle JDeveloper
- ☐ 27 Oracle Migration Workbench
- ☐ 28 Oracle9i AS Portal
- ☐ 29 Oracle Warehouse Builder
Oracle Services
- ☐ 30 Oracle Outsourcing
- ☐ 31 Oracle Consulting
- ☐ 32 Oracle Education
- ☐ 33 Oracle Support
- ☐ 98 Other
- 99 ☐ None of the above

⑦ WHAT OTHER DATABASE PRODUCTS ARE IN USE AT YOUR SITE? (check all that apply)
- ☐ 01 Access
- ☐ 02 Baan
- ☐ 03 dbase
- ☐ 04 Gupta
- ☐ 05 IBM DB2
- ☐ 06 Informix
- ☐ 07 Ingres
- ☐ 08 Microsoft Access
- ☐ 09 Microsoft SQL Server
- ☐ 10 PeopleSoft
- ☐ 11 Progress
- ☐ 12 SAP
- ☐ 13 Sybase
- ☐ 14 VSAM
- ☐ 98 Other
- 99 ☐ None of the above

⑧ WHAT OTHER APPLICATION SERVER PRODUCTS ARE IN USE AT YOUR SITE? (check all that apply)
- ☐ 01 BEA
- ☐ 02 IBM
- ☐ 03 Sybase
- ☐ 04 Sun
- ☐ 05 Other

⑨ DURING THE NEXT 12 MONTHS, HOW MUCH DO YOU ANTICIPATE YOUR ORGANIZATION WILL SPEND ON COMPUTER HARDWARE, SOFTWARE, PERIPHERALS, AND SERVICES FOR YOUR LOCATION? (check only one)
- ☐ 01 Less than $10,000
- ☐ 02 $10,000 to $49,999
- ☐ 03 $50,000 to $99,999
- ☐ 04 $100,000 to $499,999
- ☐ 05 $500,000 to $999,999
- ☐ 06 $1,000,000 and over

⑩ WHAT IS YOUR COMPANY'S YEARLY SALES REVENUE? (please choose one)
- ☐ 01 $500, 000, 000 and above
- ☐ 02 $100, 000, 000 to $500, 000, 000
- ☐ 03 $50, 000, 000 to $100, 000, 000
- ☐ 04 $5, 000, 000 to $50, 000, 000
- ☐ 05 $1, 000, 000 to $5, 000, 000

100103